Neurointerventions and the Law

OXFORD SERIES IN NEUROSCIENCE, LAW, AND PHILOSOPHY

Series Editors
Lynn Nadel, Frederick Schauer, and Walter P. Sinnott-Armstrong

Conscious Will and Responsibility
Edited by Walter P. Sinnott-Armstrong and Lynn Nadel

Memory and Law
Edited by Lynn Nadel and Walter P. Sinnott-Armstrong

Neuroscience and Legal Responsibility
Edited by Nicole A Vincent

Handbook on Psychopathy and Law
Edited by Kent A. Kiehl and Walter P. Sinnott-Armstrong

A Primer on Criminal Law and Neuroscience
Edited by Stephen J. Morse and Adina L. Roskies

Bioprediction, Biomarkers, and Bad Behavior
Edited by Ilina Singh, Walter P. Sinnott-Armstrong, and Julian Savulescu

Finding Consciousness: The Neuroscience, Ethics, and Law of Severe Brain Damage
Edited by Walter Sinnott-Armstrong

The Neuroethics of Biomarkers: What the Development of Bioprediction Means for Moral Responsibility, Justice, and the Nature of Mental Disorder
By Matthew L. Baum

Neurointerventions and the Law: Regulating Human Mental Capacity
Edited by Nicole A Vincent, Thomas Nadelhoffer, and Allan McCay

Neurointerventions and the Law

Regulating Human Mental Capacity

Edited by

NICOLE A VINCENT, THOMAS NADELHOFFER,
AND ALLAN MCCAY

OXFORD
UNIVERSITY PRESS

OXFORD
UNIVERSITY PRESS

Oxford University Press is a department of the University of Oxford. It furthers
the University's objective of excellence in research, scholarship, and education
by publishing worldwide. Oxford is a registered trade mark of Oxford University
Press in the UK and certain other countries.

Published in the United States of America by Oxford University Press
198 Madison Avenue, New York, NY 10016, United States of America.

Library of Congress Cataloging-in-Publication Data
Names: Vincent, Nicole A, editor. | Nadelhoffer, Thomas, editor. | McCay, Allan, editor.
Title: Neurointerventions and the law : regulating human mental capacity /
Nicole A Vincent, Thomas Nadelhoffer, Allan McCay (editors).
Description: New York, NY : Oxford University Press, 2020. |
Series: Oxford series in neuroscience, law, and philosophy |
Includes bibliographical references and index.
Identifiers: 2019048935 (print) | 2019048936 (ebook) | ISBN 9780190651145 (hardback) |
ISBN 9780190667979 (epub) | ISBN 9780190651169
Subjects: LCSH: Mental health laws. | Law—Psychological aspects. |
Criminal psychology. | Neurology—Law and legislation
Classification: LCC K3608 .N48 2020 (print) | LCC K3608 (ebook) | DDC 344.04/4—dc23
LC record available at https://lccn.loc.gov/2019048935
LC ebook record available at https://lccn.loc.gov/2019048936

1 3 5 7 9 8 6 4 2

Printed by Sheridan Books, Inc., United States of America

Contents

Contributors

Jan Christoph Bublitz, LLB, JD, PhD
Postdoctoral Researcher
University of Hamburg
Hamburg, Germany

William Bülow, PhD
Postdoctoral Researcher
Stockholm Centre for the Ethics of
    War and Peace
Stockholm University
Stockholm, Sweden

Adrian Carter, PhD
Associate Professor
School of Psychological Sciences
Faculty of Medicine Nursing and
    Health Sciences
Monash University
Victoria, Australia

Jennifer Chandler, LLM, LLB
Professor of Law
University of Ottawa
Ottawa
Canada, ON

Paul Sheldon Davies, PhD
Professor of Philosophy
College of William & Mary
Williamsburg, VA

Andrew Dawson, PhD
Strategic Project Adviser
    (Community & Government)
Turner Institute for Brain and
    Mental Health Medicine,
    Nursing and Health Sciences
Monash University
Victoria, Australia

Susan Dodds, PhD
Deputy Vice-Chancellor and
    Vice-President
Research and Industry
    Engagement
La Trobe University
Victoria, Australia

Alexandre Erler, DPhil
Research Assistant Professor
Philosophy and Bioethics
Chinese University
    of Hong Kong
Hong Kong, SAR

Harvey L. Fiser, JD
Associate Professor of Law
Else School of Management
Millsaps University
Jackson, MS

Farah Focquaert, PhD
Professor
Philosophical Anthropology
Ghent University
Ghent, Belgium

Colin Gavaghan, LLB, PhD
Associate Professor
Law and Policy
University of Otago
Dunedin, New Zealand

Frédéric Gilbert, PhD
Senior Lecturer in Philosophy
Philosophy and Gender Studies
University of Tasmania
Hobart, Australia

Walter Glannon, PhD
Professor of Philosophy
University of Calgary
Vancouver, BC, Canada

Daniela Goya-Tocchetto, PhD
PhD Student in Management and
    Organizations
Fuqua School of Business
Duke University
Durham, NC

Wayne Hall, PhD
Professor
Centre for Youth Substance Abuse Research
University of Queensland
St. Lucia, Australia

Valerie Gray Hardcastle, PhD
St. Elizabeth Healthcare Executive Director
Institute for Health Innovation and Vice
    President for Health Innovation
Northern Kentucky University
Highland Heights, KY

Patrick D. Hopkins, PhD
Professor
Department of Philosophy, Millsaps College
Professor
Department of Psychiatry and Human
    Behavior & Center for Bioethics and
    Medical Humanities
University of Mississippi Medical Center
Jackson, MS

Neil Levy, PhD
Professor of Philosophy
Macquarie University and Senior
    Research Fellow
Uehiro Centre for Practical Ethics
Oxford University
Sydney, Australia

Allan McCay, PhD
Teacher
University of Sydney Foundation Program
    and Affiliate Member of the Centre for
    Agency, Values and Ethics
Macquarie University
Sydney, Australia

Quinn McGuire
MPS Student
Sports Industry Management
Georgetown University
Washington, DC

Thomas Nadelhoffer, PhD
Associate Professor
Philosophy, Psychology, and Neuroscience
College of Charleston
Charleston, SC

**Christopher James Ryan, MBBS, MHL,
    FRANZCP**
Clinical Associate Professor of Psychiatry
University of Sydney, and Honorary
    Associate at Sydney Health Ethics
Westmead, Australia

Katrina L. Sifferd, JD, PhD
Professor of Philosophy
Elmhurst College
Elmhurst, IL

Sigrid Sterckx, PhD
Professor of Ethics and Political
    and Social Philosophy
Ghent University
Ghent, Belgium

Kristof Van Assche, PhD
Research Professor in Health Law &
    Kinship Studies
Antwerp University
Antwerp, Belgium

Andrew Vierra, MA
J.D. Candidate
University of Michigan Law School
Ann Arbor, MI

Nicole A Vincent, PhD
Senior Lecturer
Faculty of Transdisciplinary Innovation
University of Technology Sydney, and
    Honorary Fellow and Affiliate Member
    of the Centre for Agency, Values and
    Ethics, Department of Philosophy
Macquarie University
Sydney, Australia

Jennifer Cole Wright, PhD
Associate Professor of Psychology
    and Philosophy
College of Charleston
Charleston, SC

1

Law Viewed Through the Lens
of Neurointerventions

Nicole A Vincent, Thomas Nadelhoffer, and Allan McCay

Introduction

The development of modern diagnostic neuroimaging techniques led to discoveries about the human brain and mind that helped give rise to the field of neurolaw. This new interdisciplinary field has led to novel directions in analytic jurisprudence and philosophy of law by providing an empirically informed platform from which scholars have reassessed topics such as mental privacy and self-determination, responsibility and its relationship to mental disorders, and the proper aims of the criminal law. Similarly, the development of neurointervention techniques that promise to deliver new ways of altering people's minds (by intervening in their brains) creates opportunities and challenges that raise important and rich conceptual, moral, jurisprudential, and scientific questions. The specific purpose of this volume is to make a contribution to the field of neurolaw by investigating the legal issues raised by the development and use of neurointerventions (actual, proposed, and potential).

To locate this volume's theme within a broader context, we offer a sketch of how advances in diagnostic neuroimaging techniques have instigated debates that have, in turn, created what has come to be known as the field of neurolaw. In a nutshell, we shall argue that to the extent that the law[1] aims to regulate human behavior, advances in technologies such as diagnostic neuroimaging have (a) expanded our understanding of the brain function and psychology of the subjects whose behavior the law aims to regulate and (b) provided glimpses of potential new techniques that legal actors might one day use to support more empirically informed legal assessments and arguments.

---

[1] The scope of this book is not restricted to one jurisdiction. In fact, a variety of different kinds of legal systems are discussed in this volume. In this introductory chapter, when we refer to "the law," this should not be understood as making a claim about all legal systems but instead is generally to be understood as one or more particular legal systems.

Nicole A Vincent, Thomas Nadelhoffer, and Allan McCay, *Law Viewed Through the Lens of Neurointerventions*
In: *Neurointerventions and the Law*. Edited by: Nicole A Vincent, Thomas Nadelhoffer, and Allan McCay,
Oxford University Press (2020). © Oxford University Press 2020
DOI: 10.1093/oso/9780190651145.001.0001

This background is relevant to the specific content of this volume because, in addition to advances in diagnostic neuroimaging techniques, during the past few decades we have also witnessed significant advances in neurointervention techniques. So, in the next section, we offer an account of what the term *neurointervention* means. Our approach in this section will be partly ostensive and partly conceptual. Our approach will be ostensive in the sense that we will offer examples of what we take to be core and penumbral examples of neurointerventions, and we will contrast these with what, in our view (or at least for our purposes), are not examples of neurointerventions. However, our approach will also be conceptual in the sense that we will draw on the work of neurolaw scholars, including those whose work has been included in this volume, to explain why we think that the things we cite as core and penumbral examples of neurointerventions are such—and why we also think it makes good sense to focus on them—and to contrast them with other ways of changing minds that, in our view, are not examples of neurointerventions.

With a working definition of "neurointerventions" on the table, the re-maining four sections of this chapter will cover the following ground. We will provide an overview and discuss a range of legal challenges (and associ-ated ethical questions) raised by the (actual, proposed, and foreseeable) use of neurointerventions by those who are subject to the law, in a range of so-cial settings and contexts. Next, we discuss issues raised by legal actors' own (actual, proposed, and potential) use of neurointerventions to achieve their ends—for instance, to make defendants sane enough to stand trial, to make condemned prisoners fit enough for execution, and to help convicted offenders reform themselves by damping down their aggressive urges or increasing their ability to benefit from education. We then explore the debate over whether neurointerventions give us reason to think the law either should or will undergo fairly radical change. Finally, we offer our conclusion.[2]

Background and Context: Law, Neurolaw, and Neurointerventions

Whatever else the law might be, it is also a tool or instrument that society uses to regulate human behavior (we include the behavior of corporations and other "artificial persons" under this broad heading). The law regulates human behavior

---

[2] Unlike most introductions, we will not be discussing each chapter in order. Instead, they will be grouped together thematically given our own way of thinking about the relationship between neurointerventions and the law. The goal is to use the chapters to say something interesting about neurointerventions.

through a range of methods. Familiar examples include (a) specifying prohibitions against certain behaviors (e.g., to not harm others in certain ways, like killing them or taking their possessions), (b) creating obligations to engage in other behaviors (e.g., duties of medical professionals toward their patients or so-called Good Samaritan laws that create obligations to help bystanders in certain kinds of distress), and (c) empowering people to voluntarily engage in other behaviors (e.g., to enter into enforceable contractual relationships with others or to marry one another). The law also specifies responses or remedies that may become available if the law's rules are violated (e.g., punishment or damages), the purposes of those responses and remedies (e.g., to deter undesirable behavior through the threat of sanction or by ensuring that victims are compensated), and who must or may initiate those responses or remedies (e.g., prosecutors or victims). Furthermore, because the law is not a static entity but something that changes over time, and the changes are things that are ultimately put into place by people, the law also sets out its own internal principles to regulate how—that is, through what processes, by whom, and in what ways—its contents may be altered.[3]

Given that the law is an instrument for the regulation of human behavior, its rules and regulations are intimately intertwined with a range of presuppositions about human agency. For instance, the notion that people deserve punishment for some of their wrongdoings is often thought to rest on the idea that at least some, if not most, people have the ability to control their behavior (unsurprisingly, children and adolescents are often treated differently in this regard). If it turned out that people do not have the ability to control their behavior (in the way that we think they have this ability) or that this ability is more restricted in some contexts and more expansive in other contexts than we previously thought, then that may be a compelling reason to alter the law. Similarly, the thought that punishment may serve the purpose of deterring people from engaging in undesirable conduct rests, at least tacitly, on the presupposition that people are aware of what the law prohibits and of what sanctions it threatens to impose on lawbreakers, that they find punishment unpleasant or in other ways aversive and hence they will be motivated to avoid it, and that this may indeed then lead them to behave in whichever way will be conducive to avoiding punishment. However, this presupposition has already been called into question (Robinson & Darley, 2004), and if our fundamental assumptions about human agency turn out to be incorrect, then it's very likely that the laws that have been put in place are not as effective as lawmakers may want them to be. Thus, to the extent that an important purpose of the law is to regulate human behavior, if humans turn out to be

---

[3] Of course, much ink has been spilled over the nature of law. Addressing this difficult philosophical topic in any detail is beyond the scope of this introduction.

very different kinds of agents than what had hitherto been assumed, then to regulate human behavior more effectively, the methods that the law uses may need to be adjusted and updated.

Against this broad background, advances in fields such as cognitive neuroscience, psychology, and behavioral genetics have led to a range of discoveries about human agency that, over the past 15 to 20 years, have given rise to the field of neurolaw. For instance, some psychological studies suggest that under certain conditions people can fail to notice important features of their situations, or that their judgment may end up being impaired, or that their degree of control may be significantly lower than what might be thought to be required for full responsibility. In cognitive neuroscience, some research suggests that human brains do not finish maturing until the mid-20s and that there appear to be significant differences between the brains of people who are typically held responsible for what they do and those who are typically not held responsible for what they do—differences that, some argue, explain why these two groups of people behave in different ways. In behavioral genetics, the pioneering work of scholars like Terrie Moffitt and Avshalom Caspi (Caspi et al., 2002) has identified genes that predispose those who have them to develop violent tendencies if they grow up in violent environments, and the work of neurocriminologists like Adrian Raine and Andrea Glenn (2014) continues to uncover the ways in which environmental, social, and even dietary factors have an impact on people's propensity toward criminal behavior.

These are but a few examples of the impressively broad range of scientific findings that have led some scholars to argue that not only should the law be changed so that it is based upon a more realistic account of what human agency is actually like, but even that core institutional responses like retributive punishment should be (and likely will be) abandoned (Greene & Cohen, 2004). According to some skeptical views, the gathering data show that people are in fact not morally responsible in a desert-based way for what they do. Naturally, other scholars in the field of neurolaw such as Michael Moore (2014), Stephen Morse (2007), and David Hodgson (2000) also engage to varying extents with this growing body of empirical literature and defend at least some of the law's institutional practices against the calls for reform. In neurolaw, just as in traditional jurisprudence, there are skeptics about legal responsibility, just as there are those who defend the status quo. However, the distinctive contribution[4] from neurolaw suggests that the debate will at least partly hinge on scientific developments and not simply on further refinements when it comes to philosophical and

---

[4] We do not mean to suggest that those engaged in contemporary neurolaw discussions are the first to note that developments in science are relevant to debates about responsibility.

jurisprudential speculation. In short, making progress on this front will be an interdisciplinary affair, which is built into the very word *neurolaw*.

The previous paragraph briefly recounted some examples of ways in which scientific discoveries about the human brain and mind have prompted both calls for legal reform (on the basis that the humans the law aims to regulate, or at least some of them, are significantly different kinds of agents than what the law had hitherto assumed), and responses from those who believe that those calls for reform should be resisted for one reason or another. Importantly, though, many of the recent scientific discoveries about the human mind have been made possible through progress in behavioral genetics and, perhaps to a greater extent, the development of modern diagnostic neuroimaging techniques—for example, magnetic resonance imaging (MRI), functional MRI, diffusion tensor imaging, computed axial tomography, positron emission tomography, electroencephalography, and magnetoencephalography—that made it possible to observe and study how the brain works, as well as the structural and functional differences that exist from person to person. Put simply, advances in genetic and diagnostic neuroimaging techniques have led to an expanded understanding of the relationship between the human brain and mind, and this new understanding has, in turn, given rise to debates about whether and how the law should be changed.

However, the potential to use genetic and diagnostic neuroimaging techniques as legal tools has also created a lot of excitement and debate among neurolaw scholars. For instance, the potential to use functional neuroimaging techniques like functional MRI and electroencephalography to detect deception has created hope among some and fear among others that in the future the criminal law may acquire better tools to assess when people are telling the truth and maybe even to directly read the contents of people's minds by scanning their brains. Some have also proposed that either functional or structural (e.g., MRI and computed axial tomography) neuroimaging techniques might now or at least one day help courts to assess whether a given person suffers from a mental disorder—one that either reduces the degree of their culpability for the offense that they committed or that informs the court's decision regarding whether they are indeed competent (or fit) to make certain decisions for themselves, to enter into contracts with others, or even to stand trial or be punished.[5]

The potential to develop techniques to measure how much and what kind of pain a person feels has also created excitement among some neurolaw scholars. The possibility that something that has hitherto been unobservable—namely, the degree of people's pain and suffering—may one day become observable and

---

[5] For examples of the way some courts are already responding to neuroimaging evidence see the Australian Neurolaw Database (https://neurolaw.edu.au/), which contains publicly accessible summaries of both civil and criminal neurolaw cases.

measurable has led to debates about (a) whether this could perhaps be used in legal proceedings to more accurately assess the appropriate damages for pain and suffering that a person should be paid and (b) how much pain and suffering different offenders might experience if sentenced to the same prison term and whether criminal sentences ought to be sensitive to these individual psychological differences. By revealing new things about human agency and by creating new tools that the law can now (or might one day) use, advances in diagnostic neuroimaging techniques and technologies have led to the creation of the field of neurolaw—a field that is squarely situated at the crossroads of genetics, neuroscience, philosophy, and the law.

Neurointerventions—Core and Penumbral Examples

In addition to advances in genetic testing and neuroimaging, the past few decades have also witnessed significant advances when it comes to neurointervention techniques—that is, very roughly, techniques that enable us to modify people's minds by altering their brains.[6] Since the purpose of this volume is to explore how advances in neurointervention techniques also create new opportunities and challenges for the law, before proceeding, in this section we will explain what we mean by the term "*neurointerventions*" and why we think that, as a category of ways of changing people's minds, neurointerventions raise interesting and important questions. However, our central claim in this section will be that although neurointerventions do raise genuinely novel issues for the law, the same (or very similar) issues are also raised by ways of changing minds that, strictly speaking, are *not* neurointerventions in the previously described narrow sense. We thus think that it is preferable to define the term "*neurointerventions*" in a way that allows for core and penumbral examples (as a cluster concept) rather than in a clear-cut way that provides necessary and jointly sufficient criteria.

That said, let us start with what one might call core or paradigmatic examples of neurointerventions. Core cases include (a) pharmaceuticals (e.g., antidepressants, attention-deficit/hyperactivity disorder [ADHD] medications, and oxytocin), (b) "electroceuticals" and "magnetoceuticals" (e.g., electroconvulsive therapy, transcranial direct current stimulation, and transcranial magnetic stimulation), (c) invasive procedures (e.g., deep brain stimulation [DBS], implanted brain–computer interfaces [BCIs], and neurosurgery), and

---

[6] We are not adopting a dualist conception of the mind–brain relation here. It could be that the mind and the brain are identical or that the latter is reducible to the former. For our purposes, we need only be committed to the claim that neurointerventions influence the mind by influencing the brain. We remain agnostic concerning the relationship between the two.

(d) external BCIs. In each of these cases, the intervention directly and un-equivocally causes changes in brain capacity and function[7]—changes that could be readily identified, manipulated, and measured. These core cases of neurointervention bring about behavioral changes via direct structural or neuro-chemical changes to the brain itself. Moreover, these techniques are clearly brain interventions in the conventional sense that raise a range of important clinical, ethical, and legal issues.

When these methods are contrasted with traditional ways of changing minds (e.g., talking to people, giving them reasons, etc.), it seems clear that the same range of clinical, ethical, and legal issues are not raised. While all behavioral intervention is mediated by the brain in some important respect, not all such modifications influence the brain via the same causal route. It's the difference between trying to convince someone they should behave in a particular way—an external form of attempted behavioral modification—and directly acting upon the neural mechanisms that bring about the desired behavior. The former way of manipulating behavior requires appealing to people's practical reasoning, and the latter way involves the capacity to bypass their conscious deliberation altogether.

However, although the previous two paragraphs provide what seem like clearly different ways of changing minds, matters become significantly more complicated when we consider a third category of methods for changing minds that do not fit comfortably into either the neurointervention category or the tra-ditional category. And yet the issues that they raise often seem very similar, if not identical, to those raised by neurointerventions. We shall refer to these as "penumbral" cases. Consider, for instance, the following forms of behavioral intervention: brainwashing, indoctrination, subliminal advertising, and prop-aganda. These interventions share important features with many of the core neurointerventions in that they, too, may bypass people's conscious awareness. But these more suspicious forms of behavior modification are still external—that is, they do not exert their influence on the mind by changing the brain di-rectly. As such, these are not neurointerventions in the same sense as the core/paradigmatic examples since they do not literally involve *direct contact with* and *direct manipulation* of the brain through magnetic or electrical signals or through chemical means.[8] However, as is often the case in philosophy, there is

---

[7] This volume considers various forms of neurotechnology, including BCIs that allow for the con-trol of an external device. The brain of a person who acts to control an external device by way of BCI acts alongside the interface to provide novel capacity and function, and, of course, this novel capacity may lead to changes in behavior. We have included such BCIs as core examples of neurointervention, though we are open to the possibility that they could also be classified as penumbral examples, which we discuss below.

[8] But then again, pharmaceuticals modify the brain indirectly too—through the stomach.

not a bright line to be drawn here. So, any attempt to carve out the domain of neurointerventions in terms of necessary and jointly sufficient conditions is likely to fail.

Consider, for example, Neil Levy's (2007) claim that the means whereby an agent intervenes in his or her mind, or the minds of others, is irrelevant when it comes to assessing the moral status of the intervention. On this view—known as the parity principle—what matters is the influence or effect the intervention has on the agent. The parity principle states that "unless we can identify ethically relevant differences between internal and external interventions and alterations, we ought to treat them on a par. . . . [T]he mere fact that one kind of intervention is internal is not a ground for objection" (p. 62). If we take this principle to be true, then if two methods of changing a person's mind—one behavioral and the other biomedical—produce precisely the same mental effects and there are no other relevant moral differences between them, then there can be no principled reason to prefer the behavioral method over the biomedical method. If all else remains equal—for instance, as long as biomedical techniques do not produce unwanted side effects—then on Levy's account there can be no reason to prefer one method over the other.

If this view were correct, then the distinction we drew earlier between the direct manipulations involved in core cases of neurointervention and the indirect manipulations involved in penumbral cases may not make a significant moral difference. According to Levy, because (a) indirect interventions can be no less destructive than direct manipulations and (b) indirect interventions are presently more threatening than direct manipulations (at least for the foreseeable future), the distinction between direct and indirect interventions doesn't provide us with practical guidance when it comes to morality, the law, or public policy.

Having developed his argument for the parity principle, Levy proceeds to defend it from some common objections, including a critique put forward by Jan Christoph Bublitz and Reinhard Merkel (2014). On their view,

> [p]ersons have most control over interventions whose sensual substrates they perceive, particularly those rising to the level of conscious awareness. We can think about what we see and hear, we can modify and process it. [However, c]ontrol is reduced when stimuli are subconsciously processed (subliminal stimuli)[, but that even here] persons have more control . . . than over direct interventions. (p. 69)

They also argue that while "indirect interventions . . . leave traces in the brain, [the] transformations are somehow more in accordance with the existing personality structure and preserve the authenticity of the individual [, whereas] direct interventions 'distort' our relations to the world or to ourselves" (p. 70).

According to Bublitz and Merkel, it is not that there is a clear-cut metaphysical distinction between behavioral and biomedical interventions with regard to how each impacts authenticity and responsibility. For example, they recognize that priming and hypnosis may seriously compromise our responsibility even though they involve behavioral techniques. Similarly, despite the fact that a good diet (which improves our mental functioning) and perfumes (which can powerfully elicit memories) both achieve their effects through biomedical means, neither is usually thought to challenge authenticity or responsibility. Nevertheless, Bublitz and Merkel argue that although exceptions clearly exist, what is significant about the direct/indirect distinction—and what Levy's parity principle fails to take into account—is that this distinction roughly tracks (provides a guide to, is a rule of thumb for) an important normative distinction between generally unfair and generally fair ways of interacting with one another. The reason why, on their account, direct interventions typically challenge (whereas indirect interventions do not) agency and responsibility is because the former involve changing our minds in unfair ways, and Levy's parity principle leads us to overlook this point.

In his contribution to this volume, Neil Levy argues that Bublitz and Merkel's failure to appreciate both the extent to which indirect interventions can undermine responsibility and autonomy and just how prevalent indirect interventions are in comparison to direct interventions undermines the punch of their normative claims. To demonstrate the troubling nature of many indirect interventions, Levy cites examples like priming, the strategic placement of items in shops to influence our buying choices, and the phenomenon of ego depletion. We are exposed to these indirect ways of changing our minds extremely often, and they pose serious challenges to our autonomy and responsibility. To support the claim about the untroubling nature of many direct interventions, Levy cites the examples of exposure to sun light, good nutrition, iodine in salt, and folic acid, all of which can have marked effects on our thinking. Despite the fact that these methods of changing our minds involve direct intervention, nobody complains about them because they are familiar to us and we view them as beneficial. Given the explicitly normative focus of Bublitz and Merkel's argument, Levy's response comes in the form of the equally normative conclusion that "[a] concern for justice mandates ignoring the causal route whereby interventions work and instead assessing them on the basis of their effects on agents and on their autonomy" (2020, p. 46).

In his contribution to this volume, Christoph Bublitz (2020) rejects Levy's parity principle. On Bublitz's view, the first problem with the parity principle is that it seriously mischaracterizes what the law currently allows and prohibits when it comes to interventions. The law's focus is not on the effects, but on the protection of important rights such as free speech and freedom of thoughts.

Hence, the first reason why Bublitz rejects the parity principle is that he believes that the first premise of Levy's analogical argument for this principle seriously mischaracterizes current legal practice. According to Bublitz, this mischaracterization is enough to render Levy's argument unsound. Bublitz then goes on to claim that Levy's mischaracterization of the law leads him to overlook important normative differences between behavioral and direct brain interventions, which further undermines his argument from analogy. Analogies only work when the items being compared are sufficiently similar in relevant respects. However, while behavioral ways of changing minds have important normative features (e.g., they involve important rights that the law aims to protect), Bublitz argues that direct brain interventions lack these features. Thus, since the items in Levy's analogy are not sufficiently similar in relevant respects, Bublitz argues that this further undermines the argument for the parity principle. Not only does Bublitz think that neurointerventions and traditional interventions should be treated differently, conceptually speaking, but he also thinks this makes a practical difference. For instance, on his view, nonconsensual direct interventions into other minds should be, with few exceptions, prohibited by law. Given the unique potential harms that can arise in this context, Bublitz thinks that as a matter of law and policy neurointerventions should be treated with extreme caution.

In their chapter, Farah Focquaert, Kristof Van Assche, and Sigrid Sterckx take a different approach. On their view, given the wide array of medications and neuromodulation techniques that are being developed, the criminal justice system should consider allowing neurointerventions for the purposes of treating antisocial and criminal behavior—especially in the context of parole, probation, and mitigation of sentence—so long as certain moral and legal protections are in place. Focquaert and colleagues nevertheless think that compulsory neurointerventions are problematic under other circumstances (e.g., as part of an offender's sentence or when an offender has already served out his prison term) unless the neurointerventions in question are benign and without side effects. What they say on this front dovetails nicely with the debate between Levy and Bublitz. After all, if a given neurointervention is safe, effective, and voluntary, it's hard to see why the law should prohibit it. If, on the other hand, a neurointervention raises moral red flags, then it makes sense that the law would not permit its use (especially when the intervention is coerced or compelled). Here, as elsewhere, the focus is not on neurointerventions per se, but rather the specific neurointerventions and their associated costs and benefits.

That we should approach the issue of neurointerventions on a case-by-case basis is further evidenced by the fact that there is bound to be a range of core neurointervention techniques that will not of necessity raise any of the sorts of ethical and legal issues with which the chapters of this book concern themselves. For instance, imagine a person who lost a significant amount of cerebrospinal fluid, which then needed to be replaced with a synthetic alternative. If the synthetic cerebrospinal fluid made no difference to how the person's brain now functions, then it would not be a case of interest to us. Alternatively, imagine that with advances in science and technology, we developed synthetic neurons that could be used to replace natural neurons and that could be configured to have precisely the same connections as the ones that they replaced. Furthermore, imagine that a whole module of such neurons could be connected to replace a failing part of a person's brain—for instance, a synthetic hippocampus. If the synthetic hippocampus contained all of the same encoded information as the natural one that it replaces and if it would function no differently to it, then this, too, would not raise any of the sorts of concerns with which this book deals. Naturally, if the synthetic cerebrospinal fluid or the synthetic hippocampus malfunctioned, then this would bring up rich conceptual, ethical, and legal issues. However, our point is just that if the changes made by the synthetic replacements do not make a functional difference, then these would be examples of neurointerventions that may not raise any specific ethical, legal, and conceptual problems of the sort that are raised by the core and penumbral examples discussed above.

What we hope that the above discussion highlights is that by focusing exclusively on paradigmatic neurointerventions (e.g., DBS), we run the risk of failing to notice that many other mundane and familiar ways of changing minds (e.g., propaganda) may also raise the same range of issues. If this is right, it would seem somewhat arbitrary and unhelpful to exclude these penumbral and borderline cases from analysis and consideration. Furthermore, many novel/extraordinary direct brain interventions, like the ones discussed in the immediately preceding paragraph, do not raise any particular ethical or legal concerns of the sort with which the chapters of this book engage. The concern will arise when a way of changing minds has ramifications for agency, which means that for our purposes what matters is to define the category of neurointerventions expansively (i.e., by including both core and penumbral examples as long as they can have ramifications for agency) rather than narrowly (since not all neurointerventions will of necessity have an impact on agency). Consequently, although our discussion will often focus on neurointerventions that bear the most similarity to our core examples, the various issues, questions, problems, and solutions that are discussed in this volume also arise in the context of ways of changing minds that have more in common with examples from our penumbral list. That said, with this discussion of what we mean by *neurointerventions* on the table, we now turn to the three topics foreshadowed in the introduction to this chapter.

Regulating and Responding to People's Use
of Neurointerventions

The law sometimes regulates the production, provision, and consumption of neurointerventions that alter human minds. For instance, licenses are required to manufacture, prescribe, and sell—and prescriptions are required to purchase and consume—psychotropic medications like Prozac, lithium, methylphenidate, and modafinil. Nonpharmaceutical ways of altering minds, such as invasive surgical procedures, electroconvulsive therapy, and transcranial magnetic stimulation may also be subject to regulation. And neurointerventions that combine a number of unregulated items—e.g., the recent surge of interest in do-it-yourself transcranial direct current stimulation devices—present additional regulatory challenges. In this section, we discuss this range of legal challenges raised by the (actual, proposed, and foreseeable) use of neurointerventions in a range of social settings and contexts, by drawing on examples from several of this volume's chapters. In so doing, we consider how the law has, how it might, or how it ought to respond to problematic conduct from those who make use of neurointerventions, as well as raise questions reflecting on issues relating to the neurointerventions themselves.

For instance, in February 2015, a New Jersey court ruled that it is illegal to offer "gay conversion therapy" on grounds that being gay is not a disease and because it is fraudulent to make such offers since there is currently no way to alter people's sexual preference. But in the future, there *might* be ways of altering these preferences. After all, scientific progress happens constantly—and what then? If sexual preferences could be intentionally altered, should gay people be allowed to turn themselves straight if they so desire, regardless of whether their reasons are good and regardless of whether being gay is a disease or not? How about straight people—should they be allowed to turn themselves gay?

Because homosexuals are a political minority and because minorities lack political clout, it is important to put in place protections to safeguard their interests. Much of the attention on this front has tended to drift to the morality of interventions that would turn gay people straight. But Andrew Vierra asks whether there would be anything objectionable about straight people using neurointerventions to temporarily induce in themselves same-sex preferences. Although initially it may seem as if this use of novel neurointervention-based conversion therapies couldn't be objectionable, Vierra's chapter argues that this too would be an objectionable use of such neurointerventions. On Vierra's account, a pill that temporarily changed someone's sexual preference from opposite-sex to same-sex attraction—which he calls a "gay-for-a-day pill"— could enable heterosexual people to further misunderstand and trivialize gay people's lived experiences and to appropriate, perpetuate, and even strengthen toxic homophobic stereotypes.

Vierra's analysis has critically important implications for how prohibitions against so-called gay conversion therapy are justified and for constitutional debates about such matters as the contemporary marriage equality debate. On the former point, even if sexual preference could be altered through neurointerventions (i.e., even if the effectiveness criterion was satisfied) and even if doing this were not unpleasant, painful, or medically harmful (i.e., even if the safety criterion was satisfied), gay conversion therapy still should not be allowed since it does not actually turn a gay person straight. According to Vierra, if constructivists are right that same-sex attraction is neither necessary nor sufficient for being gay, then debates about marriage equality that predicate the matter of whether same-sex couples should be granted a legal right to marry on whether sexual preference is innate and immutable, innate but mutable, or chosen in fact does not bear on the matter at hand, since sexual preference is not what makes people heterosexual or homosexual in the first place.

Another example of how neurointerventions create new regulatory challenges for the law comes from two chapters that focus on the debate about cognitive enhancement. Before recounting the relevant content of those chapters, it may be helpful to offer some background. In March 2015 the Presidential Commission for the Study of Bioethical Issues recommended that once safe and effective cognitive enhancers are developed, measures should be taken to ensure everyone has equal access to cognitive enhancement so that the poor and disadvantaged are not further marginalized. But what if employers, keen to maximize their employees' productivity and performance, start requiring their employees to cognitively enhance themselves? Should workplace laws and regulations permit such practices—keeping in mind that we are only considering cognitive enhancement methods that are safe as well as effective—or would there still be reasons to prohibit employers from making the use of cognitive enhancers a condition of employment?

In his contribution to this volume, Alexandre Erler considers whether the use of neurointerventions in the context of employment might lead to a "new normal" in which employers expect that their employees are enhanced in ways that make them more able to perform their work. Thus perhaps employers might expect doctors, air traffic controllers, and military pilots to use some form of neuroenhancement to improve their work performance. Maybe those in occupations where agreeableness is thought to be a workplace asset might be expected to ensure that they are indeed agreeable employees by way of neurointervention. Would this be morally problematic? Should the law aim to avoid this kind of pressure on employees perhaps by way of a tax on neurointerventions or even a prohibition? For Erler, the answer to these questions depends on the precise nature of the neurointervention.

In supporting this conclusion, Erler argues that "indirect coercion" from employers, in which the need to enhance is neither explicit nor implicit but flows *indirectly* from expectations about job performance, is not necessarily any more ethically problematic than the pressure to use devices such as mobile phones that might result in a similarly indirect way from employers' expectations of the kind mentioned earlier. According to Erler, there doesn't seem to be anything particularly morally problematic about an organization that fails to accommodate the preferences of Neo-Luddites—those who have negative views toward modern technology and are thus opposed to the use of mobile telephones or computers. Erler argues that, at least in some cases, it would be similarly unproblematic for an organization to fail to accommodate the wishes of those who are opposed to the use of neurointerventions.

However, this is not the case for all neurointerventions. According to Erler, there are considerations (e.g., relating to the safety of neuroenhancements) that might count against making it permissible for employers to require their use by employees. Erler's overall conclusion is that the prospect of a "new normal" that results from widespread use of neuroenhancements in the workplace should not of itself give rise to moral concerns so long as the pressure to enhance is derived from indirect coercion rather than more direct forms of coercion in which, for example, the enhancement obligation is a condition of an employment contract. Erler's analysis has a regulatory upshot: there are no grounds for legal intervention *merely* to avoid the arrival of a new normal. Rather, regulation should aim to avert some of the pitfalls that Erler identifies (such as safety issues).

Erler's philosophical work might thus be thought to offer some useful guidance to those who are engaged in law reform. Referring back to the title of this section, the way that the law regulates and responds to people's (including perhaps those of a corporate nature as is the way with many employers) use of neurointerventions should pay careful attention to the precise nature of the neurointervention and should be wary of any tendency to lump categories of neurointerventions together that do not belong together. Perhaps the issue of defining neurointerventions that we have already averted to in this chapter might also support Erler's prescription for the law to examine the specifics of any neurointerventions. A broadly based definition of *neurointervention* in a piece of employment legislation or in case law might bring more of its fair share of confusion in subsequent development of the law as well as possibly subsuming the problematic and unproblematic into the same class.

Patrick Hopkins and Harvey Fiser's chapter also engages with issues relating to neurointerventions and employment, but it does so with a more pronounced legal orientation. Hopkins and Fiser rightly point out that much of the neurolaw scholarship has thus far engaged with neurointerventions in the context of the criminal justice system. However, many more people are affected by employment issues than criminal justice issues, and if neurointerventions have implications in the domain of employment (as they do), there is good reason to engage in more consideration of that context. Hopkins and Fiser note the many and competing ways that neurointerventions might be of interest to the stakeholders in employment relationships. These range from verifying potential employees' abilities, to the enhancement of the abilities of employees, and the monitoring of work. These and other issues may be a concern for employers, employees, and those who create and enforce the relevant laws. In setting out their analysis, Hopkins and Fiser are always mindful of the comparison between business law—more specifically, employment law—and the criminal justice context, and they provide an analysis of the way that the regulation of antisocial conduct by criminal justice systems is different from the regulation of employment relations, both generally and with reference to the specific context of neurointerventions.

One thing that emerges from the chapter is that a key difference between the criminal law and business law contexts relates to contractual agreement. In business law, a key question (and one that bears some relationship to some of the issues in Erler's chapter) is the question of what limits should be placed on an individual's ability to voluntarily engage in contracts with employers. However, one does not generally voluntarily and explicitly agree to be bound by the criminal law—one simply finds oneself subject to obligations under it. It is the contractual question—that of the proper limits of what employees can contract to—that those who are concerned with neurointerventions in the workplace will need to substantially engage with.

Hopkins and Fiser use a striking hypothetical example to illustrate some of the differences between the criminal law context and that of employment law. They use the example of implantable contact lenses, which involve the implantation of a lens into the retina, which they note to be generally thought of as part of the brain. They claim that such implantable contact lenses could potentially monitor blood alcohol levels, track movement, or even record that which is seen by the person who has the implants. Hopkins and Fiser explain that as such implants go into the retina, which is part of the brain, it could be thought of as a neurointervention, and they argue that one should not be too rigid in classifying what counts as a neurointervention thereby contributing to the somewhat persistent definitional concern that we highlighted above.

The workplace issues highlighted both by Erler and by Hopkins and Fiser suggest that neurointerventions may generate work for those engaged in employment law (in law schools, business schools, and legal practice). And in light of the significance of employment in many people's lives, there may be a need for scholars to attend to neurointervention issues when it comes to the preparedness for the emergence of litigation or debates about law reform.

While the topics of employment law and business law are underrepresented in published research on neurolaw scholarship—in particular that scholarship that focuses on the topic of neurointerventions—the law has and will need to respond to the antisocial conduct of those who are affected by or even act via some form of neurointervention. In what now follows, we examine possible scenarios in which various neurotechnologies play a role in the commission, or prevention, of offenses.

Neurotechnologies have a variety of purposes that range from intervening on the mental states of the person whose brain is interfaced with the technology (e.g., in DBS) to allowing control of external devices (perhaps controlling a cursor on a screen) without the need for a bodily action as traditionally conceived (such as using a mouse to control the cursor by way of movement of one's hand). Also, perhaps one day storing memories in a digital form rather than in the organic substrate of the brain that memories are currently stored in our brains (hippocampal prosthetics) might become a reality. Neurotechnologies might thus be used for prosthetic or enhancement purposes.

A day may come (if it has not come already) in which some form of neurotechnology plays a role in the commission of a crime. Upon the commission and subsequent detection of such crimes, courts will need to consider how to respond. In some such cases the actus reus component of the crime will have involved the perpetrator acting by way of a BCI, instead of engaging in a bodily action as traditionally conceived, and this will raise important issues for criminal liability. For instance, the defendant might argue that the device malfunctioned and that this is what led them to behave in a manner that is prohibited by the criminal law. Should this give rise to an argument for exculpation based on such a malfunction? Even if the BCI didn't malfunction, is there any reason to believe that a defendant is not criminally responsible for what has happened because one of the elements of criminal responsibility was not present? How should the law respond where a neurotechnological failure has led to the agent forgetting to do something that they were obliged to do under the criminal law?

In his chapter, Allan McCay examines questions of criminal liability in contexts where BCIs are involved. Using the example of an abusive online behavior that has come to be known colloquially as "revenge porn," together with an actual piece of legislation that criminalizes such conduct, McCay crafts a hypothetical scenario in which a person commits a revenge porn offense by way of BCI ("neurobionic revenge porn"). Reflection on the neurobionic revenge porn hypothetical scenario leads McCay to argue that although under this legislation a defendant *could* be convicted of the respective offense, courts would still face a very challenging question related to the actus reus component of this offense. Namely, in the absence of an overt physical bodily movement in this BCI-mediated offense, what precisely should be identified as the conduct that constitutes the actus reus—a component that would normally have an overt bodily manifestation in criminal offenses?

Should conduct constituting the actus reus be taken by the courts to be a mental act? Could the neural activity associated with a mental act be thought of as the relevant conduct? Could it be the flow of electrical signal into the BCI? Or some combination of the aforementioned? After canvassing various options that courts might pursue, McCay argues that none of these sit entirely comfortably within the body of criminal law that has developed over the centuries. In this way, McCay proposes, BCI-mediated criminal offenses present a truly novel challenge for a fundamental element of criminal law doctrine—that of how actus reus should be conceptualized.

McCay's analysis is to some extent a traditional legal analysis as it considers a specified set of facts (those from the hypothetical) in the context of an actual piece of legislation. However, as the chapter proceeds, the novelty of the technology and the strangeness of the options for response that are available to the courts lead him to engage with ideas that are more commonly discussed by philosophers than in legal practitioners. By contrast, in his chapter, Walter Glannon has a more substantial engagement with the philosophical literature, and while McCay's analysis is restricted to functioning BCIs, Glannon considers both functioning and malfunctioning BCIs, which he argues raise a range of important questions pertaining to defenses and thus to exculpation. Unlike McCay's specific focus on the actus reus element of criminal offenses, Glannon's focus is both wider ranging and more theoretically orientated, his aim being to challenge a commonly held view that forms of brain manipulation always necessarily undermine responsibility. To prosecute his argument, Glannon uses examples of neurotechnologies (e.g., deep brain stimulation, BCIs for controlling external devices, and hippocampal prosthetics used to artificially store memories) to show that notwithstanding the fact that they are significant interventions on the brain, they do not necessarily diminish the control of the agent whose action is influenced or mediated by the technology. In the course of his analysis, Glannon observes challenges to notions that are important to the criminal law, including issues that have some relationship to those raised by McCay, but also others that go beyond McCay's narrow concerns with actus reus. In light of this, Glannon calls for a more general reconsideration of the criteria for criminal responsibility.

While the kind of devices that McCay considers are already available, some sections of Glannon's work peer further into the future. Hippocampal prosthetics may one day be developed that generate questions about responsibility for omissions. Even though the criminal law often aims to prevent criminal acts, it also sometimes aims to punish failures to act (where there is a duty to act).

Thus, for example, where a doctor is grossly negligent in failing to engage in some treatment, perhaps by forgetting it needed to be done, and her failure leads to the death of her patient, in some jurisdictions she might be found guilty of manslaughter by criminal negligence (or in others, some similar offense). But what if a malfunction in a hippocampal prosthetic led to the failure to remember? According to Glannon, question about liability depends on whether the prosthetic failed to retrieve or encode the memory, the latter providing a more persuasive case for exculpation.

The work by both McCay and Glannon generates questions about the boundaries of what might constitute a neurointervention. To take the example of a BCI that is used to control an external device (which features in both chapters) one might note that this seems very different in kind from a performance-enhancing drug used in the workplace. Irrespective of whether such control devices are regarded as core cases of neurointerventions or penumbral forms, they seem to generate legal questions to which the courts will need to respond moving forward.

In their chapter, Frederic Gilbert and Susan Dodds raise the possibility of a form of neurotechnology that could intervene to prevent criminal conduct. While they focus primarily on the prevention of recidivism, one can imagine a variety of situations where such neurotechnology might one day be used. A person might be concerned that they may commit an offense and voluntarily decide to make use of such a preventative device. Or after committing an offense it seems possible that a person might reflect on their bad behavior, and approach their sentencing having had the neurotechnology implanted or otherwise fitted. Perhaps a community protection-minded judge might even order that an offender, or person thought likely to offend in the future, make use of this kind of preventative neurotechnology if the legal sources permitted the making of such an order.

Gilbert and Dodds note that such a preventative device could detect brain states that may be precursors to antisocial conduct and then either *warn* the agent so they can take preventative action such as leaving the situation or *automatically* intervene on the brain by way of a therapeutic response to prevent the undesirable conduct. They argue that the former advisory system could increase the agent's autonomy, but where the neurotechnology initiates the latter automatic therapeutic response and it has been coercively or involuntarily implanted in the offender by authority of the state, this would result in a diminution of autonomy. Thus, for Gilbert and Dodds, automated intervention presents greater concerns than advisory systems. Consequently, although advisory systems might be less effective in preventing violent behavior, they have greater value in virtue of enhancing autonomy. On account of this, Gilbert and Dodds argue that the state should wherever possible avoid authorizing the implantation of devices that carry out such automated interventions and only authorize their implantation in the most extreme circumstances.

Gilbert and Dodds thus join McCay and Glannon in expanding debates about neurointerventions and the criminal law to include neurotechnology. However, Gilbert and Dodds envisage a neurotechnological device that may detect the need to intervene and then to automatically administer a therapeutic response such as medication or electrical stimulation or, in the morally preferable circumstance, may keep the agent who might commit a criminal offense in the loop, perhaps by advising them to take some medication or to leave a volatile situation.

In respect to both the advisory and automated systems, Gilbert and Dodds conceive of an artificially intelligent system that interfaces with the brain and detects the need for intervention (based on patterns of neural activity) to prevent crime. As previously noted, one possibility is that the person who might offend is out of the loop (in the case of automated response). However, it is interesting to note that in both the automated and advisory systems, *the neurointervener* is out of the loop in the immediate decision about whether to issue advice, deliver medication, or engage in brain stimulation. That "decision" is left to an artificially intelligent system that interfaces with the brain of the person concerned.

Perhaps future scholarship might consider the way that debates about neurointerventions may connect up with discussions about the proper role of artificial intelligence in criminal justice systems of the future. As has just been noted, there are a variety of ways or paths that might lead a person to make use of neurotechnology that might prevent recidivism and one of them comes through an order of a judge. This possibility transitions nicely to the next section, which considers yet more ways in which neurointerventions might one day be, or have already been, made use of by the law.

The Law's Use of Neurointerventions

In addition to *regulating* the use of neurointerventions, the law also *employs* neurointerventions to alter human minds. For instance, in some jurisdictions antipsychotic medications are administered to mentally ill criminal defendants to make them fit to stand trial or to be executed. Similarly, convicted sex offenders must sometimes submit themselves to regimes of treatment with testosterone-blocking medications to diminish their sex drive as a condition of their safe release back into society. Even people who have not committed criminal offenses may in some circumstances face legal consequences if they fail to take psychotropic medications. For instance, individuals diagnosed with conditions like epilepsy, diabetes, or schizophrenia may expose themselves or others to unacceptable risks if they engage in certain activities, or more generally go about their lives unmedicated. For this reason, society reserves the right to civilly commit and forcibly medicate people deemed to pose dangers that are sufficiently serious. In this section, we discuss some of the ways in which neurointerventions may (or may not) be used within the law to achieve its own purposes. So, in what follows, we might learn about what the law's aims are by looking at what effects it is hoping to achieve by medicating someone in a given legal context and whether the use of neurointerventions (even if they could be assumed to be effective) can be justified on moral, legal, and political grounds.

One immediate issue that arises when it comes to whether or not neurointerventions ought to be used for the purposes of the law is what the public thinks about these neurointerventions. After all, while the law need not be beholden to public opinion, at least in democratic societies and perhaps to some extent even authoritarian regimes, the citizenry's ordinary attitudes, beliefs, and behavior serve as feasibility constraints on the implementation of certain legal policies and practices. It is for this reason that Thomas Nadelhoffer, Jen Wright, Daniela Goya Tocchetto, and Quinn McGuire investigate American lay people's judgments about the law's use of neurointerventions. After all, as they point out, the criminal law could (and in some cases does) avail itself of a range of different methods for changing people's minds (e.g., psychotherapy vs. brain surgery). The criminal law may do these things to achieve a variety of different aims. For instance, the goal might be to reduce the risk that dangerous offenders pose to society, other inmates, or themselves; to help convicted offenders to reform; to restore defendants' competence for trial or punishment; or to reduce racial bias in judges and juries. However, in doing any of these (and potentially other) things, Nadelhoffer and colleagues think that the law should not step too far out of line with common-sense intuitions (although it need not be a slave to those intuitions). For instance, if the law steps out of line with common-sense intuitions about issues such as the severity of punishments that it inflicts or the people onto whom it inflicts them, then this might breach the common legal prohibition against cruel and unusual punishment in both domestic and international law. Similarly, procedural guidelines and human rights might require that certain ways of changing people's minds (e.g., very painful or medically risky ones, or perhaps ones that are very invasive) are not permitted. The thought here is not that common-sense folk morality should be the only guide to what the law does and does not do, but that it might at least provide some constraints or guides to what should and should not be done given people's beliefs and attitudes.

Across three vignette-based online studies, Nadelhoffer and colleagues probed lay people's intuitions about issues related to neurointerventions, and what they found was often a startling lack of convergence between lay intuitions, philosophical views, and legal standards and practices. First, study participants were generally not that concerned about just how invasive a technique was (i.e., therapy vs. medications vs. brain implants) nor about its potential side effects (i.e., adverse vs. low). Second, the only purpose for which they seemed willing to grant the state authority to forcibly medicate convicted offenders (and only them) was to reduce violent impulsivity. The prospect of making convicted offenders more prosocial or of requiring nonoffenders like judges or juries to control their racial bias through the use of any techniques was seen as beyond the state's authority. Furthermore, study participants were generally ambivalent about the state's authority to forcibly restore competence to either be punished or to stand trial. In short, by highlighting places where public opinion and legal practices converge and diverge, these studies provide important grist for the mill for current debates about what mental competencies are needed for different contexts and whether, how, and when these competencies can be altered for legal purposes.

The main issue highlighted by Nadelhoffer and colleagues is whether and when neurointerventions should be used for legal purposes, which ties directly into several of the chapters in the volume that explore the use of neurointerventions for the purposes of the criminal law. For instance, in their chapter, Andrew Dawson, Jennifer Chandler, Colin Gavaghan, Wayne Hall, and Adrian Carter explore the role that neuropsychiatric evidence does and should play as a potential mitigating factor in sentencing. The two cases Dawson and colleagues focus on are (a) drug- and gambling-addicted offenders and (b) offenders prescribed dopaminergic medication for a movement disorder. Their goal throughout is to explore the current legal state of play when it comes to neuropsychiatric evidence in these types of cases, with a focus on whether such evidence should be considered a mitigating factor. In light of their research, Dawson and colleagues suggest that neuropsychiatric evidence—and the medical model of disease that underlies it—has "not been widely or consistently used as a mitigating factor in the sentencing of drug- or gambling-addicted individuals who have committed a criminal offense related to their addiction" (2020, p. 234). Instead, it is more common for jurists to be guided by the moral model of addiction, whereby drug addicted offenders are responsible for both their addiction and for any actions influenced by their addiction. The other class of offenders considered by Dawson and colleagues is offenders who (a) suffer from Parkinson disease and (b) who subsequently develop addictive behaviors like pathological gambling, hypersexuality, and addiction after taking dopamine agonists such as pramipexole, ropinirole, and pergolide. In this context, the evidence is mixed. It appears that judges are more willing to take this type of neuropsychiatric evidence to be mitigating.

One obvious difference between the two cases is that alcoholics and drug addicts are responsible for their condition in a way that people with Parkinson disease are not. Presumably, this partly explains why judges are inclined to treat the two cases differently. It is easier to motivate the medical model in the case of Parkinson disease and harder to motivate the moral model, which in turn helps explain the differential treatment of garden-variety addictions and compulsions and therapeutically induced addictions and compulsions. As Dawson and colleagues point out, another difference is that in the case of therapeutically induced compulsions, it tempting for judges to conclude that the medication *compelled* or *coerced* the offender's behavior. But Dawson and colleagues suggest that this is a mistake. On their view, the mere fact that an offender's behavior was influenced or caused by a medication doesn't mean the offender was compelled to act as he did. Mere causation is not a proper legal excuse. As such, Dawson and colleagues think judges should be more, rather than less, critical when it comes to neuropsychiatric evidence introduced for the purposes of mitigation. Current practices are purportedly driven more by consequentialist theories of punishment than a sound understanding of the evidence itself—evidence that is more tenuously tied to criminal responsibility than some jurists and theorists assume.

While Dawson and colleagues focus on the role that neuropsychiatric *evidence* should play when it comes to *sentencing*, they do not explore the legal *use* of neurointerventions for the purposes of *changing behavior*. This is a related topic that several contributors addressed in their respective chapters. For instance, in his chapter, William Bülow explores whether prison inmates who suffer from ADHD should receive a psychopharmacological intervention like methylphenidate for their condition. Bülow views this issue through the lens of a communicative theory of punishment—that is, a view that might be interpreted as justifying punishment in terms of the positive consequences it brings about such as rehabilitation. On this approach, medicating inmates with ADHD is a way of facilitating the communicative function of the law by maximizing the likelihood that they repent for their behavior, reconcile with those they've harmed, and embark on a process of moral reformation. Neurointerventions like methylphenidate help facilitate these ends of punishment by helping to address the neurophysiological deficits that make it difficult for some inmates to both repent and start the process of self-reformation. Given that these are important ends of punishment—at least on a communicative view—then making it more likely inmates will achieve these ends is an important function that neurointerventions can play in the law. As such, Bülow believes that if neurointerventions can help achieve the ends of the law, then they should be available on a voluntary basis. On his view, using neurointerventions to facilitate these penological ends does not render the achievement of these ends any less authentic. The changes can be real even if the methods used to assist these changes to come about are artificial in some sense. The important thing is the end result. So long as voluntary neurointerventions help bring about the right kinds of penological consequences (e.g., penance, reformation, and reconciliation) they are justified. To the extent that these interventions help inmates maximize their potential, Bülow suggests that the law ought to embrace their use.

However, it is important to reckon with the possibility that a particular neurointervention may not achieve the end that it is intended to achieve. In his chapter, Christopher Ryan explores the ethical implications of prescribing antiandrogens (also known as "androgen depletion treatment," "antilibidinal treatment," or, more colloquially, "chemical castration") to sex offenders in an effort to increase their ability to control their impulses and hence reduce the likelihood of recidivism. The two most common of these neurointerventions are cyproterone acetate (marketed as Androcur and Cyprostat) and medroxyprogesterone acetate (marketed as Provera), although there are several other drugs used for similar purposes. The key question Ryan addresses is, Should the law facilitate the voluntary use of these types of antilibidinal neurointerventions by sex offenders? He suggests that answering this question depends on several empirical issues; for example, do antiandrogens actually decrease recidivism in sex offenders, what are the side effects, and do the benefits of using antiandrogens for the purposes of reducing recidivism outweigh potential costs?

On Ryan's view, these empirical issues should be at the forefront of the debate about the legal uses of antiandrogens. However, he suggests they do not receive the attention they deserve in the philosophical, legal, and clinical literature. Instead, scholars tend to simply assume (based on intuition and insufficient evidence) the efficacy of antiandrogens and assume that cost–benefit analysis supports their use. According to Ryan, neither assumption is self-evident. Indeed, on the contrary, Ryan suggests that the empirical data call both assumptions into question, thereby problematizing the legal use of antiandrogens. As he points out, several meta-analyses and systematic reviews suggest that the alleged efficacy of antiandrogens for reducing recidivism in sex offenders has been overstated. Consequently, Ryan closely examines the six studies that are often appealed to in justifying using hormonal therapy in sex offenders, and he shows that each is methodologically flawed, which thereby undermines the empirical support for our current practices involving antiandrogens. This is especially problematic given the well-known negative side effects of this neurointervention; for example, "effects on bone mineral density and fracture risk, effects on glucose and lipid metabolism, and a variety of miscellaneous other ill-effects" (2020, p. 286). Given both the side effect profile of antilibidinal therapy and the lack of solid evidence that it reduces recidivism in sex offenders, Ryan thinks our current practices lack support. Not because there is solid evidence that these practices do not work, but because there is a lack of solid evidence to warrant us in proceeding on the assumption that they do work.

Ryan's chapter on the problems associated with the practice of using antiandrogens for the purposes of the law is directly related to the chapter by Katrina Sifferd on whether the practice can be justified in terms of the traditional justifications for punishment. Rather than looking at the efficacy and effectiveness of antiandrogens, which is Ryan's focus, Sifferd looks at the issue of chemical castration throughs the lens of the philosophy of punishment. On her view, neurointerventions involving antiandrogens do not serve the common ends of retribution, deterrence, or incapacitation (albeit for different reasons in each case). Sifferd nevertheless thinks that antilibidinal therapy could, in principle, serve rehabilitative ends, just not given the way it is currently implemented in the criminal justice system. As things stand, she thinks that chemical castration is used too broadly. However, Sifferd thinks that the state could be justified in using neurointerventions on sex offenders for rehabilitative purposes so long as these treatments target the specific psychological states that led to the offense and where these states raise legitimate concerns concerning recidivism. Because current uses of antiandrogens don't satisfy these two narrow criteria, Sifferd finds our reliance on these neurointerventions to be problematic. Sifferd suggests instead that our response to sex offenders should follow the approach taken by the highly successful drug courts (another diversion court, just like Valerie Hardcastle discusses) where we assess whether a disorder is present in the defendant, whether the disorder caused the defendant's behavior, and whether the disorder is treatable. Only when these conditions are satisfied, can chemical castration be justified.

Both Ryan and Sifferd address using neurointerventions for the purposes of restoring moral competency to sex offenders, an issue that is explored more broadly by Paul Sheldon Davies in his chapter. On his view, one aim of neurointerventions used within a criminal law context is to make people fully responsible (again)—that is, to make it such that they have the right mental competencies to be fully responsible moral agents. However, Davies argues that our folk psychological views about what mental competencies are required in this context are at best inaccurate and at worst they are simply a fiction. Davies cites work on the global workspace model of consciousness, studies of children with anancephalia, and other relevant studies to demonstrate several pertinent discrepancies in the folk psychological model presupposed by much responsibility theory and what we are actually like. For instance, first, the things that rise to our consciousness often fail to capture important features of what we ought to know to be fully responsible. Second, this is a straightforward consequence of the human brain's architecture, the way that we're wired. Third, the way we reason and what moves us to actions is often swayed or even determined by affective processes that have little relevance to what ought to sway and determine our actions. And finally, there is little we can do to address these and many other things, and so it's not even the case that we are negligent for failing to improve our epistemic and cognitive position.

Consequently, on Davies's account, as long as we keep trying to restore the competencies exalted by common sense, we will not even stand a chance of achieving this aim of neurointervention—that is, of making people responsible (again)—because those are not the competencies required for responsiblility. Davies thinks that we currently have insufficient knowledge of what actual capacities or competencies are required, which is why what we first need to do is study ourselves more carefully to learn what actually drives moral and immoral behavior. On his view, unless and until we acquire this knowledge, we cannot possibly know which neurointerventions we would be warranted in using to restore moral competency.

For instance, when the law treats condemned insane inmates with antipsychotic medications to make them sane enough to stand trial or for execution, what empirical evidence is there that the medications actually work? Come to think of it, what is it precisely that the law even hopes those medications will achieve? What mental capacities are these neurointerventions intended to restore, and why must defendants who stand trial and inmates who are about to be executed possess those mental capacities? And how does all this illuminate what a fair trial aims at and the aims that punishment are meant to promote? Similarly, recent studies on aggression suggest that certain psychotropic medications (e.g., selective serotonin reuptake inhibitors) may damp down offenders' aggression and in this way help them to control their aggressive impulses. And, as discussed earlier, for a long time now antiandrogens have been prescribed to convicted sex offenders to dampen their sexual appetites. But in these latter two cases, how does the law know when someone's moral competency has been adequately restored? What is the appropriate baseline? How would the law know whether a neurointervention has worked or whether its benefits outweigh its associated costs?

Davies's primary point is that we need a better understanding of the core competencies that undergird moral competency and responsibility before we will be in a position to know whether the benefits associated with a particular neurointervention outweigh any potential costs. In this respect the theme of his chapter runs through all of the chapters we have discussed in this section. Whether we are going to use neurointerventions to treat ADHD, sexual impulsivity, antisocial behavior, or other legally relevant disorders and behaviors, we need to first have a firm sense of what we take to be the foundational cognitive, affective, and volitional capacities required for acceptable behavior. We also need a firm understanding of the costs and benefits associated with the types of neurointerventions that are used to make it more likely that people will conform their behavior to the mandates of the law. For even if a particular neurointervention is effective in improving behavior and reducing recidivism, it may nevertheless be problematic to use it for legal purposes. Figuring out whether a particular neurointervention is problematic is partly an empirical issue and partly a theoretical issue, but that is not all. To tie this back to where this section began, knowing how judges, juries, and the public are likely to view neurointerventions will be another important factor in calculating the relevant cost–benefit analyses and figuring out whether a particular neurointervention is, on the balance, fit for legal use. In this respect, moral and legal philosophy, science, and public opinion all play an important role when it comes to utilizing neurointerventions for the purposes of the law.

Radical Change or More of the Same?

As we have seen, the law regulates neurointerventions, and it also regulates human mental capacity through the use of neurointerventions. And the chapters in this volume investigate scientific, medical, social, legal, moral, and conceptual issues that arise from these practices. One question that immediately arises in this context is whether it is time for the law to undergo a major change. While some scholars suggest that a revolution is already underway (or at least should be), others think that the traditional orientation of the law is on firm theoretical and normative footing. Whether one thinks that a legal revolution or the status quo (or something in between) is merited will depend on one's background assumptions about the nature and purpose of the law. Neurointerventions help highlight these issues by potentially putting pressure of some of our traditional beliefs and practices.

On one reading of the contributions to this volume, what is needed is a radical rethink or at least a fundamental reappraisal of the law. However, in her chapter, Valerie Hardcastle develops an analysis of the common trend of creating diversionary courts—youth courts, drug courts, and, in the case of her chapter, American war veterans' courts—which suggests that more minor and incremental change may instead be in order. On her view, these alternative courts, which cater to ever more specific subpopulations of the broad category "criminal offender," suggest that piecemeal change is already happening and that the law is already slowly moving in a better direction. According to Hardcastle, what is needed is more incremental reform around the margins, not radical changes that affect the procedures, structures, and purposes of the law more globally.

For instance, Hardcastle points out that in recent years, returning American war veterans who commit criminal offenses have been offered the option "to enter mental health treatment programs for infractions, instead of jailing them"

(2020, p. 159). A justification for this practice is the recognition that war veterans, as a subcategory of all criminal offenders, have a disproportionately high incidence of brain injuries (acquired in combat) and that these injuries appear to be causally implicated in their higher incidence of criminal offending. The thought, presumably, is to recognize the high likelihood that their criminal conduct is caused by their brain injuries and to offer them treatments for those brain injuries rather than punishing them for their misconduct. A similar thought also motivates the creation of diversionary courts that cater to other subcategories of criminal offenders. For instance, the view that young offenders are not yet a lost cause—that reform and perhaps even redemption is still within their reach since they are, after all, still in the process of being formed—leads a significant number of criminal justice systems to funnel them into special tribunals and youth courts designed to divert them away from a criminal process designed primarily to punish.

However, Hardcastle asks, what makes us think that we are justified in differentiating "returning combat vet[eran]s with [traumatic brain injury] or with other mind/brain disorders from other offenders" (2020, p. 150)? Can this differential treatment of criminal offenders, based as it is on their occupation or social category, really be justified? Presumably, everybody's actions are caused, but that hardly leads us to divert everyone away from the criminal justice system and to offer everyone medical treatment rather than punishment. Hardcastle conjectures that because we (society, courts) do not yet know how to handle the dissonance between the medical/scientific and the legal/moral views of the springs of human behavior (including criminal conduct), we are instead tackling this problem through the sideways move of siphoning off categories of defendants into diversion courts and then offering them treatments instead of just imprisoning them. However, this does not tackle the dissonance but merely ignores it, since if anyone is offered a diversionary path and treatment, then why not admit that this should be offered to everyone? It surely can't be adequate to hide behind the fact that we can't yet diagnose all causes nor offer medical treatments for them, since those are only epistemic and practical shortcomings of ours, not anything to do with defendants.

One way to understand Hardcastle's point is that in light of scientific discoveries (what is now known) and technological advances (what can now be done), institutional responses to crime are slowly and in a few isolated pockets becoming more sophisticated and morally appropriate—closer to the ideal end-point in virtue of being more justifiable, more correct in various ways (e.g., pragmatically, morally, legally, and conceptually). She writes that "[w]e believe that we can provide a 'neurointervention' of some sort that will transform the criminal into a law-abiding citizen[, and so] we divert them into forced treatment" (2020, p. 163). This reading of Hardcastle is suggested by her citing the "wide acknowledgment that the war on drugs and mandatory sentencing were misguided failures" and her claim that the shift toward individualized sentencing reflects that "we know better now what individual differences are relevant" (2020, p. 163).

However, we suspect that this reading undersells and underappreciates the historical element of Hardcastle's analysis. On our view, a useful way to understand what Hardcastle is also doing is as follows: What we are seeing is *not* a radical departure from an incumbent conventional morality (a wholescale revolution, the product of our modern enlightenment), the abandonment of retributive foundations in criminal justice, and their replacement with insurgent reformative, rehabilitative, or some other possibly incommensurable principles that support aims that can only be counterweighed against the aims of the incumbent principles. Rather, this is merely the latest iteration of an ongoing process in which the criminal justice system, in light of developments in science and technology and in response to sociopolitical pressures and changes, attempts to reassess how to define and respond to "crime."

Moreover, given the occurrence of crime, society has to decide what institutional responses it wishes to deploy and for what purpose it wishes to deploy them and perhaps even to reassess the very role of the criminal justice system itself. On this reading, the increasing number of diversionary courts (and their often radically different procedures) is part of an iterative and ongoing process through which the criminal justice system helps society to figure out what the law might want to do given what is now known and what can be done and to help society reassess what things it values (e.g., safety, liberty, retribution, compensation, distributive justice, rehabilitation, reform, or just helping the guilty to rejoin society as productive members of the community). If this is right, then neurointerventions should not be viewed (and used) as tools for the purpose of engendering a radical legal revolution. Instead, neurointerventions are more properly viewed (and used) as tools for assisting the law in making the incremental changes that have always been an integral part of how the law slowly makes progress, step by step.

Human Malleability and Synthetic Jurisprudence

The preceding sections discussed the upshots that the use of neurointerventions—by people in society and by agents of the law—might have for the law. However, at a conceptual level, it is also fruitful to explore the law through the lens of neurointerventions. Neurointerventions turn what may have seemed like constants—immutable background features of situations that set the stage on which our thinking must take place—into yet further variables for us to take into account. Put another way, reflection on legal and moral problems within the context of neurointerventions offers a prized opportunity to reveal hidden assumptions that have implicitly informed our theorizing—assumptions about the human condition so ubiquitous that we may not even have noticed them or their impact on our thinking. In this way, viewing the law through the lens of neurointerventions provides a novel methodology for testing existing moral and jurisprudential theory by uncovering factors of which we were unaware, that have the potential to sway our intuitions in ways we may not reflectively endorse.

By looking closely at neurointerventions, we get a valuable opportunity to see how hitherto-unexplicated presuppositions about the nature of human subjects—for example, that we feel pain, that we cannot alter some things about ourselves such as our sexuality and our conscience, and that we act in the world by moving our bodies—influence a range of our intuitions that inform our thinking in philosophy of law and jurisprudence. As a methodology, this is useful because it enables us to tease apart truly *analytic* jurisprudential claims from what might be called *synthetic* jurisprudential claims—that is, those that are ultimately contingent on what humans happen to currently be like. It is also useful practically, because to the extent that the law aims to regulate human behavior, it must pay close attention to what human nature is like. But in a world in which human nature becomes malleable, these features can no longer be taken for granted.

In this way, neurointerventions have a bidirectional relationship with the law. On the one hand, the law influences how we think about and interact with neurointerventions. Here the law can both facilitate and constrain our relationship with current and future techniques for manipulating behavior by manipulating the brain. Whether it's deep brain stimulation or chemical castration, the law has an integral role to play in defining our relationship with these technologies. On the other hand, neurointerventions provide us with the opportunity to redefine ourselves, which in turn provides us with the opportunity to reconsider some of the fundamental concepts that have traditionally served as the bedrock of the law. After all, at the end of the day, even if it has some other aims, the law is certainly a tool for influencing human behavior in prosocial ways. Given that neurointerventions hold out the promise to shape human behavior in hitherto unforeseen ways, they hold out the promise of remaking various features of the law. It is precisely this important interplay between neurointerventions and the law that motivated us to put together the present volume—a volume that we hope sheds interesting new light on both phenomena (and in both directions).

References

Bublitz, J. C., & Merkel, R. (2014). Crimes against minds: On mental manipulations, harms and a human right to mental self-determination. *Criminal Law and Philosophy*, *8*, 51–77.

Caspi, A., McClay, J., Moffitt, T. E., Mill, J., Martin, J., Craig, I. W., . . . Poulton, R. 2002. Role of genotype in the cycle of violence in maltreated children. *Science*, *297*, 851–854.

Dawson, A., Chandler, J., Gavaghan, C., Hall, W., & Carter, A. (2020). Judicious Use of Neuropsychiatric Evidence When Sentencing Offenders With Addictive Behaviors. In N.A Vincent, T. Nadelhoffer & A. McCay (Eds.), *Neurointerventions and the Law: Regulating Human Mental Capacity* (pp. 233–253). New York, NY, USA: Oxford University Press.

Glenn, A. L, & Raine, A. (2014). Neurocriminology: Implications for the punishment, prediction, and prevention of criminal behavior. *Nature Reviews Neuroscience*, *15*(1), 54–63.

Greene, J., & J. Cohen. (2004). For the law, neuroscience changes nothing and everything. *Philosophical Transactions of the Royal Society, B: Biological Sciences*, *359*, 1775–1785.

Hardcastle, V. G. (2020). Diversion Courts, Traumatic Brain Injury, and American Vets. In N.A Vincent, T. Nadelhoffer & A. McCay (Eds.), *Neurointerventions and the Law: Regulating Human Mental Capacity* (pp. 150–169). New York, NY, USA: Oxford University Press.

Hodgson, D. (2000). Guilty mind or guilty brain? Criminal responsibility in the age of neuroscience. *Australian Law Journal*, *74*, 661–680.

Levy, N. (2007). *Neuroethics. Challenges for the 21st century*. Cambridge, England: Cambridge University Press.

Levy, N. (2020). Cognitive Enhancement: Defending the Parity Principle. In N.A Vincent, T. Nadelhoffer & A. McCay (Eds.), *Neurointerventions and the Law: Regulating Human Mental Capacity* (pp. 233–253). New York, NY, USA: Oxford University Press.

Moore, M. (2014). Compatibilism(s) for neuroscientists. In E. Villanueva (Ed.), *Law and the philosophy of action* (pp. 1–59). Amsterdam, the Netherlands: Brill/Rodopi.

Morse, S. J. (2007). The non-problem of free will in forensic psychiatry and psychology. *Behavior Sciences and the Law*, *25*, 203–220.

Robinson, P. H., & Darley, J. M. (2004). Does criminal law deter? A behavioral science investigation. *Oxford Journal of Legal Studies*, *24*(2), 173–205.

Ryan, C. J. (2020). Is It *Really* Ethical to Prescribe Antiandrogens to Sex Offenders to Decrease Their Risk of Recidivism? In N.A Vincent, T. Nadelhoffer & A. McCay (Eds.), *Neurointerventions and the Law: Regulating Human Mental Capacity* (pp. 272–295). New York, NY, USA: Oxford University Press.

PART I

CONCEPTUAL, ETHICAL, AND JURISPRUDENTIAL ISSUES

2

Cognitive Enhancement

Defending the Parity Principle

Neil Levy

Introduction

In earlier work, I defended what I called the *parity principle* (Levy, 2007a, 2007b): the thesis that when we assess whether or not interventions into the mind are ethically problematic—and therefore ought to be banned, regulated, or judged inappropriate—we should ignore the question of the nature of the intervention (whether it is novel or familiar, invasive or noninvasive, high or low tech, targeting the brain directly or indirectly) and instead focus on its costs and benefits, broadly construed. Adopting the parity principle, I claimed, would lead to a dramatic rethinking of the debate over cognitive enhancements: some of the paradigm technologies we think of as enhancements would be seen to be innocuous, while some much more familiar practices would be seen as ethically worrisome.

In this chapter, I will sketch and defend the parity thesis once more, prior to turning to recent work by Jan Christoph Bublitz and Reinhard Merkel that argues for a conflicting view. Bublitz and Merkel (2014) argue that means matter morally, at least so far as techniques that enhance cognition are concerned. The kinds of technologies that people typically have in mind when they think about cognitive enhancement are *direct* interventions into the brain. These direct interventions into the brain are ethically much more problematic than indirect interventions, because they reduce the degree to which resulting thoughts and behavior are controlled by the person and expressive of who they genuinely are. I will argue that the direct/indirect distinction does not track an ethically worrisome/ethically benign distinction. It is not even a good heuristic, because far more injustice stems from indirect interventions than from direct, and this is not a situation that is likely to alter in the foreseeable future.

Neil Levy, *Cognitive Enhancement* In: *Neurointerventions and the Law.* Edited by: Nicole A Vincent, Thomas Nadelhoffer, and Allan McCay, Oxford University Press (2020). © Oxford University Press 2020
DOI: 10.1093/oso/9780190651145.001.0002

Cognitive Enhancement: A Case for Parity

The nature of the relationship between mind and brain is controversial. Some thinkers hold that the mind is identical to the brain; others deny this. But almost all serious thinkers today accept that the mind *supervenes* on the brain, or on the brain plus other, equally physical, stuff (whether that be the central nervous system or, for proponents of the extended mind thesis, pieces of paper, computers or tools). To say that the mind supervenes on the brain is to say that there are no mental differences without corresponding neural differences; every change of mind, every thought, every emotion, every piece of information processing is correlated with some corresponding event or process in the brain (those who hold that the mind supervenes on the brain plus something else might look outside the brain for the corresponding events and processes. For the moment, I will ignore extraneural correlates of thought for the sake of simplicity).

The fact that the mind supervenes on the brain entails that it is possible to alter aspects of cognition by changing the brain. There are many familiar examples: almost all of us have experienced some kind of alteration in mental functioning that is chemically induced, whether that be from alcohol, illegal psychoactive drugs or just the increase in mental alertness that stems from coffee drinking. More dramatically, brain injuries and lesions have predictable, sometimes devastating, effects on cognitive function. For instance, damage to the right inferior parietal cortex may produce hemiplegia (paralysis on one side of the body) together with anosognosia (denial of illness). In anosognosia, the person denies that they are paralyzed.

Since the mind depends on the brain, in a way these examples illustrate, it possible not only to induce deficits in cognition by altering the brain, but also to improve its functioning. As is the case with any complicated machine, it is much easier to damage the brain than to improve it. Anyone can take a hammer to a clock or a computer and impair its functioning, but improving its functioning requires specific tools and a great deal of expertise. Similarly, although we have long known how to produce deficits in cognition in the human mind, until very recently our powers to improve cognition using direct interventions into the brain have been limited to the side effects of substances consumed for recreational purposes (coffee, tea, kava, coca, etc.). Today, the number and variety of potentially cognition-enhancement substances is much greater.

Consider three examples:

1. Modafinil, a drug developed to promote wakefulness (mainly as a treatment for narcolepsy), has also been suggested as a possible cognitive enhancer (Turner, Clark, Dowson, Robbins, & Sahakian, 2004), and there is evidence that it already used by some scientists to this end. (Sahakian &

Morein-Zamir, 2007). Modafinil appears to enhance the ability to concentrate on a single task for a sustained period of time.

2. Methylphenidate, a drug used for the treatment of attention-deficit/hyperactivity disorder, appears to enhance spatial working memory in normal adults (Mehta et al., 2000). Working memory is closely related to what psychologists call fluid intelligence; increasing working memory capacity may have the effect of boosting general intelligence.

3. Transcranial direct current stimulation (tDCS), a technique in which low voltage electrical stimulation is applied by electrodes to the scalp, appears to make learning faster and more efficient (Kadosh, Soskic, Iuculano, Kanal, & Walsh, 2010). It thereby allows people who without it would be functioning at a normal level to function at even higher level, at least in one domain.

These are three paradigm cases of cognitive enhancement: new, apparently unprecedented, techniques of improving aspects of cognitive function by directly intervening into the brain. For many people, these techniques are far more worrisome than older methods of intervening into the mind (say, by teaching a student formal logic), even though these older methods also have the effect of improving aspects of cognitive function.

Note, however, that the fact that mind supervenes on brain entails that *some* kind of parity principle is true. Since the mind supervenes on the brain, any successful means of improving (or even just changing) any aspect of cognition must also change the brain. When someone learns formal logic, certain alterations occur in the brain; this learning is encoded or realized by changes in connections between neurons. Even reading this very paragraph alters the brain. Psychotherapy and antidepressants are both possible treatments for depression; both work, when they work, by changing the brain. Reasoned argument and the direct alteration of beliefs by altering wiring, should that ever become possible, would also both work by changing the brain. So why is the newer technology so much more controversial than the old? Is there is a fundamental difference between different kinds of interventions, and is that difference genuinely morally significant?

The Debate over Cognitive Enhancement

Many different arguments have been offered purporting to show that the newer technologies are more problematic than the old. In this section, I will briefly review some of the more influential arguments. I will claim that although some of them have some force, none of them provides even a prima facie case for thinking that the paradigm cognitive enhancements are more problematic than more familiar ways of changing the brain. Far from helping to constitute evidence against the parity principle, I will argue, these arguments strengthen it, when we think them through.

Authenticity

Some thinkers have worried that mental states produced by new technologies like tDCS or psychopharmaceuticals would not authentically belong to the person. As Carl Elliott (1998) has influentially written, "it would be worrying if Prozac altered my personality, even if it gave me a better personality, simply because it isn't *my* personality" (p. 182). The idea, roughly, is that the new personality would be alien to how I really am; a mask that falls over my face, obscuring its true nature, not an expression of my being. While the charge is more naturally made with regard to affective enhancements or alterations, it might carry over to cognitive enhancements too: I am not *really* the sharp-witted person I pass myself off as.

It is easy to think of cases in which the inauthenticity charge has bite. Suppose that I cannot sustain the outgoing sunny disposition Prozac® grants me. In such a case, there seem to be grounds for saying that while I act out of character—out of my previous and future character, that is—I act inauthentically. However, it is difficult to see why a permanent alteration, and especially an alteration in cognition, would count as inauthentic. Moreover, it is very difficult to see how certain uses of paradigm cognitive enhancements could conceivably count as inauthentic or as producing results that are inauthentic. Consider tDCS, which simply makes the process of learning somewhat more efficient. How could the fact that I have learned something somewhat more quickly than I would have without it, or that the acquired knowledge is somewhat easier to recall, cast doubt on the authenticity of the knowledge itself or of the agent?

Cheating

Many people have worried that the use of new cognitive enhancers might constitute cheating by users (see Schermer, 2008, for discussion). In some contexts, the worry is appropriate: if it is against the rules to use a technology in a competitive context, the person who gains an advantage through its use seems to be cheating. So if someone does better at an examination than other people, in significant part because they use modafinil or methylphenidate, they cheat. But this point does not get us very far. In particular, it does not answer the question whether the use of paradigm cognitive enhancers should be prohibited in the first place.

Perhaps it might be said that a deeper worry underlies the concern about cheating: whether or not methylphenidate (for instance) is prohibited, the user has an unfair advantage over nonusers (that fact might constitute a reason for banning the enhancement). The problem with this line of thought is that unfair advantages are completely ubiquitous. The capacity to concentrate is distributed across the population. This distribution reflects two things: (a) variation in genes involved in producing the systems deployed in concentration and (b) variation in training and other formative influences that also play a causal role in agents' capacities. Neither of these factors is responsive to desert; no one deserves better genes or a better upbringing. Methylphenidate would be one more source of unearned advantage and probably not an especially powerful one, compared to others.

Of course, it may be responded that the fact that there are already multiple sources of unearned advantage in the world is no reason to introduce one more. In response, I want to make two points. The first is simply to point out that not all goods are *positional* goods; that is, goods that get their value from the way they boost the status of the individual relative to others. Some goods are intrinsically valuable, and intelligence is very plausibly among them. Someone might choose to enhance aspects of their cognition due to the intrinsic value of being able to do better science or to have a better grasp of the world. Outside a competitive context, however, cheating and undeserved disadvantage are not charges that have an application. The second point I want to make in response must wait until I have outlined a third objection to the use of cognitive enhancement.

Inequality

A third reason to worry about cognitive enhancements is closely linked to the undeserved advantage worry. It is this: cognitive enhancements cost money and require other resources (time and knowledge). For that reason, these enhancements will be available preferentially to those who are already better off: the wealthier, the better informed, the more leisured. For that reason, they can be expected to increase the gap between rich and poor, within countries and between countries. Worse still, since cognitive enhancements can be expected to have financial payoffs, in terms of productivity and innovation, their use might create a vicious circle, in which the wealthier get ever wealthier and the poor fall further behind.

These concerns are worth taking seriously. Nevertheless, there is countervailing evidence suggesting that cognitive enhancements might help to reduce inequality, rather than produce it. At least with regard to existing psychopharmaceuticals, the benefits seem to be subject to a diminishing return: the better one's baseline cognitive capacities prior to their use, the smaller the benefit derived. For instance, while methylphenidate has been shown to enhance spatial working memory and sustained attention in healthy adults, the better the individual performed on working memory tasks prior to ingestion, the smaller the benefit to him or her (Mehta et al., 2000). There is evidence for a similar declining marginal utility of modafinil (Randall, Shneerson, & File, 2005). Moreover, cognitive enhancements may not be prohibitively expensive. If they bring genuine benefits, they may be made available by governments in the developed world and nongovernmental organizations in the developing. This is especially true with regard to tDCS: the apparatus may be built for less than $1,000 and then reused indefinitely, on many different people, making the per use cost negligible.

But there is another point worth making about inequality (and here I return to the question of unearned advantages as previously promised). Although there may be good reason to reject particular uses of cognitive enhancing technologies on the ground that they risk increasing the gap between the rich and the poor or because they provide yet another source of unearned advantage, these concerns are by no means unique to cognitive enhancers. Rather, if we should be concerned about inequality and unearned disadvantage (and we certainly should), we should be concerned about them no matter what their source. But the major sources of unearned inequality in the world today have nothing whatsoever to do with the paradigm cognitive enhancers; indeed, the major source of cognitive inequality in the world have nothing to do with these new technologies. Intelligence positively correlates with affluence. Higher socioeconomic status is already associated with higher intelligence (Hunt, 1995). Environmental enrichment, for instance, is already unequally distributed and causes predictable differences in cognitive capacity. Contemporary neuroscience is accumulating evidence that even within developed counties, socioeconomic status causes differences in intelligence and cognitive control (Hackman, Farah, & Meaney, 2010; Noble, McCandliss, & Farah, 2007). Much of these differences are due to differences in parenting and in the amount of stimulation given to infants (Farah et al., 2008). If we should be concerned about inequality and unearned disadvantage, there is no particular reason to be concerned about paradigm cognitive enhancers: they account for a tiny proportion of existing inequality and their contribution is likely to remain insignificant at very least for decades to come. We ought to be concerned with unearned inequality wherever we find it; to my mind, this fact powerfully supports the parity principle.

Objections to the Parity Principle

To this point, I have been reviewing the existing debate over cognitive enhancement and suggesting that the genuine worries that arise with regard to some cognitive enhancers arise much more powerfully with regard to more familiar practices and social arrangements; we ought, I contended, to be much more worried about these familiar sources of inequality than about attention-grabbing new technologies. I now want to consider a new and powerful argument against the parity principle.

Jan-Christoph Bublitz and Reinhard Merkel (2014) note that many of the new technologies that raise so much concern among neuroethicists apparently differ from more familiar techniques and practices in one central way: how *directly* they change the brain. Whereas tDCS changes the brain directly, by altering neuronal excitability, and Prozac® directly increases the amount of serotonin available at synapses, reasoned argument alters the state of the brain only by way of being processed by systems designed (by evolution) to respond to stimuli like this. They argue that the direct/indirect distinction not only maps onto the new technology/familiar practice distinction, it also gives us ethical guidance; direct interventions are ethically more problematic than indirect. Indirect interventions (by others) are normally permissible, while direct interventions are prima facie prohibited.

Bublitz and Merkel's (2014) main contention is that indirect interventions are distinctively different because they alone are *psychologically mediated*. As a result, Bublitz and Merkel suggest, two things follow: (a) agents have more control over how they respond to indirect interventions than over direct, and (b) the response is more properly reflective of the agent's identity.

The idea behind the lack of control claim is simple and highly intuitive. If you rewire my brain to make me selfish, say, I have no chance to assess whether I ought to be selfish. I just find myself more selfish. But if you present me with the collected works of Ayn Rand, I can assess the value of her arguments for myself. I can come to a rational judgment as to how good her case for the virtue of selfishness is and act accordingly. Similarly, if you pump oxytocin into the air, I simply find myself being more trusting of you, whereas if you make me a promise, I can assess how trustworthy you are in the light of your past behavior.

One might object that even with a direct intervention, we normally get the chance to assess the new mental state. Suppose you rewire my brain so that I am more trusting. Won't I notice the difference and assess whether I should act accordingly? As Dennett (1978) has argued, it won't be enough to wire in a single belief; if we want to get someone to accept something. Rather, we need to wire in a whole set of supporting beliefs (and that may be impossible in principle, let alone with today's crude techniques). Similarly, one may think, it won't be possible to wire in trust or wire out (as it were) memories.

While considerations like this may indeed limit the effectiveness of direct interventions, they won't prevent them from being effective in very many cases. The reason is that people seem readily to accept states that are implanted. There have been multiple case reports of movements elicited by direct brain stimulation in awake patients (stimulation is necessary to map out what parts of the brain are serving vital functions prior to neurosurgery). When this happens, the patient will often, although not always, confabulate a reason for the action. "I just felt like stretching," "I thought I heard a sound over there," or, in the case of someone made to laugh, "You guys look so funny dressed like that." It seems that we expect our behavior to be responsive to reasons, so we automatically assume that there is a reason even when there isn't one. In many cases of direct intervention, we can expect a similar process to occur.

Bublitz and Merkel's (2014) second ground for distinguishing direct interventions from indirect concerns the degree to which they will produce effects that are reflective of who the person is. Again, the idea is simple and intuitive. If I was made selfish by a direct brain interventions, I have been grossly manipulated. Perhaps prior to the intervention I was a decent person: no matter, the manipulation has its effect anyway. But things are very different if I am convinced of the virtues of selfishness. If the idea takes root, it must be because it found fertile soil in my psychology. Perhaps I did not previously *behave* selfishly, yet the fact that I accepted Rand's arguments shows something about me—my lack of compassion for others, say.

There is an obvious objection that Bublitz and Merkel (2014) are quick to address: indirect interventions may be unconscious. We are constantly bombarded by messages and stimuli that change our behavior without our recognizing this fact. Consider priming, for instance. It is very well established that it is possible to make people have certain thoughts by presenting them with information of which they are not conscious. In masked priming, a stimulus—a word or a picture—is presented extremely briefly, followed by a mask to prevent the image persisting on the retina. Below a certain threshold, subjects report that they saw nothing (if the stimulus is presented for a slightly longer time, they report they saw something, but they don't know what). However, we can show that they processed the content with which they were presented. It makes semantically related words more accessible: a subject presented with an image of a face will think of face related words more rapidly than face unrelated words, for instance. Changing minds like this is using an indirect means, yet does it not produce a result that is not reflective of the agent (and, indeed, over which the agent exercises no control)?

Bublitz and Merkel (2014) dismiss the worry on the grounds that even in these cases, the stimuli are processed psychologically. When we are conscious of the content of a stimulus, it is processed by a broader range of the different mechanisms that make up the mind, they claim (here they signal their acceptance of a model of the mind according to which it consists of separate information-processing mechanisms, a model that I share with them). But even when we are not conscious of the content, it is still processed psychologically; that's why it has the effects it has, like making semantically related content more accessible. People have more control over these contents, and their effects are more deeply reflective of who they are, because these contents are "run through 'filters' and are 'checked' against or aligned with existing psychological states and preferences" (Bublitz & Merkel, 2014, p. 70).

Together, these claims constitute a powerful case for a principled distinction between direct and indirect interventions. Despite its power and plausibility, however, I remain unconvinced. I shall argue that indirect interventions often produce effects that bypass agents' capacities for control and produce results no more reflective of the agent than direct. Further and more significantly, I shall argue that indirect interventions are responsible for far more injustice, more harm, more inequality, than direct and that this situation is extremely unlikely to change in the foreseeable future.

It is no part of my case to reject the claim that many direct interventions give rise to the problems that Bublitz and Merkel (2014) identify or that many indirect interventions are free from these concerns. My claim is rather that we cannot map indirect and direct interventions onto the categories of unproblematic and problematic, in the manner suggested. Some direct interventions are morally unproblematic, I will suggest, and some indirect interventions are morally problematic. Bublitz and Merkel may acknowledge this claim and insist that nevertheless the direct/indirect distinction is a good heuristic for whether we ought to worry about an intervention—that it gets things right often enough to be worth utilizing. I will argue that the fact that more injustice is the produce of indirect interventions than direct entails that the distinction is not even a good heuristic.

I begin by addressing Bublitz and Merkel's (2014) argument that we have more control over indirect interventions, starting with contents of which we are not conscious. Let's consider, first, some spectacular cases in which people lack consciousness of stimuli. In a range of conditions, people may continue to act in the absence of consciousness. This occurs in somnambulism (sleep walking), absence seizures, and perhaps psychotic fugue states. In these states, agents continue to act; sometimes, they even do terrible things. Take the famous case of Ken Parks (Broughton et al., 1994). Ken Parks rose from the sofa where he had fallen asleep in 1987 and drove 23 kilometers to his parents'-in-law house. On arrival, he let himself in with a key and stabbed them both. He then drove himself to the police station, where he told police he thought he had killed some people. Parks claimed to be somnambulistic from the time he rose from the couch to the time he found himself in the police station. Both a lower court and the Canadian Supreme Court accepted his defense, finding him not guilty of murder and assault charges.

More typically, agents in these cases perform much more innocuous, and yet puzzling, behaviors. They drive cars, they play musical instruments, and so on—typically, they continue to perform whatever action in which they were already engaged prior to the onset of the state. This is puzzling because it seems mysterious how agents *can* perform such complex actions while lacking consciousness. What is going on?

I suggest that in cases like this behaviors are driven by *action scripts*, which are motor representations of overlearned (very well-practiced) behaviors. Because we engage in these behaviors habitually, we have scripts for running them, which can operate automatically. These scripts are sensitive to aspects of our environment—your driving script incorporates routines for scanning the road conditions—but they are sensitive only to information which they are habituated to expect. That's why behavior in these states is inflexible and stereotyped (Levy, 2014).

This lack of flexibility causes a consequent diminution of control. We control our behavior, as Fischer and Ravizza (1998) have argued, when we are capable of being receptive to (i.e., understanding) and reacting to reasons. But agents who lack consciousness are receptive and reactive to a very small number of reasons. There is a wide range of reasons which Parks himself would (were he conscious of them) take be sufficient reasons to inhibit or modulate his behavior, but to which he is entirely unresponsive, because his behavior is driven by an action script that is not sensitive to these reasons. Parks controls the sphere of behavior that falls within the range of his action script—though even here his control is very limited, since he doesn't possess the capacity to modulate this script in ways that are novel—but he possesses no control over how he responds to anything which falls outside this range.

Lack of consciousness also dramatically reduces the extent to which the behavior is reflective of the agent. It reflects only the narrow range of processes that are online. It may reflect nothing more than responsiveness to what psychologists call "affordances"—the manner in which objects suggest themselves for use, responsiveness to which is acquired by learning. A knife is *for cutting*; that is one of its affordances. Parks, the man who loved his parents-in-law, was not expressed in his behavior; only some attitudes constitutive of him (which, because they are so widely shared, are not reflective of *him*) are expressed.

Of course, it might be objected that we should not generalize from a pathological case like this one to ordinary cases in which agents lack consciousness of something. I think we should, because the mechanisms involved are the same in the pathological and the ordinary cases. When an ordinary agent process a content without being aware of it, it is processed by only a narrow range of the mechanisms constitutive of the person, and therefore they lack control over its content, and their response may not be reflective of who they are. Bublitz and Merkel (2014) do recognize that consciousness of what we perceive raises control relative to unconscious processing. But, in actual fact, consciousness of stimuli is not sufficient for control over how we respond; we can unconsciously process contents we consciously perceive. Think of behavioral priming: for instance, priming with the "elderly" stereotype, by getting subjects to solve puzzles that contain words suggestive of elderly people, slows people's movements down (Bargh, Chen, & Burrows, 1996). In this case, they are conscious of the words, but not conscious of the effects the words have on them.

Here's an example showing how nonconscious processing of contents perceived consciously reduces control in normal subjects. Uhlmann and Cohen (2005) asked subjects to rate the suitability of two candidates for police chief, one male and one female. One candidate was presented as "streetwise" but lacking in formal education while the other one had the opposite profile. Uhlmann and Cohen varied the sex of the candidates across conditions, so that some subjects got a male streetwise candidate and a female well-educated candidate while other subjects got the reverse. In both conditions, subjects considered the male candidate significantly better qualified than the female, justifying their choice by the importance of the qualification that the male candidate possessed. Obviously, a preference for a male police chief was driving subjects' views about which characteristics are needed for the job, and not the other way round. We might say that the choice had a sexist content. But neither that content, nor the implicit attitude that caused subjects to make the choice, was conscious. Rather, what was conscious was the confabulated criterion.

The confabulated criterion, which came up for assessment in light of the agents' beliefs, values and other attitudes, was plausible (it took careful experimentation to show that it was a confabulation). Subjects may reasonably have concluded that their choice was justified, given that the fact that the criterion was generated unconsciously. Indeed, they may even have explicitly asked themselves whether their choice was sexist and concluded, sincerely, that it was not. What subjects could assess for consistency with their attitudes was innocuous, and the morally significant drivers of the criterion did not come up for assessment. So while the choice had a sexist content, this content was not an expression of agents' all things considered attitudes. Rather, it expressed only their implicit sexism, to which they may not have been committed. Further, agents could not control the fact that the choice had a sexist content: they failed to fulfil the epistemic conditions on control.

These considerations show, I claim, that indirect interventions can be morally very problematic: people can deliberately manipulate others using these interventions just as effectively as they can using oxytocin or propranolol. Indeed, effective targeting of an intervention usually requires that direct interventions be combined with indirect: without the person engaging in recall of something for instance, propranolol has no effect on memory reconsolidation. Further, I think that many direct interventions lack the features that Bublitz and Merkel (2014) see as problematic. Take tDCS, which has been shown to promote mathematical learning. That's all that it does: make learning more efficient. For the intervention to have any effect on cognition, it must be combined with an indirect intervention (in this case, asking subjects to engage in some mathematical tasks). It is hard to see this as any less respectful of the person or as any more reducing of their control, than say classroom math in schools.

Even when direct interventions entirely bypass psychological processes, they need not be problematic. Suppose your friend is depressed. One way you might help him is by exposing him to sunlight, which is sometimes effective with regard to mild to moderate depression. This is a direct intervention that entirely bypasses the psychological level, but because it is so familiar few people will find it genuinely troubling. This is not an isolated example: rather, direct interventions are widely used right now in ways we do not find troubling. Think of adding iodine to food. Iodine deficiency remains a significant cause of mental retardation in developing countries, but it has been largely eliminated in the developed world thanks to the addition of iodine to table salt. Adding iodine to food to enhance mental capacities does not seem different, in principle, to using methylphenidate or modafinil to the same end. Similarly, supplementation with folic acid improves average function in a way that cannot reasonably be regarded as a treatment (Durga et al., 2007) and yet is uncontroversial.

Given these facts, it is implausible that the direct/indirect distinction reliably tracks moral significance. Still, it is open to Bublitz and Merkel (2014) to claim something weaker: that the distinction is a good heuristic to use in judging whether an intervention is morally problematic. It may not always get the cases right, but it will do well enough to make it useful for most purposes. I don't think this is right, either. The direct interventions that worry Bublitz and Merkel, and so many neuroethicists, are exciting and fascinating. But their use on any scale to alter people's minds without their consent—the kind of use that Bublitz and Merkel are concerned about—is highly speculative. Right now, however, all of us are manipulated on a daily basis, in ways to which we do not consent, using indirect interventions. This is far more worrying than the speculative concerns about the application of technologies most of which have relatively small effects in the best cases.

Think, for example, of the techniques that marketers use today to encourage consumption (i.e., to encourage people to buy more than they need, as well as to shift their buying preferences). It has long been known that how goods are positioned, for instance, affects consumer behavior. Putting the most popular goods in the middle of aisles maximizes exposure to the products: such placement requires people to walk past other goods they had not contemplated buying, whereas if the more popular buys are placed at either end of the aisle, customers may not need to walk down its length. Similarly, essential items are often placed at the back of the shop to increase traffic past nonessential goods. Products may be ordered in terms of price, with more expensive goods placed where they will be encountered earlier. The result is that cheaper goods are perceived as good buys, in comparison with more expensive goods. More counterintuitively, pricing in multiple lots can encourage greater buying, and once the buying pattern is established, it tends to be maintained (Wansink, Kent, & Hoch, 1998).

Now, marketers might tell you that all these techniques are merely designed to expand consumer choice. By making consumers walk past goods, they are made aware of their existence. Special offers give people choices to buy in multiple lots, thus expanding their options. It should be admitted that these responses have some degree of plausibility. Certainly, these techniques don't *look* particularly threatening. Unlike direct interventions, they appear to leave the agent, with her powers of resistance and choice, unaffected. The fact that they are so familiar disarms our critical faculties, but these indirect interventions, which work by structuring our environment to change our minds, are powerful and sometimes subversive of agency.

The intuition that direct interventions are more threatening than direct is probably caused, in part, by a distinction I believe to be untenable (and pernicious), between agents and their environments. Agency is, in fact, scaffolded by the world. Evolution seeks the cheapest and most efficient routes to fitness-conducive traits and behaviors; that sometimes involves the outsourcing of tasks that could in principle be accomplished by the brain to the external environment. For instance, this is good evidence that we outsource representational duties to the world: rather than forming detailed internal maps of our surroundings, we use low fidelity models, relying on perceptual access for details as needed. Hence, our susceptibility to change blindness (when we fail to notice large changes in the environment); because we don't have detailed representations of the aspects changed, we fail to notice them (Levy, 2007b).

This kind of outsourcing is adaptive; it is an efficient use of cognitive resources. Arguably, we should see the ways in which we scaffold our agency as supporting our rationality under a range of conditions (Levy, 2017). However, the same mechanisms that support rationality can also be hijacked to undermine it. For example, it is adaptive to rely on the testimony of those who give appear to share our values. But once we know what the cues for appearing benevolent are, we can mimic them (Levy, 2019). Similarly, it is obviously adaptive to defer to those who manifest cues for expertise, but these cues can be faked by those who wish to take advantage of us (Guerrero, 2017). Because our agency is extended into (or embedded in) the world, these indirect interventions subvert rational agency as much as do direct, and they do so more powerfully and more pervasively than any of the kinds of direct interventions currently available or envisaged.

No doubt direct interventions can be as agency subversive as indirect—perhaps even more so. Right now, however, indirect subversion is an all too pervasive and all too powerful feature of the world we live in, whereas there are no actual or envisaged direct interventions likely to produce effects as powerful or as widespread. The direct/indirect distinction therefore does not map onto anything of ethical significance, nor does it serve as a useful heuristic for identifying interventions that are likely to be especially problematic.

For these reasons, I remain unconvinced by Bublitz and Merkel's (2014) case against the parity principle. Moreover, there is a powerful positive reason to accept it: accepting the parity principle allows us to see that neuroethical concerns—concerns, especially about the apparent injustices that cognitive enhancements threaten, given that they will be available only to an elite—apply today, in spades, to some of the most dramatic and important injustices in the world. I have in mind the set of injustices caused by the massive inequality between the global north and south. Cognitive enhancement via direct intervention is relatively ineffective and has a quickly declining marginal utility (i.e., the greater your cognitive capacity prior to enhancement, the smaller the benefit to you). But indirect interventions, via learning and teaching and the provision of an enriched environment, as well as direct interventions we all accept as unproblematic, like good nutrition, are very effective at producing better cognitive functioning. And all of this is very unequally distributed, of course, both within and, especially, between nations.

Direct interventions are not especially problematic. They are often obviously unproblematic in themselves (iodine, vitamins, sunlight); when it is less obvious, reflection shows them to be unproblematic (tDCS). Indirect interventions, on the other hand, are often very problematic. Further and importantly, indirect interventions play a very significant role in injustices that outweigh any foreseeably likely consequence of the use of new direct interventions. A concern for justice mandates ignoring the causal route whereby interventions work and instead assessing them on the basis of their effects on agents and on their autonomy.

References

Bargh, J. A., Chen, M., & Burrows, L. (1996). Automaticity of social behavior: Direct effects of trait construct and stereotype activation on action. *Journal of Personality and Social Psychology, 71,* 230–244.

Broughton, R., Billings, R., Cartwright, R., Doucette, D., Edmeads, J., Edwardh, M., . . . Turrell, G. (1994). Homicidal somnambulism: A case report. *Sleep, 17,* 253–264.

Bublitz, J. C., & Merkel, R. (2014). Crimes against minds: On mental manipulations, harms and a human right to mental self-determination. *Criminal Law and Philosophy, 8,* 51–77.

Dennett, D. (1978). Brain writing and mind reading. In *Brainstorms: Philosophical essays on mind and psychology* (pp. 39–50). London, England: Penguin Books.

Durga, J., van Boxtel, M .P., Schouten, E. G., Kok, F. J., Jolles, J., Katan, M. B., & Verhoef, P. (2007). Effect of 3-year folic acid supplementation on cognitive function in older adults in the FACIT trial: A randomised, double blind, controlled trial. *The Lancet, 369*(9557), 208–216.

Elliott, C. (1998). The tyranny of happiness: Ethics and cosmetic psychopharmacology. In E. Parens (Ed.), *Enhancing human traits: Ethical and social implications* (pp. 177–188). Washington, DC: Georgetown University Press.

Farah, M. J., Betancourt, L., Shera, D. M., Savage, J. H., Giannetta, J. M., Nancy, L., . . . Hurt, H. (2008). Environmental stimulation, parental nurturance and cognitive development in humans. *Developmental Science, 15,* 793–801.

Fischer, J. M., & Ravizza, M. (1998). *Responsibility and control: An essay on moral responsibility.* Cambridge, England: Cambridge University Press.

Guerrero, A. A. (2017). Living with ignorance in a world of experts. In R. Peels (Ed.), *Perspectives on ignorance from moral and social philosophy* (pp. 156–185). New York, NY: Routledge.

Hackman, D. A., Farah, M. J., & Meaney, M. J. (2010). Socioeconomic status and the brain: Mechanistic insights from human and animal research. *Nature Reviews Neuroscience, 11,* 651–659.

Hunt, E. (1995). The role of intelligence in modern society. *American Scientist, 83,* 356–368.

Kadosh, R. C., Soskic, S., Iuculano, T., Kanal, R., & Walsh, V. (2010). Modulating neuronal activity produces specific and long-lasting changes in numerical competence. *Current Biology, 20,* 2016–2020.

Levy, N. (2007a). *Neuroethics: Challenges for the 21st century.* Cambridge, England: Cambridge University Press.

Levy, N. (2007b). Rethinking neuroethics in the light of radical externalism. *American Journal of Bioethics (AJOB-Neuroscience), 7,* 3–11.

Levy, N. (2014). *Consciousness and moral responsibility.* Oxford, England: Oxford University Press.

Levy, N. (2017). Nudges in a post-truth world. *Journal of Medical Ethics, 43,* 495–500.

Levy, N. (2019). Due deference to denialism: Explaining ordinary people's rejection of established scientific findings. *Synthese, 196*(1), 313–327.

Mehta, M. A., Owen A. M., Sahakian B. J., Mavaddat, N., Pickard, J. D., & Robbins, T. W. (2000). Methylphenidate enhances working memory by modulating discrete frontal and parietal lobe regions in the human brain. *Journal of Neuroscience, 20,* 65.

Noble, K. G., McCandliss, B. D., & Farah, M. J. (2007). Socioeconomic gradients predict individual differences in neurocognitive abilities. *Developmental Science, 10,* 464–480.

Randall, D. C., Shneerson, J. M., & File, S. E. (2005). Cognitive effects of modafinil in student volunteers may depend on IQ. *Pharmacology Biochemistry and Behavior, 82,* 133–139.

Sahakian, B. J., & Morein-Zamir, S. (2007). Professor's little helper. *Nature, 450,* 1157–1159.

Schermer, M. (2008). On the argument that enhancement is "cheating." *Journal of Medical Ethics, 34,* 85–88.

Turner, D. C., Clark, L., Dowson, J., Robbins, T. W., & Sahakian, B. J. (2004). Modafinil improves cognition and response inhibition in adult ADHD. *Biological Psychiatry, 5,* 1031–1040.

Uhlmann, E. L., & Cohen, G. L. (2005). Constructed criteria: Redefining merit to justify discrimination. *Psychological Science, 16,* 474–480.

Wansink, B., Kent, R. J., & Hoch, S. J. (1998). An anchoring and adjustment model of purchase quantity decisions. *Journal of Marketing Research, 35,* 71–81.

3

Why Means Matter

Legally Relevant Differences Between Direct and Indirect Interventions into Other Minds

Jan Christoph Bublitz

There is nothing in the mind that has not been in the senses—except the mind itself.

—Gottfried Wilhelm Leibniz

Introduction

Are direct interventions into brains and minds, especially novel neurotechnological ones, inherently different to indirect ways of changing minds? This is a key question of neuroethics that any legal regulation of mind-interventions—old or new, natural or technological—has to face.[1] I wish to provide an affirmative answer supportive of such differences. This requires a twofold argument. It has to show, first, that there are differences between direct (or synonymously, biological or physiological) and indirect (psychological) interventions which are not based on crude mind–brain dualisms or dubious properties such as the naturalness of an intervention. Second, it has to demonstrate why these differences (should) matter for the law. This is the program for this chapter. In a nutshell, I propose understanding indirect interventions as stimuli that persons perceive through their external senses and direct interventions as those that reach brains and minds on different, nonperceptual routes. Interventions thus primarily differ in virtue of their causal pathways, because of which persons have different kinds and amounts of control over interventions. Direct interventions change minds by *bypassing resistance and control* of recipients, quite unlike mind-changes caused by perceptual inputs. In addition, direct interventions differ

[1] This paper clarifies and expands upon previous work co-authored with Reinhard Merkel (Bublitz & Merkel, 2014). It greatly benefited from critical remarks especially by Neil Levy, Thomas Douglas, Nicole Vincent, and Allan McCay. I wish to thank all of them and address some of their points in due course. The epigraph by Leibniz (1709) commemorates the 300th anniversary of his death at the time of this writing.

Jan Christoph Bublitz, *Why Means Matter* In: *Neurointerventions and the Law.* Edited by: Nicole A Vincent, Thomas Nadelhoffer, and Allan McCay, Oxford University Press (2020). © Oxford University Press 2020
DOI: 10.1093/oso/9780190651145.001.0003

from indirect ones in the way they relate to the ordinary functions of the mind–brain system, if applied without consent, they *misappropriate* mechanisms of the brain. These differences bear normative relevance in light of what I suggest to be the guiding normative principle in this domain, the human right to mental self-determination (or cognitive liberty). As a consequence, I propose the law should adopt a rough normative—not ontological—dualism between interventions into other minds: nonconsensual direct interventions into other minds should be prohibited, with few exceptions. By contrast, indirect interventions should be prima facie permissible, primarily those that qualify as exercises of free speech or other protected rights of interveners. Nonetheless, indirect interventions may require further context specific evaluations, and some may flout mental self-determination of targets to an extent that indicates a need for their restriction (e.g., subliminal stimuli).

Put differently, I forward the claim that assessments of direct and indirect interventions touch upon relevant normative considerations to different degrees. Typical justifications for direct and indirect interventions run differently, indirect ones usually fare better in light of applicable norms. Therefore, treating direct and indirect interventions on a par, as famously suggested by Neil Levy (2007, defended in chapter 2 in this volume), is neither normatively warranted, nor heuristically helpful, at least in more fine-grained evaluations of neurointerventions which legal regulations require.

To set the stage, it is worthy to note that people change each other's minds all the time. Humans are social cognizers, naturally reading and influencing other minds. Some consider the capacity to shape minds as the linchpin of the human cognitive system (Zawidzki, 2013). At least, it is a key feature that sets it apart from those of other species (Tomasselo, 2016). Accordingly, humans regularly alter beliefs, elicit emotions, or modulate various mental states and processes in others.[2] Sometimes people change others' minds intentionally, sometimes through trickery, and sometimes unexpectedly or accidentally. Regularly, people alter others' minds through words and at times, through more sophisticated means from psychotherapy to pharmaceuticals or novel neurotechnological devices. The primary aim of such interventions is altering some aspect of the mental world of addressees by producing rather specific or more diffuse mental effects. The question is whether particular means—or classes of means—to intervene into minds are normatively more problematic than others. Public opinion commonly draws a distinction between direct and indirect interventions whereby the former are conceived as more problematic than the

---

[2] For brevity's sake, I speak of mental states, but this includes all kinds of mental events or processes, conscious or nonconscious. Also, *recipients, addressees,* and *targets* of interventions are used interchangeably.

latter. Direct interventions comprise psychotropic drugs (pharmaceuticals), psychosurgery, electric or magnetic brain stimulation (through techniques such as transcranial direct current stimulation [tDCS], transcranial magnetic stimulation [TMS], deep brain stimulation [DBS]),[3] and, less familiar, methods such as ultrasound (Martin, Jeanmonod, Morel, Zadicario, & Werner, 2009) and possibly optogenetic tools in the future (Anderrson et al., 2016). These biological or physiological interventions are often contrasted with supposedly less unsettling indirect interventions, from verbal communication over psychotherapy to visual stimuli or music.[4] However, especially the pioneering work of Levy has cast doubt on the plausibility of distinctions between direct and indirect interventions and their ethical relevance. He argues that many of the criteria for drawing distinctions between interventions are misleading for empirical, metaphysical or normative reasons. Consequently, he claims that the nature of an intervention (direct–indirect, traditional–novel, natural–artificial) is irrelevant for its ethical assessment. Only the *effects* of interventions matter. Accordingly, he proposes that different (classes of) interventions should be treated on a par as long as their effects are relevantly similar. Levy's so-called parity principle strikes a chord because it rightfully exposes concerns with neurobiological interventions, which often remain vague and seem to be driven by bioconservative sentiments. However, although Levy forcefully shows that many worries over direct interventions are ill-founded, I wish to claim that not *all* of them are. The following seeks to stake out a third position, situated between the parity principle and bioconservative rejections of allegedly antinatural interventions. I will thus vindicate the public skepticism about direct intervention, but on different grounds. Normatively, my position is based in the idea of mental or psychological self-determination, and formally in an understanding of mind-interventions as social interactions between different persons with legitimate interests on either side. Therefore—and this might be a more general methodological point—the formal (legal) relations between interveners and addressees, or senders and receivers, with rights and interests on either side have to recognized. Arguments and evaluations that dwell only one-sidedly on effects on recipients and neglect relational considerations and rights of senders miss important aspects and are prone to draw misleading analogies or generalizations. For instance, different norms may apply in evaluations of what

---

[3] A comprehensive recent introduction to the varieties of brain stimulation methods is Reti (2015). For its dark history, see Valenstein (1973).

[4] This asymmetry permeates public debates over therapeucitc or enhancing drugs. Its appeal is confirmed by a recent study by Specker, Schermer, and Reiner (2017). The distinction also partially mirrors the disciplinary divide between psychology and psychiatry (and their respective treatment modalities). Traces of the distinction can also be found in the law. One example is a dualism found in criminal law which often provides strong protection to bodies against harmful interventions, but only fragmentarily to minds (Bublitz & Merkel, 2014).

people do to themselves, what parents do to their children, or the state does to criminal offenders. Accordingly, direct interventions might be less problematic in one case and more in another. Moreover, indirect interventions regularly fare better because some rights entitle interveners to alter other minds indirectly, most notably the right to freedom of speech, whereas there are usually no rights that entitle people to directly intervene into other minds. In other words, direct interventions usually do to not manifest legally protected interests, but indirect ones do. The divergence of rights on either side is a key difference between direct and indirect interventions and flows from my proposed understanding of mental self-determination. Appreciating these dissimilarities undermines the parity principle and opens the view for more nuanced evaluations of particular interventions. Levy raises some objections to (previous formulations of) my account in the previous chapter to which I respond in the final section.

At the outset, it is helpful to contextualize the dispute. In the long run, legal scholars and policymakers are interested in assessing whether the use of particular means for particular ends in specific contexts is morally or legally (im) permissible. The law has to develop respective norms and doctrines that clearly convey to potential interveners which means of changing minds are permissible and which are not. Correspondingly, the law has to define whether and under which conditions affected persons can legitimately complain about—or even forcefully resist—unwanted alterations of their minds and the conditions under which the state is obliged to provide protection against unwanted interventions. Answering these questions requires developing a legal taxonomy of permissible and impermissible mind-interventions. It has to accommodate a range of broad as well as context-specific considerations. The distinction between direct and indirect interventions is just one of them. Therefore, even if the normative dualism suggested here holds, it may still be the case that, all things considered, some direct interventions are unproblematic in some instances whereas indirect ones are objectionable in others. What is legitimate in romantic seduction might, for instance, turn out to be illicit in political campaigning. Please note that because of the range of considerations, final assessments of specific interventions become increasingly complex—too complex, in fact, to present a comprehensive evaluation of any normatively challenging intervention in the confines of this chapter. But I will provide some sketches. My primary aim is to tease out differences between *classes* of interventions. The following is thus not a strike-down argument against direct interventions in every context, but a set of interrelated considerations that place a substantial burden on justifying their nonconsensual imposition on others. A burden heavy enough to warrant a normative dualism as the default rule for the law. Although the argument proceeds from a legal perspective, the reasons favoring indirect interventions also apply to ethics. Of course, depending on one's further commitments in ethics, these reasons may come to bear differently. But any full ethical theory of mind-interventions has to accommodate them in some way. I thus hope to contribute to the discussion in ethics as well.

Evaluating Interventions and the Ethics of Consciousness

Claims about things of a certain type being preferable to, or less worrisome than, things of another type are comparative. The comparative claim of interest here is that one class of interventions, indirect ones, fare better than another, direct ones.

This of course does not entail that every member of that class is preferable to those of the other. For practical purposes, the main interest does not lie in abstract comparisons between classes of interventions, but in choosing a specific interven-tion over another under given circumstances. Should parents give methylphen-idate to their kids or change schools? Should I take antidepressants or enroll in psychotherapy? Should the state administer drugs or cognitive behavioral therapy to criminal offenders? Should method A or B be deployed (or none)? Answers require knowledge about the pros and cons, costs and benefits, of each inter-vention. The most important individual element in this are its *effects*, the good and bad, desired and unwanted. To clarify the further discussion, some words about effects upfront. Most importantly, effects are highly specific to individual interventions and therefore do not allow for class-comparisons. There are surely indirect interventions that are much more powerful and with stronger side-effects than direct interventions. Also, effects are of course a contingent empirical matter that cannot be dealt with here. Therefore, the most important aspect in evaluating specific interventions is not in the foreground of the following discussion (but will resurface indirectly at some point). The discussion rather revolves around the question whether there are any *other* normatively relevant aspects, apart from effects and side-effects. To this, the following provides an affirmative answer.

It is nonetheless helpful to understand that assessing effects of a specific in-tervention is already fraught with difficulties. For one, empirical data is often inconclusive, even with respect to means available for some time (see, e.g., con-troversies over selective serotonin reuptake inhibitor antidepressants or can-nabis).[5] This might be partially due to shortcomings of industry-sponsored

---

[5] For the latest on selective serotonin reuptake inhibitors effectiveness in major depression, see Jakubovski, Varigonda, Freemantle, Taylor, and Bloch (2016).

(pharmaceutical) research. But it is largely a consequence of the challenging nature of the task. Mental effects are often subtle and hard to detect; people respond differently to interventions (e.g., pharmacogenomics), and it proves hard to control for other confounding factors such as cross-effects in studies (they require high n-numbers). More broadly, anyone involved in psychological testing is painfully aware of the enormous difficulties in measuring mental states and processes, not only because of their peculiar epistemological accessibility, but also because a comprehensive model of the mind and its parts is missing.

Apart from these general problems of empirical research about minds, further difficulties arise when it comes to evaluating the pros and cons of an intervention. *Kinds* and *strengths* of effects have to be evaluated, and this requires norms. Whether strength is favorable depends, for instance, on whether the intervention is wanted or unwanted by affected persons. Evaluating kinds of effects requires *valuing* mental states, those modified and those newly brought about. It is remarkable that almost hardly any criteria exist for ascribing (dis)value to mental states. Although some appear beneficial and others detrimental, evaluations are regularly not as straightforward as it seems. Even paradigmatic negative mental states as fear or worries are beneficial in some situations. Evaluations require an—as yet, outstanding—comprehensive ethics of consciousness, a theory that provides criteria for valuing mental states.[6] It faces a range of intriguing questions such as whether positive valenced emotions are ipso facto good, (likely not), whether and to which extent self-critical thoughts are better or worse than self-affirmative ones, or how improvements in one domain may be traded against impairments in another. It may also need to distinguish between mental domains, broadly construed. Different criteria might apply to affective states and to cognitive processes.

Discussions about nosology and mental disorders in psychiatry exhibit some parallels to such an ethics of consciousness, but they derive mainly from a limited set of normative premises around concepts of illness. An ethics of consciousness has to be more comprehensive. It cannot solely rely on subjective appreciations because humans are not well-versed in introspectively grasping how mental elements—thoughts, emotions, moods, dispositions—relate to and affect one another. A science-based ethics of consciousness has to rely on (longitudinal) psychological and phenomenological studies. We are far from having such an ethics of consciousness, its, development is a task for neuroethics in the coming decades. Without it, assessing mind-interventions lacks a stable foundation.

---

[6] I borrow the term from Metzinger (2010).

Distinctions between Interventions

Misleading Distinctions

Once pros and cons of specific interventions are evaluated, they can be compared to others. One of the key problems is that many interventions are on a first glance incommensurable, they simply produce different effects in different domains. How to compare the mental changes caused, say, by placing children in a different social environment or administrating them pharmaceuticals? Common standards needs to be created, but they inevitably neglect many facets of the richness of changes caused by interventions.

Instead of such complex comparisons, formal attributes or secondary properties of interventions such as their direct/indirect, natural/artificial, invasive/non-invasive nature are often alluded to. Such formal properties then stand in as proxies for the truly important but hard to assess criteria; they are uses as a heuristic as an *attribute substitution* (Kahneman & Frederick, 2002). This is problematic since attributes are often suggestive or misleading. For instance, some interventions are viewed with suspicion because they allegedly cause "permanent" or "irreversible" changes, or "alter the personality" of persons. In light of the brain's plasticity (and potentially neurogenesis), such claims are empirically questionable. But even if some physiological effects are more durable than others, or touch upon more central characteristics of a person, does it matter? These attributes are used in an evaluative sense, but their normative premises remain implicit. For all we know, if spelled out fully, they may likely turn out to be unpersuasive. After all, higher education or bonding in intimate relationships, to take two examples, likely (and hopefully) cause long-lasting and hard-to-reverse mental (and neuronal) effects, but this hardly raises moral concerns. Permanence, reversibility, or strength of connections are thus no clearly favorable or unfavorable attributes.

Perhaps the most pervasive misleading attribute that needs to be mentioned concerns the fact that direct interventions *rewire* or *change the brain.*[7] Worries based on the brain changing nature of interventions (at least tacitly) seem to presuppose that other interventions leave the brain unchanged. Such imagined less worrying interventions allegedly only alter the mind (they work "purely psychologically"). Equally misleading are allusions to "rewiring," which supposedly means creating or strengthening (or weakening or discarding) connections between neurons or changes in higher-level connections of the

---

[7] This argument seems impossible to overcome in public discourse. At the day of writing, the science pages of the *New York Times* express excitement over the fact that hypnosis "is not only in the mind" but changes the brain (Goode, 2016).

connectome (Seung, 2012). The glaring problem with such claims is that they rely on unpersuasive mind–brain dualisms that presuppose that some mental effects are causable without changes in the brain or without rewiring neuronal connections. Although the relation between the mind and brain is still a metaphysical mystery, we have ample reason to assume that every mental change is—depending on your favorite theory—caused, realized, accompanied, or supervening upon changes in the brain.[8] No mental changes without physical changes. Even innocuous interventions change brains: reading these words triggers a cascade of neuronal processes in the brain of you, dear reader, and every time you remember something, you recall (and reproduce) an alteration of synaptic connections in your brain. Meditation, exercise, or psychotherapy demonstrably change the brain. Eric Kandel (2007) remarks that the deeper aim of his lectures is altering brain cells of his students.[9] Evaluations of interventions—or distinctions between them—based on the mere fact that some change the brain are nonstarters.[10]

Equally unfeasible are distinctions between "invasive" or "noninvasive" interventions. In medicine, *invasive* denotes interventions that enter or invade the body, either by puncturing the surface of the skin or "going within" through body orifices.[11] Electric stimulation through tDCS, for instance, counts as noninvasive according to this nomenclature. But since all interventions, even the most "psychological", change the brain, all "go within" and possess the problematic feature of causing changes within the body. Without further explication, these terms are more suggestive than helpful (Davis & van Koningsbruggen, 2013). The same is true for "internal" or "external" interventions: at some point, every intervention is external (to the body) and at another, it causes internal changes (in brain and mind). Many evaluative claims over particular interventions appear innocently unaware of these difficulties and warrant suspicion. However, despite the shortcomings of these distinctions, there might be other, more relevant ones. So, if two interventions, A and B, cause sufficiently similar effects, is there anything else of normative relevance?

---

[8] As an introduction to the mind–brain problem, see Chalmers (2002) and Kim (2011).

[9] For changes in the brain caused by psychotherapies, see Linden (2006); for meditation see, Davidson et al. (2003).

[10] Moreover, the legal literature sometimes speaks about "morphological" brain changes and neuroscience about "structural" or "functional" ones. These attributes are equally inept to designate relevant differences because they primarily depend on the technologies used to detect them. *Morphological* stems from the days when brains were dissected and examined by eye or under microscopes; *structural* and *functional* refer to neuroimaging techniques. These methods measure diverging properties of the brain in different modes and temporal and spatial resolutions but do not denote qualitatively different physiological effects.

[11] Cf. Merriam-Webster's (n.d.) medical definition of *invasive*: "1. tending to spread; especially tending to invade healthy tissue; 2. involving entry into the living body (as by incision or by insertion of an instrument).

Levy's Parity Principle

I claim that, apart from effects, the causal pathways or (parts of) the *modus operandi* of interventions are normatively relevant and that in virtue of this, indirect interventions are markedly less worrisome than direct ones. This normative asymmetry between interventions stands in contrast to Levy's parity principle. In his book *Neuroethics*, he formulates a weak and a strong version and adds several specifications (Levy, 2007). I have to leave the subtleties of his profound account aside here. My target is a simpler and more common version of the principle, which can be summarized as follows: Different means to alter minds should be treated legally (or ethically) on a par because there are, apart from effects, no intrinsic differences between means of ethical or legal relevance. Accordingly, what matters in evaluations of mind-interventions is not their nature (direct or indirect, physiological or psychological) but only their effects. Challenging the parity principle thus requires a twofold argument:

1. Presenting a meaningful distinction between direct and indirect interventions that neither falls prey to metaphysical objections, nor contravenes empirical findings about the workings of the mind.
2. Demonstrating why this difference bears normative significance.

Before pointing to the weaknesses of the parity principle, however, I wish to give it due credit. It is a useful prima facie test, insofar as it helps to expose the many just mentioned unpersuasive distinctions abound. A good share of the louder voices in public discourse seems biased against the novel, the neuro, and the nonnatural. As a tool to elucidate such biases, the parity principle is commendable and has become an anchor in neuroethics. It presses for justification whenever interventions are treated differently. Here is a legal example. The law regulates various means to alter minds through different frameworks: some drugs and pharmaceuticals fall under strict and tightly enforced international narcotic control regimes, others under more lenient domestic rules, while neurotools such as tCDS and TMS are considered medical devices and are therefore much easier legally accessible. However, since these are all means to alter minds, potentially effective and with side effects, such a piecemeal regulatory approach is unpersuasive, especially as different normative criteria apply to them (Bublitz, 2016). The parity principle calls for justifications of such different treatment. Therefore, it helps to see the general in the particular. It is not false, but too broad and becomes unsustainable in specific cases. Identifying similarities and differences between interventions depends on the level of analysis. The parity principle remains on the surface; it highlights the former and levels the latter.

Proposed Distinction: Sensory Perception versus Purely Physiological Interventions

Making the case for legally relevant differences requires defining more precisely what qualifies as a direct or an indirect intervention. As everything resembles everything else in some sense and differs in another, many distinctions between interventions might be drawn (for other recent approaches see Focquaert & Schermer, 2015; Dahaner, 2019). I would like to suggest the following distinction:

> Interventions are indirect or psychological if affected persons perceive (including nonconsciously). Stimuli through their outward senses—vision, hearing, taste, smell, touch.
>
> Direct interventions are those that reach the brain/mind through other, nonperceptual ways (i.e., purely physical-biological processes), such as magnetic or electrical stimulation of the brain. They comprise, but are not restricted to, interventions traditionally considered invasive, including substances that undergo metabolic processes before they cross the blood–brain barrier (e.g., psychotropic drugs).

Admittedly, this is a rough distinction that immediately prompts a set of intriguing questions. So here are some clarifications: These two modalities might not be exhaustive. It is probably useful to consider *genetic* interventions as a further category sui generis. The same might be true for bodily activities of persons, such as deep breathing or exercise, which induce psychological changes. They seem distinct from, at least in light of normative considerations, interventions that affect body and mind from the outside, through the administration of substances, physical forces or "energies", or external stimuli.[12] I am only concerned with such latter interventions. In addition, it is useful to draw further subdistinctions. For instance, pharmaceuticals or brain stimulation methods may have distinct peculiarities that merit special attention. The direct–indirect distinction does not oppose such further distinctions; in fact, finer ones with respect to indirect interventions will be drawn in the following discussion.

With respect to the perceptual nature of indirect interventions, it should be noted that the nature of perception—as well as the senses—are still subject to

---

[12] Surely, the effects of exercise might be similar to drugs, see Vina, Sanchis-Gomar, Martinez-Bello, and Gomez-Cabrera (2012). However, as it is an illustrative example, when the authors write that "exercise can be considered as a drug," they are close to a category mistake. Exercise may have similar effects to some drugs in the brain. But that does not negate the many differences between drugs and exercise. One of them, relevant here, might be that the potential effects of exercise are much more restricted than those of drugs and emerge only from internal bodily processes, whereas potent drugs might override such processes.

many discussions. For instance, it is not even clear how many senses human possess and how they should be individuated (Macpherson, 2011). The present argument is confined to the classic five senses that take up information from the external world (taste, sight, touch, smell, sound);it leaves internal senses aside (Macpherson, 2011). This presupposes that exogenous sense experiences are conceptually and phenomenologically sufficiently distinct and discernible from internally generated ones (bodily sensations such as pain, hunger, fatigue). Furthermore, some implications of this distinction may appear counterintuitive: the afternoon tea counts as a direct intervention. Eating chocolate to lift one's mood counts as a direct intervention if its effects are due to the pharmacological actions of its ingredients, but as an indirect one if caused by its taste.[13] Direct interventions thus comprise a broad range of interventions, even mundane ones. People directly intervene into their minds on a daily basis. Such a broad definition may appear misguided and neglectful of the specific worries about neurobiological high-tech interventions. However, this objection seems already caught up in questionable preconceptions. Doing justice to mind-interventions requires acknowledging that there might only be gradual differences between a cup of tea and a neurodevice. The broadness of the definition also indicates that reasonable normative assessments require finer differentiations in virtue of additional considerations. But, despite grey areas, sensory perception is the most plausible candidate for a distinguishing criterion that captures normatively relevant differences between the two classes of interventions.

Here is why: let us step back from philosophical questions and Mosaic pieces of empirical sciences and consider some basic facts about humans. They possess a cognitive machinery, physically located in the brain (possibly spread out to other parts such as the gastrointestinal tract and maybe the rest of the body). The cognitive machinery is partially open to the environment. As part of the organism, it relies on bodily processes and requires oxygen, energy, etc. In addition, it is open to the environment in another distinct way: through the senses. Like other animals, humans perceive the external world through their senses. Senses are the organism's gateways to the outside, its receptors to take up external information. Sensory perception detects and processes external stimuli. Sensuously perceived stimuli can thus be understood as *informational inputs* into the cognitive machinery (which contain sense data). The cognitive machinery is adapted to process such stimuli through a cascade of psychological mechanisms that decode, filter, and engage with incoming information. A subgroup of informational input consists of symbolic and conceptual or communicative inputs, which form a normatively salient category ("speech" or "expression").

---

[13] For chocolate's effects, see Scholey and Owen (2013).

Both apertures—the sensory and the bodily—can be used to access and alter the cognitive machinery, and both ways involve biological processes. Vision works through electromagnetic waves, touch and hearing work through pressure, and smell and taste work through chemical reactions. Every intervention is thus physical-biological. However, only our sensory modalities acquire and process information. For instance, magnetic or electric forces stimulating brain cells cannot be described as informational inputs (they do not bear informational content), nor is the organism's reaction to them describable as perception.[14] Therefore, direct interventions are no informational inputs into the cognitive machinery, but rather physical alteration of its neuronal substrate. In this view, common distinctions that pitch "purely psychological" against "physiological" interventions frame the contrast from the wrong end. Rightly put, direct interventions are purely physiological whereas indirect ones are physiological *and* psychological.[15]

Functions

Let us look a bit more closely at two further distinctions between direct and indirect interventions. The first concerns their relation to the ordinary functions of the cognitive machinery. Irrespective of the perplexing philosophical problems of perception—and so I hope, without getting entangled in the deep controversies around "ordinary functioning" in psychiatry—I suggest that one may fairly say that the ordinary function of the perceptual system is to acquire and process sense data, information from the external world. At least, this is a fairly uncontroversial claim if one assumes, as I will here, that one of the ordinary functions of the brain is information processing. Then, sensitivity of brain cells and brain

---

[14] If direct interventions (e.g., electric currents) cause sensory feelings (e.g., itching), the latter would count as an indirect intervention because it is sensually perceived. But this effect is a by-product, not the causally effective part of interest. This main effect is produced a direct intervention. Furthermore, direct interventions might be used to convey information. One may use TMS stimulation ("zappings") as a code (e.g., three failures of working memory may be the signal that working hours are over). This interaction can now be described as *informational*. But on a closer look, there are two interventions. The zapping is a direct intervention because it does not produce its effect (memory lapses) through perception (nor through informational content). In addition, the zapping is used as an informational exchange. In that case, both interventions have to be evaluated on their own.

[15] A usual objection against this distinction states that it still involves a residual dualism as it speaks about psychological processes as distinct from physiological ones. However, if one entertains a physicalist position that does not allow for independent psychological processes, the burden of argument is to show how physical processes instantiate those processes that psychology and cognitive science speak about. As long as they are not explained away (e.g., eliminativist positions), the described psychological processes exist. This remains true even if they are fully reducible to physical processes.

areas to sensory input is a necessary part of its ordinary functioning. By processing such stimuli, the system simply performs this function. In this view, perceptible stimuli engaging the cognitive system thus neither impair its functioning, nor interfere with its integrity.

Whereas one can say with some confidence that one of the functions of the networks of connected brain cells is signaling or conveying information, one cannot, with the same confidence say that picking up and reacting to magnetic fields or electric currents (TMS, tDCS) emanating from sources outside of the skull is. Responsiveness to such stimuli is *not* necessary for the functioning of the cognitive machinery, but rather a contingent feature due to the particular physical realization of the cognitive machinery in humans. Possibly, the neurobiological substrate of the mind, the brain, could have been realized physically in other ways. Functionally equivalent systems running on a different hardware (e.g., insensitive to magnetism) are easily conceivable. Sensitivity to direct interventions is thus not necessary for ordinary functioning. The effects of direct interventions may sometimes even be conceived as distorting interferences with the integrity of the system. When, for instance, neurons increase or decrease "firing" rates because of electrical stimulation of nearby tissue, ordinary signaling is altered. That is the very point of the intervention. Thereby, ordinary functioning is disrupted, at least insofar as signaling no longer works appropriately. Thus, unlike perceptual stimuli, direct interventions may well be described as functional alterations of the system and sometimes as impairments of ordinary functioning. This is an interesting difference with potential normative ramifications.[16] I concede though that the argument may not work if direct interventions restore ordinary functioning (e.g., as in some coerced medical treatments).

Furthermore, I do not wish to purport that this juxtaposition is purely descriptive. Terms such as *integrity, should behave*, or *ordinary functioning* are nonneutral ascriptions. Ascribing functions requires reference to a goal (Krohs & Kroes, 2009; McLaughlin, 2000).Whereas the function of technical artefacts depends on the purposes for which they were designed or for which they are used, nature is free from intentionality, teleology, or predestined purpose. In nature things simply happen. In the absence of goals, ascribing (mal)functions to biological systems is problematic. Yet, ascribing the function of perception to the senses, or information signaling to cells, is unsuspicious, as long as it does *not* imply that utilizing the brain for different functions, as add-ons or expansions, is not (and by extension, ethically or legally impermissible).

---

[16] It is surely conceivable that neuroscience develops additional sensory modalities for humans—for example, echolocation or senses for electric or magnetic fields that some animals (fish) possess. As long as these are sufficiently analogous to the native senses, especially in the ways in which sense data are processed and integrated, such neosensory inputs would presumably count as indirect interventions.

this requires a normative argument that is yet to come. To anticipate it: persons should be entitled to choose the functions of their organism. They may voluntarily turn their brain into, for example, a receptor for electromagnetic waves, and they may equally deny and close such pathways into their minds. Interveners who nonetheless avail themselves of these pathways then *misappropriate* the mechanisms of the brain (in the sense of making use of them without permission)—and that constitutes an interference with mental self-determination.

Control

Arguments about functions are concededly controversial. Although the previous section reveals a significant difference between interventions, nothing in the more general argument hinges on the point about functions. Sceptics are invited to disregard further references to functions. My main argument draws on another difference between perceptual and psychological interventions: the kind and amount of *control* that affected persons have over it. Control is not a purely descriptive concept either, it designates a relation between a controlling subject and a controlled object. Normatively interesting concepts of control are accordingly tied to notions of a subject, a particularly thorny issue with respect to the mind, which cannot be unpacked here.[17] The term *control* is used variously in psychology (e.g., Hassin, 2005). Nonetheless, even without a clear-cut definition, it is possible to approximate relevant features, distinguish between kinds and degrees of control, and eventually formulate a tentative definition of control that suffices for our purposes. In general, the notion of control over one's mind is broad and includes, for instance, powers and capacities for mental actions. They are often limited. For instance, we often fail to direct our thoughts, or stop the wandering of our minds, and may appear more as passive observers to our stream of consciousness than its directors. A bit provocatively, Thomas Metzinger writes that "for two thirds of their conscious lifetime, human beings do not possess mental autonomy" (Metzinger 2013, p. 14).

---

[17] It invites questions as to who the subject that controls unconscious mechanisms is. It cannot be the "conscious I." Answers require no less than a construal of the notion of the subject in light of recent findings of cognitive sciences (see Wegner, 2005). While philosophically intriguing the absence of such a concept does not call the suggested normative distinction into question. For our purposes, a concept of the subject that comprises the organism including higher-level mental functions and consciousness suffices. By contrast, accounts that confine control to conscious awareness become implausible in light of the fact that most psychological activities are unconscious. While cognitive sciences may not leave much room for strong metaphysical concepts of subjects, they do *not* call into question differentiations between various kinds and degrees of control.

Our present interest, however, lies more narrowly in control over interventions. My main claim is that the relevant forms of control concern the abilities to detect, engage with, and counteract interventions, and that they typically differ in quality and quantity with respect to direct and indirect interventions. Importantly, the degree of available control negatively correlates with the strength of an intervention. Some interventions are weak and easily resistible; others might be literally irresistible. But strength, as previously mentioned, depends on contingent empirical features of specific interventions and is not a criterion to differentiate *classes* of interventions. The relevant claim in this respect is that the degree of control over interventions *also* correlates with respect to their causal pathways.

Control over Indirect Interventions

Let us first look at indirect interventions, sensuously perceived stimuli. Apart from vision, we cannot shut down our senses or block uptake of information. Through our senses, we are constantly connected to the world (online) to some degree. However, we have some mental control further down the pathway.

A first distinction that suggests itself runs between those stimuli of which persons become consciously aware at some point and those that are merely nonconsciously processed. We have the greatest degree of control over stimuli that rise to conscious awareness. Despite limits, we have mental capacities to engage with these stimuli by giving attention to or distracting us away from them. We can relate to their content, evaluate the information, compare it to pre-existing knowledge and experiences, and categorize or discard it. We have less control over stimuli that remain non-conscious.

This folk psychological approximation is supported by a rough view at the architecture of the mind: although still subject to debate, a picture stable enough for our purposes has emerged. It views the mind as a complex network of specialized modules with different properties that process different types of information in different ways. Some parts of this network run through consciousness; most parts work nonconsciously. It is likely one of the functions of consciousness to enable distribution and integration of information from various modules throughout the network. Through becoming conscious, information is made available to other modules (e.g., global workspace model, Baars, 1997). If this view is correct, one can say that persons have the highest (although still limited) degree of control over consciously available information, because more modules can access and process and engage with it. Nonetheless, all incoming perceptual stimuli are first processed by non-conscious mechanisms. Non-conscious processing is the default mode of operation. The larger share of the myriad of stimuli constantly entering our senses remains nonconscious, only salient stimuli are elevated to conscious awareness. But of course nonconscious information is also further relayed, processed, and engaged with, it may even translate into action

(Bargh & Williams, 2006).[18] All conscious mental activity is grounded in many nonconscious processes "under the hood" that prepare and process information. My suggestion is that even this form of information processing provides some sort of control. Not conscious control, but engagement with stimuli through non-conscious mechanisms and modules. Stimuli are, for instance, checked against available knowledge, predictions, and expectations and are filtered for relevance. Perception itself is likely shaped by thoughts, beliefs, and desires.[19] Persons thus relate to the informational content of such stimuli at least in some way. Because of this, nonconscious stimuli do not prompt random or irrational effects, but rather trigger preset responses, which may often be helpful and adequate. These mechanisms are, to some extent, adaptive and modifiable through learning and novel experiences. Accordingly, I suggest that even these nonconscious processes provide a basal form of control over stimuli, although less control than over conscious stimuli.

There is another angle from which one may approximate relevant aspects of mental control and that complements the conscious/nonconscious distinction. A large body of work from several disciplines converges on dual-process models of the mind.[20] Although varying in detail, the common idea is that the mind comprises of two systems that can roughly be discerned: System 1, the evolutionary older one, works fast and parallel, nonconscious, automatic and relies on simple information processing strategies such as heuristics. System 2 works slowly and has only limited capacities but is more deliberate and can access explicit memory. System 1 provides quick and preset responses whereas System 2 enables higher-functioning, reflective thought, and more complex and varied response. Incoming data are first processed in System 1, and some is relayed to System 2. Both systems interact and integrate information; details of their interplay are unclear (Evans and Stanovich, 2013). But despite gaps in the precise understanding of different systems, the dual-process view is illuminating as it explains phenomena such as typical failures of reasoning through properties of various psychological processes. The distinction can also be utilized for present purposes and allows for a tentative conclusion with respect to control: Persons have greater control over stimuli processed by System 2 and less over those processed only by System 1.[21] How the distinction between the two

---

[18] The idea of unconscious perception has long troubled philosophers. But empirical science clearly demonstrates its possibility (see Prinz, 2016).

[19] The extent of this influence ("cognitive penetration") remains hotly contested. See, for example, Stokes (2012).

[20] For a good overview see Evans and Frankish (2009) and Kahneman (2011).

[21] One way of framing the distinction between the system makes this difference in control particularly salient. In analogy to a photo camera, Joshua Greene (2014) speaks of System 1 as the automatic mode and System 2 as the manual mode. The manual mode requires more effort and takes much longer than the automatic mode but allows for more fine-grained control. Although a metaphor, it points in the same direction as the current argument.

systems maps onto the conscious–nonconscious divide is an intricate question and depends on how systems are delineated (Frankish, 2009). Contents only processed by System 1 can rise to conscious awareness, so System 2 processing is not necessary for consciousness. System 2 processing probably requires conscious awareness of some of the stimuli. It therefore seems best to view the distinctions between systems and conscious–nonconscious processing as different dimensions of mental control which overlap nut are not co-extensive. But details do not need to concerns us here. The main suggestion is that a relevant notion of control can be explicated by drawing on features of the presented picture of the mind. Here is a tentative definition: *the extent of control a person possesses over an intervention correlates with the extent and type of her mental capacities and mechanisms available to engage with it.* As a consequence, control over indirect interventions comes in degrees, with more control over conscious than over nonconscious stimuli and more control o System 2 is activated rather than merely System 1.

Further empirical findings could be adduced to render this picture more precise, but its present form suffices to tease out differences to control over direct interventions.

Control over Direct Interventions

Let us contrast this with control over direct, physiological interventions. Their causal pathways differ, as they do not run through the just described psychological systems, processes, filters, or mechanisms at all; their route is one of biophysical, (chemical, electrical) processes alone. Whether direct interventions are effective solely depends on biophysical events in the brain.[22] Roughly, one can put one contrast in this way: direct interventions are mainly about biophysical interactions of the person with the intervention, whereas indirect interventions are about the interplay with the physically embedded information.

Because of different pathways, the kind of control over direct and indirect interventions differs. People can counteract onset and impact of direct interventions to varying degrees. We are accustomed to working against hunger, fatigue, or alcohol, but our powers are limited. The same is likely true for our control over the impact of magnetic fields, electric currents, or pharmaceuticals on the cognitive system. Although not necessarily irresistible, the amount of

---

[22] To be more precise, the received wisdom of drug experiments and psychiatry suggests that effects of psychoactive substances are influenced by "set and setting" (Hartogsohn 2016; Zinberg 1984)—that is, the internal psychological conditions (expectation, motivation) of consumers and context of consumption (perhaps similar to placebo effects).Effectiveness might not only be about biophysical processes alone, it is also about the mental state of the recipient, and it this sense, she may have some residual control.

control over such forces is quite low. Moreover, the kind of control over direct interventions categorically differs from control over perceptive stimuli; the former requires exercising different mental strategies (and, in a sense, mobilizing different mental "energies").Accordingly, direct interventions often seem to bypass mental control of targeted persons.[23]

This aspect seems to be one of the reasons for the personality transforming potential of some direct interventions. Although sensuously perceived stimuli can cause deep effects (e.g., witnessing a traumatizing event), their effectiveness seems to depend on predispositions and the pre-existing state of perceivers to a much greater degree. Sensory perceptions some haw have to find traction with person, have to resonate with her, play to her beliefs, hopes, fears, or traits. Accordingly, even drastic indirectly induced personality changes seem to be more in line with the personality and might often be more fittingly described as a reaccentuation rather than a thorough transformation. By contrast, direct interventions are more powerful because they bypass the processes with which indirect stimuli resonate; they directly modify a neuronal configuration and bypass the personality of recipients; more concretely, all the innumerous mental mechanisms that make up who we are. This is illustrated by the fascinating reports of severely depressed patients unresponsive to therapies whose moods are apparently alterable within minutes through DBS (Mayberg et al., 2005; Schlaepfer & Lieb, 2005; for more recent developments see Dougherty, 2015; Morishita, 2014). Conceptualizing such cases by merely saying that DBS is more effective than other therapies is too simple. DBS is more effective precisely because it operates on a different causal route, because it does not resonate with the personality of the patient and her cognitive machinery in a "depressive mode," but rather reconfigures the neuronal parameters of the cognitive machinery itself.

In conclusion, a crucial difference between direct and indirect interventions lies in their causal pathways. Indirect interventions pass through the ordinary perceptive mechanisms of the cognitive system, direct interventions alter it. Control over one's mind is limited and comes in degrees. The form of control persons can exert over sensuously perceived stimuli, especially those rising to conscious awareness, differs in kind and extent from control over purely physiological interventions. Control over sensory stimuli can be further

---

[23] Concededly, this is a rough and oversimplified picture that fails, for instance, to differentiate between sensory modalities. Think about the lack of control over sensory perceptions of smells, due to the fact that olfactory stimuli are not relayed to the thalamus. Nonetheless, if one agrees with the idea that we possess less control over smells than over other perceptible stimuli, one affirms my general suggestion that control depends on pathways of stimuli. Moreover, both direct and indirect interventions can trigger further equally hard to control effects (e.g., smells evoking memories). But such further effects are not our concern here.

differentiated in virtue of conscious/nonconscious and System 1/System 2 processing.

Of course, the overall amount of control of a person over interventions depends on additional factors including her general abilities, further circumstantial factors, as well as the strength of interventions. While these empirical variables become relevant in evaluations of specific methods, they do not allow identifying principled differences between classes of interventions and must be held fixed for our present inquiry. Thus, ceteris paribus, persons have more control over indirect than direct interventions.

Normative Relevance of Differences

Against this backdrop, we can turn to the normative part: Why should these differences matter? Answers require normative criteria. A legal, rights-based perspective focuses on legal relations between persons, more concretely, on legal relations that pertain to minds. What is the legal relation of a person to the mind of another; which actions potentially altering another's mind are (im) permissible? The legal relation of a person to the mind of another is secondary to a more fundamental relation: the one between a person and her own mind. Are persons legally entitled to alter their own minds, can others—or the state—keep them from doing so? And what rights do persons have against unwanted alterations of their mind?

The law rarely addresses these intriguing questions in abstract. While many legal doctrines regulate how to treat bodies, our own or those of others, few explicitly concern minds.[24] Even regulations of mind-altering tools such as drugs are not formulated in light of a general theory over rights to minds, but are piecemeal legislation mainly based on considerations of harmfulness.[25] The mind is a largely unchartered area of the law. Filling the void and evaluating mind-interventions adequately requires developing a full-fledged legal theory over rights to minds. In the following, I shall present some cornerstones, especially a (human) right to mental self-determination, which is not yet accepted in many jurisdictions, but should be incorporated in the catalogues of international human rights. This is the normative premise of the argument.

---

[24] One might think that rights to the body encompass rights to minds, because minds are realized in brains. However, legally, rights to the body do not fully capture interventions into minds. For several reasons, distinct doctrines for the protection of the mind have to be developed (cf. Bublitz & Merkel 2014).

[25] The international drug convention, for instance, do not even consider a right of users to alter their minds (Bublitz, 2016).

Different Legal Relations

Before elaborating on the substance of the right, I wish to make a methodological suggestion: assessments of interventions should pay attention to different formal relations between interveners and targets (cf. Merkel, 2007). Because of them, generalizations, and analogies might not be easily drawn. The failure to observe these differences befalls many contemporary discussions of the issue. Senders and receivers of mind-altering interventions can stand in different formal relations to another, and these relations affect corresponding rights and duties. Next is an overview of the most important types.

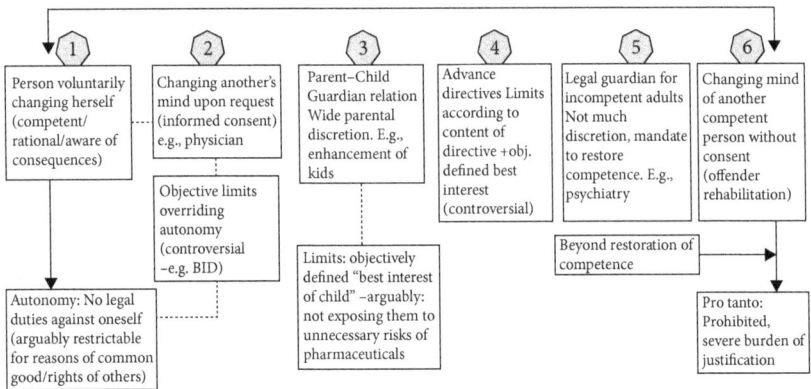

1	2	3	4	5	6
Person voluntarily changing herself (competent/rational/aware of consequences)	Changing another's mind upon request (informed consent) e.g., physician	Parent–Child Guardian relation Wide parental discretion. E.g., enhancement of kids	Advance directives Limits according to content of directive +obj. defined best interest (controversial)	Legal guardian for incompetent adults Not much discretion, mandate to restore competence. E.g., psychiatry	Changing mind of another competent person without consent (offender rehabilitation)

Objective limits overriding autonomy (controversial –e.g. BID)

Beyond restoration of competence

Autonomy: No legal duties against oneself (arguably restrictable for reasons of common good/rights of others)

Limits: objectively defined "best interest of child" –arguably: not exposing them to unnecessary risks of pharmaceuticals

Pro tanto: Prohibited, severe burden of justification

In the first case (upper left), a competent person voluntarily alters her own mind. Here, intervener and receiver are identical, whereas all other cases involve (at least) two persons. Accordingly, the first case concerns legal limits to alter one's *own* mind, whereas the other cases concern rights and limits to alter *other* minds. In a legal view, these cases differ categorically because a right barring mind-interventions only obliges *other* persons, not rightholders themselves.[26] Consequently, the only question in the first case is whether there are any limits to mental freedom (and how they can be justified). In cases concerning *other* minds, the specific relation between intervener and recipient strongly influences whether and to which extent interventions are permissible. Different substantive rules and considerations apply. They derive from general considerations, are not peculiar to mind-interventions and are controversial in all case types. The reason for introducing these distinctions is of methodological nature: Because diverging rules apply to different relations, the dissimilarities between direct and indirect interventions may play out differently in various case types. The most salient example concerns the paradigmatic case of enhancement: A competent person voluntarily enhancing herself (1) is in

---

[26] One of the reasons lies in the nature of rights: rights and duties against oneself arguably cannot exist (as rightsholder and dutybearer would be identical).

light of mental self-determination less unsettling than parents enhancing children (3), which is less unsettling than criminal justice systems "enhancing" competent offenders against their will (6). Worries over direct interventions in the latter case may not apply to the former. And reversely, even though one comes to conclusion that direct interventions are permissible in voluntary self-enhancements (1), it does not follow that they are equally so in (6). Case-based reasoning in neuroethics often fails to distinguish between various case types. It could gain precision by becoming sensitive to these distinctions. The most problematic cases in which differences between interventions are mainly relevant are unwanted interventions (especially 5 and 6). I will only be concerned with interventions into other minds (i.e., not case types 1, 2, and 4).

Rights against Mind-Interventions

We can now turn to the substance of affected rights. The key one, I suggest, is the right to mental self-determination or, as often called in the United States, cognitive liberty. Although not (yet) acknowledged by most legal systems nor found in legal textbooks, I claim it is a fundamental human right. It draws upon the guarantee of freedom of thought, enshrined in many human rights treaties[27] and is a logical prerequisite to many more specific human or constitutional rights.[28] It may be viewed as a logical expansion of the right to bodily autonomy and flows from the idea that individuals should decide self-regarding matters for themselves, a basic premise of liberal legal orders (widely endorsed in western jurisdictions). It would be hardly conceivable if autonomy stopped at what is most central to the person: her mind. Mental self-determination has to be the starting point for legal assessments of mind-interventions. But as here is not the place to provide a deeper theoretical justification for the right, I have to direct the reader to discussions elsewhere.[29] Let me, however, sketch my view on content and scope of the right: as the name suggests, it confers upon its holder the liberty to self-determine or control what is in and on her mind. This entails the permission to alter one's own mind at will. It further implies, by the logic of norms *that others do not have claims over the content of the rightsholder's mind.* No one can legally demand that the rightsholder entertains a specific thought, feels a certain way, or possesses or exercises particular mental capacities. The importance of this claim will become evident in a minute. Additionally, the right implies a claim against others to refrain from altering minds of rightsholders against their will (therefore, interventions in case types 5 and 6 are pro tanto impermissible).

---

[27] E.g. Art. 18 Universal Declaration of Human Rights; Art. 19 International Covenant on Civil and Political Rights; Art. 9 European Convention on Human Rights.
[28] Boire, 2001.
[29] See Bublitz/Merkel, 2014; Bublitz (2014a,b).

Three clarifications are warranted. The right may have limits. Moreover, rightsholders have the power to consent to mind alterations (relevant for case types 2 and 4). Furthermore, a right to mental self-determination does not imply or presuppose that humans are ideally self-determined or self-controlled beings. We are not. As a legal right, mental self-determination pertains to relations *between* persons, not to psychic or bodily forces within a person. It guarantees negative liberties against interferences by others.

To render the scope more precise, let us image how the world and social interactions would become if the duty to refrain from altering other minds were strictly observed. Then, we would be obliged to refrain from sending mind-altering stimuli to others, which means that we could not even speak to one another without obtaining prior permission. Such a strict construal of the right is implausible. The law is, after all, interested in finding norms for a reasonable social order of which cooperation and communication are essential elements. Blanket prohibitions to alter other minds are thus neither practically conceivable nor politically desirable. While withdrawal from social interactions might be a legitimate conception of a good life, and social interactions should not be imposed on those who seek solitude, a Thoreauen lifestyle cannot serve as a model for normative orders for contemporary societies. Everyone who seeks to transcend solipsism desires and depends on social interaction. The law's task is to enable and promote meaningful and useful forms of interaction while curbing those forms that undermine mental self-determination in a troubling way. Therefore, the scope of the right against mind-interventions has to be confined to interferences that undermine mental self-determination to a degree that fails a test of what is reasonable in a highly cooperative, interactive, and communicative society. And this, I claim, is true of interventions that bypass mental control. Most of the myriad of stimuli entering our senses everyday, by contrast, fall outside of the scope of the right. In light of this normative premise, the relevance of mental control and integrity—and the direct versus indirect distinction—becomes evident. The more control, the better. In addition, mental self-determination entitles persons to define the functions of their cognitive machinery for themselves. Those wishing to utilize their brains as receptors for magnetic fields outside of their skull may ascribe this function to them. Magnetic receptivity then becomes a feature of their cognitive system. Those, by contrast, who do not wish to open such a pathway into their minds may reject this function. Using this pathway against the will of the person amounts to illicitly appropriating another's cognitive system.[30]

The upshot is this: everyone has a right against unwanted mind-interventions. It correlates with a duty of interveners to respect mental control and to refrain from altering minds of rightsholders. Interventions undermining or bypassing mental control, or appropriating functions of other brains, are particularly troublesome.

---

[30] The same cannot be said with respect to ordinary sense functions. If person A talks to B against the latter's will, it seems implausible to say that A has misappropriated B's sense functions.

Let us tie this together with the previous analysis and recapitulate: Interventions can be differentiated in terms of control. Persons have more control over stimuli processed by System 2 that rise to conscious awareness, less over those processed nonconsciously or by System 1 only, and even less control over direct interventions. In light of the right to mental self-determination, the latter are thus more problematic than the former. Respecting mental self-determination thus commands refraining from altering minds through direct interventions or through problematic control-undermining indirect interventions (only nonconscious or System 1 processing).

Rights to Intervene into Other Minds

At this stage, I hope to have shown why—in light of a reasonable construal of the applicable norm—the law should draw distinctions between interventions. Yet so far, only rights *against* mind-interventions have been taken into account. Perhaps, however, interveners may invoke rights *favoring* interventions. After all, mind-interventions are social interactions. Rights against interventions are only one side of the equation. If a conflict between rights for and against interventions emerges, rights have to be reconciled through the applicable method (e.g., balancing). This conflict plays hardly any role in current debates, but only its appreciation allows grasping the full scale of the normative issues at stake. Which rights could interveners invoke? Potentially several, especially in special circumstances (e.g., case types 3–6). But rather than elaborating on such specific rights, I wish to draw attention to another structural difference between direct and indirect interventions in this regard. The following discussion might get a bit tricky. In the previous section, I argued that interveners do not possess rights over minds of targets ("No claims over rightsholders' minds"). Therefore, interveners cannot *justify* mind-altering interventions by a claim that the target is under a legal duty to be in the mental state which the intervention produces. However, interventions might be justified by *other* considerations, primarily by rights permitting interveners potentially mind-altering *actions*. Free speech is the prime example. It can be conceived as a permission to send potentially mind-altering stimuli of a particular form, communicative stimuli. While it entitles interveners to send stimuli, it does not guarantee that the message be heard or appreciated. Senders may speak, but recipients do not have to listen. The key to solve the conflict between free speech as a permission to send stimuli and mental self-determination as a right against receiving them lies in distinguishing between *actions* and *effects*. Interveners have a right to speak but no claim that speech produces the desired effects in listeners. Free speech may justify communicative mind-interventions if they turn out successful, but it does not guarantee the conditions necessary for success.

More has to be said about the scope and strength of free speech and finer distinctions be drawn with respect to particular situations (e.g., "captured audiences" who cannot escape exposure to unwanted speech), means and purposes of communication (e.g., advertising), and atypical cases. It is worth noting here that usually only indirect interventions give rise to such conflicts since direct interventions are usually *not* protected by rights such as free speech because interveners do not pursue (legally) legitimate ends with their action. They primarily seek to alter targeted minds—to which they are *not* entitled because of recipients' right to mental self-determination. To illustrate: regularly, the only aim and interest of an intervener spraying a psychotropic substance such as oxytocin in a room or applying a magnetic field to another's forehead is altering the mental world of affected persons. Targets can reject tampering with their minds because of their right to mental self-determination. They could not, by contrast, bar interveners from speaking to them (because of free speech of interveners). More generally: The action of directly intervening (e.g., pushing a button) is, by itself, regularly not valuable for intrinsic or social reasons; whereas the action of indirect interventions (expression) is. Accordingly, a structural difference in the justification of direct and indirect interventions emerges: some indirect interventions are exercises of strong rights; direct interventions are usually not.[31]

In cases in which a right to the intervening actions such as free speech exists, it has to be balanced against the countervailing right to mental self-determination. This requires context-specific considerations. Effects and strength of interventions play a key role, weaker ones undermining mental self-determination to a lesser degree are easier justifiable than stronger ones. But strength is not the only decisive factor. Highly effective, even irresistible interventions which are doubtlessly permissible are easily conceivable. The prime example is a persuasive argument that cannot but make (a rational) listener change her opinions or beliefs. This is the "forceless force" of the better argument, and it differs substantially from the force of, for example, a chemical intervention targeting opinions or beliefs. Rational and justifiable beliefs require a particular mode of acquisition and transformation: reason or evidence (Crutchfield, 2016). Of course, communication regularly involves more than rational exchange of reasons. The law draws distinctions among various forms (e.g., manipulation, coercive persuasion, undue influence). Communicative interventions fall on a spectrum. Habermasian ideal speech situations in which statements are formulated free from emotional influences or distracting associations in contexts devoid of power lie on one end. There, only better arguments prevail. On the opposing end lie communicative forms deploying psychological trickery and exploiting psychological weaknesses of recipients. Lines of moral and legal significance run even between these poles. A parity principle obfuscates them.

---

[31] Note that in exceptional cases, the norm "No claims over minds of another" is false, because other persons do have such claims, most notably, parents over children (case type 3). Parents not only have a right; they are even under a *duty* to shape their kids' minds (e.g., education and development of mental skills). The same might be true for the state or guardians with respect to noncompetent persons, or even, most controversially, with respect to criminal offenders. These case types require finer discussion. Here, I only wish to reiterate the previously made methodological point that such atypical cases do not allow for generalizations.

Where precisely the boundaries between permissible speech and undue per-suasion are best drawn is a challenging question that dates back to Greek debates over the ethics of rhetoric. Instead of providing answers, I can only note that it is a shortcoming of legal theory and philosophy to not offer more concrete guid-ance about "undue influence" or "illicit manipulation," concededly a complex matter in which empirical and normative considerations are deeply interwoven (see Coons and Weber, 2014). Especially (social) psychology, cognitive sciences, and "marketing studies" have produced a wealth of findings that needs to be ana-lyzed in light of ideas of mental self-determination and free speech, such as the role of emotions in attitude formation and communicative strategies appealing to them (see Cialdini, 2007, 2016). History has shown the effectiveness of propa-ganda by indirect means stirring emotions of the masses, and instilling fear and insecurity still seems to be a winning strategy of political campaigns at this very moment in the United States and Europe.[32] In the dawning age of "posttruth" and "alternative facts," the primacy of opinion change through rational discourse tends to be replaced by vindication of intuitions, ideologies, and sentiments. We should insist on the importance of justifiable beliefs and the primacy of argu-ment in opinion formation as it forms the bedrock of societies, which wish to engage with each other on, by and large, rational ways. Therefore, a default policy for a social order of reasonable citizens has to hold that beliefs should be altered through evidence and argument and not by interventions bypassing reasons and reasoning. Challenging work about the normative limits of communicative in-fluence awaits to be done, and some sophisticated forms of persuasion (e.g., in advertising or political campaigning) might have to be restricted more strongly. But that opens a long debate about the value and limits of free speech, which would lead us astray here. But it indirectly proves my point. To reiterate: a key difference between direct and indirect interventions is that restricting the latter leads into thorny issues of free speech; restricting the former does not.

Free speech is the most salient example of the asymmetrical relation between di-rect and indirect interventions and suffices to casts doubts on the parity principle. Taking parity seriously entails losing criteria to distinguish between communicative and other interventions. But what about other forms of influences via the senses that we send and receive all the time? Given their ubiquity and manifoldness, it is impos-sible to survey them here. But the structure of their assessment is the same: rights of interveners have to be reconciled with mental self-determination of recipients. A brief and basic example: Imagine an ordinary conversation between A and B in which the former is strongly influenced by the latter's appearance—her style, dress, look, posture, tone of voice, and social standing. While A remains largely unaware of these influences, B uses her charms intentionally. These nonrational

---

[32] See Bargh (2017) for some astonishingly simple experiments that change political attitudes by evoking emotions of fear and security.

factors change A's mindset, so that he finds her arguments persuasive. B's noncommunicative influences are no instances of free speech. Do they violate A's mental self-determination? Arguably not. The way a person appears and presents herself to others and behaves are expressions of her personality and protected by rights to the person. They may justify B's impact on A's mind.

In this way, other noncommunicative influences need to be analyzed. Further rights may come into play, as well as further consideration such as implicit consent. In many cases, a right to send influential indirect stimuli might be absent, and in some instances, they clearly run afoul of mental self-determination (e.g., subliminal stimuli, see Dijksterhuis, Aarts, and Smith, 2005). Many of them, however, are also inevitable manifestations of social life. They unavoidably accompany cherished forms of social practices and thus cannot be restricted without curbing these practices, which seems unattractive in many cases. Every mundane communicative intervention is befallen with nonrational influences just mentioned. But, nonetheless, whereas indirect interventions regularly accompany desirable forms of social interventions, direct interventions seem to be only rarely inevitable by-products of desirable social interactions.

Consequences

What follows from this? In light of mental self-determination, indirect interventions fare better than direct ones for several interrelated reasons: Indirect interventions leave the integrity of the cognitive system intact. Regularly, they neither misappropriate functions, nor bypass control capacities of affected persons. Furthermore, insofar as they are instances of communication, they enjoy free speech protection. Direct interventions, by contrast, bypass control capacities, may misappropriate functions, and legal rights justifying them are regularly absent since no one has claims over another's mind. Indirect interventions of noncommunicative nature require further context specific evaluation. As long as they inevitably accompany ordinary interactions, they are likely the kind of mutual influence that social life entails and that escapes reasonable regulation. Still, some forms might be illicit. This allows ranking interventions in an ascending order of normative concern, with prior ones being normatively preferable to subsequent ones. The following are some paradigmatic instances.

1. Perceptual stimuli, available for conscious and System 2 processing, of communicative nature
2. Perceptual stimuli, available for conscious and System 2 processing, of noncommunicative nature but protected by rights
3. Perceptual stimuli, only available for nonconscious or System 1 processing, inevitably accompanying desirable social interactions (e.g., priming)

4. Perceptual stimuli, only available for nonconscious and System 1 processing, avoidable (e.g., subliminal stimuli)
5. Direct interventions, avoidable

Herewith, some progress to the overall aim of developing a taxonomy of
mind-interventions is made. Of course, empirical facts such as strengths of
interventions and further normative criteria have to be added to complete such a
taxonomy. But it allows for some conclusion. First, suppose a prospective intervener (e.g., policymaker, advertiser, or therapist) asks for guidance on whether
and by which means they should change the mind of someone else? The parity
principle denies differences. But that surely does not reflect the best answer. The
advice must be, Respect mental self-determination. This might imply to not intervene at all. And if so, through the means that leave recipients with the highest
degree of mental control.

Second, we can further specify the prospects for direct interventions into
other minds. They are, cum grano salis, only permissible in a narrow range
of cases: For one, there might be cases in which interveners do have a right
to alter minds (either to the action or action and effects), because the right
to mental self-determination is *limited*. Whether and where limits may run
is a question I cannot address here. But, if at all, limits will be restricted to
exceptional cases, such as legally incompetent persons or rehabilitation of
offenders.[33] A second category concerns unavoidable direct interventions.
For instance, eating at a restaurant regularly involves direct interventions
(through psychotropic properties of food—think only of glucose; Wenk,
2015). While restaurants should surely respect mental self-determination
of customers (and inform them about possible psychotropic effects of
meals), this is a good example of socially accepted (and low-intensity) direct interventions. There might be similar examples in other domains of
life. But apart from such exceptions, direct interventions into other minds
are impermissible—regardless of their strength (provided they are effective
above a de minimis threshold).

Where finer lines should between indirect interventions should be drawn,
especially between sophisticated forms of communicative persuasion involving
appeals to emotion, depends on further value decisions. The key question
is this: What should be the default mode of engaging with other minds, and
which modes undermine mental control to a degree so disquieting that the
legal system should step in? After all, as a guiding line, it suggests itself to bar
those interventions which severely undermine mental self-determination and

---

[33] I argue against such coercive interventions in the minds of offenders in Bublitz 2018. For opposing views, see Douglas (2014, 2018).

fail to serve legitimate ends. This entails banning direct interventions. And here we have arrived at the asymmetry between interventions that this chapter sought to demonstrate. The following figure shows the relevant questions schematically:

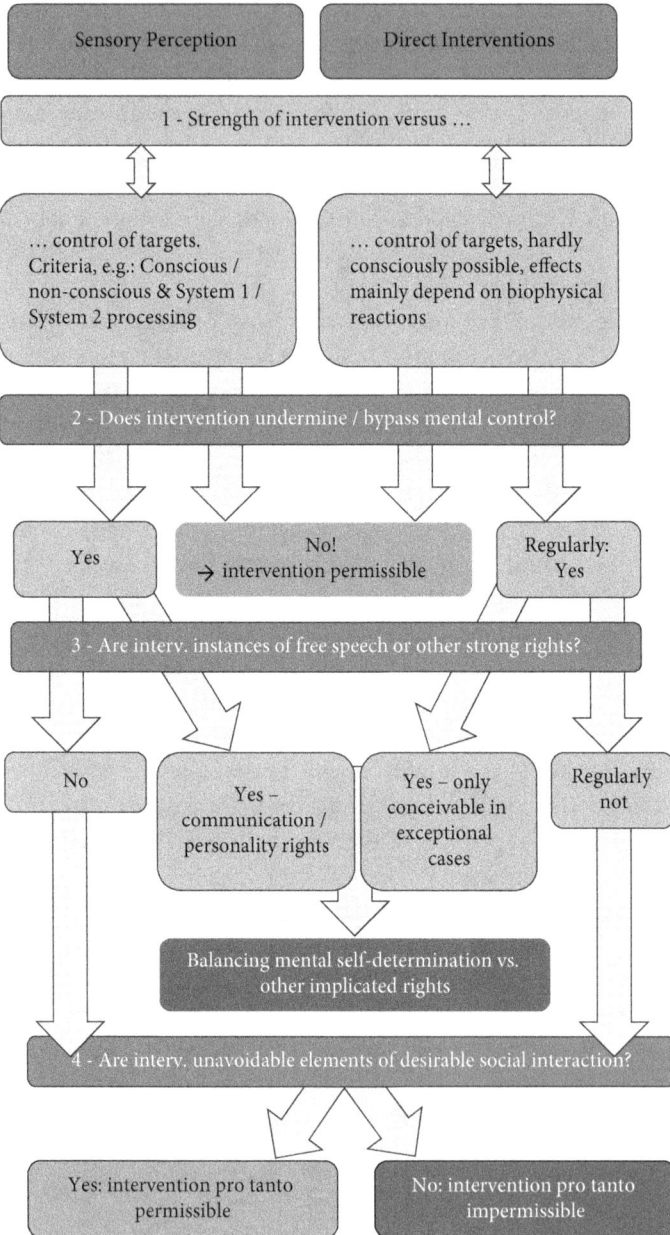

More Complex Interventions

The foregoing analysis was confined to *single* interventions. More complex interventions may comprise a range of various stimuli. For instance, therapies in psychiatry often involve a combination of drugs and talk therapies. Or, more sinister, consider gaslighting, or brainwashing, a vague concept for a set of severe manipulative interventions exploiting mental weaknesses and instabilities (Taylor, 2006). Although not necessarily involving direct interventions, the latter are paradigmatic examples for illicit attacks on mental self-determination of victims. Similarly, methods such as aversive conditioning based on uncontrollable learning mechanisms that associate unrelated stimuli (e.g., aversive conditioning in *Clockwork Orange*) may infringe upon mental self-determination. More benign, psychotherapies may trigger hard to control emotional dynamics or nonconscious processes such as (counter)transference (Lemma, 2016).[34] Likewise, sophisticated audiovisual installations or immersive virtual realities can be powerful influences. Conversely, experiments showed that sensory *deprivation* of external stimuli had massive effects on the mind (Grassian & Friedmann, 1986). Also, indirect stimuli might be harder to control under specific external (social) circumstances that weaken mental control, from time pressure to situational factors. In combination, interventions consisting of several, by themselves, innocuous stimuli can amount to massive intervention into minds, and, if imposed involuntarily, mental self-determination speaks in favor of their ban.

Environmental Interventions

Against this backdrop, we can assess some recently discussed cases. The first concerns advertisements in public places. Imagine a billboard featuring the actress Jennifer Aniston. Perceiving it creates a visual representation of Aniston in the perceiver, which triggers further thoughts about her. Moreover, Nicole Vincent suggested a garden in which the neuropeptide oxytocin is released, making visitors more open, trusting, and more intimately conversing. Thomas Douglas challenges my distinction with a case in which the walls in an institution (a ward or prison) are painted in a color that calms and soothes people, who remain unaware of the influence (Douglas, 2018). As the paint manipulates persons to the same degree than direct interventions may, Douglas considers the

---

[34] Transference is a process in the relation between patient and therapist in psychoanalytic therapy. In theory, the patient transfers feelings and attitudes of older interpersonal relation on the therapists. Therapies may make use of this nonconscious process.

direct–indirect distinction unpersuasive. Finally, a common objection against the distinction refers to nudging through choice architecture.

Let us assume the interventions in these cases are effective. They are peculiar because they are not confined to one-to-one situations but alter public places and potentially affect a broader audience. Let us call them *environmental interventions*. Normatively, they raise questions as to how environments should be designed, by whom, and about the extent to which affected persons may legitimately complain about the world being designed in a specific way. That environmental conditions alter behavior is among the central tenets of behaviorism. To Skinner and in a somewhat strange relation, the leftist movement of the 1960s and 1970s, the environment was the decisive causal factor (Skinner, 2002, cf. Wheeler, 1973). Interventions accordingly aim at changing the environment (including social conditions), which may then change people. Even though the scientific demise of behaviorism was mainly due to its overemphasis on the environment, it is beyond doubt that environmental stimuli can effectively alter behavior (Chomsky, 1971). And, on my account, normatively, evaluating environmental interventions requires balancing countervailing rights and interests in the manner previously outlined, with the difference that social or public considerations come to the fore.

Take the Aniston billboard. Perceiving means picking up information from the external world, to which we are constantly connected. Perception thus necessarily implies that minds of perceivers may be altered through perceived stimuli. Thus, our existential mode of being connected to the world through our senses brings alterations of our minds with it. Normatively, this suggests (although not necessarily entails) that perceivers usually cannot complain about alterations of their minds through perception. As long as perceptions are veridical, perceivers acquire knowledge about the world through perception. They may only complain about the existence of particular stimuli (or about the existential mode of being connected through the world via perception, but that is not a legally relevant complaint).

Whether complaints are warranted is a normative question that has to accommodate several aspects, among others, strength of stimuli and effects on mental self-determination. In addition, it involves normative considerations over the design of public spaces. Because people share the external world, no individual can claim priority of her particular interests over those of others, and that includes her mental reactions to perceiving the social sphere. The design of public places is therefore a res publica. Options range from a low stimuli environment—say, painting everything in grey—to high-stimuli environments such as Times Square. Communities have good reasons to choose the latter, to paint walls colorfully or put up boards for communicative exchange. In the design decision, mental self-determination of perceivers has to be recognized, but only as one among several relevant factors. Accordingly, beholders of a billboard cannot complain about having a visual representation (i.e., what perceiving implies), nor about perceiving female faces in public or Aniston in persona. They could only complain about the particular representation on the board. The setback of this intervention into their minds has to be weighed against the legitimate democratic prerogative over designing public spaces, and the interests putting up such billboards pursies. In this case, the effects on mental self-determination through the Aniston stimulus are so trivial that community interests to afford spaces for visual communication prevail. However, not all forms of public advertisements appear beyond scrutiny. More intensive and systematic interventions—imagine a city plastered with Aniston pictures, for instance—may violate mental self-determination.

But, in any case, billboards contrast with direct interventions: In experiments with epilepsy patients, neuroscientists discovered "concept cells" (as it were of Aniston). These findings suggest that concepts are stored in individual cells, which function as building blocks of memory (Quiroga, 2012; Quiroga, Reddy, Kreiman, Koch, & Fried, 2005). Imagine that instead of a billboard, a device is installed that stimulates the concept neuron of Aniston whenever a person walks by, triggering the same mental effects as the board. This direct intervention interferes with mental self-determination as there is no reason to have a visual representation of Aniston walking by that spot. Further, installing the device does not serve legitimate interests of the community (here, again, the right to mental self-determination bars legal protection of interests in other persons entertaining specific thoughts). The difference between the billboard and the device—although both have identical effects—is that good reasons of the community may speak for putting up the former, but none for the latter.

Surely, one may wonder why we should not enrich the environment with such direct interventions. This brings us Vincent's oxytocin garden. There is no principled objection against such places as long as affected persons consent to exposure. Visitors aware of the oxytocin may be deemed to consent by entering. Without consent, oxytocin impinges upon mental self-determination. We can also view the Aniston case through the lens of consent. A person walking with eyes wide open through an urban environment can be deemed to consent to the impressions she perceives, inasmuch as they remain within the range of the expectable. Likewise, if instead of oxytocin, the garden was full of splendid flowers inducing a warm and opening mood, perceivers lack grounds to complain as this is a typical and expectable response to an environment designed in a socially adequate way.

Consent is also one of the problems in Douglas' case. The wall color is a sensual indirect intervention. In fact, a shade of pink, Baker-Miller pink, is suspected of reducing aggressive behavior. Some prisons cells were painted in the tone, but its effectiveness is unclear (Genschow, 2015). More generally, physical environments, spaces, architecture, and color can exert influence, in the way that visiting awe-inspiring buildings does. But while effective, I suspect that strength should not be overstated. According to the previously described distinctions, sensory perception leaves perceivers with some form of control (this might be testable empirically). The arising normative question is how places as prisons should be designed. As any design of such institutions will inevitably have some effects, they are, as such, not avoidable. An inhospitable clinical setting would also effect people. So, if one designs a prison which alters minds of inmates in any case, why not in a way creating an atmosphere in which people feel secure, comfortable, and at ease? If all spaces affect people, designing them conducive to their functions seems appropriate. Particularly influential forms are nonetheless troubling. The example in point is the Panopticon as described by Foucault (1995). Cells of inmates are constantly visible because of the setup of the building. The constant exposure to surveillance lets inmates internalize a feeling of being surveilled and, thereby, alters minds and behaviors. However, these effects touch upon further issues such as privacy in corrective settings. To avoid these additional complexities, let us assume Baker-Miller pink has considerable mind-altering effects quite unlike ordinary colors, is effective without awareness, and can neither be avoided nor resisted by affected persons. Then, the paint amounts to a constant indirect intervention and may interfere with mental self-determination. However, exposing prisoners to it might be justifiable by the special conditions of incarceration, and this seems to do some of the argumentative work in the example. While prisons lack claims over minds of inmates, they have a right—and a duty—to enforce compliant *behavior* that includes, in perilous situations, physical restraints or even direct mind-interventions (e.g., a sedative). One might argue the institutional interest in reducing aggressive behavior justifies less-invasive means such as a calming paint. The crucial aspect is thus not the perceptible nature of the intervention but its inescapable omnipresence and potential justifiability.

Finally, consider a basic case of choice architecture (e.g., positioning and pricing of goods in a supermarket). To Sunstein and Thaler, such nudges do not interfere with liberties or rights of affected persons at all (Thaler &Sunstein, 2008). This is why their idea of "libertarian paternalism" is so intriguing. If they were correct, the legal difference to direct interventions is evident: the latter surely interfere with rights such as mental self-determination. However, according to my construal of the right, choice architecture does appear worrisome. Positioning of goods in supermarkets is not a matter of free speech. It may be an expression of shop owners' rights to property or business that allows them to set up stores how they see fit. However, they are obliged to respect mental self-determination of customers. Choice architecture falls within the tension of these rights. While one may say that placing goods in a particular order only rearranges existing stimuli, it is also an intentional attempt to steer decisions and behavior in ways of which customers are not aware. Respecting mental self-determination implies not exploiting mental weaknesses. Balancing rights may yield the compromise that costumers have to be informed about these influences. Awareness might empower them to consciously (System 2) reconsider their choices (although indications are that people also succumb to nudges they are made aware of; Sunstein, 2016). At the same time, a duty to inform about choice architecture does not severely infringe rights of shop owners. They can still arrange goods as they please. Yet again, choice architecture differs from direct interventions (e.g., releasing an odorless substance with similar mind-altering effects). Directly influencing choices is something to which shop owners are not entitled, because it does not serve legitimate interests in running their business. Their only aim is altering choices, and that, as such, is off limits to them due to customers' right to mental self-determination. To sum up, while some of these environmental interventions give grounds for concern, they often require further context specific considerations. In any case, they do not disprove relevant differences between direct and indirect interventions.

Reply to Levy

With the previous discussion in place, let me finally address some objections Levy raises in Chapter 2 of this volume against (an earlier version of) my account. I concur with his criticisms of ill-founded distinctions between interventions and with large parts of his present argument. Still, and somewhat surprisingly, we reach diverging normative conclusions. Broadly, Levy seeks to dismiss the relevance of the distinction by showing that many indirect interventions are worrying precisely for the same reason as direct interventions are—namely, because they undermine control or alter central characteristics of persons. In such general terms, I agree. Our disagreement, though, seems partly due to the methodological point I raised earlier. Levy presents the example of a moderately depressed person who exposes herself to sunlight or adds iodine to her diet. I agree that there is nothing to demur to absorbing sunlight or iodine. Voluntarily changing one's own mind through direct interventions is often unproblematic and the right to mental self-determination not even implicated because it only obliges others (it does not create duties against oneself). However, if persons are exposed to sunlight or mind-altering foods against their will, the right kicks in (imagine a prison inmate is put on a mandatory diet to reduce aggression). Analogies between cases of voluntary self-change to nonvoluntarily interventions are misleading (see the distinction between case *supra*).

Furthermore, in the foregoing chapter, Levy objects to the "lack of control" criterion for two reasons. For one, persons may have "the chance to assess the new mental state" produced by direct interventions in the same ways as those produced by indirect ways. I agree, but we seem to talk past each other. My argument pertains the kind and degree of control persons have over interventions from the moment of first contact until their effects set in (where that endpoint is remains concededly a bit blurry). It does not pertain to more downstream effects and how (easily) reversible they are (largely a matter of strength). Levy further argues that people may not have full control even over consciously perceived stimuli. He notes in the previous chapter that "consciousness of stimuli is not sufficient for control over how we respond." This well-chosen example demonstrates that we can be "conscious of words, but not of the effects the words have" on us. Again, I agree. But this does not undermine the relevance of the direct–indirect distinction. I do not wish to suggest, nor does my account presuppose, that humans are anything near ideally self-controlled agents. Large parts of our psychological operations remain opaque to us, we post hoc rationalize and confabulate. Such weaknesses render us vulnerable to exploitation by others. Yet, the existence of such weaknesses does not imply or suggest the truth of the parity principle. The priming examples nicely illustrates this. Susceptibility to conceptual or perceptual priming is a feature of our psychological system, priming occurs in ordinary situations and conversations. Because it is effective, one may call for an "ethics of priming." Attempts to regulate priming, however, face the problem of its ubiquity and raise free speech–related difficulties. Some priming effects (e.g., in a rhetorically skilled speech) seem to be legitimate exercises of this right. More generally, unless one is prepared to severely obstruct communication (e.g., by obliging speakers to choose words in ways devoid of priming effects, if possible at all), it largely escapes regulation. Perhaps special forms or contexts might be regulatable (e.g., masked priming, advertisement), but priming as such is just not restrictable across the board. So, whereas Levy is right that priming is not beyond concern, his conclusion is questionable: the existence of hard-to-regulate control undermining influences such as priming does not imply that other, equally effective, *direct interventions* that exploit psychological weaknesses should also remain unregulated across the board.

More generally, showing that indirect interventions can produce equally normatively worrisome effects than direct ones is a strategy insufficient to validate the parity principle. The unfortunate existence of some influences does not justify retaining or putting into place further suspect influences. Consider this analogy. The inability to control all toxins in the air does not justify more emissions. Levy correctly writes that "people can manipulate others through [indirect interventions] just as effectively as they can using oxytocin" or other direct interventions (previous chapter). But what follows from this? I claim that *even though* two interventions cause sufficiently similar effects, assessments may differ, frequently along the direct–indirect divide, because *other* normative considerations come into play—the many finer-grained considerations of the sort outlined in this chapter. This claim cannot be falsified by showing (dis)similarities of effects. Instead, it would have to be shown that other considerations are normatively *irrelevant*.

Taking Levy's argument further, one may deny the significance of the direct–indirect distinction by holding that the by far strongest influences on everyone, inescapable and potent to shape deep levels of personalities, are upbringing, education, media, and culture. Indeed, cultural forces (and the industry creating them) shape our thoughts, desires, and even self-conceptions probably to a far greater degree than most direct interventions ever can. Nevertheless, although the right to mental self-determination is not blind to the social and cultural forces shaping everyone these forces largely escape meaningful legal regulation, at least as long as one seeks social participation. The right suggests scrutinizing particular cultural practices detrimental to mental self-determination (e.g., effects of photoshopped models on the self-image of adolescents). Stronger regulation seems warranted, and mental self-determination provides a strong argument to this end. However, the influence of such practices pales in comparison to the powers of broader social and cultural forces. The law is often impotent to capture, let alone regulate, dynamics and effects at these levels. But, nonetheless, given that everyone is exposed, even subjected to a range of such overwhelming influences—should therefore other (direct) interventions be permissible *as well*?

I don't think so. I join Levy in lamenting social injustices such as lack of education and nutrition and their effects on mental development. I wish to add that the unequal distribution of means to change minds (e.g., the lacking access of millions of marginalized people to have their voices heard in the forums of political power) significantly contributes to this malaise (see Paulo & Bublitz, 2019). But I fail to see why a "concern for justice mandates ignoring the causal route whereby interventions work" (foregoing chapter). Society should not stop at banning direct interventions for wrongly assuming other forms of influence are ineffective, but begin by banning those that clearly undermine mental self-determination.

After all, as Levy seems to share the normative premise of mental self-determination, and as I agree with his descriptive claims, I can only account for our diverging conclusions by a final intuition: In a consequentialist framework, effects are all that matters *per definitionem* whereas rights-based frameworks usually insist on the importance of factors overriding consequences. It might not be a coincidence that a structurally similar contrast emerges here. Perhaps we are simply witnessing another variation of differences in more general positions of normative ethics.

Conclusion

In conclusion, if one seeks to secure an inner citadel from physiological or psychological influences, any of these proposed regulations are insufficient. But that aim is futile. Reasonable regulations for real minds start with accepting that the human mind is malleable and manipulable on diverse ways, many of which are hardly regulatable. Normatively, every person has a right against mind-interventions and, correlatively, a duty to respect mental self-determination of others. What this means more precisely is a complex question. Contemporarily, the ideal of mental self-determination is accorded an adequate role neither in legal or ethical theory, nor in practice. In its light, interventions into other minds that undermine or bypass control are particularly worrisome. Whether this is the case depends on the strength and mode of an intervention. Blanket prohibitions of all mind-altering stimuli, including sensory ones, are inconceivable in cooperative and communicative societies. For good reasons, particular forms of social interaction are considered desirable. This is reflected in specific rights to send mind-altering stimuli, primarily freedom of speech. Ultimately, we have to accept that social life necessarily involves influencing others and being influenced by others. Reasonable regulation has to pick out the most worrisome interventions. The distinction between physiological and psychological interventions is central and suggests a normative dualism: prima facie direct interventions are impermissible, whereas indirect interventions are permissible. Nonetheless, some forms of indirect interventions (e.g., akin to psychological trickery) may also be regarded as illicit. As I have hopefully urged enough in this chapter, finer distinctions with respect to particular contexts and means are necessary. The parity principle unfortunately gets in the way of seeing the necessity for systematically developing more nuanced distinctions.

References

Andersson, M., Avaliani, N., Svensson, A., Wickham, J., Pinborg, L., Jespersen, B., . . . Kokaia, M. (2016). Optogenetic control of human neurons in organotypic brain cultures. *Scientific Reports, 6*, 24818.

Baars, B. J. (1997). *In the theater of consciousness: The workspace of the mind.* New York, NY: Oxford University Press.

Bargh, J. (2017). *Before you know it.* New York, NY: Touchstone.

Bargh, J. A., & Williams, E. L. (2006). The automaticity of social life. *Current Directions in Psychological Science, 15*(1), 1–4.

Boire, R. G. (2001). On cognitive liberty. *The Journal of Cognitive Liberties, 2*(1), 7–22.

Bublitz, C. (2014a). Cognitive liberty or the international human right to freedom of thought. In N. Levy & J. Clausen (Eds.), *Springer handbook of neuroethics* (pp. 1309–1333). Dordrecht, The Netherlands: Springer.

Bublitz, C. (2014b). Freedom of thought in the age of neuroscience. *Archiv fuer Rechts- und Sozialphilosophie, 100*, 1–25.

Bublitz, C. (2016). Drugs, enhancements & rights: Ten points for lawmakers to consider. In F. Jotterand. & V. Dubljevic (Eds.), *Cognitive enhancement: Ethical and policy implications in international perspective* (pp. 309–328). New York: Oxford University Press.

Bublitz, C. (2018). "The soul is the prison of the body"—Mandatory moral enhancement, punishment & rights against neuro-rehabilitation. In D. Birks & S. Thomas (Eds.), *Treatment for crime: Philosophical essays on neurointerventions in criminal justice* (pp. 289–320). Oxford, England: Oxford University Press.

Bublitz, C., & Merkel, R. (2014). Crimes against minds: On mental manipulations, harms, and a human right to mental self-determination. *Criminal Law and Philosophy, 8*(1), 51–77.

Chalmers, D. (2002). Consciousness and its place in nature. In S. P. Stich & T. A. Warfield (Eds.), *The Blackwell guide to philosophy of mind* (pp. 102–142) Malden, MA: Blackwell.

Chomsky, N. (1971). The case against BF Skinner. *The New York Review of Books, 17*(11), 18–24.

Cialdini, R. (2007). *Influence: The psychology of persuasion*. New York, NY: HarperCollins.

Cialdini, R. (2016). *Pre-suasion: A revolutionary way to influence and persuade*. London, England: Random House.

Coons, C., & Weber, M. (2014). *Manipulation: Theory and practice*. Oxford, England: Oxford University Press.

Crutchfield, P. (2016). The epistemology of moral bioenhancement. *Bioethics, 30*(6), 389–396.

Dahaner, J. (2019). Why internal moral enhancement might be politically better than external moral enhancement. *Neuroethics, 12*(1), 39–54.

Davidson, R. J., Kabat-Zinn, J., Schumacher, J., Rosenkranz, M., Muller, D., Santorelli, S. F, . . . Sheridan, J. F. (2003). Alterations in brain and immune function produced by mindfulness meditation. *Psychosomatic Medicine, 65*(4), 564–570.

Davis, N. J., van Koningsbruggen, M. G. (2013). "Non-invasive" brain stimulation is not non-invasive. *Frontiers in Systems Neuroscience, 7*, 76.

Dijksterhuis, A., Aarts, H., & Smith, P. (2005). The power of the subliminal: On subliminal persuasion and other potential applications. In R. Hassin & J. Uleman (Eds.), *The new unconscious* (pp. 77–106). Oxford, England: Oxford University Press.

Dougherty, D. D., Rezai, A. R., Carpenter, L. L., Howland, R. H., Bhati, M. T., O'Reardon, J. P & Cusin, C. (2015). A randomized sham-controlled trial of deep brain stimulation of the ventral capsule/ventral striatum for chronic treatment-resistant depression. *Biological Psychiatry, 78*(4), 240–248.

Douglas, T. (2014). Criminal rehabilitation through medical intervention: Moral liability and the right to bodily integrity. *The Journal of Ethics, 18*, 101–122.

Douglas, T. (2018). Neural and environmental modulation of motivation: What's the moral difference? In D. Birks & T. Douglas (Eds.), *Treatment for crime: Philosophical essays on neurointerventions in criminal justice* (pp. 280–223). Oxford, England: Oxford University Press.

Evans, J., & Frankish, K. (2009). *In two minds: Dual processes and beyond.* Oxford, England: Oxford University Press.

Evans, J., & Stanovich, K. E. (2013). Dual process theories of higher cognition: Advancing the debate. *Perspectives on Psychological Science, 8*(3), 223–241.

Focquaert, F., & Schermer, M. (2015). Moral enhancement: Do means matter morally? *Neuroethics, 8*(2), 139–151.

Foucault, M. (1995). *Discipline and punish: The birth of the prison.* New York, NY: Second Vintage Books.

Frankish, K. (2009). Systems and levels: Dual-system theories and the personal-subpersonal distinction. In J. Evans & K. Frankish (Eds.), *In two minds: Dual processes and beyond* (pp. 89–107). Oxford, England: Oxford University Press.

Genschow, O., Noll, T., Wänke, M., & Gersbach, R. (2015). Does Baker-Miller pink reduce aggression in prison detention cells? A critical empirical examination. *Psychology, Crime & Law, 21*(5), 482–489.

Goode, E. (2016, July 29). Is hypnosis all in your head? Brain scans suggest otherwise. *The New York Times.* http://www.nytgimes.com/2016/07/30/science/hypnosis-brain-changes.html

Grassian, S., & Friedman, N. (1986). Effects of sensory deprivation in psychiatric seclusion and solitary confinement. *International Journal of Law and Psychiatry, 8*(1), 49–65.

Greene, J. (2014). Beyond point-and-shoot morality: Why cognitive (neuro)science matters for ethics. *Ethics, 124,* 695–726.

Hartogsohn, I. (2016). Set and setting, psychedelics and the placebo response: An extra-pharmacological perspective on psychopharmacology. *Journal of Psychopharmacology, 30*(12), 1259–1267.

Hassin, R. (2005). Nonconscious control and implicit working memory. In R. Hassin & J. Uleman (Eds.), *The new unconscious* (pp. 196–223). Oxford, England: Oxford University Press.

Jakubovski, E., Varigonda, A., Freemantle, N., Taylor, M., & Bloch, M. H. (2016). Systematic review and meta-analysis: Dose-response relationship of selective serotonin reuptake inhibitors in major depressive disorder. *American Journal of Psychiatry, 173*(2), 174–183.

Kahneman, D. (2011). *Thinking, fast and slow.* New York, NY: Farrar, Straus and Giroux.

Kahneman, D., & Shane, F. (2002). Representativeness revisited: Attribute substitution in intuitive judgment. In T. Gilovich, D. Griffin, & D. Kahneman (Eds.), *Heuristics and biases: The psychology of intuitive judgment* (pp. 49–81). New York, NY: Cambridge University Press.

Kandel, E. (2007). *In search of memory: The emergence of a new science of mind.* New York, NY: W. W. Norton.

Kim, J. (2011). *Philosophy of mind.* Boulder, CO: Westview Press.

Krohs, U., & Kroes, P. (2009). *Functions in biological and artificial worlds: Comparative philosophical perspectives.* Cambridge, MA: MIT Press.

Leibniz, G. W. (2008). Letter to Friedrich Bierling. In C. I. Gerhardt (Ed.), *Die philosophischen Schriften von G. W. Leibniz* (Vol. 7). Hildesheim, Germany: Olms. (Original work published 1709)

Lemma, A. (2016). *Introduction to the practice of psychoanalytic psychotherapy.* Malden, MA: Wiley.

Levy, N. (2007). *Neuroethics: Challenges for the 21st century.* Cambridge, England: Cambridge University Press.

Linden, D. (2006). How psychotherapy changes the brain—The contribution of functional neuroimaging. *Molecular Psychiatry, 11*, 528–538.

Macpherson, F. (2011). Individuating the senses. In F. Macpherson, *The senses: Classical and contemporary philosophical perspectives* (pp. 3–45). New York, NY: Oxford University Press.

Martin, E., Jeanmonod, D., Morel, A., Zadicario, E., & Werner, B. (2009). High-intensity focused ultrasound for noninvasive functional neurosurgery. *Annals of Neurology, 66*, 858–861. doi:10.1002/ana.21801

Mayberg, H., Lozano, A. M., Voon, V., McNeely, H. E., Seminowicz, D., Hamani, C., . . . Kennedy, S. H. (2005). Deep brain stimulation for treatment-resistant depression. *Neuron;45*(5), 651–660.

McLaughlin, P. (2000). *What functions explain: Functional explanation and self-reproducing systems.* Cambridge, England: Cambridge University Press.

Merkel, R. (2007). Treatment—Prevention—Enhancement: Normative foundations and limits. In R. Merkel, G. Boer, J. Fegert, & T. Galert (Eds.), *Intervening in the brain: Changing psyche and society* (pp. 289–382). Heidelberg, Germany: Springer.

Merriam-Webster. (n.d.). Medical definition of *invasive*. Retrieved from https://www.merriam-webster.com/dictionary/invasive

Metzinger, T. (2010). *The ego tunnel: The science of the mind and the myth of the self.* New York, NY: Basic Books.

Metzinger, T. (2013). The myth of cognitive agency: Subpersonal thinking as a cyclically recurring loss of mental autonomy. *Frontiers Psychology, 4*, 931.

Morishita, T., Fayad, S., Higuchi, M., Nestor, K. A., & Foote, K. D. (2014). Deep brain stimulation for treatment-resistant depression: Systematic review of clinical outcomes. *Neurotherapeutics, 11*(3), 475–484. doi:10.1007/s13311-014-0282-1

Nussbaum, M. C. (1995). Objectification. *Philosophy & Public Affairs, 24*(4), 249–291.

Paulo, N., & Bublitz, C. (2019). Pow(d)er to the people? Voter manipulation, legitimacy, and the relevance of moral psychology for democratic theory. *Neuroethics, 12*, 55–71.

Prinz, J. (2016). Unconscious perception. In M. Matthen (Ed.), *The Oxford handbook of philosophy of perception* (pp. 371–389). Oxford, England: Oxford University Press.

Quiroga, R. Q. (2012). Concept cells: The building blocks of declarative memory functions. *Nature Reviews Neuroscience, 13*(8), 587–597.

Quiroga, R. Q., Reddy, L., Kreiman, G., Koch, C., & Fried, I. (2005). Invariant visual representation by single neurons in the human brain. *Nature, 435*(7045), 1102–1107.

Reti, I. (Ed.). (2015). *Brain stimulation: Methodologies and interventions.* Hoboken, NJ: Wiley.

Schlaepfer, T., & Lieb, K. (2005). Deep brain stimulation for treatment of refractory depression. *The Lancet, 366*(9495), 1420–1422.

Scholey, A., & Owen, L. (2013). Effects of chocolate on cognitive function and mood: A systematic review. *Nutrition Reviews, 71*(10), 665–681. doi:10.1111/nure.12065

Seung, S. (2012). *Connectome: How the brain's wiring makes us who we are.* Boston, MA: Houghton Mifflin Harcourt.

Skinner, B. F. (2002). *Beyond freedom and dignity.* London: Hackett.

Specker, J., Schermer, M., & Reiner, P. (2017). Public attitudes toward moral enhancement: Evidence that means matter morally. *Neuroethics, 10*, 405–417.

Stokes, D. (2012). Perceiving and desiring: A new look at the cognitive penetrability of experience. *Philosophical Studies, 158*(3), 477–492.

Sunstein, C. (2016). Do people like nudges? *Administrative Law Review, 68*(2), 177–232.

Sunstein, C., & Thaler, R. (2003). Libertarian paternalism is not an oxymoron. *University of Chicago Law Review, 70*(4), 1159–1202.

Taylor, K. (2006). *Brainwashing: The science of thought control.* Oxford, England: Oxford University Press.

Thaler, R., & Sunstein, C. (2008). *Nudge: Improving decisions about health, wealth and happiness.* New Haven, CT: Yale University Press.

Tomasello, M. (2016). *A natural history of human morality.* Cambridge, MA: Harvard University Press.

Valenstein, E. (1973). *Brain control: A critical examination of brain stimulation and surgery.* New York, NY: Wiley.

Vina, J., Sanchis-Gomar, F., Martinez-Bello, V., & Gomez-Cabrera, M. C. (2012). Exercise acts as a drug: The pharmacological benefits of exercise. *British Journal of Pharmacology, 167,* 1–12.

Wegner, D. (2005). Who is the controller of controlled processes? In R. Hassin & J. Uleman (Eds.), *The new unconscious* (pp. 19–36). Oxford, England: Oxford University Press.

Wenk, G. (2015). *Your brain on food: How chemicals control your thoughts and feelings.* Oxford, England: Oxford University Press.

Wheeler, H. (Ed.). (1973). *Beyond the punitive society.* San Francisco, CA: W. H. Freeman.

Zawidzki, T. (2013). *Mindhaping: A new framework for understanding social cognition.* Cambridge, MA: MIT Press.

Zinberg, N. (1984). *Drug, set, and setting: The basis for controlled intoxicant use.* New Haven, CT: Yale University Press.

4

Neuroprosthetics, Behavior Control, and Criminal Responsibility

Walter Glannon

Introduction

Philosophers and legal theorists argue that moral and criminal responsibility for actions require autonomous agency. The bodily movements with which the actions are identified must be voluntary and must issue from mental states the person endorses following critical reflection. In addition, the action must not involve any physical or psychological coercion, compulsion, or constraint (Dworkin, 1988; Frankfurt, 1988a, 1988b, 1988c; Mele, 1995). Many also argue that moral and legal responsibility for actions presuppose that they do not result from causal routes that bypass the agent's mental states as the direct causes of her actions (Davidson, 2001a, 2001b; Mele, 1995, 2009). Agents have to act from their "own mechanisms, which cannot be formed by pills, *electronic stimulation of the brain* or brainwashing" (Fischer & Ravizza, 1998, p. 236, emphasis added; also see Bublitz & Merkel, 2013). Being morally responsible for one's actions excludes "severe manipulation of the brain, hypnosis and the like" (Fischer, 2006, p. 53). These conditions would seem to undermine responsiveness to reasons as a necessary condition for responsibility.

If the previous discussion is right, however, then it may seem that in bypassing, replacing, or modulating damaged neural circuits mediating motor and mental functions, neuroprosthetics undermine the conscious control necessary for autonomous and responsible agency. Mechanisms other than the person's own normally functioning brain-mind seem to undermine the control necessary for responsibility because they seem to cause nonvoluntary or involuntary actions. Yet when they operate effectively, neuroprosthetics surely do not undermine but restore control of motor and mental functions when they have been lost through brain injury or impaired by neurodevelopmental or neurodegenerative disorders (Glannon, 2015; Schermer, 2015; Vincent, 2015). They enable varying degrees of voluntary agency and responsibility by restoring varying degrees of the requisite motor and mental capacities. For this reason, whether or to what extent a person with a device implanted in his brain can be criminally responsible for an action,

Walter Glannon, *Neuroprosthetics, Behavior Control, and Criminal Responsibility* In: *Neurointerventions and the Law.* Edited by: Nicole A Vincent, Thomas Nadelhoffer, and Allan McCay, Oxford University Press (2020). © Oxford University Press 2020
DOI: 10.1093/oso/9780190651145.001.0004

omission, or a consequence of an action or omission will depend on the extent to which he can control the device and the thought and behavior it is designed to regulate.

In this chapter, I consider three different neuroprosthetics: deep brain stimulation (DBS), implantable brain–computer interfaces (BCIs), and hippocampal prosthetics (HPs). DBS modulates dysfunctional neural circuits associated with neurological and psychiatric disorders through electrical stimulation of targeted circuits in the brain. This device can restore some motor, cognitive, affective and volitional capacities. BCIs can allow people with extensive paralysis or brain injury to bypass the site of injury and restore a more limited range of motor functions. By restoring the capacity to form new memories, HPs can improve the retention of information necessary to plan actions and foresee their probable consequences. Even when they are therapeutic, the effects of all three of these devices could be described as "severe manipulation of the brain." Contrary to the intuition that an artificial device implanted in one's brain undermines or impairs agency, the shared control between the subject and these devices provides a sufficiently robust sense of autonomous agency for one to be responsible for one's actions, omissions, and their consequences. In principle, it does not matter whether neural and mental processes are generated and sustained artificially or naturally, provided that the agent endorses these states and events as her own and they move her to perform desired actions. Artificial devices implanted in the brain to modulate thought and behavior are not necessarily "alien" to an agent and impediments to autonomous agency but enabling devices that can be considered as a form of expanded or extended embodiment. The neuromodulating mechanisms associated with the device can be the agent's own. What matters for autonomous agency and moral and criminal responsibility is not whether one has a device implanted in one's brain, but whether or to what extent it generates and sustains the motor and mental capacities necessary to control one's behavior (Morse, 2006; Vincent, 2008). I take brain and mind to be interacting and interdependent processes of a person, or human organism, as a unitary system. Lower-level neural processes and higher-level mental processes influence and are influenced by each other in a series of re-entrant loops designed to enable flexible behavior and adaptability to the environment (Feinberg, 2001).

Neuroprosthetics are significantly different from psychotropic drugs in altering the brain because they involve a more focused means of neuromodulation. They modulate, bypass, or replace specific sites in specific neural circuits regulating different behaviors. Their direct mechanism of action is in contrast to the distributed and nondiscriminating effects of drugs. In motor disorders such as Parkinson's disease or essential tremor, the effects of these devices on motor functions can be immediate. In psychiatric disorders, the effects of stimulating the brain on mental functions may be immediate but, in most cases, can be delayed for weeks. In this regard, these effects may not be significantly different from the effects of drugs for these disorders. Overall, though, neural prosthetics can more effectively modulate brain and mental functions and provide an agent with a greater degree of control of his thought and action.

I present actual and hypothetical cases of brain implants to explore the extent to which individuals with these devices control their behavior in the way they operate them. This, in turn, can influence normative assessments of that behavior. Brain implants that alter motor and mental functions should make us reconsider standard interpretations of mental and physical criteria of criminal responsibility. In DBS one can be responsible for an action over which one has no control at a later time depending on how one uses the device at an earlier time. In some uses of BCIs, one can be responsible for an action—such as moving a computer cursor or robotic arm—even when it does not correspond to a voluntary bodily movement. One may have the requisite mens rea but not the typical actus reus and still be responsible for an action and its consequences. With BCI-mediated actions, the mental states of the agent that are the basis of responsibility play a greater role in determining the content of responsibility than in cases where one is able to voluntarily move one's body. HPs may influence assessments of responsibility for omissions depending on the extent to which they restore the capacity for memory formation. In general, neural prosthetics reveal the complex effects that manipulation of the brain-mind have on the control we need for moral and legal responsibility. The effects of these devices question the view that any type of manipulation of the source of our thought and behavior always undermines this control. They recommend a broader interpretation of autonomous agency control and responsibility. In particular, DBS and HPs may generate obligations regarding behavior that people with a device implanted in their brains would not have but for a neurological or psychiatric disorder. This raises questions about fairness in normative judgments between people with normal brain function and those with brain dysfunction needing devices to restore the relevant capacities to normal levels. In exploring the normative implications of neuroprosthetics, I demonstrate that some brain-mind manipulations, even those deemed problematic by philosophers and legal theorists, can support rather than undermine responsibility.

Deep Brain Stimulation

DBS has the widest range of applications among neuroprosthetics. It can be used as both a probe and modulator of activity in dysfunctional neural circuits implicated in neurological and psychiatric disorders (Benabid, 2003, 2007; Lozano &

Lipsman, 2013). Probing the brain with electrodes while patients are awake can locate the crucial circuits and determine the extent to which they are dysfunctional. In its modulating function, DBS has been used to restore motor control in Parkinson's disease and other movement disorders and improve cognition, mood, and motivation in major depressive disorder (Holtzheimer & Mayberg, 2011) and obsessive-compulsive disorder (Figee et al., 2013; Mallet et al., 2008). This technique has also improved learning and spatial working memory in some patients with early-stage Alzheimer's disease (Laxton et al., 2010; Laxton & Lozano, 2013). In DBS, electrodes are implanted unilaterally or bilaterally in a particular region of the brain. The electrodes are connected to leads through which electrical current can be delivered by a pulse generator implanted in the abdomen or under the collarbone. The frequency and intensity of the voltage of the generator can be increased or decreased by the operation of a handheld programmable device.

In the disorders I have mentioned, the neuromodulating effects of DBS can re-establish and sustain optimal levels of neural function, preventing extremes of deficit or surfeit in the relevant neural circuits and neurotransmitters (Glannon, 2015; Lipsman & Lozano, 2015). This balance facilitates the formation and execution of action plans and promotes flexibility in adapting to the demands of the environment. Overstimulating targeted circuits, or stimulating the wrong circuits, in an attempt to release physical and mental constraints imposed on agents by certain neuropathologies could result in different pathologies and have equally disabling effects on agency and behavior control. In Parkinson's disease, for example, electrical stimulation of the subthalamic nucleus (STN) or globus pallidus interna can resolve hypodopaminergic activity causing motor, cognitive, and emotional inhibition. But imprecise stimulation of these brain circuits may induce hyperdopaminergic activity and result in impulsivity, hypersexuality, and addiction (Castrioto, Lhommee, Moro, & Krack, 2014; Christen, Bittlinger, Walter, Brugger, & Muller, 2012; Frank, Samanta, Moustafa, & Sherman, 2007; Muller & Christen, 2011). The problem is that the basal ganglia of which the subthalamic nucleus and globus pallidus interna are components involve not only circuits mediating motor functions but cognitive and emotional functions as well. Many of these are interconnected and may not be entirely segregated. It can be challenging to produce salutary neurological and psychiatric effects with DBS without also producing any deleterious effects. Similarly, in major depression overstimulation of a dysfunctional nucleus accumbens in the reward system associated with anhedonia and avolition can cause hyperdopaminergic effects in these circuits and result in pathological behaviors of euphoria (hypomania) and mania (Christen et al., 2012; Synofzik, Schlaepfer, & Fins, 2012). The risk of causing these sequelae can be reduced by more precise stimulation of circuits at the right frequency and intensity.

Even when DBS performs its neuromodulating functions safely and effectively, it raises the question of autonomous agency. Having control of one's behavior presupposes that conscious mental processes have some causal role in this behavior. Yet, the fact that DBS operates outside of one's awareness and without any apparent conscious contribution from the subject seems to threaten this control. This is different from nonconscious habitual behavior that develops over time from conscious mental states and actions. Although it is not conscious in a moment-to-moment way, one can control habitual behavior provided that it displays responsiveness to reasons. How could one be in control of one's behavior if one is a passive recipient of the effects of neurostimulation rather than an agent who induces these effects? The neuromodulating function of the device appears to undermine autonomous agency, with the person's actions traceable to an artificial source. It seems that the device rather than the person is in control of her behavior (Klaming & Haselager, 2013). When behavior is caused by a brain-mind machine, "who is responsible for involuntary acts?" (Clausen, 2009, p. 1080).

Autonomy consists of two general capacities: competency and authenticity (Dworkin, 1988; Frankfurt, 1988a, 1988b; Mele, 1995; Taylor, 1991). The first involves the cognitive and affective capacity to critically reflect on the mental states that issue in one's actions. The second involves the cognitive and affective capacity—and the actual exercise of that capacity—to identify with or endorse these mental states following a period of critical reflection. The idea of identification or endorsement is captured by Harry Frankfurt's concept of a second-order desire, which is a general desire to have particular first-order desires move one to perform certain actions (Frankfurt, 1988b). The process of reflecting on and identifying with one's mental states and actions is what makes them one's *own*. Mental states with which one does not identify or endorse may be considered "alien" to the agent. Through reflection and identification, an autonomous agent is able to regulate the motor and mental springs of her actions. Autonomous agency is synonymous with this self-regulating process and being in control of one's behavior.

The fact that DBS operates outside of a person's awareness does not undermine but instead supports behavior control by modulating dysregulated neural circuits that generate and sustain thought and action (Lipsman & Glannon, 2013; Glannon, 2015; Schermer, 2015). The subject's implicit knowledge that electrodes are implanted and activated in the brain does not figure in the explicit content of her awareness. By not interfering with but enabling the formation and translation of conscious intentions into actions, DBS promotes effective decision-making. Most normal brain processes are not transparent to us. We have no direct access to our afferent and efferent pathways between the central and peripheral nervous systems, for example, and only experience the sensorimotor consequences of our nonconscious motor plans. It is not significant whether these consequences are produced by a natural or artificial system. Provided that a prosthetic device connects in the right way with the neural inputs and outputs that regulate behavior, it allows the subject to initiate and execute action plans. Insofar as the device ensures that the subject has the motor and mental capacities necessary to perform actions she wants to perform, she can identify the device as her own, as an extended or expanded feature of her brain-mind.

Having a DBS system implanted in one's brain does not mean that one is not an autonomous agent, has no control of one's behavior and cannot be responsible for it. Neurostimulation does not undermine but can restore the behavior control that has been lost or impaired from neurological and psychiatric disorders. It is the brain disease rather than the prosthetic that impairs or undermines control and autonomous agency. Although it operates outside of a person's conscious awareness, the device does not replace him as the source of his actions but enables voluntary and effective agency by restoring the functional integrity of the neural circuits that mediate the relevant mental capacities. The shared behavior control between the conscious subject and the artificial device is not fundamentally different from the shared behavior control between the conscious subject and naturally occurring unconscious processes in her normally functioning brain. As I pointed out in the discussion of sensorimotor functions, the performance of many actions does not require conscious reflection. The fact that these actions do not issue from conscious intentions does not mean that they are involuntary. Moreover, DBS can modulate neural circuits in a way that can make them amenable to cognitive-behavioral therapy or other psychotherapies. The bottom-up effects of neurostimulation can allow top–down rewiring effects from mental states to cortical circuits. The operation of the device outside of the patient's reflective thought can induce changes in the brain that can have salutary effects on reflective thought and how it issues in voluntary actions.

Although I have defended the idea of shared behavior control between the subject and a DBS device, the ability to turn the stimulator on and off is one component of this control that lies entirely with the subject. The decision to turn it off indicates that at least some of the behavior of a person with a neural prosthetic involves reflective thought. Among other reasons, this is necessary for a person with a brain implant to pass through airport security without triggering alarms. Crucially, this presupposes that the individual knows when to turn the stimulator back on and that doing this is necessary to restore modulation of motor, affective, and volitional functions. Retaining this cognitive capacity while the stimulator was off would be necessary for the individual to retain control through a period in which there were no neuromodulating effects from the device. But the greater degree of control of his behavior this possibility offers him appears to generate obligations that would not be generated if he did not have a neuropsychiatric disorder for which the device is used. He would have an obligation to keep the device on to prevent self-harm and harm to others. If he lost control of his motor, cognitive, and volitional capacities and thus lost some or all behavior control after turning it off, then it could be argued that he would be criminally responsible for the consequences if they involved harm to others. He could be responsible both for negligence in failing to turn the device back on and for the consequences of this omission. If he willfully refused to turn it back on, then he would be responsible for this action in addition to its consequences. Because of its critical role in behavior control, a person with a neuroprosthetic would have an obligation to use it in a way that did not entail any risk of harm to others.

Some with severe psychiatric disorders may not have sufficient competence to appreciate the potentially harmful consequences from turning off the device. This may reduce a patient's obligation to use it in a responsible way. At the same time, it may entail an obligation of device makers and physicians who implanted the device to monitor the patient's use of it and prevent this situation from occurring. This might suggest that it was not the patient but others who would control the device and its effects on her thought and action. Any such obligation to monitor the device would have to be consistent with the patient's cognitive and affective liberty in not having others completely control her mental processes and behavior. First- and third-person control of the device could be a matter of degree, depending on the patient's level of competence. But any professional obligation to monitor the device would have to be balanced against the patient's own capacity for behavior control, even if it was limited by a psychiatric disorder. These considerations should be framed by a more general point about the connection between options for action and control. Presumably, the more options one has, the more control one has over one's behavior. This does not necessarily follow, though. Sometimes acquiring more options can be disabling by causing cognitive overload and interfering with the exercise of one's executive capacity and the completion of action plans. They may reduce rather than increase control. Having some constraints on action may be more of a blessing than a burden if the constraints enable more narrowly focused attention and effective agency.

In a different scenario, a person may keep the stimulator on but increase the frequency and intensity of the electrical current delivered to his brain beyond what he knows is an optimal level. If this increase resulted in hypomania or mania causing him to lose control of his cognitive and volitional capacities, and if this loss of control resulted in harm to others, then he could be responsible for the action and its consequences. While he lacked control at the time of a harmful action or omission, responsibility would transfer from the earlier time when he had cognitive control in foreseeing the probable harmful sequence of events to the later time when he lacked control. Lacking control at the later time alone would not be sufficient to excuse him from responsibility for the consequences. This assessment is similar to a situation in which a person cognitively impaired from driving under the influence of alcohol is held criminally responsible for injuring a pedestrian in a crosswalk. Like the case of the person who turns off the stimulator, a person who wants to increase its voltage to enhance his mental capacities would be obligated to use the device in a way that would avoid the risk of harm to others. This risk could be avoided by restricting the operation of the device to a clinical setting under the supervision of a medical professional. But allowing a competent patient to regulate the device on her own would increase the control she had of her thought and action and thus her responsibility for them.

Even if it is reasonable to claim that operating a neurostimulating device on one's own is not unduly burdensome, it raises the question of whether it would be fair to hold people with neuroprosthetics to a higher standard of behavior control than those without brain disease or injury who do not need them for this purpose. Why should a device that ensures the same sort of control that people without the device have generate an obligation to use it in a certain way that would not apply to people with healthy brains? I will return and respond to this question following a discussion of several cases.

The potential for self-harm and harm to others from tinkering with neurostimulation is illustrated in an actual case of a patient with a history of generalized anxiety and obsessive-compulsive disorder (Synofzik, Schlaepfer, & Fins, 2012). The case did not involve the patient turning off the stimulator on his own but instead the psychiatrist increasing the voltage of the device at the patient's request. Following continuous stimulation of the nucleus accumbens in the reward system of his brain, the patient experienced improved mood and motivation. He told his psychiatrist that he wanted to feel even better and asked him to increase the voltage of the stimulator. This caused him to feel "unrealistically good" and "overwhelmed by a feeling of happiness and ease" (Synofzik et al., 2012, p. 32). Despite the euphoria, he retained insight into his condition and enough cognitive capacity to know that a pathological level of mood from the higher voltage entailed a risk of irrational and harmful behavior. Accordingly, he asked the psychiatrist to adjust the stimulation parameters to maintain optimal levels of mood and motivation. If the psychiatrist maintained the stimulation at a pathological level and the patient performed harmful actions, then the psychiatrist would be responsible for these actions as well as for failing to prevent them because of the control he had over this sequence of events in operating the device.

The ability of a competent patient to operate the stimulator on his own could have important implications for responsibility for his actions and its consequences. Suppose that the patient I just described could operate the DBS device on his own without monitoring and adjustment of the stimulation parameters by his psychiatrist. Suppose further that he increased the frequency and intensity to feel even better. He did this when his modulated mental states were within a normal range. This would ensure that the action was voluntary and within his cognitive, sensorimotor, affective, and volitional control. If this caused dopaminergic hyperactivity in the nucleus accumbens, euphoria and impaired rationality and led to reckless driving of a motor vehicle that killed another driver, then it could be argued that he would be criminally responsible for negligent homicide. He would be responsible for the consequence even though he lacked cognitive control when it occurred. The consequence was causally sensitive to his action in the sense that it would not have occurred but for his act of increasing the frequency and intensity of the stimulator. He would be responsible because, when he voluntarily requested the increase, he had the cognitive capacity to foresee a high probability of a harmful outcome from his action. The control and responsibility he exercised at the earlier time in voluntarily increasing the stimulation would transfer to the later time, even though he lost his cognitive capacity to reason about which actions to perform or refrain from performing. The harmful outcome of his reckless driving fell within the known risk of becoming euphoric. He could have prevented it by not increasing the stimulation. On the other hand, one could argue that the person would not be fully responsible for the consequence because the manufacturer of the device could have programmed it to limit the amount of electrical stimulation the device could deliver to the brain. The manufacturer could have ensured that, once the stimulation reached an optimal level, it would not be possible for the user to increase it. Given the probability of some patients deliberately or inadvertently increasing the voltage and inducing hypomanic or manic states, this would be a reasonable expectation about the social responsibility of the device maker. However, knowledge of this limitation might cause the patient to feel even less in control of his thought and behavior, which the modulating effects of the device already regulate to a considerable extent. Although this mechanism would ensure control, it could undermine the patient's belief that control is shared between him and the device. Increasing the stimulation above an optimal level may not be a rational decision, even if the patient were competent when he increased it (Brock & Wartman, 1990). Yet not having this option may limit the extent of control the patient would want to have. Still, the value of having this choice would have to be weighed against the potential of harm to himself and others from exercising it.

There are equally significant implications of turning off the stimulator for criminal responsibility. Consider a hypothetical case of a patient with a stimulating device implanted in his brain to downregulate neural hyperactivity causing an impulse control disorder (Micieli, Lopez-Rios, Plata-Aguilar, Botero-Posada, & Hutchison, 2017). This manifests in pathological gambling, hypersexuality, and outbursts of anger. These symptoms have appeared *as a result of* DBS in some cases of patients with Parkinson's disease by overstimulating the brain's reward circuitry. But the technique could prevent impulsivity as a primary symptom by targeting the right neural circuits at the right frequency in modulating dopamine dysregulation in these circuits. The ability to regulate one's impulses depends on connectivity between the prefrontal cortex, which underpins rationality, and the limbic system, which underpins basic desires and emotions. This connectivity is dysfunctional in impulse control disorders, and DBS can restore normal connectivity and allow the prefrontal cortex to inhibit limbic function. The stimulator enables the person to control his impulses. He turns off the stimulator, though, and shortly thereafter resumes his pathological behavior. During an argument with another person, he becomes angry, assaults, and kills him. Charged with the criminal offense of second-degree murder, the accused argues that he was unable to control his impulse. Because he lacked the requisite volitional control to refrain from performing the action, he claims that he was not criminally responsible for it.

Criminal responsibility for an action generally presupposes what are described as "cognitive" (understanding) and "control" (volitional) conditions. The first says that one must have the capacity to recognize and respond to reasons indicating the wrongfulness of the action (Fischer & Ravizza, 1998, Chapter 3; M'Naghten's Case, 1843). The second says that one must have the capacity to control one's conduct so that it conforms to the requirements of the law (Model Penal Code, 1985, 4.01). Some jurisdictions influenced by the M'Naghten test have only a cognitive condition for the insanity defense. Other jurisdictions influenced by the Model Penal Code have both cognitive and control conditions. Although they are not explicit about the legal implications of their theory of moral responsibility, John Martin Fischer and Mark Ravizza seem to take the general capacity to recognize and respond to reasons to involve both cognitive and volitional dimensions. The cognitive capacity to understand reasons alone is not sufficient to translate reasons into actions. This account can be extended to criminal responsibility. Combined cognitive and volitional capacities offer a more satisfactory account of rational and moral agency. Indeed, in the case at hand, the extent to which reason-related frontal regions and impulse-related limbic regions interact suggests that cognitive and control conditions may not be separable. In this case, the impulse appears to override the agent's rational capacity to restrain it. Yet, if he has the cognitive capacity to know that turning off the device would stop the neuromodulating effects on his dysregulated frontal-limbic network, that it entailed a high probability of an inability to resist his violent impulse, and he had a choice to keep the device on or off, then he might have enough cognitive control over the sequence of events resulting in the criminal act to be responsible for it.

An agent may be morally and often criminally responsible for an action he is physically unable to resist or prevent at a later time if, at an earlier time, he is cognitively able to foresee that performing a particular action would incapacitate him. As in the case of the euphoric patient, the agent with the impulse control disorder need not approve of the behavioral changes resulting from turning off the stimulator to be responsible for them. His ability to foresee them as the probable consequence of an earlier voluntarily action or omission is sufficient for him to be criminally responsible (Merkel et al., 2007; Bublitz & Merkel, 2009). He had the ability to prevent the criminal act by not performing the action, or performing a different action, at the earlier time. Cognitive control over a sequence of events can make one responsible for an action within that sequence even if the action is an involuntary bodily movement. Behavior control and responsibility transfer from the earlier to the later time. If one accepts this claim, then self-induced incapacitation may not be an excusing condition for the consequences of the impairment. Yet some jurisdictions might consider this incapacitation a mitigating condition even if it was caused by a voluntary act and even if the consequences of the act were foreseeable. The criminal law is inconsistent on the tracing of later actions and consequences back to earlier actions or omissions and what this implies for criminal responsibility.

Stephen Morse (2006) points out that

an agent will be *prima facie* criminally responsible if the agent acts with the appropriate mental state, *mens rea*, required by the definition of the offense, such as purpose, knowledge, recklessness or negligence. Criminal law typically defines an act as an intentional bodily movement performed by an agent whose consciousness is reasonably intact. (p. 399; also see Morse, 2011, 2015).

In the same vein, Shaun Gallagher (2006) states that "if my bodily movement is not intentional, then it is mere behavior, something like reflex behavior. If my bodily movement is determined by something other than my own reflective thought, then it is an involuntary movement but not an action" (p. 110). The impulsive action of the agent in my example was not intentional. But he had the cognitive and physical ability to prevent himself from acting impulsively by reactivating the stimulator, which he failed to do. He had the requisite mens rea to be responsible for a negligent omission and its consequence—the impulsive act of killing another person. Although he may have lacked the cognitive and volitional capacity to restrain his impulse to kill at the time of his action, at an earlier time he had the cognitive capacity to prevent himself from being in a situation where he lacked the capacity to restrain the impulse.

In the one actual and two hypothetical cases I have presented, the cognitive and physical control the stimulator provides these agents and the known probable harmful consequences of not operating it appropriately constitute reasons for keeping the stimulator on and at an optimal level of frequency and intensity. The device substitutes or compensates for dysfunctional unconscious brain processes that would mediate motor and mental capacities in a normally functioning brain. When it functions properly, the DBS system provides the agent with the same control of her behavior as any agent would have without it. There is nothing unduly burdensome about her having to keep it on at a certain frequency and intensity of electrical current. The fact that a device is implanted in these agents' brains does not impair but enables them to have the requisite control and thus does not mitigate or excuse but makes them fully criminally responsible for their actions. Moreover, they need not approve of the behavioral changes caused by willfully increasing the voltage or turning off the stimulator to be criminally responsible for them (Bublitz & Merkel, 2009; Merkel et al., 2007). If the individual had the cognitive capacity to foresee these changes as a probable consequence of his action or omission, then he could be morally and criminally responsible for them. Still, the idea that the device gives people general control over which particular actions they perform or fail to perform at specific times may put them in a more compromised position that those who can control their behavior without it. This could be a mitigating factor regarding their responsibility.

Earlier, I raised the question of whether it would be unfair to hold these subjects to what appears to be a higher standard of obligation and responsibility than that of healthy subjects who do not need brain implants to restore normal motor and mental functions. But if subjects with neuropsychiatric disorders are able to voluntarily turn the device on or off and have the cognitive capacity to know what these actions entail, then in principle it would not seem unfair to hold them morally and criminally responsible for their actions and omissions and the consequences of these events. The crucial point is that the stimulating device provides them with a sufficient degree of control over their bodily movements and mental states. The neurobiological difference between a functional brain and a stimulating device implanted in a dysfunctional brain does not necessarily involve a morally and legally significant difference. Yet if they are forced to turn off the device in some situations and then turn it back on to regulate their actions, a conscious process in which people with healthy brains do not have to engage, then it *could* be unduly burdensome. This points to the more general normative issue of the ramifications of allocating behavioral burdens in the criminal law and what would constitute a fair allocation of such burdens.

Another factor to consider is the possibility of "brain-jacking" by hackers violating neural implant security (Pycroft et al., 2016). Third parties could gain unauthorized access to the DBS implant system through various physiological attack vectors and externally manipulate the implanted pulse generator. This type of intervention could undermine the intended therapeutic neuromodulating effects of DBS. It could cause patients and research subjects to carry security devices with them in addition to the DBS system. This would clearly be an inconvenience and unduly burdensome for them. It could generate a disincentive to keeping the stimulator on, possibly leading to nonadherence and a return of neurological or psychiatric symptoms. These situations could warrant attributions of mitigated rather than full responsibility for what those with brain implants do or fail to do. The expectation and obligation to keep the stimulator on while aware of possible interference is something they would not have but for their brain disease. People with healthy brains would not have to confront these problems. Nevertheless, the ability of the device to restore some degree of control of their behavior and their ability to control the device make them deserving of at least some degree of responsibility for their behavior.

As noted, there is the potential for unintended adverse outcomes of DBS. More precise targeting of dysfunctional circuits will reduce the incidence of these outcomes. This may be difficult to achieve if patients can operate devices away from monitoring by medical practitioners and can activate, deactivate, and increase or decrease the stimulation they deliver to the brain on their own. But this would increase the control that people with this neuroprosthetic have over their behavior and increase the content of responsibility for what they do or fail to do with the device.

BCIs for Motor Control

Brain-computer interfaces (BCIs), or brain-machine interfaces (BMIs) involve real-time direct connections between the brain and a computer (Lebedev, 2014; Lebedev & Nicolelis, 2006; Wolpaw & Wolpaw, 2012). Bidirectional feedback between the user and the system produces physical changes in the brain that can restore some degree of motor control for people with lost limbs, extensive paralysis, or neurodegeneration (Hochberg & Cochrane, 2013). By providing the subject with the relevant type of feedback, the system may allow her to translate intentions into physical actions despite the inability to perform intentional voluntary bodily movements. Depending on their ability to operate the interface in forming and translating their intentions into actions, a BCI can bypass the injured or dysfunctional brain regions that ordinarily enable these movements. The actus reus of moving a computer cursor or robotic arm may include physical actions that go beyond the typical physical (bodily) actions necessary for one to be responsible. Although the extent of agency of a person using a BCI is limited, use of this technique can expand the content of moral and legal responsibility beyond standard interpretations of this content. Because BCI-mediated actions require more mental effort in forming and executing action plans than in standard accounts of agency, the mental states and thus the mens rea of the agent play a greater role in shaping assessments of criminal responsibility than in cases where one can perform voluntary bodily movements.

There are two types of feedback with BCIs. The first involves feedback about the outcome of a self-initiated, BCI-mediated action. It provides only indirect feedback about brain activity. The second type involves direct feedback about the level of brain activity itself. The first is more pertinent to the potential to restore behavior control in the sense that the subject can perceive the success or failure of her mental act of intending or trying to move the cursor or robotic arm.

BCIs utilize wired or wireless systems to detect and transmit signals in the brain's motor and parietal cortices into different actions. There are three main types of BCIs. One consists of scalp-based electrodes that are part of the equipment in an electroencephalograms (EEG). Because they do not involve intracranial surgery and implantation of a device in the brain, they do not entail a risk of infection or hemorrhage. At the same time, though, they may not readily read signals from the motor cortex because the cranium can deflect or "smear" them. In electrocorticography (ECoG), electrodes are implanted above (epidurally) or below (subdurally) the brain's dura mater just under the skull. They can decode motor and parietal cortical signals more readily than scalp-based electrodes because they are not susceptible to cranial smearing (Leuthardt, Schalk, Wolpaw, Ojemann, & Moran, 2004). But they involve some risk of infection and hemorrhage. Like noninvasive scalp-based systems, both forms of electrocorticography BCIs impose constraints on the subject's movement because of the wires running from the electrodes to the machine.

Wireless systems consisting of a microelectrode array implanted in the motor area of the brain avoid this problem. Because they can decode and transmit neural signals from this region more directly, implanted arrays are more likely to facilitate the execution of the subject's motor intentions in actions. Still, this depends on the particular features of the neurological deficit and the patient's ability to operate the BCI. Risks in wireless systems include the possibility of infection, edema, and hemorrhage from the implant. There are also questions about biocompatibility between the implant and surrounding neural tissue. The implant could cause adverse changes in the brain, or it could become damaged and rendered dysfunctional from exposure to organic brain tissue. In addition, wireless systems may be vulnerable to hacking from external sources. This could interfere with forming and translating intentions into actions and constrain subjects from acting or coerce them into performing undesired actions. These are the main limitations of implantable microchips in the brain, requiring careful monitoring and the need to develop advanced devices that would be immune to hacking. Compared with other devices, though, implanted microchips that can decode and transmit neural signals through a BCI more effectively promote agency in subjects whose ability to act is severely limited by a damaged brain.

The ability or inability to move an external prosthetic through mental and neural activity may vary among subjects. Depending on how injury or disease affects their brains and which cognitive and volitional capacities are intact, some subjects may be more capable than others to be trained to operate a BCI to produce physical movements. Ordinarily, most motor skills are performed unconsciously and automatically following an initial period of conscious attention and learning. These skills are maintained in procedural memory. For those with extensive paralysis, considerable conscious mental effort is required to effectively operate the interface in performing motor tasks. Subjects whose cognitive and volitional capacities have been impaired by injury to the central nervous system may have difficulty translating their thoughts into actions or fail to do so. Planning is a critical component of moving a prosthetic device with the aid of the interface. The subject must indicate with his brain-mind how the cursor or robotic arm should move before executing the intention to move it. This complex cognitive task requires sustained focus, attention and effort. This is all part of the operant conditioning of the subject by the trainer in learning how to use a BCI. Not all severely paralyzed subjects have the necessary degree of these mental capacities to effectively use the system. Indeed, the rate of BCI illiteracy may be as high as 30% even among healthy subjects (Birbaumer, Gallegos-Ayala, Wildgruber, Silvoni, & Soekadar, 2014). Failure to meet the desire and expectation to move a cursor or robotic arm may cause distress and psychological harm to some subjects by defeating their interest in recovering a limited degree of motor control.

For those who are able to move a prosthetic device external to their body by forming and translating motor intentions into actions, the unconscious conditioning resulting from knowing how to operate the BCI and the conscious intention and effort of the subject are critical components of this process. The second aspect of learning how to use the interface shows that the subject has some control over moving the device. Despite technological and operational differences between DBS and a BCI, like the first, the second is an enabling device. There is shared motor control between the subject and the interface system, which supports rather than replaces the subject's intact cognitive and volitional capacities. Provided that there is proprioceptive and somatosensory feedback from the robotic hand or arm to the brain, the subject can experience these external prosthetics and the internal neuroprosthetic to which they are linked as forms of extended or expanded embodiment and part of her self (Gallagher, 2005). Studies suggest that prosthetic limbs controlled by a subject using a BCI can become incorporated into the brain's representation of the body (Lebedev, 2014, p. 108).

The subject can perceive the prosthetic as her own, and her moving it can be an autonomous act.

Suppose that a subject paralyzed from a severe brain injury is frustrated about the time and effort it takes him to move a prosthetic arm. But he is able to move it. He takes his frustration out on his trainer by moving the limb so that it strikes him in the head, seriously but not fatally injuring him and causing significant harm. A justified attribution of moral and criminal responsibility for the assault would require proof that the subject was able to control the movement of the prosthetic with his thought and that striking the trainer was not a random occurrence caused by BCI dysfunction. To rule out the possibility of the arm moving unexpectedly and unintentionally, device experts and the research group using the BCI with the subject could rely on his history of success or failure in operating the device. They could also rely on functional neuroimaging showing brain activity while the subject was engaged in certain cognitive and motor tasks to confirm that he had the capacity to move the arm as he did. And they could analyze data from the implant at the time of the actions. These three criteria would be sufficient to establish that he had the capacity to move the arm and that his particular mental states at the time of the action constituted probable cause. This could establish that he was causally responsible for the action. In addition, the content of the malevolent intention necessary to establish moral and criminal responsibility for the action could be inferred from the way in which the subject caused the prosthetic to move. He could be criminally responsible for assaulting the trainer despite the fact that he was unable to perform a voluntary bodily movement. The complex actus reus is assaulting the trainer by moving the prosthetic arm. The complex mens rea is the intention to move the arm to assault the trainer. Because of the paralysis, the subject not only has to plan to move the prosthetic but also to actually move it so that it strikes the trainer. These mental acts in the sequence of events resulting in the assault are necessary for the subject to move the artificial limb and be criminally responsible for the assault in virtue of moving it. This raises the question of how advances in neurotechnology could influence the evolution of the distinction between actus reus and mens rea in the criminal law. Actual cases similar to the hypothetical case I have presented might eventually resolve it, though it is still very much an open question (Bublitz et al., 2019).

There are two main implications of this hypothetical case. First, the actus reus in the content of responsibility may involve something other than a voluntary bodily movement. Second, the mens rea is more complex and plays a more critical role than in cases where subjects have normal motor capacities in performing actions and exercise these capacities unconsciously as a matter of course. The subject must not only form and execute an intention to harm the trainer but also form and execute the prior intention to move the robotic arm necessary to carry out his primary action plan. Two pairs of two distinct but related mental acts of forming and executing intentions constitute the mental basis of responsibility. Nevertheless, unlike normal brain function and even DBS, where motor functions are modulated outside of one's conscious awareness, the fact that the subject had to put more effort into executing the action plan through the BCI would not be a mitigating factor in assigning responsibility to him. This form of premeditation might even be an aggravating factor. The control the subject has in using the BCI, albeit limited, may enable him to translate at least some intentions into actions. Also, the content of responsibility would include only actions enabled by the BCI and which the subject could perform by using it. Insofar as the subject can control whether he assaults or refrains from assaulting the trainer with the robotic arm, he could be criminally responsible for this action.

Hippocampal Prosthetics

Some people lose the ability to encode and store memories from newly learned information. This can be caused by impaired or lost function of the hippocampus—or, more precisely, the circuit consisting of the hippocampus and entorhinal cortex—from brain injury or infection. While adverse effects on this memory circuit prevent the formation of new episodic memories, they can also impair semantic and working memory, both of which utilize information derived from episodic memory (Eichenbaum, 2012, Section 3; Hasselmo, 2012). This can disrupt agency by disrupting the capacity to anticipate the future and form action plans. An HP, or hippocampal-entorhinal (H-E) prosthetic, consists of a multisite electrode array implanted in the area encompassing the H-E circuit (Berger et al., 2011; Hampson et al., 2013; Hampson et al., 2018). The array is linked to a very large-scale integration biomimetic model providing the necessary inputs and outputs for memory encoding. HPs have been used in animal models and have only recently been tested in humans. While they are at a developmental stage and may be ready for implantation in the human brain in the next 5 years, they remain a hypothetical neural prosthetic.

For those with severe anterograde amnesia from damage to the H-E and adjacent neural circuits, an HP might be able to restore the brain's ability to retain information through the encoding of new episodic memories. It could have significant therapeutic potential because this circuit is a key component of the episodic memory system and one of the first neural structures to undergo cellular loss associated with pathology of amyloid beta and tau protein in Alzheimer's disease. Artificial reconstruction of neuron-to-neuron connections with a biomimetic microchip model replacing a damaged H-E circuit could improve or restore short- and long-term episodic memory and its effects on semantic and working memory. It could improve planning and decision-making by providing an adequate amount of information to the subject and thus improve her capacity for agency.

It would not matter whether memory functions were maintained through natural or artificial means, provided that an HP maintained the neural inputs and outputs necessary for these functions. But the prosthetic would have to integrate into the brain in such a way as to be sensitive to activity in multiple cell fields in other circuits mediating declarative (conscious) and nondeclarative (unconscious) memory systems to which the H-E circuit was connected. This would require sensitivity to interaction between episodic and emotional memory systems mediated by circuits in limbic and frontal regions of the brain, while not adversely affecting the independent procedural memory system mediated by circuits in the striatum and cerebellum. Because of its potential to restore memory and the critical role of this cognitive capacity in agency, an HP could have significant implications for moral and criminal responsibility. In particular, this prosthetic may influence attributions of responsibility for omissions in the form of failing to remember earlier actions, as well as for the consequences of these omissions.

On a sweltering afternoon in June 2013, in the town of Milton, Ontario, Canada, Leslie McDonald left her two-year-old grandson, Maximus Huyskens, inside a car for several hours. The toddler died from hyperthermia, and McDonald was charged with criminal negligence causing death (Rogers, 2013). Maximus had been left in the care of his grandmother while his father was at work and his mother was at an appointment. Together with purposefulness, knowledge, and recklessness, negligence is one of four culpable states of mind within the Model Penal Code. Despite being deaf, McDonald appeared to have the mens rea of negligence because she was able but failed to pay attention to the situation when she was creating a substantial risk for the child. In November 2013, McDonald was found guilty of criminal negligence causing death for failing to recognize this risk and failing to act to prevent the tragic outcome.

Either Leslie McDonald forgot that she had left her grandson in the car or mistakenly believed that doing so did not create a substantial risk for him. If one accepts the first account, then the question arises as to whether she lacked the capacity to remember leaving the child in the car or had this capacity but failed to exercise it. The psychological explanation that she was overloaded with information while performing multiple cognitive tasks and was unable to pay attention would not be convincing because a reasonable person would have had the toddler and the risk foremost in her mind. No scans of McDonald's brain were taken and thus were not introduced in court by the defense as evidence of a brain abnormality. There were no behavioral indications that her negligence was due to dementia or amnesia from a brain disorder.

Suppose that she had been experiencing anterograde amnesia from a brain injury and unable to form new memories. An HP was implanted in her brain, restoring a normal capacity to encode new information in her episodic, semantic, and working-memory systems. Would it have made any difference to the criminal negligence charge and conviction if she had an HP implanted in her brain and the device malfunctioned? Would this have supported excusing her in the same way that a neuropathology impairing her capacity to reason would have constituted an excuse? Insofar as this neuroprosthetic enables one to form new memories rather than retrieve them once they have been encoded and stored in the hippocampal formation (short-term) and neocortex (long-term), the claim that McDonald was unable to *retrieve* the memory of leaving her grandson in the car because of device malfunction would not have much moral or legal weight. This claim would not be addressing the critical question of whether she was criminally negligent. Prosecution could argue that she was able to retrieve the memory but failed to because she was not sufficiently attentive to the situation and aware of the potential for hyperthermia and death. But a malfunctioning HP designed for memory encoding could mean that she was unable to form a memory of leaving the child in the car, and she could not *recall* the event and attend to it if she could not *form* a memory of it. In that case, she could be excused from the charge of criminal negligence causing death because the HP malfunction would imply that she lacked the cognitive content necessary for negligence. This is different from the claim that she lacked access to stored information in her brain, as suggested by the idea that she had the capacity for retrieval but had a cognitive lapse at the critical time. There was no memory for the accused to retrieve because the information was not encoded in her brain, and so she could not have been negligent in failing to retrieve it. Device manufacturers and memory researchers could confirm that the HP malfunction precluded McDonald's ability to form a memory of her action and that this precluded her from knowing that she had left her grandson in the car.

It would not be unfair to hold this person to the same standard of responsibility as others with normal memory if the device restored the capacity for memory formation. Unlike DBS and BCIs, the fact that an HP functions completely outside of the subject's thought and actions puts no burden on her regarding its operation. Moreover, provided that it restores the capacity for memory formation, simply having a device implanted in one's brain does not constitute a morally or legally significant difference from those with normal memory function and no need for an implant. The implant itself would not be a mitigating factor. What might be a mitigating, factor, however, is if the implant restored memory capacity to only to a certain extent and left some impairment. One might be responsible to a lesser extent in such a case. Still, judgments about full or partial responsibility would have to be made on the basis of the person's behavior as a manifestation of the extent of the device's memory-restoration function. Device malfunction would impair one's cognitive control in acting and mitigate or excuse one from responsibility for actions. This, in principle, would not be different from cases of impaired memory encoding from a brain disorder affecting the hippocampus or entorhinal cortex. Still, the hypothetical description of the McDonald case is an example of how the function or malfunction of a neuro prosthetic could have ethical and legal consequences when it is used to treat a disorder of memory capacity and its effects on rational, moral and legal agency.

Conclusion

As the examples I have presented and discussed illustrate, there are six respects in which neuroprosthetics should make us reassess criteria of moral and criminal responsibility. First, they challenge the view that manipulation of the brain and mind always undermines the control of thought and behavior necessary for responsibility. Second, the ways in which these devices alter neural and mental processes indicate the need for broader interpretations of agency, autonomy, and behavior control. Neuroprosthetics that restore some degree of the motor, cognitive, and volitional capacities necessary for agency are not alien to subjects but are forms of extended or expanded embodiment that become part of the agent's self. The shared behavior control between the subject and the neuroprosthetic promotes rather than impairs or undermines autonomous agency. Some people with neural implants may not identify with them as constitutive of their extended selves but as devices they have to tolerate and live with because of their neuropathology. This would not absolve them of responsibility for their actions and omissions. What determines whether persons are responsible for their behavior is not so much whether they identify with a neuromodulating device but more so whether it restores, maintains, or enhances the capacity to respond to reasons. They could be responsible *because of* the device's capacity to restore responsiveness to reasons rather than *in spite of* it. Third, neuroprosthetics raise questions about the standard interpretation of the actus reus in criminal law as a voluntary bodily movement and highlight the need for more fine-grained descriptions of actions. Fourth, the neural and mental capacities necessary to move a prosthetic limb with the aid of a BCI to perform a criminal act warrant a broader understanding of mens rea that includes at least two distinct pairs of mental acts in forming and executing intentions. Fifth, the control a person has with a DBS device may generate moral and legal obligations about its use that they would not have but for the neurological or psychiatric disorder the device is designed to regulate. Sixth, the possibility of "brain-jacking" through third-party unauthorized access in external manipulation of an implanted pulse generator or microchip could create the need to carry security devices in addition to the implants and an additional burden for the user. Depending on the context of action, having the device or chip in one's brain may constitute a mitigating factor in assessing responsibility for one's actions or omissions.

A more general philosophical concern is that development of more sophisticated neuroprosthetics could gradually replace natural neural circuits in the brain and turn it into a completely artificial organ. This could transform us into cyborgs or complete mechanisms in a transhuman world. One could question whether or how we could retain normative practices and institutions in such a world. But the idea that advanced neuroprosthetics could seamlessly integrate into the human body and brain does not imply that they will explain away the mental capacities on the basis of which we hold people responsible. These devices will likely continue to compensate for neural and mental dysfunction while supplementing rather than supplanting normal functioning neural circuits and the mental states they mediate. Initiatives such as the Human Brain Project, whose original goal was to simulate the entire brain by constructing an artificial version of it, would not likely be able to replicate the complex interactions between the brain, body and environment and how these interactions influence the content of our mental states (Markram et al., 2011). In light of some organizational problems, the Project now has the more modest goal of developing platforms for neurocomputing and neurorobotics research and development. Any fear that these devices might cause us to lose our personhood and capacity to act and be responsible for what we do or fail to do would be unfounded. The brain is not a self-contained organ. Persons are constituted by their brains but are not identical to and thus cannot be defined solely in terms of them. They are also constituted by their bodies and mental states, the content of which is not only shaped by their brains but also by the natural and social environment in which they are embedded. This content involves brain–body–environment interaction, which cannot be captured by a reductionist model based entirely on neural circuitry. Normative questions about how brain disease and injury impair the capacity for responsible behavior and how neuroprosthetics can restore this capacity need to be informed by factors inside and outside the brain.

Acknowledgments

This chapter is based on a presentation I gave at the Neurointerventions and the Law Conference at Georgia State University, Atlanta, on September 14, 2014. I am grateful to the audience for their thoughtful questions and discussion. I am especially grateful to Nicole Vincent and Allan McCay for extensive and very helpful comments on earlier versions of the chapter.

References

Benabid, A.-L. (2003). Deep brain stimulation for Parkinson's disease. *Current Opinion in Neurobiology, 13,* 696–706.

Benabid, A.-L. (2007). What the future holds for deep brain stimulation. *Expert Reviews of Medical Devices, 4,* 895–403.

Berger, T., Hampson, R., Song, D., Goonawardena, A., Marmarellis, V., & Deadwyler, S. (2011). A cortical neural prosthesis for restoring and enhancing memory. *Journal of Neural Engineering, 8,* e046017.

Birbaumer, N., Gallegos-Ayala, G., Wildgruber, M., Silvoni, S., & Soekadar, S. (2014). Direct brain control and communication in paralysis. *Brain Topography, 27,* 4–11.

Brock, D., & Wartman, S. (1990). When competent patients make irrational choices. *The New England Journal of Medicine, 322,* 1595–1599.

Bublitz, C., & Merkel, R. (2009). Autonomy and authenticity of enhanced personality traits. *Bioethics, 23,* 360–374.

Bublitz, C., & Merkel, R. (2013). Guilty minds in washed brains? Manipulation cases and the limits of neuroscientific excuses in liberal legal orders. In N. Vincent (Ed.), *Neuroscience and legal responsibility* (pp. 335–374). Oxford, England: Oxford University Press.

Bublitz, C., Wolkenstein, A., Jox, R., & Frierich, O. (2019). Legal liabilities of BCI-users: Responsibility gaps at the intersection of mind and machine? *International Journal of Law and Psychiatry, 65,* doi:10.1016/j.ijlp.2018.10.002

Castrioto, A., Lhommee, E., Moro, E., & Krack, P. (2014). Mood and behavioral effects of subthalamic stimulation in Parkinson's disease. *The Lancet Neurology, 13,* 287–305.

Christen, M., Bittlinger, M., Walter, H., Brugger, P., & Muller, S. (2012). Dealing with side effects of deep brain stimulation: Lessons learned from stimulating the STN. *AJOB-Neuroscience, 3*(1), 37–43.

Clausen, J. (2009). Man, machine and in between. *Nature, 457,* 1080–1081.

Davidson, D. (2001a). Actions, reasons and causes. In D. Davidson, *Essays on actions and events* (2nd ed., pp. 3–10). Oxford, England: Clarendon Press.

Davidson, D. (2001b). Mental events. In D. Davidson, *Essays on actions and events* (2nd ed., pp. 207–224). Oxford, England: Clarendon Press.

Dworkin, G. (1988). *The theory and practice of autonomy.* New York, NY: Cambridge University Press.

Eichenbaum, H. (2012). *The cognitive neuroscience of memory: An introduction* (2nd ed.). New York, NY: Oxford University Press.

Feinberg, T. (2001). *Altered egos: How the brain creates the self.* New York, NY: Oxford University Press.

Figee, M., Luigjes, J. Smolders, R., Valencia-Alfonso, C., Van Wingen, G., de Kwaastemiet, B., . . . Denys, D. (2013). Deep brain stimulation restores frontostriatal network activity in obsessive-compulsive disorder. *Nature Neuroscience, 16,* 366–387.

Fischer, J. M. (2006). *My way: Essays on moral responsibility.* New York, NY: Oxford University Press.

Fischer, J. M., & Ravizza, M. (1998). *Responsibility and control: A theory of moral responsibility.* New York, NY: Cambridge University Press.

Frank, M., Samanta, J., Moustafa, A., & Sherman, S. (2007). Hold your horses: Impulsivity, deep brain stimulation and medication in Parkinsonism. *Science, 318,* 1309–1312.

Frankfurt, H. (1988a). Coercion and moral responsibility. In H. Frankfurt, *The importance of what we care about* (pp. 26–46). New York, NY: Cambridge University Press.

Frankfurt, H. (1988b). Free will and the concept of a person. In H. Frankfurt, *The importance of what we care about* (pp. 11–25). New York, NY: Cambridge University Press.

Frankfurt, H. (1988c). Identification and externality. In H. Frankfurt, *The importance of what we care about* (pp. 58–68). New York, NY: Cambridge University Press.

Gallagher, S. (2005). *How the body shapes the mind.* Oxford, England: Clarendon Press.

Gallagher, S. (2006). Where's the action? Epiphenomenalism and the problem of free will. In S. Pocket, W. Banks, & S. Gallagher (Eds.), *Does consciousness cause behavior?* (pp. 109–124). Cambridge, MA: MIT Press.

Glannon, W. (Ed.). (2015). *Free will and the brain: Neuroscientific, philosophical and legal perspectives.* Cambridge, England: Cambridge University Press.

Hampson, R., Song, D., Opris, I., Santos, L., Shin, D., Gerhardt, G., . . . Deadwyler, S. A. (2013). Facilitation of memory encoding in primate hippocampus by a neuroprosthetic that promotes task-specific neuronal firing. *Journal of Neural Engineering, 10,* e66013.

Hampson, R., Song, D., Robinson, B., Fetterhoff, D., Dakos, A., Roder, B., et al. (2018). Developing a hippocampal neural prosthetic to facilitate human memory encoding and recall. *Journal of Neural Engineering, 15,* 036014, doi:10.1088/1741-25521

Hasselmo, M. (2012). *How we remember: Brain mechanisms of episodic memory.* Cambridge, MA: MIT Press.

Hochberg, L., & Cochrane, T. (2013). Implanted neural interfaces: Ethics in treatment and research. In A. Chatterjee & M. Farah (Eds.), *Neuroethics in practice* (pp. 235–250). Oxford, England: Oxford University Press.

Holtzheimer, P., & Mayberg, H. (2011). Deep brain stimulation for psychiatric disorders. *Annual Review of Neuroscience, 34,* 289–307.

Klaming, L., & Haselager, P. (2013). Did my brain implant make me do it? Questions raised by DBS regarding psychological continuity, responsibility for actions and mental competence. *Neuroethics, 6,* 527–539.

Laxton, A., & Lozano, A. (2013). Deep brain stimulation for the treatment of Alzheimer's disease and dementias. *World Neurosurgery, 80,* S28.e1–S28.e8.

Laxton, A, Tang-Wai, D., McAndrews, M., Zumsteg, D., Wennberg, R. Keren, R., . . . Lozano, A. M. (2010). A phase 1 trial of deep brain stimulation of neural circuitry in Alzheimer's disease. *Annals of Neurology, 68,* 521–534.

Lebedev, M. (2014). Brain-machine interfaces: An overview. *Translational Neuroscience, 5,* 99–110.

Lebedev, M., & Nicolelis, M. (2006). Brain-machine interfaces: Past, present and future. *Trends in Neurosciences, 29,* 536–546.

Leuthardt, E., Schalk, G., Wolpaw, J., Ojemann, J., & Moran, D. (2004). A brain-computer interface using electrocorticographic signals in humans. *Journal of Neural Engineering, 1,* 63–71.

Lipsman, N., & Glannon, W. (2013). Brain, mind and machine: What are the implications of deep brain stimulation for perceptions of personal identity, agency and free will? *Bioethics, 27,* 465–470.

Lipsman, N., & Lozano, A. (2015). Implications of functional neurosurgery and deep brain stimulation for free will and decision-making. In W. Glannon (Ed.), *Free will and the brain: Neuroscientific, philosophical and legal issues* (pp. 191–204). Cambridge, England: Cambridge University Press.

Lozano, A., & Lipsman, N. (2013). Probing and regulating dysfunctional circuits using deep brain stimulation. *Neuron, 77,* 406–424.

Mallet, L., Polosan, M., Nematollah, J., Baup., N, Welter, M.-L., Fontaine, D., . . . Aouizerate, B. (2008). Subthalamic nucleus stimulation in severe obsessive-compulsive disorder. *The New England Journal of Medicine, 359,* 2121–2134.

Markram, H., Meier, K., Lippert, T., Grillier, S., Frackowiak, R. Dehaene, S., . . . Saria, A. (2011). Introducing the Human Brain Project. *Procedia Computer Science, 7,* 39–42.

Mele, A. (1995). *Autonomous agents: From self-control to autonomy.* New York, NY: Oxford University Press.

Mele, A. (2009). *Effective intentions: The power of conscious will.* New York, NY: Oxford University Press.

Merkel, R., Boer, G., Fegert, J., Galert, T., Hartmann, D., Nuttin, B., . . . Rosahl, S. (2007). *Intervening in the brain: Changing psyche and society.* Berlin, Germany: Springer.

Micieli, R., Lopez-Rios, A., Plata-Aguilar, R., Botero-Posada, L., & Hutchison, W. (2017). Single-unit analysis of the human posterior hypothalamus and red nucleus during deep brain stimulation for aggressivity. *Journal of Neurosurgery, 126,* 1158–1164.

M'Naghten's Case. (1843). 8 Eng. Rep. 718, 722. Cited in the Report of the Committee on Mentally Abnormal Offenders. London, Her Majesty's Stationery Office, 1975, 217.

Model Penal Code. (1985). *Official draft and commentaries.* Philadelphia, PA: American Law Institute.

Morse, S. (2006). Brain overclaim syndrome and criminal responsibility: A diagnostic note. *Ohio State Journal of Criminal Law, 3,* 397–412.

Morse, S. (2011). Lost in translation? An essay on law and neuroscience. In M. Freeman (Ed.), *Law and neuroscience: Current legal issues* (Vol. 13, pp. 529–562). Oxford, England: Oxford University Press.

Morse, S. (2015). Neuroscience, free will and criminal responsibility. In W. Glannon (Ed.), *Free will and the brain: Neuroscientific, philosophical and legal issues* (pp. 251–286). Cambridge, England: Cambridge University Press.

Muller, S., & Christen, M. (2011). Deep brain stimulation in Parkinsonian patients— Ethical evaluation of cognitive, affective and behavioral sequelae. *AJOB-Neuroscience, 2*(2), 3–13.

Pycroft, L., Boccard, S., Owen, S., Stein, J. Fitzgerald, J, Green, A., & Aziz, T. (2016). Brainjacking: Implant security issues in invasive neuromodulation. *World Neurosurgery, 92,* 454–462.

Rogers, K. (2013, July 5). Grandmother charged in death of Milton, Ont. Toddler left in hot car. *Globe and Mail.* http://www.theglobeandmail.com/news/national/grandmother-charged-in-death-of-milton-toddler-left-alone-in-hot-car/article/013019696

Schermer, M. (2015). Reducing, restoring or enhancing autonomy with neuromodulation techniques. In W. Glannon (Ed.), *Free will and the brain: Neuroscientific, philosophical and legal issues* (pp. 205–228). Cambridge, England: Cambridge University Press.

Synofzik, M., Schlaepfer, T., & Fins, J. (2012). How happy is too happy? Euphoria, neuroethics and deep brain stimulation of the nucleus accumbens. *AJOB-Neuroscience, 3*(1), 30–36.

Taylor, C. (1991). *The ethics of authenticity.* Cambridge, MA: Harvard University Press.

Vincent, N. (2008). Responsibility, dysfunction and capacity. *Neuroethics, 1,* 199–204.

Vincent, N. (2015). Assessment and modification of free will via scientific techniques: Two challenges. In W. Glannon (Ed.), *Free will and the brain: Neuroscientific, philosophical and legal issues* (pp. 168–188). Cambridge, England: Cambridge University Press.

Wolpaw, J., & Wolpaw, E. (Eds.) (2012). *Brain–computer interfaces: Principles and practice.* New York, NY: Oxford University Press.

5

Is There Anything Wrong With Using AI Implantable Brain Devices to Prevent Convicted Offenders from Reoffending?

Frédéric Gilbert and Susan Dodds

Introduction

New predictive brain implants operated by artificial intelligence (AI) have been tested with significant success for the first time in a human clinical trial (Kingwell, 2013). These new brain implants use AI to not only predict neuronal events and related biochemical events before they occur, but they can also forewarn, or advise, implanted people that these events are imminent. Because the neuronal event can be predicted, the implants offer the prospect of instigating or triggering a specific course of action that can minimize, or even avoid, the negative effects of the neuronal event. For instance, a clinical trial using continuous electroencephalography (EEG) recordings from a patient's brain activity has successfully shown that such implants can predict epileptic seizures by learning the brain activity patterns of an individual based on AI techniques (Gardner, Krieger, Vachtsevanos, & Litt, 2006). The implant then sends a signal to advise the patient that they will soon experience a seizure through an SMS message or a wearable monitor (Cook et al., 2013; Kingwell, 2013), allowing the patient to take precautionary steps in advance of the seizure. The patient, may be able to prepare for, or even prevent the oncoming seizure, by instigating a certain course of action (e.g. by taking antiseizure medications). Let us define the predictive and advisory brain device as an AI technology designed to forecast specific neuronal events and translate raw neuronal data into information that an individual can access immediately allowing them to prevent or mitigate the effects of otherwise unforeseen neuronal events.

In a pilot study conducted with epilepsy patients implanted with these predictive and advisory devices (Gilbert, 2015; Gilbert & Cook, 2015), one of us raised the possibility that this technology could be developed further to incorporate automated therapeutic activation. For example, the AI device could

Frédéric Gilbert and Susan Dodds, *Is There Anything Wrong With Using AI Implantable Brain Devices to Prevent Convicted Offenders from Reoffending?* In: *Neurointerventions and the Law.* Edited by: Nicole A Vincent, Thomas Nadelhoffer, and Allan McCay, Oxford University Press (2020). © Oxford University Press 2020 DOI: 10.1093/oso/9780190651145.001.0005

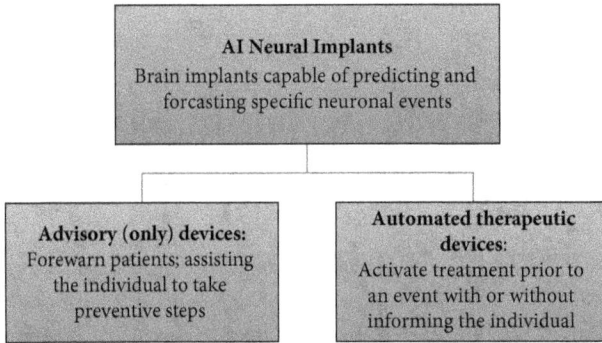

Figure 5.1. Illustration of the two categories of AI predictive devices. On the left, an automated therapeutic response with notification; on the right, an automated therapeutic response without notification.

advise the patient of an impending seizure and then also automatically administer electric stimulation, drug discharge, light activation, or whatever other treatment is necessary to avert or minimize the seizure. We call the devices that couple diagnostic prediction with automatic triggering of a therapy "automated therapeutic response systems." We thus distinguish two types of AI predictive technologies: advisory systems and automated therapeutic response systems (see Figure 5.1).

This leads us to consider how we should respond to an AI device that did not just forewarn or advise an implanted person about a potentially harmful neuronal event, but also identify an impending neuronal event and discharged a therapeutic response to prevent a particular set of harmful behaviors or symptoms from occurring. We have to add that the therapeutic response come without requiring any further decision or action by the implanted individual; it operates similar to the way that an implantable cardioverter defibrillator monitors a patient's heart rate and delivers an electrical shock if abnormal heart rhythm is detected to restore a normal heart rate (Di Marco, 2003). This suggestion could bring with it a raft of new applications leading to challenging ethical questions.

As an illustration of how brain activity could be detected and stopped by an AI automated brain device before manifesting itself, consider how certain forms of aggressive and violent behaviors occur in a neurobiologically similar manner to the onset of epilepsy, in particular temporal or frontal lobe seizures (Jobst et al. 2000; Marsh & Krauss, 2000; Shih, Thabele, Germano, & Gerpen, 2009). We can also consider the current, targeted use of deep brain stimulation within experimental trials for reducing aggressiveness (Franzini, Broggi, Cordella, Dones, & Messina, 2012) or its suggested use for diminishing sexual urges in paraphilic individuals (De Ridder, Langguth, Plazier, & Menovsky, 2009; Fuss, Auer, Biedermann, Briken, & Hacke, 2015).[1] Hypothetically, one could argue that predicting specific brain disturbances or changes before aggressive symptoms occur (that could otherwise result in criminal behaviors) would be clinically useful in some individuals and allow targeted treatment to prevent these aggressive behaviors from happening.

The potential use of predictive AI brain implants raises questions about the moral, legal, and medical obligations to prevent foreseeable and harmful aggressive or illegal behaviors, especially among violent offenders. Should we contemplate the possibility of implanting advisory technologies or automated therapeutic response technologies in convicted violent offenders as a means of reducing the risk of recidivism or of violent assault?

We acknowledge that even if AI implantable device were free of side effects such as postoperative personality changes (as observed in a minority of patients treated with invasive brain technologies; Gilbert, 2015; Gilbert et al., 2017, 2019), the ability to use neural implants to effectively prevent a complex and specific behavior before it happens (e.g., precrime) belongs to the realm of science fiction. It is generally agreed that organized, purposeful, goal-directed criminal acts are unlikely to be something that can be read off an EEG. The speculation that it might in the future be possible to use AI and brain implants to identify a special pattern of brain activity that accurately presages an aggressive attack is highly unlikely given the current state of the science. Nevertheless, it is not fanciful to think that in the near future, some refractory aggressive behavioral outbursts or intermittent explosive aggressive disorder (McElroy, Soutullo, Beckman, Taylor, & Keck, 1998) might become targeted by these sorts of predictive implant technologies, given deep brain stimulation already has been tested in an attempt to address these behaviors (Franzini, Broggi, Cordella, Dones, & Messina, 2012). Consequently, the purpose of this chapter is to assess the ethical implications of the potential use of advisory and automated therapeutic responses as ways of reducing the risk of reoffending in light of the potential impact these could have on the moral autonomy of the implanted offender. Can these technologies be seen as a way to increase the convicted offender's autonomy, capacities, and control of harmful urges? Or as undermining the offender's autonomous agency. This chapter will offer some preliminary answers to such questions.

---

[1] Of course, the effectiveness of these experimental trials remains open to vigorous debate; in this regard, please refer to Gilbert, Viana and Vranic (2016), Gilbert and Vranic (2015), and Gilbert, Vranic, and Hurst (2013). However, for the sake of our argument, let us imagine a world where brain implants are effective at controlling violent behaviors with few side effects.

Advisory (Only) Devices

The use of predictive advisory therapeutic implants as a primary means of inhibiting specific behaviors could have a beneficial impact on an individual's ability to engage effectively in sustained decision-making. Advisory brain implants could be used to monitor urges that indicate a higher risk that the individual will commit a crime during incarceration or in a postimprisonment environment or even to support some sort of community-based sentence—as a diversion from incarceration.[2] For instance, if a convicted offender with a history of violence struggles to control impulses, that individual could be implanted with an advisory device and could learn from the device to control their responses to neurological events, by avoiding patterns of responses that result in violent behavior toward others. If the device could forewarn the individual by signaling in advance that the individual is undergoing neuronal patterns indicative of an impending aggressive outburst, then the implanted individual could learn to react appropriately (e.g., leaving the environment that has triggered the neuronal change, taking medication, etc.). The continuous monitoring of brain activity by the advisory device could assist the individual to learn to identify precursors, such as biological signals or various phenomena, that normally lead that person to aggressive outbursts and to develop strategies to avoid them.

In this scenario, assuming that the offender has freely chosen to be implanted with the advisory device, the implant does not coercively prevent reoffending or aggressive behavior; rather, it would serve as a means for this person to increase her autonomous control over harmful urges and her capacity to interrupt patterns of action.[3] By extending one's capacities to deflect violent urges, the advisory system could be viewed as increasing individual moral decision-making capacity and autonomy. By being alert to the neuronal signs and deciding to respond by leaving a situation likely to lead to violence, the implanted individual strengthens and increases his or her moral decision-making capacity to act as an autonomous moral agent. In this case, the assumption is that the implanted individual does not wish to act violently and has been struggling to control her responses to the triggers for her aggression. She is more autonomous in

---

[2] The decision about which kinds of criminal behaviour could justify use of brain implants to prevent or reduce the risk of harm occurring is highly contentious. For the purposes of this chapter, we are assuming two points. First, harms resulting from the acts of individuals who are known to be moved to violent rage might be the kind of behaviour that might be targeted for these kinds of implants. Second, it might be possible to neurologically detect, with a sufficiently high level of accuracy, the precursor warnings that an individual is on the verge of violent rage and that at that point there is the possibility of some kind of intervention that would stop the changes in the brain leading to the harmful outcome.

[3] However, if the state required offenders at risk of recidivism to accept an implant as a condition of release from prison, then the requirement for released offenders to be implanted *would* be coercive.

responding to the warning given by the implanted device to the degree that she wishes to increase her control over her violent impulses and the degree to which she chose the implant as a way of bolstering her capacity to act in accordance with her avowed commitments.[4] As a result, the moral autonomy of implanted individuals may be enhanced because their capacity to control their behavior is improved by the advanced warning provided by the device.

Some could argue that individuals are morally obliged to always act in accordance with the best available evidence. For the sake of argument, let us assume that the AI used in the neural implants to predict likely impulsive violence is reliable *and* that the individual has the capacity to take steps to prevent harmful actions occurring after the device provides advance warning. Then the advisory information may be an individual's only reliable evidence capable of playing an epistemic and informative role in their decision-making at that moment. If the individual has the power to choose otherwise, but decides contrary to that reliable available evidence to do nothing about the warning, then they would be allowing the prediction to come to fruition.

For this reason, if individuals are forewarned by their implant that their neural state is such that they are predisposed at that time to engage in immoral or illegal actions, could we hold them more accountable or culpable for their subsequent illegal actions if they ignore the advice and commit an offense? By not acting in accordance with the advice from the predictive device, implanted individuals are knowingly acting at least negligently, and potentially recklessly, by failing to take steps to prevent an outburst of potentially violent aggression to occur in the face of a forewarning by the implanted device (Danaher, 2013). However, if the device was faulty and failed to provide the correct prediction, then the individual would be no more culpable[5] for their violent behavior than individuals who have not been implanted and do not know how to anticipate or control their violent urges.

If one is pathologically prone to sudden blind rages, this would likely entail that one has diminished autonomy. From this perspective, people who have been implanted with an AI advisory device will likely experience increased autonomy because it increases their capacity to control their actions in accordance with their values. By comparison, those who lack control over their violent rages and do not have access to the information provided by an implanted device would be less responsible for their enraged actions than those who have greater control on

---

[4] Having extra choices does not always increase one's capacity to achieve one's goals. "Binding oneself" to a future course of action is sometimes a valuable tool for achieving one's ends and thus the capacity to deprive ourselves of choices contributes to our autonomy, this is discussed further later in the chapter. Thanks to Robert Sparrow for raising this point.

[5] An implanted patient could potentially be less culpable. Because the individual tried the implant as an approach to reducing the risk of offending (they try anything in their power to reduce risk unlike the individual who did not even have an implant). Should the AI device be faulty, then it would seem to be bad luck. Thanks to Allan McCay for this suggestion.

account of having received an implant.[6] A person who has no history of being overtaken by a pathologically violent rage would be less culpable for her unexpected violent reactions (assuming that the violent reaction was not controllable by the person at the time) than someone who knows that they can't control their anger.

Normally, we assume that someone with limited cognitive capacities (e.g. a child, a cognitively impaired person) would be held less responsible than someone with greater cognitive capacities, given their more limited capacity for the practical reasoning and agential control associated with moral and legal responsibility (Vincent, 2011, 2015). Given that an implanted individual is forewarned when the implant detects brain state patterns typically associated with impending violent aggression, it stands to reason that they are likely to have more opportunity and greater capacity to refrain from enacting the behavior than relevantly similarly situated individuals who are not implanted. On this basis, to what extent could implanted individuals be seen as having greater responsibility for their subsequent violent action(s) given that they receive a forewarning of such? In these circumstances, does responsibility depend on the predictive capacities of the AI implant, or on the degree of control that the agent has in choosing to act on the predictive advice?

A number of factors need to be understood to link predictive capacities to degrees of responsibility. If an individual ignores his or her AI device's warning about an upcoming aggressive outburst and the individual then causes severe harm to another person (assuming the aggressiveness contributed to the incident to the extent that the incident would not have occurred if the individual had not ignored the advisory warning from the device), then the question becomes whether ignoring device warnings should increase to the degree of responsibility for the offense. By contrast, it seems implausible to suggest that an individual who ignores the warning from the device, but does not commit an aggressive action could be held responsible for ignoring the warning. That is, we do not think that an individual who does not commit harm should be viewed as culpable, if they simply fail to attend to a predictive brain device warning.

Where harm has been caused by the aggressive actions of an individual who ignores a device warning, the implanted individual's act of ignoring the warning is arguably negligent or reckless and blameworthy. That is, the individual has

---

[6] Here we are only discussing and comparing the accountability of pathologically violent individuals implanted with predictive brain technologies on the assumption that there is capacity to act to break the link between the brain activity that signals a likely violent outburst and the actual occurrence of violence, and we are not comparing those people to nonviolent citizens who are not prone to pathological violence. It is possible that the extra choices made possible to pathologically violent individuals through being implanted may simply restore their relevant capacities to a 'normal' citizen level.

breached his or her duty of care to take steps to avoid harm, by responding to the warning from the AI device to defuse the situation likely to lead to harmful aggression, or the individual has recklessly ignored the warning and likely outcome. A person is likely found to be guilty of negligence if harm occurs—and they failed to take appropriate care to avoid harm that she had a duty to protect another against. A person may be found to have been reckless if he or she knew that he or she was prone to causing harm due to pathological violence and acted with indifference or disregard to the likely risk of harm provided by the predictive device, meaning that the individual knew, or should have known, that his or her subsequent actions were likely to cause harm. It follows, then, that where an individual has increased capacity to exercise autonomy (through improving the individual's information about risk or his or her capacity to control his or her actions), that increased autonomy is paralleled by an increase in the degree of moral or legal responsibility. In other words, the implanted individual would be responsible for causing harm as a result of ignoring the device's warning. An implanted individual would be blameworthy for ignoring a warning and liable in degree for the harmful consequences of doing so.

Automated Therapeutic Devices

If we accept the prospect that brain activity could be detected and then interfered with (e.g., by direct drug delivery) so that impulses could be shut down before they manifest in behavior as a result of a therapeutic intervention triggered by a predictive signal, then questions arise that may call for a revision to some aspects of our moral and medical responses to harmful behavior. Imagine that an individual could have an AI brain implant that both predicts that a harmful consequence is likely to occur due to a particular pattern of neuronal behavior and can deliver a drug, electrical stimulation, or another targeted therapy immediately that prevents the harmful consequence of the changed brain states from occurring. The responsibility and culpability of the individual for what happens as a result appears to depend, to some degree on whether the release of the preventative therapy is within the direct control of the individual (on noting the warning of a change in brain activity, the individual can act to send a signal to the implant to release the preventative therapy), or it is an automated feature of the AI of the device (ensuring that the individual is prevented from acting in a harmful way as a result of the changed brain state).

Imagine, then, that an AI device could be implanted in the brains of pathologically violent individuals and, in addition to monitoring their EEG to detect a change in brain activity that is associated with that individual becoming violent and causing harm, it can immediately and automatically deliver a therapeutic treatment to prevent those harmful effects from occurring, without the individual becoming aware that this is happening in his or her brain. In other words, the device could trigger an inhibiting response before a harmful urge could become an action and can do so without warning the implanted individual and without the individual being aware of the therapeutic response. In contrast to advisory devices that provide signals to the individual and allow the individual to choose how to respond, automated therapeutic devices are automatically activated, allowing no possibility for the individual to decide to act or to interfere in the activation process. Would being implanted with one of these automated AI therapeutic devices, which prevent harmful actions from occurring once a neuronal change has been detected, undermine the individual's autonomy? Would it affect the person's moral autonomy? We understand moral autonomy as involving, to some degree, the possession and capacity to deploy a range of competencies relating to self-discovery, self-definition and self-direction (Meyers, 1989) so that one acts in accordance with one's own values. Bearing in mind that these devices are being programmed to identify neural patterns associated with behaviours (e.g., criminal violent urges) not compatible with societal values, to what extent does preventing predicted behaviours threaten an individual's freedom of choice and action?

Some would ask to what extent using these types of inhibiting therapeutic responses challenges the core notion of moral decision-making or autonomy. The use of these devices for this purpose may be viewed as failing to respect and undermining the individual's agency. In other words, by setting into action an automatic therapeutic response before harmful urges crystallize into acts, predictive brain devices close off opportunities for individuals to demonstrate virtuous character traits by closing the "window of moral opportunity" for them to choose at all, including choosing to do the right thing in the face of urges to do otherwise (Smilansky, 1994a). After all, if the device were only to warn the person that it is highly probable that they will commit a harmful act, an individual might be able to respond in such a way as to inhibit their harmful urges without the help of an automatic therapeutic system (e.g., by taking inhibitive medication). In this instance, self-control is praiseworthy and ultimately grounded in a personal and free choice that overcomes a harmful impulse.

An individual might be thought to merit moral praise and to have acted autonomously (at least to some degree) if she decided to be implanted because she knows that she really struggles to control her urges and recognizes that acting on them is wrong. As a form of volitional "bootstrapping" in the face of akratic action, she could exercise (relative) moral virtue by choosing to make herself unable to make poor choices or to fail to overcome (for her) irresistible urges. Her autonomy (and virtue) would be straightforwardly constrained, however, if the state imposed the automated therapeutic device on her without her consent.

Ethically, automated therapeutic devices differ significantly from devices that implement advisory warning systems because, while the automated devices guarantee reduction in harmful behavior (reducing bad outcomes) by preventing the person from acting on impulses, at the same time they curb the individual's capacity to exercise autonomous self-control and agency. If the devices are implanted by the state as way of preventing harmful behaviours, and not chosen by the individual, then they involve the state prospectively limiting individual freedom of action.

A problem with automated therapeutic responses is that the process, in effect, outsources decisional capacities to the AI within devices. The inhibition of a violent urge would be the result of a technological intervention by the device, not the agent. The problem with outsourcing inhibitions to AI implants is that doing so fails to treat the individual as a moral agent, undermines autonomy and moral responsibility. The implanted individual cannot control the technology that administers therapeutic responses prior to any wrongdoing and the implanted individual cannot control the behavior response caused by the therapeutic intervention. This impedes the individual's autonomy and may lead to reduced self-control. For example, it might lead a person to think: "This device will always intervene, so I needn't really reflect on my own impulses and actions." Having the device set to "auto-pilot" might cause implanted individuals to fail to reflect on their actions at all and therefore produce a false sense of moral security; the person might come to believe "I am incapable of doing wrong."

Some could ask whether implanting a person with a device that delivers an inhibiting response prior to any harmful action occurring is, in fact, a form of preventative punishment (Smilanky, 1994a, 1994b; Zedner, 2010). Preventative punishment occurs when a person who is thought to be prone to offend is prevented from acting in a way that could lead to the offense occurring. The use of automatic predictive brain devices that prevent the agent from acting immorally can be understood as preventative punishment or punishment without a crime (unless one argues that the onset of brain activity itself is culpable[7]). However, is the stopping of impulses that presage a crime a form of punishment, if the implanted individual has chosen to be implanted with the device? It is difficult to conceive that a brain device stopping an agent from doing X is actually a form of punishment; it seems rather more a type of behavioral regulation than a form of punishment. However, if the individual has been implanted by the state, then the situation may be different.

Whether automated intervention that prevents harmful actions from occurring can be understood as a punishment may substantially depend on (a) whether it is justified by an authority imposing it with reference to past wrongdoing and

---

[7] This would be hard to do given that brain activity per se is not controllable by the individual.

(b) whether or not the implant has been voluntarily chosen by the individual or coercively forced upon the individual by an authority. Preventing an individual from wrongdoing, in a case where the patient is unable to control his or her impulses could be understood as behavioral regulation rather than punishment. But if the justification for preventing the action is to prevent recidivism or to prevent individuals whose neural activity suggests a proclivity to criminal harm, then it could be understood as constituting a preventative sanction or a punishment.

In addition to these concerns, automated interventions rely on estimating the likelihood of harmful actions based on a device monitoring a plurality of signals indicative of particular brain activity and then estimating the time frame before harmful behavior is expected to occur (Osorio et al., 2001). Statistically, it is possible for the predictions to provide false positives and false negatives, meaning that an intervention may be given even though the device has provided a false reading. Depending on the nature of the intervention option (e.g., chemical, electrical etc.), the intervention may be more harmful than therapeutic. We can easily think that for public safety, a personalized-algorithm may determine in favor of minimizing risk to society, thus increasing the probability that inhibiting interventions are administered in error (erring on the side of protecting potential victims). On the other hand, there could also be cases where the predictions are wrong, for instance, when the device does not provide a "treatment" when it should have. Who should be accountable for not having stopped the harmful behavior from occurring? Should the individual be fully blamed, or should some of the blame rest on the manufacturer of the device for not having inhibited the harmful action? If an individual was found to be legally incompetent to control their pathological aggressive outbursts without the implant and for that reason he or she would be considered (from a legal perspective) not to be accountable for these actions, then it could be argued that cases where the device failed to administer the treatment and harm occurs, and then device manufacturers could in some cased be held accountable for the resultant harms.[8,9]

---

[8] The responsibility of a device manufacturer will depend on what the manufacturer has claimed about reliability. If they claimed that the device will only reduce the risk of outbursts by 20%, and this holds across the population that uses the device, then it would be unfair to hold them accountable should the device fail in a particular instance (unless the failure was the result of negligence relating to the particular device). For these reasons, the reliability of devices would need to be assessed before they could be reasonably used where there is a high risk of harm resulting from false negatives. Thanks to Allan McCay for suggesting this nuance.

[9] Another potential problem with automated therapeutic activation systems would be for those cases in which an aggressive response is justified or morally appropriate and the system automatically prevented the implanted individual from reacting in this way. For instance, if the implanted individual is attacked and, consequently, needs to become aggressive to defend himself, what should be the therapeutic prescription in this context? It may even be the case that the action is nullified, thus putting the individual at personal risk. Not all socially adverse behaviors are adverse in every context. In an ideal world, a suitably sophisticated device would be able to distinguish between these different scenarios—unprompted aggression versus prompted aggression.

Conclusion

The purpose of this chapter was to examine the ethical implications of the potential use of neural implants that use AI to provide advisory or automated therapeutic responses as a means of reducing the risk of reoffending, in particular with respect to the potential effects on the moral autonomy of the implanted offender.

As argued in this chapter, advisory devices could potentially increase moral decision-making capacity and moral autonomy, assuming that the individual is free to choose or refuse to be implanted in the first place. An individual who is forewarned that her or his brain state indicated a propensity for harmful behaviors, the individual could learn to develop strategies to avoid aggressive outbursts by recognizing precursors or phenomenon that usually lead to them. In the long run, this is likely to extend the implanted person's capacity to control harmful urges and increase the capacity to refrain from causing harm.

By contrast, automated therapeutic interventions pose a direct challenge to individual moral autonomy, where the patient is coercively implanted. From our discussion, it appears that devices that deliver automated therapeutic interventions may diminish individual moral decision-making capacity and moral autonomy through the outsourcing of personal control to the AI in brain devices. As previously discussed, the automated therapeutic delivery system is intended to stop violent behaviors that are likely to cause some kind of harmful consequences ahead. We have observed that a person would be considered praiseworthy if they were capable of using advisory devices to assist them in inhibiting their harmful urges without the intervention of an automatic therapeutic system. The automatic activation of treatment to prevent harmful behaviors diminishes autonomy and agency, taking away the capacity to autonomously control one's actions, including those that are morally appropriate.

Our examination indicates that it would be ethically premature to pursue automated therapeutic response devices as a means of addressing criminal behavior, even in extreme cases (De Ridder et al., 2009; Franzini et al., 2012; Fuss et al., 2005; Jobst et al., 2000; Marsh & Krauss, 2000; Shih et al., 2009).[10] At this point in time, development of devices that can support individuals to avoid harmful behavior through advisory warnings are potentially more valuable, given the importance we place on moral and legal responsibility and autonomous agency. If

---

[10] In addition to previously discussed ethical issues, a perfectly functional technology developed to target some extreme cases could exacerbate existing psychiatric problems, alter cognitive capacities, and develop unintentional neuropsychiatric effects as has been observed with other invasive brain implants (Gilbert, 2012, 2013a, 2013b, 2014).

automated activation is eventually considered as an option of last resort for some rare cases of pathological compulsion, it should only be utilized in conjunction with rigorous monitoring, ideally within a supervised environment prior to the individual being released from custody.

Further questions remain to be explored. Among these, did the individual voluntarily choose the AI advisory device as a way to improve her or his moral decision-making and reduce the likelihood of causing harm? Under what circumstances may she or he negotiate disengagement of the system? Given neural plasticity, if the advisory devices are used successfully by patients to change their behavior after receiving the warning, would the devices still be considered accurate in predicting the risk of harmful behavior? Would the AI be able to predict new (and potentially harmful) brain states for an individual in light of changes to their psychological environment and provide new warnings? What is the best model for assessing the responsibility of manufacturers for detection errors? Further research will be required to address these questions.

Acknowledgments

The authors would like to thank Robert Sparrow and Allan McCay for comments on early versions of this chapter. Dr. Frederic Gilbert is the recipient of an Australian Research Council Discovery Early Career Researcher Award (project number DE150101390). Funding from the Australian Research Council Centre of Excellence Scheme (Project Number CE 140100012) and the National Science Foundation (NSF Award #EEC-1028725) for this research is gratefully acknowledged.

References

Cook, M., O'Brien, T., Berkovic, S., Murphy, M., Morokoff, A., Fabinyi, G., . . . Himes, D. (2013). Prediction of seizure likelihood with a long-term, implanted seizure advisory system in patients with drug-resistant epilepsy: A first-in-man study. *Lancet Neurology*, *12*(6), 563–571.

Danaher, J. (2013). Enhanced control and criminal responsibility. In E. Hildt & A. G. Franke (Eds.), *Cognitive enhancement: An interdisciplinary perspective* (pp. 283–308). Dordrecht, The Netherlands: Springer.

De Ridder, D., Langguth, B., Plazier, M., & Menovsky, T. (2009). Moral dysfunction: Theoretical model and potential neurosurgical treatments. In J. Verplaetse, J. de Schrijver, S. Vanneste, & J. Braeckman (Eds.), *The moral brain: Essays on the evolutionary and neuroscientific aspects of morality* (pp. 155–183). Dordrecht, The Netherlands: Springer.

Di Marco, J. P. (2003). Implantable cardioverter–defibrillators. *The New England Journal of Medicine, 349,* 1836–1847. doi:10.1056/NEJMra035432

Franzini, A., Broggi, G., Cordella, R., Dones, I., & Messina, G. (2012). Deep-brain stimulation for aggressive and disruptive behavior. *World Neurosurgery, 80,* S29.e11–S29.e14. doi:10.1016/j.wneu.2012.06.038

Fuss, J., Auer, M. K., Biedermann, S. V., Briken, P., & Hacke, W. (2015). Deep brain stimulation to reduce sexual drive. *Journal of Psychiatry and Neuroscience, 40*(6), 429–431. doi:10.1503/jpn.150003

Gardner, A. B., Krieger, A. M., Vachtsevanos, G., & Litt, B. (2006). One-class novelty detection for seizure analysis from intracranial EEG. *Journal of Machine Learning Research, 2*(7), 1025–1044.

Gilbert, F. (2014). Self-estrangement & deep brain stimulation: Ethical issues related to forced explanation. *Neuroethics, 8*(2), 107–114. doi:10.1007/s12152-014-9224-1

Gilbert, F. (2012). The burden of normality: From "chronically ill" to "symptom free." New ethical challenges for deep brain stimulation postoperative treatment. *Journal of Medical Ethics, 38*(7), 408–412.

Gilbert, F. (2013a). Deep brain stimulation and postoperative suicidability among treatment resistant depression patients: Should eligibility protocols exclude patients with history of suicide attempts and anger/impulsivity? *American Journal of Bioethics: Neuroscience, 4*(1), 28–35. doi:10.1080/21507740.2012.740143

Gilbert, F. (2013b). Deep brain stimulation for treatment resistant depression: Postoperative feelings of self-estrangement, suicide attempt and impulsive-aggressive behaviours, *Neuroethics, 6*(3), 473–481. doi:10.1007/s12152-013-9178-8

Gilbert, F. (2015). A threat to autonomy? The intrusion of predictive brain implants. *American Journal of Bioethics Neuroscience, 6*(4), 4–11.

Gilbert, F., & Cook, M. (2015). Are predictive brain implants an indispensable feature of autonomy? *Bioethica Forum, 8*(4), 121–127.

Gilbert, F., Cook, M., O'Brien, T., & Illes, J. (2019). Embodiment and estrangement: Results from a first-in-human "intelligent BCI" trial. *Science & Engineering Ethics, 25*(1), 83–96. doi:10.1007/s11948-017-0001-5

Gilbert, F., Goddard, E., Viaña, J. N. M., Carter, A., & Horne, M. (2017). "I miss being me": Phenomenological effects of deep brain stimulation. *American Journal of Bioethics Neuroscience, 8*(2), 96–109. doi:10.1080/21507740.2017.1320319

Gilbert, F., Viaña, J. M. N., & Vranic, A. (2016). Acquired paedophillia and moral responsibility. *American Journal of Bioethics Neuroscience, 7*(4), 209–211. doi:10.1080/21507740.2016.1244221

Gilbert, F., & Vranic, A. (2015). Paedophilia, invasive brain surgery, and punishment, *Bioethical Inquiry, 12,* 521–526. doi:10.1007/s11673-015-9647-3

Gilbert, F., Vranic, A., & Hurst, S., (2013). Involuntary & voluntary invasive brain surgery: Ethical issues related to acquired aggressiveness. *Neuroethics, 6,* 115–128. doi:10.1007/s12152-012-9161-9

Jobst, B. C., Seigel, A. M., Thadani, V. M., Roberts, D. W., Rhodes, H. C., & Williamson, P. D. (2000). Intractable seizures of frontal lobe origin: Clinical characteristics, localizing signs, and results of surgery. *Epilepsia, 41,* 1139–1152.

Kingwell, K. (2013). Implantable device advises patients with epilepsy of seizure likelihood. *Nature Reviews Neurology, 9,* 297. doi:10.1038/nrneurol.2013.94

Marsh, L., & Krauss, G. L. (2000). Aggression and violence in patients with epilepsy. *Epilepsy Behavior, 3,* 160–168.

McElroy, S. L., Soutullo, C. A., Beckman, D. A., Taylor, P., & Keck, P. E. (1998). DSM-IV intermittent explosive disorder: A report of 27 cases. *Journal of Clinical Psychiatry, 59*(4), 203–210.

Meyers, D. (1989). *Self, society and personal choice.* New York, NY: Columbia University Press.

Osorio, I., Frei, M. G., Manly, B. F. J., Sunderam, S., Bhavaraju, N. C., & Wilkinson, S. B. (2001). An introduction to contingent (closed-loop) brain electrical stimulation for seizure blockage, to ultra-short-term clinical trials, and to multidimensional statistical analysis of therapeutic efficacy. *Journal of Clinical Neurophysiology, 18*(6), 533–544.

Shih, J. L., Thabele, L. M., Germano, F., & Gerpen, J. V. (2009). Behavior in front lobe epilepsy: A video-EEG and ictal SPECT case study. *Neurology, 73*(21), 1804–1806.

Smilansky, S. (1994a). The time to punish. *Analysis, 54*(1), 50–53.

Smilansky, S. (1994b). Determinism and prepunishment: The radical nature of compatibilism. *Analysis, 67*(296), 347–349.

Vincent, N. (2011). Enhancing responsibility. In L. Nadel, F. Schauer, & W. Sinnott-Armstrong (Eds.), *Legal responsibility and neuroscience.* New York, NY: Oxford University Press.

Vincent, N. (2015). A compatibilist theory of legal responsibility. *Criminal Law and Philosophy, 9,* 477–498.

Zedner, L. (2010). Pre-crime and pre-punishment: A health warning, *Criminal Justice Matters, 81*(1), 24–25.

6

Offering Neurointerventions to Offenders With Cognitive-Emotional Impairments

Ethical and Criminal Justice Aspects

Farah Focquaert, Kristof Van Assche, and Sigrid Sterckx

Introduction

Imagine that effective neurointerventions (i.e., biological or biopsychological interventions targeting our brain functioning and thereby our behavior) would exist that could partly or fully restore moral functioning and behavior and further imagine that such interventions would provide a better long-term risk-minimizing strategy compared to imprisonment.[1] Such potential neurointerventions may range from being noninvasive (e.g., food and vitamin supplements, brain training, neurofeedback, magnetic brain stimulation, drugs to combat addiction) to invasive with moderate to severe side effects (e.g., androgen deprivation therapy, electroconvulsive therapy, deep brain stimulation) or even very invasive and extremely risky (e.g., neurosurgery). While some of these interventions are standard medical treatment for certain disorders (e.g., androgen deprivation therapy for prostate cancer, drugs to combat addiction, antipsychotics for chronic aggression), they may also be used off label as a means to reduce violent, deviant behavior (e.g., androgen deprivation therapy for offenders with pedophilia). Moreover, some of these interventions are in the investigational phase and may not be considered as treatments at present (e.g., magnetic, direct current, or deep brain stimulation for addiction, or food and vitamin supplements to reduce aggressive behavior).

A wide variety of medications (e.g., selective serotonin reuptake inhibitors and antipsychotics) can be successful in lowering impulsivity and aggression in adults and children (De Deyn & Buitelaar, 2006; Pappadopulos et al., 2006), and

---

[1] Our focus is explicitly on restoring moral functioning and behavior in the sense of treating mental illnesses, cognitive-emotional impairments and addictions. We understand enhancement as any "deliberate intervention . . . which aims to improve an existing capacity that most or all human beings typically have, or to create a new capacity" (Buchanan, 2011, p. 23). Enhancement of normal moral capacities is beyond the scope of our chapter.

Farah Focquaert, Kristof Van Assche, and Sigrid Sterckx, *Offering Neurointerventions to Offenders With Cognitive-Emotional Impairments* In: *Neurointerventions and the Law.* Edited by: Nicole A Vincent, Thomas Nadelhoffer, and Allan McCay, Oxford University Press (2020). © Oxford University Press 2020
DOI: 10.1093/oso/9780190651145.001.0006

neuromodulation techniques such as neurofeedback are being investigated to manage risk factors for deviant behavior, such as attention deficit hyperactivity disorder (Gevensleben et al., 2009) and substance use disorders (Arani, Rostami, & Nostratabadi, 2010; Sokhadze, Cannon, & Trudeau, 2008). A recent review study (Balia, Carucci, Coghill, & Zuddas, 2018) concluded that their findings partially support adding pharmacotherapy (e.g., stimulant medications and atypical antipsychotics) as a potentially useful therapeutic approach for aggressive behavior in children with a primary diagnosis of conduct disorder without co-morbid disorders who do not respond to psychoeducational or psychological interventions. Large effect sizes have been reported for aggressive behaviors in children with a primary diagnosis of attention-deficit/hyperactivity disorder, and co-morbid conduct disorder and/or oppositional defiant disorder (Pappadopulos et al., 2006). Also, recently, small-scale investigational studies involving noninvasive neurostimulation such as transcranial direct current stimulation and transcranial magnetic stimulation seem to show some promise for the management of addictions (17 studies, medium effect size). Magnetic stimulation that targets the prefrontal cortex may increase cognitive control mechanisms, decrease craving levels, or both (Conti & Nakamura-Palacios, 2014; Jansen et al., 2013). However, it must be kept in mind that, at present, most of these interventions are in the early stages of research and development.

If certain neurointerventions can restore impaired moral decision-making and behavior in offenders, should the criminal justice system then be permitted to use such neurointerventions and, if so, under which conditions? Could it be ethical to offer probation, parole or reduced prison sentences including neurointerventions as one of the conditions?[2] To what extent would it make a difference that the proposed neurointerventions are invasive, risky, and/ or nonreversible? Similarly, could it ever be ethical to force neurointerventions as part of an offender's sentence, either during incarceration or as a postprison requirement?

In this chapter, we will argue that it *can* be ethical to offer neurointerventions to offenders as a condition of probation, parole, or sentence reduction provided that the following minimal ethical conditions are met: (a) the status quo is in no way cruel, inhuman, degrading or in some other way *wrong*; (b) the neurointervention itself is in no way cruel, inhuman, degrading, or in some other way *wrong*; (c) the neurointervention respects the well-being of the offender; (d) the neurointervention targets one or more risk factors for recidivism; and (e) the neurointervention is voluntary: the offender is formally required

---

[2] For example, this includes the circumstance where a judge imposes a prison sentence that is reduced because, upon completion of the prison sentence, the offender will be subjected to residential or nonresidential treatment.

to give his or her free and informed consent upon acceptance, and, if appropriate, a court-appointed guardian his or her authorization.[3] We go into detail concerning the specific implications of each condition and discuss potential counterarguments to our view. The conditions that we stipulate are targeted at reversible neurointerventions that may have moderate to severe side effects.

In this chapter, we will argue that it can be ethical to offer neurointerventions to offenders as a condition of probation, parole, or sentence reduction, provided that the fulfillment of five minimal conditions is verified on a case by case basis. For example, our conditions require the absence of cruel, inhuman, degrading, or in some other way *wrong* offers, while we acknowledge that answers to the questions of what constitutes a cruel, inhuman, and/or degrading intervention, and whether or not the element of reversibility is a determining factor may not be exactly the same for everyone. We further argue that forcing *invasive and/ or risky* neurointerventions as part of an offender's sentence is both ethically and practically problematic. Moreover, although forcing *noninvasive* therapies as part of an offender's sentence may be considered ethical by some experts, their implementation may remain problematic from a practical point of view and especially so in the case of offenders with psychopathy. It is likely that many neurointerventions will require the offender's willingness to undergo the intervention to achieve successful therapy outcomes and to effectively reduce recidivism. For example, an unwillingness to undergo a given intervention may result in the use of countermeasures by the offender (e.g., getting testosterone online in the case of androgen deprivation treatment). Moreover, treatment outcomes focusing on changing behavior are usually better when individuals are motivated to undergo treatment (Simpson, Joe, & Rowan-Szal, 1997).

We discuss some of the reasons why the offer of neurointervention can be a more morally acceptable option as compared to imprisonment, both for society and for the offender. Next, we discuss how both the status quo (imprisonment) and the neurointervention itself need to be in no way cruel, inhuman, degrading, or in some other way wrong for the offer to adequately address the issue of (potential) coercion within criminal justice settings. We further discuss how the third condition, in combination with the first two conditions, ensures maximum concern for the well-being of the offender as a way to prevent morally unacceptable practices. In our view, concern for the well-being of offenders with mental health needs and forensic patients minimally implies that the least invasive option is considered first, that the intervention is psychologically or clinically indicated,

---

[3] This condition requires that the offender gives his or her free and informed consent upon acceptance, or, where the person concerned is not deemed to be legally competent, authorization is provided by that person's legal representative, the offender does not object, and the offender takes part as far as possible in the authorization procedure.

that the intervention is not disproportional in a way that the severity of the neurointervention outweighs the severity of the crime, and that it offers a good risk-to-benefit ratio in and of itself. It should constitute standard medical treatment outside of correctional settings. Moreover, we discuss how the need to safeguard the well-being of the offender, in combination with the need to target one or more risk factors for recidivism, prevents the illicit use of neurointerventions as a means of social behavior control. Then, we argue why voluntariness is both ethically and practically preferable to forced neurointerventions, although non-invasive interventions *without any side effects* could be considered exceptionally acceptable.

Punishment versus Rehabilitation

Stephen J. Morse (2008) has convincingly argued that offenders with severe psychopathy should be civilly committed rather than given a sentence due to their impaired moral rationality (i.e., their inability to be responsive to moral reasons due to cognitive and affective impairments in moral reasoning and decision-making). In line with their impaired moral rationality, recent neurobiological findings show both structural and functional brain impairments in psychopaths in regions of the brain that are implicated in the normal development of moral reasoning (Focquaert, Glenn, & Raine, 2015). Hence, offenders who do not satisfy the required criteria for legal culpability and who therefore cannot be deemed legally responsible should not be sentenced and should instead receive adequate mental health treatment that may or may not involve involuntary civil commitment.

The reality is such however that, in many countries, offenders with personality disorders (e.g., psychopathy, schizotypal personality disorder) and/or other mental health impairments (e.g., substance abuse disorders, schizophrenia, sexual disorders) are more often than not considered to be *legally sane* and are therefore given a prison sentence rather than being civilly committed. The reluctance to civilly commit certain offenders with psychiatric disorders may be partially explained by the rather grim prospect of successful behavioral treatment for some of these disorders depending on their severity or nature (e.g., psychopathy; Focquaert & Raine, 2011). For certain severe and violent psychopathic offenders, for example, this basically means that their release into society will not be warranted from a public safety perspective and may thus result in lifelong civil commitment in forensic long-term care facilities. Hence, for severe psychopathic offenders, getting a prison sentence will likely lead to an earlier release compared to civil commitment. At the same time, giving offenders with serious personality disorders or other mental health impairments a prison sentence without any kind of treatment is problematic from the standpoint of public safety (these individuals will re-enter society at some point), as well as from the standpoint of offenders' human rights.[4]

There are several reasons why providing adequate treatment rather than imprisonment can be a more defensible option for many offenders. First, individuals with mental health disorders have a basic human right to receive adequate mental health treatment, regardless of whether these individuals are offenders or law-abiding citizens.[5] Second, treatment may increase autonomy in offenders who are suffering from conditions that negatively impact their self-governance due to irresistible thoughts and impulses that accompany the disorder in question. As we have previously argued, androgen deprivation treatment for sexual disorders can substantially diminish the deviant thoughts and compulsions that are common in individuals with such disorders, and thereby increase autonomy, and adequate substance abuse treatment (e.g., methadone maintenance treatment, heroin maintenance treatment, long-acting naltrexone abstinence treatment) helps individuals to overcome their addictive urges and is more effective in reducing crime in comparison to sanctions without treatment (Hall & Carter, 2013). Third, adequate treatment rather than imprisonment allows for the maximal preservation of one's freedom, personal relations, employment, and career prospects and of one's position as a member of the community (Focquaert & Raine, 2011; Rosati, 1994). Stigmatization and loss of one's professional and personal relations upon re-entry in society is a common difficulty faced by many offenders and often precludes successful reentry (Kleinig, 2008). For example, many offenders responsible for drug-related crimes have experienced the option of treatment rather than imprisonment as a welcome opportunity (Stevens et al., 2005). Fourth, several studies indicate that adequate treatment results in lower recidivism rates in comparison to sanctions without treatment (e.g., Hall & Carter, 2013; MacKenzie, 2006; Mears, 2010; White, Saunders, Fisher, & Mellow,

---

[4] Note that, both for offenders that have been sentenced to a term of imprisonment and for those that have been civilly committed, general safeguards are stipulated in international legal instruments. These include, at the level of the United Nations, the *Principles of Medical Ethics relevant to the Role of Health Personnel, Particularly Physicians, in the Protection of Prisoners and Detainees against Torture and Other Cruel, Inhuman or Degrading Treatment or Punishment* (1982), the *Body of Principles for the Protection of All Persons under Any Form of Detention or Imprisonment* (1988), the *Basic Principles for the Treatment of Prisoners* (1990), and the *Optional Protocol to the Convention against Torture and other Cruel, Inhuman or Degrading Treatment or Punishment* (2002). At the level of the Council of Europe these, in addition, include *Recommendation No R(82)17 concerning Custody and Treatment of Dangerous Prisoners* (1982), *Recommendation No R(98)7 concerning the Ethical and Organisational Aspects of Health Care in Prison* (1998), and *Recommendation No R(2006)2 on the European Prison Rules* (2006).

[5] Unfortunately, even civil commitment does not guarantee adequate mental health treatment. For instance, in Belgium, before the establishment of two forensic psychiatric centers in 2014 and 2017, many offenders who were civilly committed ended up in prison due to an alarming shortage of available beds in forensic mental health facilities (Vandevelde et al., 2011).

2012). Studies also suggest that less severe sanctions are more likely to reduce recidivism (Cochran, Mears, & Bales, 2014). Cochran and colleagues suggest that this may be due to the fact that less severe sanctions, such as community-based sanctions rather than imprisonment, involve more rehabilitative services, treatment, and community support and more readily allow for community reintegration. Alternatively, a higher reduction in recidivism may be due to the fact that less severe sanctions reduce one's exposure to potentially *criminogenic* environments such as prisons (Nagin, Cullen, & Jonson, 2009). Bales and Piquero's (2012) study comparing incarceration to nonincarcerative sanctions (probation or intensive probation) supports the overall conclusions of prior literature (for a review, see Nagin et al., 2009), namely, that imprisonment has a criminogenic effect on reoffending in comparison to nonincarcerative sanctions. Incarceration delays and often problematizes desistance (Canton, 2017).

Although controversial and ethically questionable, in several U.S. states, androgen deprivation therapy is mandated as a condition of probation or parole for certain sexual offenders. In some states (e.g., Florida) androgen deprivation therapy is even mandated as part of the sentence, does not require informed consent, and may result in additional punishment if the offender does not comply.[6] Such practice is highly controversial and ethically dubious because: (a) it disregards the offender's autonomy; (b) it involves a kind of therapy that may result in serious, irreversible side effects, especially in case of long-term use; and (c) treatment outcomes are potentially compromised due to the forced nature of the intervention (Thibaut et al., 2010). Moreover, in up to 20 U.S. states, violent sexual offenders may face both a prison sentence and subsequent civil commitment (i.e., under sexually violent predator statutes), which, of course, significantly increases the length of incarceration. Although the rationale behind such civil commitment is treatment and the protection of society, its implementation, especially in cases where the civil commitment is lifelong, can be questionable. The decision to civilly commit an offender under a sexually violent predator statute is typically based on clinical or actuarial risk assessments performed by forensic practitioners (psychiatrists and clinicians), who need to determine the presence or absence of volitional control impairments directly arising from a clinical condition. Unfortunately, the currently used validated tools for such risk assessments are not suited to decisively establish such impairments (Rogers et al., 2005). Similarly problematic is the fact that the predictive value of forensic

---

[6] Pursuant to Section 794.0235 of the Florida statutes, the court has the possibility to sentence a person convicted of sexual battery to be treated with medroxyprogesterone acetate. Where that person has a prior conviction of sexual battery, the court is under the obligation to impose that sentence. If the convict refuses to allow the administration of the product, he or she will additionally be held guilty of a felony of the second degree that is punishable by a term of imprisonment not exceeding 15 years and a fine not exceeding $10,000 (Florida Legislature, 2019).

Psychopathy Checklist–Revised assessments of psychopathy for example, which are often performed by clinicians in the field, may differ considerably from the predictive value obtained in controlled research studies where evaluations are performed by trained research staff (Murrie, Boccaccini, Caperton, & Rufino, 2012). Hence, there is both a substantial risk of false positives and false negatives and this is a very serious matter since it may result in the improper lifelong civil commitment of a given individual. At the same time, for certain violent offenders with psychopathy, especially severe psychopathy, the recidivism risk and threat to society do not warrant their release into society.

The Netherlands allows a judge to impose a prison sentence followed by post-prison mandated mental health treatment, either residential or nonresidential, of mentally ill offenders provided that such treatment has been deemed necessary at the time of sentencing. For nonviolent crimes, the maximum duration is for four years after the offender has completed his or her prison sentence. For violent crimes, the duration may be extended if certain conditions are met.[7] Such postprison treatment, possibly involving neurointerventions such as psychopharmacological treatment, might provide a better "solution" for individuals with personality disorders (e.g., mild to moderate psychopathy or schizotypal personality disorder) in comparison to a prison sentence without any type of therapy, support, or skills training. Two things are essential for this to work: (a) the offender's willingness to cooperate in the treatment/rehabilitation; and (b) successful treatment/rehabilitation options. We now turn to the five minimal conditions that we propose are needed for the offer of neurointerventions as a condition of probation, parole or sentence reduction to be ethically acceptable.

Neurointervention as a Condition of Probation, Parole, or Sentence Reduction

If the neurointerventions are sufficiently safe (e.g., they have no moderate or severe side effects) and if recidivism risk is adequately addressed (by effectively targeting biological or biopsychological risk factors for criminal behavior), then the offer of such interventions as part of an alternative and/or reparative sanction may be considered ethically acceptable by some (Greely, 2007; Rosati, 1994). Nevertheless, some and perhaps many will argue that offenders will feel pressured into accepting the interventions out of fear of serving a lengthy prison sentence. If prisoners feel unduly pressured into accepting a specific intervention, offering it would threaten their autonomy and invalidate their free and informed consent.

---

[7] See Dutch Criminal Code (1881, Articles 37–38u) and Dutch Code of Criminal Procedure (1921, Articles 509o to 509x).

The element of coercion in judicial settings, in combination with the requirement that the intervention respects the well-being of the incarcerated individual, urges us to be extremely cautious when offering neurointerventions to offenders. Indeed, the ethical worries loom large when moderate to severe side effects are possible, especially in cases of irreversible interventions, even if the recidivism risk can be adequately addressed by such interventions. However, the question arises as to whether, if offenders would indeed feel quasi-coerced to a greater or lesser degree into accepting the offer of some type of neurointervention, this would *necessarily* constitute a sufficient reason to withhold the offer?

Where an offender is offered an alternative to prison, in the form of a neurointervention that targets risk factors for recidivism, this offer may be seen as a form of quasi-coercion. Thus, although the offender may give formal consent to the intervention and may have the right to withdraw that consent, since the offer is made within a judicial context one must question whether the consent is the result of a truly voluntary choice and thus whether it is valid. Quasi-coercion is problematic for many experts—some consider it to be unconstitutional,[8] a violation of the offender's rights, while others have a more pragmatic viewpoint, seeing the neurointervention as a practical response to crime or as a humane alternative to prison for offenders with mental health disorders (Focquaert & Raine, 2012; Stevens et al., 2005). Indeed, for such offenders, some experts have argued that neurointervention may enhance or restore the offender's autonomy, a positive outcome for the offender that justifies a temporary disregard for autonomy. In this context, Caplan (2006) has argued that, subject to certain safeguards, it is ethically acceptable to offer psychopharmacological treatment to offenders with substance abuse disorders as an alternative to prison. Likewise, we have previously argued for the offer of androgen deprivation therapy to offenders with sexual disorders (Douglas, Bonte, Focquaert, Devolder, & Sterckx, 2013; Focquaert, 2014). Multiple studies have reported low levels of perceived coercion in correctional mental health settings (e.g., Moser et al., 2004; Poythress, Petrila, McGaha, & Boothroyd, 2002; Redlich, Hoover, Summers, & Steadman, 2010; Rigg, 2002). However, perceived coercion and actual coercion are not necessarily the same, and an offender's account of the presence or absence of coercion does not necessarily indicate actual (un)coerced treatment (Rigg, 2002).

However, while coercion as such is clearly morally problematic, there is a substantial and important difference in the case of an offender offered the choice

---

[8] It has been argued that legislation authorizing the use of chemical or physical castration of (repeat) sex offenders in some U.S. states may violate the sex offender's First Amendment right to entertain sexual fantasies, the Eighth Amendment's ban on cruel and unusual punishments, and the Fourteenth Amendment's guarantee of due process and equal protection (Beckham, 1998; Druhm, 1997; Scott & Holmberg, 2003; Vanderzyl, 1994). However, other commentators have vehemently denied that this would be the case (Gimino, 1997; Tullio, 2009).

between prison and "treatment" (Focquaert & Raine, 2012). Indeed, many offenders responsible for drug-related crimes have experienced the option of treatment as a welcome opportunity (Stevens et al., 2005). Coercion is not an all-or-nothing phenomenon—there are many degrees of coercion from the mild to the extreme, and, to some extent at least, there is a degree of coercion in many medical treatments (Cosyns, 1999; Group for the Advancement of Psychiatry, 1994).[9] In the context of a judicial decision concerning treatment of an offender, coercion, to some degree, will be present: the relevant question is whether it is present to such a degree that *the validity of the offender's consent* must be cast into doubt, that is, whether the offender's decision was indeed an expression of his or her free and autonomous decision-making. Can an offender, faced with prison as the only other alternative, indeed voluntarily opt for a neurointervention? Some might look to the analogy of a patient offered treatment for a severe or life-threatening condition, when the treatment on offer comes with its own risks, for example, of death or debilitating side effects. This analogy suggests that valid consent can be given for a "least worst" option (Bomann-Larsen, 2013). But in the offender's case we may be looking not at the choice between status quo and medical treatment, but at the choice between different "punishments." Hence, it can be argued that the medical treatment analogy is somewhat different since in the offender's case *both* the status quo and the neurointervention offered derive from decisions by others (i.e., the judicial authorities), others who could offer different alternatives that the offender might more willingly accept.[10] To safeguard voluntary consent and secure the ethical permissibility of offering neurointerventions to offenders, specific minimal conditions will need to be met over and above the necessity of obtaining free and informed consent.

Discussing the moral acceptability of "internal punishment" (i.e., an offered nonfatal, physically invasive neurointervention), Rosati (1994) argues that "it is rational to opt for a sentence that maximally preserves one's freedom and autonomy" (p. 145).[11] Moreover, Rosati observes that circumstances can force individuals to make difficult choices but that those circumstances do not necessarily

[9] Every patient's medical decision happens within a specific context comprising external and/or internal factors that influence that person's decision-making: "Coercion must not be considered a particular quality that is present in some therapeutic situations and absent in others. It is a matter of degree, and it can be found in most, if not all, treatment situations (Group for the Advancement of Psychiatry, 1994). Therapists use prestige and power in their interaction with clients, and this can be seen as coercion. The source of coercion may be external, as is commonly the case in the treatment of sexual abusers. It may also be internal, with the person seeking treatment because of the disastrous consequences of his untreated paraphilia" (Cosyns, 1999, p. 405).

[10] We would like to thank an anonymous reviewer for this valuable remark.

[11] Rosati (1994) gives the examples of surgical castration as a condition of probation for sexual crimes and long-term, reversible contraconception as a condition of probation for child abuse. These examples are not intended as a defense of these interventions. Rosati argues that offering permanent, irreversible interventions is not morally acceptable.

make the choice irrational or involuntary (Bomann-Larsen, 2013). Key to this, at least in part, is the status quo—what the individual will experience if the choice for treatment is not made. Foddy and Savulescu (2006) argue that where the status quo is left as one of the two options, then making the offer, in itself, does not harm the individual; it does not put the offender under irresistible pressure to agree, and it does not necessarily call the validity of one's consent into question. Although their analysis may be convincing in case of medical decision-making, the situation is different within the judicial system as the government has the option of providing different ways to respond to crime (e.g., retributive punishment in comparison to a human ecological approach as implemented in Bastoy prison in Norway or nonretributive mental health courts).

What might call the validity of one's consent into question within correctional contexts, in our view, are the conditions under which the offer is made—whether the status quo is itself ethically permissible or is itself "unfair, unjust, harmful or in some other way wrong" (Foddy & Savulescu, 2006, p. 7). We have in mind those situations where the status quo is oppressive to the extent that the offender or forensic patient cannot but submit to the proposed neurointervention. For example, if a prisoner is incarcerated in conditions that are physically and mentally abusing, any kind of offer will be accepted as a means to escape that situation. Although it can be rational to opt for extremely invasive interventions that might be (or appear to be) less worse than the status quo, it remains ethically problematic to offer such interventions because one is coerced to accept interventions that one might otherwise despise. Hence, if the status quo is morally unacceptable, offering a "lesser evil" coerces that individual to opt for the neurointervention.

It follows that an offer that is irresistible—presumably one that no rational person would decline relative to the status quo—could indeed call the validity of the consent into question due to the coercive nature of the decision-making context. It is questionable whether one's consent can be free and informed under such conditions. It follows that offering neurointerventions with potentially moderate to severe side effects is acceptable provided that the prison conditions that an offender faces if he declines are not cruel, inhuman, degrading, or otherwise wrong.[12]

---

[12] The increase in autonomy that likely results from opting for an alternative that is not cruel, inhuman, or degrading does render the offer morally acceptable even if free and informed consent cannot be fully guaranteed. Under those circumstances, it would be immoral to deny those offenders the option of having a better future solely because the status quo is unacceptable. It follows that it is morally acceptable to offer benign neurointerventions without moderate to severe side effects (e.g., vitamin and food supplements, neurofeedback) even if the status quo involves cruel, inhuman, or degrading prison circumstances. Inevitably some neurointerventions will occupy a gray zone.

Foddy and Savulescu (2006) flag the potential for an individual's vulnerability being exploited unfairly,[13] which leads, in our view, to the requirement that the treatment offered must not be unfair, unjust, harmful, or otherwise wrong. This aligns with Rosati's (1994) argument that the treatment offered must not be cruel or inhuman and must promote the offender's overall well-being.

These requirements laid down by Rosati (1994; in the context of criminal justice) and by Foddy and Savulescu (2006; in the context of research ethics) are of crucial importance to neurointerventions for immoral or deviant behavior. It can be argued that offering an intervention in the context of criminal justice that can be effective and would (arguably/presumably) promote the overall well-being of the offender may nevertheless be cruel or inhuman due to the nature of the possible side effects. For example, deep brain stimulation, which could be used to treat aggression or potentially even antisocial personality disorder (De Ridder et al., 2009; Gilbert, Vranic, & Hurst, 2013), involves some risk of serious (e.g., surgery-related) side effects.

We propose that the morally suspect aspects of the offer itself can be acceptably addressed, if it is the case that a rational individual would consider the offer to be increasing his or her well-being. Thus, for the neurointervention to be an acceptable option, it must be medically, psychiatrically, and/or psychologically indicated and offer a good benefit-to-risk ratio in and of itself. Thus, it should constitute standard medical treatment outside of correctional settings. In general, the offender must wish to be free of his or her compulsion toward socially deviant behavior which is inherently undesirable (rather than simply contrary to contemporary mores). Although for many offenders there can be such a wish to be free of their compulsions in and of itself, it will be the case that for some offenders the ability to avoid imprisonment will be an additional motivating factor. However, if the imprisonment is not in itself of such a nature that it makes the alternative option (neurointervention) irresistible, then it can be rational to opt for a situation in which one maximally preserves one's freedom and autonomy (Rosati, 1994). Out of respect for the well-being of the offender and forensic patient, one should always start with the least invasive neurointervention that can be expected to be effective. Moreover, the neurointervention may never be disproportional to the offense in a way that the severity of the neurointervention

---

[13] "Imagine we offer a starving man the choice of doing nothing (and dying of starvation) or some food but only if he also takes part in sloppily designed clinical trial in which there is a 1% chance of death. Assume that no reasonable person in a reasonable situation would choose to take part in this trial. Though this offer makes the starving man better off, it arguably also exploits his vulnerable situation in an unfair way. His starvation forces him to accept a compensation for the experiment's risk which is unfairly small. The problem in these situations is that the participant is *insufficiently* compensated, and not that the participant is somehow choosing (in his situation) irrationally or unfreely. He gets something but he should get *more*." (Foddy & Savulescu, 2006, p. 8, emphasis in original).

outweighs the severity of the crime (e.g., androgen deprivation treatment or physical castration for exhibitionism, as happened in the Czech Republic).[14]

If the previously mentioned conditions are not respected, then aberrant, morally unacceptable practices such as ablative surgery for heroin addiction in China (Ge et al., 2013) or physical castration for exhibitionism in the Czech Republic (European Committee for the Prevention of Torture, 2009) are a real threat. Last but certainly not least, to maximally prevent the illicit use of neurointerventions as a means of social behavior control (Persson & Savulescu, 2008; Savulescu & Persson, 2012) rather than as a means to benefit both society and the offender, it is necessary that the neurointervention targets one or more risk factors for behavior that can justifiably be defined as criminal behavior and that it does not target psychological or other traits that are not conducive to criminal behavior. For example, treatment to counteract aggression or sexual disorders such as pedophilia are distinct from treatments to counteract homosexuality or religious heterodoxy. In general, this demand entails that any intervention that is offered to offenders strictly addresses risk factors for criminal behavior and does not aim to change the personality of the offender as such. It rules out so-called moral enhancement practices that directly or indirectly aim to conform individuals to existing societal or cultural norms.[15]

The judicial setting of the point at issue in this chapter, in combination with the demand that the neurointervention respects the well-being of the offender, urges us to be extremely cautious when offering such interventions to offenders with impaired mental facilities, including moral decision-making capacities. The ethical worries are particularly pressing where moderate-to-severe side effects are foreseeable—and especially so when the effects of the intervention are irreversible. Even though, under the right conditions, a choice between incarceration and neurointervention can be made rationally and autonomously, we consider that the increased risk of coercion invalidating consent in this context should speak against any offer being made of risky or irreversible neurointerventions.[16] In the case of incompetent and/or severely mentally impaired offenders, authorization should be sought from a court-appointed guardian and the offender

---

[14] Note that, following the international human rights law prohibition on inhuman or degrading treatment or punishment, the concept of proportionality is in many countries accepted as a key principle in sentencing. It entails that a punishment will be unjust if its duration or type does not fit the crime and the specific circumstances of the offender (van Zyl Smit, 1995).

[15] We would like to thank Nicole Vincent for highlighting the ethical unacceptability of coerced societal or cultural *normalization*.

[16] We are aware that in case of fully mentally competent offenders there may be a gray area as to what constitutes cruel and inhuman treatment, and for some ethicists, irreversibility may be acceptable under certain, exceptional circumstances. An in-depth discussion of this issue exceeds the aims of this chapter.

should as far as possible take part in the authorization procedure and should not object.

Provided certain minimal ethical conditions are met (which will need to be determined on a case-by-case basis), it can be ethical to offer neurointerventions to offenders as a condition of probation, parole or sentence reduction. These conditions can be summarized as follows: (a) the status quo is in no way cruel, inhuman, degrading, or in some other way *wrong*; (b) the offered neurointervention is in no way cruel, inhuman, degrading, or in some other way *wrong*; (c) the neurointervention respects the well-being of the offender; (d) the neurointervention targets one or more risk factors for recidivism; and (e) the neurointervention is voluntary: the offender is formally required to give his or her free and informed consent upon acceptance and, if appropriate, a court-appointed guardian his or her authorization. If the offender, after having given his or her free and informed consent, subsequently fails to comply with the treatment or chooses to withdraw from treatment, then (the remainder of) the prison sentence will need to be served. In sum, if the offer of a given type of neurointervention satisfies these conditions, then an offender can be given the choice between the intervention and (further) incarceration.

However, even if these conditions are met, an additional ethical issue needs to be considered. It is doubtful that sentencing that is restricted to alternative sanctions involving effective neurointerventions will provide sufficient closure and healing for the victims of the crime. For that reason, it is of the utmost importance that the criminal justice system pays considerable attention to the needs and concerns of the victims, as well as to the legitimate concerns of other relevant actors in society. To assure that the rights of victims are upheld, it is necessary that alternative sanctions are prescribed by law and include appropriate reparation toward victims and other relevant actors in society (Focquaert & Raine, 2012).

In the next section, we discuss why voluntary neurointerventions (Condition 5) are ethically and practically preferable to forced interventions during incarceration or as postprison requirements, with the potential exception of noninvasive interventions without side effects (e.g., vitamin and food supplements).

Forcing Neurointerventions within Criminal Justice Settings

What about forcing neurointerventions as part of an offender's sentence, either during incarceration or as a postprison requirement? The rationale behind this would, of course, be to prevent criminal behavior within prison and to decrease the recidivism risk after the offender is released from prison. Governments and the criminal justice system indeed have a duty to protect their citizens, but at what price and to what extent? Does this duty allow the state and the criminal justice system to disregard individual autonomy? In Western judicial systems, it is generally considered *fair* to deprive individuals from their right to free movement (temporarily or even lifelong) if they are convicted of a (serious) crime. However, it is generally considered unfair to invade an individual's bodily privacy, even if an individual has made him or herself "liable" to incarceration by committing a crime. Overall, the offender's right to refuse mental health treatment (e.g., electroconvulsive therapy) outweighs the state's interests regarding crime prevention and public safety. Disrespecting individual autonomy in medical decision-making violates an individual's basic human rights, whether these individuals are offenders or law-abiding citizens.

Some ethicists suggest that forced (bio)medical interventions and deprivation of the right to free movement are comparable responses to crime, thereby holding that liability to incarceration implies liability to (some forms of) forced (bio)medical intervention (e.g., Carter, 2017; Douglas, 2014a, 2014b; Peterson, 2018; Petersen & Kragh, 2017). Douglas (2014b) understands liability to incarceration as liability to the hypothetical scenario of "minimal incarceration":

> Suppose that offenders could be held in institutions that placed serious and constant constraints on free movement and association, but otherwise exposed offenders to no greater risks to their health and security than average members of the unincarcerated society, and took all reasonable steps to safeguard opportunities for political participation, legal representation and education. (p. 105)

According to Douglas (2014a), if we regard locking individuals up in prison for a long period of time as justifiable, then by the same rationale, requiring these individuals to undergo safe and effective neurointerventions should also be considered acceptable.

> I have been developing the argument that if locking offenders in prison for a long period of time is justified, then it's difficult to see why requiring prisoners to undergo some type of safe and effective neurointervention couldn't also be acceptable. In many cases neurointervention may be less intrusive and harmful, and potentially more effective in preventing reoffending, which is normally at least one of the purported purposes of incarceration. (Douglas, 2014a)

However, there are several reasons why this and similar views may be problematic. First, forcing neurointerventions violate an individual's right to bodily integrity and the forced nature of the intervention in and of itself can be experienced as invasive, degrading, and humiliating. In reply, Douglas argues that the violation in the case of mandatory drugs is hardly greater and most likely less than in the case of (minimal) incarceration. While this may be the case for certain drugs (e.g., selective serotonin reuptake inhibitors, drugs for addiction) as compared to some incarceration practices, it most definitely is not the case for all types of neurointervention. Forced neurointerventions (e.g., antipsychotics, androgen deprivation therapy, transcranial magnetic stimulation, electroconvulsive therapy, deep brain stimulation) can easily result in greater bodily intrusions compared to prison time, even under the comparative demand of "minimal incarceration." While deprivation of the right to free movement may be experienced as more intrusive by some individuals compared to certain *forced* biomedical interventions, the invasiveness of either measure will, at least in part, depend on the circumstances and the needs and preferences of the individual in question. It will be nearly impossible to outline general rules of practice based on the level of intrusiveness.

Second, Bublitz and Merkel (2014) have convincingly argued that all individuals, including offenders, have a right to mental integrity. Such a right is violated if offenders are forced to undergo neurointerventions that impact their cognitive, affective, and motivational capacities. A recent study by Petersen and Kragh (2017) argued that an offender's "freedom of thought" is potentially equally violated by forced biomedical interventions as by forced incarceration practices. Although current incarceration practices are often problematic, I disagree that incarceration violates an offender's "freedom of thought" in the same way forced neurointerventions can violate it (e.g., chemical castration). Freedom of thought refers (in part) to our ability to rationally reflect on the many influences that impact us, and our ability to endorse, reject, or object to these influences. Biomedical interventions may overrule our capacity to reflect upon the changes it brings about and can remove our ability to gradually endorse, reject, or object to the alterations of our self. It can silence those who receive these interventions (e.g., electroconvulsive therapy or deep brain stimulation) if proper free and informed consent is lost and especially if these interventions are mandated by the criminal justice system (Focquaert & Schermer, 2015).

Third, any nondesert-based account of criminal justice, in addition to arguing against most existing incarceration practices around the world, which may include being exposed to rape, violence, solitary confinement, supermax prisons, lack of adequate health treatment, etc., will have difficulties defending a liability to (minimal) incarceration as the default answer to crime. Douglas (2014b) mentions that incarceration may be hard to justify given prevailing prison conditions, but nevertheless contends that a liability to what he calls "minimal incarceration" would be widely accepted. According to Ryberg and Petersen (2017), there is a prima facie tension

> between contending, on the one hand, that it is unacceptable to violate the autonomy of the criminal [i.e., in the context of forced medical interventions]

while holding, on the other, that it is acceptable (or morally required) to place the criminal behind bars for five or ten years—or perhaps even for life—against his or her will. (pp. 375–376).

We agree that there is such a tension for those experts who argue that incarceration is morally legitimate or *deserved*. However, free will skeptics see incarceration as a necessary harm that is ultimately unjust and reject *mass* incarceration practices as an ethically defensible solution to crime. For example, according to Pereboom (2014), an intuitively legitimate theory of crime prevention can be drawn based upon an analogy between the treatment of carriers of communicable diseases and the treatment of criminals. According to such a theory, similar to society's right to isolate carriers of dangerous, communicable disease (e.g., Ebola), society has the right to isolate the criminally dangerous. However, it does not have the right to treat criminals more harshly than is needed for society to be protected from the dangers posed by these individuals. Such a theory would also demand a degree of concern for the rehabilitation and well-being of the offender that is absent in most criminal justice settings today; it would not allow for incarceration unless necessary, and it would not allow morally questionable practices such as the death penalty or excessively harsh environments such as supermax prisons.

Fourth, Ryberg and Petersen (2017) argue that the goal of applied ethics is to provide answers to challenges that arise in existing practices, such as the current criminal justice system, and in those cases "it will not always do to consider how agents ought to act under ideal circumstances" (p. 379). Indeed, we need to be able to answer how we will address existing challenges and prevent moral wrongs from happening in nonideal, real world circumstances. "Minimal incarceration" as envisioned by Douglas (2014b) is not a real-world possibility. It is definitely not what prisons are like today and unlikely how prisons will be in the near or even distant future, however worrisome that fact is. In the real world, liability to incarceration implies being locked up in prisons that do not satisfy the ethical demand of "minimal incarceration." We need to provide answers to those real-world scenarios. Moreover, even if forced neurointerventions are less intrusive compared to real-world incarceration, which remains to be determined on a case-by-case basis, that does not make them ethically defensible in themselves. It merely implies that the moral wrong that they convey is a lesser wrong. Arguing that a liability to minimal incarceration is comparable to a liability to neurointerventions under ideal circumstances may fail to address the worrisome and potentially devastating real-world side effects that biomedical interventions may bestow upon individuals.

Under real-word circumstances, it is problematic to see incarceration as the *default* answer to crime, and it is also problematic to *force* neurointerventions upon offenders as both approaches may and often do infringe upon the ethical values of autonomy, dignity, bodily integrity, and mental liberty (Canton, 2017). Our argumentation does not imply that incarceration is better as incarceration may be criminogenic rather than rehabilitative for many individuals. All four worries that we have voiced provide reasons to question either forced incarceration or forced neurointerventions as the default. If an adequate level of safety can be guaranteed, our analysis argues in favor of *offering* various options to offenders as this maximally respects offenders' autonomy, bodily integrity, and mental integrity increases the motivation for and effectiveness of the sanction in question and has the potential to reduce the criminogenic effects of imprisonment (Focquaert & Raine, 2012).

Some arguments could nevertheless be given in favor of noninvasive, benign neurointerventions without side effects as part of an offender's sentence. First, the level of intrusion that is posed by certain forms of noninvasive neurointerventions (e.g., neurofeedback using computer games or vitamin and omega 3 supplements) may be so small or even nonexistent that one could argue that the benefits in terms of violence reduction outweigh the costs as no harm or only minimal harm toward the offender is involved. Second, we generally do not regard an individual's right to refuse medically indicated treatment as absolute. Specific circumstances exist in which forced medical treatment is considered ethical. For instance, it is considered ethical to initially treat burn victims against their will instead of withholding treatment (which would result in death due to medical complications), because most of these patients voluntarily want to continue treatment after the initial shock of their situation has disappeared (Caplan, 2006). Forced treatment of individuals who are experiencing psychotic episodes and pose a direct harm to themselves or others constitutes another example. Moreover, parental refusal of life-saving treatment for their children is not respected (e.g., Jehovah's Witnesses refusing blood transfusions for their children in life-threatening situations or pediatric oncology patients who are not given evidence-based treatment), and the state may mandate such treatment. Some countries quasi-mandate certain vaccinations (e.g., in Belgium, Italy, and Poland, parents can be fined if they do not comply with the child vaccination program, and in France, Spain, and the United States children cannot enroll for school unless they have received certain vaccinations) because the risk to public health is enormous and because vaccinations are only effective if almost everyone is vaccinated. Refusing vaccination is often considered unethical by experts because individuals who are refusing vaccination are free-riding upon the moral sense of duty of individuals who accept vaccination (Nuffield Council on Bioethics, 2007). These situations are, of course, substantially different, but they nevertheless show that we do not consider an individual's right to refuse medical treatment as absolute under all circumstances, at least not from an ethical perspective.

Even if it could be considered ethically permissible to force benign neurointerventions without side effects, one important issue remains. Forced treatment is often not effective or not as effective as voluntary treatment simply due to its forced nature which undermines trust, cooperation and a sense of justice. For example, it is likely to be particularly ineffective in psychopaths who are known to refuse treatment unless enrolling in treatment directly benefits them (e.g., as a requirement of probation or parole), who are typically unwilling to cooperate within treatment settings and who tend to drop out at a higher rate compared to offenders without psychopathy (Hare, 2006; Skeem et al., 2002). For most mental health treatments treatment compliance will be essential to effectively reduce recidivism.

Conclusion

It can be ethical to *offer* neurointerventions to offenders as a condition of probation, parole, or sentence reduction provided certain minimal ethical conditions are met. The following conditions need to be investigated on a case-by-case basis: (a) the status quo is in no way cruel, inhuman, degrading, or in some other way *wrong*; (b) the intervention is in no way cruel, degrading, or in any some other way *wrong*; (c) the intervention respects the well-being of the offender; (d) the neurointervention targets one or more risk factors for recidivism; and (e) the neurointervention is voluntary: the offender is formally required to give his or her free and informed consent upon acceptance, and, if appropriate, a court-appointed guardian his or her authorization. If the offender agrees but subsequently fails to comply with the neurointervention or chooses to withdraw, (the remainder of) the prison sentence needs to be served. *Forcing* invasive and/or risky neurointerventions as part of an offender's sentence is both ethically and practically problematic. Although forcing benign neurointerventions as part of an offender's sentence may be considered ethical by some experts, we argue that their implementation remains questionable from a practical point of view, with the possible exception of neurointerventions without side effects such as vitamin and omega 3 supplements. It is likely that many (if not most) neurointerventions will require the offender's willingness to undergo the intervention to achieve successful treatment outcomes and effectively reduce recidivism.

Acknowledgments

We would like to thank the researchers at the Department of Bioethics (National Institutes of Health) for their insightful comments on an earlier version of this paper.

References

Arani, F. D., Rostami, R., & Nostratabadi, M. (2010). Effectiveness of neurofeedback training as a treatment for opioid-dependent patients. *Clinical EEG and Neuroscience, 41*(3), 170–177.

Bales, W. D., & Piquero, A. R. (2012). Assessing the impact of imprisonment on recidivism. *Journal of Experimental Criminology, 8,* 71–101.

Balia, C., Carucci, S., Coghill, D., & Zuddas, A. (2018). The pharmacological treatment of aggression in children and adolescents with conduct disorder: Do callous-unemotional traits modulate the efficacy of medication? *Neuroscience and Biobehavioral Reviews, 91,* 213–238. doi:10.1016/j.neubiorev.2017.01.024

Beckham, L. (1998). Chemical castration: Constitutional issues of due process, equal protection, and unusual punishment. *West Virginia Law Review, 100,* 853–894.

Bomann-Larsen, L. (2013). Voluntary rehabilitation? On neurotechnological behavioural treatment, valid consent and (in)appropriate offers. *Neuroethics, 6,* 65–77.

Bublitz, J. C., & Merkel, R. (2014). Crimes against minds: On mental manipulations, harms, and a human right to mental self-determination. *Criminal Law and Philosophy, 8,* 51–77.

Buchanan, A. (2011). *Beyond humanity?* Oxford, England: Oxford University Press.

Canton, R. (2017). *Why punish? An introduction to the philosophy of punishment.* New York, NY: Palgrave.

Caplan, A. L. (2006). Ethical issues surrounding forced, mandated, or coerced treatment. *Journal of Substance Abuse Treatment, 31,* 117–120.

Carter, S. (2017). Could moral enhancement interventions be medically indicated. *Health Care Analysis, 25*(4), 338–353.

Cochran, J. C., Mears D. P., & Bales, W. D. (2014). Assessing the effectiveness of correctional sanctions. *Journal of Quantitative Criminology, 30,* 317–347.

Conti, C. L., & Nakamura-Palacios, E. M. (2014). Bilateral transcranial direct current stimulation over dorsolateral prefrontal cortex changes the drug-cued reactivity in the anterior cingulate cortex of crack-cocaine addicts. *Brain Stimulation, 7,* 130–132.

Cosyns, P. (1999). Treatment of sexual abusers in Belgium. *Journal of Interpersonal Violence, 14,* 396–410.

De Deyn, P. P., & Buitelaar, J. (2006). Risperidone in the management of agitation and aggression associated with psychiatric disorders. *European Psychiatry, 21,* 21–28.

De Ridder, D., Langguth, B., Plazier, M., & Menovsky, T. (2009). Moral dysfunction: Theoretical model and potential neurosurgical treatments. In J. Verplaetse, J. de Schrijver, S. Vanneste, & J. Braeckman (Eds.), *The moral brain: Essays on the evolutionary and neuroscientific aspects of morality* (pp. 155–183). Dordrecht, The Netherlands: Springer.

Douglas, T. (2014a). Blurred lines: Neurointerventions in crime prevention. *The University of Otago Magazine.* http://www.otago.ac.nz/bioethics/news/otago082730.html

Douglas, T. (2014b). Criminal rehabilitation through medical intervention: Moral liability and the right to bodily integrity. *The Journal of Ethics, 18,* 101–122.

Douglas, T., Bonte, P., Focquaert F., Devolder, K., & Sterckx, S. (2013). Coercion, incarceration, and chemical castration: An argument from autonomy. *Journal of Bioethical Inquiry, 10,* 393–405.

Druhm, K. W. (1997). A welcome return to draconia: California penal law 645, the castration of sex offenders and the constitution. *Albany Law Review, 61,* 285–343.

Dutch Code of Criminal Procedure. (1921, January 15). Retrieved from http://www. wetboek-online.nl/wet/Wetboek%20van%20Strafvordering.html

Dutch Criminal Code (1881, March 3). Retrieved from http://www.wetboek-online.nl/ wet/Wetboek%20van%20Strafrecht.html

European Committee for the Prevention of Torture and Inhuman or Degrading Treatment or Punishment. (2009). *Report to the Czech Government on the visit to the Czech Republic carried out by the European Committee for the Prevention of Torture and Inhuman or Degrading Treatment or Punishment (CPT).* Strasbourg: The Council of Europe. http://www.cpt.coe.int/documents/cze/2009-08-inf-eng.pdf

Florida Legislature. (2019). Florida Statutes Annotated, Title XLVI, Chapter 794, 794.0235—Administration of medroxyprogesterone acetate (MPA) to persons convicted of sexual battery. Retrieved from http://www.leg.state.fl.us/statutes/index. cfm?App_mode=Display_Statute&Search_String=&URL=0700-0799/0794/Sections/ 0794.0235.html

Focquaert, F. (2014). Mandatory neurotechnological treatment: Ethical issues. *Theoretical Medicine and Bioethics, 35,* 59–72.

Focquaert, F., Glenn, A., & Raine, A. (2015). Psychopathy and free will. In W. Glannon (Ed.), *Free will and the brain: Neuroscientific, philosophical and legal perspectives* (pp. 103–120). Cambridge, England: Cambridge University Press.

Focquaert, F., & Raine, A. (2011). Antisocial personality disorders. In W. Chambliss (Ed.), *Key issues in crime and punishment* (pp. 13–28). Thousand Oaks, CA: SAGE.

Focquaert, F., & Raine, A. (2012). Ethics of community-based sanctions. In S. M. Barton-Bellessa (Ed.), *Encyclopedia of community corrections* (pp. 144–148). Thousand Oaks, CA: SAGE.

Focquaert, F., & Schermer, M. (2015). Moral enhancement: Do means matter morally? *Neuroethics, 8,* 139–159.

Foddy, B., & Savulescu, J. (2006). Addiction and autonomy: Can addicted people consent to the prescription of their drug of addiction? *Bioethics, 20,* 1–15.

Ge, S., Chang, C., Adler, J. R., Zhao, H., Chang, X., Gao, L., . . . Gao, G. (2013). Long-term changes in the personality and psychopathological profile of opiate addicts after nucleus accumbens ablative surgery are associated with treatment outcome. *Stereotactic and Functional Neurosurgery, 91,* 30–44.

Gevensleben, H., Holl, B., Albrecht, B., Schlamp, D., Kratz, O., Studer, P., . . . Heinrich, H. (2009). Distinct EEG effects related to neurofeedback training in children with ADHD: A randomized controlled trial. *International Journal of Psychophysiology, 74*(2), 149–157.

Gilbert, F., Vranic, A., & Hurst, S. (2013). Involuntary and voluntary invasive brain surgery: Ethical issues related to acquired aggressiveness. *Neuroethics, 6,* 115–128.

Gimino, P. J. III. (1997). Mandatory chemical castration for perpetrators of sex offenses against children: Following California's lead. *Pepperdine Law Review, 15,* 67–105.

Greely, H. T. (2007). Neuroscience and criminal justice: Not responsibility but treatment. *The University of Kansas Law Review, 56,* 1103.

Group for the Advancement of Psychiatry. (1994). *Forced into treatment* (Report No. 137). Washington, DC: American Psychiatric Press.

Hall, W., & Carter, A. (2013). How may neuroscience affect the way that the criminal courts deal with addicted offenders? In N. Vincent (Ed.), *Neuroscience and legal responsibility* (pp. 278–301). Oxford, England: Oxford University Press.

Hare, R. D. (2006). Psychopathy: A clinical and forensic overview. *Psychiatric Clinics of North America, 29*, 709–724.

Jansen, J. M., Daams, J. G., Koeter, M. W. J., Veltman, D. J., van den Brink, W., & Goudriaan, A. E. (2013). Effects of non-invasive neurostimulation on craving: A meta-analysis. *Neuroscience and Biobehavioral Reviews, 37*, 2472–2480.

Kleinig, J. (2008). *Ethics and criminal justice.* Cambridge, England: Cambridge University Press.

MacKenzie, D. L. (2006). *What works in corrections: Reducing the criminal activities of offenders and delinquents.* Cambridge, England: Cambridge University Press.

Mears, D. P. (2010). *American criminal justice policy.* Cambridge, England: Cambridge University Press.

Morse, S. J. (2008). Psychopathy and criminal responsibility. *Neuroethics, 1*, 205–212.

Moser, D. J., Arndt, S., Kanz, J. E., Benjamin, M. L., Bayless, J. D., Reese, R. L., . . . Flaum, M. A. (2004). Coercion and informed consent in research involving prisoners. *Comprehensive Psychiatry, 45*, 1–9.

Murrie, D. C., Boccaccini, M. T., Caperton, J., & Rufino, K. (2012). Field validity of the Psychopathy Checklist–Revised in sex offender risk assessment. *Psychological Assessment, 24*, 524–529.

Nagin, D. S., Cullen, F. T., & Jonson, C. L. (2009). Imprisonment and reoffending. *Criminal Justice, 38*, 115–200.

Nuffield Council on Bioethics. (2007). Infectious diseases. In *Public health: Ethical issues.* London, England: Author. https://nuffieldbioethics.org/publications/public-health/guide-to-the-report/infectious-disease

Pappadopulos, E., Woolston, S., Chait, A., Perkins, M., Connor, D. F., & Jensen, P. S. (2006). Pharmacotherapy of aggression in children and adolescents: Efficacy and effect size. *Journal of the Canadian Academy of Child and Adolescent Psychiatry, 15*(1), 27–39.

Pereboom, D. (2014). *Free will, agency, and meaning in life.* Oxford, England: Oxford University Press.

Persson, I., & Savulescu., J. 2008. The perils of cognitive enhancement and the urgent imperative to enhance the moral character of humanity. *Journal of Applied Philosophy, 25*(3), 162–177.

Petersen, T. S. (2018). Should neurotechnological treatments offered to offenders always be in their best interests? *Journal of Medical Ethics, 44*, 32–36.

Petersen, T. S., & Kragh, K. (2017). Should violent offenders be forced to undergo neurotechnological treatment? A critical discussion of the 'freedom of thought' objection. *Journal of Medical Ethics, 43*(1), 30–34.

Poythress, N. G., Petrila, J., McGaha, A., & Boothroyd, R. (2002). Perceived coercion and procedural justice in the Broward mental health court. *International Journal of Law and Psychiatry, 25*, 517–533.

Redlich, A. D., Hoover, S., Summers, A., & Steadman, H. J. (2010). Enrollment in mental health courts: Voluntariness, knowingness, and adjudicative competence. *Law and Human Behavior, 34*, 91–104.

Rigg, J. (2002). Measures of perceived coercion in prison treatment settings. *International Journal of Law and Psychiatry, 25*, 473–490.

Rogers, R., & Jackson, R. L. (2005). Sexually violent predators: The risky enterprise of risk assessment. *Journal of the American Academy of Psychiatry and Law, 33*, 523–528.

Rosati, C. S. (1994). A study of internal punishment. *Wisconsin Law Review, 123*, 123–170.

Ryberg, J., & Petersen, T. S. (2017). Neuroethics and criminal justice. In K. Lippert-Rasmussen, K. Brownlee, & D. Coady (Eds.), *A companion to applied philosophy* (pp. 370–382). Oxford, England: Wiley.

Savulescu, J., & Persson, I. (2012). Moral enhancement, freedom and the God Machine. *Monist, 95*(3), 399–421.

Scott, C. L., & Holmberg, T. (2003). Castration of sex offenders: Prisoners' rights versus public safety. *Journal of the American Academy of Psychiatry and the Law, 31*, 502–509.

Simpson, D. D., Joe, J. W., & Rowan-Szal, G. A. (1997). Drug abuse treatment retention and process effects on follow-up outcomes. *Drug and Alcohol Dependence, 47*, 227–235.

Skeem, J. L., Monahan, J., & Mulvey, E. P. (2002). Psychopathy, treatment involvement and subsequent violence among civil psychiatric patients. *Law and Human Behavior, 26*, 577–603.

Sokhadze, T. M., Cannon, R. L., & Trudeau, D. L. (2008). EEG biofeedback as a treatment for substance use disorders: Review, rating of efficacy, and recommendations for further research. *Applied Psychophysiology and Biofeedback, 33*, 1–28.

Stevens, A., Berto, D., Heckmann, W., Kerschl, V., Oeuvray, K., Van Ooyen, M., . . . Uchtenhagen, A. (2005). Quasi-compulsory treatment of drug dependent offenders: An international literature review. *Substance Use & Misuse, 40*, 269–283.

Thibaut, F., De La Barra, F., Gordon, H., Cosyns, P., Bradford, J. M. W., & WFSBP Task Force on Sexual Disorders. (2010). The World Federation of Societies of Biological Psychiatry (WFSBP) guidelines for the biological treatment of paraphilias. *World Journal of Biological Psychiatry, 11*, 604–655.

Tullio, E. M. (2009). Chemical castration for child predators: Practical, effective, and constitutional. *Chapman Law Review, 13*, 191–219.

Vanderzyl, K. A. (1994). Castration as an alternative to incarceration: An impotent approach to the punishment of sex offenders. *Northern Illinois University Law Review, 15*, 107–140.

Vandevelde, S., Soyez, V., Vander Beken, T., De Smet, S., Boers, A., & Broekaert, E. 2011. Mentally ill offenders in prison: The Belgian case. *International Journal of Law and Psychiatry, 34*, 71–78.

van Zyl Smit, D. (1995). Constitutional jurisprudence and proportionality in sentencing. *European Journal of Crime, Criminal Law and Criminal Justice, 3*, 369–380.

White, M. D., Saunders, J., Fisher, C., & Mellow, J. (2012). Exploring inmate reentry in a local jail setting: Implications for outreach, service use, and recidivism. *Crime Delinquency, 58*, 124–146.

7

Diversion Courts, Traumatic Brain Injury, and American Vets

Valerie Gray Hardcastle

Introduction

The U.S. Center for Disease Control (CDC; 2013a) reports that there are almost two million traumatic brain injuries (TBIs) per year in the United States, ranging from mild concussions to the most severe form of trauma. TBIs occur at a rate of roughly four every minute in the United States. In addition, the Department of Defense (2014) Special Report on Traumatic Brain Injury claims: "Traumatic brain injury is one of the invisible wounds of war, and one of the signature injuries of troops wounded in Afghanistan and Iraq."

TBI is also highly correlated with criminal behavior. The CDC (2013b) estimates that over a third of prison inmates experienced TBI in the past year—a much, much higher rate than in the general population. But how the medical and scientific communities understand the origins of behavior clashes with how our justice system does. U.S. law assumes that all adults are rational beings who act for specific reasons and that, in each instance, an individual could have done otherwise had he or she chosen to. In contrast, medicine, psychiatry, neuropsychology, and neurology all hold that diseases, injuries, and deformities in the brain influence and even determine a person's thoughts, desires, impulses, and ability to control one's behavior. From the perspective of brain science, our legal system's underlying theory of human behavior is not only lacking, but is grossly at odds with our best data.

Historically, the legal system has recognized that when in the throes of severe mental illness, we may not be rational or in control of our impulses. The American court system is beginning to differentiate returning combat vets with TBI or with other mind/brain disorders from other offenders. As I describe in this chapter, several districts have created special diversion courts for veterans accused of a variety of crimes.

Several questions arise from this practice. Should vets be treated differently than other noncombatant defendants with similar brain injuries? Should mental or brain disorders affect how we assign or understand legal responsibility? How

Valerie Gray Hardcastle, *Diversion Courts, Traumatic Brain Injury, and American Vets* In: *Neurointerventions and the Law*. Edited by: Nicole A Vincent, Thomas Nadelhoffer, and Allan McCay, Oxford University Press (2020).
© Oxford University Press 2020
DOI: 10.1093/oso/9780190651145.001.0007

do we square diversion courts with the standards for not guilty by reason of insanity? I shall argue that we are starting to experience a sea change in how our legal system understands and assigns blame, how we connect data regarding neural interventions with punishment and remediation, and how we distinguish "mad" from "bad."

This chapter examines the impact of including neuroscience data in the legal system where defendants might have had a TBI, both for civilians and for our new and growing population of TBI victims, returning combat veterans. We are starting to see trends that suggest significant revisions in how courts view punishment and culpability, due largely, I believe, to a greater neurobiological understanding of brain disorders that affect cognition and behavior, like TBI.

Incidence of Traumatic Brain Injuries

Public attention has been focused intently on TBI over the past several years, due largely to a heightened media focus on the long-term health outcomes among professional football players and other athletes (Sahler & Greenwald, 2012). New specialty clinics and rehabilitation facilities have sprung up for both the general public and the military to aid in the remediation of patients affected by TBI. The Department of Defense has invested millions of dollars in new treatment centers for TBI in the combat theaters and throughout the United States. In addition to that, the Army's medical research division has invested $700 million in basic TBI research (Office of the Surgeon General, 2013). They and others have been carefully tracking outcomes for TBI patients (e.g., Department of Defense, 2014; Dijkers, Harrison-Felix, & Marwitz, 2011; Lamberty, Nelson, & Yamada, 2013), and our understanding of the long-term implications of TBI has substantially improved (Silver, McAllister, & Yudofsky, 2011).

We know that TBI is the leading cause of death in children and adolescents, and the second leading cause of injury and death in adults (after general trauma; CDC, 2010, Decuypere & Klimo, 2012). A review of TBI studies in Europe suggests that there are about 235 TBI incidents per 100,000 people, with the average death rate of about 15 per 100,000 (Tagliaferri, Compagnone, Korsic, Servadei, & Kraus, 2006). Over five million Americans and almost eight million Europeans live with some disability or functional deficit caused by TBI, ranging from severe impairment of consciousness to more subtle cognitive effects, such as attentional difficulties, impulsivity, impaired decision-making, decreased cognitive endurance, challenges with multitasking, and slowed processing speeds (Lux, 2007; Roozenbeek, Maas, & Menon, 2013).

If we look specifically at the almost three million Americans who have now served in Iraq or Afghanistan—whose numbers, incidentally, rival those who served in Vietnam—conservative estimates are that about 12% of veterans returning from the combat theaters suffer from at least mild TBI (Schneiderman, Braver, & Kang, 2008). The Department of Defense's count of medically diagnosed TBI among servicemen from 2010 through the second quarter of 2014 is well over 300,000 (Defense and Veterans Brain Injury Center, 2014). However, the Institute of Medicine (2012) of the National Academies' report on veterans and posttraumatic stress disorder (PTSD) indicates that at least half of those suffering from brain injuries do not report them or seek medical care for their symptoms (see also Logan, Goldman, Zola, & Mackey, 2013). Moreover, even when they do attempt to get help, they often will not admit to their psychological symptoms until a year or more after deployment (Polusny et al., 2011; Vanderploeg et al., 2012). The RAND Corporation estimates that military members who have sustained a TBI might be as much as three times higher than official counts (Tanielian & Jaycox, 2008). Therefore, the official estimates should be taken as marking the very low end for the number of TBI among vets.

It should not be surprising that soldiers on active duty get injured, but the number of TBI among our Iraqi and Afghan veterans is much more than what we saw with previous military actions. There are several reasons for this increase. First, soldiers are able now to survive blasts that previously would have been fatal because military armor and field medical care have improved significantly (Okie, 2005; Warden, 2006). Second, the chosen weapon for rebel fighters is the improvised explosive device, so much so that over half of the combat injuries in Operation Enduring Freedom in Afghanistan and Operation Iraqi Freedom were due to explosive blasts (Sayer et al., 2008). And third, these veterans are seeing significantly more tours in combat zones than ever before. In Vietnam, for example, one 12-month tour was the standard; sometimes soldiers re-upped for a second. In our current conflicts, we now have soldiers who have experienced 8, 9, 10, even 11 or 12 tours of duty. This is true especially for our elite forces, who are the most likely to be engaged in combat situations.

It is well known that TBI is correlated with social, cognitive, and psychological difficulties for civilians. Not surprisingly, we see the same patterns among veterans. Ommaya et al. (1996) found that veterans diagnosed with a mild TBI were almost two times more likely to be discharged for behavioral problems. Moreover, the moderate TBI group was over five times more likely to be discharged for alcoholism or drug use than discharges considered as a whole, and not surprisingly, the severe TBI group had the highest rate of discharge for medical reasons. Veterans with moderate or severe TBI also seek outpatient treatment at a higher rate than veterans without similar injuries, despite being extremely disinclined to get any sort of help at all (Galarneau et al., 2008).

In addition, veterans with diagnosed TBI are at greater risk for additional neuropsychiatric disorders, such as chronic pain, depression, anxiety, or PTSD, which also have behavioral implications (Fann, Katon, Uomoto, & Esselman, 1995; Fenton, McClelland, Montgomery, MacFlynn, & Rutherford, 1993; Lew et al., 2009). In fact, Lew and colleagues conclude that using a single diagnosis of postconcussive syndrome may not turn out to be clinically useful for veterans. Hoge et al. (2008) found that the primary factors associated with disability in soldiers with a history of TBI were, in fact, PTSD and depression. The RAND study estimates that, among those diagnosed with postconcussive syndrome, a third had co-occurring depression while another third had PTSD (Tanielian & Jaycox 2008). Crooks, Zumsteg, & Bell (2007) document that, among those with TBI, depression and anxiety were present in up to 40% of soldiers who still had postconcussion symptoms three months after the incident. Of course, there are distinct TBI symptoms that cannot be tied to other psychiatric conditions, such as headaches, balance and coordination difficulties, and eye-tracking abnormalities. Nonetheless, it can be a challenge to separate out post-TBI symptoms in vets, since they rarely exist in isolation from other overlapping syndromes.

Given the challenge of co-occurring mental disorders in vets, can we tie criminal behavior to a history of TBI in our veteran population? Although the conclusions are relatively controversial and the data supporting them rather weak, the answer appears to be that, yes, we can. We already know that both male and female inmates are more likely to have a history of TBI than the general population, especially from childhood (CDC 2013b). Lifetime TBI rates in inmates are estimated to be approaching 90% (Timonen et al. 2002), which stands in strong contrast to the general population, which is estimated to have a TBI rate of less than 1 in a 10 (CDC 2013b). (There are some cautions, however, that the rate of TBI is substantially underestimated for urban African American men (Turkstra, Jones, & Toler, 2003). A large longitudinal study from Finland found that TBI in childhood or adolescence was significantly predictive of later mental disorders and criminality in men (Timonen et al., 2002). And a related study also found that TBI in childhood increases criminality among adolescence as well (Luukkainen, Riala, Laukkanen, Hakko, & Räsänen, 2012). We can find the same trends among veterans. Although the connections are currently indirect, they appear to be real. For example, inmates with recent TBI score significantly worse on tests for anger and aggression (Slaughter, Fann, & Ehde, 2003). We find the same pattern for veterans. Vietnam veterans with a history of TBI scored higher on tests for violence than did healthy veteran controls who were matched by age, educational level, and length of experience in Vietnam (Grafman et al., 1996).

The issue now is whether and how to use research on TBI, and its relation to poor behavioral outcomes, in the courtroom, either as exculpatory or mitigating evidence, for civilians or our veterans. But before I can respond to that, I need to rehearse briefly how brain data have been used in recent times in our legal system. This will set the appropriate context in which to consider this matter.

Brain Data and TBI in Courts

The exact frequency of admission of neuroimaging evidence into legal contexts is unknown (Morse, 2012), although both surveys of clinical neuropsychologists and data from case citations in the legal database Lexis Nexis Academic involving neuropsychologists show that neuropsychological testimony and evidence have become fairly routine (Kaufmann, 2009; Sweet, Giuffre Meyer, Nelson, & Moberg, 2011; Sweet & Guidotti Breting, 2013), and their use is steadily increasing (Shen, 2013). In particular, structural neuroimaging data (e.g., computed tomography [CT], positron emission tomography, [PET], or magnetic resonance imaging [MRI]) are routinely admitted as evidence of certain neural diseases or of physical damage to the brain (Moriarty, 2008), and structural neuroimaging is also the modality of choice for TBI assessment (Davis, Wippold, Cornelius, Aiken, Angtuaco, et al., 2012).

Historically, courts had been hesitant about using expert testimony, long before psychology or neuroscience got a foothold as a discipline (cf. *Winnans v. N.Y. Erie Railroad Co.*, 1859). But, as psychology became legitimized as a science and as it began to demonstrate useful results, courts began to recognize that experts in psychology might be helpful to juries making decisions (*People v. Hawthorne*, 1940).

Jenkins v. United States (1962) is the first significant case that recognized the expertise and potential contribution of clinical psychologists to proffering whether a defendant had a "mental disease or defect" (p. 647). To be admissible, the testimony would have to pass a two-part test. First, the subject matter about which the expert would be testifying must be related to some occupation, profession, business, or science "beyond the ken of the average layman" (p. 643). Second, the expert must have "skill, knowledge, or experience in that field" (p. 643). *Simmons v. Mullins* (1975) extended the test to neuropsychology, when a psychologist was found competent to testify "as an expert on organic brain injury" (p. 897; see also Kaufmann 2009). Today, neurological, and neuropsychological data are increasingly common in criminal trials (Kaufmann & Greiffenstein, 2013; Larrabee, 2012).

In *People v. Weinstein* (1992), an early and now infamous PET scan case, the court was willing to let a psychiatrist testify about the defendant's lack of cognitive ability to understand the nature and consequences of his conduct or to appreciate its wrongfulness. Weinstein was accused of strangling his wife and pushing her out of the 12th floor window of their apartment as a way to hide the murder as a probable suicide. Claiming that his patient lacked criminal responsibility due to a mental disease or defect, his psychiatrist proffered testimony that Weinstein had a cyst within the arachnoid membrane of the brain that caused "metabolic imbalances" in the other areas of the brain. The psychiatrist used data from PET scans to support his claims. This case is controversial because it is not at all clear that an arachnoid cyst, which often begins prenatally and generally has few to no cognitive symptoms, could be causally connected to Weinstein's violent behavior.

More PET scans in courtroom quickly followed. For example, in *People v. Williams* (2004), Elton Williams's defense team used PET scan evidence to support the claim that the degree of homicide should be reduced in the charge. The defendant's expert used PET scans to show a pattern of abnormal activity in a variety of Williams' brain areas that is associated with impaired reasoning and difficulties regulating aggression. Ultimately, Williams was convicted of a lesser charge of second-degree murder, which suggests that the PET scan evidence might have influenced the jury's reasoning and decision.

Use of structural MRI and CT scans in courts followed soon thereafter. In *State v. Kuehn* (2007), the Nebraska Supreme Court upheld the trial court's decision that expert testimony about MRI images and CT scans depicting subdural hematoma, atrophy, or diffuse brain damage met the reliability requirements laid out in *Daubert v. Merrell Dow Pharmaceuticals* (1993), the so-called Daubert standard. This standard has been modified twice since the 1993 Supreme Court ruling, and the current standard for admitting expert scientific testimony is

> A witness who is qualified as an expert by knowledge, skill, experience, training, or education may testify in the form of an opinion or otherwise if:
> (a) The expert's scientific, technical, or other specialized knowledge will help the trier of fact to understand the evidence or to determine a fact in issue;
> (b) The testimony is based on sufficient facts or data;
> (c) The testimony is the product of reliable principles and methods; and
> (d) The expert has reliably applied the principles and methods to the facts of the case. (As amended Apr. 17, 2000, eff. Dec. 1, 2000; Apr. 26, 2011, eff. Dec. 1, 2011)

This standard now holds in the U.S. federal courts as well as in over half of its states. But regardless of the standard used, courts across the country and in various jurisdictions have found structural MRI and CT scans to be both reliable and relevant in supporting the claim of a brain injury (Moriarty, 2008).[1]

---

[1] Indeed, courts have gone further than that. In *Allen v. Bloomfield Hills School District* (2008), the court concluded, "a mental or emotional trauma can . . . result in physical changes to the brain." A runaway train ran into a school bus, injuring its driver. The train driver, Allen, was subsequently diagnosed with PTSD and sued the city. By statute, he was required to establish that he suffered "bodily injury" from the accident to win his claim. The municipality filed a motion for a summary judgment, alleging that PTSD did not constitute bodily injury. Allen's attorney submitted an affidavit from a physician that claimed that Allen's brain scan showed "decreases in frontal and subcortical activity consistent with depression and post-traumatic stress disorder." It also stated that "the

But the courts have also recognized that brain scans have their limits. In *Forrest v. Steele* (2012), the U.S. District Court asserted that a PET scan "cannot show the cause of damage, nor can it demonstrate the existence of diminished capacity, predict future behavior, or establish a person's state of mind." Therefore, failing to obtain a PET scan, even though a later scan confirmed both brain damage and chemical injury, does not mean that there was ineffective assistance of counsel. Other cases have made similar rulings; for example, *Trimble v. Bobby* (2012) found that an expert's statement that a PET scan "could have" been helpful in diagnosing brain abnormalities was insufficient to establish ineffective assistance of counsel, and *Rogers v. State* (2012) also ruled that failing to obtain a PET scan did not constitute ineffective counsel because it would not have added anything to the process as the trail court already found that the defendant had brain damage.

On the other hand, failing to present evidence of brain injury or brain damage, if available, could be construed as ineffective counsel. TBIs that differentially affect the frontal or temporal lobes are more likely to be introduced in criminal contexts because of their connection to executive functioning, impulse control, memory, and affect regulation. Because defendants in capital cases can present just about any sort of mitigating evidence they care to during the sentencing phase, they are more likely to present this type of evidence then (Blume & Johnson, 1999). The U.S. Court of Appeals for the Eleventh Circuit recently held that because mitigating evidence of an inmate's childhood TBI, which left the defendant with behavioral difficulties and impaired cognition, was not presented during the penalty phase of his trail, he had received ineffective counsel (*Evans v. Secretary*, 2012). The court underscored that "undisputed brain damage resulting from a TBI is inherently mitigating" (p.77).

However, and not surprisingly, brain deficits are not always considered mitigating factors. Peter Nong Le was accused of killing his brother's girlfriend and daughter for disrespecting him and his elderly parents. In *Nong Le v. Barnes* (2012), his defense attorney claimed that he was not guilty by reason of insanity, due to previous TBI and PTSD. A soldier who fought for the South Vietnamese during the Vietnam War, Nong Le was part of the contingent that was forced to march the Ho Chi Min trail in 1972 and was brutalized as a prisoner of war in the re-education camps of North Vietnam. Nong Le immigrated to the United States after his release from North Vietnam and had moved into his parents' home a month before the killings. A neuropsychologist testified that brain scans revealed brain damage associated deficits in "problem solving, divided attention,

---

abnormalities . . . are quite pronounced and are clearly different in brain pattern from any of the normal controls and . . . are consistent with an injury" to plaintiff's brain. On the basis of this affidavit, the court ruled that an emotional trauma could be a bodily injury.

multi-tasking, and nonverbal learning and memory." In addition, Nong Le "displayed clinically elevated levels of anxiety, interpersonal insensitivity, depression, hostility, paranoid ideation, suspiciousness, and delusions" (*Nong Le v. Barnes*, 2012). The first jury deadlocked, with 1 juror agreeing with the defense that Nong Le was not sane and 11 holding that he was. A second jury ultimately rejected the insanity defense and found him criminally responsible for the double homicide. He was sentenced to life in prison without parole plus 25 years.

State v. Stanko (2013) is yet another case of documented brain injuries failing to mitigate. Stephen Christopher Stanko was sentenced to death for shooting an elderly friend, Henry Turner, in the back, using a pillow as a silencer, then hitting him the back of the head, and then fatally shooting him in the chest. At his trial, a neuropsychologist and a neurologist both testified that Mr. Stanko had suffered significant damage to his frontal lobes, from two separate injuries. The first occurred at birth, when he was deprived of oxygen; the second was a TBI, when he was hit on the back of the head with a beer bottle as a teenager. As a result, his gray matter was 4 standard deviations below normal in his right hemisphere. The experts concluded that "this injury . . . would significantly compromise and impair an individual's ability to exercise judgment, impulse control, control of aggression." On appeal, the South Carolina Supreme Court ruled that while the "appellant certainly presented evidence which could have reduced, mitigated, or excused the Victim's murder," thereby invalidating the trial judge's instructions, it was not enough to reverse the original jury's final decision that Mr. Sanko was sane at the time of the crime. Mr. Stanko currently sits on death row at the Leiber Correctional Institution in Ridgeville, South Carolina.

Connecting the Brain to the Mind

Why do we see this conflicting pattern of results, in which some brain injuries are mitigating, but other virtually identical ones are not? No doubt part of the answer lies in the individual circumstances of each case, but there also appears to be a common belief among judges that they (and juries) are capable of accurately assessing the mental states and motivations of a defendant based on the defendant's previous and current behavior without any additional expert contributions. A Massachusetts trial judge excluded such testimony, saying the jury and he did not need an expert to make a voluntariness determination because that is "something that the ordinary person can determine on all the evidence in this case" (cf. *Commonwealth v. Crawford*, 1999). (This finding was overturned on appeal.) The Supreme Court of Minnesota made similar judgment in *Bixler v. State* (1998), as did the New Jersey Supreme Court in *State v. Free* (2002). In fact, the most common reason for excluding evidence from the mind and brain sciences is not failing to meet the Daubert standard, but failing to assist the trier of fact (34% of the cases), with being unreliable and irrelevant coming in close second (33%) and third (27%; Shapiro, 2012; see also Slobogin, 2003). Such evidence is excluded, by and large, because courts conclude that they do not need it to carry out their charges.

Medicine, psychiatry, neuropsychology, and neurology all hold that diseases, injuries, and deformities in the brain influence and can even determine a person's thoughts, desires, impulses, and ability to control one's behavior. In contrast, Western law presumes that adults are rational beings who act for specific reasons and that in each instance, an individual could have done otherwise had he or she chosen to. In other words, courts do not care about issues of impulse control, emotional lability, and the like. They focus on rational thought and means–ends reasoning instead. The neuroscience behind criminality might tell us something about the brains of criminals, but it does not tell us anything about a person's reasons for acting. And it is the reasons themselves that are important for legal culpability and the justification of punishment. Neuroscience and the law simply have different frames of reference, which prevent one from informing the other. Our human institutions do not dovetail with our scientific ones.

In short, the U.S. legal system relies on some version of folk psychology,[2] while a scientific perspective leaves less room, if any, for rational decision-making to have a place in explaining behavior. There has been some discussion in the literature regarding whether neuroimaging might be able to capture legal constructs like intentionality, reason, responsibility, or truthfulness instead of the less helpful (from a legal point of view) neurobiological and psychological constructs like impulsivity, aggression, or impaired executive function (Buller, 2006; Gazzaniga, 2006; Gazzaniga & Steven, 2005; Greene & Cohen, 2004; Farah, 2005; Jedlička, 2005; Schaffner, 2002; Thompson, 2007). And indeed, some progress has been made on using neuroimaging to determine whether one is lying or whether a memory is genuine (Canli & Amin, 2002; Illes, Kirschen, & Gabrilei, 2003). But, in many respects, this is simply the wrong perspective to be taking. For it is clear that, from a neuroperspective, the legal system's folk theory of human behavior is not supported by our best scientific data. Brain scans will not be able to unearth the brain correlates for things like "reasons" as these simply do not exist as the law assumes.

In addition, it has become somewhat of a cottage industry in psychology to demonstrate how inaccurate human folk are at "reading" one another. For

[2] Here I am referring to the collection of platitudes about the mind that ordinary people use to predict and explain one another's behavior. The idea that this collection of platitudes resembles a theory dates back to David Lewis (1966, 1970, 1972). Philosophers call this idea "folk psychology"; psychologists often refer to the same idea as "naïve psychology."

example, a recent meta-analysis of over 200 published studies (which included over 23,000 participants) testing our ability to distinguish truth-telling from deception found that we are successful, on average, just 54% of the time—barely above chance (Bond & DePaulo, 2006). Studies have shown over and over again that "the ordinary person" is simply no good at divining others' motivations and emotions based on their behavior. The folk theories we rely on to hypothesize about the reasons for or causes of others' behavior are just not up to that task.

That our folk theories of human behavior are false does not matter most of the time—they are good enough to get the job done in our routine social interactions. I can use them to navigate meeting a colleague at 3:00 on Thursday afternoon, for example. But a trial is not a routine social interaction, and in this venue there is less room to be sloppy or inaccurate in one's assessment of others' mental states and behavior. Here, it should be preferable to rely on actual scientific data instead of homilies learned at mothers' knee or extrapolated from one's personal experiences.

Importantly, though, the legal system is starting to change. As discussed in the previous section, courts now admit, on occasion, that brain abnormalities can mitigate and, in some cases, even fully explain, someone's behavior. At some point in the near future, the cognitive dissonance currently in the court system between brain data and theoretical legal assumptions will have to be resolved. But in the meantime (the previously discussed cases excepted), it is largely managing the conflict by simply diverting those defendants with mental disorders out of the traditional legal system. In other words, it is coping with the fundamental incompatibility between brain data and legal constructs by channeling the problematic cases that might highlight the irreconcilability though a special process that does not presume defendants' rational means–ends reasoning produced their behavior.

Since their inception in the late 1990s, so-called diversion courts have played an increasingly large role in managing defendants accused of criminal behavior. In particular, the American court system is starting to distinguish returning combat vets with TBI or with other mind/brain disorders from other defendants. Several districts have created special diversion courts for veterans accused of a variety of crimes, ranging from minor misdemeanors up to violent felonies. These courts allow some military members to enter mental health treatment programs for infractions, instead of jailing them. In many cases, Veterans Treatment Courts allow veterans to remain in the community as they complete treatment, and, if they complete successfully, the original charges are dropped. (If they do not complete their assigned program successfully, then normally their diversion ends, and they are sent back to their original docket.)

We are also finding other diversion courts that help treat addicts and perpetrators with mental disorders instead of simply punishing them for behaviors that, in a very real sense, may have been beyond their control. Although these courts are relatively new, preliminary data suggest that defendants who go through this system are more likely to become productive and law-abiding citizens than those who are warehoused in our prisons and jails (Marlowe, 2010).

Still, unanswered questions arise from this practice. Should vets be treated differently from other noncombatant defendants with similar brain injuries? Should mental or brain disorders affect how we assign punishment? Is there perhaps such a thing as a "semi-voluntary" act (cf. Denno, 2002, 2003)? At the present time, the details regarding how diversion can be made to fit with traditional notions of responsibility and culpability is still being sorted out.

I am just going to take it as obvious that, from a legal standpoint, there is nothing special about being a brain-injured veteran over being any other sort of brain-injured defendant. Hence, any diversion out of the normal court structure that vets are allowed should be extended to civilians (and such opportunities are increasingly occurring with civilians). I fully expect that, if Veteran Treatment Courts continue to be successful in reintegrating their clients back into society, then ever more similar courts will become available for the general population.

Both traditional courts and diversion courts have as their goal an orderly society with law-abiding citizens, but the similarities between them end there. The idea of "therapeutic justice," which informs diversion courts, is a misnomer in that it subverts conventional notions of justice. "Justice" includes the concepts of retribution and compensation; therapeutic justice does not. Even though diversion treatments result in a loss of rights for defendants, they are not punishment in any traditional sense. While they may be consequentialist, similar to some views on punishment, in that one goal is to prevent further lawlessness, they are not concerned with deterrence, which traditional consequentialist views of punishment include. Indeed, if anything, their aim is the antithesis of deterrence: to encourage more citizens to seek treatment for mental disorders.

Our legal system is slowly moving beyond a system of punishment to one centered on therapy and rehabilitation, one that leaves time-honored views of punishment as justified retribution for behavior far behind. I suggest that diversion courts have significantly changed how we assign punishment. But they have done so by skirting the legal system and its folk psychological presumptions instead of engaging directly with the issues.

Another way of making the same point is to notice that diversion courts belie the legal system's traditional notions of responsibility, for they are predicated on the idea that the criminal behavior is explained by something outside of traditional folk psychological notions of reasons, beliefs, and desires. The traditional legal verdict of not guilty by reason of insanity requires that defendants either have delusions so severe they cannot comprehend what they are doing or they cannot distinguish right from wrong at the time of the act. Normally, these criteria hold even if we understand what is happening biologically in an individual at the time of the crime. However, diversion courts are based on the notion that their defendants, while not delusional, are still not as culpable as "normal" defendants. Perhaps it would make sense to describe them as semi-rational or semi-responsible or having committed semi-voluntary acts, although in many respects, how we describe responsibility is less important than recognizing the fundamental conceptual shifts taking place. In these courts, biological explanations for behavior now implicitly take precedence over reasons-based explanations. And, as our science of behavior grows more sophisticated, it encroaches more and more on the territory covered by folk psychology, which means that the scope of our regular criminal courts will cover less and less over time. If we believe our brains cause our behavior, and our brains are the way they are because of our genetic composition, chemical infusion, or life experiences, it becomes difficult to maintain that understanding behavior in terms of means–ends reasoning is coherent. From science's perspective, it is no longer clear what mens rea would refer to, in at least many cases.

Although this would be another essay, I believe we are seeing the same sort of change occurring across the board in our culture. Lawrence Friedman (1993) is surely right when he wrote: "Methods of punishment are related to what is happening in the larger world" (p. 315). Brains and brain data are increasingly becoming part of our everyday vernacular, as demonstrated by everything from the covers of popular magazines (*Time Magazine*, February 3, 1997; May 10, 2004; January 29, 2007) to the surging popularity of brain-training apps and programs, to President Obama's public announcement of an $18 billion BRAIN initiative, which follows President Bush's announcement of the 1990s as the "Decade of the Brain." As a result, the brain and its functioning have, for better or worse, become pop-culture fixtures in the 21st century (Thornton, 2011). And our current cultural fascination with things brain-based cannot help but influence how brains and brain data are viewed in the courtroom.

The real challenge is where to draw the line around those who are eligible for diversion. One can easily imagine a future in which all defendants get diverted because we would be able to identify something in their brains somewhere that influenced their criminal behavior. We would then remediate everyone, as no one has perfect self-control. In this case, no one is responsible for anything, and our system of criminal law would effectively cease to exist. Is this the natural outcome of the trends we are seeing now?

I would like to suggest perhaps a different perspective, however. I do not believe that our legal system is on the verge of collapse. Nor do I believe that all defendants will be diverted in the near future. Instead, perhaps, we should understand recent trends as a deep separation occurring between our notions of guilt and responsibility, on the one hand, and our sense of punishment, on the other.

What to Do with the Guilty?

Defendants who get diverted are all guilty. They all did something bad, or at least they did something illegal, and in being diverted, they are publicly affirming that prima facie they did something wrong. Everyone involved in the process, from the magistrates to the attorneys for both sides to the physicians and social workers to the defendants themselves, believes and accepts that the defendants are guilty—that they did what they are being accused of doing (and that they were aware of what they were doing when they did and that what they were doing was wrong). In that sense, the defendants are responsible. What is different with diversion is how the so-called punishments are meted out. What is different is what justice looks like.

In a recent House Appropriations Subcommittee on Financial Services and General Government, U.S. Supreme Court Justice Anthony Kennedy remarked, "The corrections system is one of the most overlooked, misunderstood institutions we have in our entire government" (March 23, 2015). He went on to reprimand the legal profession for being focused solely on questions of guilt and innocence and not on what comes after. But I do believe that we are seeing pockets of change; we are starting to focus more on what comes next, once someone has been found guilty.

What is the best way to respond to the guilty? Our answers have evolved over time. The history of penology in the United States is a history of great change, from the public pillorying and branding of the colonial era to the advent of the prison system in the 19th century through the hope of rehabilitation and the rise of prisoners' rights in the mid-twentieth century, and the wave of massive incarceration of past 30 years, to where we are today, with a recent emphasis on preventing recidivism (although this may be changing under Trump's administration). Diversion courts are just the latest incarnation of how we manage the guilty.

In the early years of 20th century, parole, probation, and indeterminate sentences started as way to individualize punishment to ensure that each prisoner received exactly what he or she deserved, given the totality of the circumstances (Friedman, 1993). But, prisons at that time were quite inhumane. In 1908, Kate Bernard, Oklahoma's Commissioner of Charities and Corrections, found brutality common in the prisons of the day: floggings, water torture, and extended confinement to small spaces were standard procedures (cf. Hougen, 1989). In 1913, a grand jury in Westchester County, New York, censured Sing Sing prison, noting that its cells were "infested with vermin" and "unfit for the housing of animals, much less human beings" (Tannenbaum, 1933, pp. 6–7). There was no running water nor any toilet facilities, only slop buckets. Joseph F. Fishman, who purportedly visited 1,500 jails in the United States at around the same time, decried penitentiaries as "human dumping grounds" (Fishman, 1923, p. 21). A jail in Phoenix, Arizona, had a hundred prisoners jammed in "foul cage" crawling with vermin that was supposed to house only 40 people (p. 42). All this, in addition to the notorious Southern chain gangs, groups of prisoners who were permanently shackled together and worked long hours in the hot sun.

What followed in the mid-century were attempts to make the criminal justice system more protective of individual rights and liberties. There began a movement for "prisoners' rights" and away from so much judicial discretion in sentencing. In the 1940s, the third circuit court found Georgia's chain gangs amounted to cruel and unusual punishment (*Johnson v. Dye*, 1949). In 1969, *Talley v. Stephens* held that Arkansas could not whip prisoners without "appropriate safeguards," and then in 1970, a federal court declared that the whole state penitentiary system in Arkansas was unconstitutional (*Holt v. Sarver*). Other decisions and changes swiftly followed. As a result, the penal system became more differentiated, with maximum-, medium-, and minimum-security prisons, along juvenile detention centers and women's prisons. We had shifted from paying more attention to the offense in determining punishment to focusing more on the offender.

Then, in the latter part of the 20th century, we shifted back again. We stacked victim's rights against prisoners' rights. And, crime rates climbed rapidly, a virtual panic about criminality and criminals swept the nation. As a society, we were no longer interested in rehabilitation or reform; we wanted deterrence and incapacitation. Our focus was to get bad people off the streets and to keep them off. We began a perhaps ill-advised "war on drugs." We switched to mandatory sentencing guidelines and did away with parole for many offenses. The penal system became partially privatized and relatively lucrative.

Now, once again, the tide is turning. Crime rates have been declining steadily, and folks are turning their attention again to what is going on in prisons, to rehabilitation and recidivism rates, and to whom is being incarcerated. There is wide acknowledgment that the war on drugs and mandatory sentencing were misguided failures, and we perhaps created criminals through our administrations of so-called justice. We are turning back to a more individualized approach to punishment. Diversion courts are just yet another differentiation in our criminal justice system, as we know better now what individual differences are relevant.

This is where we are today. We want to help the guilty, if we can, so that they can rejoin society as productive members, if at all possible. We believe that we can provide a "neurointervention" of some sort that will transform the criminal into a law-abiding citizen. So, we divert them into forced treatment. This is the new face of justice. (I'm going to leave aside the fact that we actually have very few effective treatment options for TBI, not to mention PTSD and addiction.)

Philosophers have been bickering about whether folk psychology is salvage-able for decades now without resolution. It is time to set aside that debate in this arena, for we all already know that the legal system has been struggling with an incorrect and inappropriate perspective on human behavior. Perhaps the issue of how to understand responsibility is a red herring. The question is what to do with the guilty. We should be focusing our energy and efforts on helping those interested in remediation to get it right—whom can we help and why? Our best path forward then is to acknowledge what is already happening in the judicial system and for the scientific community to do its collective best to educate the lay public, judges, and lawyers about what we can fix in the brain and the psyche, and what we cannot, to help them understand whom to divert and how.

References

Allen v. Bloomfield Hills School District, 760 N.W.2d 811 (Mich. App. 2008), appeal dismissed, 779 N. W.2d 793 (Mich. 2010).

Bixler v. State. (1998). 582 N.W.2d252, 256 (Sup.Ct.Minn.)

Blume, J. H., & Johnson, S. L. (1999). *The Fourth Circuit's "double-edged sword": Eviscerating the right to present mitigating evidence and beheading the right to the assistance of counsel.* Cornell Law Faculty Publications. Paper 235. Retrieved from http://scholar-ship.law.cornell.edu/facpub/235.

Bond, C. F., & DePaulo, B. M. (2006). Accuracy of deception judgments. *Personality and Social Psychology Review, 10*, 214-234.

Buller, T. (2006). Brains, lies, and psychological explanations. In J. Illes (Ed.), *Neuroethics: Defining the Issues in theory, practice, and policy* (pp. 51–60). New York, NY: Oxford University Press.

Canli, T., & Amin, Z. (2002). Neuroimaging of emotion and personality: Scientific evidence and ethical considerations. *Brain and Cognition, 50*, 414–431.

Centers for Disease Control and Prevention. (2010). Ten leading causes of death and injury. Retrieved from http://www.cdc.gov/injury/wisqars/leadingcauses.html

Centers for Disease Control and Prevention. (2013a). Traumatic brain injury & concussions. Retrieved from https://www.cdc.gov/traumaticbraininjury/

Centers for Disease Control and Prevention. (2013b). Traumatic brain injury in prisons and jails: An unrecognized problem. Retrieved from http://www.cdc.gov/traumaticbraininjury/pdf/prisoner_TBI_Prof-a.pdf

Commonwealth v. Crawford. (1999). 429 Mass. 60.

Crooks, C. Y., Zumsteg, J. M., & Bell, K. R. (2007). Traumatic brain injury: A review of practice management and recent advances. *Physical Medicine and Rehabilitation Clinics of North America, 18*, 681–710.

Davis, P. C., Wippold, F. J. II, Cornelius, R. S., Aiken, A. H., Angtuaco, E. J., Berger, K. L., ... Coley, B. D. (2012). Expert panel on neurologic imaging. ACR Appropriateness Criteria® head trauma. Reston, VA: American College of Radiology (ACR). Retrieved from http://www.guideline.gov/content.aspx?id=37919.

Decuypere, M., & Klimo, P. Jr. (2012). Spectrum of traumatic brain injury from mild to severe. *Surgical Clinics of North America, 92,* 939–957.

Defense and Veterans Brain Injury Center. (2014). DOD worldwide numbers for TBI. DOD Office of Responsibility. Retrieved from http://dvbic.dcoe.mil/dod-worldwide-numbers-tbi

Department of Defense. (2014). Traumatic brain injury: Department of Defense special report. Retrieved from http://www.defense.gov/home/features/2012/0312_tbi/

Denno, D. W. (2002). Crime and consciousness: Science and involuntary acts. *Minnesota Law Review, 87,* 269–399.

Denno, D. W. (2003). A mind to blame: New views on involuntary acts. *Behavioral Sciences and the Law, 21,* 601–618.

Dijkers, M. P., Harrison-Felix, C., & Marwitz, J. H. (2011). The traumatic brain injury model systems: History and contributions to clinical service and research. *Journal of Head Trauma Rehabilitation, 25,* 81–91.

Evans v. Secretary, DOC (2012), 2013 U.S. App. LEXIS 296.

Fann, J. R., Katon, W. J., Uomoto, J. M., & Esselman, P. C. (1995). Psychiatric disorders and functional disability in outpatients with traumatic brain injuries. *The American Journal of Psychiatry, 152,* 1493–1499.

Farah, M. J. (2005). Neuroethics: The practical and the philosophical. *Trends in Cognitive Sciences, 9,* 34–40.

Fenton, G., McClelland, R., Montgomery, A., MacFlynn, G., & Rutherford, W. (1993). The postconcussional syndrome: Social antecedents and psychological sequelae. *British Journal of Psychiatry, 162,* 493–497.

Fishman, J. F., with V. Perlman. (1923). *Crucibles of crime: The shocking story of the American jail.* New York, NY: Cosmopolis Press.

Forrest v. Steele, 2012 WL 1668358 (W.D. Mo May 11, 2012)

Friedman, L. M. (1993). *Crime and punishment in American history.* New York, NY: Basic Books.

Galarneau, M. R., Woodruff, S. I., Dye, J. L., Mohrle, C. R., & Wade, A. L. (2008). Traumatic brain injury during Operation Iraqi Freedom: Findings from the United State Navy–Marine Corps combat trauma registry. *Journal of Neurosurgery, 108,* 950–957.

Gazzaniga, M. S. (2006). Facts, fictions, and the future of neuroethics. In J. Illes (Ed.), *Neuroethics: Defining the issues in theory, practice, and policy* (pp. 141–148). New York, NY: Oxford University Press.

Gazzaniga, M. S., & Steven, M. S. (2005). Neuroscience and the law. *Scientific American Mind, 16,* 42–49.

Grafman, J., Schwab, K., Warden, D., Pridgen, A., Brown, H. R., & Salazar, A. M. (1996). Frontal lobe injuries, violence, and aggression: A report of the Vietnam head injury study. *Neurology, 46,* 1231–1238.

Graham v. Florida, 560 U.S. 48, 130 S. Ct. 2011 (2010).

Hoge, C. W., McGurk, D., Thomas, J. L., Cox, A. L., Engel, C. C., & Castro, C. A. (2008). Mild traumatic brain injury in US soldiers returning from Iraq. *The New England Journal of Medicine, 358,* 453–463.

Holt v. Sarver, 309 F. Supp. 362 (E.D. Ark., 1970).

Hougen, H. R. (1989). Kate Bernard and the Kansas penitentiary scandal, 1908–1909. *Journal of the West, 17,* 9.

Illes, J., Kirschen, M. P., & Gabrilei, J. D. E. (2003). From neuroimaging to neuroethics. *Nature Neuroscience, 6,* 250.

Jedlička P. (2005). Neuroethics, reductionism, and dualism. *Trends in Cognitive Sciences, 9,* 172.

Jenkins v. United States, 307 F.2d 637 (D.C. Cir. 1962).

Johnson v. Dye, Warden, 175 Fed 2d 250 (C.A. 3, 1949).

Kaufmann, P. M. (2009). Protecting raw data and psychological tests from wrongful disclosure: A primer on the law and other persuasive strategies. *The Clinical Neuropsychologist, 23,* 1130–1159.

Kaufmann, P. M., & Greiffenstein, M. F. (2013). Forensic neuropsychology: Training, scope of practice, and quality control. *National Academy of Neuropsychology Bulletin, 27,* 11–15.

Lamberty, G. J., Nakase-Richardson, R., Farrell-Carnahan, L. V., McGarity, S., Bidelspach, D., Harrison- Felix, C., & Cifu, D. X. (2014). Development of a TBI model system within the VA polytrauma system of care. *Journal of Head Trauma Rehabilitation, 29*(3), E1–E7. DOI: 10.1097/HTR.0b013e31829a64d1

Lamberty, G. L., Nelson, N. W., & Yamada, T. (2013). Effects and outcomes in civilian and military traumatic brain injury: Similarities, differences, and forensic implications. *Behavioral Sciences and the Law, 31,* 814–832.

Larrabee, G. (Ed.) (2012). *Forensic Neuropsychology: A Scientific Approach (2nd ed.).* New York: Oxford University Press.

Lew, H. L., Otis, J. D., Tun, C., Kerns, R. D., Clark, M. E., & Cifu, D. X. (2009). Prevalence of chronic pain, posttraumatic stress disorder, and persistent postconcussive symptoms in OIF/OEF veterans: Polytrauma clinical trial. *Journal of Rehabilitation Research and Development, 46,* 697–702.

Lewis, D. (1966). An argument for the identity theory. *Journal of Philosophy, 63,* 17–25.

Lewis, D. (1970). How to define theoretical terms. *Journal of Philosophy, 67,* 427–446.

Lewis, D. (1972). Psychophysical and theoretical identifications. *Australasian Journal of Philosophy, 50,* 249–258.

Logan, B. W., Goldman, R. T., Zola, M., & Mackey, A. (2013). Concussive brain injury in the military: September 2001 to the present. *Behavioral Sciences and the Law, 31,* 803–813.

Luukkainen, S., Riala, K., Laukkanen, M., Hakko, H., & Räsänen, P. (2012). The association of traumatic brain injury with criminality in adolescent psychiatric inpatients in Northern Finland. *Psychiatric Research, 200,* 767–772.

Lux, W. E. (2007). The neurocognitive basis of compromised autonomy after traumatic brain injury: Clinical and ethical considerations. *Neurotherapeutics, 4,* 525–530.

Marlowe, D. B. (2010). Research update on adult drug courts. *National Association of Drug Court Professionals.* Retrieved from http://www.nadcp.org/sites/default/files/nadcp/Research%20Update%20on%20Adult%20Drug%20Courts%20-%20NADCP_1.pdf

Moriarty, J. C. (2008). Flickering neuroadmissibility: Neuroimaging evidence in U.S. Courts. *Behavioral Sciences and the Law, 26,* 29–49.

Morse, S. J. (2012). Neuroimaging evidence in law: A plea for modesty and relevance. In J. R. Simpson (Ed.), *Neuroimaging in forensic psychiatry: From the clinic to the courtroom* (pp. 341–358). Chichester, England: Wiley-Blackwell.

Nong Le v. Barnes, 2012 WL 6147895 (C.D. Cal. 2012), report and recommendation adopted, Le v. Barnes, 2012 WL 6178433 (C.D. Cal. Dec. 10, 2012)

Office of the Surgeon General. (2013). TBI talking points 2013. Washington, DC: Author.

Okie, S. (2005). Traumatic brain injury in the war zone. *The New England of Journal of Medicine, 352,* 2043–2047.

Ommaya, A. K., Salazar, A. M., Dannenberg, A. L., Ommaya, A. K., Chervinsky, A. B., & Schwab, K. (1996). Outcome after traumatic brain injury in the U.S. military medical system. *The Journal of Trauma: Injury, Infection, and Critical Care, 41,* 972–975.

People v. Hawthorne, 291 N.W. 205, 208 (Mich. 1940).

People v. Weinstein, 591 N.Y.S.2d 715 (N.Y.S.Ct. 1992).

People v. Williams, 2004 WL 740049 (Cal. App. 4th Dist. 2004), as modified (April 13, 2004), review denied (June 23, 2004)

Polusny, M. A., Kehle, S. M., Nelson, N. W., Erbes, C. R., Arbisi, P. A., & Thuras, P. (2011). Longitudinal effects of mild TBI and PTSD comorbidity on post-deployment outcomes in National Guard soldiers deployed to Iraq. *Archives of General Psychiatry, 68,* 79–89.

Rogers v. State, 97 So.3d 824 (Fla. 2012).

Roozenbeek, B., Maas, A. I., & Menon, D. K. (2013). Changing patterns in the epidemiology of traumatic brain injury. *Nature Reviews Neurology, 9,* 231–236.

Sahler, C. S., & Greenwald, B. D. (2012). Traumatic brain injury in sports: A review. *Rehabilitation Research and Practice,* https://doi.org/10.1155/2012/659652

Sayer, N. A., Chiros, C. E., Sigford, B., Scott, S., Clothier, B., Pickett, T., & Lew, H. L. (2008). Characteristics and rehabilitation outcomes among patients with blast and other injuries sustained during the Global War on Terror. *Archives of Physical Medicine and Rehabilitation, 89,* 163–170.

Schaffner, K. F. (2002). Neuroethics: Reductionism, emergence, and decision-making capabilities. In: S. Marcus (Ed.), *Neuroethics: Mapping the field* (pp. 27–33). New York, NY: The Dana Foundation.

Schneiderman, A. I., Braver, E. R., & Kang, H. K. (2008). Understanding sequelae of injury mechanisms and mild traumatic brain injury incurred during the conflicts in Iraq and Afghanistan: Persistent postconcussive symptoms and posttraumatic stress disorder. *American Journal of Epidemiology, 167,* 1446–1452.

Shapiro, D. L. (2012). What is all the fuss about *Daubert*? A re-analysis. *Psychological Injury and Law, 5,* 202–207.

Shen, F. X. (2013). Neuroscience, mental privacy, and the law. *Harvard Journal of Law and Public Policy, 36,* 653–653.

Silver, J. M., McAllister, T. W., & Yudofsky, S. C. (2011). *Textbook of traumatic brain injury* (2nd ed.). New York, NY: American Psychiatric Publishing.

Simmons v. State, 105 So.3d 475 (Fla. 2012).

Slaughter, B., Fann, J. R., & Ehde, D. (2003). Traumatic brain injury in a county jail population: Prevalence, neuropsychological functioning, and psychiatric disorders. *Brain Injury, 17,* 731–741.

Slobogin, C. (2003). Pragmatic forensic psychology: A means of "scientizing" expert testimony from mental health professionals? *Psychology, Public Policy, and Law, 9,* 275–300.

State v. Free (2002). 798 A.2d 83 (N.J. Super. Ct. App. Div.)

State v. Kuehn, 728 N.W.2d 589 (Neb. 2007).

State v. Stanko, 741 S.E.2d 708 (S.C., 2013) rehearing denied (Apr. 3, 2013), Petition for Certiorari filed July 2, 2013.

Sweet, J. J., Giuffre Meyer, D., Nelson, N., & Moberg, P. (2011). The TCN/AACN "Salary Survey": Professional practices, beliefs, and incomes of U.S. neuropsychologists. *The Clinical Neuropsychologist, 25,* 12–61.

Sweet, J. J., & Guidotti Breting, L. M. (2013). Symptom validity test research: Status and clinical implications. *Journal of Experimental Psychopathology, 4,* 6–19.

Tagliaferri, F., Compagnone, C., Korsic, M., Servadei, F., & Kraus, J. (2006). A systematic review of brain injury epidemiology in Europe. *Acta Neurochirugica, 148,* 255–268.

Talley v. Stephens. 247 F. Supp. 683 (E.D. Ark., 1965) at 689.

Tanielian, T. E., & Jaycox, L. H. (Eds.). (2008). *Invisible wounds of war: Psychological and cognitive injuries, their consequences and services to assist recovery.* Santa Monica, CA: RAND Corporation.

Tannenbaum, F. (1933). *Osborne of Sing Sing.* Chapel Hill: University of North Carolina Press.

Thompson S. K. (2007). A brave new world of interrogation jurisprudence? *American Journal of Law and Medicine, 33,* 341–357.

Thorton, D. J. (2011). *Brain culture: Neuroscience and popular media.* Piscataway, NJ: Rutgers University Press.

Timonen, M., Miettunen, J., Hakko, H., Veijola, J., von Wendt, L., & Räsänen, P. (2002). The association of preceding traumatic brain injury with mental disorders, alcoholism, and criminality: The Northern Finland 1966 Birth Cohort Study. *Psychiatric Research, 113,* 217–226.

Trimble v. Bobby, 2012 WL 3852040 (N.D. Ohio 2012).

Turkstra, L., Jones, D., & Toler, H. L. (2003). Brain injury and violent crime. *Brain Injury, 17,* 39–47.

Vanderploeg, R. D., Belanger, H. G., Horner, R. D., Spehar, A. M., Powell-Cope, G., Luther, S. L., & Scott, S. G. (2012). Health outcomes associated with military deployment: Mild traumatic brain injury, blast, trauma, and combat associations in the Florida National Guard. *Archives of Physical Medicine and Rehabilitation, 93,* 1887–1895.

Warden, D. (2006). Military TBI during the Iraq and Afghanistan Wars. *Journal of Head Trauma Rehabilitation, 21,* 398–402.

Winnans v. N.Y. & Erie Railroad Co., 62 U.S. 88 (U.S. 1859).

8

Neurobionic Revenge Porn and the Criminal Law

Brain–Computer Interfaces and Intimate Image Abuse

Allan McCay

Introduction

Technological change sometimes leads to new kinds of wrongs, which, in turn, may be met by new responses from the criminal law. One such relatively new wrong is the phenomenon that has become informally referred to as "revenge porn," in which intimate images (which may sometimes have been initially obtained with the consent of the person whose image is used) are nonconsensually distributed, perhaps via social media over the Internet, to humiliate a former lover after a break-up. In recognition of the harm done to victims (those people, intimate images of whom are nonconsensually distributed, in the aforementioned and other ways and for revenge or other reasons), many jurisdictions have now passed legislation criminalizing intimate image abuse (McGlynn, Rackley, & Houghton, 2017).[1]

However, advances in neurotechnology create new possibilities for the commission of intimate image abuse (and other offenses), by way of brain–computer interfaces (BCIs). Either by way of an implanted device or some form of external sensor, BCI technology exists that allows people to interact with the external world by mental rather than bodily action. Such technology can currently assist some with disabilities to regain autonomy, for example, by controlling a device such as a wheelchair. A BCI may also restore the capacity to communicate where a medical condition (such as locked-in syndrome) make it otherwise impossible. Outside the medical context, BCI technology can be used for a variety of purposes, including playing electronic games and controlling flying drones.[2]

---

[1] The term *intimate image abuse* would include revenge porn but is more expansive including abuse that is not motivated by revenge (e.g., motivated by extortion) (Australian Legal and Constitutional Affairs Reference Committee, 2016).

[2] For a useful overview of these and other uses of BCIs, see Steinert, Bublitz, Jox, & Friedrich (2019).

Allan McCay, *Neurobionic Revenge Porn and the Criminal Law* In: *Neurointerventions and the Law.* Edited by: Nicole A Vincent, Thomas Nadelhoffer, and Allan McCay, Oxford University Press (2020). © Oxford University Press 2020
DOI: 10.1093/oso/9780190651145.001.0008

The range of possibilities for these technologies is impressive, and there is considerable commercial excitement about them. Indeed, in a special feature, *The Economist* magazine has discussed the commercial possibilities (The Next Front ier: Neurotechnology, 2018).

BCIs come in a number of forms and are used for a variety of purposes. I will not try to survey the range of such uses but focus instead on the use of BCIs to control a cursor and thus interact with a computer and the Internet, by a mental rather than bodily act (such as a hand moving a computer mouse).

Like Internet (and other) technologies, BCI technology is at some stage likely to be used for the purposes of committing crimes (if it has not already been so used). While there has been some scholarly attention paid to such possibilities and the way the criminal law might or should respond to them (Gurney, 2018; Haselager, 2013; Ienca & Haselager, 2016; Steinert, Bublitz, Jox, & Friedrich, 2019; Weinberger & Greenbaum, 2016; see also Chapter 4 of this volume), to my knowledge, no one has yet been charged with or convicted of an offense that they committed by mental act via BCI. In this chapter, I will consider the possibility of committing an intimate image abuse offense via a BCI. I will use a hypothetical example to make things more specific and tractable to analysis.

Unlike much of the work that has been done thus far in relation to BCIs and criminal responsibility, my analysis will involve a significant engagement with legislation and some engagement with case law. So, although the chapter involves an unusual topic, when considered from a methodological perspective, it might be thought of as traditional legal analysis. However, as will be seen, the novelty of the issues presented by my hypothetical example seems to nudge lawyers into territories that have thus far been more often visited by philosophers.

One reason to pick the example of intimate image abuse to work with is that it is a striking example of a relatively new form of offense, which may one day be committed in a novel way (via BCI). I will refer to such offenses as BCI intimate image abuse (BCIIIA). The connection between the defendant's brain and the Internet in relation to BCIIIA leads to some interesting questions about the criminal law's conceptualization of the boundaries of the person.

However, another reason to consider BCIIIA relates to the aforementioned commercial excitement. It seems that interaction with social media by way of BCI is being pursued by what is perhaps the most significant social media company: Facebook. It has been reported that Facebook has plans to allow users to interact with their services via BCI (*Thought experiments; Brains and machines,* 2018) and they have been hiring staff with skills in BCI technology (*Facebook has 60 people working on how to read your mind,* 2017). It is notable that Facebook has been a platform for intimate image abuse and the company is taking steps to address this problem (*Facebook asks users for nude photos in project to combat "revenge porn.",* 2017). Thus, the possible future combination of BCI and social media, through Facebook or some other online platform, would seem to raise the possibility of BCIIIA issues.

I will argue that it is unclear how the law might respond to BCIIIA and, more generally, to crime committed by way of BCI. This is very unfamiliar legal territory and the terrain raises questions about the law's concept of actus reus, a concept that is central to the criminal law. In this chapter, I will paint a picture of uncertainty about this central legal concept as the criminal law grapples with neurobionic action in cyberspace.

Thus, my focus is not on the *ethics* of the criminalization of BCIIIA, but on the *legal* uncertainties given the existing structure of the criminal law; my aim is to demonstrate that there are indeed significant uncertainties. As Brownsword, Scotford, and Yeung (2017) have noted, new technologies can be "legally disruptive" and "[e]stablished legal frameworks, doctrines, and institutions are being, and will be, challenged by new technological developments" (p. 8). In particular they claim that "long-standing doctrinal rules may require re-evaluation" (p. 8). This was, of course, the case in respect of Internet technologies, but my goal here is to demonstrate the potentially disruptive nature of BCIs and consider possibilities for re-evaluation.

While from a legal perspective BCIIIA is both perplexing and challenging, in a broader context, the response to neurobionic revenge porn under consideration here may be thought of as demonstrating one (legal) instance of the way that technological change may put a strain on existing social practices that have their origins in some earlier times. It is often said in respect to new technologies that it is worth starting to consider responses before any issues emerge, and I will endeavor to do that here.

A Novel Way of Offending

To understand the novelty of BCIIIA, it is useful to start by considering the question of what sort of things have traditionally been criminalized. While the law has sometimes criminalized *omissions* or even *status* (such as being a member of a terrorist organization[3]), most of those who appear in court are there to face charges as a direct result of some *bodily action* that they ought not to have performed such as throwing a punch or sending a fraudulent email by way of the bodily action of moving a hand controlling a computer mouse. One of the things that makes BCIIIA somewhat unusual is that it is not a crime of omission or a

---

[3] Crimes Act 1900 (NSW) s301 J.

status crime, yet it does not involve bodily action (at least as traditionally conceived). This does not seem to fit straightforwardly into the law's way of thinking about offenses.

To fully appreciate the novelty of BCIIIA as seen from the law's perspective, it is useful now to turn to the hypothetical example. My hypothetical example is of a person with a BCI that is implanted[4] in their brain, who uploads intimate images of another person onto social media without that person's consent. As the person who engages in the upload makes use of an implanted BCI, the offense might be thought of as being committed by a bionic person (a person who is part machine). More specifically the offense is neurobionic,[5] the bionic element being located in the brain, and that is why the title of the chapter refers to *neurobionic revenge porn* (an informal reference to a subcategory of BCIIIA).

To examine the possibility of BCIIIA, I will pick a jurisdiction to site my hypothetical example. One jurisdiction that has fairly recently criminalized intimate image abuse is New South Wales (NSW), Australia, and I will focus on the possible criminal liability of a person[6] who has nonconsensually uploaded intimate images onto social media from NSW by way of an implanted BCI.

It will be argued that a BCI-mediated offense could be prosecuted under NSW law and may lead to conviction. However, as suggested earlier the analysis of the hypothetical scenario raises some interesting questions concerning the nature of the conduct constituting the actus reus. Perhaps this is not surprising because as Heersmink (2013) has noted, BCIs provide "a new way of acting on the world" (p. 208). It would be surprising if legal rules that were created with the regulation of bodily action, omissions, and offenders' statuses in mind, easily transitioned to the regulation of neurobionic agents who at least sometimes act in cyberspace by way of BCI-mediated mental action. It will be seen that the law's unfamiliarity with the technology leads to the canvassing of legal possibilities that are novel and strange.

Brain–Computer Interfaces

The form of BCI that is of interest here is the type that allows control of a cursor by way of mental action. Such BCIs operate by way of the detection of neural activity associated with intentions. In essence, the BCI detects intentions from

---

[4] The various kinds of BCIs and the reasons for my choice of an implanted BCI will emerge later.

[5] Rosenfeld and Wong (2017) use this term in the context of BCIs.

[6] While of others have considered questions relating to the liability of BCI manufacturers (Burwell, Sample, & Racine 2017), I will not focus on such questions here.

neural activity associated with mental action and then endeavors to put them into effect—in the case of the hypothetical scenario, by electronically moving a cursor. It thus could enable a person to actively participate in social media by way of mental action and, where it functions properly, could be a useful way of communicating.

BCIs may be implanted in the agent's brain or onto the surface of the brain, or it may operate from a position external to the agent's scalp, operating by way of electrodes placed on the scalp.[7] While commercial applications of BCI technology often make use of external electrodes, the focus for implanted interfaces has been on those who for medical reasons have mobility or communication issues. Of course, brain implants involve surgery, and the risks of complications give reasons not to engage in such treatment except in exceptional circumstances. This may change one day, and implanted technology might become more prevalent and not confined to those whose medical condition creates a need for it. It is hard to predict what direction this technology may ultimately take and a variety of directions are actively being pursued (*Thought experiments: Brains and machines*, January 2018).

The focus of this chapter is on implanted BCI technology (the reason for this will emerge later and relates to the significance of implantation for the conduct constituting the actus reus). In my hypothetical scenario, an agent with an implant acts by way of the device in the following manner. The agent looks at a computer screen on which a cursor is visible and instead of using their hand to control a mouse or trackpad (and thereby the cursor), they perform the mental acts of *imagining* particular bodily movements to move the cursor in various directions or select text, or click on virtual icons.[8] The BCI detects the neural activity related to these acts of imagination and moves the cursor in accordance with what is imagined, as the different acts of imagination produce neural activity in different parts of the brain which can be detected and interpreted by the BCI. Thus, the BCI might be programmed to move the cursor left in response to a particular act of the imagination and right in response to another different act of imagination. The agent receives visual feedback from the screen, which demonstrates whether the act of imagination has led to the desired outcome (moving the cursor left or right).

While the primary focus of this paper is on a *properly functioning* BCI, it is worth noting that BCIs can malfunction. As noted by Weinberger and Greenbaum (2016, p. 150), BCIs[9] can fail to correctly detect intention. This

---

[7] For a more detailed explanation of these three types of interface, see Chapter 4 of this volume).

[8] The ways in which BCIs operate are developing, but this means is not particularly unusual. For an overview of BCI operation, see Heersmink (2013).

[9] Weinberger and Greenbaum use the term *brain-machine interface*, which refers to the same type of devices termed *BCI*, as used in in this chapter.

might result from signal noise that confuses the device or might even involve a predictive failure on the device's part (a failure to accurately predict intention in a way analogous to the way that predictive text on word processor sometimes gets things wrong). BCI technology may make use of artificial intelligence that may detect intention, but such technology is subject to the possibility of failure (Weinberger & Greenbaum, 2016, p. 150). Some have considered the possibility of hacking a BCI and yet another reason why a BCI might malfunction might be that it was hacked by a malicious programmer (see Chapter 3 in this volume; Ienca & Haselager, 2016).

Another issue is that the device might detect neural activity related to an intention and act upon it *prior* to the accused person being consciously aware of the intention (Weinberger & Greenbaum, 2016, p. 150). Some research suggests that where an agent intends to act, there is preconscious neural activity associated with the action. The research suggests that prior to conscious awareness of an intention to perform an act unconscious neural processes begins. As noted by Weinberger and Greenbaum (2016, p. 150), a BCI may initiate an action on the world based on preconscious neural activity. Such an action may be completed *prior to conscious awareness of the intention* in the mind of the agent.

Thus, it seems that there are three interesting possibilities for the law to consider in the context of BCIIIA:

1 The BCI *correctly* detects an intention to upload and uploads the images *after* the agent is consciously aware of the intention.
2 The BCI *wrongly* detects an intention to upload and uploads the images based on this error.
3 The BCI *correctly* detects an intention to upload and uploads the images *before* the agent is consciously aware of the intention.

All these possibilities merit scholarly consideration, but herein I will primarily focus on the first one (postconscious upload), and my primary hypothetical scenario addresses this situation. The reason for this focus (rather than a consideration of all three) relates to the large number of issues that would require discussion. The first possibility might seem to be the most straightforward of the three, but it is striking that *even that possibility* generates much that is of legal interest, and there is merit in starting with the relatively unproblematic case of postconscious upload.

In the course of focusing on the first scenario, there will be a brief mention of issues relating to second scenario, but I will leave the latter two scenarios for proper consideration at some later time. I will now explain the intimate image offense that is to be applied to the hypothetical scenario used here.

The Crimes Amendment (Intimate Images) Act 2017 (NSW)

In 2017, the NSW Parliament passed intimate image abuse legislation that, among other things, inserted a new section into the Crimes Act 1900 (NSW):

91Q
(1) A person who intentionally distributes an intimate image of another person:
  (a) without the consent of the person, and
  (b) knowing the person did not consent to the distribution or being reckless as to whether the person consented to the distribution, is guilty of an offence.
  Maximum penalty: 100 penalty units[10] or imprisonment for 3 years, or both.

For purposes of the current analysis, it is not necessary to explore the boundaries of what constitutes an intimate image, but, as an example, this would typically include an image of a person's private parts or of them engaged in a sex act.[11] Of more interest in relation to the context of BCIs is the definition of *distribute*, which, according to s91N(1), includes the following:

(a) send, supply, exhibit, transmit or communicate to another person, or
(b) make available for viewing or access by another person, whether in person or by electronic, digital or any other means

It is worth noting that the other person does not have to have actually seen the image as s91N(2) states: "A person may be regarded as having distributed an image to another person whether or not the other person views or accesses the image." In short, this legislation criminalizes the intentional, nonconsensual distribution of intimate images and imposes a maximum penalty of three years imprisonment for the crime.

A Hypothetical Scenario

It is now necessary to further describe my hypothetical example. The example involves a person in NSW, who has used an implanted BCI to control a cursor to engage in intimate image abuse. This person has been charged with the s91Q(1) offense and is alleged to have composed some text by way of BCI manipulation of a cursor, to have assembled some intimate images on the screen to be uploaded

---

[10] "Penalty units" are a means of calculating fines.
[11] S91N(1) provides a definition of what constitutes an intimate image.

(in the same manner and knowing that the person appearing in the images did not consent to distribution), and then used the BCI to manipulate the cursor to select an icon on the computer screen that says "upload," thereby making the images and text available to many people on social media.

The last step, which triggers the upload, involves imagining waving one's right hand.[12] The BCI is programmed to recognize this act of the imagination as signaling the accused person's intention to select the icon on the screen marked "upload," and the accused is aware that the device will upload after this icon is selected in that manner.

The accused imagines waving their right hand, and *after* this act of the imagination is consciously experienced by the accused, the BCI triggers upload. It triggers the upload because it has *correctly* detected their intention to select the icon on the screen marked "upload." I will refer to this as "postconscious upload."

Clearly there are some interesting evidential questions that relate to my hypothetical, but I will put those to one side and will assume for the purposes of discussion that credible evidence supporting the facts outlined in the hypothetical has been put forward, and the court accepts it as credible. Such evidence might come from a credible accused, expert evidence from a neuroscientist and neural engineer or other expert, and/or evidence of the circumstances of upload and prior history of the operation of the BCI.

For reasons of space and scope, I will not be considering the issue of at what stage the accused's conduct (perhaps prior to upload) amounts to an *attempt* to commit a s91Q(1) offense but will focus only on whether they have committed the *completed* offense. However, questions relating to neurobionic attempts may merit further analysis and may also generate some interesting questions.

Postconscious Upload: The BCI Correctly Detects Intention and Uploads after the Intention Has Formed in the Accused's Mind

In this section I will ask whether a person who engages in BCIIIA could be convicted under the legislation passed by the NSW Parliament. I will consider whether postconscious upload might constitute an offense under s91Q(1).

---

[12] One could imagine the BCI system being programmed to upload after a hand-wave is imagined twice with a delay between the first and second act of the imagination to reduce the risk of unintended upload. However, that would just make the second act of imagination the mental act that actually triggers the upload. There might still be a risk of unintended upload in a situation where the person assembles the images, composes the text, imagines the hand-wave once, and then deliberates about whether to imagine it for a second time to trigger the upload.

There seems to be nothing in the section to suggest that intentional transmission, communication, or making available requires bodily action. In fact, it seems quite possible for the prosecution to argue that the BCI mediation involved making available to others by "electronic, digital, or any other means." As the uploading person in the example was aware of the lack of consent of the victim, it seems quite likely that given sufficient evidence of intention (whether by way of confession, expert evidence in relation to the device, or other) that the prosecution could successfully argue that a s91Q(1) offense had been committed and that the offender should be convicted notwithstanding the use of a BCI. The wording of the s91Q(1) offense appears to be neutral as to the matter of whether the offense must be committed by BCI or bodily action. The NSW legislature, perhaps inadvertently, thus appears to have adopted a position of neurotechnological neutrality in this instance, and perhaps the issue of neurotechnological neutrality is worth bearing in mind for those engaged in drafting future legislation.

But what was the conduct constituting the actus reus? As will be seen, this is where the uncertainty arises.

What Was the Conduct That Constitutes the Actus Reus?

The actus reus of an offense (sometimes known as the external element or elements) relates to the defendant's conduct. This conduct must be voluntary (and not, for example, a reflex action). The mens rea is the guilty mind or mental state of the defendant (e.g., intention or recklessness). In respect of serious offenses, the prosecution must generally prove both the actus reus and mens rea, beyond reasonable doubt. These concepts are at the very heart of the criminal law and central to the way it is understood, taught and practiced. So, let us now try to identify the mens rea and actus reus in the hypothetical scenario.

The mens rea is the intention to distribute intimate images, knowing that the person did not consent or being reckless as to his or her consent to the distribution, and it seems there is nothing especially problematic in understanding this mens rea in the context of BCIIIA. If a person used their hand to move a computer mouse on a mousepad to upload and was charged with s91Q(1) offense, the prosecution would need to show that at the time of the bodily action (movement of the mouse), they intended to distribute the intimate images and that they knew the person was not consenting or was reckless as to consent to the distribution. In the case of BCIIIA, the prosecution would need to first identify the BCIIIA conduct constituting the actus reus (more on this shortly) and show that at that time the accused intended to upload the intimate images, knowing the person was not consenting or being reckless as to consent to the distribution.

Before moving on to actus reus, one technical point relating to BCIs is worth noting together with its significance for the law. As the technology stands at the moment, it is not possible to have a mens rea detector. No device exists that could identify a mental state as complex as intention to distribute intimate images, knowing that the person did not consent or being reckless as to his or her consent to the distribution. Current technology is much less sophisticated and can only detect mental states that are far simpler, such as a person imagining a hand-wave.

If one day it did become possible for a device identify the relevant knowledge and the intention to distribute and then automatically uploaded without any further mental step, then the law might be very hard pressed to identify an actus reus. Could the automatic process following the detection of the mens rea really be considered by the law to be an action? As noted earlier, the law says that the conduct constituting the actus reus must be voluntary (rather than say a bodily spasm), but could such an automatic process be said to be a voluntary? Is it even the *defendant's* conduct? It is not necessary to answer these questions at present as this form of detection is not a technical possibility. However, given the pace of technological change, it may be a question worth flagging for future consideration.

I will now return to currently possible technology and consider the conduct constituting the actus reus in the hypothetical example. While on the facts given in the hypothetical, the issue of mens rea may be unproblematic, the tricky part is identifying conduct constituting the actus reus.

In this respect, it is worth noting that there is a sense in which BCIIIA is very similar to more orthodox forms of intimate image abuse that involve a bodily action, in which a human hand controls a mouse on a mousepad. In BCIIIA, the BCI detects neural activity associated with intentions to control a cursor on a screen. In the more traditional bodily form of intimate image abuse, a similar result is achieved by a different, more organic method in which the agent's nervous system has a role in controlling the movement of a human hand and, thereby, a mouse on a mousepad to control a cursor. In both cases the agent just controls a cursor to engage in intimate image abuse.

However, part of the skill of a lawyer is in picking up on what are sometimes seemingly small distinctions between fact situations to mount an argument that is advantageous to their client (e.g., this might happen when trying to distinguish an inconvenient precedent that might otherwise be followed by the court). So notwithstanding there being significant similarity at some level between traditional and BCI-mediated intimate image abuse, the criminal law may well have to address and respond to arguments that highlight the way that BCIIIA is *different.* It is possible that a particular fact situation may make it advantageous to at least one side of a case, to highlight this difference and to put forward an argument involving a nontraditional view of the conduct constituting the actus reus (in fact, as will be seen shortly, none of the possibilities seem truly traditional). The court would then have to respond to this nontraditional view of conduct, and due to the novelty of the options that may be presented, one cannot be sure of the response.

Prior to moving to consider options for determining that conduct, I will consider a legal distinction relating to actus reus that is useful to bear in mind. The law distinguishes between offenses in which the actus reus involves just a form of *conduct* and those offenses that require that a specific *consequence* occur. Thus, driving offenses such as speeding just focus on the specific conduct of exceeding the speed limit, whereas the offense of murder criminalizes a more varied form conduct (e.g., stabbing, shooting, poisoning) that causes a specific consequence (the death of a person). If the victim does not die, there has been no murder.

It is worth considering whether s 91Q(1) criminalizes a specific form of conduct, conduct causing a particular consequence, or both. It seems at least arguable that "distribute" might be either be just conduct or conduct causing a consequence. As mentioned before, section 91 N(1)(b) includes "make available" in the definition of "distribute." It seems that "making available" requires a consequence of an act, and one does not make something available to someone unless it is actually available to them (perhaps available for download from a server in relation to the hypothetical scenario). However, it may be that under s91N(1) (b) (which is an alternative leg to the definition of "distribute") "send" could be argued to be conduct. So, it might be argued that one has sent a letter to someone before it arrives, even if it never arrives. On this view, you could send something to another person without it ever actually becoming available to them.

The act of sending might be argued to be the act of inserting the letter into the post box. Perhaps something analogous might be argued to be true of an email and perhaps the act of sending in this case is selecting the icon that says "send." So arguably, one has sent the email whether or not it ultimately becomes available for download by its intended recipient. I will not further delve into the technicalities of such a legal argument as it distracts from the main purpose of the discussion but from now on, I will assume that "distribute" might either be a specific form of conduct including sending or, in the law's terms, conduct causing a consequence—that is, making available.

With this distinction in mind, I will now canvas the possibilities for the conduct constituting the actus reus *working first on the assumption that the images have become available to another person (a consequence)* and we are looking for the *conduct* that caused them to become available. Then I will consider the possibility that "distribute" might be just conduct and briefly consider the legal difficulties that might emerge from this view.

If distribute is construed to be a consequence that requires the availability of the images to another person (perhaps on a server awaiting download), in the absence of a bodily movement, there seem to be four possibilities. The possibilities are as follows:

A. the *mental act* of imagining a hand-wave is the conduct constituting the actus reus (I will refer to this as "mental act").
B. the *neural activity* associated with the mental act of imagining a hand-wave is the conduct constituting the actus reus (I will refer to this as "neural activity").
C. the *flow of electrical signal* through the implanted wire is the conduct constituting the actus reus (I will refer to this as "flow of electrical signal").
D. the conduct constituting the actus reus is some combination of A, B, and C (I will refer to this as "combination").

Mental Act

An obvious possibility might be to view the mental act of imagining the hand-wave as the conduct constituting the actus reus. This makes some sense as it is that act of imagination that seems to take the place of a hand depressing a mouse to upload, and a court might be persuaded to regard this voluntary mental act, for the purposes of determining criminal liability, as somewhat analogous to a more traditional form of conduct constituting actus reus (i.e., a voluntary hand movement). Thus, although the device focuses on the neural activity associated with an imagined waving of one's hand and uses that to detect intention to select the relevant icon, perhaps the mental act of imagining waving could itself be thought of as the *mental* conduct that constitutes the actus reus. This would be a somewhat radical step for the law insofar as an act of the imagination now takes the place of bodily action in justifying an ascription of criminal responsibility.[13]

While this mental act approach does not lead to the embrace of pure thought-crime (in the situation being considered here the mental acts criminalized have effects in the world; i.e., they "make available"), perhaps the radical nature can be appreciated when considering the question of control. As O'Brolchain and Gordijn (2014, p. 167) have noted in the context of their work on BCIs, it may be that agents may have less control over their mental conduct than bodily action. Perhaps in at least in some circumstances, mental action is indeed more difficult to control than bodily action. It is hard to be sure about this as, to my knowledge, there is no comparative research[14] on the topic, but O'Brolchain and Gordijn's contention seems to be worth considering as due to the former opacity of our

---

[13] This may just be a limitation of currently available technology, and it may be that in future the manufacturers of BCIs may find other mental ways of acting to control BCIs.

[14] Such research may be methodologically challenging.

thought processes, the training of young people by their carers is focused primarily on control over bodily action, rather than control over mental action.[15] So perhaps it wouldn't be surprising if it turned out that people have less control over their mental action than bodily action. Because of this control issue, it might be thought to be a significant step for the criminal law to move toward the criminalization of mental conduct without bodily action.

It is worth also noting that in the particular instance here, crime is partly an imaginary phenomenon. In some circumstances (like in the hypothetical scenario), wrongful imaginings could thus lead to criminal liability.

If the law were to embrace the possibility of mental conduct as constituting actus reus, then the common law would need to find a principled way of determining the subset of mental acts that could be regarded as actus reus. While possible, this would require the development of some new legal principles, which although assisted by existing legal doctrine, would require something of a creative rethink of the criminal law.

In relation to the hypothetical scenario, it is also worth noting that the final act of imagination, namely, the hand-wave, is the last in a series of mental acts. If the temporal frame of the conduct constituting the acts reus were to be expanded backwards incorporating these earlier mental acts this would not help deal with the issue of the lack of traditional bodily act, as none of the earlier acts are bodily either.

Neural Activity

Perhaps a less appealing option might be for the courts to deem the conduct constituting the actus reus to be the *neural activity* associated with the imagined hand-wave. This might be thought of as a reductive approach to actus reus. One might think of particular parts of defendant's brains as *body parts* that respond by way of neural activity to certain mental triggers such as imaginary hand waves. So perhaps, for example, one's motor cortex might be thought of as a body part that one voluntarily "moves" by imagining a hand-wave.

The law has often been said to subscribe to a problematic form of dualism in which the mental and physical are radically different in nature and, and although failing to retain a traditional bodily movement-based notion of conduct constituting actus reus, the neural activity view would at least keep the conduct itself (rather than the voluntariness of it) firmly in the domain of physical events (those physical events being neural events in this instance).[16]

---

[15] Although perhaps some meditative or religious traditions might emphasize control over mental action to a greater extent.

[16] See Fox and Stein (2015) for a discussion of dualism and the law in the context of American jurisprudence.

This neural activity approach would require a principled way of identifying the neural activity that is to be criminalized in such a way as could be incorporated into legal doctrine. This may be somewhat challenging to and would again require something of a rethink of a concept at the heart of the criminal law.

If this view were embraced, one might then ask whether the conduct constituting the actus reus of crimes committed *without* the use of a BCI should also now be regarded as the neural activity associated with the with the initiation of bodily movement and, if not, why not. An advocate of the neural activity approach to actus reus should have a principled answer to this question.

A further problem with the neural activity approach is that as suggested earlier neural activity associated with action may precede conscious awareness of intention. An advocate of the neural activity approach to the conduct constituting actus reus would need to consider the question of *at what point* in the duration of the neural activity the relevant criminal conduct has taken place (as will be seen later some legal doctrine sees the timing of the actus reus as significant).

Perhaps this view just seems to create new problems without much in the way of benefit over the mental act approach from the last section, so it is worth examining the other potential candidate, a candidate which is perhaps also somewhat unattractive.

Flow of Electrical Signal

Perhaps the right way of thinking about an implanted BCI is to see it as *part of the agent* in something like the way that an arm with artificial parts (such as pins inserted into bones to hold them in place after an accident) is part of an agent or in the way that a fully prosthetic arm is also arguably part of the agent.[17] On this view, the BCI is the part of the agent that interacts with cyberspace (like a hand or mouth). It is not a tool that the agent uses.

So, an agent might interact with cyberspace by manipulation of a cursor by bodily movement involving an arm and hand on a mousepad, by a voice command involving a bodily action, which primarily involves the mouth, or through the transmission of signal through a wire. As on the current view the wire is part of the agent's body (a body that is partly organic and partly inorganic), the transmission of signal is something the agent *does*, rather than something that happens after they have acted. Thus, the agent might be thought of as a cyborg[18] or bionic whole comprised of biological tissue and an inorganic BCI rather than an unmodified human using a BCI as a tool.

---

[17] I do not mean to suggest that it might not be argued that an external BCI could not be seen as part of the agent, but it is not necessary to deal with this issue here.

[18] Warwick (2014) uses the term *cyborg* of those with BCIs and considers the possibility of human enhancement in that context.

On this view, the next possible candidate for the conduct constituting the actus reus is the flow of electrical signal. So, the relevant conduct might be thought of as the flow of electrical signal through the implanted wires. Unlike the moving of a hand to control a mousepad, it would thus be a visually imperceptible bodily action and unlike the voice command it would not be audible, but it would be no less a bodily action. One might say that the defendant "flowed signal" into cyberspace using the part of their body that is a wire.

But then where does the conduct end and consequences of the conduct begin? One possibility might be that the conduct ended after signal had flowed beyond the scalp of the agent, and everything after that was the result of the conduct. However, this seems somewhat arbitrary. The flow of electrical signal view seems to raise questions about the criminal law's conception of the boundaries of the criminal actor. One might wonder where defendants end and the devices they use, or even cyberspace, begins.[19]

A further issue with this view would be the difficulty of finding a principled way of delineating the subset of electrical signal that could constitute the conduct constituting the actus reus, in a way that could be incorporated into legal doctrine. Again, this may be challenging for lawyers.

Combination

Yet another approach would be to adopt a combination of mental act, neural activity, and flow of electrical signal, as the conduct constituting the actus reus. Thus, the relevant conduct would be composite in nature.[20] Depending on the combination selected, such an approach might have different strengths and weaknesses, but a problem with this approach is that it might create even greater complexity in an area that is already somewhat confusing from the perspective of the criminal law. However, it must be acknowledged that the courts might ultimately pursue some form of combination approach.

One thing to note after considering these four options (mental act, neural activity, flow of electrical signal and combination) is the uncertainty that remains. Perhaps the first option, mental act, is the most appealing but even that seems strange in the context of the existing criminal law, and a lawyer preparing to argue a case would be working in an area with significantly less guidance from legal authorities than may normally be available. Perhaps in these circumstances

---

[19] For a discussion of and references to some philosophical literature concerning the boundaries of agency, see Klein et al. (2015, p. 16).

[20] A combination of A and B might be something analogous to what in philosophy of mind has been referred to as dual aspect theory, in which "a living human brain is not just a physical object, but is rather an entity with two distinct aspects, namely a physical or objective aspect as a brain, and a mental or subjective aspect as a conscious mind" (Hodgson, 2012, p. 56). However, it is worth noting that there is already both a mental and physical aspect to actus reus: to satisfy the actus reus requirement of an offense, a bodily movement must be voluntary, thereby importing a mental aspect.

it might be useful to turn to the work of those philosophers who have considered related issues to construct a legal argument, but I will leave consideration of such a possibility for another occasion.[21]

Perhaps the Actus Reus Is a Form of Conduct Rather Than a Consequence

Before moving on, it is worth remembering that as suggested earlier perhaps "send" is *conduct* rather than a consequence. That view seems even more troubling in the context of BCIs. I will not go through all the possibilities for conduct but simply focus on mental act as one such possibility. If the actus reus is conduct, that conduct is the act of sending, and the act of sending is constituted by imagining a hand-wave, then the crime is *completed* as soon as the hand-wave has been imagined. If one imagines the BCI failing to detect or transmit signal, then there would be no effect on the external world, but *nonetheless the defendant would be guilty of a completed offense* (not a mere attempt). This seems to involve the criminalization of a pure form of mental action, and perhaps the troubling implications of this might lead a court to prefer to favor an approach to statutory interpretation that would see "send" as requiring some external consequence.

A Theoretical Issue

In relation to the facts under consideration here, what has been considered in the preceding sections might be thought of as being of a somewhat theoretical nature since earlier I argued that the defendant might be convicted notwithstanding the neurobionic dimension. However, it is possible to imagine scenarios where questions concerning the nature of the act constituting the actus reus issue might force itself into judicial consideration.

The Australian High Court has confirmed that mens rea and actus reus must coincide.[22] This is what is often referred to as the temporal coincidence rule. If while engaged in careful driving one accidentally killed someone, and then later on, believing they were still alive and one formed an intent to kill them, then there would be no temporal coincidence between the actus reus and the mens rea and thus no crime of murder.

However, there are some cases where a strict application of the temporal coincidence rule has not been followed, and flexibility on the issue has been displayed

---

[21] The concept of the "extended mind" (Clark & Chalmers, 1998) may be worth considering in this respect.

[22] *Meyers v R* (1997).

in judicial reasoning. In a Privy Council case that could have strongly persuasive influence in Australia, *Thabo Meli v R* (1954), the accused, while executing a plan to kill the victim, hit him on the head and then, wrongly thinking he was dead, rolled him over the edge of a cliff. The unconscious victim later died of exposure at the base of the cliff. It was argued by the accused that the intention to kill had ceased before the act causing death (one cannot intend to kill a person who one thinks is dead), and thus there was no temporal coincidence of mens rea and actus reus. However, the court held that this was really one series of acts, and it was not appropriate to divide up the acts in the way argued by the accused. Thus, temporal coincidence might occur at some point during the series of acts. This case seems to indicate a judicial willingness to sometimes avoid the rigidity of the temporal coincidence rule where the facts make it seem appropriate to do so.

I will now consider a variation of the hypothetical scenario, which is one of BCI malfunction on the assumption that "distribute" requires causation of a consequence. Consider the following BCIIIA case. The accused decided to upload the images and imagined the hand-wave to perform the upload *but the BCI malfunctioned and failed to detect the intention to select the "upload" icon and failed to upload at that time.* Later on, the accused tried to hide the forensic trail back to him as uploader by performing some deletion of files and, in the course of that process, the BCI wrongly detected an intention to select the "upload" icon and uploaded the intimate images.

There would now be an issue of temporal coincidence and to consider the issue the court would need to consider what the conduct constituting the actus reus was. It seems possible that the opposing parties to the case might differ in their view of the relevant conduct constituting the actus reus—the prosecution might see one view of conduct constituting actus reus as advantageous to them and argue for that, and the defense might prefer another view. Thus, what may have been considered to be a theoretical question would become a question that the court would need to answer. I will not attempt to consider how the courts might respond, my point is merely to show that to address an argument about temporal coincidence, the court might need to decide the nature of neurobionic actus reus. So perhaps there might be a factual situation in which the discussion in the preceding sections might have a practical application in the determination of a case and perhaps lead to new doctrine.

Jettison Actus Reus?

In light of these issues, a radical view might suggest that the law needs to transform such that some crimes can be committed by mens rea alone without the need for an actus reus. But this way of thinking seems illiberal. Surely a liberal state should not be engaged in criminalizing intentions *without any associated actions* and perhaps few theorists (or practitioners) would be happy to jettison the actus reus requirement.

It seems that none of possible approaches to the conduct constituting actus reus comes without something of a rethink. Perhaps the difficulties which have just been highlighted might lead us to ponder a much larger question relating to the criminal law's relationship with the human condition. Is it just a contingent feature of how human agency has thus far tended to have been exercised—by way of bodily action—that it makes sense for the law draw the distinction it does between the mens rea and actus reus? Perhaps the possibility of acting by way of BCI draws attention to this contingency.

Conclusion

All of the neurobionic options seem to generate new questions about the right way of thinking of the actus reus element of a criminal offense. They seem to challenge a central concept in criminal law theory, that of the conduct capable of constituting the actus reus, which is often thought to be either bodily action (as conventionally conceived), omission, or a status, rather than one or more of non-traditional options considered here.

When the question of the nature of neurobionic actus reus is forced into judicial consideration, the law will no doubt find a way of adapting. In fact, significant adaptation may be required, and it is possible that there will be important downstream consequences for subsequent jurisprudence and criminal law theory.

But in the meantime, although it seems that a person accused of BCIIIA could be convicted of the offense under consideration here, it is unclear what the court might deem to be the conduct constituting actus reus. If one imagines the scope of criminal behavior that might conceivably be committed by way of BCI, this may one day become a significant issue of for the criminal law and, perhaps, one that ranges from computer-based offenses to the control of physical objects to commit assault, murder, and a variety of other offenses.

Acknowledgments

I thank Andre Van Schaik, Gail Mason, Arlie Loughan, Andrew Dyer, Marcello Ienca, Richard Heersmink, Eric Sellers, Carolyn Mackay, Richard Campbell, Andrew Dyer, Nicole Vincent, Thomas Nadelhoffer, students of the 2018 neurolaw class at Macquarie University, and the participants at my 2018 presentation to the members of the Sydney Institute of Criminology.

References

Australian Legal and Constitutional Affairs References Committee. (2016). Phenomenon colloquially referred to as "revenge porn." Retrieved from https://www.aph.gov.au/Parliamentary_Business/Committees/Senate/Legal_and_Constitutional_Affairs/Revenge_porn/Report

Brownsword, R., Scotford, E., & Yeung, K. (2017). Law, regulation, and technology: The field, frame and focal questions. In *The Oxford handbook of law, regulation and technology* (pp. 3–40). Oxford, England: Oxford University Press.

Burwell, S., Sample, M., & Racine, E. (2017). Ethical aspects of brain computer interfaces: A scoping review. *BMC Medical Ethics, 18*(60), 1–11.

Clark, A., & Chalmers, D. (1998). The extended mind. *Analysis, 58*(1), 7–19.

Crimes Act 1900 (NSW). Retrieved from http://www8.austlii.edu.au/cgi-bin/viewdb/au/legis/nsw/consol_act/ca190082/

Fox, D., & Stein, A. (2015). Dualism and doctrine. *Indiana Law Journal, 90*, 975–1010.

Gurney, D. (2018). Killer robot arms: A case-study in brain–computer interfaces and intentional acts. *Minds and Machines, 28*(4), 775–785.

Haselager, P. (2013). Did I do that? Brain–computer interfacing and the sense of agency. *Minds and Machines, 23*(3), 405–418.

Heersmink, R. (2013). Embodied tools, cognitive tools and brain–computer interfaces. *Neuroethics, 6*(1), 207–219.

Hodgson, D. (2012). *Rationality + Consciousness = Free Will*. Oxford: Oxford University Press.

Ienca, M., & Haselager, P. (2016). Hacking the brain: Brain–computer interfacing technology and the ethics of neurosecurity. *Ethics and Information Technology, 18*(2), 117–129.

Klein, E., Brown, T., Sample, M., Truitt, A. R., & Goering, S. (2015). Engineering the brain: Ethical issues and the introduction of neural devices. *Hastings Center Report, 45*(6), 26–35.

McGlynn, C., Rackley, E., & Houghton, R. (2017). Beyond "revenge porn": The continuum of image-based sexual abuse. *Feminist Legal Studies, 25*(1), 25–46.

Meyers v R. (1997). HCA 43.

O'Brolchain, F., & Gordijn, B. (2014). Brain–computer interfaces and user responsibility. In G. Grubler & E. Hildt (Eds.), *Brain-computer-interfaces in their ethical, social and cultural contexts* (pp. 163–182). Dordrecht, The Netherlands: Springer.

Rosenfeld, J. V., & Wong, Y. T. (2017). Neurobionics and the brain–computer interface: Current applications and future horizons. *Medical Journal of Australia, 206*(8), 363–368.

Steinert, S., Bublitz, C., Jox, R., & Friedrich, O. (2019). Doing things with thoughts: Brain-computer interfaces and disembodied agency. *Philosophy & Technology, 32*(3), 457–482.

Thabo-Meli v R. (1954) 1 WLR 228.

The Crimes Amendment (Intimate Images) Act 2017 (NSW). Retrieved from https://www.legislation.nsw.gov.au/#/view/act/2017/29/sch1

The Economist. (2018, January 6). The next frontier: Neurotechnology.

The Economist. (2018, January 6). Thought experiments; Brains and machines.

The Guardian. (2017, April 20). Facebook has 60 people working on how to read your mind. Retrieved from https://www.theguardian.com/technology/2017/apr/19/facebook-mind-reading-technology-f8

The Guardian. (2017, November 8). Facebook asks users for nude photos in project to combat "revenge porn." Retrieved from https://www.theguardian.com/technology/2017/nov/07/facebook-revenge-porn-nude-photos

Warwick, K. (2014). The cyborg revolution. *Nanoethics, 8*(3), 263–273.

Weinberger, S., & Greenbaum, D. (2016). Are BMI prosthetics uncontrollable Frankensteinian monsters?" *Brain-Computer Interfaces, 3*(3), 149–155.

PART II
PUNISHING PEOPLE

9

Folk Jurisprudence and Neurointervention

An Interdisciplinary Investigation

*Thomas Nadelhoffer, Daniela Goya-Tocchetto, Jennifer Cole Wright,
and Quinn McGuire*

Introduction

Because neuroethics is a relatively new field, there are plenty of unexplored (and underexplored) issues in need of philosophical and empirical investigation. For present purposes, our focus will be on a cluster of related issues pertaining to legal competency (e.g., the competence to stand trial or to be executed), on the one hand, and neurointerventions (e.g., using medication to forcibly[1] restore competence, reduce violent impulsivity, or even decrease racial bias), on the other hand. Given the number of potential moral quandaries that arise on these fronts, we think this cluster of topics offers fertile ground for interdisciplinary research. For while legal scholars, legal decision makers, legislators, and forensic psychiatrists have been wrestling with these issues for some time,[2] philosophers

---

[1] For the studies we will be discussing, our focus is on compelled treatment (e.g., forcibly medicating someone against their wishes to make them competent to stand trial) and mandated treatment (e.g., making treatment a necessary condition for judges and jurors). The difference is that in the former cases, the actors being medicated have no choice in the matter. In the case of mandatory treatment, the legal actors could always refuse to participate in the trial. Problems arise in both contexts. There are similar issues with coerced, pressured, and even some forms of seemingly voluntary treatment, but we will not be discussing these forms of treatment in this chapter.

[2] You can find discussions about competency in the common law literature as early as Blackstone in the 18th century (Blackstone, 1916). The issue concerning the moral and legal status of involuntary medication, while more recent, is also well traveled. While there is no agreement about whether the courts should have the authority to use forcible medication (e.g., Caplan, 2006; Hayes, 2004; Heilbrun & Kramer, 2005; Melton, Petrila, Poythress, & Slobogin, 1997; Morse, 2003, 2011; Slobogin, 2006), there is evidence of a not-infrequently held belief that forcible medication is a "clear and resounding success" when it comes to restoring competency (Cochrane, Herbel, Reardon, & Lloyd, 2013).

Thomas Nadelhoffer, Daniela Goya-Tocchetto, Jennifer Cole Wright, and Quinn McGuire, *Folk Jurisprudence and Neurointervention* In: *Neurointerventions and the Law*. Edited by: Nicole A Vincent, Thomas Nadelhoffer, and Allan McCay, Oxford University Press (2020). © Oxford University Press 2020
DOI: 10.1093/oso/9780190651145.001.0009

and social psychologists have arrived relatively late to the debate—a shortcoming we hope to mitigate in the following pages.[3]

In this chapter, our primary task is to report findings from three studies that explore people's beliefs and attitudes about a number of issues concerning neurointervention and the law across several scenarios—scenarios that have been discussed in the neuroethics literature. These scenarios include (a) requiring judges and jurors to use medications to minimize their implicit racial bias, (b) forcibly medicating dangerous inmates to minimize their dangerousness, (c) giving convicted offenders pills that increase prosocial behavior (and reduce antisocial behavior), and (d) forcibly medicating inmates to restore their competency for execution or even their basic competency to stand trial. While some cases involve noninvasive pharmacological neurointerventions, other cases involve either more traditional treatment modalities (e.g., cognitive behavioral therapy) or more radical modalities (e.g., invasive brain implants).

To set the stage for our investigation, we first briefly survey some landmark American legal cases pertaining to mental competency and explore a few of the ethical issues that arise in this context. Next, we discuss some of the background assumptions that animate our present project—for example, the view that data about common sense morality is important for philosophers interested in nonideal theory building in neuroethics (and elsewhere). Having placed our metaphilosophical and methodological cards on the table, we present the results from our three studies. Lastly, we discuss some shortcomings and limitations of our present studies and consider some future avenues of research before offering some concluding remarks.

Our overarching goal in what follows is to discuss how potential legal decision makers view the kinds of issues that are already being debated in academic journals and in the popular press when it comes to legal competency, forcible medication, and the relationship between neuroscience and the law more generally. For on our view, understanding the boundaries of common sense morality and folk jurisprudence will help build bridges between our preferred moral, legal, and political theories and public policy. In addition to contributing to the philosophical and empirical literature on neurointervention, we also hope our studies make a practical contribution by providing some preliminary insight into public views concerning both when and why neurointerventions may be used in the criminal law. And while neither philosophical theories nor decisions about public policy *must* track these folk beliefs, we nevertheless think that how people ordinarily think about neurointerventions (for better or worse) ought to be taken into consideration by philosophers, judges, and policy makers alike.

---

[3] For recent work by philosophers, see Garasic (2013), Vincent (2014), and Whiting (2015). For some earlier work by psychologists, see Robinson and Darley (1995), Ghetti and Redlich (2001), Grisso (1996), and Pescosolido, Monahan, Link, Stueve, and Kikuzawa (1999), although it is worth mentioning that much of the empirical work on folk jurisprudence focuses on people's beliefs about the death penalty, juvenile responsibility, and the insanity defense, respectively.

Setting the Stage: Competency, Therapy, and Neurointervention

As recently as December 2, 2015, a hearing was held in Maine concerning the mental competency to stand trial of Leroy Smith III—a 29-year-old man charged with murdering, dismembering, and burying his father.[4] Because Smith suffers from schizophrenia but refuses to take medications, his attorneys argued that he wasn't competent to stand trial. Having considered the facts of the case, on January 8, 2016, Justice Donald Marden sided with the defense in finding Smith incompetent. However, to remedy the situation, Justice Marden ordered that he be forcibly medicated to restore his competency—an authority vested in the court by a relatively new law in Maine that allows for involuntarily medicating defendants to restore their competency so long as (a) important state interests are at stake, (b) the treatment is "substantially likely" to render the defendant competent to proceed, and (c) the treatment is "unlikely" to produce side effects that would further interfere with the defendant's ability to assist his in his defense. If Smith's competency is restored, his trial will re-commence, and he will be called upon to account for the criminal charges against him.

While Smith's case is new, the underlying ethical issues are not. There are long-standing, thorny problems that arise when it comes to competency and the law. In 1835 Richard Lawrence attempted to assassinate American President Andrew Jackson but was later deemed incompetent to stand trial, which set off a controversy at the time (*United States v. Lawrence*, 1835). By the late 1800s, however, the recognition that competency should play an essential role in the criminal law was widely shared. One federal court expressed the sentiment by stating,

> [It is] fundamental that an insane person can neither plead to arrangement, be subjected to a trial, or, after trial, receive judgment, or, after judgment, undergo punishment; to the same effect are all common law authorities . . . it is not "due process of law" to subject an insane person to trial upon an indictment involving liberty or life (*Youtsey v. United States*, 1899).

Judges have nevertheless continued to wrestle with the problem of competency up to the present day. Consider, for example, *Dusky v. United States* (1960). Milton

---

[4] For details of this ongoing case, see http://www.pressherald.com/2016/01/08/gardiner-man-accused-of-killing-dismembering-father-to-be-involuntarily-medicated/. In the United States of America, the case of *Sell v. United States* (2003) set the stage for forced medication to restore competence to stand trial cases To this day, *Sell*'s effect seems to be that more nor less forced medication orders are made and upheld. As Susan A. McMahon (2013) argues, "the involuntary medication of nondangerous defendants, predicted [in *Sell*] to be a 'rare' occurrence, has instead become routine." (p. 389) The fear that this was going to happen was expressed by commentators almost immediately after *Sell* was decided (e.g., see Gerbasi & Scott, 2004). More recently, Mounia Rhoulam (2016) suggests that the feature of *Sell* that accounts for this is that the key term "serious crime" is too vague, and in particular because courts don't adequately take into account the defendant's liberty interests in assessing seriousness.

Dusky was a 33-year-old-man charged with assisting in the kidnapping and rape of an underage female. Despite evidence that Dusky was suffering from schizophrenia at the time of the trial, he was nevertheless found competent to stand trial. Dusky was eventually found guilty and later sentenced to 45 years in prison. His attorney claimed that his conviction should be reversed on grounds that he was incompetent during his trial—a claim that eventually made its way to the U.S. Supreme Court. The Court's decision in the case established criteria for determining whether a defendant is competent to stand trial.

According to the Court, "the test [for competency] must be whether he [the defendant] has sufficient present ability to consult with his attorney with a reasonable degree of understanding and a rational as well as factual understanding of the proceedings against him" (*Dusky v. United States*, 1960). On this view, regardless of whether a defendant was sane when he committed an offense, the defendant must be competent during his trial. Because the Court found that the brief mental status examination used in Dusky's original trial was insufficient for determining competency, his case was remanded for retrial. Dusky subsequently received a reduced sentence of 20 years.

Ford v. Wainwright (1986) is another landmark case that shaped our current understanding of competency in the law. Alvin Bernard Ford was convicted of murdering a police officer in 1974 and sentenced to death. While waiting for execution, Ford started displaying increasingly odd behavior—for example, referring to himself as Pope John Paul III, claiming to have thwarted a Ku Klux Klan conspiracy to bury dead inmates inside the walls of prisons, and boasting that he personally appointed nine new justices to the Florida Supreme Court. Despite evidence that Ford was suffering from paranoid schizophrenia, a panel of three psychiatrists nevertheless found him sufficiently competent to be executed. Ford's attorneys appealed and the case made its way to U.S. Supreme Court.

At the outset, the Court made a preliminary finding that executing an inmate who is incompetent would constitute "cruel and unusual punishment" (in violation of the Eighth Amendment). They also found that Florida's procedures for making determinations of competency were inadequate. In the wake of the Court's ruling, Ford was transferred to a psychiatric facility, where he was deemed to be incompetent to execute. He was subsequently detained, forcibly medicated, and successfully treated for schizophrenia.[5] By 1989, a federal judge

---

[5] It is worth noting that the standards for "successful treatment" in the legal system are not the same as standards in nonforensic settings. So, just because an offender has been rendered sufficiently competent to stand trial, it doesn't mean that the offender is cured, satisfied with what has been done to him, etc. The bar for legal competence is fairly low and the state has wide latitude when it comes to forcibly medicating people. We may end up unwittingly forcibly medicating a defendant like Smith who could be innocent at the end of the day. But that is a worry for another day.

ruled that Ford was sufficiently competent to be executed, and Ford was sent back to death row where he died at the age of 37, although not by execution but due to natural causes while awaiting his execution.

Cases like these raise a host of important questions at the crossroads of philosophy, psychiatry, law, and public policy. Because so many people who have compromised competency of one sort or another (e.g., to stand trial, to be executed) suffer from schizophrenia, the most common medications used for restoring competency are antipsychotics, which are well-known to have adverse side effects. This raises serious concerns about whether the state should have the authority to forcibly medicate defendants to render them competent to stand trial or competent for execution, given the likelihood of these adverse effects. But as we previously noted, the U.S. Supreme Court, especially in more recent competency cases such as *Washington v. Harper* (1990), *Riggins v. Nevada* (1992), *Sell v. United States* (2003), and *Panetti v. Quarterman* (2007), continues to give states pretty wide latitude in how to resolve this thorny problem.

Not all states have responded in the same way. In the wake of *Perry v. Louisiana* (1990), for instance, the Supreme Court of Louisiana found that forcibly medicating inmates to restore their competency for execution violates the Louisiana State Constitution's prohibition against cruel and unusual punishment (among other things). As a result, the practice isn't permitted in Louisiana. In Arkansas and Maine, on the other hand, courts have the authority to forcibly restore competence for the purposes of execution—an authority they are not afraid to use, as evidenced by our earlier discussion of Leroy Smith III.[6]

While competence and forcible medication are important issues in their own right, they also interest us in part because they tie into broader discussions about neurointervention (the topic of the present volume). After all, legal decision makers, criminal offenders, and defendants aren't the only potential targets for neurointervention. For instance, if we could use safe and effective medications to reduce implicit racial bias in judges and jurors or to increase prosocial behavior in inmates (see the following discussion for details), then we could presumably also at some stage have to consider whether it would be warranted to require use of similar medications by police officers, witnesses, victims, and maybe even in the general population.

Although we will not explore the vast range of considerations that might put us on the slippery slope from endorsing the use of neurointerventions in

---

[6] See also *Singleton v. Norris* (2003) for the legislative and judicial history of the approach adopted by Arkansas.

the criminal justice system to endorsing their (potentially mandatory) use in nonforensic contexts, we take it that there is a real potential that we could find ourselves on a troubling slippery slope, nonetheless. Pandora has already been let out of the box, as they say, when it comes to neurointerventions and the law. So, it's hard to see ourselves turning back. The legal tides have already turned. The question we now face is, How should we, as a society, regulate and circumscribe the use of neurointerventions (both within the court system and in society more generally)? This is obviously a very complex question. It's no surprise then that we won't be answering it in this single book chapter! Instead, we simply try to fill in a few of the empirical pieces that are needed before we will be in the position to answer the question before us.

Neuroethics and Common Sense Morality

Given the gravity of the issues we've been examining, it is unsurprising that a lot of ink has been spilled when it comes to how society ought to respond. However, our goal in this chapter is not to take a stand on this normative issue. Instead we set for ourselves a descriptive task that we nevertheless believe has normative implications—namely, to develop a better understanding of how people ordinarily think about the neuroethical issues that arise when it comes to competence, forcible medication, and neurointerventions more generally. This is a goal that is admittedly driven by several controversial background assumptions which we do not have the space to adequately defend here.

We nevertheless want to pause to place our metaphilosophical and methodological cards on the table. First, we have a preference for nonideal theory building in moral, political, and legal philosophy. In this respect, we agree with Wiens (2015) that ideal principles designed with little regard for feasibility considerations do not provide an appropriate target for real world reforms and are ill suited for comparative evaluations amongst feasible possible worlds.[7] So, while we are interested in first-order philosophical theorizing, we also think philosophers should give serious thought to how to get from their preferred theories to public policy (at least in moral, legal, and political philosophy).

Second, we believe that folk intuitions, attitudes, and beliefs are relevant when it comes to nonideal theory building even if just as starting points of our investigations or as potential impediments that may need to be overcome when it

---

[7] For some excellent work on the relationship between philosophy and public policy, see Wolf (2011).

comes to getting from theory to practice. In the case of the law and public policy, we believe data about folk jurisprudence both can and should play a role. At a minimum, we need to be aware of any tensions or contradictions that may exist between philosophical theory, legal code, and community standards (for further discussion, see Robinson & Darley, 1995).

Third, we agree that "too many moral philosophers and commentators on moral philosophy . . . have been content to invent their psychology or anthropology from scratch" (Darwall Gibbard, & Railton, 1997, pp. 34–35). Accordingly, we wanted to explore the intuitions that interest us in a controlled and systematic way. This methodological commitment is one of the unifying forces behind much of the recent work that has been done in experimental philosophy.[8] It is also a commitment that animates our present investigation.

No doubt, for those who do not share our background assumptions, this may seem like a philosophically pointless enterprise (e.g., Bengson, 2013; Cullen, 2010; Deutsch, 2010; Ichikawa, 2011; Kauppinen, 2007; Ludwig, 2010; Sosa, 2007, 2010). But that is a debate for another day. For now, let it suffice for us to say that we are pluralists both when it comes to what counts as philosophy and when it comes to what counts as philosophically relevant or important. On our view, given that philosophers have different interests, goals, and methodologies—which we believe is a good thing—we wouldn't expect data about folk intuitions or common sense morality to be relevant to *every* philosophical project. But at the same time, we reject the view that these types of empirical data are uniformly irrelevant *no matter* what interests or goals a particular philosopher may have.

Moreover, it is not as if the assumptions that undergird our own approach are philosophically novel (even if the methodologies we use may be new). Henry Sidgwick (1974/2011) once argued that one of the primary goals of ethical theorizing is to "make explicit the implied premises of our common moral reasoning" (p. 163). Because we, too, believe that cataloging and understanding people's beliefs about ethical issues is an important task for moral philosophers, our present focus will be on the views about competency, forced medication, and neurointervention that are embedded in common sense morality. And while empirical data about folk jurisprudence are unlikely to straightaway *solve* any debates in neuroethics, we nevertheless believe that these data can *inform* (and perhaps even *constrain*) our philosophical theorizing—especially for those who have joint interests in theory and public policy.

---

[8] For an overview of the various goals and methods adopted by experimental philosophers, see Nadelhoffer and Nahmias (2007) and Knobe and Nichols (2008).

Three Preliminary Studies

Study 1

The materials for Study 1 were uploaded to Qualtrics—an online survey company. Participants were 354 people recruited through Amazon's Mechanical Turk (MTurk) service and paid $1 each for completing the survey. Participants had to be at least 18 years of age and living in the United States. Fifty-three percent of participants ($n = 191$) reported being male, and 47% ($n = 163$), female. Participants reported being represented by the following ethnicities: Black/African American ($n = 25$), Asian/Pacific Islander ($n = 21$), White/Caucasian ($n = 286$), Native American ($n = 2$), and Hispanic/Latino ($n = 20$). Each participant was randomly assigned to one of the six conditions we will discuss below.

One goal we had for Study 1 was to make our materials as ecologically valid as possible (given the limitations of vignette-based paradigms). So, we developed three cases that were based on recent news stories we came across in the popular press. The first case focused on research that suggests that drugs known as beta-blockers can be used to reduce implicit (although not explicit) bias.[9] The second case focused on using pharmacological interventions to decrease impulsive violence among both juvenile and adult inmates. Banner (2014) served as the inspiration for our second case. The third case was based on research that suggests that the neurotransmitter oxytocin can increase pro-social behavior (and decrease antisocial behavior). Potter (2014) served as the inspiration for our third case. All of the names from the original news stories were changed. Moreover, because we needed the treatments in these cases to have the same name, we made one up and used it consistently across conditions (and across studies).[10]

We also wanted to see how sensitive people's judgments are to whether a given neurointervention is described as having minimal versus more adverse side effects. So, each of the cases had a "low side effect" condition and an "adverse side effect" condition (see the following discussion). Next, we also wanted to explore people's intuitions about neurointerventions both inside and outside the law. So, while the racial bias and impulsive violence cases involve legal actors—judges and jurors versus inmates, respectively—the so-called morality pill we discuss in the third case involves the use of neurointerventions by the general public.

---

[9] The article that served as the inspiration for our first case can be found here: http://www.ox.ac.uk/news/2012-03-08-drug-reduces-implicit-racial-bias-study-suggests

[10] We opted for Lombrossic as a nod to Cesare Lombrosso—the controversial founding father of criminology and one of the first scholars to develop a biological account of criminality.

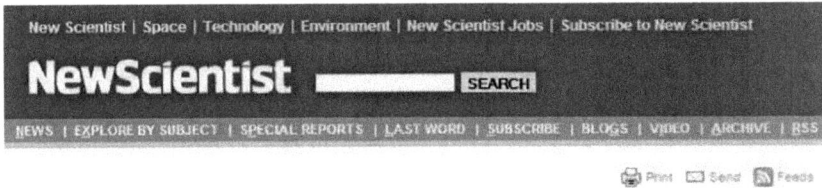

Figure 9.1. Mock news banner

Each participant received only one of the six possible cases and was then asked to record her level of agreement with a series of statements (see the following discussion). To increase the likelihood that participants took themselves to be reading an actual news story rather than a made-up vignette, we included a banner from *New Scientist* with each case (see Figure 9.1)—a strategy that has been used in previous studies on people's judgments about the relationship between free will, responsibility, and advances in neuroscience (e.g., Schooler, Nadelhoffer, Nahmias, & Vohs, 2014; Shariff et al., 2014). Because some deception is involved with this approach, participants were debriefed afterward and told that while the stories they read were based partly on recent events or stories, these stories were nevertheless modified to suit the ends of our present investigation. We also provided participants with a link to the original story upon which their vignette was based.

Here are the cases (with two conditions each) along with the statements participants received as part of Study 1.

Racial Bias Case

New Drug Reduces Implicit Racial Bias By Julia Reed

Taking a recently developed medication called Lombrossic can affect a person's subconscious attitudes towards race, a team of ethicists, psychiatrists and psychologists at Oxford University has found. In a study published in Psychopharmacology, researchers gave 18 people the drug Lombrossic and 18 people a placebo and found that the Lombrossic group scored significantly lower on the Implicit Attitude Test into subconscious racial bias—a standard test for testing subconscious racial attitudes. There was no significant difference in the groups' explicit attitudes to other races.

Lombrossic blocks activation in the peripheral 'autonomic' nervous system and in the area of the brain implicated in fear or emotional responses. The researchers believe Lombrossic reduced implicit racial basis because such bias is based on automatic, non-conscious fear responses, which the drug blocks.

Sylvia Smith, lead author and experimental psychologist at Oxford University, said: "Our results offer new evidence about the processes in the brain that shape implicit racial bias. Implicit racial bias can occur even in people with a sincere belief in equality. Given the key role that such implicit attitudes appear to play in discrimination against other ethnic groups, our findings are also of considerable ethical interest."

She added: "Many people with medical conditions are probably already on drugs which affect subconscious bias and more research is needed into how drugs which affect our nervous system affect our moral attitudes and practices."

Professor Jeff Bilford of Oxford University's Faculty of Philosophy, a co-author, added: "Such research raises the tantalizing possibility that our unconscious racial attitudes could be modulated using drugs, a possibility that requires careful ethical analysis. Biological research aiming to make people morally better has a dark history. And Lombrossic is not a pill to cure racism. But given that Lombrossic may have 'moral' side effects, we at least need to better understand what these effects are."

One issue that is raised by this research is whether the state has the authority to forcibly[11] medicate judges and jurors with Lombrossic in order to minimize the well-documented effects that implicit racial biases have on legal decision-making.

> [Low side effect condition] Given that Lombrossic is inexpensive, effective, and has very few side effects, there is going to be an increasing temptation to put it to use in the courtroom.
>
> [Adverse side effect condition] Despite the fact that Lombrossic has some well-documented negative side effects—e.g., slurred speech, extreme weight gain, and trembling—there is nevertheless going to be an increasing temptation to put it to use in the courtroom.]

Is this a good idea? If not, why not? If so, what are the limitations of the state's authority to forcibly medicate otherwise law abiding citizens? How do we balance individual freedom with the state's interest in ensuring that defendants receive a fair and impartial trial by a jury of their peers? These are just some of difficult questions we must ask in the wake of recent scientific advances in psychopharmacology.

---

[11] We should have used "mandated" here rather than "forcibly." For something to be mandated, it is merely a necessary condition. In this case, if you want be a judge or if you are going to serve on a jury, then you must take the racial bias pill. But someone could always just refuse to be a judge or serve on a jury. In the case of forcible medication, there is no means of escape for the offeder. He has no means of escape. It is not clear whether the participants would have tracked this subtle difference. It is worth testing this down the road. Thanks to the Nicole Vincent for bringing this distinction to our attention.

Statements for Racial Bias Pill (1–Strongly Disagree to 7–Strongly Agree)

1. It is appropriate for the legal system to force jurors and judges to take Lombrossic to reduce the influence of implicit racial bias on legal decision making.
2. It is appropriate for the court system to offer jurors and judges the choice of taking Lombrossic on a voluntary basis.
3. The state has a compelling interest to do whatever is necessary to ensure that defendants receive a fair and impartial trial.
4. The moral costs of forcibly medicating judges and jurors outweigh the moral cost of implicit bias in legal decision making.
5. The state does not have the authority to forcibly medicate law abiding citizens.
6. Using drugs like Lombrossic to change human behavior undermines the importance of free will—which is an important cornerstone of civil society.
7. While reducing implicit racial bias is an important goal, medication is the wrong way of bringing about this goal.

Impulsive Violence Case
New Drug Reduces Impulsive violence By Julia Reed
On May 23, 2013, the New York Department of Corrections released 27-year-old Daniel St. Hubert, a paranoid schizophrenic who had served five years in prison for the attempted murder of his mother. Within a week of St. Hubert's release, he reoffended by killing a woman and a child and he savagely attacked another child and an elderly woman. Shortly thereafter, St. Hubert was apprehended and charged with two counts of murder and two counts of attempted murder. Before his release, St. Hubert's sister had begged authorities to assist her in getting treatment for her brother, who was thrice declared unfit for trial and thrice institutionalized in a mental-health facility and had a history of violent crimes. Despite that history, St. Hubert apparently did not qualify for outpatient mental-health treatment under New York's "Kendra's Law," a law named for a young woman who was pushed in front of a subway by a mentally ill man who was not undergoing treatment.

Obviously, this situation spotlights the role of mental-health treatment in the arena of criminal law, a problem that has long plagued the criminal-justice system. Courts have consistently struggled with the issue of whether to forcibly medicate mentally ill defendants or convicts after they complete their terms of incarceration. For instance, in *Washington v. Harper* the Supreme Court ruled that it is not a violation of due process to forcibly medicate an inmate if that inmate is a danger to himself and others, and if the medication is in the inmate's medical interest. But this ruling deals with the forcible medication of inmates and defendants. They do not address what should be done about a mentally ill inmate who completes his or her sentence or becomes eligible for parole and therefore is released into the general public. Obviously this issue has no easy resolution.

Indeed, this issue may have just gotten even more complicated in the wake of the recent discovery of a drug that greatly reduces impulsive violence in criminal populations. A team of researchers at Harvard Medical School led by Dr. Edward Gage have developed a new drug—called Lombrossic—that reduces activity in the parts of the brain that are believed to cause violent impulses. In a recent clinical trial, inmates who were given Lombrossic were 50% less likely to commit violent offenses while they were in prison and 35% less likely to reoffend upon release.

[Low side effect condition] Given that Lombrossic is inexpensive, effective, and has very few side effects, the court system is already taking notice.

[Adverse side effect condition] Despite the fact that Lombrossic has some well-documented negative side effects—e.g., slurred speech, extreme weight gain, trembling, and disorientation—the court system is already taking notice.]

If nothing else, the research by Dr. Gage and his collaborators holds out the promise that we may finally have more powerful pharmacological tools for treating criminals who have problems with impulsive violence. But a number of important moral questions remain. For instance, does the state have the authority to forcibly medicate these criminals against their wishes (whether they are presently incarcerated or being released)? If not, why not? If so, what are the limitations of this authority? No matter how you answer these questions, it's clear that if the New York Department of Correction had access to Lombrossic when they released St. Hubert, several lives may have been saved. But if we give the state the power to deny criminals the right to refuse medical treatment, how do we ensure this power doesn't get abused? These are just some of difficult questions we must ask in the wake of recent scientific advances in psychopharmacology.

Statements for Impulsive Violence Pill (1–Strongly Disagree to 7–Strongly Agree)

1. It is appropriate for the legal system to forcibly medicate inmates with Lombrossic to reduce their violent impulsivity.
2. It is appropriate for the legal system to forcibly medicate parolees with Lombrossic as a condition for their release.
3. It is appropriate for the legal system to forcibly medicate children and juveniles with Lombrossic when they display violent impulsivity at a young age.

4. The state has a compelling interest to do whatever is necessary to keep society safe from violent offenders.
5. The moral costs of forcibly medicating inmates and parolees outweigh the moral costs of violence on society.
6. While the state has the authority to forcibly medicate criminals with Lombrossic, it does not have the authority to forcibly medicate law abiding citizens.
7. Using drugs like Lombrossic to change human behavior undermines the importance of free will—which is an important cornerstone of civil society.
8. While reducing impulsive violence is an important goal, medication is the wrong way of bringing about this goal.

Prosocial Behavior Case
New Drug Improves Moral Behavior By Julia Reed

A new drug called Lombrossic has been used to alter users' personalities to make them "better" people, a neuroscientist has claimed. At a London conference on how science could be used to improve human brain function, Sylvia Smith, a neuroscientist at Oxford University, explored the possibility of using Lombrossic to alter deeply rooted human personality traits, in a way that was previously limited to fiction like RL Stevenson's Strange Case of Dr. Jekyll and Mr. Hyde. "At the time this was science fiction but recent studies have shown that by shifting people's brain chemistry you can change people's personalities," said Dr. Smith.

Lombrossic—which has already been dubbed the "morality pill"—has been documented to have an effect on decision making when subjects are presented with moral dilemmas. For instance, Dr. Smith said that half of a test group was given Lombrossic and the other half was given a placebo. The members of the test group who received Lombrossic were subsequently more likely to engage in pro-social behavior (e.g., helping others) than the members of the control condition. They were also less likely to engage in anti-social behavior (e.g., cheating and lying). These findings have already been replicated several times.

Dr. Smith said that for some this showed that the drug could act to enhance moral qualities, but others might disagree. "This is less a scientific Statement, than it is a philosophical Statement," said Dr. Smith. "I think the place to start is that there are probably certain types of moral behaviors that we would want people to want to do," she said, adding that drugs that led to people making a small sacrifice to help other people would probably be described as moral enhancers by most, and further tests could show the effect of Lombrossic on enhancing these qualities.

However, she said that the question of when to administer Lombrossic was also one for ethical debate, rather than scientific research.

[Low side effect condition] For instance, if researchers are able to enhance moral behavior with drugs such as Lombrossic that are inexpensive, effective, and have very few side effects, there will be a temptation for the state to use these pills to increase pro-social behavior and decrease anti-social behavior.]

[Adverse side effect condition] For instance, despite the fact that these new "morality pills" have some well-documented negative side effects—e.g., slurred speech, extreme weight gain, and trembling—there is nevertheless going to be a temptation for the state to use these pills to increase pro-social behavior and decrease anti-social behavior.]

But does the state have the authority to forcibly medicate individuals who are prone to immoral behavior—e.g., criminals? If not, why not? If so, what are the limitations of this authority? If medicating criminals becomes the norm, why not think non-criminals will eventually be forcibly medicated as well. After all, wouldn't the world be a better place if we are all a bit more moral? These are just some of difficult questions we must ask in the wake of recent scientific advances in psychopharmacology.

Statements for Prosocial Pill (1–Strongly Disagree to 7–Strongly Agree)

1. It is appropriate for the legal system to forcibly medicate inmates with Lombrossic to reduce their antisocial behavior.
2. It is appropriate for the legal system to forcibly medicate children and juveniles with Lombrossic when they display antisocial behavior at a young age.
3. The state has a compelling interest to do whatever is necessary to keep society safe from antisocial individuals.
4. The moral costs of forcibly medicating people outweigh the moral costs of antisocial behavior on society.
5. While the state has the authority to forcibly medicate criminals, it does not have the authority to forcibly medicate law abiding citizens.
6. Using drugs like Lombrossic to change human behavior undermines the importance of free will—which is an important cornerstone of civil society.
7. While reducing antisocial behavior and increasing prosocial behavior are important goals, medication is the wrong way of bringing about these goals.

Results
The first thing we did was test for main effects, running a mixed-factor design with Statement as a within-participant variable and Goal (Reduce Racial Bias/

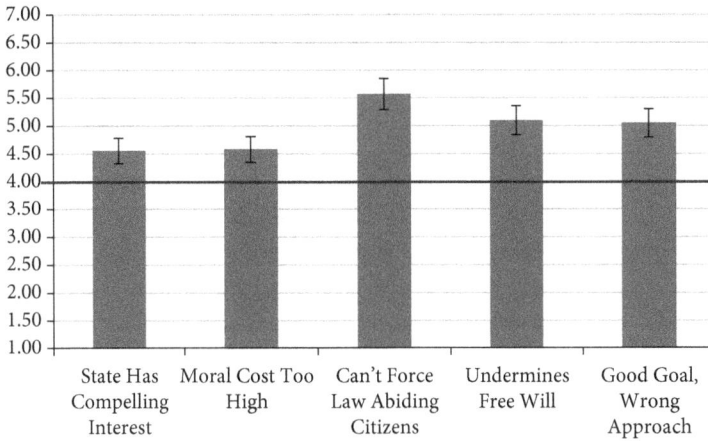

Figure 9.2. Main effect for statement. We didn't include the statements about forcing medication here because they differed too much across the scenarios. There were nonetheless some differences worth noting. For instance, participants were more supportive of forcibly medicating inmates who suffered from violent impulsivity than those who displayed antisocial behavior, especially when it was unsafe: Violence (Safe/Unsafe) = Ms 4.51/4.84, SE = 0.23/0.21, and Morality (Safe/ Unsafe) = Ms 3.02/2.46, SE = 0.24/0.21. And, although less enthusiastic, they were also more supportive of forcibly medicating violent children/juveniles than antisocial ones: Violence (Safe/Unsafe) = Ms 3.22/3.14, SE = 0.23/0.23, and Morality (Safe/Unsafe) = Ms 2.28/1.95, SE = 0.19/0.17. These results also suggest that participants were generally more supportive of forcing medication on adults than children/juveniles. And, as a whole, participants were very unsupportive of forcibly medicating jurors and judges, especially when unsafe: Ms = 2.6/1.8, SEs = 0.23/0.17.

Reduce Violence–Impulsivity Reduction/Promote Prosocial Behavior) and Pill Safety (Low Side Effects/Adverse Side Effects) as between-participant variables. This revealed a main effect for Statement, $F(4,1320) = 24.2$, $p < .001$, $\eta^2 = 0.068$, and for Goal, $F(2,330) = 50.3$, $p < .001$, $\eta^2 = 0.234$ (see Figures 9.2 and 9.3, respectively).

Several things can be gleaned from the results displayed in Figure 9.2. First, participants appear to appreciate the tension between the state's interests in keeping society safe and the moral appropriateness of using neurointerventions to accomplish this goal. While participants agreed (across conditions) that the state has a compelling interest to do whatever is necessary to keep people safe from antisocial individuals, they also agreed (indeed, even more strongly and across conditions) that the moral cost of using neurointerventions outweighs the benefits. This tension between state interests and individual rights permeates our moral, legal, and political landscape these days in contexts ranging from abortion to the death penalty—which is why we included these statements in the materials.

Second, most participants are opposed to using neurointerventions on law abiding-citizens, even if they are more sympathetic with using interventions on legal actors. Third, these findings suggest that people think that using neurointerventions to alter human behavior challenges or undermines the notion of free will, which is once again what we expected based on past research (e.g., Goodwin et al., in prep; Nadelhoffer & Goya-Tocchetto, 2013; Nahmias, Coates, & Kvaran, 2007) and our past experiences talking about these issues with students. Just as people perceive a tension between state interests and individual rights, they also seem to perceive a tension between free will and neuroreductive accounts of human agency.

Finally, participants agreed (across conditions) that while we may be able to use neurointerventions to change human behavior for the better, these methods don't bring these changes about *in the right way*—yet another common response we hear in the classroom. On this view, even if neurointerventions work, they do so by bypassing more appropriate means for bringing about behavioral changes such as therapy, undermining people's autonomy, manipulating them as agents, etc. In each case, the efficacy of neurointerventions doesn't justify their use. There are many possible side effects—both on the individual and society more generally—each of which might undermine the justified use of these interventions.

The results displayed in Figure 9.3 show that participants' overall judgments differed across the three conditions—that is, the three different contexts and types of neurointerventions elicited different responses. Participants were less

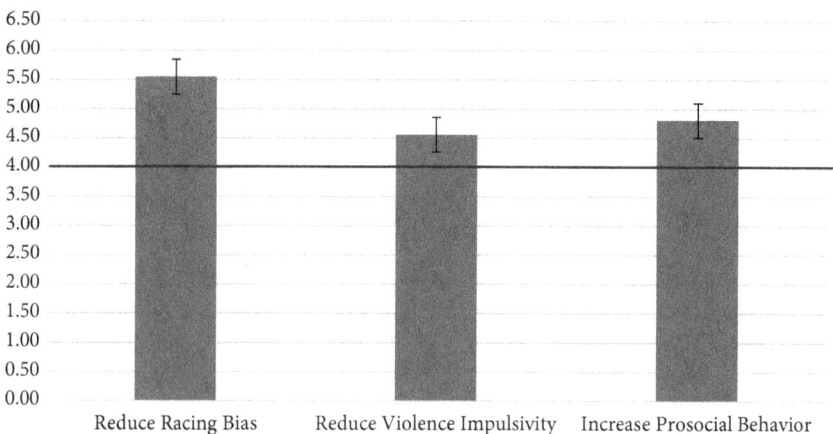

Figure 9.3. Main effect for goal

worried about the use of neurointerventions to reduce impulsive violence than to improve moral judgment or diminish racial bias. Participants in the racial bias condition seemed the most concerned. The prospect of using neurointerventions on judges and jurors to control their implicit racial bias was viewed as more alarming or problematic than using neurointerventions on dangerous inmates to control their violent behavior or on people for the purposes of inducing pro-social behavior (and discouraging antisocial behavior). Perhaps this is because people view implicit racial bias as less problematic than violent impulsivity or antisocial behavior. Another possibility is that people found mandating that judges and jurors take medication is problematic not because implicit bias isn't sufficiently problematic but because judges and jurors haven't done anything wrong that would trigger the requirement that they use medications.[12] Either way, using neurointerventions in the former context may be deemed as too extreme or intrusive given the problem it is trying to solve. More work would need to be done to figure out precisely why.

All of these results are in line with our previous work. However, we were surprised to find no main effect for Pill Safety, $F(4,330) = 1.2$, ns. We expected that participants (across conditions) would find neurointerventions with well-documented negative side effects to be more problematic than interventions with very few side effects. There was some influence, however—as revealed by a three-way interaction between Statement, Goal, and Pill Safety, $F(8,1320) = 2.6$, $p = .007$, $\eta^2 = 0.016$ (Figure 9.4).

This more fine-grained analysis reveals that pill safety ended up making a difference. For instance, while participants thought that the moral cost of using unsafe neurointerventions to reduce impulsive violence was too high, using safe interventions was viewed more favorably in these circumstances. Similarly, participants were much less comfortable using unsafe "morality" pills to induce prosocial behavior in law abiding citizens than using safe pills—even though in both cases participants on average agreed that using neurointerventions for this purpose is morally problematic. Finally, when it came to participants' responses to whether using pills to reduce implicit bias in judges and jurors is the wrong means to an otherwise acceptable end, we find that while agreement is high in both the safe and unsafe conditions, it is strongest in the latter case. Each of these three findings about the relevance of pill safety to people's beliefs and attitudes comport with our original expectations.

We find a similarly complicated picture when we look more closely at the issue of free will. In both the racial bias and the prosocial conditions, people strongly agreed that using pills (whether safe or unsafe) undermined the notion of free

---

[12] Thanks to Nicole Vincent for highlighting this alternative explantion.

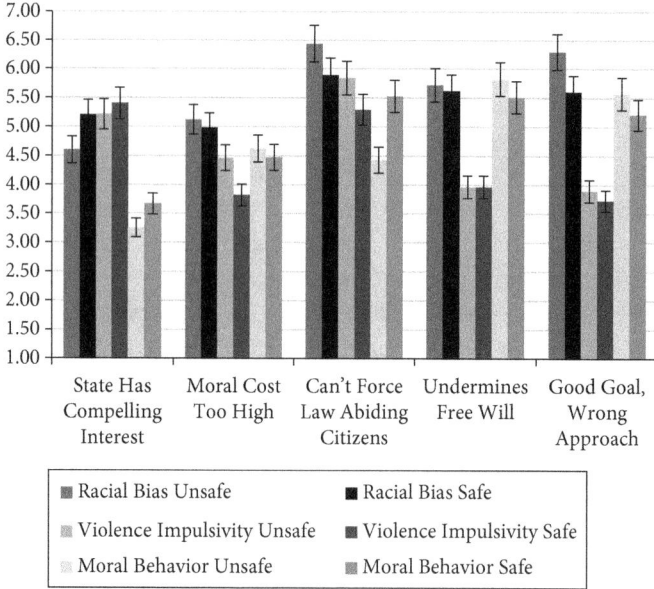

Figure 9.4. Three-way interaction between Statement, Goal, and Pill Safety

will. However, participants in the impulsive violence conditions were unsure about the relationship between neurointervention and free will. Perhaps this is because dangerous inmates who struggle with impulsive violence are viewed as having less free will to begin with than judges, jurors, or people from the general population. Testing this hypothesis would require more research on people's moral beliefs and attitudes about violent criminals and punishment (see Goodwin et al., in prep; Nadelhoffer et al., 2013, for some earlier work on this issue). For now, we can only gesture toward a plausible explanation of our preliminary findings.

The next analysis we conducted was a mixed-factor design with Who Forced (Inmates/Child-Juvenile Delinquents) as a within-participant variable and Goal and Pill Safety as between-participant variables. This revealed a main effect for Who Forced, $F(1,220) = 108.6$, $p < .001$, $\eta^2 = 0.331$, as well as for Goal, $F(1,220) = 61.1$, $p < .001$, $\eta^2 = 0.217$. There was once again not a main effect for Pill Safety, $F(1,220) = 0.68$, ns. Participants were significantly more supportive of forcing medication on inmates ($M = 3.7$, $SE = 0.112$) than they were of forcing medication on children/juvenile delinquents ($M = 2.6$, $SE = 0.105$). They were also significantly more supportive of forcing medication in the Impulsive violence case ($M = 3.9$, $SE = 0.136$) than in the Prosocial Behavior Goal ($M = 2.4$, $SE = 0.135$). Both main effects were qualified by a two-way interaction between

Who Forced and Goal, $F(1,220) = 18.1$, $p < .001$, $\eta^2 = 0.076$ (Figure 9.5), which showed that people find forcibly medicating inmates less problematic than forcibly medicating children or juvenile delinquents, especially when these inmates are displaying violent impulsivity.

Finally, we ran independent-samples t-tests which revealed that participants were more supportive of medicating inmates for violent impulsivity than they were medicating judges and jurors against racial bias, $t(221) = 11.5$, $p < .001$. They were also (a) more supportive of medicating inmates for violent impulsivity than they were medicating inmates for moral behavior, $t(222) = 8.6$, $p < .001$, and (b) more supportive of medicating inmates for moral behavior than they were medicating judges and jurors against racial bias, $t(223) = 2.5$, $p = .012$ (although much less so than in the case of impulsive violence).

All told, we found some interesting results in Study 1, some of which were expected and some of which were not. Our primary goal was to get preliminary data concerning people's baseline intuitions about the use of neurointerventions for different purposes and on different target populations. We think our efforts were largely successful. By using a variety of statements about the issues surrounding neurointervention (e.g., state interests, individual rights, and free will), we managed to shed some light on the contours of people's beliefs and attitudes. Overall, we found that participants were conflicted about the moral status of neurointervention (both inside and outside of the law). Whether the goal was to use pharmacological treatment modalities to reduce implicit racial bias in judges or increase prosocial behavior in criminal offenders and noncriminal-offenders,

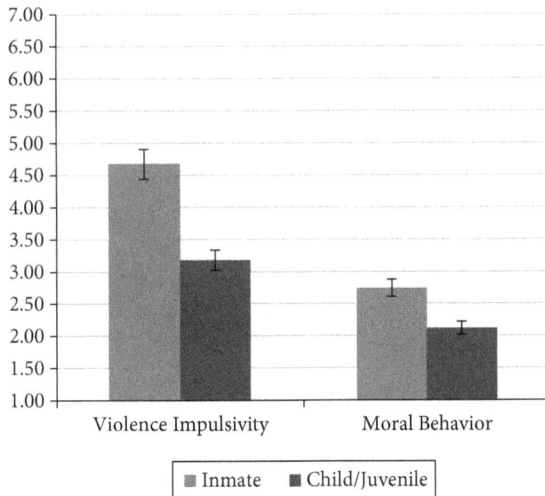

Figure 9.5. Two-way interaction between Who Forced and Goal

participants tended to have worries about using neurointerventions to bring about behavioral changes—worries that included the state overstepping its moral authority, the importance of free will, and using misguided means to achieve otherwise laudable ends.

But there was less ambivalence among participants when it came to forcibly medicating dangerous inmates who struggle with impulsive violence—a practice a number of participants embraced. Given that this is a context that arises commonly in the legal system, our findings on this front are especially relevant from the standpoint of the law and public policy. Moving forward, the temptation by legislators and judges to rely on neurointerventions to change abnormal or dangerous behavior is only likely to increase (especially as the biotechnologies improve). Knowing what people ordinarily think about these issues is relevant in this context. If most people find the practice acceptable and it is already legally protected and legislatively mandated (at least in some jurisdictions),[13] it is going to be difficult to reverse the trend, or to stem the coming neuropharmacological tide if we have reason to suppose this practice is problematic. This is not to suggest that one should simply defer to the dictates of public opinion! It is just to say that one needs to understand what one is up against if common sense morality is standing in between one's preferred theory and policies on the ground.

Study 2

For Study 2 we once again uploaded our materials to Qualtrics. Participants were 798 people recruited through Amazon's MTurk service and paid $1 each for completing the survey. Participants had to be at least 18 years of age and living in the United States. Of the participants, 50.6% percent ($n = 406$) reported being male, and 49.5% ($n = 398$), female. Participants reported being represented by the following ethnicities: Black/African American ($n = 72$), Asian/Pacific Islander (n = 51), White/Caucasian ($n = 632$), Native American ($n = 9$), and Hispanic/Latino ($n = 37$). Each participant was randomly assigned to one of the nine conditions we will discuss in the following text.

Because we did not find a main effect for pill safety in Study 1, in Study 2 we eliminated it as an issue; instead, the treatment in each condition was described as being "effective, inexpensive, and having very few side effects." This time our

---

[13] It's not clear which way the causal arrow goes here. It could be that public policy and legal decisions track folk views or it could be that once a practice is adopted by legislators and legal decision makers, this influences folk views. Parsing this would require more empirical work. Thanks to the Nicole Vincent for highlighting these two possibilities.

goal was to explore people's intuitions about different *types* of treatment modalities. So, we simply reused the three primary cases from Study 1—the racial bias, impulsive violence, and prosocial cases. However, for Study 2, we added three conditions for each case—cognitive behavioral therapy, a pill, and a brain implant. Also, we once again used the same mock news design as well with the same banner from Figure 9.1.

Based on our experiences discussing cognitive enhancement with students, we had reason to predict that participants would have different views about noninvasive behavioral therapy, noninvasive pharmacological therapy, and invasive implant therapy (even if the outcome, safety, and efficacy of the treatments are the same). Time and time again, students worry that even if the goal of a particular enhancement is laudable—reducing racial bias or increasing prosocial behavior—some methods of bringing this about are more appropriate and less problematic than others. These students tend to think that while therapy and counseling represent the right way to facilitate behavioral change, pills and neural implants are inappropriate shortcuts.

So, in Study 2 we wanted to see whether the *type* of intervention (e.g., therapy, pill, or implant)—and not just the *goal* of the intervention (e.g., reducing racial bias vs. reducing impulsivity) or the *target* of the intervention (e.g., judges vs. prison inmates)—mattered. As such, there were three cases in Study 2, with three conditions per case. For brevity's sake, we are only going to describe the parts of the conditions that were new to Study 2 (see Study 1 for details of the cases). The following conditions were added, respectively, to the beginning of the racial bias, impulsive violence, and prosocial behavior cases from Study 1.

Racial Bias Cases
Therapy Condition
Going through a new cognitive behavioral therapy program called the Lombrossic Program can affect a person's subconscious attitudes towards race, a team of ethicists, psychiatrists and psychologists at Oxford University has found. In a study published in Psychotherapy, researchers had 18 people undertake the Lombrossic Program and 18 people in a control group did not participate in the program. They found that the Lombrossic group scored significantly lower on the Implicit Attitude Test into subconscious racial bias—a standard test for testing subconscious racial attitudes. There was no significant difference in the groups' explicit attitudes to other races.

The Lombrossic Program works by training people how to control activation in the peripheral 'autonomic' nervous system and in the area of the brain implicated in fear or emotional responses. The researchers believe Lombrossic reduced implicit racial basis because such bias is based on automatic, non-conscious fear responses, which the treatment program helps people to consciously control.

Pill Condition

Taking a recently developed medication called Lombrossic can affect a person's subconscious attitudes towards race, a team of ethicists, psychiatrists and psychologists at Oxford University has found. In a study published in Psychopharmacology, researchers gave 18 people the drug Lombrossic and 18 people a placebo and found that the Lombrossic group scored significantly lower on the Implicit Attitude Test into subconscious racial bias—a standard test for testing subconscious racial attitudes. There was no significant difference in the groups' explicit attitudes to other races.

Lombrossic blocks activation in the peripheral 'autonomic' nervous system and in the area of the brain implicated in fear or emotional responses. The researchers believe Lombrossic reduced implicit racial basis because such bias is based on automatic, non-conscious fear responses, which the drug blocks.

Implant Condition

Researchers have recently shown that a brain implant—called the Lombrossic implant—can affect a person's subconscious attitudes towards race, a team of ethicists, psychiatrists and psychologists at Oxford University has found. In a study published in Frontiers of Neuroscience, researchers installed the Lombrossic implant in 18 people and another 18 people did not receive the implant. They found that the Lombrossic group scored significantly lower on the Implicit Attitude Test into subconscious racial bias—a standard test for testing subconscious racial attitudes. There was no significant difference in the groups' explicit attitudes to other races.

The Lombrossic implant blocks activation in the peripheral 'autonomic' nervous system and in the area of the brain implicated in fear or emotional responses. The researchers believe Lombrossic reduced implicit racial basis because such bias is based on automatic, non-conscious fear responses, which the implant blocks.

Impulsive Violence Cases

Therapy Condition

Indeed, this issue may have just gotten even more complicated in the wake of the recent discovery of a cognitive behavioral program that greatly reduces impulsive violence in criminal populations. A team of researchers at Harvard Medical School led by Dr. Edward Gage have developed a new treatment—called the Lombrossic Program—that has been shown to reduce activity in the parts of the brain that are believed to cause violent impulses. In a recent clinical trial, inmates who underwent the Lombrossic Program were 50% less likely to commit violent offenses while they were in prison and 35% less likely to reoffend upon release. Given that the Lombrossic Program is inexpensive, effective, and has very few side effects, the court system is already taking notice. If nothing else, the research by Dr. Gage and his collaborators holds out the promise that we may finally have more powerful cognitive behavioral tools for treating criminals who have problems with impulsive violence.

Pill Condition

Indeed, this issue may have just gotten even more complicated in the wake of the recent discovery of a drug that greatly reduces impulsive violence in criminal populations. A team of researchers at Harvard Medical School led by Dr. Edward Gage have developed a new drug—called Lombrossic—that reduces activity in the parts of the brain that are believed to cause violent impulses. In a recent clinical trial, inmates who were given Lombrossic were 50% less likely to commit violent offenses while they were in prison and 35% less likely to reoffend upon release. Given that Lombrossic is inexpensive, effective, and has very few side effects, the court system is already taking notice. If nothing else, the research by Dr. Gage and his collaborators holds out the promise that we may finally have more powerful pharmacological tools for treating criminals who have problems with impulsive violence.

Implant Condition

Indeed, this issue may have just gotten even more complicated in the wake of the recent discovery of a neural implant that greatly reduces impulsive violence in criminal populations. A team of researchers at Harvard Medical School led by Dr. Edward Gage have developed a new brain implant—called the Lombrossic implant—that reduces activity in the parts of the brain that are believed to cause violent impulses. In a recent clinical trial, inmates who received a Lombrossic implant were 50% less likely to commit violent offenses while they were in prison and 35% less likely to reoffend upon release. Given that the Lombrossic implant is inexpensive, effective, and has very few side effects, the court system is already taking notice. If nothing else, the research by Dr. Gage and his collaborators holds out the promise that we may finally have more powerful neurological tools for treating criminals who have problems with impulsive violence.

Prosocial Behavior Cases
Therapy Condition

A new cognitive therapy program called the Lombrossic Program has been used to alter users' personalities to make them "better" people, a psychologist has claimed. At a London conference on how science could be used to improve human brain function, Sylvia Smith, a psychologist at Oxford University, explored the possibility of using the Lombrossic Program to alter deeply rooted human personality traits, in a way that was previously limited to fiction like RL

Stevenson's Strange Case of Dr. Jekyll and Mr. Hyde. "At the time this was science fiction but recent studies have shown that by shifting people's conscious brain states you can in turn influence their brain chemistry and change people's personalities," said Dr. Smith.

Pill Condition

A new drug called Lombrossic has been used to alter users' personalities to make them "better" people, a neuroscientist has claimed. At a London conference on how science could be used to improve human brain function, Sylvia Smith, a neuroscientist at Oxford University, explored the possibility of using Lombrossic to alter deeply rooted human personality traits, in a way that was previously limited to fiction like RL Stevenson's Strange Case of Dr. Jekyll and Mr. Hyde. "At the time this was science fiction but recent studies have shown that by shifting people's brain chemistry you can change people's personalities," said Dr. Smith.

Implant Condition

A brain implant called the Lombrossic implant has been used to alter users' personalities to make them "better" people, a neuroscientist has claimed. At a London conference on how science could be used to improve human brain function, Sylvia Smith, a neuroscientist at Oxford University, explored the possibility of using Lombrossic implants to alter deeply rooted human personality traits, in a way that was previously limited to fiction like RL Stevenson's Strange Case of Dr. Jekyll and Mr. Hyde. "At the time this was science fiction but recent studies have shown that by shifting people's brain chemistry you can change people's personalities," said Dr. Smith.

After being presented with one of these nine conditions, participants in Study 2 were presented with a series of statements and asked to report their level of agreement. The statements were identical to those used for the cases in Study 1 except that the statements for Study 2 refer to cognitive therapy, pills, or implants (respectively).

Results

We once again first tested for main effects, running a mixed-factor design with Statement as a within-participant variable and Goal (Reduce Racial Bias/Reduce Impulsive Violence/Increase Prosocial Behavior) and Intervention Type (Pill/Therapy/Implant) as between-participants variables. This revealed a main effect for Statement, $F(6,4284) = 172.1, p < .001, \eta^2 = 0.194$, and Goal, $F(2,714) = 53.5, p < .001, \eta^2 = 0.130$ (see Figures 9.6 and 9.7, respectively).

The results provide further evidence that participants detect the tension between the state's interest in keeping society safe and the moral appropriateness of using neurointerventions in their efforts to do so. While people strongly agree that the state has a compelling interest in keeping society safe by curbing dangerous behavior, it doesn't have the moral authority to intervene however it sees fit (and it certainly doesn't have the authority to forcibly intervene in the lives and minds of law-abiding citizens). Indeed, participants (across conditions) agreed (a) that the moral costs of forcible interventions are too high even when it comes to adult inmates who are dangerous, (b) that forcible interventions threaten to undermine the importance of the notion of free will, (c) forcible interventions are an inappropriate means to an otherwise laudable goal, and (d) that the moral costs of forcible intervention are too high to outweigh the benefits.

All of the results from Figure 9.6 are roughly in line with what we found in Study 1. The same cannot be said about the results from Figure 9.7. In Study 2, as in Study 1, we once again found an overall difference in how people responded to the impulsive violence case and how they responded to the prosocial/antisocial case. However, this time around the relationship was inverted. In Study 1, people were more against neurointervention in the prosocial/antisocial conditions than in the impulsive violence condition. In Study 2, the opposite was the case. It's not clear why that is. We suspect it is because each case in Study 2 involved three

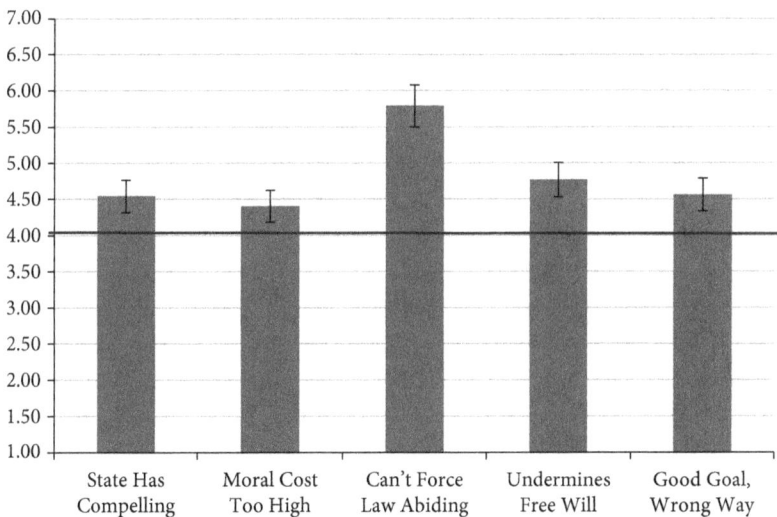

Figure 9.6. Main effect for statement. As in Figure 9.2, we once again left out the statements about forcing medication here because they differed too much across the scenarios. However, we saw the same general trends as before, with there being more support for forcing medications on violently impulsive than anti-social inmates, parolees, and children/juveniles—and more supportive of medicating adults than children/juveniles.

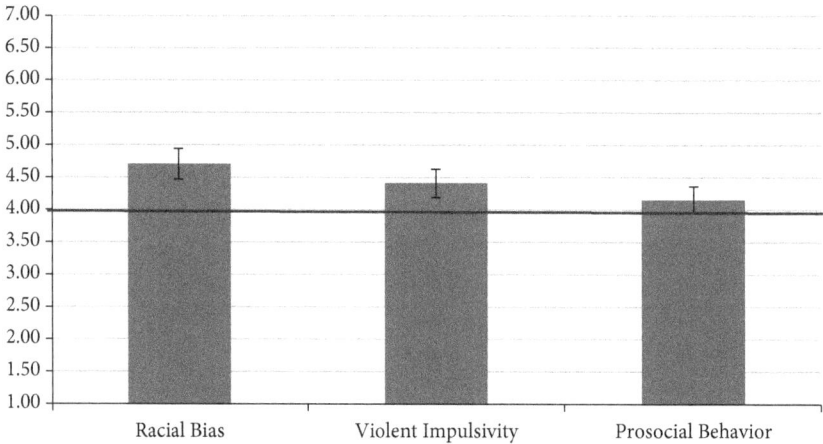

Figure 9.7. Main effect for goal

conditions—including conditions involving voluntary and involuntary behavioral therapy programs. In Study 1, on the other hand, each case involved an explicit neurointervention—namely, a pill. Because we broadened the scope of the investigation in Study 2 to include multiple treatment modalities, we expected that the results would be more complicated—which is what you see if you compare Figure 9.7 with Figure 9.3. There are nevertheless lots of commonalities between the two data sets (as we previously discussed). So, at least thus far, our empirical house is mostly in order.

However, the biggest surprise in Study 2 is that there was not a main effect for Intervention Type, $F(2,714) = 0.02$, ns. Given that exploring people's intuitions about different kinds of interventions was central to this particular study, we decided to take a closer look at the responses, which revealed an interactive effect. Specifically, we found a two-way interaction between Statement and Intervention Type, $F(12,4284) = 22.4$, $p < .001$, $\eta^2 = 0.059$ (Figure 9.8).

This analysis (see Figure 9.8) revealed that intervention type did make a difference under certain circumstances; for example, participants were most concerned about brain implants and least concerned about cognitive behavioral therapy (with pills falling somewhere in between). It also appears that participants, like our students, tended to think that cognitive therapy was a way of bringing about behavioral changes without at the same time challenging the notion of free will. Pills and implants, on the other hand, were found to be more problematic when it comes both to free will and to the state's authority to forcibly alter beliefs and behaviors. Yet, while participants (across conditions) viewed therapy more favorably, they nevertheless tended to think that forcibly using any of the three methods was problematic. Indeed, even the notion of giving people

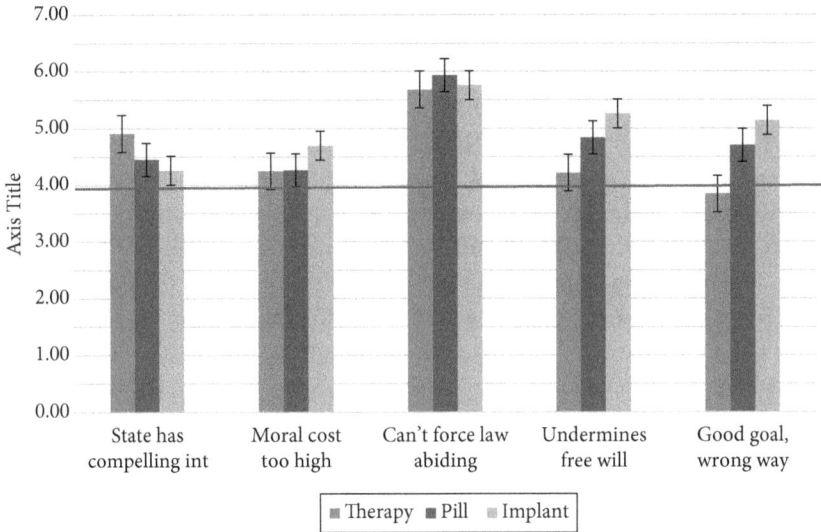

Figure 9.8. Two-way Interaction between Statement and Intervention Type

the *option* of using these interventions was met by participants with resistance (in the case of pills and implants) or uncertainty (in the case of therapy).

Study 2 yielded some interesting results. First, we were able to successfully replicate several of the findings from Study 1 concerning people's baseline beliefs about neurointerventions in different contexts; for example, in both studies participants were (a) strongly opposed to using neurointervention on the general population and (b) strongly opposed to using neurointervention (or any intervention, for that matter) to reduce racial bias in judges and jurors—to name but a few of the commonalities between the findings of the two studies. Second, we were able to shed light on how people view the use of different types of interventions—namely, cognitive behavioral therapy, pills, and brain implants—both inside and outside the law. While the type of intervention didn't have as widespread an influence on people's beliefs and attitudes as we expected, people were nevertheless sensitive to the issue.

Looking at both Study 1 and Study 2 together, the overarching finding seems to be that people are generally suspicious when it comes to the state's authority to use the kinds of neurointerventions that we discussed in the vignettes. While people agree that the state does (and presumably should) have the authority to use neurointerventions under some circumstances (e.g., in the case of impulsively violent inmates), they also recognize that there are limits to this authority and that using this authority raises a host of important moral, legal, political, practical, and even metaphysical issues (e.g., the problem of free will).

Study 3

For Study 3, we once again uploaded the materials to Qualtrics. Participants were 354 people at least 18 years of age, living in the United States recruited through Amazon's MTurk service and paid $1 each for completing the survey. Fifty-three percent of participants ($n = 191$) reported being male, and 47% ($n = 163$), female. Participants reported being represented by the following ethnicities: Black/African American ($n = 25$), Asian/Pacific Islander ($n = 21$), White/Caucasian (n = 286), Native American ($n = 2$), and Hispanic/Latino ($n = 20$). Each participant was randomly assigned to one of six of the aforementioned conditions.

In Study 3, we wanted to turn our attention to the issue that we used as a springboard for discussion at the start of this chapter—namely, the two types of competency and forcible medication. So, we constructed two cases based partly on the actual facts from *Ford v. Wainwright* (see the section Setting the Stage for details). In the first case, the issue we raised is whether the state should be able to forcibly medicate "Bernard Johnson" to restore his *competency to be executed*. In the second case, it was whether the state should be able to forcibly medicate "Bernard Johnson" to restore his *competency to stand trial*. Based on the findings from Study 2, we also decided to include three conditions for each case in Study 3—a cognitive therapy condition, a pill condition, and a brain implant condition. Each condition began with the following:

> Bernard Johnson was convicted of murder in 1997 and sentenced to death in the state of Florida. During the trial, Johnson was deemed by the jurors to be free of mental illness when he committed the crime. However, in 2010, while on death row, Johnson's mental health diminished to a point resembling paranoid schizophrenia: Johnson began referring to himself as Pope John Paul III, and reported such accomplishments as thwarting a vast Ku Klux Klan conspiracy to bury dead prisoners inside the prison walls; foiling an attempt by prison guards to torture his female relatives inside the prison; and personally appointing nine new justices to the Florida Supreme Court. Johnson also claimed he was "free to go whenever [he] wanted", because he theorized that anyone who executed him would in turn be executed.

The participants were then presented with one of the following cases.

Execution Case
A panel of three psychiatrists was eventually called to examine Johnson's behavior, and concluded that while Johnson suffered from psychosis and various mental disorders, he was still capable of understanding the nature of the death

penalty and the effect that such a penalty would have on him. The governor of Florida, Bob Graham signed a death warrant for Johnson in 2010.

The case made its way to the United States Supreme Court. The Supreme Court determined that executing mentally ill patients like Johnson violates the Eight Amendment's prohibition of "cruel and unusual" punishment. So, the ruling overturned Governor Graham's death warrant. According to the Court, unless and until Johnson's sanity was restored, he was not eligible for the death penalty.

[Therapy condition] In response, Florida decided to force Johnson to undergo a recently developed and highly effective behavioral therapy regiment called the Lombrossic Program in order to make him sane enough to execute,

[Pill condition] In response, Florida decided to forcibly medicate Johnson with a recently developed and highly effective anti-psychotic medication called Lombrossic in order to make him sane enough to execute,

[Implant condition] In response, Florida decided to force Johnson to receive a recently developed and highly effective brain implant called the Lombrossic implant in order to make him sane enough to execute,

which is a practice that had been previously deemed acceptable by the Supreme Court in an earlier case. In 2014, Johnson was executed for his crime.

Trial Case

For the trial conditions, the first paragraph was the same as the first paragraph of the execution cases. The only differences occurred in the second paragraph— which is what we will include here as follows.

A panel of three psychiatrists was eventually called to examine Johnson's behavior, and concluded that while Johnson suffered from psychosis and various mental disorders, he had been sane when he committed the crime and he was presently sane enough to understand the trial proceedings. Johnson appealed the panel's decision. His attorneys denied that he was sane enough to stand trial. The case made its way to the United States Supreme Court. The Supreme Court determined that making mentally ill patients like Johnson stand trial violates the Fifth Amendment's guarantee of "due process." According to the Court, because Johnson's sanity was sufficiently compromised he had not been eligible to stand trial even if he had been sane when he committed the original murder.

[Pill condition] In response, Florida decided to forcibly medicate Johnson with a recently developed and highly effective anti-psychotic medication called Lombrossic so he would be sane enough to stand trial,

[Therapy condition] In response, Florida decided to force Johnson to undergo a recently developed and highly effective behavioral therapy regiment called the Lombrossic Program so he would be sane enough to stand trial,

[Implant condition] In response, Florida decided to force Johnson to receive a recently developed and highly effective brain implant called the Lombrossic implant so he would be sane enough to stand trial,

a practice which had already been previously deemed acceptable by the Supreme Court in an earlier case. Johnson was subsequently tried for the murder he committed (while sane) in 1992. A jury found Johnson guilty of murder and sentenced him to die. He was executed in 2014.

After being presented with one of these six conditions, participants in Study 3 were presented with a series of statements and asked to report their level of agreement or disagreement. To save space, we have combined the statements across conditions (while highlighting the differences). Participants received the statements that corresponded to the specific condition they received.

Study 3 Statements (1–Strongly Disagree to 7–Strongly Agree):

1. Johnson should have stood trial for the crime he committed.
2. Johnson should have been punished for the crime he committed.
3. Johnson should have been executed for the crime he committed.
4. People who were legally guilty when they committed their crimes should be punished even if they are presently legally insane.
5. That Johnson developed a serious mental illness *after* he committed the crime is irrelevant to [(a) whether he should have been executed for the crime he committed, (b) whether he should have stood trial for the crime he committed].
6. The state both *does* and *should* have the authority [(a) to forcibly medicate Johnson with Lombrossic, (b) to force Johnson to undergo behavioral therapy like the Lombrossic program, (c) to force Johnson to receive the Lombrossic brain implant] in order to make him mentally competent enough to [(a) execute for his crime, (b) stand trial for his crime].
7. People should be mentally competent to be executed.
8. The death penalty is sometimes justified.

Results

We once again first tested for main effects, running a mixed-factor design with Statement as a within-participant variable and Competency Type (Trial/Execution) and Intervention Type (Pill/Therapy/Implant) as between-participants variables. This revealed a main effect for Statement, $F(7,2457) = 99.6$,

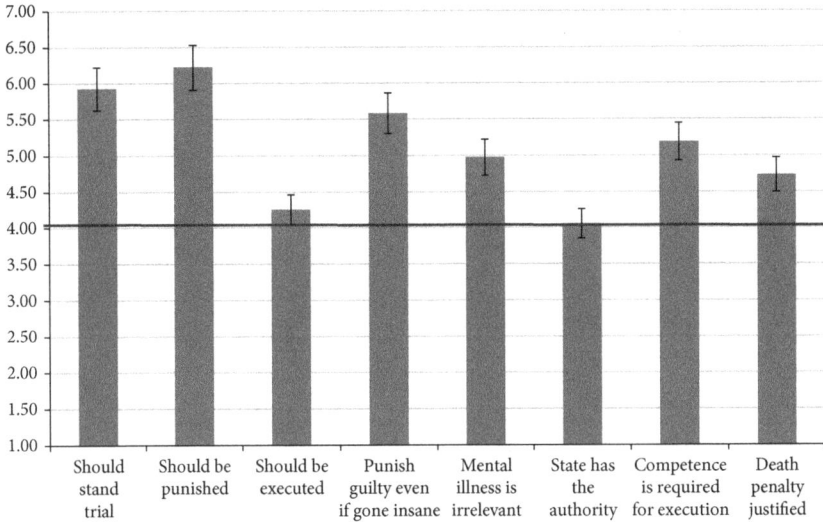

Figure 9.9. Main effect for statements

$p < .001$, $\eta^2 = 0.221$ (Figure 9.9), with no main effect for Competency Type or Intervention Type.

In short, participants across conditions were strongly supportive of the notion that Bernard Johnson should stand trial and be punished for his crime—and that guilty people should be punished for their crimes more generally, even if they subsequently become incompetent or insane. But, they were more ambivalent when it came to the moral appropriateness of the death penalty (both in Johnson's case and in general) and when it came to whether the state has the authority to use forcible treatment to restore competency.[14]

Participants also seemed surprisingly insensitive to the relevance of mental illness to punishment and execution. This certainly represents a divergence from the received view in the literature—namely, that current incompetence can serve as a temporary (and perhaps even permanent) grounds for not being able to prosecute or punish an alleged offender. In this case, participants across conditions agreed that Bernard Johnson should stand trial, be punished, and even be executed despite the fact that he was described as having symptoms associated with paranoid schizophrenia both during and after his trial. It seems

---

[14] It's not clear what is driving this ambivalence. It could be that people don't think competency matters for punishment more generally or it could be that people don't think we should be forcibly restoring competency for the purposes of punishment more generally. In short, it may be that the ambivalence we find in these cases involving capital punishment—which is an especially harsh form of punishment—is being driven by people's background beliefs about punishment.

that for most participants, the most important factor for justified punishment is sanity and guilt at the time of the commission of the offense. Becoming mentally incompetent after the fact doesn't get offenders off the hook from having to stand trial and answer for what they did and from being eligible to be punished for what they did (at least for most of our participants). In this respect, it seems that people may not share some of the foundational assumptions about competency that are embedded in the common law tradition—for example, that it is cruel and unusual per se to execute inmates who are mentally incompetent.

At the same time, participants nevertheless thought that the state has the authority to forcibly restore competence for the purposes of holding offenders accountable for their crimes. In this sense, our results also suggest that current legal practice converges with common sense morality at least when it comes to the state's authority to forcibly restore competency. So, in this respect, what the courts are doing to Leroy Smith III in Maine falls within the scope of legitimacy when it comes to folk jurisprudence. As we mentioned earlier, this doesn't mean that we ought to bend our theoretical wills to the pressures of public opinion. If one's philosophical theories are incompatible with these common beliefs and practices, then one should roll up one's sleeves. The road from theory to practice will be a hard interdisciplinary row to hoe. That is not to say that this is not the road we ought to travel either normatively or practically speaking. But on our view, we think researchers should know what lies ahead for their views when it comes to the navigable but inescapable forces of public opinion.

Our analysis also revealed two 2-way interactions—one between Statement and Competency Type, $F(7,2457) = 5.9$, $p < .001$, $\eta^2 = 0.017$, and the other between Statement and Intervention Type, $F(14,2457) = 3.3$, $p < .001$, $\eta^2 = 0.019$ (see Figures 9.10 and 9.11, respectively).

The findings in Figure 9.10 reveal that participants treated the competency to stand trial and the competency to be executed as largely similar. The two places where participants' responses diverged were (a) the issue of whether the state both does and should have the authority to forcibly medicate for the purposes of restoring competency and (b) the relevance of mental illness to the two different types of competency. On one hand, while participants in general mildly agreed with forcibly restoring competency to stand trial, they also mildly disagreed with forcibly medicating to restore competency for execution. On the other hand, people were more worried about mental illness in the context of competency to be executed than they were in the context of competency to stand trial. Given that the stakes are much higher in one context than the other, these findings are unsurprising.

In Figure 9.11, we see that participants largely agreed that (a) Johnson should stand trial, (b) Johnson should be punished, (c) offenders who were sane and guilty when they committed an offense should be punished (even if they are no longer competent), (d) whether a guilty offender is presently mentally ill

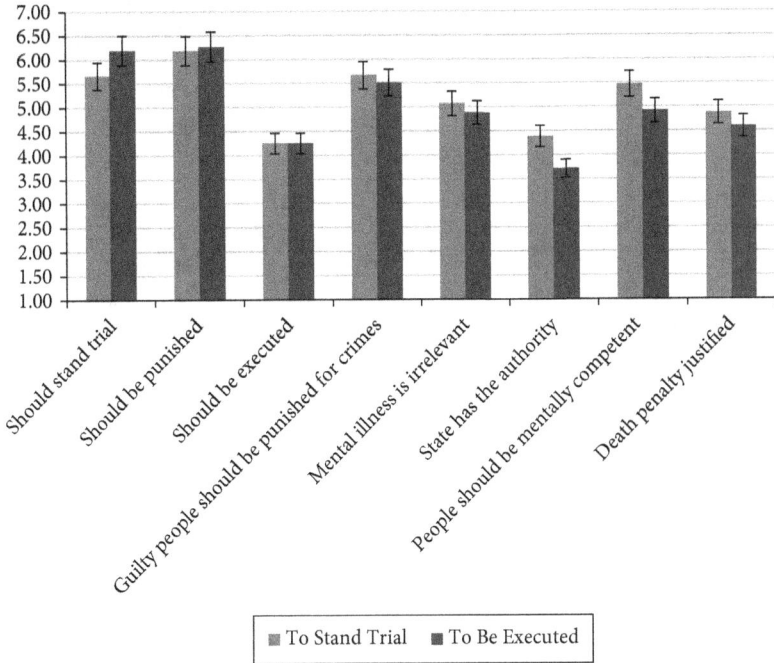

Figure 9.10. Two-way interaction between Statement and Competency Type

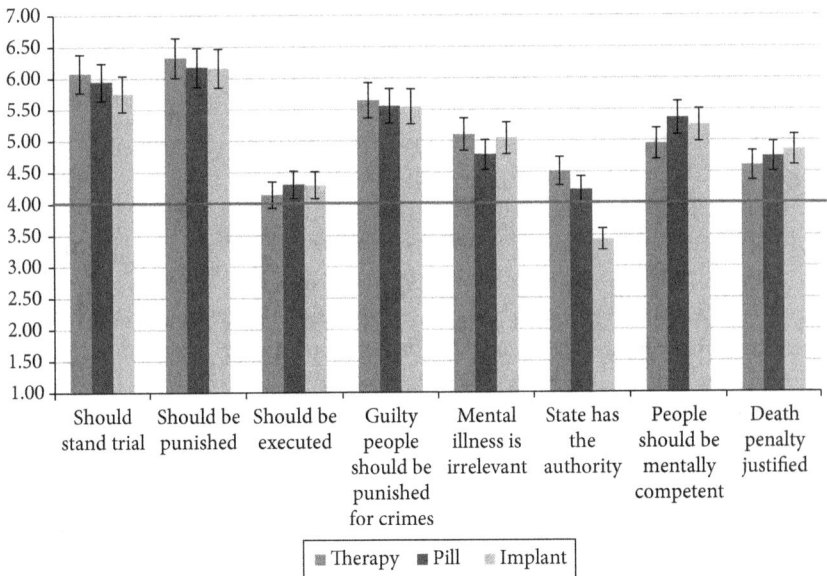

Figure 9.11. Two-way interaction between Statement and Intervention Type

is largely irrelevant to whether he should be punished, and (e) the state nevertheless has the authority to forcibly restore competence if need be. But here again, participants were less convinced when it came to the death penalty (both in Johnson's case and in general). Given that public opinion is divided when it comes to the death penalty more generally (at least in the United States), these findings are similarly in line with our expectations.

Perhaps the biggest surprise was that people's intuitions about these cases seemed largely insensitive to the different treatments. While we found mixed results in Study 2 on this front, given the high stakes in the cases used in Study 3, we expected people to be more sensitive overall this time to the different kinds of treatments. Other than the issue of whether the state has the authority to forcibly restore competence—where participants' judgments about implants strongly diverged from their judgments about pills and cognitive behavioral therapy—treatment modality did not make a pronounced difference in people's judgments about how Johnson (and other offenders) ought to be treated by the courts. While participants were less willing to agree that the state has the authority to forcibly intervene with brain implants than pills or cognitive behavioral therapy, the intervention type didn't yield different responses to the other statement types.

We nevertheless think that the findings from Study 3 were illuminating—especially because they highlight the way that data on common sense morality and folk jurisprudence can be relevant to philosophical theorizing. In particular, our participants were more punitive and less sensitive to competence and mental illness than judges, legal scholars, and legislators have assumed. On this ordinary view, so long as someone committed an criminal offense while sane, he ought to be punished (and perhaps even executed)—regardless of whether he happens to be presently suffering from a serious mental illness like paranoid schizophrenia. Should this more extreme view about the relationship between punishment and competency be reflected in the law simply in virtue of the fact that it is the majority view? That is not a question we can tackle here.

For present purposes, let it suffice for us to say that we have our own philosophical axes to grind when it comes to common sense morality, the current system of punishment, the death penalty, and the current practice of forcibly medicating people to restore their competency for trial (or execution). We also take issue with several other views commonly expressed by our participants. But defending our own views was not our present goal. Instead, our task was to present data on folk intuitions about these and related issues—data we believe are important for moral and legal philosophers who have an interest in public policy. Figuring out how these data should shape our philosophical theories and our public policies is a task for another day.

On our view, much more empirical work on folk beliefs about neuro-intervention is needed before we will be in the position to make informed decisions concerning which philosophical theories we should adopt and which policy decisions we should make. In this chapter, we have merely presented the results of some preliminary findings. While we believe this is an important first step toward bridging the gap between empirical research, philosophical theorizing, and more practical legal and political concerns, a number of important questions about folk views concerning neurointervention remain unanswered. Filling in these missing details is an interdisciplinary task for another day.

Present Limitations and Future Research

Before closing, we wanted to first acknowledge that there are several shortcomings and limitations when it comes to our three studies. For starters, with the benefit of hindsight we know that the design of our cases and statements could have been improved. However, these three studies represented our first pass at trying to empirically investigate this topic, and we will further refine our materials moving forward. We will also continue to analyze the data we have already collected, only some of which was discussed in this chapter. Apart from some empirical work that was done in the late 1990s on the "public view" of legal issues surrounding competence, forcible medication, etc. that implemented an interview approach, there is scant other systematically collected and analyzed data on how people think about these issues (Pescosolido et al., 1999). Not surprisingly, given the relative recency of this modality, there is even less data on people's attitudes and beliefs about competence, forcible medication, and neurointerventions, whether inside or outside the law. And while we think our findings were probative (even if sometimes surprising), we hope to improve upon and extend our research moving forward.

Another obvious limitation of our present studies is that we focused narrowly on the intuitions and beliefs of Americans. So, when we spoke throughout the paper about "our ordinary moral language and practices," "folk jurisprudence," "folk intuitions," "common sense morality," and the like, we were using those terms as shorthand for the moral beliefs and practices of U.S. citizens. We have recently been working with colleagues in Brazil on similar issues with the hopes of obtaining cross-cultural data. Either way, we realize that cross-cultural studies and historical analyses would need to be run to determine whether our findings are robust and stable. If they are, then our findings may have revealed something deep and interesting about human psychology. If not, then they would still be interesting and useful from a more local standpoint and for the formulation of public policy in the United States.

Finally, another limitation of our present studies is that we only focused on *folk* jurisprudence—that is, the beliefs and attitudes of *laypersons*. Because these laypersons are themselves potential legal decision makers (i.e., jurors), we believe our findings are morally and legally relevant. However, it would also be illuminating to have data on how judges, defense attorneys, prosecutors, parole board members, prison wardens, forensic psychiatrists and lawmakers view these issues as well. So, another logical extension of our present research would be to not only collect data from other cultures, but to also collect data from a variety of actual legal decision makers (Cox et al., 2012). From vignette-based studies to full-blown mock trials, there are several methods we could adopt in extending our research in this direction. For present purposes, however, we limited our attention to laypersons since we believe their beliefs and attitudes are also relevant to the broader societal project of deciding how and when to use neurointerventions to forcibly change people's thoughts and behaviors.

Concluding Remarks

Our overarching goal in this chapter was to view the moral, legal, and political issues associated with neurointervention through the lens of folk jurisprudence. In short, we wanted to see how potential legal decision makers view the kinds of issues that are already being debated in academic journals and in the popular press when it comes to legal competency, forcible medication, and the relationship between neuroscience, law, and society more generally. We think that having a better understanding of the shape of common sense morality and folk jurisprudence is no less important for public policy than conceptual, analytic, and normative work in moral, legal, and political philosophy. At a minimum, we think that data on folk intuitions can serve as helpful feasibility considerations to inform the formulation of policy.

Consider, for instance, some of our main findings. First, people don't tend to think that the state has the authority to forcibly medicate legal decision makers or the general population (even if doing so would bring about positive consequences like reducing implicit racial bias or promoting prosocial behavior). People have even deeper worries when it comes to forcibly medicating children and adolescents than when it comes to adults (even if the former are deemed to be dangerous). In these contexts, we find a convergence between folk jurisprudence, the consensus views in philosophy, and our current legal practices. However, when it comes to adult inmates (especially those who struggle with impulsive violence), the situation is more complicated. Here people are less confident when it comes to whether the state has the authority to use forcible medication for the purposes of reducing violent impulsivity. Moreover, so long as offenders were sane at the time of their crimes, people tend to think that they should be tried, punished, and even executed, even if they are presently incompetent owing to mental illnesses like schizophrenia. In these contexts, we find a striking rift between public opinion, philosophy, and the law. So, in the event that philosophers, judges, or legislators want to insist that we protect the currently mentally ill from legal harm (and that we not rely on forcible neurointerventions), they will have public opinion to contend with at some point along the way.

It is this connection to public policy that we believe gives empirical data on laypersons' intuitions about competence, forcible medication, neurointerventions, etc. their philosophical value. Insofar as one is jointly interested in philosophical theory and public policy—that is, insofar as one is interested in taking a genuinely interdisciplinary approach to doing philosophy, rather than just *applying* philosophy done from the armchair to other disciplines—one ought to be interested in how people ordinarily think about the underlying issues. For illustrative purposes, consider what we'll call "the problem of neurointervention"—for instance, whether and when neurointerventions are morally permissible. This is a complex and multi-faceted issue that spans (a) moral, legal, and political theory; (b) legal, penological, political, and forensic practice; and (c) public opinion about the underlying moral, legal, and political issues at stake.

Adequately addressing the problem of neurointervention is beyond the scope of any one chapter, volume, or book. What we tried to do instead is contribute our own little piece to this broader interdisciplinary project. While our main goal was to present some data on folk jurisprudence, we also hope to have shown how these findings might be philosophically relevant given certain methodological commitments and certain interests in practical ethics and public policy.

Acknowledgments

First, we would like to thank the audience at The Atlanta Neuroethics Consortium's Neurointerventions and the Law Conference (2014, at Georgia State University). We got some helpful feedback on some of the earlier studies for this project. Second, we would like to thank Nicole Vincent for proving us with invaluable feedback. Addressing her commentary greatly improved the paper. Whatever mistakes and errors remain are ours alone.

References

Banner, A. (2014, June 27). Daniel St. Hubert and why the criminal-justice system needs more mental-health oversight. HuffPost. Updated August 27, 2014. Retrieved from https://www.huffpost.com/entry/daniel-st-hubert-and-why-_b_5485853

Bengson, J. (2013). Experimental attacks on intuitions and answers. *Philosophy and Phenomenological Research, 86*(3), 495–532.

Blackstone, W. (1916). *Commentaries on the law of England* (W. Jones, Ed.). San Francisco, CA: Bancroft-Whitney Company.

Caplan, A. (2006). Ethical issues surrounding forced, mandated, or coerced treatment. *Journal of Substance Abuse and Treatment, 31*, 117–120.

Cochrane, R., Herbel, B., Reardon, M., & Lloyd, K. (2013). The *Sell* effect: Involuntary medication treatment is a "clear and convincing" success. *Law and Human Behavior, 37*(2), 107–116.

Cox, J. M., Goldstein, N., Dolores, J., Zelechoski, A., & Messenheimer, S. (2012). The impact of juveniles' age and levels of psychosocial maturity on judges' opinions about adjudicative competency. *Law and Human Behavior, 36*(1), 21–27.

Cullen, S. (2010). Survey-driven romanticism. *Review of Philosophy and Psychology, 1*(2), 275–296.

Darwall, S., Gibbard, A., & Railton, P. (Eds.). (1997). *Moral discourse and practice: Some philosophical approaches.* New York, NY: Oxford University Press.

Deutsch, M. (2010). Intuitions, counter-examples, and experimental philosophy. *Review of Philosophy and Psychology, 1*(3), 447–460.

Dusky v. United States, 362 U.S. 402 (1960).

Ford v. Wainwright, 477 U.S. 399 (1986).

Garasic, M. D. (2013). The Singleton case: Enforcing medical treatment to put a person to death. *Medicine, Health Care and Philosophy: A European Journal, 16*(4), 795–806.

Gebrasi, J. B., & Scott, C. L. (2004). "*Sell v. U.S.*: Involuntary medication to restore trial competency—A workable standard? *Journal of the American Academy of Psychiatry and the Law, 32*(1), 83–90.

Ghetti, M. A., & Redlich, A. D. (2001). Reactions to youth crime: Perceptions of accountability and competency. *Behavioral Science and the Law, 19*, 33–52.

Goodwin, G., Gromet, D., Tang, S., Nadelhoffer, T., & Sinnott-Armstrong, W. (in prep). Mind, brain, and character: How neuroscience affects people's views of wrongdoing. University of Pennsylvania.

Grisso, T. (1996). Society's retributive response to juvenile justice: A developmental perspective. *Law and Human Behavior, 20*(3), 229–247.

Hayes, J. (2004). *Sell v. United States*: Is competency enough to forcibly medicate a criminal defendant? *The Journal of Criminal Law and Criminology, 94*(3), 657–686.

Heilbrun, K., & Kramer, G. (2005). Involuntary medication, trial competence, and clinical dilemmas: Implications of *Sell v. United States* for psychological practice. *Professional Psychology: Practice and Research, 36*(5), 459–466.

Ichikawa, J. (2011). Experimentalist pressure against traditional methodology. *Philosophical Psychology, 25*(5), 743–765.

Kauppinen, A. (2007). The rise and fall of experimental philosophy. *Philosophical Explorations, 10*(2), 95–118.

Knobe, J., & Nichols, S. (2008). An experimental philosophy manifesto. In J. Knobe & S. Nichols (Eds.), *Experimental philosophy* (pp. 3–14). Oxford, England: Oxford University Press.

Ludwig, K. (2010). Intuitions and relativity. *Philosophical Psychology, 23*(4), 427–445.

McMahon, S. A. (2013). It doesn't pass the *Sell* test: Focusing on "the facts of the individual case" in involuntary medication inquiries. *American Criminal Law Review, 50*, 387–416.

Melton, G., Petrila, J., Poythress, N., & Slobogin, C. (1997). *Psychological evaluations for the courts: A handbook for mental health professionals and lawyers* (2nd ed.). New York, NY: Guilford Press.

Morse, S. (2003). Involuntary competence. *Behavioral Sciences and the Law, 21*, 311–328.

Morse, S. (2011). Mental disorder and criminal law. *Journal of Criminal Law and Criminology, 101*, 886–967.

Nadelhoffer, T., & Goya-Tocchetto, D. (2013). The potential dark side of free will: Some preliminary findings. In G. Carusso (Ed.), *Exploring the illusion of free will and moral responsibility* (pp. 121–140). Lanham, MD: Lexington Books.

Nadelhoffer, T., Gromet, D., Goodwin, G., Nahmias, E., Sripada, C., & Sinnott-Armstrong, W. (2013). The mind, the brain, and the criminal law. In T. Nadelhoffer (Ed.), *The future of punishment* (pp. 193–211). Oxford, England: Oxford University Press.

Nadelhoffer, T., & Nahmias, E. (2007). The past and future of experimental philosophy. *Philosophical Explorations, 10*(2), 123–149.

Nahmias, E., Coates, J., & Kvaran, T. (2007). Free will, moral responsibility, and mechanism: Experiments in folk intuitions. *Midwest Studies in Philosophy, 31*, 214–242.

Panetti v. Quarterman, 551 U.S. 130 (2007).

Perry v. Louisiana, 498, U.S. 38 (1990).

Pescosolido, B., Monahan, J., Link, B., Stueve, A., & Kikuzawa, S. (1999). The public's view of the competence, dangerousness, and need for legal coercion of persons with mental health problems. *American Journal of Public Health, 89*, 1339–1345.

Potter, T. (2014, May 17). "Morality pills" close to reality, claims scientist. International Business Times. Retrieved from https://www.ibtimes.co.uk/morality-pills-close-reality-claims-scientist-1448977

Rhoulam, M. (2016). Due process and serious crime: The vague term that promotes the forcible medication of countless incompetent defendants, trumping their fundamental liberty. *Civil Rights Law Journal, 26*(2), 255–291.

Riggins v. Nevada 504, U.S. 127 (1992).

Robinson, P. H., & Darley, J. M. (1995). *New directions in social psychology.* Justice, liability, and blame: Community views and the criminal law. Boulder, CO: Westview Press.

Schooler, J., Nadelhoffer, T., Nahmias, E., & Vohs, K. (2014). Measuring and manipulating beliefs and behaviors associated with free will: The good, the bad, and the ugly. In A. Mele (Ed.), *Surrounding free will* (pp. 72–94). New York: Oxford University Press.

Sell v. United States, 539 U.S. 166 (2003).

Shariff, A. Z., Greene, J. D., Karremans, J. C., Luguri, J. B., Clark, C. J., Schooler, J. W., Baumeister, R. F., & Vohs, K. D. (2014). Free will and punishment: A mechanistic view of human nature reduces retribution. *Psychological Science, 1*–8.

Sidgwick, H. (2011). *The method of ethics* (J. Bennett, Ed.). Retrieved from http://www.earlymoderntexts.com/ (Original work published 1874)

Singleton v. Norris, 319 F. 3d, Court of Appeals, 8th Circuit (2003).

Slobogin, C. (2006). *Minding justice.* Cambridge, MA: Harvard University Press.

Sosa, E. (2007). Experimental philosophy and philosophical intuition. *Philosophical Studies, 132*(1), 99–107.

Sosa, E. (2010). Intuitions and meaning divergence. *Philosophical Psychology, 23*(4), 419–426.

United States v. Lawrence, 26 F. Cas. 887 (D.C. Cir. 1835).

Vincent, N. A. (2014). Restoring responsibility: Promoting justice, therapy and reform through direct brain interventions. *Criminal Law and Philosophy, 8*(1), 21–42.

Washington v. Harper 494, U.S. 210 (1990).

Wiens, D. (2015). Against ideal guidance. *Journal of Politics, 77*(2), 433–446.

Whiting, D. (2015). Evaluating medico-legal decisional competency criteria. *Health Care Analysis*, *23*(2), 181–196.

Wolf, J. (2011). *Ethics and public policy: A philosophical inquiry.* New York, NY: Routledge.

Youtsey v. United States, 97 F. 937, 940-41 (6th Cir. 1899).

10

Judicious Use of Neuropsychiatric Evidence When Sentencing Offenders With Addictive Behaviors

Implications for Neurointerventions

Andrew Dawson, Jennifer Chandler, Colin Gavaghan, Wayne Hall,
and Adrian Carter

Introduction

In a widely discussed clinical case (Burns & Swerdlow, 2003), a 40-year-old male patient exhibited pedophilic behavior after developing a tumor in his right orbitofrontal cortex. He developed a strong interest in child pornography, despite reporting no previous sexual attraction to children. He also made sexual advances toward his prepubescent stepdaughter that resulted in his legal removal from the family home and a conviction for child molestation. He was expelled from a court-ordered rehabilitation program for repeated sexual harassment of staff and was to receive a prison sentence. The evening before sentencing, he experienced severe and persistent headaches. Magnetic resonance imaging revealed a prominent tumor in the patient's right orbitofrontal cortex. The tumor was surgically removed and the patient's sexual urges ceased. Sometime later the sexual urges returned, and a brain scan revealed that he had another tumor. It was subsequently resected with the same effect, and his sexual urges one again ceased.

This case raises complex neurolaw issues. If the neuropsychiatric evidence[1] had been available at trial, could the patient have relied on a defense that his impulses were "irresistible" (Penney 2012)? A common intuitive response is "yes"—it wasn't "him"; it was the tumor. Yet some of his conduct was inconsistent with someone acting on irresistible impulses. For several weeks the patient concealed his child pornography collection and a sexual advance toward

[1] We define neuropsychiatric evidence as expert testimony or peer-reviewed publications that involve neurological, neurobiological, or neuropsychological research.

Andrew Dawson, Jennifer Chandler, Colin Gavaghan, Wayne Hall, and Adrian Carter, *Judicious Use of Neuropsychiatric Evidence When Sentencing Offenders With Addictive Behaviors* In: *Neurointerventions and the Law*. Edited by: Nicole A Vincent, Thomas Nadelhoffer, and Allan McCay, Oxford University Press (2020). © Oxford University Press 2020 DOI: 10.1093/oso/9780190651145.001.0010

his stepdaughter from his wife. This sort of deliberate conduct may not fit well with our first impression of an out-of-control offender. Moreover, the patient reported that the "pleasure principle" *overrode* his impulse control, not that it *eradicated* it. In fact, he was able to successfully inhibit motor responses on a neuropsychological test of impulse control prior to resection (Burns & Swerdlow, 2003). The dissonant cognitive and behavioral evidence suggests that the patient's capacity for impulse control may not have been totally compromised and that a legal defense grounded in absence of volition may have failed. Yet among neurolaw commentators, there appears an understandable consensus that this striking case is as close as we might come to seeing a causal connection between prefrontal pathology and aberrant behavior (Glenn & Raine, 2014).

Cases in which more subtle neural abnormalities arise from repeated, noncoerced ingestion of a drug are similarly complex, even if they do not appeal to our intuitions as powerfully as the just discussed case. Given the prevalence of addiction-related criminal offending,[2] and our growing understanding of the neuropsychiatric basis of addictive behaviors, neurolaw scholars must grapple with whether neuropsychiatric evidence can be a mitigating factor in cases where offenders suffer from compulsive behaviors such as drug or behavioral addictions, or whether neurointerventions (e.g., psychopharmacologies or brain stimulation) are needed to respond to addictive behaviors.

In this chapter, we consider how commonwealth courts[3] have used neuropsychiatric evidence in the sentencing of criminal offenders with drug-induced addictive behaviors or compulsions. We first examine how neuropsychiatric evidence has influenced the historical "medical versus moral model" drug addiction debate (Hall, Carter, & Forlini, 2015; Leshner, 1997). We then illustrate how neuropsychiatric evidence, and the medical models it supports, has not been widely or consistently used as a mitigating factor[4] in the sentencing of drug- or gambling-addicted individuals who have committed a criminal offence related to their addiction. In addition, neuropsychiatric evidence has not been the basis

---

[2] Addition-related offending could reflect a drug- or gambling-addicted individual: consuming a prohibited drug, committing crimes (e.g., theft, assault or embezzlement) to support his or her drug or gambling addiction, and committing crimes indirectly related to his or her drug or gambling addiction (e.g., involuntary manslaughter; Taylor 2002).

[3] We limit our focus to commonwealth jurisdictions because (a) the two cases of medication-related offending were heard in Australia and Canada, (b) space is too limited to consider the relevant drug and gambling addiction case law across all the jurisdictions of the United States, and (c) the United States may be heading down an overtly "medicalized" path in terms of sentencing offenders with addictive behaviors (see *United States v Hendrickson* (2014).

[4] Mitigating factors alleviate, abate or diminish the severity of punishment imposed by the law (Husak & Murphy, 2013). Descriptive mitigating factors "officially" have this impact, while normative mitigating factors arguably have this impact. They are not defenses, which preclude any imposition of penal liability.

for mitigation for the few courts that have adopted a more medical perspective when sentencing drug- or gambling-addicted individuals.

We contrast this with commonwealth courts' use of neuropsychiatric evidence as a mitigating factor in two cases where criminal offending was linked to addictive behaviors that developed in a "therapeutic" context. Specifically, we consider two cases where addictive behaviors were induced by dopaminergic medication prescribed to treat Parkinson's disease (PD) and restless leg syndrome (RLS).

A degree of inconsistency is evident between the courts' approach to defendants whose offending takes place against a background of different forms of addiction or compulsive behavior. Specifically, there is some evidence that those whose addictive behavior has arisen either in the context of a clear pathology (such as a brain tumor) or in a therapeutically sanctioned program are treated more sympathetically than those whose addiction has arisen from non-medical drug use. There may be sound reasons for this differential treatment, (although as we discuss later in the chapter, these may often cut across rather than between categories), but it is not clear that relevant neuropsychiatric evidence is one of them. It is essential that courts are explicit about the basis for distinguishing these classes of defendant in the sentences that they impose. Doing so will help ensure courts are not needlessly restricted in their intervention options when faced with the rare case of an offending patient who refuses to cease taking medication upon release.

Addiction Neuropsychiatry and the Law

Central to debates about the nature of addiction is whether addicted individuals can make rational choices about whether to use a drug or gamble. Two views have dominated recent public debates about addiction, particularly drug addiction.[5] Medical models construe addiction as "a chronic, relapsing disease of the brain" (Leshner, 1997, p. 46) that severely reduces an individual's rational decision-making and control over their drug use. In contrast, moral models describe both drug addiction and criminal acts committed to support it as freely chosen acts for which individuals should be held fully responsible. In sentencing drug-addicted offenders, courts must consider drug-addicted individuals' voluntariness (Husak & Murphy, 2013)—that is, their ability to exercise conscious control over their criminal actions.

---

[5] Due to scope and the more limited state of the neuropsychiatric literature on behavioral addictions (e.g., pathological gambling), we only focus on how neuropsychiatric evidence informs medical and moral models of drug addiction.

Medical and Moral Models of Drug Addiction

Proponents of medical models claim that chronic drug use "hijacks" brain regions in addicted persons that are involved in reward valuation, rational deliberation, and self-control, rendering their drug use irresistible (Leshner, 1997; Volkow, Koob, & McLellan, 2016). Addiction neuroimaging has identified differences in the neural function and structure of drug-addicted individuals that advocates argue explains the pathological desire for drug rewards, irrationality, and loss of control over drug use (Goldstein & Volkow, 2011).

The strong claim that drug addiction is a brain disease that eliminates individuals' ability to control their drug use, however, is difficult to reconcile with a number of clinical and epidemiological observations (Hall et al., 2015; Lewis, 2015). Despite drug-addicted individuals' documented impairments of cognitive control, many drug-addicted individuals manage to take unassisted "time-outs" from drug use to reduce their tolerance or discontinue their drug use in response to external events (e.g., birth of a child, threat of job loss, or changes in substance availability and price; Heyman, 2009). Many drug-addicted individuals also appear capable of sophisticated planning to obtain their desired substance and avoid arrest (Foddy & Savulescu, 2006). Drug-addicted individuals have also been shown to be responsive to small incentives (e.g., small monetary rewards) in exchange for reduced substance use (Higgins & Petry, 1999; Prendergast, Podus, Finney, Greenwell, & Roll, 2006). This choice pattern might only reflect switching from one immediate, certain reward (i.e., the drug) to another (i.e., money), but such flexibility in preferences, even if short-sighted, seems inconsistent with a strong brain disease view. Lastly, in contrast to the view promulgated by "brain disease" supporters, most drug-addicted individuals manage to overcome their addiction without treatment (Heyman, 2009).

Proponents of the moral model argue that chronic drug use is simply a free, albeit often irrational, choice. They argue that those who claim to be "dependent" or 'addicted' are doing so to avoid taking responsibility for their behavior and its consequences (Davies, 1997). This view downplays the maladaptation in neural function and structure observed in drug-addicted individuals and ignores the environmental factors (e.g., poverty, social stress, and lack of community treatment facilities) that can interact with genetic vulnerabilities to produce problematic drug use and make it much more difficult to overcome addiction (Young-Wolf, Enoch, & Prescott, 2011). In short, strong forms of the medical model and the moral model do not accurately reflect the confluence of neurobiological, psychological, clinical and epidemiolog-ical evidence.

Sentencing Drug- and Gambling-Addicted Offenders: Incarcerate or Treat?

In commonwealth jurisdictions, the sentences imposed on drug- and gambling-addicted offenders reflect a strong emphasis on moral models (Brooks & Blaszczynski, 2011; Taylor, 2002). For example, in the Australian case of *R v Henry* (1999), Chief Justice Spigelman established that drug addiction is not of itself a mitigating circumstance in New South Wales. Spigelman referred with approval to the reasons of Chief Justice King in *R v Spiero* (1979):

> One feels sympathy for the person who has become entangled in drug addiction, but the courts cannot treat addiction as an excuse, or even a mitigating factor, in relation to serious crime. Those who are addicted to drugs must understand that if they allow their addiction to lead them into serious crime, they must expect to receive the same serious punishment as would be received by others. (p. 549)

Spigelman also suggested that invoking gambling or sex addiction as a basis for mitigation will fail. This was supported in subsequent Australian cases, including *R v Chapman* (2001), *R v Foley* (2001), and *R v Grossi* (2009). Similarly, in the English case of *R v Lawrence* (1988), Justice Simon Brown was unequivocal:

> Their Lordships could not make it too plain what the principle was to be followed. It was no mitigation whatever that a crime was committed to feed an addiction, whether it be drugs, gambling, sex, fast cars or anything else. If anyone hitherto had been labouring under the misapprehension that it was, then the sooner and more firmly it was disabused the better. (p. 464)

In *R v Brewster* (1998), English courts later reinforced their stance that self-induced drug or gambling addiction cannot be relied on as mitigation. With regard to Canadian cases, the Alberta Court of Appeal in *R v McIvor* (1996) held that

> an addiction to or an obsession with gambling is neither an exceptional circum-stance justifying the imposition of a non-custodial sentence nor a mitigating

factor warranting a sentence of less than what would otherwise be fit and proper. Similarly, neither addiction to alcohol nor to drugs is recognised as an exceptional circumstance or a mitigating factor in cases of embezzlement (p. 287).

McIvor has been cited in subsequent Canadian cases that also rejected gambling addiction as a mitigating factor: *R v Holmes* (1999), *R v McTighe* (2005), *R v Smith* (2015), and *R v Ayorech* (2012). It should be noted, however, that some Commonwealth courts have occasionally accepted an offender's drug and gambling addiction as a mitigating factor (Taylor, 2002, 2004). In Canada, in the case of *R v Horvath* (1997), Judge Bayda of the Saskatchewan Court of Appeal provided an endorsement of medical models of pathological gambling and dismissed an appeal against a conditional sentence:

> The offences were the products of a distorted mind—a mind seriously diseased by a disorder now recognized by the medical community as a mental disorder. The acts committed at the command of that mind were not acts of free choice in the same sense as are the acts of free choice of a normal mind. A pathological gambler does not have the same power of control over his or her acts as one who does not suffer from that complex disease. Accordingly, where those acts constitute criminal offences, the moral culpability—moral blameworthiness—and responsibility are not of the same order as they would be in those cases where the mind is not so affected. (p. 129)

It is not clear, however, that the main impact of the medical model was the mitigation of moral blame in *Horvath*. Bayda's reasoning reflected as much an embrace of a medical model of pathological gambling as a recognition that "one pathological gambler will not be deterred by putting another pathological gambler in jail" (p. 46):

> Common sense tells us the best way to prevent a pathological gambler from committing offences designed to raise money that will be used to feed a potent gambling addiction is to emasculate the addiction by curing it or where no cure is available, by providing long-term care. Putting a pathological gambler in jail for a short period is not a cure. (p. 44).

Australian and English courts have occasionally placed some weight on drug and gambling addictions as mitigating factors: *R v Nolan* (1998), *R v Rainford* (2003), and *R v Hatzenratz* (1997). The sentences in these scattered Australian and English cases might have reflected courts' more general realization that legally coerced treatment is generally a more effective and economical means of rehabilitation and reducing recidivism than imprisonment (Hall & Carter, 2013).

Medication-Related Sex Offenses in Parkinson's Disease

In 2012, an instructive criminal case was heard in the Australian state of Tasmania, *Tasmania v Martin* (2011, 2012).[6] Terrence Martin, a former parliamentarian who was diagnosed with PD, was found guilty of one count of sexual intercourse with a young person under the age of 17 and one count of producing child exploitation material.[7] In a separate proceeding, Martin also pled guilty to one count of possessing child exploitation material. On the counts of sexual intercourse with a young person and producing child exploitation material, Martin received a custodial sentence of 10 months, which was suspended for two years. On the count of possessing child exploitation material, Martin received a custodial sentence of one month, which was suspended for 21 months.

Martin is one of a small but significant number of PD patients who develop addictive behaviors, such as pathological gambling, hypersexuality, compulsive shopping and binge eating, after taking dopamine agonists (DAs; e.g., pramipexole, ropinirole, and pergolide). DAs are prescribed to alleviate the motor symptoms of PD, a neurodegenerative disorder characterized by dopaminergic cell loss in the substantia nigra pars compacta of the midbrain (Kish, Shannak, & Hornykiewicz, 1988). PD symptoms can also be treated with the dopamine precursor levodopa, a medication that is more commonly associated with other addictive behaviors, such as dopamine dysregulation syndrome (developing a dependence on levodopa) and punding (rigid and repetitive stereotyped behaviors; Averbeck, O'Sullivan, & Djamshidian, 2014).

In *Martin*, expert testimony from two neurologists and a psychiatrist was presented to support claims for general causation between DAs and addictive behaviors and specific causation between DAs and Martin's hypersexuality. The Crown did not challenge this expert testimony or present its own neurological or psychiatric experts.

General Causation: Can DAs Cause Addictive Behaviors?

A causal relationship between DAs and addictive behaviors is plausible when judged against standard epidemiological criteria such as the strength of association, temporal consistency of the relationship, biological gradient, specificity and biological plausibility, and coherence (Ambermoon, Carter, Hall, Dissanayaka, & O'Sullivan, 2011). In terms of strength of association, around one in seven

---

[6] Sentencing comments from this case are referred to in the text without specific references.

[7] The underage girl was a 12-year-old female at the time. She was advertised as an 18-year-old prostitute by her mother and another male.

PD patients taking DAs present with an addictive behavior (Weintraub et al., 2010), with around 7% of PD patients on DAs presenting with pathological gambling (Voon et al., 2006). This compares to a pathological gambling prevalence rate of 0.5% in the general community (Petry, Stinson, & Grant, 2005). DAs have also been shown to induce pathological gambling in RLS (Evans & Butzkueven, 2007).

In terms of consistency, addictive behaviors in PD typically occur after the patient begins taking DAs, or significantly increases their dose, and generally resolve once the patient reduces the dose or ceases taking Das (Averbeck et al., 2014). The question of biological gradient is unresolved. While increasing doses often results in the emergence of addictive behaviors, a large cohort study of over 3,000 individuals was unable to find a dose-dependent relationship between DAs and addictive behaviors (Weintraub et al., 2010).

There is a plausible neurobiological mechanism that could underpin the development of addictive behaviors following dopamine replacement therapy (DRT). Dopaminergic medication gradually sensitizes the mesolimbic dopamine system and ensures that known, proximate, and accessible rewards (e.g., food, sex, money, material goods, and the medication itself) become imbued with incentive salience and pathologically "wanted" (Robinson & Berridge, 2008). While plausible, this hypothesis awaits further confirmation.

Specific Causation: Did DAs Cause Martin's Sexual Behavior?

Martin's aberrant behaviors initially arose after he began taking prescribed DAs for PD and his hypersexual symptoms significantly worsened after his DA doses increased in 2007. He reported these hypersexual symptoms to his prescribing doctor in 2008, who changed his prescription to another DA, but the behaviors re-emerged. Between January 2007 and October 2009 Martin engaged 162 sex workers on 506 occasions at a cost of approximately $150,000. The events leading to the charge of sexual intercourse with the underage girl occurred in 2009. Martin's hypersexual symptoms ceased after he stopped taking DAs in late 2009.

Both Justice Porter and Justice Blow accepted the expert neurological and psychiatric testimony at sentencing. Justice Porter concluded that a suspended sentence was justified because there was a "direct causal link between the medication prescribed for Mr Martin's PD and the offending . . . what Mr Martin suffered was really an illness." Justice Blow concluded that Martin "would not have committed any crimes if he had not taken those drugs." Later, we consider whether this strong use of neuropsychiatric evidence as a mitigating factor was warranted.

Medication-Related Alcohol Abuse in
Resting Leg Syndrome?

In 2012, an instructive criminal case was heard in the Canadian province of Manitoba (*R v Henderson*, 2011). It blends elements of the *Martin* case with a more common drug-related offence, alcohol impaired driving causing bodily harm. In April 2008, Joan Henderson was playing video lottery terminals (similar to slot machines) and drinking alcoholic beverages at a bar in Winnipeg, Manitoba. After the bar closed, she went to her car to drive home. While driving home, Henderson collided with a city street-cleaning truck. A city employee, Michael Pacheco, was placing road signs into the back of the truck at the time and was violently pinned between the truck and Henderson's car. He suffered devastating injuries to his legs and was taken to hospital in critical condition. After emerging from the vehicle, Henderson reportedly struggled to walk and talk. Her blood-alcohol reading was 0.20, two and a half times the legal limit in Manitoba. In her statement, she revealed to police that she was taking the DA Mirapex® (pramipexole) for RLS, a medication also prescribed for PD. Henderson reportedly did not drink or gamble before taking Mirapex®.

Henderson pled guilty to *impaired driving causing bodily harm* in the Manitoba Court of Queen's Bench (*R v Henderson*, 2011). At sentencing, her defense submitted expert evidence from a clinical neuropsychologist stating that it is "well-documented in the peer review literature" (p. 16) that Mirapex is associated with increased alcohol consumption, "poor judgment" (p. 16) and addictive behaviors such as pathological gambling. The defense chose not to expressly frame Henderson's alcohol consumption as compulsive or inevitable. It noted that Mirapex® can "promote compulsive behavior" (p. 24) but argued that the decision to drink and drive excessively stemmed from "a decision that she wouldn't ordinarily have made"—that is, poor judgement—as "opposed to involuntariness" (p. 24). The Crown did not contest the expert evidence or question the neuropsychologist's credentials, but argued that Henderson's decision to drive was voluntary and not medication-induced. The Crown also emphasized the importance of general deterrence and denunciation in drink driving cases, Pacheco's vulnerability as a city employee and Henderson's high blood-alcohol level.

On one hand, Justice Keyser considered the terrible impact of the incident on Pacheco and his family and Henderson's high, and therefore aggravating, blood-alcohol level. On the other hand, Justice Keyser took into account a lack of clear guidance from case law on the appropriate range of sentence; Henderson's guilty plea, apparent remorse, and lack of criminal record; and the "specific factors that caused [the accused] to drink" (p. 29)—namely, "the drug [that] caused her to drink compulsively that day" (p. 29). Justice Keyser decided to sentence

Henderson to two years' supervised probation because of the "exceptional circumstances" of the case. Exceptional circumstances must be established to justify a noncustodial sentence in cases of impaired driving causing bodily harm.

The Crown appealed the sentence on the grounds that Justice Keyser erred in both fact and principle. With regard to fact, the Crown argued that Mirapex® may have explained why Henderson drank excessively, but did not explain why she drove under the influence. With regard to principle, the Crown argued that the sentence did not fulfil the sentencing aims of denunciation and general deterrence and that recent criminal law developments meant that a term of imprisonment was the most appropriate sentence.[8]

The Court of Appeal first outlined the trial judge's crucial findings of fact: Henderson did not normally drink alcohol; she was taking Mirapex® for RLS; Mirapex® is linked with compulsive behavior; Mirapex® "caused the accused to drink compulsively that day" (p. 49); and her choice to drive was an impaired choice by someone who had not chosen to become impaired. It relied upon the "uncontroverted" (p. 50) neuropsychological testimony that Mirapex® led to Henderson's alcohol use and "poor judgment" (p. 16) in reducing Henderson's moral blameworthiness. Ultimately, the Court of Appeal decided that Justice Keyser was correct in concluding that Mirapex led the accused to drink compulsively and impaired her judgment, prompting her to drive while intoxicated. This, rather than Henderson's good character and remorse, constituted the exceptional circumstances required for Henderson to avoid a term of imprisonment as a penalty.

Are DAs Linked to Alcohol Abuse?

There is very little evidence to support the assertion of the defense neuropsychologist that DAs increase the risk of alcohol abuse. There are very few case reports of alcohol abuse in patients receiving DAs in the literature. Dodd et al. (2005) report a single patient using alcohol more frequently following ropinirole, a DA also used in the treatment of RLS and PD. Friedman and Chang (2013) also reported a single case of alcohol abuse following ropinirole, although this study was not published at the time of *R v Henderson* (2011). In contrast, a study of over 3,000 individuals treated for PD did not report a significant increase in alcohol consumption in those taking DAs (Weintraub et al., 2010). Moreover, alcohol abuse is not identified in the prescribing information provided by the manufacturer. In *Henderson*, the expert neuropsychologist provided the Court an

---

[8] A discussion of the alleged errors of principle is beyond the scope of this chapter.

appendix detailing the various studies supporting his testimony that Mirapex® is linked to pathological gambling, compulsive shopping, alcohol consumption and "poor judgment" (p. 16). Given the lack of evidence in the literature, we are surprised that the Crown did not contest this judgement or engage its own expert neuropsychologist.

Justifying Differential Treatment of Offenders With Addictive Behaviors

Our analysis highlights the differential treatment of offenders with common drug or gambling addictions and those with therapeutically induced addictive behaviors. One justification of the differential treatment of the classes of offenders with addictive behaviors is to trace responsibility back to prior choices for which the actor *was* responsible. On a standard account, a drunk driver who kills a pedestrian after voluntarily consuming over the legal limit is in a different position from a drunk driver who was forced to consume alcohol and put behind the wheel. Applying that approach to addictive behaviors would mean that, while the defendant may not be able to control his present behavior because of the addiction, he may bear at least some measure of responsibility for having developed that addiction in the first place or, perhaps, for failing to seek treatment for it: "To the extent that addicted people are to blame for their own predicament, they are not entitled to cite their predicament as an excuse" (Kennett, Vincent, & Snoek, 2015, p. 1074). The extent to which responsibility can be traced back to the addiction's origins may depend on a range of factors. It seems reasonable, for example, that someone who voluntarily tried a substance known to them to be highly addictive might bear more responsibility for their subsequent addiction than someone who sampled the substance with no such knowledge. Factors such as immaturity and influence from others may also be relevant. All of this seems relatively uncontentious. Less clear, however, is whether this approach provides a straightforward basis on which to distinguish medical from recreational addiction.

With regard to the risk of addiction, this seems more likely to vary *within* categories, rather than distinguish between them. While the popular media may offer up a narrative whereby even the most casual experimentation with recreational drugs inevitably leads to addiction, the reality is that most drug users never become addicted (Kennett et al., 2015). Someone experimenting with recreational drugs may be aware that they are running a risk of addiction but believe that the likelihood of addiction is not especially high. They have not chosen to become addicted but, rather, chosen to accept a risk that varies with the kind of drug involved.

This is also true of prescription drugs. Most users, even of relatively risky drugs, will never become addicted. However, the risk of addiction has in some cases transpired to be far higher than once previously recognized. The significant number of people addicted to prescription opioids, for instance, has been widely publicized in recent years (Centers for Disease Control and Prevention, 2016; Moghe, 2016). Furthermore, it could even be argued that someone taking prescription opioids is likely to be more aware of those dangers than someone taking recreational drugs, given that prescribing doctors are presumably more likely than drug dealers to explain those risks and the warning signs to look out for. Pharmaceutical information sheets are provided with these medications outlining these risks.

In all such cases, responsibility might plausibly be thought to vary with how much is known. In the case of Oxycontin®, information about the risk of addiction was withheld from patients and their doctors, a factor that would seem to mitigate their responsibility quite considerably. The knowledge factor, though, seems likely to vary across both prescription and recreational drug use, rather than offering a clear point of division between them.

The age at which the addicted person first used the substance in question may also be a relevant consideration in attributing responsibility. Decisions made during childhood or adolescence are generally less blameworthy than those made by adults. Again, this seems likely to be a factor that varies within the two categories, rather than offering a clear dividing line between them. Addiction to recreational drugs is more common among preadult users than addiction to prescription drugs (Centers for Disease Control and Prevention, 2016).

There are other factors that seem plausibly to have a bearing on responsibility for addiction. For instance, it might be thought that seeking treatment for the addiction, or taking other diachronic steps to prevent the addicted behavior, might reasonably be expected of the addicted individual. As Morse (2006) has argued, "almost all addicts have lucid, rational intervals between episodes of use during which they could act on the good reasons to seek help quitting or otherwise to take steps to avoid engaging in harmful drug-related behavior" (p. 193).

Once again, though, it seems likely that there will be addicted individuals among both the prescription and the recreational cohorts who have taken such steps, and others among both cohorts who have not. To whatever degree the medication taken by the defendants in *Martin* (2011, 2012) and *Henderson* (2011) enhanced their respective desires or diminished their executive control over them, questions can still be asked about the possibility to take diachronic steps—most obviously, by reporting the aberrant desires to their doctors. In other cases, the aberrant behavior may be more sudden, affording little opportunity to anticipate or avoid it. Evidence and argument will be required in each case, but again, these factors seem unlikely to offer a clear dividing line between prescription and recreational drug use.

There is, however, one factor that might have a bearing on responsibility for addiction that also offers a reason to view recreational and prescription drug use differently. This relates to the justification for taking the drug in the first place, or "onset responsibility." While both the recreational and prescription drug users might be taking similar risks, their reasons for taking those risks are not equivalently valid. Someone taking a risky drug for the purposes of prolonging their life, avoiding extreme suffering, or maintaining or restoring basic functionality is, we might think, in a different position to someone taking a risky drug for enjoyment or social acceptance. This is especially the case if following the advice of a respected authority, such as a medical professional.

This plausible distinction was noted in both *Martin* (2011, 2012) and *Henderson* (2012). That said, patients who are warned of, or become aware of, the possible effects of DAs but who fail to take adequate steps to manage risk (e.g., by pursuing self-exclusion contracts with casinos) might fare differently in court. In Martin's case, he arguably would have realized that the second medication he was prescribed was responsible for his hypersexuality, given he had already reported this to his doctor after taking his original medication and he had likely begun collecting child exploitation material.[9] He could have chosen to stop taking it and sought assistance from a medical professional. He could have also taken steps to avoid encounters with salient sexual stimuli and seek treatment for his hypersexuality (Bartlett, Hall, & Carter, 2013).

There is a further reason why we might think that this is a distinction that operates within as well as between categories. Malingerers notwithstanding, everyone taking a prescription drug may have a valid reason for taking it, but they will not invariably be reasons of equal validity. Not everyone taking prescription drugs are doing so to prolong their life, avoid extreme suffering or maintain or restore basic functionality; some are aimed at treating considerably lesser degrees of pain or discomfort, much in the same way that some use "recreational" drugs. Would it be valid for a court to consider the seriousness of the user's condition or extent of their suffering? Justification may be a valid consideration, but it may not be a binary one. Moreover, the fact that a drug was originally taken on

---

[9] If this was the case, the influential House of Lords *R v Kingston* (1994) becomes pertinent. Here, the defendant, who had pre-existing pedophilic tendencies, had his drink spiked with Valium and sexually abused a 15-year-old youth. He claimed he would not have committed the abuse "but for" the drug and thus did not have the requisite mental state for the offense. The Court rejected this defense in light of his pedophilic tendencies, which it deemed to constitute the intent to offend. If Martin collected child exploitation material before switching to the second medication, the facts would be analogous to *Kingston* and any consideration that Martin would not have offended "but for" the medication (Blow J) may not have factored into his suspended sentence.

prescription does not preclude the possibility that it was subsequently abused or misused.

The extent to which blame may fairly be attributed for such nonmedical use is impossible to determine without further information. There are, no doubt, in many cases blurred borders between the "legitimate" use in accordance with the prescription, and the "illegitimate" nonmedical use that followed. Addiction does not generally advertise its arrival, and legitimate users may not realize it was heading toward them until it has arrived. On the other hand, as we previously noted, it is likely that many users of prescription drugs have been warned of such dangers and advised of diachronic steps to avoid it. The extent to which they are responsible for that addiction will vary from case to case.

That goes precisely to our point. It is dangerous to make sweeping assumptions about broad categories of addicted individuals based on a single factor. A range of variables will plausibly bear on the question of responsibility for addiction, and it is quite possible that some offenders who first came into contact with the substance through prescription use might bear more responsibility—either for the addiction or for failure to seek help for it—than some of those whose first contact was recreational.

The Misapplication of Irrelevant Neuropsychiatric Evidence

As we have seen, in sentencing drug- and gambling-addicted individuals, commonwealth courts' willingness to use addiction as a mitigating circumstance has been inconsistent and their explicit use of neuropsychiatric evidence as a mitigating factor has been minimal. In most cases, courts will also be able to rely on other justifications for treating offenders with brain tumors or movement disorders differently from offenders with drug or gambling addictions. It is not clear, then, why the courts in *Martin* (2011, 2012) and *Henderson* (2011) needed to invoke neuropsychiatric evidence at all. It is also not clear why the courts did not take greater care in evaluating and applying this evidence after deciding to make it a core plank of their sentencing judgments. As we illustrate in the following discussion, these courts might have been wise to adhere to their more traditional strategy of treating with suspicion neuropsychiatric evidence deployed in service of reducing offender culpability.

Conflation of Causation with Compulsion

The court in *Martin* (2011, 2012) saw DRT as compelling Martin's hypersexuality, with Justice Porter arguing for a "direct *causal* link" between DRT and

Martin's offending. In *Henderson* (2011), Justice Keyser concluded that Mirapex "*caused* [Henderson] to drink compulsively," and the Court of Appeal subsequently endorsed this view: Mirapex® "*caused* the accused to drink compulsively that day." This was despite Henderson framing her defense in terms of a reduced capacity for rational deliberation and self-control, rather than a medication-induced compulsion to drink. This kind of rationale arguably rests on a misinterpretation of the neuropsychiatric evidence and represents "the fundamental psycholegal error" (Morse, 2013, p. 508)—treating evidence of causation, which will presumably be everywhere within good scientific explanations of human behavior, as if it were equivalent to evidence of compulsion. DRT only "causes" addictive behavior (which prima facie does *not* include alcohol abuse) according to epidemiological criteria. This causal relationship does not entail the conclusion that individual patients are *compelled* to perform these aberrant behaviors. Undoubtedly, patients strongly desire particular rewards, but the pursuit of these rewards, while difficult to resist, is not rendered inevitable by the medication.

No Empirical Scrutiny of Claims of Compromised Capacity and Control

In *Martin* (2011, 2012), Justice Blow concluded that Martin sexually offended "only because his capacity for self-control was substantially diminished as a result of him taking medication as prescribed." Justice Martin concluded that Martin's "sexual inhibitions were markedly lessened by the medication and his capacity to make proper judgments adversely affected." Similarly, in *Henderson* (2011), the Court of Appeal referred to Henderson's "impaired capacity" and "poor judgment" (p. 16) as the exceptional circumstances that led to a noncustodial sentence.

This argument is not supported empirically in the case of PD patients with addictive behaviors. Various neuropsychological studies show that PD patients with addictive behaviors demonstrate no more robust impairment on cognitive and motor control tasks than PD patients without addictive behaviors or healthy controls (e.g., Claassen et al., 2015; Djamshidian, O'Sullivan, Lees, & Averbeck, 2011; Wylie et al., 2012). This evidence accords with particular goal-directed aspects of Martin's behavior, such as his meticulous record-keeping of his sexual encounters and his careful attempts to avoid detection when engaging the victim. Although neuropsychological studies examining RLS patient performance on motor and cognitive control tasks are scarce, this empirical picture is also consistent with Henderson's apparent capacity to control her alcohol use in particular environments. Henderson volunteered to the police that she was taking Mirapex®. In her view, this was why she had not been drinking before going to the bar.

It is difficult to understand what the neuropsychologist for the defense meant by "poor judgment" (p. 16) in *Henderson* (2011). The Court of Appeal appeared to take it to refer to risky decision-making in light of Henderson's decision to drive while intoxicated. This is obviously not the only cognitive process to which "poor judgment" (p. 16) could refer, but evidence that DAs increase risky decision-making in laboratory settings is weak. The vast majority of studies have not found more risky decision-making in PD patients with addictive behaviors compared to PD patients without addictive behaviors (e.g., Cera et al., 2014; Claassen et al., 2011; Djamshidian et al., 2010).

Invoking Irrelevant Neuropsychiatric Evidence: Implications for Coerced Neurointerventions

Martin and Henderson voluntarily ceased their medication regime to be released on a suspended sentence. A minority of vulnerable patients in future might prefer to maintain their medication regime to avoid losing motor function or experiencing a DA withdrawal syndrome (DAWS; Mestre, Strafella, Thomsen, Voon, & Miyasaki, 2013; Nirenberg, 2013). DAWS is similar to withdrawal in drug addiction and can involve significant anxiety, dysphoria, and even suicidal thoughts.

When faced with this situation, we suggest that any court that takes the view that medication has *compelled* the addictive behaviors could offer patients two "coerced choices" as to interventions. These choices would be broadly inspired by the established practices of drug courts (Hall & Carter, 2013). The first choice for patients would be to accept a suspended sentence or conditional discharge with terms of probation including either ceasing taking their medication or undertaking risk mitigation strategies. For example, assuming them to be effective, risk mitigation strategies could hypothetically include agreeing not to drive or access the Internet, or submitting to surveillance of Internet use. Deep brain stimulation (DBS) might also be considered a potential risk mitigation strategy. Martin's decision to undergo DBS was noted at sentencing as a factor that reduced his likelihood of reoffending.

However, we doubt courts would coerce patients to undergo neurosurgery. DBS is also a common procedure for movement disorders that often allows some reduction of medication and thus likelihood of addictive behavior. The second choice would arise if the patient refuses to either stop their medication or to submit to other risk mitigation measures: incarceration or hospitalization if a person poses a substantial risk of serious injury to the public. If courts adjust their stance with regard to the influence of medication on behavior (in line with our previous critique), a third choice emerges for patients: the gradual reduction of medication together with close monitoring by a specialist with strong care-giver involvement. This choice is by no means ideal, but seems a sensible inter-vention that courts might offer in these complex cases.

Complete cessation of medication will likely confirm vulnerable patients' le-gitimate fears about loss of motor function or DAWS. The benefits of medication in terms of motor function is obvious to anyone who has observed a Parkinsonian patient go from their "off" state to their "on" state. Likewise, the seriousness of DAWS cannot be dismissed because it can involve anxiety, panic attacks, de-pression, dysphoria, agitation, nausea, pain, and suicidal ideation that lasts for months and sometimes years. It is also more common in PD patients with ad-dictive behaviors (Nirenberg, 2013). For these reasons, we suggest that courts ordering the cessation of medication would be imposing the kind of "cruel and unusual" treatment against which numerous international and Commonwealth charters seek to protect offenders: Universal Declaration of Human Rights (1948, Article5) and Canadian Charter of Rights and Freedom (1982, Section 12). While upholding the sentencing aims of deterrence and public protection, this choice would not aid the offender's rehabilitation and arguably goes far beyond denunciation into cruelty.

A patient might understandably not wish to cease their medication. Yet if courts are committed to the view that medication compels addictive behaviors, they will be left with no option but to send the patient to a secure psychiatric facility. This would protect the community from the further harm but with doubtful rehabilitative value. There are few psychosocial treatments for addictive behaviors in PD with any empirical support (Zhang et al., 2016). It is also an open question whether commitment in a psychiatric facility sufficiently denounces the crime and deters others.

Neither of these choices is entirely desirable from either the offender's or the community's perspective. Yet, as far as we can tell, these are the only choices avail-able to patients who appear before a court that equates causality with compul-sion. What if a court took a more critical view of the neuroscientific evidence, as we have argued that they should? Would the court be able to offer an additional "coerced choice" to patients? We think so. As a rough sketch, courts could deliver a suspended sentence on the conditions that the patient (a) reduce their addic-tive desires (and only some motor function) by gradually reducing their medica-tion under the very strict specialist supervision; (b) trial other medications that might assist in reducing addictive behaviors (e.g., amantadine); (c) involve their caregivers or social workers in monitoring their behavior to minimize the chance that their addictive desires will be translated into addictive behaviors (e.g., care-giver monitoring of internet usage); and (d) engage in cognitive behavioral therapy.

We emphasize that this demanding, multifaceted regimen does not represent a perfect solution. For example, it might require additional buffering to ensure community protection; it fails to sufficiently denounce the crime; and it would involve a lot of 'trial and error' to maintain reasonable motor function in the face of medication reduction. Nevertheless, it would be a pragmatic "least of all evils" approach that, it should be remembered, will only be required in very rare cases.

Conclusion

We have argued that (a) commonwealth courts do not tend to see drug or gambling addictions as mitigating factors in cases of addiction-related offending; (b) when these courts have made exceptions and adopted a medical lens in sentencing drug- and gambling-addicted individuals, the approach has arguably been driven by consequentialist reasoning, rather than acceptance of claims made by addiction neuropsychiatry; (c) in two instructive cases of medication-related criminal offending, there has been an explicit use of neuropsychiatric evidence to suggest compulsion, reduced self-control, and diminished moral blame and thus endorsement of a medical model in sentencing; and (d) this use of neuropsychiatric evidence was unnecessary as there are other rationales for treating medicated offenders differently from offenders with drug and gambling addictions. This conclusion should be welcomed by future courts that wish to maintain a degree of pragmatic flexibility when determining an appropriate intervention for a medicated offender unwilling to cease medication.

References

Ambermoon, P., Carter, A., Hall, W. D., Dissanayaka, N. N. W., & O'Sullivan, J. D. (2011). Impulse control disorders in patients with Parkinson's disease receiving dopamine replacement therapy: Evidence and implications for the addictions field. *Addiction, 106*(2), 283–293.

Averbeck, B. B., O'Sullivan, S. S., & Djamshidian, A. (2014). Impulsive and compulsive behaviours in Parkinson's disease. *Annual Review of Clinical Psychology, 10*(1), 553–580.

Bartlett, F., Hall, W. D., & Carter, A. (2013). *Tasmania v Martin* (No 2): Voluntariness and causation for criminal offending associated with treatment of Parkinson's disease. *Criminal Law Journal, 37*(3), 330–341.

Brooks, G., & Blaszczynski, A. (2011). Judicial decisions on cases involving problem gambling and crime in England and Wales. *International Gambling Studies, 11*(1), 81–92.

Burns, J., & Swerdlow, R. H. (2003). Right orbitofrontal tumor with pedophilia symptom and constructional apraxia sign *Archives of Neurology, 60*(3), 437–440.

Centers for Disease Control and Prevention. (2016, March 16). Prescription opioids. Retrieved from https://www.cdc.gov/drugoverdose/opioids/prescribed.html

Cera, N., Bifolchetti, S., Martinotti, G., Gambi, F., Sepede, G., Onofrj, M., . . . Thomas A. (2014). Amantadine and cognitive flexibility: Decision-making in Parkinson's patients with severe pathological gambling and other impulse control disorders. *Neuropsychiatric Disease and Treatment, 10*, 1093–1101.

Claassen, D. O., van den Wildenberg, W. P. M., Harrison, M. B., van Wouwe, N. C., Kanoff, K., Neimat, J., & Wylie, S. A. (2015). Proficient motor impulse control in Parkinson disease patients with impulsive and compulsive behaviors. *Pharmacology, Biochemistry and Behavior, 129*, 19–25.

Claassen, D. O., van den Wildenberg, W. P. M., Ridderinkhof, K. R., Jessup, C. K., Harrison, M. B., Wooten, F., & Wylie, S. A. (2011). The risky business of dopamine agonists in Parkinson disease and impulse control disorders. *Behavioral Neuroscience, 125*(4), 492–500.

Davies, J. B. (1997). *The myth of addiction* (2nd ed.). Amsterdam, The Netherlands: Harwood Academic.

Djamshidian, A., Jha, A., O'Sullivan, S., Silveira-Moriyama, L., Jacobson, C., Brown, P., . . . Averbeck, B. B. (2010). Risk and learning in impulsive and nonimpulsive patients with Parkinson's disease. *Movement Disorders, 25*(13), 2203–2210.

Djamshidian, A. O'Sullivan, S., Lees, A., & Averbeck, B. B. (2011). Stroop test performance in impulsive and nonimpulsive patients with Parkinson's disease. *Parkinsonism and Related Disorders, 17*(3), 212–214.

Dodd, M. L., Klos, K. J., Bower, J. H., Yonas, E. G., Josephs, K. A., & Ahlskog, J. E. (2005). Pathological gambling caused by drugs used to treat Parkinson disease. *Archives of Neurology, 62*(9), 1377–1381.

Evans, A. H., & Butzkueven, H. (2007). Dopamine agonist-induced pathological gambling in restless leg syndrome due to multiple sclerosis. *Movement Disorders, 22*(4), 590–591.

Foddy, B., & Savulescu, J. (2006). Addiction and autonomy: Can addicted people consent to the prescription of their drug of addiction? *Bioethics, 20*(1), 1–15.

Friedman, J. H., & Chang, V. (2013). Crack cocaine use due to dopamine agonist therapy in Parkinson disease. *Neurology, 80*(24), 2269–2270.

Glenn, A. L., & Raine, A. (2014). Neurocriminology: Implications for the punishment, prediction and prevention of criminal behaviour. *Nature Reviews Neuroscience, 15*(1), 54–63.

Goldstein, R. Z., & Volkow, N. D. (2011). Dysfunction of the prefrontal cortex in addiction: Neuroimaging findings and clinical implications. *Nature Reviews Neuroscience, 12*(11), 652–669.

Hall, W. D., & Carter, A. (2013). How may neuroscience affect the way that the criminal courts deal with addicted offenders? In N. Vincent (Ed.), *Neuroscience and legal responsibility* (pp. 279–302). New York, NY: Oxford University Press.

Hall, W. D., Carter, A., & Forlini, C. (2015). The brain disease model of addiction: Is it supported by the evidence and has it delivered on its promise? *The Lancet Psychiatry, 2*(1), 105–110.

Heyman, G. M. (2009). *Addiction: A disorder of choice*. Cambridge, MA: Harvard University Press.

Higgins, S. T., & Petry, N. M. (1999). Contingency management: Incentives for sobriety. *Alcohol Research & Health, 23*(2), 122–127.

Husak, D., & Murphy, E. (2013). The relevance of the neuroscience of addiction to criminal law. In S. J. Morse & A. L. Roskies (Eds.), *A primer on criminal law and neuroscience: A contribution of the law and neuroscience project, supported by the MacArthur Foundation* (pp. 216–239). New York, NY: Oxford University Press.

Kennett, J., Vincent, N. A., & Snoek, A. (2015). Drug addiction and criminal responsibility. In J. Clausen & N. Levy (Eds.), *Handbook of neuroethics* (pp. 1065–1083). Dordrecht, The Netherlands: Springer.

Kish, S. J., Shannak, K., & Hornykiewicz, O. (1988). Uneven pattern of dopamine loss in the striatum of patients with idiopathic Parkinson's disease: Pathophysiologic and clinical implications. *The New England Journal of Medicine, 318*(14), 876–880.

Leshner, A. I. (1997). Addiction is a brain disease, and it matters. *Science, 278*(5335), 45–47.

Lewis, M. (2015). *The biology of desire: Why addiction is not a disease.* Brunswick, NJ: Scribe.

Mestre, T. A., Strafella, A. P., Thomsen, T., Voon, V., & Miyasaki, J. (2013). Diagnosis and treatment of impulse control disorders in patients with movement disorders. *Therapeutic Advances in Neurological Disorders, 6*(3), 175–188.

Moghe, S. (2016, October 14). Opioid history: From "wonder drug" to abuse epidemic. *CNN.* Retrieved from https://www.cnn.com/2016/05/12/health/opioid-addiction-history/index.html

Morse, S. J. (2006). Addiction, genetics, and criminal responsibility. *Law and Contemporary Problems, 69*(1), 165–207.

Morse, S. J. (2013). A good enough reason: Addiction, agency and criminal responsibility. *Inquiry: An Interdisciplinary Journal of Philosophy, 56*(5), 490–518.

Nirenberg, M. (2013). Dopamine agonist withdrawal syndrome: Implications for patient care. *Drugs & Aging, 30*(8), 587–592.

Penney, S. (2012). Impulse control and criminal responsibility: Lessons from neuroscience. *International Journal of Law and Psychiatry, 35*(2), 99–103.

Petry, N. M., Stinson, F. S., & Grant, B. F. (2005). Comorbidity of DSM-IV pathological gambling and other psychiatric disorders: Results from the National Epidemiologic Survey on Alcohol and Related Conditions. *Journal of Clinical Psychiatry, 66*(5), 564–574.

Prendergast, M., Podus, D., Finney, J., Greenwell, L., & Roll, J. (2006). Contingency management for treatment of substance use disorders: A meta-analysis. *Addiction, 101*(11), 1546–1560.

R v Ayorech, ABCA 82 (2012).

R v Brewster, 1 Cr App R 220 (1998).

R v Chapman, NSWCCA 457 (2001).

R v Foley, ACTSC 109 (2001).

R v Grossi, VSCA 51 (2008).

R v Hatzenratz, EWCA Crim 232 (1997).

R v Henderson, MBCA 9 (2011).

R v Henry, 46 NSWLR 346 (1999).

R v Holmes, 237 AR 146 (1999).

R v Horvath, 117 CCC (3rd) 110 (1997).

R v Kingston, 3 All ER 353 (1994).

R v Lawrence, 10 Cr App R (S) 463 (1988).

R v McIvor, 106 CCC (3rd) 285 (1996).

R v McTighe, 193 CCC (3rd) 522 (2005).

R v Nolan, VSCA 135 (1998).

R v Rainford, VSCA 49 (2003).

R v Smith, BCSC 1267 (2015).

R v Spiero, 22 SASR 543 (1979).

Robinson, T. E., & Berridge, K. C. (2008). The incentive sensitization theory of addiction: Some current issues. *Philosophical Transactions of the Royal Society of London: Series B Biological Sciences, 363*(1507), 3137–3146.

Tasmania v Martin (Sentencing comments, Supreme Court of Tasmania, Porter J, 29 November 2011).

Tasmania v Martin (Sentencing comments, Supreme Court of Tasmania, Blow J, 16 February 2012).

Taylor, G. (2002). Should addiction to drugs be a mitigating factor in sentencing? *Criminal Law Journal, 26*(6), 324–343.

Taylor, G. (2004). Is addiction to gambling relevant in sentencing? *Criminal Law Journal, 28*, 141–159.

United States v. Hendrickson, 25 F. Supp. 3d 1166 (N.D. Iowa 2014).

Volkow, N. D., Koob, G. F., & McLellan, A. T. (2016). Neurobiologic advances from the brain disease model of addiction. *The New England Journal of Medicine, 374*(4), 363–371.

Voon, V., Hassan, K., Zurowski, M., de Souza, M., Thomsen, T., Fox, S., . . . Miyasaki J. (2006). Prevalence of repetitive and reward-seeking behaviors in Parkinson disease. *Neurology, 67*(7), 1254–1257.

Weintraub, D., Koester, J., Potenza, M., Siderowf, A. D., Stacy, M. A., Voon, V., . . . Lange, A. E. (2010). Impulse control disorders in Parkinson disease: A cross-sectional study of 3090 patients. *Archives of Neurology, 67*(5), 589–595.

Wylie, S. A., Claassen., D. O., Huizenga, H. M., Schewel, K. D., Ridderinkhof, K. R., Bashore, T. R., & van den Wildenberg, W. P. M. (2012). Dopamine agonists and the suppression of impulsive motor actions in Parkinson disease. *Journal of Cognitive Neuroscience, 24*(8), 1709–1724.

Young-Wolff, K. C., Enoch, M.-A., & Prescott, C. A. (2011). The influence of gene-environment interactions on alcohol consumption and alcohol use disorders: A comprehensive review. *Clinical Psychology Review, 31*(5), 800–816.

Zhang, S., Dissanayaka, N. N., Dawson, A., O'Sullivan, J. D., Mosley, P., Hall, W., & Carter, A. (2016). Management of impulse control disorders in Parkinson's disease. *International Psychogeriatrics, 28*(10), 1597–1614.

PART III

HEALING PEOPLE

11

"It Will Help You Repent"

Why the Communicative Theory of Punishment Requires the Provision of Medications to Offenders With ADHD

William Bülow

Introduction

Attention-deficit/hyperactivity disorder (ADHD) is common among prison inmates. According to Ginsberg, Hirvikoski, Grann, and Lindefors (2012), the estimated population of adult prison inmates with ADHD in several European countries is in the range of 25% to 45%. In comparison, ADHD is estimated to affect 2% to 5% of adults in the general population. ADHD is also associated with coexisting psychiatric disorders where substance use disorder and antisocial personality disorder are common, both of which increase the risk of delinquency. Among prison inmates with ADHD, it is most often combined with conduct disorder, usually childhood onset conduct disorder, which in turn is believed to be the dominating risk factor in mediating the later development of antisocial behavior and delinquency, not ADHD alone (Ginsberg et al., 2012, p. 706).

Individuals with ADHD suffer from problems with attention, hyperactivity, and/or acting impulsively (Ginsberg et al., 2012, p. 705). One form of treatment for ADHD is methylphenidate, a central nervous system stimulant that has been shown to be effective in reducing the severity of symptoms in prison inmates with this condition (Ginsberg & Lindefors, 2012). In turn, this sort of treatment might help to increase the autonomy and self-control needed to successfully participate in rehabilitation and education programs.[1]

As ADHD is prevalent among prison inmates, it is reasonable that this would also affect discussions on the ethics of punishment. Recently, overlapping discussions about criminal justice ethics and neuroethics have addressed the question of whether the use of biomedical and neuropsychiatric interventions

---

[1] According to Ginsberg (2013), it is important to bear in mind that methylphenidate is in itself not sufficient for offender rehabilitation, but must be accompanied with traditional rehabilitation programs, such as learning, work training, and cognitive therapy.

William Bülow, *"It Will Help You Repent"* In: *Neurointerventions and the Law.* Edited by: Nicole A Vincent, Thomas Nadelhoffer, and Allan McCay, Oxford University Press (2020). © Oxford University Press 2020
DOI: 10.1093/oso/9780190651145.001.0011

(henceforth *neurointerventions*) should be encouraged within criminal justice systems. One part of these discussions has focused on the moral permissibility of offering treatment as an alternative to imprisonment, or as a condition of early release (Bomann-Larsen, 2013; Ryberg, 2012, 2015; Ryberg & Petersen, 2013).[2]

My aim in this chapter is not to suggest that medical interventions should replace or reduce the time of incarceration. Rather, I suggest that at least some neurointerventions, such as providing methylphenidate to offenders with ADHD, should be encouraged for the sake of achieving certain penological ends. More specifically, I focus on the *communicative theory of punishment* and its implications for this area. In the contemporary context, this theory, although a species of retributivism, has become a familiar alternative to traditional theories in the philosophy of punishment such as the deterrence theory, the rehabilitative theory, and traditional forms of retributivism. Within the more prominent version of this theory, famously advocated by Antony Duff, criminal punishment is understood as a form of *secular penance*. Criminal law declares that certain conduct is wrong, punishment is imposed on offenders who commit criminal offences, and as an upshot the criminal offender may become repentant and begin to reform, eventually reconciling with whom they wronged (Duff, 2001, p. 106). Though this theory has attracted serious attention,[3] less has been said about the recent achievements in neuroscience in relation to this theory. I argue that this theory provides compelling nonmedical reasons to offer methylphenidate to offenders with ADHD. As a general conclusion, I propose that my discussion shows that the distinction between rehabilitation on the one hand and punishment on the other is far from obvious. To the contrary, different forms of treatment (including pharmacological) and punishment can be understood as mutually and equally important aspects within in a single penal framework, rather than two conflicting paradigms of criminal justice.

I will proceed as follows. First, I will introduce the communicative theory of punishment and its main features. In the process, I pay specific attention to how the theory can conceptualize certain forms of treatment programs as instances of communicative punishment. I then problematize two of the central concerns within this theory: the relationship between repentance and self-reform. I argue

---

[2] If morally acceptable, medical interventions could provide a promising alternative to standard punishment. Rather than incarcerating offenders for a long period of time, psychopharmacological treatment should be considered, since it in turn could be hypothesized to assist in reducing recidivism. From a pure consequentialist perspective, this should be strongly encouraged. On the other hand, a proponent of a retributivist view could argue that the justifying aim of punishment is for the offender to suffer in proportion to the harm he or she has inflicted upon his or her victims. Since this is the aim, it could be argued that direct treatment of any sort is not a legitimate substitute for the punishment, although reform or specific deterrence may be a side effect of harsh treatment (Ryberg, 2015).

[3] For instance, in his recent introduction to philosophical theories of punishment, Thom Brooks (2012) devotes a large part of a chapter to communicative theories of punishment (pp. 103–122).

that the connection between these two is not as evident as one might think and that both aims may be hindered by the symptoms associated with an ADHD diagnosis. I suggest that to overcome these hindrances and achieve the aims of communicative punishment, prison inmates should be provided with the option to undergo pharmacological intervention consisting of taking methylphenidate for their ADHD. I then discuss one potential objection to my argument concerning the authenticity and moral worth of pharmacological treatment. In the final section, I summarize and discuss my general conclusions.

The Communicative Theory of Punishment

According to its most prominent advocate, Antony Duff, the communicative theory of punishment (or communicative theory for short) states that the justification of criminal punishment lies in its communicative purpose, where the justifying aim of punishment is to communicate to the offender the censure he or she deserves for committing the crime (Duff, 2001, p. 30). Duff maintains that criminal offenses are *public wrongs*, that is, wrongs in which the public as a whole has a proper interest (pp. 60–61). This proper interest motivates an authoritative and communal condemnation of such a wrong, which in turn merits a communal response. Understood as public wrongs, criminal wrongdoings are not only wrongs to the victim, but to the society as a whole. The victim is not wronged solely in virtue of being a freestanding individual, but is wronged also as a member of the community. Thus, crimes are always wrongs against the community according to Duff (p. 63).

As a way of communicating the censure that an offender deserves, criminal punishment, on the communicative theory, is warranted as an attempt at persuading the offender that what he or she has done was wrong (Duff, 2001, p. 30). In Duff's own terms, criminal punishment can be understood as a form of *secular penance*. On his view, criminal punishment is imposed on the offender for the crime through which he or she will become repentant, begin to reform, and, eventually, reconcile with those whom the offender has wronged (p. 106). Thus, on the communicative theory, criminal punishment aims at the goals of *repentance, reform*, and *reconciliation*, where a truly successful penal communication occurs where each of these aims are fulfilled.

An act of repentance is an authentic recognition that one has done wrong. It is acknowledgement of a particular act as wrongful and something that one wishes to be undone. Repentance is also necessarily painful, since it pains one to recognize and admit that what one has done was wrong (Duff, 2001, p. 107). According to the communicative theory of punishment, repentance is not finished easily and must, therefore, occupy the wrongdoer's attention, thoughts, and emotions for some considerable length of time (p. 107). The second part of secular penance is reform. Duff claims reform— more specifically, *self-reform*—is an implication of repentance. The repentance of a wrong involves the recognition that one should avoid doing the same wrong in the future (p. 108). The third aspect, reconciliation, is what a repentant wrongdoer seeks from those whom he or she has wronged. According to Duff, reconciliation often requires more than a verbal apology, especially where grave wrongs have been committed. In such cases, it can take the form of reparation for the harm one has done, either to the victim or to the community as a whole. An apology could also consist of the willingness to undergo a penitential burden that expresses the repentance and recognition of one's wrongdoing to those people concerned (p. 109).

One attractive feature of Duff's theory of criminal punishment, I believe, is how it accounts for both forward-looking and backward-looking components of punishment. It is backward-looking in the sense that punishment is justified as deserved censure. Unlike traditional retributivist accounts, however, it is forward-looking in its focus on reform and reconciliation where the aim is to restore the relationship between the offender and the community. Another attractive feature of the theory is how it is inclusive rather than exclusive, and that the offender is regarded as an equal moral agent and as a member of the normative community. In this sense, Duff's account avoids a common critique to traditional consequentialist theories of punishment, as it succeeds in acknowledging the possible good effects of punishment on offenders without treating them as mere means to ends (see, e.g., Boonin, 2008; Golash, 2005).

The aim of secular penance can be accomplished in various ways. Among Duff's (2001) own examples are probation programs and requiring offenders to undergo certain rehabilitation programs. One implication of Duff's account is that at least some forms of rehabilitation programs are not seen as therapy.[4] Rather, they qualify as instances of communicative punishment (Duff, 2001, p. 103). One of Duff's own examples of a program that fulfills his criteria of punishment is the CHANGE Project[5] (pp. 102–104). CHANGE, a treatment

---

[4] The notion of reform, rehabilitation, and therapy are occasionally used interchangeable in philosophical discussion on legal punishment. It is important, however, to recognize that they are somewhat different. Reform involves a change in an individual's dispositions, attitudes, and commitments. This is something that communicative punishment may bring about. In contrast, therapy and rehabilitation does not have to involve any change in this sense. Rather, rehabilitation is a means of helping the offender becoming more compliant with the law and to better function in society. For example, working programs may count as a form of rehabilitation program, where the aim is to make the offender prepared for the working market and thus become adjusted to society, but does not have to involve any change in that offenders' values or dispositions. That being said, there are examples where rehabilitation, therapy, and reform overlap.

[5] A program very similar to the CHANGE project is being used in Swedish Correctional Care—the Integrated Domestic Abuse Program—with a specific focus on domestic abuse (Kriminalvården, 2015).

program targeting male offenders sentenced for domestic abuse, was established in Scotland in 1989 and operates with the theoretical assumption that violence occurs because of issues of power and control between men and women in intimate relationships. From this perspective, domestic violence is embedded in everyday conflicts—such as jealousy, domestic work, childcare, money, and alcohol—and the ordinary mundane aspects of everyday life are held to be fundamental to the perpetration of this violence (Dobash & Dobash, 2000, p. 258). The program is based on cognitive behavioral therapy and asserts that violence is a form of learned behavior. In essence, the program focuses on ways of thinking about intimate relationships and ways of behaving in relation to issues of conflict and disagreements. The fundamental focus is on violence, and the CHANGE program seeks to challenge the offenders to bring them to accept their responsibility for the offense and to help them to change their behavior (Dobash & Dobash, 2000, pp. 258–259). This is done through a series of confrontational group sessions that involve both reenactment and discussion (Duff, 2001, p. 103).

Duff (2001) holds that it is because of its intentional focus on the offending man as responsible for his violence and his need to change that makes participation in a rehabilitation program such as CHANGE, in conjunction with probation or a prison sentence, appropriate as a form of communicative punishment.[6] First, treatment programs are imposed on offenders for their criminal offenses as an appropriate response to their wrongdoing. As a response, it seeks to persuade the offender to recognize his actions and his conduct as a transgression of the community's moral norms and, therefore, accept that the rehabilitation program is a justified response to his crime. This corresponds to the goal of repentance on Duff's account of penitential punishment. Repentance is in itself burdensome, and according to Duff, these sorts of rehabilitation programs are also deliberately burdensome or painful in the sense that they aim to confront the offender with his previous wrongdoing (p. 107). Having to attend a rehabilitation program can be burdensome in itself, and Duff maintains that we should see this burden as part of the offender's punishment and not merely as an inevitable side effect of therapy (p. 103). Rehabilitation programs such as CHANGE are also forward-looking in the sense that they aim to persuade the offender that he has done wrong, as well as helping the offender from committing additional wrongs and to refrain from violence (p. 103). This aspect of rehabilitation programs corresponds to the second goal of punishment: reform. As I have already indicated, to recognize and to repent from one's previous wrongdoings is to recognize that one needs to avoid doing the same wrong in the future (p. 108). Reform, in this sense, is then necessarily self-reform, since the reformation must be based on the

---

[6] It should be acknowledged that violent offenders can be female too. However, as CHANGE is a program targeting male offenders, I will to use the pronoun *he* as I discuss this particular program.

offender's own repentance from his past behavior. In the end, repentance and reformation can also lead to the third goal of punishment, reconciliation, and make the participation in the program an appropriate apology.

This way of conceptualizing treatment programs is of special interest to my focus on offenders with ADHD. The reason, or so I will argue, is that offenders suffering from ADHD might fail to grasp the communicative message their participation in the sort of treatment programs exemplified in the previous discussion is meant to communicate. I will now turn to this issue in greater detail.

Communicative Punishment and ADHD Treatment: A Case for Methylphenidate

On the face of it, Duff's (2001) theory is attractive. If we assert that his theory is the correct one, what are its implications for the issue at hand with regards to offenders with ADHD? On Duff's view, communicative punishment is justified as an attempt at persuading offenders that what they have done is wrong and to bring about repentance, reform, and reconciliation. In this section, I argue that severe ADHD may hinder two aims of successful penal communication— namely, repentance and reform—and thus undermine the communicative aim of punishment.

Even though the attempt to bring about repentance and reform is the internal aim of communicative punishment, Duff (2001) acknowledges that at least some offenders will remain unpersuaded by the message of punishment (pp. 121–124). There are, of course, various possible reasons why this might happen. Some offenders will not listen seriously to the message that their punishment is intended to communicate, while others will listen but remain unpersuaded. Some might fail to listen or remain unpersuaded because they do not care about the rightness or wrongness of their conduct. Another possibility is that the offender is committed to other values than the shared values sanctioned by their community. The latter kind is exemplified by what Jonathan Jacobs (2007) has referred to as morally unreachable agents—that is, agents who are fixed in their moral characters, who do not fully acknowledge their offense, and thus who have very little or no moral motivation for self-correction (p. 18). In this case, we might have strong reasons to suppose that the aim of communicative punishment will inevitably fail. However, according to Duff, we might be justified in an attempt that we know will fail. We are justified in such an attempt partly because it is owed to the victim and to the community that share in the wrong that the offender has exceeded. Also, in either case the offender has, in virtue of being an autonomous moral agent, the right not to listen to the message of the punishment. One virtue of seeing communicative punishment as an attempt at persuading the offender that he or she has done wrong, according to Duff, is that the offender is rightly treated as a moral agent (p. 123).

Yet another possibility, and the one in which I am interested here, is the offender who is impeded by conditions associated with a particular mental impairment. An offender suffering from ADHD, for instance, may be an agent who could listen to the message communicated by punishment and become persuaded by it, but fails to do so due to different forms of distractions, such as the lack of attentiveness. *This is different from actively choosing not to listen to the message of punishment.* Rather, impulsive behavior and hyperactivity may very well limit an offender's capacity to listen carefully to the message of his or her communicative punishment, rendering the person less autonomous to freely choose to either accept or refute the message. This is specifically true when the punishment involves the participation in a probation program that demand high levels of concentration, working memory, and self-regulation. As an illustration, we may introduce a possible distinction between external and internal interferences that may undermine a person's autonomy. Paradigmatic examples of external interferences are brainwashing, deception, or manipulation. *These interferences are all caused by other agents.* In contrast, as Jonathan Pugh (2014) points out, autonomy can be inhibited without direct interference by other agents. One example is an agent who only acts on the basis of his or her impulsive desires (p. 373). For instance, it is fairly uncontroversial to assume that a drug addiction may undermine an individual's autonomy. One explanation is that an addict acts on impulsive desires that, given some form of critical reflection, the individual would wish that he or she didn't have. However, the same is often true for cognitive conditions such as ADHD, associated with a high level of impulsivity and lack of control (pp. 373–374). In contrast to brainwashing or deception, this and other symptoms associated with ADHD are not dependent on interferences by other agents; they can be understood as internal interferences that might undermine a person's autonomy.[7]

In cases where both external and internal interferences are absent, it is indeed reasonable to say that one has a right not to listen to the message of punishment. However, in the case of ADHD, which is associated with hyperactivity and

---

[7] According to Pugh (2014), giving methylphenidate to individuals suffering from ADHD to increase their autonomy calls into question whether there is an ethically relevant distinction between enhancement and treatment (p. 375). This distinction has been widely discussed in bioethics on whether it is morally permissible to enhance mental and physical capacitates beyond "normal" function (see, e.g., Kamm, 2005; Sandel, 2004). Of course, some might disagree, although I believe that we have good reason to accept Pugh's conclusion. For my purpose, however, this doesn't seem to be much of a problem, since we could accept that providing individuals suffering from ADHD with methylphenidate is not an instance of cognitive enhancement, but a form of treatment aimed at restoring certain capacities, such as concentration and impulse control, to "normal" functioning. As few deny that treatment of this sort is permissible, they should be agreeable to providing methylphenidate to prisoners suffering from ADHD.

strong impulsive behavior, the level of autonomy grounding the right to either listen or refute the message is not obviously fulfilled or at least can be improved.[8] The remedy to this situation, I believe, could be to provide methylphenidate for ADHD to prisoners suffering from this condition. Doing this would be warranted in so far as we see punishment as a form of secular penance.

Besides hindering repentance, and thus the communicative aim of punishment, ADHD may also hinder reform. As I previously emphasized, Duff (2001) describes reform (or more precisely *self-reform*) as an implication of repentance. To repent for one's wrongdoings, one must recognize the need to avoid doing those things in the future. Still, this is far from the easy task it might initially appear to be. The fact that you repent from your criminal wrongdoing, and thus recognize the need to change your behavior in the future, is not the same as ensuring that you actually succeed in changing your ways. For many people, it is not enough to repent from a previous act to change. This may be due to various constraints or limitations (e.g., learning difficulties) one might have. Some constraints might be socio-economic. If one is not given the opportunity to work, housing, education, etc., it might be hard for a criminal offender to actually realize self-reformation and to stay out of trouble, even though he or she may very well be repentant for previous crimes. Other obstacles might involve various forms of addiction such as drug abuse. To support and assist self-reformation among repentant offenders, it is arguable that one equally should assist and help them from relapsing into crime. However, there are other examples of obstacles that have less to do with external factors. ADHD is one such example. As ADHD includes problems of attention, hyperactivity, and/or acting impulsively, these could very well undermine the prospects of self-reformation as many treatment programs in correctional care include high demands on concentration, working memory, and self-regulation (Ginsberg, 2013, p. 406). It is important to bear in mind that many of the offenders suffering from ADHD need assistance not only during their time in prison or during probation but also postrelease. Thus, in so far as we wish to induce reform, we should be willing to subsidize ADHD medicine for these offenders postrelease.

If methylphenidate can assist in achieving the communicative aim stated by the communicative theory one might, of course, question why this should only be optional. Why shouldn't it be mandatory for offenders to take methylphenidate if they are diagnosed with ADHD? One reason why a proponent of the communicative theory of punishment might accept mandatory psychopharmacological interventions of this sort for offenders with ADHD is because

---

[8] That said, it is not necessarily so that impulsive behavior undermines such a right. As Pugh (2014) points out, high impulsivity is not always inimical to an agent's autonomy. Some individuals value impulsivity and spontaneity. However, this is a case where the impulsiveness and spontaneity are not something that distracts the agent from leading a life of his or her own choosing, but is a constitutive part thereof.

it facilitates the possibility for secular penance. Since this is the aim of punishment, the conditions of one's punishment (such as the prison conditions) should also reflect this aim. For instance, if it were the case that little contact with people outside of the prison system undermines the prospects for repentance and self-reform, then proponents of the communicative theory of punishment should be willing to endorse more permeable prisons or perhaps earlier parole. Analogously, if offenders with ADHD render the possibility for successful secular penance less probably, then why shouldn't the communicative theorist accept mandatory psychopharmacological intervention?

The communicative theorist could stress that undergoing pharmacological ADHD treatment is not part of the punishment, and for that reason it shouldn't be imposed. There is an important distinction between what is imposed as part of the punishment and what may be offered to the offenders to assist or help them (see Duff, 2001, p. 150). Punishment—on the communicative theory—is justified as deserved censure and as an attempt at persuading offenders about the wrongfulness of their conduct. What is part of the punishment must therefore be directed only at their criminal conduct (which is true of CHANGE in the case of men sentenced for domestic abuse). In contrast, psychiatric care, including psychopharmacological treatment, is not primarily targeting the criminal in the sense prescribed by the communicative theory. Rather, psychiatric treatment is intended as a way of reducing the symptoms associated with a diagnosis and/or to help the offender cope with various problems. That is, psychological treatment during a prison sentence is not part of the punishment, but could be offered to offenders to help them cope with different problems and needs. These measures may very well help facilitate and assist both repentance and self-reform. Nevertheless, even though a treatment may help facilitating these ends, it would be wrong to conclude the treatment should be made mandatory or that they are just a part of the imposed punishment.

Another reason why mandatory treatment should not be accepted under the communicative theory of punishment is because such coerced pharmacological interventions could violate the normative constraint of treating offenders as autonomous moral agents. Even though the symptoms associated with ADHD may, as I have previously noted, sometimes hinder autonomous and voluntary behavior (especially so when it comes to listening to the message communicated to them by types of punishment that presupposes abilities of concentration, self-regulation, and working memory), it would be too strong a claim to make that people suffering from ADHD completely lack autonomy or that they aren't moral agents capable of making any autonomous decisions.[9] By and large, most of us

---

[9] I assert, without argument, that moral agency presupposes the ability to act autonomously and voluntarily. Besides this ability, the capacity for moral agency also involves responsiveness to moral considerations.

do from time to time fail to act autonomously. We would then violate this constraint if we were to force anyone to undergo treatment because it would be false to suggest that people who suffer from ADHD are nonautonomous agents in the sense that they may never act autonomously or voluntarily. This is something that Duff (2001) also considers an important normative constraint on the institution of punishment. Therefore, to avoid violating this important moral constraint, the communicative theory of punishment could demand that we ought to recognize and treat the offender as a moral agent who is capable of making autonomous decisions about treatment. This would constrain us from requiring prison inmates to undergo such a treatment, even though it would be permissible to make it available and maybe even to encourage them to avail themselves of it.[10] For sure, there are reasons why one may wish not to take methylphenidate, since one might very well perceive that one's mental condition has an impact on or is intertwined with one's personality in a way that makes treatment with methylphenidate undesirable or improper.[11] Thus, whether or not one wishes to undergo treatment should be left up to one's own choice.[12]

A counterargument, however, is that methylphenidate might be needed to make offenders eligible for that kind of punishment. After all, if punishment is imposed and (as in Duff's, 2001, own CHANGE example) part of the deliberate burden imposed by the punishment lies in it inducing repentance, the offenders' eligibility for that punishment will partly hinge on whether they indeed could repent. If this is right, then would this not entail that we must ensure that offenders that are held responsible for their crimes will experience the burdens associated with repentance?

Thus far, I have steered away from reaching a final verdict about whether the communicative theory would warrant mandatory or optional treatment. I am inclined to contend that pharmacological interventions are not part of the punishment, and for that reason, they should not be imposed. Therefore, I will assume

[10] It is arguable, however, that an offender who makes an autonomous decision not to undergo medical treatment for ADHD also bears responsibly for foreseeable consequences of his or her condition.

[11] In an interview study with adults suffering from ADHD carried out in the Netherlands, most of the respondents were said to have difficulties separating their personality or character from their mental condition. As the authors of this study indicate, this shows that questions about identity and authenticity sometimes play an important and sometimes problematic role in the experience of ADHD adults (Bolt & Schermer, 2009).

[12] Some may, of course, argue that even though one is given the option, this would still be coercive, since the willingness to do so can be framed as an indication of good behavior for which one may later be rewarded, for instance, in terms of increased chances for extended visits from family or the possibility of permitted furloughs. Thus, even though the coercion is never direct, but rather indirect, it is still coercive. This is a question that goes beyond the scope of this paper, but I wish to stress that although I recognize this possible objection, I do not believe that it can be paired with the question about more direct coercive offers, such as where undergoing medical treatment is rewarded with prerelease (as discussed in Bomann-Larsen, 2013; Ryberg & Petersen, 2013).

that at least when providing inmates with the choice of undergoing pharmaco-logical treatment for their ADHD, it is reasonable that the overall aim of pun-ishment as secular penance can be successfully achieved, while at the same time respecting the offenders as moral autonomous agents. In the following section, I will discuss a possible objection to my argument thus far, namely, whether the secular penance facilitated by methylphenidate might be less authentic.

A Less Authentic Moral Improvement?

A possible objection to the line of argument I have previously outlined is that the repentance and self-reform made possible by pharmacological treatment is of less moral value than its nonpharmacological alternative on account that they would be less authentic. The idea, then, is that even though an offender might wish to undergo psychopharmacological treatment and, as a result, may success-fully achieve the communicative aims of punishment, the resulting moral gains would be less valuable. This concern could be summarized by the slogan: "It is not you; it's your drugs!" as it could be argued that it is the drugs, not the of-fender, that does the work.

The notion of authenticity is closely related to autonomy. To be an autono-mous agent means that one is self-govern and is living in accordance with one's basic desires and values. It involves having the capacity to choose among dif-ferent alternatives in a free and deliberate way. As such, autonomy is a matter of degrees, and one may lead a more or less autonomous life. It is possible to dis-cern different components of autonomy, including will, decision, and actions. How autonomous a person is depends on all of these aspects (Sjöstrand & Juth, 2014, p. 116). Authenticity is about the extent to which one really is one's own. Authenticity can be attributed to different objects, including desires, preferences, and achievements. The claim, as I understand it, is that even though an offender with ADHD wishes to take methylphenidate for his or her condition to change his or her ways, his or her achievement will be unauthentic as it is the drugs that does the work. On one interpretation, it is so because the change in one's beha-vior is not due to one's own effort.

It is hard to deny that we take great interest and pride in our own efforts. For instance, an amateur runner finishing a marathon in under three and a half hours does, at least, have subjective value to the person who succeeds in doing so. This value would arguably be undermined if it was shown that this is not a result of one's own effort, such as one who has secretly been given performance-enhancing drugs by someone else (Sandel, 2004). However, we evidently do not dismiss all sorts of assistance. For instance, I can employ the services of a personal trainer and dietitian to help me train to succeed in my goal of running a marathon, and there seems little reason to suppose that this would diminish the value of my finishing the marathon in under three and a half hours in comparison to if I had not had their assistance. The same, it seems, holds for self-reformation, since for it to be successfully achieved, we sometimes need assistance from others. But this should not lead us to the conclusion that the self-reformation has less value.

Alternatively, this concern could also be important if there was reason to suppose that the moral improvement and self-reform were solely or dominantly attributable to the psychopharmacological treatment. However, it is far from obvious that this would be so in this case. Methylphenidate would not morally enhance per se, but rather it would improve cognitive capacities needed to achieve this end. In this sense, it doesn't limit the offender's autonomy or take away any particular realm of decision-making.[13] Moreover, whether the offender is improved is largely dependent on whether the offenders come to accept the message communicated to them by their punishment. If they are to change, this will be an effect of successful penal communication where the offenders are experience repentance and a need to reform themselves.

To appreciate this point, I wish to consider another discussion on self-improvement where a moderate acceptance of cognitive-enhancing drugs has been shown to be important. In her discussion on cognitive enhancement and virtue ethics, Barbro Fröding (2011) points out that virtue ethics has often been criticized for being an elitist moral theory.[14] According to this argument, to become a fully virtuous agent is overly demanding, and for many people, the virtuous life is an unattainable ideal. This is, Fröding argues, in part due to biological and genetic limitations. From her virtue ethical perspective, Fröding argues that certain forms of human enhancement—and, notably, cognitive enhancement—can be beneficial for most of us to live virtuous and flourishing lives. Cognitive enhancement may, as Fröding puts it, "make an important contribution by helping to lift agents to a starting point where they would have a reasonable chance at instilling the virtues" (p. 229). Still, Fröding argues, human enhancement should not—in fact, cannot—replace the traditional way of achieving moral virtues, but only assist us. To this end, we also need a personal commitment to the virtuous life. One must want to become a virtuous person and desire the virtuous life for its own sake.

---

[13] In her discussion of criminal punishment from a virtue ethical perspective, Katrina L. Sifferd (2016) argues that chemical castration should not be morally permissible because it permanently removes a realm of decision making. In contrast, various forms of treatment, such as direct brain interventions or pharmacological treatments, are permissible only in so far as they assist the offender with changing his or her character as he or she desires. This sort of constraint is very much in line with how I argue here. For a different view on the permissibility of chemical castration, see Douglas, Bonte, Focquaert, Devolder, and Sterckx (2013).

[14] For a discussion on virtue ethics and the charge from elitism, see Svensson (2008).

I believe that Fröding's (2011) ideas are important and have interesting implications for my discussion on the communicative theory of punishment and the introduction of certain cognitive-enhancing drugs in the criminal justice context. Similar to having a commitment to a virtuous life to become fully virtuous, an offender should ideally repent from his past wrongdoing to start the process of reforming himself. But to become virtuous, some individuals may need to undergo some forms of cognitive enhancement. Similarly, some offenders might also need assistance to succeed in their reformation, and such assistance could include accepting cognitive-enhancing drugs. It is not farfetched, however, that for an individual to endorse a strong commitment to the virtuous life the individual must at least perceive this as an attainable ideal. Even if one has an initial desire to become more virtuous but fails over and over in doing so, it is not implausible that one will cease to endorse this ideal. Analogously, even though one may wish to distancing oneself from one's previous behavior, the inability to reform may seriously undermine the prospect for repentance, as one is probably less likely to repent for that behavior.

In both cases the individuals strive toward becoming a better person is to a large extent due to their own commitments and desires and is hardly attributable to the enhancement techniques alone. In the case of offenders with ADHD, methylphenidate will only lift the starting point. The repentance and reform, however, are dependent on the offenders own efforts. After all, an offender may be given methylphenidate and yet the penal communication fail due to other circumstances—such as the offenders unwillingness to accept the message communicated to him. However, in cases where the offender does repent and successfully reform, it appears that the psychopharmacological treatment does not compromise authenticity.

Concluding Remarks

Ethical questions regarding the intersection between medical intervention and criminal justice will become increasingly more prevalent in the future, especially since the range of medical interventions capable of facilitating rehabilitation is likely to expand (Douglas, 2014). Moreover, as we come to realize that a substantial number of offenders suffer from mental conditions that render them less likely to achieve reform, this should also be relevant to our assessment and application of penal theories. This chapter adds to the much needed ethical discussion on this development. More specifically, I have argued that from the standpoint of the communicative theory of punishment, there are compelling nonmedical reasons to provide methylphenidate in correctional facilities to offenders diagnosed with ADHD. This does not however warrant forced treatment with methylphenidate, but only offering it as an option to inmates. In more general terms, I believe that my discussion shows that the distinction between rehabilitation on the one hand and punishment on the other is far from obvious. Certain forms of rehabilitation techniques should be accepted as a means to foster repentance and the prospects of self-reform, which Duff's (2001) version of the communicative theory of punishment so strongly emphasizes. Thus, rather than being two conflicting paradigms of criminal justice, different forms of treatment or rehabilitation and punishment can be understood as mutually and equally important aspects within in a single penal framework.

As a final remark, I wish to stress that as proponents of a communicative theory similar to Duff's (2001) view should be willing to accept that methylphenidate should be provided to inmates with ADHD, this should not lead us to the conclusion that we must accept that any kind of psychopharmacological treatment should be given to offenders. Accepting a medical intervention should depend on whether it can help fulfill the aims of secular punishment without undermining the moral autonomy of the offender.

References

Bolt, I., & Schermer, M. (2009). Psychopharmaceutical enhancers: Enhancing identity? *Neuroethics, 2*(2), 103–111.

Bomann-Larsen, L. (2013). Voluntary rehabilitation? On neurotechnological behavioural treatment, valid consent and (in)appropriate offers. *Neuroethics, 6*(1), 65–77.

Boonin, D. (2008). *The problem of punishment.* Cambridge, England: Cambridge University Press.

Brooks, T. (2012). *Punishment.* London, England: Routledge.

Dobash, R. E., & Dobash, R. P. (2000). Evaluating criminal justice interventions for domestic violence. *Crime & Delinquency, 46*(2), 252–270.

Douglas, T. (2014). Criminal rehabilitation through medical intervention: Moral liability and the right to bodily integrity. *Journal of Ethics, 18*(2), 101–122.

Douglas, T., Bonte, P., Focquaert, F., Devolder, K., & Sterckx, S. (2013). Coercion, incarceration, and chemical castration: An argument from autonomy. *Journal of Bioethical Inquiry, 10*(3), 393–405.

Duff, A. R. (2001). *Punishment, communication, and community.* Oxford, England: Oxford University Press.

Fröding, B. (2011). Cognitive enhancement, virtue ethics and the good life. *Neuroethics, 4*(3), 223–234.

Ginsberg, Y. (2013). Kan onda cirklar brytas? Om ADHD med antisocialitet och ADHD behandling på Norrtäljeanstalten. *Socialmedicinsk Tidskrift, 90*(3), 399–409.

Ginsberg, Y., Hirvikoski, T., Grann, M., & Lindefors, N. (2012). Long-term functional outcome in adult prison inmates with ADHD receiving OROS-methylphenidate. *European Archives of Psychiatry and Clinical Neuroscience, 262*(8), 705–724.

Ginsberg Y., & Lindfors, N. (2012). Methylphenidate treatment of adult male prison inmates with attention-deficit hyperactivity disorder: Randomized double blind placebo controlled trail with open-label extension. *The British Journal of Psychiatry, 200*(1), 68–73.

Golash, D. (2005). *The case against punishment: Retribution, crime prevention, and the law.* New York, NY: New York University Press.

Jacobs, J. (2007). Character, liability, and morally unreachable agents. *Criminal Justice Ethics, 26*(2), 16–28.

Kamm. F. (2005). Is there a problem with enhancement? *The American Journal of Bioethics, 5*(3), 5–14.

Kriminalvården. (2015). Idap – för män som utövat våld i nära relation. Retrieved from http://www.kriminalvarden.se/behandling-och-vard/behandlingsprogram/vald/idap

Pugh, J. (2014). Enhancing autonomy by reducing impulsivity: The case of ADHD. *Neuroethics, 7*(3), 373–375.

Ryberg, J. (2012). Punishment, pharmacological treatment, and early release. *International Journal of Applied Philosophy, 26*(2), 231–244.

Ryberg, J. (2015). Is coercive treatment of offenders morally acceptable? On the deficiency of the debate. *Criminal Law and Philosophy, 9*(4), 619–631. doi:10.1007/s11572-013-9288-8

Ryberg, J., & Petersen, T. S. (2013) Neurotechnological behavioural treatment of criminal offenders—A comment on Bomann-Larsen. *Neuroethics, 6*(1), 79–83.

Sandel, M. (2004). The case against perfection. *The Atlantic Monthly, 293*(3), 51–62.

Sifferd, K. L. (2016). Virtue ethics and criminal punishment. In J. Webber, & A. Masala (Eds.), *From personality to virtue* (pp. 35–61). Oxford, England: Oxford University Press.

Sjöstrand, M., & Juth, N. (2014). Authenticity and psychiatric disorder: does autonomy of personal preferences matter? *Medicine, Health Care, and Philosophy, 17*(1), 115–122.

Svensson, F. (2008). Virtue ethics and elitism. *Philosophical Papers, 37*(1), 131–155.

12

Is It *Really* Ethical to Prescribe Antiandrogens to Sex Offenders to Decrease Their Risk of Recidivism?

Christopher James Ryan

Introduction

The question that forms the title this chapter (usually without the italicized "really") has been the subject of many papers over many years. In recent years the question has been asked more than ever, undoubtedly as part of a well-documented exponential increase in the number of academic papers and book chapters on the intersection of law and neuroscience (Shen, 2010). At the same time there is a significant amount of information available on the basic empirical questions that should underlie this ethical question as it might apply to the *real* world. What evidence is there that antiandrogens decrease recidivism? What harms can antiandrogens do? If antiandrogens do prevent recidivism, how effective are they?

My motivation for writing this chapter is that the answers to those empirical questions, to the extent that they are available, seem to be playing very little role in philosophical, clinical, or legal debate, and more often than not there is an assumption that antiandrogens are either effective in this role, or that they are probably effective, and a further assumption that if they are effective, they are probably very effective.

I will first, explain what antiandrogens are, and briefly survey the jurisdictions where they are used in the hope of preventing sex offender recidivism. Next, I will provide examples of the assumptions of efficacy that motivated the chapter. I will then look at why it is thought that antiandrogens might be effective in decreasing recidivism, before critically examining the empirical evidence that is often used to support the view that antiandrogens are effective in reducing sex offender recidivism.[1] Finding that evidence wanting, I will briefly review the

---

[1] I will not attempt to provide a classical systematic review of the empirical evidence around this issue. The literature already contains many such reviews, and they are referenced herein. Rather, this is a narrative review, written for those who lack expertise in interpreting meta-analyses and the

Christopher James Ryan, *Is It Really Ethical to Prescribe Antiandrogens to Sex Offenders to Decrease Their Risk of Recidivism?* In: *Neurointerventions and the Law.* Edited by: Nicole A Vincent, Thomas Nadelhoffer, and Allan McCay, Oxford University Press (2020). © Oxford University Press 2020
DOI: 10.1093/oso/9780190651145.001.0012

known harms associated with the use of antiandrogens and then make some estimate, despite the poverty of evidence available, of how effective antiandrogens might be at preventing recidivism, if they are effective at all. Finally, with the empirical ground established, I will make some comments on the ethical question that is the title of the paper.

What Is Antiandrogen Treatment and in Which Jurisdictions Is It Used?

Antiandrogen treatment—also known as androgen depletion treatment or antilibidinal treatment, is commonly known in the lay press as chemical castration. The terms refer to the administration of drugs designed either to lower a male's testosterone levels or decrease the effect of circulating testosterone. There are a number of such drugs, but in this chapter, I will focus on the two most commonly used in the hope of decreasing recidivism in sex offenders.[2] The drug most commonly prescribed in the United States is medroxyprogesterone acetate (MPA, marketed as Provera®), a synthetic progestogen usually given as an intramuscular injection (Depo Provera®). In United Kingdom, Europe, Canada, and Australia the most commonly prescribed drug is cyproterone acetate (CPA, marketed as Androcur® and Cyprostat®). CPA is an antiandrogen, available in both oral and long-acting injectable forms, that blocks the production of testosterone and opposes its action.[3]

---

like—philosophers, lawyers, judges, and politicians. Consequently, I have tried to avoid the technical jargon of formal systematic reviews, while scrupulously avoiding any notion of dumbing the evidence down.

[2] These other drugs have different mechanisms of action and include gonadotropin-releasing hormone agonists or luteinizing hormone-releasing hormone agonists or analogues. With continued use, these drugs, which include, buserelin (with the tradenames Suprefact®, CinnaFact®, and Metrelef®), leuprorelin or leuprolide (Lucrin®, Eligard®, Lupron®, Viadur®, Leuprome®), goserelin (Zoladex®), and tryptorelin (Decapeptyl®, Diphereline®, Gonapeptyl®, Trelstar®) reduce sex hormone production. They are less commonly used in sex offenders but are often mentioned as potentially effective in reducing recidivism. These agents are available as long-acting injectable formulations or implants placed under the skin.

Although a thorough review of the efficacy of these agents is beyond the scope of this chapter, it is worth noting that a 2009 review of drug treatment for paraphilic disorders found no controlled trials of these drugs directed at recidivism, and only one placebo-controlled, evaluator-blinded, crossover trial of leuprolide in pedophilia. This trial had five participants and the results suggested that while on active drug participants had fewer pedophilic urges and masturbated less to thoughts of children, although the type of pedophilic interest (age, gender) did not change (Guay, 2005; Schober et al., 2005).

[3] In recent years antidepressants, particularly selective serotonin reuptake inhibitors (SSRIs), have been increasingly prescribed in an effort to reduce recidivism in sexual offenders. These drugs are also beyond the scope of this discussion, although it is worth noting that their 2012 review of the efficacy of these agents, Baratta, Javelot, Morali, Halleguen, and Weiner (2012) could locate only one placebo controlled double-blind study of an SSRI for any similar indication. This study used the SSRI

Antiandrogens are prescribed to sex offenders in the hope that the resultant decrease in testosterone will decrease the individual's aggressiveness and/or sex drive and that this will make it easier for offenders to control their antisocial urges. The use of hormonal treatments to alter sexual impulse has a long and checkered history; a particularly disturbing example being Alan Turing's "agreement" to take "organotherapy" to avoid a prison after pleading guilty to various "acts of gross indecency," which is how English criminal law described consensual homosexual sex in 1952 (Hodges, 1983).

At the time of writing statutes in at least six U.S. states (California,[4] Florida,[5] Louisiana,[6] Montana,[7] Oregon,[8] and Wisconsin[9]) either allow for antiandrogen treatment to be given compulsorily to certain offenders or prevent parole unless sex offenders undergo antiandrogen treatment (Mancini, Barnes, & Mears, 2011).[10] Similar provisions exist in Canada (Criminal Code, RSC 1985, c C-46, ss 752-61; see also Kutcher, 2010) and at least four Australian states (Queensland,[11] New South Wales,[12] Western

citalopram to try to reduce compulsive sexual behavior in a cohort of homosexual subjects without any paraphilia. No statistically significant improvement was noted between the treated group and the control group (see also Wainberg et al., 2006).

[4]   California Penal Code §645: Permits courts to order antiandrogens for parolees, who have committed certain serious sex crimes against victims under 13 years of age. Courts must order repeat offenders to undergo treatment. Offenders may opt for surgical castration instead.

[5]   Florida Crimes Statute §794.0235: Permits courts to order MPA for offenders who have committed "sexual battery." Repeat offenders must undergo treatment. In both instances, treatment is contingent upon a court-appointed medical expert's determination that the defendant is an appropriate candidate. Offenders may opt for surgical castration instead.

[6]   Louisiana §15:538: First offenders convicted of sex crimes against minors aged 12 or younger and certain repeat offenders must have a mental health evaluation, including a treatment plan, before they are eligible for probation, parole, or a sentence reduction or suspension. The treatment plan may include an antiandrogen, although offenders may choose surgical castration instead.

[7]   Montana §45-5-512: Courts may sentence an offender who is convicted of sexual assault, rape, or incest involving a minor under age 16 and who is at least three years older than the victim to undergo antiandrogens or any other "medically safe" drug treatment that reduces sexual fantasies, sex drive, or both.

[8]   Oregon §144.625: Requires the Department of Corrections to establish a pilot program for 40–50 sex offenders per year to which offenders at risk of reoffending will be referred and those most likely to benefit treated with antiandrogens on parole. A later section (144.631) clarifies that nothing in this section prohibits the State Board of Parole and Post-Prison Supervision from requiring antiandrogen treatment for a person not on the pilot program.

[9]   Wisconsin §302.11: Enables the Department of Corrections to deny the usual presumptive release on parole to a "serious child sex offender" who refuses to participate in antiandrogen treatment.

[10]   Note too that Texas Government Code §501.061 allows certain repeat sex offenders to elect for orchiectomy, however, this cannot be a condition of probation or parole.

[11]   The Dangerous Prisoners (Sexual Offenders) Act 2003 (Queensland) provides for "the continued detention in custody or supervised release" of a class of offenders. The supervised release orders may contain requirements that the released prisoner "comply with any reasonable direction . . . given to the prisoner" by a corrective services officer about the "released prisoner's rehabilitation or care or treatment" (s16B(1)(b)).

[12]   The Crimes (High Risk Offenders) Act 2006 (New South Wales) provides for "extended supervision . . . of high risk sex offenders and high risk violent offenders so as to ensure the safety and protection of the community" after the completion of their prison term and parole (s 3). The extended

Australia[13] and Victoria[14]). Though the United Kingdom does not permit the forced application of antiandrogens, a 2007 circular by the National Probation Service (2007) described an avenue for sex offenders to be assessed and offered antiandrogens as a means of decreasing recidivism. In Europe, some form of legislation allowing antiandrogen treatment exists in at least the following countries— Denmark, Germany, Norway, Sweden, Switzerland (Wong, 2001), Poland, Macedonia ("Convicted Paedophiles," 2014), the Czech Republic, and Russia. Similar laws have been recently enacted in the Republic of Korea (Koo et al., 2013).

Assumptions of Efficacy in the Academic Literature and the Courts

Clinicians, academics, and judges often assume that antiandrogens are effective in reducing sex offender recidivism. Grubin and Beech, the psychiatrist and psychologist authors of a 2010 editorial in the *British Medical Journal*, confidently state that, "Antiandrogenic drugs and physical castration undoubtedly . . . reduce sexual reoffending" and that the effect on the risk of sexual offences is "big" (Grubin & Beech, 2010, p. 433).[15] Similarly Saleh and Guifry (2003), another psychiatrist/psychologist author pair have gone into press stating that antiandrogens have been used to "eliminate sex-offending behavior" (p. 487). In other less effusive examples, the psychiatrist Berlin has said that antiandrogens have shown themselves to be a means of "significantly decreasing sex offender recidivism rates" (Berlin, 2009, p. 61), and the authors of a 2013 paper on outcome

---

supervision orders may impose a variety of conditions including participation in "treatment and rehabilitation programs" (s 11(d)).

[13] Dangerous Sexual Offenders Act 2006 (Western Australia) allows a court "satisfied that there is an unacceptable risk that . . . the person would commit a serious sexual offence" to impose a supervision order containing "terms that the court thinks appropriate . . . for the rehabilitation or care or treatment of the person subject to the order" (ss 7, 18(2)).

[14] The Serious Sex Offenders (Detention and Supervision) Act 2009 (Victoria) provides a mechanism to require "offenders who have served custodial sentences for certain sexual offences and who present an unacceptable risk of harm to the community to be subject to ongoing . . . supervision." The court must consider imposing a variety of conditions including conditions relating to "treatment or rehabilitation programs or activities that the offender must attend and participate in" (s 17(1)(e)).

[15] Grubin and Beech (2010) go on to state: "Physical castration of sex offenders was carried out in several European countries in the first part of the 20th century, and . . . recidivism rates of less than 5% over long follow-up periods are invariably reported, compared with expected rates of 50% or more" (p. 434). In support of this claim they cite Heim and Hursch (1979). However, no thorough reading of Heim and Hursch's paper could support Grubin and Beech's claim. Indeed, Heim and Hursch clearly state (in a section of their paper titled "Pitfalls in Analyzing Recidivism Rates": "Conclusions that the chance of an uncastrated sex offender committing another sex crime is almost ten times higher than that of a castrated one are unwarranted because these statistics compare two different types of men and are therefore not valid" (p. 300).

of sex offender treatment introduce the topic by stating that there is evidence "that chemical castration with or without psychotherapy can successfully reduce recidivism rates" (Koo et al., 2013, p. 563).

In contrast to these clinicians, philosophers and academic lawyers tend to offer only muted support for the efficacy of antiandrogens in sex offender recidivism; however, most seem to write with the assumption that antiandrogens do, or at least might, provide an effective break on the rate of recidivism when administered to sex offenders (see, e.g., Greeley, 2009; Scott & Holmberg, 2003; Sifferd, 2013; Vincent, 2014).[16]

Perhaps most concerning of all, some judges making decisions around the use of antiandrogens seem convinced of their efficacy. In a recent New South Wales Supreme Court case, for example, a judge was persuaded by psychiatric expert evidence that it was "clear" that treatment with CPA was an "important aspect of the management of the Defendant's risk of further sexual offending" (*State of New South Wales v Williamson*, 2014, p. 51). Similarly in a Western Australian Supreme Court case another judge, again informed by expert opinion, stated "there are some cases, and this is one, where the safety of the community cannot be ensured unless the dangerous sexual offender agrees to and does comply with an anti-libidinal treatment regime in the community" (*Director of Public Prosecutions for Western Australia v McGarry*, 2009, p. 116).

Do Antiandrogens Decrease Sex Offender Recidivism?

There is certainly reason to suspect that antiandrogens *might* decrease the rate of sex offender recidivism. Although it is widely believed that antiandrogens render treated offenders impotent (Sifferd, 2003), this is not the case (Bancroft, 2005). There *is* evidence, though, that androgen depletion tends to decrease the degree of tumescence and the duration of erections (Bancroft, 2005) and that antiandrogens may decrease a man's reported libido.[17] Although it is not

---

[16] It is important to note that even muted support is not universal. Douglas Bonte, Focquaert, Devolder, and Sterckx (2013) state that they will assume, for the sake of their argument, that antiandrogens are effective, but they are very clear that "there is currently no robust evidence to support this assumption" (p. 398).

[17] There have been numerous studies, generally with only small numbers of participants, examining the efficacy of both CPA and MPA in terms of their effect on various penile parameters including nocturnal tumescence and responsiveness to erotic stimulation. For example, a single blind placebo controlled crossover study examining the effects of cyproterone on five pedophiles found that the number of full erections decreased by 83% and that the total number of erections fell by 37% (Cooper & Cernovovsky, 1992). A similar larger study using MPA in 48 males (including 39 sexual offenders) found 40 were affected such that they reported reductions in the frequency of sexual fantasy and arousal, and in the desire to engage in deviant behaviors. The pedophiles also reported increased control over sexual urges (Gagné, 1981). Interestingly a smaller study on eight normal middle-aged men found considerably fewer effects on libido and sexual function (Loosen, Purdon, & Pavlou, 1994).

necessary to achieve an erection for most sex crimes and although some sex offenders are impotent, it seems likely that, for some individuals at least, libidinal urges may be part of the motivation for their offenses. There is also evidence, although considerably less strong, that administration of antiandrogens may decrease aggression (Loosen et al., 1994); however, most of these data are in the context of people suffering dementia (Bolea-Alamanac et al., 2011; Loosen et al., 1994). The evidence, to the extent that it exists, that antiandrogens might actually decrease recidivism in sex offenders takes two forms—individual studies and systematic reviews. I will review both, looking first at the reviews.

Systematic Reviews of Efficacy

Meta-analyses and systematic reviews look at a number of studies together in an effort to overcome some of the limitations often presented by individual, small trials with methodological difficulties. There are a number of recent systematic reviews examining whether treatment of any sort (pharmacological or psychological or surgical) reduces recidivism among sex offenders. Each systematic review uses different criteria to include and rate studies; however, the authors of all the reviews agree that there are few good quality studies that examine this issue.

The most stringent form of review paper is that conforming to the Cochrane systematic review methodology. Cochrane reviews include only well-designed randomized controlled trials (Jadad et al., 1998). The findings of Cochrane reviews are generally regarded as extremely robust once a number of studies of sufficient quality are pooled together. However, in many fields, there are simply not enough well-designed randomized controlled trials to draw any meaningful conclusions. A 2015 Cochrane review of antilibidinal treatment found only seven small trials that met inclusion criteria; all published prior to 1995. The authors concluded that, although there were some encouraging findings in the studies they reviewed, the limitations of the studies examined did not allow firm conclusions to be drawn regarding pharmacological intervention as an effective intervention for reducing sexual offending (Khan et al., 2015).

Even systematic reviews with far laxer study quality admission criteria tend to exclude studies of antiandrogen therapy for sex offender recidivism. Hanson, Bourgon, Helmus, and Hodgson (2009) reviewed the efficacy of all treatment modalities in the reduction of sex offender recidivism using criteria specifically designed to accommodate the difficulties encountered in this field of research (Beech et al., 2007). The authors concluded that of all the 129 studies of all forms of sex offender treatment that they identified from a literature review, only one study of any form of therapy could be regarded as methodologically "strong" and only five as "good" (Hanson et al., 2009). Nineteen "weak" studies were included in their review, but no study specifically examining the efficacy of antiandrogen drugs was of sufficient quality to reach even the "weak" standard, and all of the antiandrogen studies were among the 104 studies rejected from analysis. Similar earlier systemic reviews also excluded studies examining antiandrogens (Hanson & Bussière, 1998; Hanson et al., 2002), as did a 2013 review into treatment interventions to prevent sexual abusers of children from reoffending (Långström et al., 2013).

Generally, even when studies of antiandrogens *have* been included in systematic reviews the results have tended not to support their efficacy. Gallagher, Wilson, Hirschfield, Coggeshall, and MacKenziere (1999) viewed four studies that used antiandrogens plus supplemental treatment and found an overall positive but nonstatistically significant effect: the authors concluded that the evidence did "not allow for claims of effectiveness of the hormonal treatments of sex offenders" (p. 41).

A notable exception to all of this is the 2005 systematic review by Lösel and Schmuker (2005), which is the largest and most cited.[18] It considered 69 studies reviewing controlled trails of all forms of treatment (psychological, pharmacological, and surgical) of people who had either "been convicted of a sexual offense or to have committed acts of illegal sexual behavior that would have lead to a conviction if officially prosecuted" (p. 119).[19] The authors pooled the results of studies involving over 22,000 individuals. However, of these studies, 60% had control groups that were recognized as not equivalent to the treatment group and only seven had a randomized design. Overall the authors concluded that treatment interventions were more effective than control interventions at reducing recidivism and that of the treatment interventions, surgical castration was the most effective; chemical castration, less so; and psychological interventions, least so. The authors identified only six studies that examined the efficacy of hormonal medication. A table in their result section suggests, on the basis of analysis of these studies, that, on average, those person's receiving hormones where three times less likely to reoffend than controls. This result is surprising since the four positive studies that Lösel and Schmuker use to draw this conclusion are the same four studies that Gallagher et al. (1999) used to concluded that the

---

[18] This is review is frequently cited in those making optimistic assessments of the efficacy of antiandrogens. See, for example, Grubin and Beech (2010), Koo et al. (2013), and Codispoti (2008).

[19] Lösel and Schmucker (2005) do not rigidly adhere to this condition since as noted above (and below in the section on surgical castration) some of their studies concerning antiandrogens included participants who were neither sex offenders nor would have been prosecuted for their unwanted activities. These included people with an interest in pornography, men who were unfaithful, and homosexuals.

evidence did "not allow for claims of effectiveness of the hormonal treatments of sex offenders" (p. 27).

Individual Studies of Efficacy

The different conclusions of the Gallagher et al. (1999) and the Lösel and Schmuker (2005) reviews highlight that reviews are vulnerable to both the quality of the studies examined and any bias that the reviewers themselves may bring. One way to avoid these risks is to look at the individual studies themselves and since there are so few controlled studies examining the effects of antiandrogen drugs on recidivism among sex offenders, this is easily done. Controlled studies are those that compare the effect of the intervention under investigation to the effect of another intervention or placebo. As previously noted, Lösel and Schmuker have conducted the most comprehensive recent review of the treatment of sex offenders and used an exhaustive search strategy and uncovered only six such studies (Fedoroff, Wisner-Carlson, Dean, & Berlin, 1992; Langevin et al., 1979; Maletzky, 1991; Maletzky & Field, 2003; McConaghy, Blaszczynski, & Kidson, 1998; Meyer, Cole, and Emory, 1992). I conducted a similar search as part of writing this chapter but was unable to find any additional more recent studies.

In the remainder of this section I have briefly reviewed all six of the studies included in the Lösel and Schmuker (2005) review. They illustrate the myriad difficulties with such studies. To my mind, simply reading through the studies makes it difficult to support Lösel and Schmuker's conclusions. Indeed, it becomes fairly obvious that any strong claim that antiandrogens are effective in preventing recidivism is fanciful and that even tacit assumptions of possible efficacy seem unwise.

The first study is a 1979 Canadian investigation that followed 37 exhibitionists for up to two years (Langevin et al., 1979). Only 27 of the exhibitionists had had prior forensic involvement, so 10 were arguably not actual sex offenders and therefore not strictly relevant to a question about sex offender recidivism. The authors do not reveal the exact doses of MPA given except to say that "generally 100 to 150 mg . . . was administered," with the goal to "'take the edge' off their sex drive" (Langevin et al., 1979, p. 277). The study was originally designed to compare three groups—men receiving MPA alone, men receiving assertiveness training alone, and men receiving both. The assertiveness training was administered by graduate students, so it is possible that it was not of the highest quality.

When the study began, five patients volunteered to enter the MPA-alone arm, but as the study progressed, all five withdrew their participation. In response to this, the researchers simply ignored the data from those dropouts—a maneuver strictly prohibited in research methodology, because, obviously, the participants who drop out are those most likely to have found the intervention unhelpful. All remaining 32 subjects received assertiveness training, and 15 of these volunteered to receive MPA. Remarkably, relapse (termed "recidivism" in the study) was not defined. Only 12 of the 17 patients who received assertiveness training alone completed the program. Again, the dropouts were ignored, and so it was reported that assertiveness training alone group had a 50% "recidivism" rate (6/12). Of the 15 who had volunteered for MPA in addition to their assertiveness training, only five completed the program, the other 10 were ignored, and so the MPA plus assertiveness training arm was reported as having only a 20% "recidivism" rate (1/5). The authors noted that, because of the high dropout rate, this was an unfair assessment of the effectiveness of MPA, but this did not stop Lösel and Schmuker (2005) including it in their analysis.

The second study was published in 1991 and was based in an Oregon clinic (Maletzky, 1991). The researchers retrospectively reviewed the medical records of the first 100 patients to consent to receive MPA (averaging 250 mg for two weeks for an average of five months) after antiandrogens had been recommended by their physician. The authors compared the progress of these patients to that of 100 other patients who did not receive MPA, whose files were chosen at random. Although these comparison files were matched by age, sex, and marital status, they were a very different group from those who underwent treatment. Nearly 60% of the treatment group had "aggressive sexuality," meaning they had committed rape or acts of sexual sadism, but only 9% of control group had "aggressive sexuality." Once again, it was unclear how many of those who entered the trial were actual sex offenders, nor did it seem likely that the percentage of actual sex offenders would be roughly equivalent in treatment and control groups. Both groups were extremely heterogeneous. In addition to those with "aggressive sexuality," both groups also contained pedophiles, men with a variety of paraphilias, and a grab bag of those who had experienced "frequent sexual liaisons and affairs, impaired opposite-sex relationships, frequent use of prostitutes, obsession with pornography, and presence of sexually transmitted diseases" (Maletzky, 1991, p. 123). Thirty-six percent of the treatment group, but only 12% of the control group, had "central nervous system damage from causes such as post-traumatic brain injury or developmental disability" (p. 123).

The point of having a treatment and control group is that both groups will be treated in exactly the same way, except for the treatment being investigated. In this study though, clinic patients received various combinations of behavioral, cognitive, group, and family therapies as their therapists and the clinic director felt were indicated. Reoffense was not defined and seems to have been subjectively defined in the study. The authors gave one example of "reoffense" and described it as a second-hand report of a patient with moderate developmental disability seen playing with young children and lifting girls into the air.

This was recorded as a reoffense even though heterosexual pedophilic behavior was not part of this subject's profile and despite the fact no actual offense had been committed. By the end of the three-year follow-up period, 10 patients from the treatment arm had "reoffended" (one while being prescribed the MPA) as had six patients from the control group, but again, it is impossible to interpret the meaning of this result in the face of so much uncertainty.

The third study is a 1992 Johns Hopkins paper that retrospectively reviewed the files of 46 patients with a variety of "paraphilias"—including pedophilia, voyeurism, and exhibitionism (Fedoroff et al., 1992). Only 21 of the patients had previously been arrested and were therefore actual sex *offenders*. The rest presumably were men seeking help for what they perceived as a problem. All patients received group psychotherapy, but 27 also volunteered to receive MPA (300–500 mg weekly). Of the 395 patients originally enrolled in the program, the researchers only examined patients who attended the program for five years. Those who were discharged before five years, who dropped out, who were lost to follow-up, who had been arrested earlier, or who had died were all ignored. This cherry-picking attitude to the selection of files introduces a range of biases, the most obvious of which being that it is likely that those who drop out of therapy *or those who are arrested* are those for whom therapy was not effective. Relapse was defined as "any inappropriate sexual behavior" as defined either by the patient or the researchers; however, the researchers were aware of which treatment the patients had been given when they made their subjective judgement of "relapse," making it likely that their judgements were biased to their pre-existing beliefs about the treatment's efficacy. The rate of relapse among subjects receiving MPA was 15% (4/27) whereas the rate of relapse among subjects not receiving MPA was 68% (13/19). The authors acknowledged some of the shortcomings of their study but nonetheless conclude that their "findings strongly support the hypothesis that lower relapse rates are associated with the addition of MPA to on-going long-term psychotherapy" (Fedoroff et al., 1992, p. 120). Again, in the face of such methodological squalor, this conclusion seems fanciful.

The fourth study was a 1992 retrospective review of the records of 61 patients referred to a private Texas clinic for evaluation of sex offending behavior and who were offered and strongly encouraged to take MPA (Meyer et al., 1992). Forty men agreed to take MPA at a starting dose of 400 mg per week, and these were compared to 21 who refused but complied with the rest of the offered treatment program. Although the two groups were similar in demographics and were mostly made up of pedophiles and exhibitionists, seven of the MPA arm but none of the control group were rapists. Reoffense was defined as either arrest for any offense committed since being on therapy or revelation of offending to the therapist. Twelve of the 21 patients who refused MPA reoffended, while 17 of 40 men who took MPA reoffended, 10 after they had ceased taking the drug and 7 while still taking it. Rapists and exhibitionists were those most likely to reoffend.

The final two of the six controlled studies were negative. That is, they did not find that the antiandrogens had any effect on recidivism. One was from the previously described Oregon group reporting the early results of pilot program (Maletzky & Field, 2003). The study reviewed the histories of 33 sexual offenders who had been assessed and deemed appropriate for MPA therapy while on parole. Eighteen had been commenced on MPA, while 15 had not commenced it, despite the recommendation, for a variety of reasons including cost, difficulty of locating a medical practitioner willing to prescribe MPA, and the opinion of some parole officers that MPA was not necessary in that individual case. The report compared the outcomes of the two groups nearly two years into the program and found that, at that time, no participant in either group had reoffended.

The final study, also negative, is easily the strongest methodologically and was published in 1988 (McConaghy et al., 1988). This Australian study recruited 30 men "who consecutively sought treatment for anomalous sexual urges or behaviors they felt unable to control" (McConaghy et al., 1988, p. 199). Only 19 of the men had been convicted for sexual offenses. The men were randomly allocated: 10 received MPA (150 mg per two weeks, and then monthly); 10, imaginal desensitization (a form of psychological therapy); and 10, both. All subjects were reviewed one year into treatment, but the results are clouded by the fact that only 15 of the 20 patients allocated to take MPA completed the prescribed course and that three patients requested additional treatment during the trial so that either MPA or imaginal desensitization was added to their original regime. Efficacy of the treatment was assessed by both the patient's own report of the "reduction produced in strength of anomalous urges" and by estimates of this made by a professional interviewer.[20] As such, despite being included in the Lösel and Schmuker (2005) review, this study was not truly measuring recidivism. The researchers found no significant differences in efficacy among the three treatment arms.

These six studies illustrate the myriad methodological problems typical of research used to support a claim that antiandrogen agents decrease reoffending. In such studies the term *sex offenders* does not describe a cohesive class of persons. So-called offenders have often not committed an offense, and since the overall numbers of subjects are small and the numbers of recidivists considerably smaller,[21] these studies often include and lump together a variety of obviously

[20] Subjects who had treatment added to their regime were counted in the group of their initial treatment and their results at the end of that treatment were those reported.

[21] A meta-analysis by Hanson and Bussière (1998) found less than 14% of sexual offenders had relapsed after approximately five years at risk in the community.

different types of sex offence—rape, sex offences against children, voyeurism, frotteurism, etc.—even though one might hypothesize that the possible efficacy of antiandrogens would differ significantly between each type (Bradford, Fedoroff, & Gulati, 2013). Even more important, in terms of determining efficacy, these subclasses of sex offenders are not matched between treatment and control groups.

Despite the heterogeneity of offenders, the numbers of subjects enrolled in these studies is tiny in contrast to the numbers generally admitted to pharmaceutical treatment trials. In no study were subjects or investigators blind to which treatment the subject was receiving. This will tend to bias results to favor the use of antiandrogens. It is likely that the use of subject self-report will also bias results in favor of antiandrogens as subjects from forensic referral services, particularly, are likely to be motivated to appear to be improving, and there is evidence that such subjects exaggerate their reported responses to treatment (Schober et al., 2005).

The length of follow-up differs between studies and is not the same for all offenders within a particular study. Given that it is known that different types of offender follow very different "career trajectories," these differences in follow-up period will again make individual studies and pooled analyses extremely difficult to interpret (Francis, Harris, Wallace, Knight, & Soothill, 2014; Lussier & Cale, 2013). Definitions of relapse are unclear and inconsistent across studies. In some studies, sexual reoffense is defined as reconviction; in others, it is rearrest. Some studies restrict themselves to further *sex* offenses, others include other varieties of criminal offense (Bradford et al., 2013). In still others treatment failure is simply self-reported relapse. Studies looking for a treatment effect will have the most robust findings if subjects are allocated randomly to experimental groups and if the groups include a no-treatment—or better, a placebo—control group. Only one of the previously described studies allocated subjects randomly—the Australian study with a negative result.

Conclusion: Do Antiandrogen Drugs Decrease Recidivism Among Sex Offenders?

It is very difficult to see how one could have any confidence, from examination of the studies, or of the broader systematic reviews, that antiandrogen therapy had any proven efficacy in reducing the rate of recidivism among sex offenders. The four positive studies are uninterpretable. A lack of evidence of efficacy is not the same as evidence of a lack of efficacy, and there is insufficient evidence to conclude antiandrogens are not effective. It is worth noting, though, that the two better studies in terms of methodology are both are negative.

Does Surgical Castration Decrease Recidivism Among Sex Offenders?

Although a comprehensive review of this topic is beyond the scope of this chapter, it is worth at least a brief excursion into this area. In the literature, many of the optimistic claims about the efficacy of antiandrogens are cited by a reference to a study or a review on surgical castration (see, e.g., Grubin & Beech, 2010, who cite Heim & Hursch, 1979). Having shown that there is no evidence that "chemical castration" decreases recidivism, a reader may wonder whether the evidence for surgical castration is any better.

The short answer is no, but this has not stopped numerous writers making the same optimistic claims about surgical castration; indeed, these are often more optimistic. For example, in his recent exploration of the ethical issues around surgical castration for sex offenders, McMillan (2014) concludes, "There seem to be some good reasons to think that [surgical] castration is effective at helping prevent further offending" (p. 585).

Part of the reason for McMillan's optimism is the confident assertions of efficacy set out in Lösel and Schmucker's (2005) meta-analysis, which, despite acknowledging the serious problems with all the included studies, notes "a very strong effect for surgical castration" (p. 135). Lösel and Schmucker included eight studies of surgical castration in their meta-analysis.[22] I will not review all of these in the same detail as I have the antiandrogen studies. It is worth reviewing one, probably the most cited, to illustrate that exactly the same problems arise in these studies as arose in those concerning the antiandrogens. Wille and Beier (1989) retrospectively reviewed the outcomes of 99 of the 400 people who were castrated in Germany between 1970 and 1980 and compared them to the outcomes of 35 of the more than 370 people who originally applied for castration but who then either changed their minds or were refused the operation by the "authoritative commission." The original numbers enrolled in the intervention and control groups were 104 and 53, respectively. There is very little information in the study to indicate why some of the original participants were eventually excluded, nor is there information that would allow any determination of selection bias in the original sample populations. The follow-up period averaged 11 years. It is difficult to know how exactly the authors defined recidivism. At one point, it

---

[22] The authors do not directly identify the eight studies used and a number may be among the unpublished theses listed among the "studies integrated into meta-analysis." Five of the studies are easily picked out: Wille and Beier (1989), Stürup (1953, 1968), and Cornu (1973). Despite placing no restrictions on time of publication upon their review, the authors did not include several papers published between 1930 and 1963, some of which included sex offenders forcibly castrated under the Nazi regime. The studies as recorded in Wille and Beier, are extremely difficult to obtain, and I have not been able to obtain any reports of their results (Bunsmann, 1940; Jensch, 1944; Langeluddeke, 1963; Ohm, 1960a, 1960b; Sand, 1940; Schlegel, 1935; Wolf, 1934).

is defined as any formal charge, whether or not this led to conviction, but later the authors state that "sexual offences committed by two castrated applicants and 20 non-castrated applicants were discovered which were unknown to the police or which had not led to conviction" (p. 125), suggesting that they may have included events simply reported to them by subjects or associates. Once again, those who dropped out of the study were simply excluded from analysis. The most common offenses committed by participants were sexual assault on children, which occurred in 73% of those castrated and 49% of those not. Other offenses included homicide (1% vs. 3%), rape/attempted rape/sexual assault (22% vs. 12%), exhibitionism (3% vs. 2%), and necrophilia (0% vs. 1%). Nineteen percent of the control group and 1% of the intervention group had not committed any sexual act. Of the control group who had not committed a sexual offense, three participants had requested castration for arson and another six were either psychotic or of "low intelligence" and therefore could not consent. The single participant of the intervention group who had not committed a sexual offence was a homosexual but who "suffered severely under his strong obsession for degrading sexual activity" [*sic*] (Wille & Beier, 1989, p. 116). Two thirds of all participants had IQs less than 90. One third of the intervention group, but only 10% of the control group, were formally mentally retarded.

Of the 99 castrated participants eventually evaluated only 3 were rated as offenders of a sexual offense whereas of the 35 noncastrated participants eventually evaluated 16 were so rated, representing recidivism rates for castrated and noncastrated participants of 3% and 46%, respectively. It is this extraordinary difference in outcomes that is usually quoted when this study is cited. Obviously, this difference is enormous, although, once again due to the multiple methodological problems of this study, the degree to which this can be generalized to the effectiveness of surgical castration is very unclear.

Adverse Effects of Antiandrogens

Much more is known about the adverse effects of antiandrogens than about their effectiveness in sex offenders, as it is possible to draw conclusions on this from much larger studies where antiandrogens have been used to treat a variety of other problems. Broadly speaking the adverse effects of antiandrogens can be considered under three headings: effects on bone mineral density and fracture risk, effects on glucose and lipid metabolism, and a variety of miscellaneous other ill effects.

Antiandrogen therapy causes rapid bone loss in the spine, hip and, to a lesser extent, the rest of the skeleton (Giltay & Gooren, 2009). This bone loss, far in excess of normal aging, significantly increases the risk of osteoporotic fractures. In a study of 50,000 patients treated for prostate cancer, Shahinian, Kuo, Freeman, and Goodwin (2005) compared patients who had had antiandrogens to those who had not and found, among other things, that between and one and five years after surgery, those on antiandrogens had approximately double the risk of suffering a fracture that required hospitalization. Of course, this increased in risk cannot be applied unproblematically to those who might receive antiandrogens for sex offenses. For one thing, all of the prostate cancer patients studied were over 65 and some were considerably older. Nonetheless the increase is concerning, especially when one considers that it is often suggested that the proffered preventative effects of antiandrogens in sex offenders only apply while the drugs are being taken and that the offenders' younger ages may see them taking the drugs for many years. Also at least one very small trial of sex offenders taking antiandrogens demonstrated two of the four patients treated with cyproterone developed significant osteoporosis (Grasswick & Bradford, 2003). It should also be noted that it is likely that some of the increase fracture risk can probably be offset by the use of other drugs such as calcium, vitamin D, and the bisphosphonates. The last class have been found to be effective in reducing bone loss in patients taking antiandrogens (Sharifi, Gulley, & Dahut, 2005).

Antiandrogens almost certainly adversely effect a range parameters associated with cardiovascular health including weight gain, hyperinsulinemia, hyperglycemia, and insulin resistance (Giltay & Gooren, 2009). Perhaps related to these changes, a ten-year study of 73,000 elderly men with prostate cancer found antiandrogens increased the risks of developing diabetes mellitus by 44% and the mortality of cardiovascular diseases by 16% (Keating, O'Malley, & Smith, 2006). As with the effects on bone metabolism it is important to recognize that these effects may not translate easily to effects on sex offenders, although, notably, two trials of patients with antisocial behavior and various paraphilias treated with MPA (one with 9 participants, the other with 48), demonstrated significant weight gain in around 55% of participants of between 2 and 21 kg (Gagné, 1981; Meyer et al., 1977).

Fatigue is the most commonly reported side effect, reported by over 60% of participants in some studies, and occurring for two to three days after the injection (Gagné, 1981). Hot flushes and night sweats also occur in most men and can be troublesome (Giltay & Gooren, 2009). Enlargement of breast tissue (gynecomastia), which can be painful, occurred in 20% of 300 paraphilics prescribed cyproterone acetate (Laschet & Laschet, 1975). Clinically significant depression was noted in 3 of 31 healthy young men enrolled in a double-blind placebo-controlled crossover trial who received leuprolide, a newer antiandrogen agent, over three months (Schmidt et al., 2004). A range of other adverse effects, some extremely serious, are often cited, however little or no data are available on their incidence and they are probably rare. They include deep vein thrombosis and pulmonary embolism, suppression of the adrenal stress response (Krueger, Hembree, & Hill, 2006), liver failure (reports of which have stopped U.S. Food and Drug approval for cyproterone), and psychosis (Bradford & Pawlak, 1993; Cooper, 1981; Guay, 2009).

Finally, although rarely noted as an adverse effect in this context, antiandrogens cause impotence in a minority of men, frequently cause erectile difficulties and appear to lead to variable decreases in libido (Guay, 2009).

If Antiandrogens Are Effective, How Effective Are They Likely to Be?

When one reads some of the comments with which I started this chapter, it would be easy to get the impression that not only were antiandrogens effective in decreasing recidivism, but that without them recidivism was inevitable and with them the risk of offense was only slight. Even if antiandrogens are eventually shown to be effective, neither of these assumptions is likely to be correct.

The evidence around the rate of recidivism in sex offenders is plagued by definitional and methodological difficulties. Unfortunately, it is not possible to provide a detail overview of the topic here, although several excellent reviews are available (e.g., Hanson & Bussière, 1998; Stathopoulos, 2010). It is clear, though that, once caught, the clear majority of sex offenders are not reconvicted, although the frequency of reported recidivism in sex offenders varies markedly from study to study, sample to sample, and offense to offense. Unsurprisingly, rates also vary with the length of follow-up applied. In Australia, for example, the rates of sexual offenders being rearrested or reconvicted for a sexual offense varies in studies from 2% to 16% (Lievore, 2005). These studies vary in follow-period between 4 and 12 years. They demonstrate sex crime recidivism rates for rapists of between 2% and 7% and for child molestation of between 5% and 16% (Burgoyne, 1979; Greenberg, Da Silva, & Loh, 2002). Probably the most cited review regarding recidivism rates is that by Hanson and Bussière (1998) who reviewed 61 studies of sexual offense recidivism that included 23,000 offenders. They calculated a mean estimate of the rate of re-conviction for sexual offences of 13%, ranging from 4% for incest offenders to 21% for boy victim pedophiles.

It is noteworthy that these rates of recidivism are far lower than the rates of recidivism in the control arms of the studies that supposedly demonstrated the efficacy of antiandrogens and surgical castration as previously cited. Although recidivism in those studies was often defined at a much lower threshold, the marked difference between the rates seen in treatment studies and the rates recorded in these epidemiological studies cast even further doubt upon the validity of the treatment studies.

One measure of efficacy is the number needed to treat (NNT). This is the number of people that need to take a drug so that one person may achieve the hoped for result. To make some vaguely meaningful estimate of the number of sex offenders that will need to be treated to avoid one episode of recidivism, it will be necessary to make some rather speculative assumptions.

Let us assume that rate of detected recidivism for a particular type of untreated sex offender is 15% over five years. Although this figure reflects Hanson and Bussière's (1998) mean rate, this imagined rate is toward the higher end of most rates of most sex crimes. The higher the rate of recidivism, the lower the NNT is likely to be. Then, let us also assume that, despite the paucity of evidence, antiandrogens do have an effect on the rate of sexual recidivism. Given that lack of evidence, any estimate of the size of the treatment effect must be a stab in the dark. The most-quoted figure for the size of the treatment effect is that claimed by Lösel and Schmucker (2005). They used the six studies described above to estimate an odds ratio for the effect of antiandrogens on recidivism of 3.08. This figure is almost certainly far higher than any real figure, assuming that antiandrogens have any effect at all, but it will do for our current purposes and will provide a concrete, if rather fanciful, estimate of the NNT.

If we assume the rate of untreated recidivism is 15%, then we might also assume the rate of recidivism after antiandrogen treatment is around 5%. This is a figure not very dissimilar to that found in many studies, although in such studies treatment usually consists of a number of modalities, not just antiandrogens alone. The difference between 5% and 15% would be roughly equivalent to an odds ratio of 3. In this hypothetical example then the absolute reduction in risk attributable to the use of antiandrogens would be 10% (15% minus 5%), and therefore the number of sex offenders that one would need to treat to prevent one sex offender from becoming a recidivist (the NNT) would be 10. Even with these very generous assumptions of efficacy, 9 of any 10 treated sex offenders would not have benefited from the treatment, and 1 in 20 treated sex offenders will reoffend despite treatment.

Two further things should be said about this calculation. First, as I have previously alluded to, the very generous assumptions imply that, even if, despite the lack of evidence, antiandrogens are effective, it is almost certainly the case that the true NNT will actually be much larger than 10. Second, although it would possible to decrease the number of sex offenders needlessly exposed to antiandrogens if we had good data about which sex offenders might particularly benefit from antiandrogens, at this point, no such data exist.

Ethical and Legal Implications

Although most papers concerning the ethical implications of the use of antiandrogens in sex offenders are appropriately concerned with the nature of coercion, moral autonomy, or the ethics of forcing a bodily intervention (McMillan, 2014; Ryberg & Petersen, 2014; Shaw, 2014; Sifferd, 2013; Werthiemer & Miller, 2014), the empirical information reviewed in this chapter suggests that in the real world, the world in which sex offenders are currently being prescribed antiandrogens, a more potent concern should be the paucity of evidence of efficacy of these compounds for this task.

We know that most sex offenders will not reoffend with or without antiandrogens. Despite the confident claims often made in the literature and in courtrooms, we do not know if antiandrogens have any effect at all upon the likelihood of sex offenders reoffending, and there is reason to believe that if they do have such an effect, it will be very modest. Arguments in favor of the administration of these drugs are often predicated on the protection that they may afford to the community, but it could easily be that any protection is illusory. Certainly the degree of protection seems to be being exaggerated. If the state cannot have confidence that antiandrogen administration will protect the community, and I have essentially laid out an argument to support this view, then it is hard to see how the rest of the more usually debated ethical dilemmas around antiandrogen administration should even arise. The state should not compel or even coerce (by whatever definition one wishes to use) sex offenders to take androgens, because it is very likely that society will achieve either no benefit from this action or only a very small benefit. Conceivably, if any actual benefits are oversold, as they are currently, that benefit may be offset by a false confidence that the community is being protected by what is in reality an extremely weak intervention.

The state should not authorize the compulsory or coerced use of antiandrogens, not because of concerns about bodily integrity or autonomy or the adverse effects of these agents, though all these concerns are real. The state should not authorize the compulsory or coerced use of antiandrogens to sex offenders, because, in all probability, the damn things don't work.

This analysis does not, of course, present a clear argument against the truly voluntary use of antiandrogens by sex offenders who, despite being informed of the poverty of evidence, still wish to trial the agents in the hope that they might nonetheless gain benefit themselves. It is difficult to imagine that many such people would opt for antiandrogens if honestly informed of their data on efficacy, but if an offender did, it would not be unreasonable to prescribe an agent, at least as a trial. Obviously though, the person's decision to take an antiandrogen could not be factored into any calculations about their fitness for release, beyond perhaps the notion that such a person might be demonstrating a significant commitment to nonrecidivism.

Lastly, it remains theoretically possible that antiandrogens might have a usefully large effect on the risk of recidivism in at least some sex offenders. Although it will be difficult to design trials that might demonstrate this hypothesized effect, it is not impossible. Trial sizes could be increased, and the heterogeneity of study populations decreased, by multisite collaborations. The lack of data on efficacy of the agents mean that there should be no ethical issues in using a randomized design or in the use of a placebo as a comparator if antiandrogens were added to a treatment as usual regime. While the adverse effects of the antiandrogens might make it difficult to blind participants as to whether or not they were on the active substance, it should be possible to blind investigators making judgements about relapse, if this were properly defined. Probably the biggest obstacle for researchers will be the legislative environment, but even that can be overcome and apparently was addressed in the Oregon studies where the state legislated for a pilot program (Oregon §144.625).

Even with these innovations, the practical difficulties around conducting such trials will mean that methodological difficulties will remain. However, as the two negative trials previously reviewed suggest, it may be that only a small number of methodologically stronger trials will be needed to further confirm a view that antiandrogens have no efficacy in this domain, and if that were the case, then presumably, antiandrogen treatment for sex offenders would be ceased.

References

Associated Press. (2014, February 6). Convicted paedophiles in Macedonia face chemical castration. *The Guardian.*

Bancroft, J. (2005). The endocrinology of sexual arousal. *Journal of Endocrinology, 186*(3), 411–427.

Baratta, A., Javelot, H., Morali, A. Halleguen, O., & Weiner, L. (2012). The role of antidepressants in treating sex offenders. *Sexologies, 21*(3), 106–108.

Beech, A., Bourgon, G., Hanson, R. K., Harris, A. J. R., Langton, C., Marques, J., . . . Yates, P. M. (2007, February). Sexual offender treatment outcome research: Collaborative Outcome Data Committee guidelines for evaluation. *Government of Canada.* Retrieved from http://www.publicsafety.gc.ca/cnt/rsrcs/pblctns/sxl-ffndr-trtmnt/sxl-ffndr-trtmnt-eng.pdf

Berlin, F. S. (2009). Commentary: Risk/benefit ratio of androgen deprivation treatment for sex offenders. *Journal of the American Academy of Psychiatry and Law, 37,* 59–62.

Bolea-Alamanac, B. M., Davies, S. J., Christmas, D. M., Baxter, H., Cullum, S., Nutt, D. J. (2011). Cyproterone to treat aggressivity in dementia: A clinical case and systematic review. *Journal of Psychopharmacology, 25*(1), 141–145.

Bradford, J. M., & Pawlak, A. (1993). Double-bind placebo crossover study of cyperoterone acetate in the treatment of paraphilias. *Archives of Sexual Behavior, 22*(5), 383–402.

Bradford, J. M. W., Fedoroff, P., & Gulati, S. (2013). Can sexual offenders be treated? *International Journal of Law and Psychiatry, 36*(3–4), 235–240.

Bunsmann, F. (1940). Beobachtungen an entmannten Sittlichkeitsverbrechem aus dem Zuchthaus Munster. *LW., Dt. Zscher. Germ. Med. 33,* 248–253.

Burgoyne, P. H. (1979). *Recidivism among rapists: A study of men released from custody after having served sentences for rape or attempted rape.* Melbourne, Australia: Government Printer.

Codispoti, V. L. (2008). Pharmacology of sexually compulsive behavior. *Psychiatric Clinics of North America, 31*(4), 671–679.

Convicted paedophiles in Macedonia face chemical castration. (2014, February). *The Guardian.* Retrieved from https://www.theguardian.com/world/2014/feb/05/paedophiles-macedonia-chemical-castration

Cooper, A. J. (1981). A placebo-controlled trial of the antiandrogen cyproterone acetate in deviant hypersexuality. *Comprehensive Psychiatry, 22*(5), 458–465.

Cooper, A. J., & Cernovovsky, Z (1992). The effects of cyproterone acetate on sleeping and waking penile erections in pedophiles: Possible implications for treatment. *Canadian Journal of Psychiatry, 37,* 33–39.

Cornu, F. (1973). *Katamnesen bei kastrierten Sittlichkeitsdelinquenten aus forensisch-psychiatrischer Sicht* [Follow-ups with castrated sex offenders]. Basel, Switzerland: Karger

Crimes (High Risk Offenders) Act 2006 (New South Wales).

Dangerous Prisoners (Sexual Offenders) Act 2003 (Queensland).

Dangerous Sexual Offenders Act 2006 (Western Australia).

Dennis, J. A., Khan, O, Ferriter, M, Huband, N, Powney, MJ, & Duggan, C. (2012). Psychological interventions for adults who have sexually offended or are at risk of offending. *Cochrane Database of Systematic Reviews, 12,* CD007507.

Director of Public Prosecutions for Western Australia v McGarry. WASC 226 (2009).

Douglas, T., Bonte, P., Focquaert, F., Devolder, K., & Sterckx, S. (2013). Coercion, incarceration, and chemical castration: An argument from autonomy. *Journal of Bioethical Inquiry, 10*(3), 393–405.

Fedoroff, J. P., Wisner-Carlson, R., Dean, S., & Berlin, F. S. (1992). Medroxy-progesterone acetate in the treatment of paraphilic sexual disorders. *Journal of Offender Rehabilitation, 18*(3–4), 109–124.

Francis, B., Harris, D. A., Wallace, S., Knight, R. A., & Soothill, K. (2014). Sexual and general offending trajectories of men referred for civil commitment. *Sexual Abuse, 26*(4), 311–329.

Gagné, P. (1981). Treatment of sex offenders with medroxyprogesterone. *American Journal of Psychiatry, 138*(5), 644–646.

Gallagher, C. A., Wilson, D. B., Hirschfield, P., Coggeshall, M. B., & MacKenzie, D. L. (1999). A quantitative review of the effects of sex offender treatment on sexual reoffending. *Corrections Management Quarterly, 3*(4), 19–29.

Giltay, E. J., & Gooren, L. J. G. (2009). Potential side effects of androgen deprivation treatment in sex offenders. *Journal of the American Academy of Psychiatry and Law, 37,* 53–58.

Grasswick, L. J., & Bradford, J. M. (2003). Osteoporosis associated with the treatment of paraphilias: A clinical review of seven case reports. *Journal of Forensic Sciences, 48,* 849–855.

Greely, H. T. (2009). "Who knows what evil lurks in the hearts of men?": Behavoral ge-nomics, neuroscience, criminal law, and the search for hidden knowledge. In N. A. Farahany (Ed.), *The impact of behavioral sciences on criminal law* (pp. 161–180). New York, NY: Oxford University Press.

Greenberg, D. M., Da Silva, J.-A., & Loh, N. (2002). *Evaluation of the Western Australian Sex Offender Treatment Unit (1987–1999): A quantitative analysis.* Perth: University of Western Australia.

Grubin, D., & Beech, A. (2010). Chemical castration for sex offenders. *British Medical Journal, 340*, 433–434.

Guay, D. R. P. (2009). Drug treatment of paraphilic and nonparaphilic sexual disorder. *Clinical Therapeutics, 31*(1), 1–31.

Hanson, R. K., & Bussière, M. T. (1998). Predicting relapse: A meta-analysis of sexual offender recidivism studies. *Journal of Consulting and Clinical Psychology, 66*(2), 348–362.

Hanson, R. K., Gordon, A., Harris, A. J., Marques, J. K., Murphy, W., Quinsey, V. L., & Seto, M. C. (2002). First report of the Collaborative Outcome Data Project on the Effectiveness of Psychological Treatment for Sex Offenders. *Sexual Abuse: A Journal of Research and Treatment, 14*(2), 169–194.

Hanson, R. K., Bourgon, G., Helmus, L., & Hodgson, S. (2009). The principles of effective correctional treatment also apply to sexual offenders: A meta-analysis. *Criminal Justice and Behavior, 36*(9), 865–891.

Heim, N., & Hursch, C. J. (1979). Castration for sex offenders: Treatment or punishment? A review and critique of recent European literature. *Archives of Sexual Behavior, 8*(3), 281–304.

Hodges, A. (1983). *Alan Turing. The Enigma.* Princeton, Princeton University Press.

Jadad, A. R., Cook, D. J., Jones, A., Klassen, T. P., Tugwell, P., Moher, M., & Moher, D. (1998). Methodology and reports of systematic reviews and meta-analyses. A com-parison of Cochrane Reviews with articles published in paper-based journals. *Journal of the American Medical Association, 280*(3), 278–280.

Jensch, N. (1944). *Untersuchungen an entmannten Sittlichkeitsverbrechern.* Leipzig, Germany: Thieme.

Keating, N. L., O'Malley, A. J., & Smith, M. R. (2006). Diabetes and cardiovascular disease during androgen deprivation therapy for prostate cancer. *Journal of Clinical Oncology, 24*(27), 4448–4456.

Khan, O., Ferriter, M., Huband, N., Powney, M. J., Dennis, J. A., & Duggan, C. (2015). Pharmacological interventions for those who have sexually offended or are at risk of offending. *Cochrane Database of Systematic Reviews*, 2015, CD007989.

Koo, K. C., Shim, G. S., Park, H. H., Rha, K. H., Choi, Y. D., Chung, B. H., . . . Lee, J. W. (2013). Treatment outcomes of chemical castration on Korean sex offenders. *Journal of Forensic and Legal Medicine, 20*(6), 563–566.

Krueger, R. B., Hembree, W., & Hill, M. (2006). Prescription of medroxyprogesterone ac-etate to a patient with pedophilia, resulting in Cushing's syndrome and adrenal insuffi-ciency. *Sexual Abuse: A Journal of Research and Treatment, 18*(2), 227–228.

Kutcher, M. R. (2010). The chemical castration of recidivist sex offenders in Canada: A matter of faith. *Dalhousie Law Journal, 33*(2), 193–216.

Langevin, R., Paitich, D., Hucker, S., Newman, S., Ramsay, G., Pope, S., . . . Anderson, C. (1979). The effect of assertiveness training, Provera and sex of therapist in the treatment of genital exhibitionism. *Journal of Behaviour Therapy and Experimental Psychiatry, 10*, 275–282.

Langeluddeke, A. (1963). *Die Entmannung von Sitttichkeitserbrechern.* Berlin, Germany: de Gruyter.

Långström, N., Enebrink, P., Lauren, E. M., Lindblom, J., Werko, S., & Hanson, R. K. (2013). Preventing sexual abusers of children from reoffending: Systematic review of medical and psychological interventions. *British Medical Journal, 347,* f4630.

Laschet, U., & Laschet, L. (1975). Antiandrogens in the treatment of sexual deviations of men. *Journal of Steroid Biochemistry, 6,* 821–826.

Lievore, D. (2005). Thoughts on recidivism and rehabilitation of rapists. *University of New South Wales Law Journal Forum, 11*(1), 29–32.

Loosen, P. T., Purdon, S. E., & Pavlou, S. N. (1994). Effects on behavior of modulation of gonadal function in men with gonadotrophin-releasing hormone antagonists. *American Journal of Psychiatry, 151*(2), 271–273.

Lösel, F., & Schmucker, M. (2005). The effectiveness of treatment for sexual offenders: A comprehensive meta-analysis. *Journal of Experimental Criminology, 1*(1), 117–146.

Lussier, P., & Cale, J. (2013). Beyond sexual recidivism: A review of the sexual criminal career parameters of adult sex offenders. *Aggression and Violent Behavior, 18*(5), 445–457.

Maletzky, B. M. (1991). The use of medroxyprogesterone acetate to assist in the treatment of sexual offenders. *Annals of Sex Research, 4,* 117–129.

Maletzky, B. M., & Field, G. (2003). The biological treatment of dangerous sexual offenders. *Aggression and Violent Behavior, 8*(4), 391–412.

Mancini, C., Barnes, J. C., & Mears, D. P. (2011). It varies from state to state: An examination of sex crime laws nationally. *Criminal Justice Policy Review, 24*(2), 166–198.

McConaghy, N., Blaszczynski, A., & Kidson, W. (1988). Treatment of sex offenders with imaginal desensitization and/or medroxyprogesterone. *Acta Psychiatrica Scandinavica, 77,* 199–206.

McMillan, J. (2014). The kindest cut? Surgical castration, sex offenders and coercive offers. *Journal of Medical Ethics, 40*(9), 583–590.

Meyer, W. J. III, Cole, C., & Emory, E. (1992). Depo provera treatment for sex offending behavior: An evaluation of outcome. *Bulletin of the American Academy of Psychiatry and the Law, 20,* 249–259.

Meyer, W. J., III, Walker, P. A., Wiedeking, C., Money, J., Kowarski, A. A., Migeon, C. J., & Borgaonkar, D. S. (1977). Pituitary function in adult makes receiving medroxyprogesteron acetate. *Fertility and Sterility, 20*(10), 1072–1076.

National Probation Service of the United Kingdom. (2007). Medical treatment for sex offenders. London: National Offender Management Service.

Ohm, A. (1960a). Zur Frage der Entmannung—Eine Auswertung der Berliner "Akten betr. Entmannung": I. *Zeitschrift für Psychosomatische Medizin, 61,* 21–34.

Ohm, A. (1960a). Zur Frage der Entmannung—Eine Auswertung der Berliner "Akten betr. Entmannung": II. *Zeitschrift für Psychosomatische Medizin, 62,* 106–119.

Ryberg, J., & Petersen, T. S. (2014). Surgical castration, coercion and ethics. *Journal of Medical Ethics, 40*(9), 593–594.

Saleh, F. M., & Guidry, L. L. (2003). Psychosocial and biological treatment considerations for the paraphilic and nonparaphilic sex offender. *Journal of the American Academy of Psychiatry and the Law, 31,* 486–493.

Sand, K. (1940). Die gesetzliche Kastration: 10 jahrige Erfahrungen mit gesetzlicher Kastration in Danemark. *Veroffentlichungen aus dem Gebiete des Volksgesundheitsdienstes, 54.*

Schlegel, A. (1935). Die Entmannung als Sterilisierung und Scherungsmassregel gegengefahrlich Sexualverbrecher. *OffentL Gesd. disenst, 1*, 361–365.

Schmidt, P. J., Berlin, K. L., Danaceau, M. A., Neeren, A., Haq, N. A., Roca, C. A., & Rubinow, D. R. (2004). The effects of pharmacologically induced hypogonadism on mood in healthy men. *Archives of General Psychiatry, 61*, 997–1004.

Schober, J. M., Kuhn, P. J., Kovacs, P. G., Earle, J. H., Byrne, P. M., & Fries, R. A. (2005). Leuprolide acetate suppresses pedophilic urges and arousability. *Archives of Sexual Behavior, 34*(6), 691–705.

Scott, C. L., & Holmberg, T. (2003). Castration of sex offenders: Prisoners' rights versus public safety. *Journal of the American Academy of Psychiatry and Law, 31*, 502–509.

Serious Sex Offenders (Detention and Supervision) Act 2009 (Victoria).

Shahinian, V. B., Kuo, Y-F., Freeman, J. L., & Goodwin, J. S. (2005). Risk of fracture after androgen deprivation for prostate cancer. *The New England Journal of Medicine, 352*, 154–164.

Sharifi, N., Gulley, J. L., & Dahut, W. L. (2005). Androgen deprivation therapy for prostate cancer. *Journal of the American Medical Association, 294*, 238–244.

Shaw, E. (2014). Offering castration to sex offenders: The significance of the state's intentions. *Journal of Medical Ethics, 40*(9), 594–595.

Shen, F. X. (2010). The law and neuroscience bibliography: Navigating the emerging field of neurolaw. *International Journal of Legal Information, 38*, 352–99.

Sifferd, K. (2013, January 22). Chemical castration as punishment. *Neuroethics & Law Blog.* Retrieved August 31, 2014, from http://kolber.typepad.com/ethics_law_blog/2013/01/chemical-castration-as-punishment-by-katrina-sifferd.html.

State of New South Wales v Williamson. NSWSC 939 (2014).

Stathopoulos, M. (2010). Measuring sexual offender recidivism. *Aware: Australian Centre for the Study of Sexual Assault Newsletter, 25*.

Stürup, G. K. (1953). Les délinquants sexuels et leur traitement au Danemark et dans les autres pays scandinaves [Sexual offenders and their treatment in Denmark and other Scandinavian countries]. *International Review of Criminal Policy, 4*, 1–19.

Stürup, G. K. (1968). Treatment of sexual offenders in Herstedvester Denmark. *Acta Psychiatrica Scandinavica, 43*(Suppl. S204), 5–63.

Vincent, N. A. (2014). Restoring responsibility: Promoting justice, therapy and reform through direct brain interventions. *Criminal Law and Philosophy, 8*, 21–42.

Wainberg, M. L., Muench, F., Morgenstern, J., Hollander, E., Irwin, T. W., Parsons, J. T., . . . O'Leary, A. (2006). A double-blind study of citalopram versus placebo in the treatment of compulsive sexual behaviors in gay and bisexual men. *Journal of Clinical Psychiatry, 67*(12), 1968–1973.

Werthiemer, A., & Miller, F. G. (2014). There are (STILL) no coercive offers. *Journal of Medical Ethics, 40*(9), 592–593.

White, P., Bradley, C., Ferriter, M., & Hatzipetrou, L. (1998). Managements for people with disorders of sexual preference and for convicted sexual offenders. *Cochrane Database of Systematic Reviews, 2*, CD000251.

Wille, R., & Beier, K. M. (1989). Castration in Germany. *Sexual Abuse: A Journal of Research and Treatment, 2*(2), 103–133.

Wolf, C. (1934). *Die Kastration bei sexuellen perversionen und Stttichkeitsverbrechen des Mannes.* Basel, Switzerland: Schwabe

Wong, C. M. (2001). Chemical castration: Oregon's innovative approach to sex offender rehabilitation, or unconstitutional punishment? *Oregon Law Review, 80*(1), 267–301.

13

Chemical Castration as Punishment

Katrina L. Sifferd

I begin my analysis of chemical castration as punishment with a case where a criminal defendant in Florida was sentenced to chemical castration. The case of Phu Tran illustrates the way in which current chemical castration statutes may be applied by the courts. Florida passed its statute in 1997. It authorizes trial judges to sentence *any defendant who is convicted of sexual battery* to receive medroxyprogesterone acetate (MPA). If the defendant is convicted of sexual battery and has a prior conviction for sexual battery, the statute *requires* the trial court to impose a sentence of MPA administration (Spalding, 1998, p. 120). The trial judge issuing a sentence of MPA must have a medical consult who determines that the "defendant is an appropriate candidate for treatment" (p. 123). However, the statute does not define "medical expert" or "appropriate candidate." Informed consent for the treatment is not mandated.

U.S. Chemical Castration Statutes and the Case of Phu Tran

In 2005, Phu Tran was convicted of sexual battery for digital penetration of two women while they were customers at a nail salon in (*Tran v. State*, 2007). Tran was sentenced to two consecutive terms of incarceration: 8 years in prison for one offense to be followed by 12 years of incarceration for the other offense. At the time of his sentence, the court noted that the 1997 Florida chemical castration statute made a chemical castration order mandatory, but reserved ruling pending an evaluation from an expert regarding whether Tran was a good candidate for castration. Four months later, Tran was sentenced to five years of MPA, the drug most commonly used to chemically castrate, in addition to his prison sentences.

At the court-ordered hearing to determine Tran's candidacy for castration, the state's psychiatrist, Dr. Thomas, testified that she thought Tran might be a sociopath. Dr. Thomas noted that while she was not prepared to say Tran was a "dyed-in-the-wool psychopath," Tran "certainly has some of the characteristics" (Francheschina, 2005). Dr. Thomas also told the judge that the drugs used in chemical castration were effective in curbing sexual appetite by "shutting down

Katrina L. Sifferd, *Chemical Castration as Punishment* In: *Neurointerventions and the Law.* Edited by: Nicole A Vincent, Thomas Nadelhoffer, and Allan McCay, Oxford University Press (2020). © Oxford University Press 2020
DOI: 10.1093/oso/9780190651145.001.0013

the production of testosterone," and that persons subject to chemical castration "are eunuchs for all intents and purposes." In the end, she concluded Tran was indeed a good candidate for the castrating drugs and recommended he be placed on them permanently (although, as already stated, the court gave Tran the much more limited sentence of five years of castration).

In response to Tran's sentencing appeal, the appellate court said the trial court had made a mistake when it reserved ruling on the duration of Tran's MPA treatment until four months after the sentencing hearing (Francheschina, 2005). Importantly, the court noted that chemical castration is not to be viewed as pure treatment but instead as a part of a punishment package. This means whether it is to be applied, and its duration, must be determined at sentencing so that the court can ensure that an offender's punishment package as a whole is proportional to his crime (*Tran v. State*, 2007). The court held that application of additional punishment after a Tran's sentencing hearing violated his constitutional right not to be subject to multiple prosecutions and punishments for the same criminal offense; that is, the trial court had violated the double jeopardy rule. Here is a portion of the court's ruling:

> The state contends that the MPA statute is for treatment purposes and does not constitute punishment for double jeopardy purposes. Second, the state argues that even if the statute is for punishment purposes, as long as MPA treatment is ordered at sentencing, the final determination as to the appropriateness of such treatment could be made thereafter without creating a double jeopardy violation.... We reject the state's contention that the MPA statute is for remedial treatment purposes, as opposed to punishment. The language of the entire statute speaks of MPA in terms of a sentence and a penalty. In the context of civil commitment proceedings for sexually violent predators, the Supreme Court has indicated that "[t]he categorization of a particular proceeding as civil or criminal 'is first of all a question of statutory construction." (Kansas v. Hendricks, 521 U.S. 346, 361 (1997) (quoting Allen v. Illinois, 478 U.S. 364, 368 (1986)). As a matter of statutory construction, it would appear that a sentence to administration of MPA does constitute punishment. Pursuant to the statutory scheme, the administration of MPA is imposed as part of a criminal sentence. Indeed, section 794.0235 is placed within Florida's criminal code, rather than under Florida's public health code. Compare §§ 394.910-.931, Fla. Stat. (2006) (Involuntary Civil Commitment of Sexually Violent Predators). Since the legislature has deemed MPA treatment a penalty, we conclude that it is part of the defendant's punishment and sentence. (*Tran v. State*, 2007)

In sum, the appellate court held that once Tran began serving his sentence, the trial court's subsequent order of MPA injections for a period of five years violated

Tran's constitutional rights because it amounted to additional punishment (*Tran v. State*, 2007). And because under the statute MPA treatment is a state-imposed punishment, it must be justified as such (i.e., it must serve a purpose of punishment—retribution, incapacitation, deterrence, or rehabilitation).[1]

The Florida chemical castration statute (§794.0235) under which Tran was sentenced has several interesting characteristics. Under the statute, a first-time offender convicted of sexual battery may be sentenced to castration regardless of the age of the offender's victim. This means that the statute does not target sex offenders who prey upon children, but all sex offenders. As the court in Phu Tran's case noted, chemical castration is mandatory on second offense. The statute also states that the court may sentence an offender to chemical castration, or the offender may voluntarily opt for surgical castration instead. When an offender is sentenced to MPA, this sentence of mandatory if a court-appointed medical expert determines he is a good candidate for MPA treatment (although what makes an offender a good candidate is not specified). Treatment is to begin not more than one week after a defendant who is incarcerated is released. Informed consent for treatment is not required, meaning that the offender subject to an MPA order need not be told of the many side effects of the drug (discussed in detail later in the chapter) If an offender refuses fails to show up for treatment or refuses treatment, he may be found guilty of a second-degree felony and sentenced to life in prison. Finally, a court order must specify a duration for castration, whether it is a specific term or for life (as would necessarily be the case if the offender opted for surgical castration).

A few other U.S. states have similar statutes (for an overview of U.S. castration statutes, see Scott & Holmberg, 2003). The California chemical castration statute differs from Florida's because it is aimed at sex offenders who victimize children: any person convicted of a specified sex offense—including sodomy, oral copulation, and sexual penetration—where the victim is under 13 may be punished with castration (Scott & Holmberg, 2003). Similar to Florida, California's statute stipulates that castration may be chemical or voluntary surgical, is at judicial discretion on first offense and mandatory on second offense, and is a condition of parole. However, no medical or psychiatric evaluation is required, and MPA is to be administered until the California Department of

---

[1] Model Penal Code section §1.02(2) states that the general purposes of sentencing is "to render sentences in all cases within a range of severity proportionate to the gravity of offenses, the harms done to crime victims, and the blameworthiness of offenders; and when reasonably feasible, to achieve offender rehabilitation, general deterrence, incapacitation of dangerous offenders, restoration of crime victims and communities, and reintegration of offenders into the law-abiding community, provided these goals are pursued within the boundaries of proportionality in subsection (a) (i); and (iii) to render sentences no more severe than necessary to achieve the applicable purposes in subsections (a)(i) and (a)(ii) . . . "

Corrections demonstrates to prison board treatment is no longer necessary (Scott & Holmberg, 2003).

In Louisiana, any person convicted of aggravated rape, forcible rape, second degree sexual battery, aggravated incest, or molestation of a juvenile when the victim is under the age of 13, or any repeat sex offender, may be sentenced to chemical castration (Scott & Holmberg, 2003). Castration is mandatory if a qualified mental health professional specifies it is necessary in a treatment plan (Scott & Holmberg, 2003). A particularly interesting aspect of the Louisiana statute is its stipulation that the offender must pay the ongoing costs for evaluation, treatment plan, and treatment (including MPA injections). (It is unclear what happens if the offender cannot pay for his injections—I assume he would still be subject to the drug.) In addition, in Louisiana castration is not a condition for release; it is a punishment to be applied in addition to incarceration (Scott & Holmberg, 2003).

Chemical castration works via antiandrogen drugs, often by way of large weekly injections. Depro-Provera® is the brand name for MPA, the drug most often used for chemical castration in the United States. MPA is an analogue of the female hormone progesterone, used to reduce the normal level of testosterone in a male by 50%—a level equal to the level found in prepubescent boys (Smith, 1998). MPA inhibits, through its effect upon neural pathways in the sexual system of the brain, the release of luteinizing hormone from the pituitary gland (Melella et al., 1989). Luteinizing hormone is the chemical messenger that normally stimulates the testicles to produce androgen. Hence, the ultimate effect of MPA is to reduce the level of androgen, especially testosterone, in the blood stream (Melella et al., 1989). The drug is thought to reduce sex-drive and levels of aggression in men and to reduce the capacity for an erection (Smith, 1998), although the exact impacts of the drug differ from person to person (Stinneford, 2005). MPA has significant side effects, such as osteoporosis, changes in cardiovascular health, blood fat levels, blood pressure and symptoms that mimic women's menopause (Stinneford, 2005). Although chemical castration can be applied as a temporary punishment, and the injections may be halted and offender's sexual function restored, some of these side effects have been found to linger long after injections are stopped.

There is some evidence that judges are not sentencing eligible offenders to chemical castration in the few U.S. states that allow it, even in cases where castration is made mandatory by statute.[2] However, how the statutes are currently applied is less important than how they *could be applied* in any particular case.

---

[2] One law review article notes that from the time the Florida statute was enacted in 1997 to 2005, judges had ordered chemical castration in three of 107 eligible cases (see Simpson, 2007).

Where a certain punishment is legal, the possibility remains that it may be applied to eligible offenders, and if a law is written such that it is likely to generate unjustifiable applications of criminal punishment, the law should be rewritten or repealed. Further, the lack of use means that in the rare cases where an offender is sentenced to chemical castration, his sentence is arbitrary. In his concurring opinion in *Furman v. Georgia* (1972), which found the death penalty to be unconstitutional because it application to a tiny subset of homicide defendants was necessarily arbitrary, Justice Stewart wrote:

> These death sentences are cruel and unusual in the same way that being struck by lightning is cruel and unusual. . . . I simply conclude that [the constitution] cannot tolerate the infliction of a sentence of death under legal systems that permit this unique penalty to be so wantonly and so freakishly imposed. (*Furman v. Georgia*, 1972)

My analysis here takes the three previously discussed statutes at face value. I will examine whether the aims of retribution, deterrence, incapacitation, or rehabilitation—the four most prominent aims of punishment in the U.S. criminal justice system—can be achieved by chemical castration. I conclude that the only possible aim to be met by chemical castration is rehabilitation; however, as the statutes are written, this aim is not achieved. Thus, all three statutes represent an unjustifiable use of state power.

The Functions of Punishment

Criminal sanctions, including incarceration, are designed to serve particular functions. These are often called the principles of punishment, and the four primary functions are retribution, deterrence, incapacitation, and rehabilitation.[3] According to the principle of retribution, violators of the law should get their "just deserts" such that public censure or punishment is an appropriate response to a wrongful act. The principle of deterrence attempts to influence an offender and other's decision-making with the threat of punishment. Both the general population and the specific offender who is punished may be deterred from choosing to commit criminal acts by punishment. The principle of incapacitation also aims to stop defendants from offending, but there is no attempt to influence decision-making; instead, the offender's environment is manipulated to

---

[3] Although both restoration of the victim, and reintegration of the offender into the community are mentioned in the Model Penal Code purposes section, I discuss neither here, in part because neither seem sufficiently influential in the generation of verdicts or policy in the United States.

make reoffending impossible, typically via incarceration. Finally, rehabilitation is the idea that offenders can be reformed so that they won't reoffend.

Most legal scholars agree that punishment aims to fulfill these multiple functions, although adherents of different ethical theories emphasize the importance of different functions. As Brown (2002) notes, one of the central problems in the criminal law is that it cannot be justified by a single ethical theory. Deterrence, incapacitation, and rehabilitation are easily understood as supporting the utilitarian aim of social order because they focus on the harmful consequences of crime. Deontological moralism, on the other hand, tends to stress the aim of retribution, where punishment is based upon blame and must be proportional to wrongfulness of the crime: criminal offenders deserve moral condemnation and punishment proportional to the harm caused by and/or the moral wrongfulness of their action.

I used to see the functions of punishment as a checklist where the aims were ordered by relative importance: (a) retribution, (b) deterrence, (c) incapacitation, and (d) rehabilitation. But I have come to see this as an extreme oversimplification.[4] Western systems of criminal justice seem to embrace all four of the functions listed, but the relationship between the aims is more complex than an ordered list. Although I cannot give a detailed account of interactions of the functions of punishment and justifying ethical theories here, I now feel that retribution should act as a general constraint on the total *amount* of punishment that can be applied in any case, and the other principles, especially incapacitation and rehabilitation, should primarily inform the *type* of punishment that is applied within the range of appropriate punishment proportional to the offender and his wrongdoing. That is, the total amount of punishment must be proportionate to the crime and to the type of offender (e.g. homicide vs. theft, adult vs. youth offender, offender with full mental capacity vs. diminished capacity); however, questions regarding whether the offender needs to be incapacitated via incarceration, or whether certain types of punishment are likely to deter other offenders similar to this offender in the future or whether certain punishments will rehabilitate (or will reduce the possibility of rehabilitation) should also be considered within the overall parameters of proportionality.

Norval Morris (1974) famously advocates this kind of account, often called *limiting retributivism*, and some argue that it is the consensus model of criminal punishment in the United States and Europe.[5] Limiting retributivism

---

[4] I have also come to see deterrence as a less important aim, due to the overwhelming research that offenders tend not to be deterred by threat of punishment (Mendes, 2004; Tonry, 2008) and rehabilitation as more important. Rehabilitation is an especially worthwhile principle of punishment from the virtue theory perspective (Sifferd, 2016).

[5] The recently redrafted language of the Model Penal Code's "purposes" section appears to reflect limiting retributivism (Frase, 2003).

is a hybrid theory of punishment, where retributive notions of just deserts provide an appropriate range of justified penalty within which an offender might be sentenced. Backward-looking retributive considerations of proportionality must then be balanced with forward-looking considerations of social order to create a punishment package that first and foremost is proportional to crime and offender, but that also aims to reduce recidivism and overall crime rates.

Morris's (1974) limiting retributivism specifically places strict upper limits on punishment based on desert, but no lower limit (Frase, 2003). Morris also promotes the principle of parsimony in punishment, which requires that "the least restrictive sanction necessary to achieve defined social purposes should be imposed" (Morris, 1974, p. 59). Courts ought not to impose the maximum an offender deserves unless there are very good reasons to do so and, indeed, should aim to assign lesser sentences and community-based sanctions whenever appropriate (Frase, 2003). Reasons to impose a sentence toward the more severe end of the retributive range include forward-looking considerations such as the need to incapacitate an offender considered especially dangerous.

A limiting retributive account of the aims of punishment diminishes the importance of deterrence in comparison to a pure utilitarian justification of punishment, because retributive considerations set the upper limit of punishment. However, limiting retributivism does not depend solely on notions of just deserts. Limiting retributivism is a "mixed" account of punishment that applies principles from both utilitarianism and legal moralism. Many important legal scholars have adopted some version of a hybrid theory, including H. L. A. Hart (1968), who also viewed desert as providing an upper limit on criminal sanctions (p. 237). Hart indicated that one must appeal to a retributive account of appropriateness of punishment given the crime committed, which "set[s] a maximum within which penalties, judged most likely to prevent the repetition of the crime by the offender or others, are to be chosen" (pp. 236–237).

There are worries regarding how any retributive theory, including limiting retributivism, can distinguish wrongful behavior deserving punishment from behavior which the state oughtn't punish (e.g., adultery) and how such a theory can clearly articulate degrees of wrongfulness (Kaplow & Shavell, 2002, pp. 303–305). However, I agree with Frase (2003) that the criminal law, especially U.S. state law, already does a pretty good job providing a proportional structure of offenses. There is general agreement that state criminal codes address behavior that ought to be considered criminal and deserving of criminal punishment and do so utilizing a sliding scale matching wrongfulness to degree of punishment. This is the case despite clear instances of overcriminalization of some behavior (as many would argue was the case with the United States' so-called war on drugs) and the fact that the U.S. criminal justice system as a whole may have failed meet Morris's (1974) principle of parsimony. (That is, while the scale matching wrongfulness of crime to severity of punishment may be in one sense somewhat accurate, the whole continuum of punishments is too severe.)

With regard to articulating degrees of wrongfulness, the Illinois Criminal Sexual Assault Act (720 ILCS 5/12-12, et seq.) provides a good example. Illinois's statute stipulates a wide range of possible sentences for conviction of a sex offense (defined as sexual penetration with force or threat of force) from four years to natural life, depending on the presence of aggravating circumstances. Such circumstances include whether this is a defendant's first offense, whether the victim suffered bodily harm, whether the offender used a deadly weapon, and the age of the victim (both a minor and an elderly victim enhances the sentence). Thus, a first conviction of simple sexual assault might result in anything from a 4-year to a 16-year prison sentence, and aggravating factors may further increase the range of sentence: sexual assault resulting in bodily harm or of a young victim carries a sentence of 6 to 30 years on a first conviction and natural life if the offender is being sentenced for a second sexual assault.

However, as previously indicated, Morris's (1974) limiting retributivism does not generally provide minimum sentences. The Illinois statute stipulates a four-year minimum. In addition, Morris encouraged judges to cluster sentences around the lower end of the range indicated by considerations of desert, which I can say from experience the Illinois Cook County Criminal Courts often do not do. Even so, the Illinois statute, like many state statutes can be taken as an example of limiting retributivism in action. All of the aggravating factors listed in the statute represent aspects of the crime that speak to a retributive assessment of desert and incrementally increase punishment based on these factors.

Although the Illinois statute provides an example of retributive notions of just desert acting to delimit the appropriate range of punishments, it does not invite serious consideration of forward-looking aims of punishment except those automatically achieved by incarceration (e.g., incapacitation and possibly deterrence). There are no specifically rehabilitative options available to the court sentencing a sex offender in Illinois, as there are for offenders sentenced for a drug conviction, where an Illinois drug court may order mandatory addiction treatment (see 720 ILCS 5/12-12, et seq.). I will argue that chemical castration cannot be justified as appropriate retributive punishment or as achieving the aims of deterrence or incapacitation, but might be justified as part of an punishment package by the forward-looking aim of rehabilitative treatment for a small subset of sex offenders, in the same way that coercive medical treatment for drug-addicted offenders is a justifiable punishment.

Retribution

As previously discussed, limiting retributivism aims to use considerations of just desert and proportionality to set the upper limits of a criminal sentence. Such a sentence often consists in a stint in prison, but Morris also supported community-based sanctions and treatment programs (Morris & Tonry, 1991). Indeed, Morris and Tonry wrote an entire book in support of what they called "intermediate punishments" that lie between prison and probation in response to the explosion of the U.S. prison population, advocating sentences of intensive probation, substantial fines, community service orders, residential controls, and treatment orders (Morris & Tonry, 1991, p. 4). They argued that such sentences are a more proportional response to many felonies, less expensive than traditional incarceration, and more likely to accomplish treatment objectives than prison-based treatment (Morris & Tonry, 1991). Thus, the hybrid theory of limiting retributivism is certainly compatible with sentences other than prison.

Even so, I do not think the particular sentence of chemical castration cannot be directly justified as a state-sanctioned punishment on retributive grounds. As University of Chicago law professor Dan Kahan (1996) has noted, although we seem comfortable with the notion that the purpose of sending offenders to prison is at least in part to cause suffering, European countries and the United States openly reject states using alternative means of causing suffering, especially corporal punishment. In 1978, the European Court of Human Rights found corporal punishment violated Article 3 of the European Convention on Human Rights because it was fundamentally degrading (*Tyrer v. United Kingdom*, 1978). In the United States, the last instance of state-imposed corporal punishment occurred in Delaware in 1952 (a flogging). Since this time the legal community appears to be operating as though corporal punishment violates the Constitution's prohibition against cruel and unusual punishment (although the Supreme Court has not decided the question). If chemical castration is cast as a purely retributive punishment, it seems to be the type of inhumane corporal punishment no longer practiced.

Further, retributive punishments must be proportional to the type of agent and degree of harm caused, and chemical castration would seem to be proportional in the lex talionis sense. Lex talionis punishments are retaliatory eye-for-an-eye punishments similar in kind to the crime committed. One can see lex talionis–type retributive sentiment in this statement on chemical castration found in a New York University Law School forum blog (in the blog's corpus, not in the comments): "I fail to see the problem with irreversibly invading and mutilating a child-rapist, much less causing him to suffer the side effects of menopause. In fact, there seems no more fitting a punishment for the child rapist (NYU Forum on Law, Culture, and Society, 2012). Chemical castration, at least when viewed as a retributive punishment, would seem to harken back to the days when Thomas Jefferson (1778) wrote a bill that included sentences of up to 15 lashes for witchcraft; death by poison for those who killed by poisoning; castration for men guilty of rape, polygamy, or sodomy; and a minimum half-inch hole bored in the nose cartilage of women convicted of sex crimes. Morris and Tonry (1991) refuse to even discuss the idea of retaliatory corporal punishments in their book on limiting retributivism:

> We shall not discuss corporal punishments, the lash, the birch, the chopping of hands and tongues, the slitting of lips and noses, the slicing of ears. They are less romantic than brutalizing, not only to those who suffer such punishments but—and the historical record is clear on this—to the society that applies them. (pp. 5–6)

In sum, cast as a retaliatory corporal punishment, chemical castration would seem to be degrading, brutalizing, or cruel such that it may violate the U.S. Constitution Eighth Amendment's prohibition against cruel and unusual punishment. Certainly, the punishment is unusual in that it only seven states have chemical castration statutes (Stinneford, 2005, p. 559). Scholars also argue that the practice is cruel because its aim to "exert control over the mind of the offender by rendering it incapable of experiencing sexual desire" which violates offenders' dignity and has painful, disabling, and possibly fatal long-term effects (Stinneford, 2005, p. 559), thus the practice may be seen as violating contemporary standards of decency.

In addition to these concerns, there are other, more pragmatic worries about chemical castration as retributive punishment. As famous jurist William Blackstone (1879) argued:

> Retaliation may sometimes be too easy a sentence; as if a man maliciously should put out the remaining eye of him who had lost one before, it is too slight a punishment for the maimer to lose only one of his. . . . Besides there are many crimes, that will in no shape admit of these penalties, without manifest absurdity and wickedness. Theft cannot be punished by theft, defamation by defamation, forgery by forgery, adultery by adultery, and the like. (p. 13)

One can imagine cases where castration of a sex offender might be both too easy and too tough a retributive sentence. Imagine a pedophile who is disgusted with himself for committing sex crimes against children to the point where he is suicidal. Treatment that diminishes his sexual desire for children may be a relief for this offender, not painful retaliation for his crimes. On the other hand, an undergraduate man who date-raped another undergraduate might legitimately argue that a sentence of chemical castration for even an intermediate length of time—let's say, 10 or 15 years—would be too severe a sentence, especially given that it is likely to impact his ability to obtain a partner and have children during the normal span of time within which most persons start a family.

Blackstone's worries about state "wickedness" are also important. State-endorsed physical harm of citizens can undermine the state's authority to impose legal duties and thus rule of law. A state that performs violent acts against its citizens, even in response to violence, may lose the moral high ground in the eyes of the citizenry necessary to request that citizens do not respond similarly to violence committed against them. From the perspective of the theory of law proposed by Hart (1961), state-imposed violent corporal punishment may degrade the social acceptance he claimed was vital to citizens' felt obligation to follow the law.

It seems clear that chemical castration does not achieve aim of retribution in a way acceptable to a modern liberal democracy. Retaliatory physical harm by way of direct brain manipulations ought not be considered an appropriate response to sex crimes, because such a punishment (a) is degrading, inhumane, and may be unconstitutionally cruel and unusual; (b) may constitute both too lenient and too severe a punishment, depending on the case; and (c) may undermine the state's moral authority and thus rule of law.

Therefore it seems chemical castration as a state-sanctioned criminal punishment must accomplish a forward-looking aim of punishment to be justifiable. Next I will consider whether castration achieves the aims of deterrence, incapacitation, and rehabilitation.

Deterrence

There are two ways in which a potential offender may be deterred by punishment. First, criminal punishments may reduce the overall rate of crime in the general population. This is termed *general deterrence*. Second, an offender who has experienced criminal punishment may be deterred from committing future crimes because of this experience. This is called *specific deterrence*. In both cases persons considering committing a crime are dissuaded from doing so to avoid the unpleasantness of punishment.

Deterrence anchors many utilitarian accounts of punishment. Bentham (1996) argued that more severe punishments were necessary to convince potential offenders not to commit more serious crimes (which, in many cases, have a bigger payoff for offenders), while lesser punishments were enough to convince citizens not to commit lesser crimes. Thus a fine might be enough to stop people from speeding or parking in a handicapped spot, but a hefty penalty such as a long prison sentence might be needed to convince a potential offender not to kill someone they really wanted dead. In this way some utilitarians argue the appropriate criminal punishment for a crime is (at least in part) determined by the rational calculus of costs and benefits of the crime to the potential offender.

However, this sort of utilitarian way of determining criminal penalties has been undermined by research on deterrence. Although it seems that in general the existence of a criminal justice system may deter some persons from crime, and thus societies with state-enforced criminal penalties may have lower crime rates than they would have without criminal penalties, 30 years of studies on deterrence have made clear that even very broad changes in punishment regimes have almost no effect on rates of offending (Tonry, 2008). That is, even very severe increases in punishments, such as three-strikes laws that applied life in prison sentences to an offender's third felony conviction, or the death penalty to aggravated homicides, have little or no effect on crime rates (Tonry, 2008). Even though persons who commit crimes must in some sense know that their acts may be subject to criminal punishment, the type or severity of punishment that may be applied seems to have little effect on their decision-making (Tonry, 2008).

Because of this, it is exceedingly unlikely that potential offenders within the few states with chemical castration statutes will be deterred from sex crimes by the specific threat of castration. First, many potential sex offenders in these states won't know that their act may be subject to a chemical castration statute. In this case the threat of castration can have no deterrent effect in addition to a general desire to avoid criminal punishment. Second, even if a potential sex offender knew he was committing a crime within a state with a chemical castration statute, he may not think his act in particular would be likely to result in castration: in the previously discussed case, even the judge seemed surprised that castration was a mandatory penalty for Tran because the two incidents amounted to repeat sex crimes. And, as we have already noted, many judges within the states that have chemical castration as a possible penalty fail to apply the penalty when offenders qualify. In general, sex offenders may experience less fear of criminal punishment than other types of offenders because of the large percentage of sex crimes that are not reported—the majority, according to the National Institute of Justice (2010b). An even smaller subset of sex crimes reported actually result in a criminal conviction. For all of these reasons, the particular punishment of chemical castration cannot be considered a *general deterrent* for persons who may commit qualifying sex crimes and thus cannot justify the previously discussed castration statutes.[6]

---

[6] It is unclear whether proposed penalties would have a robust deterrent effect in an ideal criminal justice system, where the application of criminal penalties was swift and 100% accurate. Even in this case, there would be epistemic and other agential limitations on deterrent effect. Given this, it is so unlikely our criminal justice system will approach ideal deterrent effect that we need not discuss the

There is a somewhat stronger likelihood that chemical castration could act as a *specific deterrent*. We might imagine a case where an offender who was chemically castrated decides not to commit another sex crime for fear of another round of MPA treatment. But this scenario assumes an offender who, like Phu Tran in Florida, is given a sentence of MPA for a limited duration. In California, however, MPA is to be administered as a condition of parole until the California Department of Corrections demonstrates to prison board treatment is no longer necessary. If the California Department of Corrections made a point of demonstrating to the prison board that MPA is no longer necessary, we might assume the offender in question is reformed such that a specific deterrent effect is unnecessary.

In Florida and Louisiana, it is possible a castrated offender might be taken off MPA and then deterred by the possibility of being recastrated. However, in both states MPA sentences can be quite long, even lifelong. And in the case of a shorter sentence, say, where the offender is given the drug until he is in his 50s, it may be that by this point in his life he is less likely to suffer from very strong sexual urges due to old age and thus would have less need for a deterrent. (Indeed, many offenders may "age out" of criminal tendencies.) Finally, it is obvious that if an offender opts for voluntary surgical castration under the Florida or California statutes, there can be no specific deterrent effect. But, in small number of cases in Florida and Louisiana, it is possible, if extremely unlikely, chemical castration could serve as a specific deterrent.

There is a deeper problem than worries about duration with the notion of castration as specific deterrent, however. To be deterred by the threat of chemical castration an offender must experience chemical castration as unpleasant, so he will choose not to commit another sex crime so as to avoid being recastrated. But this may not be the case. Some sex offenders choose to be surgically castrated because they wish to be rid of their deviant sexual urges forever, and other sex offenders feel that administration of MPA helps them become a fully responsible agent, because, as Cephalus in the Pato's *Republic* might say, it rids them of a "mad master" (Book I). If chemical castration acts as some psychiatrists and psychologists say it should, and it reduces overwhelming sexual urges so as to allow offenders to make more responsible sexual choices, it may be experienced as a positive treatment for an unwanted affliction. In this case, the drug would certainly have no specific deterrent effect, although it may have a therapeutic and possibly incapacitative effect (see the following discussion).

possibility further. (Note the difference, too, between the likelihood that a judge will unjustly apply a chemical castration statute as written in a particular case and the likelihood that our criminal justice system and possible offenders will function so as to have a better deterrent effect.)

Because chemical castration is extremely unlikely to have a general deterrent effect and because chemical castration may have a specific deterrent effect only a very small number of offenders who qualify for castration under the statutes, it seems that the Florida, California, and Louisiana chemical castration statutes cannot be justified by appeal to castration's deterrent effect.

Incapacitation

The aim of deterrence focuses on the way punishment might convince a person not to commit crimes. Punishment that incapacitates, on the other hand, *forces* an offender not to reoffend. If chemical castration incapacitates sex offenders from committing sex crimes, without the cost of keeping them in prison, then it seems this might be a good forward-looking justification for the punishment.

However, as previously discussed, under limiting retributivism (the justification of punishment manifest in the U.S. Model Penal Code), use of MPA as incapacitation of criminal offenders ought to be limited by retributive considerations of proportionality of crime and type of offender to sentence. For example, we ought not to incapacitate offenders in prison indefinitely if the proportional upper limit of punishment for their crime is a 15-year sentence, regardless of how dangerous we think they are. Partly, of course, this is because any assessment of dangerousness is only a best guess regarding an offender's likelihood of recidivism. The length of a castration sentence ought to be limited to the amount of punishment allowed by notions of just desert. The appellate court in Pho Tran's case recognized this limitation when it demanded the length of the administration of MPA be determined at sentencing: administration of MPA must be viewed as one component of a sex offender's punishment package, where the total amount of a sex offender's punishment must be made to fit within the proportional limiting range of appropriate punishments.

This means that the California statute, which indicates that MPA should be used as a condition of parole for as long as the Department of Corrections deems necessary,[7] probably consists in an unjustified use of MPA as incapacitation. In the absence of an effort on the part of the Department of Corrections to show the offender no longer needs the MPA, the default will be to continue MPA injections for the rest of his life. Thus, the length of time the offender is subject to administration of MPA is dependent not on a proportional period of time given the

---

[7] California Penal Code 645(d) reads in full: "(d) The parolee shall begin medroxyprogesterone acetate treatment one week prior to his or her release from confinement in the state prison or other institution and shall continue treatments until the Department of Corrections demonstrates to the Board of Prison Terms that this treatment is no longer necessary."

offender's offense and level of responsibility, but instead, on the Department of Corrections' determination that the treatment is "necessary" (where the reasons it might be necessary are not specified in the statute). In addition, the Florida and California statutes, which indicate that an offender may have voluntary surgical castration in lieu of administration of MPA, may also generate sentences meant to be incapacitative that violate proportionality. Surgical castration is obviously a lifelong punishment. In many cases this permanent sanction will exceed the upper limit of proportional punishment for a particular offender, regardless of whether this was his "choice."

However, there is another, more important concern regarding chemical castration as incapacitative punishment: namely, that MPA may not actually incapacitate sex offenders from sex crimes. Prison incapacitates by removing an offender from society, thus making it impossible to commit most crimes. Castration does not, however, remove an offender from situations where he may commit a sex crime; instead, it attempts to address the cause of sex crimes (sexual urges, assuming that this is indeed the cause; see the following discussion) regardless of where he is located (and often, castration is a condition of release into the community). Some proponents of chemical castration (i.e., politicians) seem to think that MPA removes an offender's ability to have an erection—although it is not clear MPA does this—and thus his ability to commit a sex offense is removed. But, of course, this is not the case, as Phu Tran's sexual assault shows (Phu Trans digitally penetrated his victims).

Studies of recidivism rates of chemically castrated offenders clearly show that MPA should not be considered incapacitative despite evidence that it reduces sexual desire (see Chapter 12 of this volume). Anecdotally, psychiatrist Chris Ryan tells me that some sex offenders experience better sexual function on MPA. But even if chemical castration severely limits sexual desire—and reduces sexual capacity to some extent—a sex offender's sexual desires and capacity may not be causally related to his past sex offense or to the likelihood he will commit another sex offense in the future. Remember the Pho Tran case. It seems likely that Tran was motivated to sexually assault the two clients of the nail salon where he worked because of the sexual desire he felt for the two women. In this case MPA may work to reduce the overwhelming sexual urges Tran feels toward women once he is released, and it *may* have an effect on reducing the likelihood of recidivism. But there are other stories we might tell about the motivations of Tran. It is at least possible that instead of experiencing overwhelming desire for sex with the women, Tran has a deep-seeded hatred of women. (Maybe he was sexually abused by a woman as a child, or maybe he was ridiculed one too many times by women in school.) On this story of Tran's crime, when Tran sexually assaulted the women, he felt no sexual desire at all, but instead felt hatred and anger and thus wanted to make the women feel powerless and under his control. Or, imagine

Tran has a low IQ and some intellectual disabilities and was raised in a very shel-
tered environment where his overbearing mother ignored his sexuality. His first
job outside of the home was at the nail salon, and a vindictive neighbor told him
that if he thought a woman was pretty, she would like it if he assaulted her. In this
case, sexual desires are one of the causes of Tran's assaults, but he isn't suffering
from overwhelming sexual desires such that administration of MPA seems to be
the best means to reduce Tran's likelihood of recidivism. Certainly, in this third
set of imagined circumstances, it makes more sense to educate Tran than to castrate him. And if his hatred for women was the primary cause of his crime, Tran
is unlikely to be incapacitated by the reduction of his sexual urges, although the
level of aggression he feels toward women might be impacted by the drugs (but
not, probably, his hatred).

I'm willing to go out on a limb and speculate that the reason why studies find
chemical castration has little to no effect on recidivism—although there is anecdotal evidence that voluntary administration of MPA can help some sex
offenders and others who suffer from sexual disorders—is because sex offenses
are committed for a plethora of reasons, and overwhelming sexual urges are just
one category of such causes. Decreasing sexual urges, and even decreasing overall
levels of aggression, may have no impact on some sex offender's likelihood of
committing a sex offense because it might not address many of the psychological causes of his past antisocial decisions and might thus also fail to address his
likelihood of recidivism. Anecdotal stories may identify a sex offender who is
plagued by strong, unwanted desires for illegal sexual partners or acts and who
can successfully use MPA as a means to decrease his attraction to illegal sex partners, along with therapy and other tools. But the larger studies identified by Ryan
(see Chapter 12 of this volume) tend to focus on administration of MPA to large
categories of offenders, where the category is defined by the type of crime an
offender committed. Within these categories many offenders may not have overwhelming sexual urges, nor the desire to alter their decision-making or access
to multiple sources of treatment. Even if administration of MPA impacts sexual
capacity, it will not incapacitate most of these offenders from sex offenses.

In sum, there is some evidence that MPA may lessen sexual desire and/or
levels of aggression, but it isn't at all clear that this creates an *incapacity* to commit
sex crimes. Studies indicate that most of the offenders who qualify for chemical
castration under the Florida, California, and Louisiana chemical statutes will
not be incapacitated by administration of MPA (or surgical castration, for that
matter). It could be that a detailed medical exam could be used to identify the
subset of sex offenders who suffer from overwhelming sexual urges and thus who
might be less likely to recidivate if given MPA. But note, even these offenders will
not be incapacitated by the drug in the same way they would be by incarceration.
Instead, it makes more sense to consider MPA a rehabilitative tool that could

help them decide not to recidivate. For these reasons, the previously discussed castration statutes cannot be justified on incapacitative grounds.

Rehabilitation

> While it is tempting to see rehabilitation as incompatible with punishment, this view is incorrect. Punishment is best understood as a *response* to crime. . . . Rehabilitation is one of many possible responses.
>
> —Thom Brooks (2012, p. 56)

A punishment is rehabilitative if it reforms an offender such that he chooses not to commit further crimes. Rehabilitative programs attempt to influence offenders' rational processes such that they are more easily able to follow legal norms, either by giving them skills that will improve situational factors and decrease their likelihood of recidivism, or, in some cases, attempt to address specific problems directly related to an offender's past crime. For example, job training or the opportunity to earn a GED (high school diploma equivalent) may make it more likely an offender will get a job upon release, and thus decrease his chance of performing illegal acts as a way to earn money. Anger management therapy or mindfulness training, on the other hand, attempts to directly impact offender's decision-making processes by teaching him to slow down and more carefully consider the consequences of behavior.

Some scholars have worried about chemical castration as punishment because it consists in a court-ordered direct brain intervention (Stinneford, 2005). However, there is another direct brain intervention already widely accepted as part of a court-based rehabilitative program: drug courts often mandate medical treatment of addicted drug offenders. A drug court is a specialized or problem-solving court that targets criminal offenders who have alcohol and other drug addiction and dependency problems. As of 2013, there were over 2,800 drug courts operating throughout the United States (National Institute of Justice, 2010a), and roughly half of them offered medication as a part of addiction treatment (Matusow et al., 2013). Such treatment is rehabilitative in that it reduces the strength of, or eliminates, persistent, intrusive psychological states directly related to offender's crime and likely to cause recidivism (e.g., cravings). Although drug treatment regimens are rehabilitative, they are also coercive in that if an offender refuses treatment he is removed from the program. Often an offender has to plead guilty to the charges against him to stay within the drug court system, but the normal penalties for the charges are held in abeyance during treatment

(Bahr, Masters, & Taylor, 2012). If the offender finishes his or her treatment successfully, the charges are dropped. If he or she fails to finish treatment, the offender is sent to jail or prison to serve their sentence (Bahr et al., 2012).

One example of a medical treatment used by drug courts is topiramate, which treats alcohol and cocaine addiction. Topiramate is thought to decrease cravings and has been found to significantly improve addiction treatment outcomes (Bahr et al., 2012). Importantly, treatment of offenders handled by drug courts is almost always initiated and guided by a medical professional (Bahr et al., 2012). Medication is often given in conjunction with therapy, which assists the offender in behavior modification to avoid triggers for their addiction and seek healthy alternatives such as exercise. The best outcomes for drug court programs are associated with a multifaceted treatment approach (Bahr et al., 2012).

I have shown that it is unlikely chemical castration can be justified by the aims of retribution, deterrence, and incapacitation. But the similarities between the overwhelmingly accepted administration of medicine to drug offenders to reduce cravings by drugs and administration of MPA to reduce overwhelming sexual urges in sex offenders indicate that chemical castration might be properly seen as rehabilitative treatment. However, as I will show, there are many difficulties fitting chemical castration within the rehabilitative treatment model. In the end, I argue that chemical castration as currently allowed under U.S. statutes cannot be considered rehabilitative treatment because of the way in which these statutes administer MPA to sex offenders.

The biggest problem with the chemical castration statutes is that there is no consistent matching between psychological disorders or symptoms and MPA as treatment for such disorders or symptoms. Let's just assume for the sake of argument that MPA acts to lessen sexual urges and urges to act aggressively. Let's also assume, as I previously argued, that sex crimes are committed for any number of (often compound) reasons, including overwhelming sexual urges; feelings of aggression, hate, frustration, and confusion; false beliefs; and plain old selfishness or narcissism. Some sex offenders captured by the chemical castration statutes probably have overwhelming sexual urges, but many do not. Some sex offenders captured by the statutes probably have strong aggressive urges, but many do not. Some sex offenders captured by the statutes may have both sorts of urges, but many may not have either. Again, even assuming the efficacy of MPA in reducing these urges on its own without supplementary treatment such as therapy— something I don't think it is safe to assume—the administration of MPA to the group of offenders that qualify for chemical castration in Florida, California, and Louisiana will treat a psychological disorder or symptom in only some (likely small) subset of these offenders.

This means the state will end up "treating" psychological states within offenders that are unrelated to his crime and unrelated to concerns that he will recidivate with regard to a similar type of crime—and this is worrying for reasons other than just MPA's inefficiency as treatment. Imagine if, once an offender was found guilty of a crime, the court was justified in targeting for rehabilitation *any* psychological aspect of the offender that the state determined was dangerous. The state could then decide to "rehabilitate" any psychological traits correlated with higher rates of recidivism with regard to any type of crime. For example, an offender convicted of theft might be coerced into anger management, or addiction treatment, or even administration of MPA, if the court determined he had psychological symptoms or disorders that might lead to future crimes.

But this would clearly be a violation of the offender's agency (and as I will argue, constitutional rights): state-sanctioned punishment is a response to a specific commission of a crime, and forward-looking aims of punishment ought to target recidivism via mandatory or coercive programming only with regard to the type of crime for which the offender was convicted. Imagine the alternative: what if a person arrested and convicted of stealing an automobile were subjected by the state to a battery of psychological tests to determine if he had a likelihood of committing other crimes, including sex crimes? What if this offender was then forced into mandatory rehabilitative programming for these proclivities (unrelated to his crime)? In this case a person arrested for theft might be subject to anger management therapy or even chemical castration during his time under state supervision resulting from his theft conviction.

I think this would be problematic for several reasons. First, forcing an offender convicted of theft to take such wide-ranging psychological tests seems to be a clear invasion of privacy and possibly an unconstitutional search.[8] The state is not entitled to review and assess the entire psychology of an offender just because he has committed a crime. Second, tailoring coercive punishment to psychological proclivities unrelated to an offender's crime would seem to violate due process.[9] The Fifth Amendment of the U.S. Constitution guarantees of due process provides that "no person shall . . . be deprived of life, liberty, or property, without due process of law." In this case, the court would seem to deny liberties (very important liberties, in the case of chemical castration) via rehabilitative programming in response to criminal proclivities without using the judicial process to find the offender guilty of a crime related to those proclivities. I would argue that there is no clear difference between the state looking

---

[8] In the United States, courts can force defendants to undergo a mental evaluation, but only in certain circumstances (e.g., cases where the defendant has claimed legal insanity or incompetence).

[9] In *Washington v. Harper* (1990), the U.S. Supreme Court held that the due process clause permits a state to treat an incarcerated inmate for a serious mental disorder with antipsychotic medication against his will only where he is dangerous to himself or others, and the medication prescribed is in his best medical interest. It thus seems likely involuntary treatment of criminal proclivities unrelated to an incarcerated offender's crime may violate due process.

for and addressing criminal proclivities unrelated to an offender's crime and the state randomly reviewing law-abiding citizens for criminal proclivities and then addressing such proclivities.

In other words, the state has no more right to address the possibility that an offender convicted of theft will commit a sex offense than they have to address a worry that an as-of-yet law-abiding citizen will commit a sex crime based upon the presence of certain psychological states. The state is not justified in coercive rehabilitative treatment in an attempt to reduce recidivism with regard to other types of crime than the one for which the offender is being punished.

This becomes even more clear when one notes that if the drug court statutes were written like the chemical castration statutes, every offender who committed certain drug crimes or committed a repeat drug crime might be mandated by statute to undergo medical treatment for addiction, *regardless of whether they have a drug addiction*. Instead, drug courts are designed by statute to identify drug-addicted offenders and to mandate treatment only for such offenders (Bahr et al., 2012). In general, drug offenders whom the court suspects are addicted undergo a medical evaluation. If the offender is found to have an addiction that led to his drug crime, the court may then offer treatment for that addiction, although again, the "offer" is coercive in that refusal will usually result the offender serving their sentence.

Of course, the state may be justified in offering offenders *volunteer* rehabilitative opportunities that may impact many aspects of their psychology, and it should: yoga, chess, gardening programs, job training in demolition, and beekeeping are all programs offered to offenders housed in the Cook County Jail (the county Chicago is located within) as a means to occupy inmates' time in a constructive way, with hopes that they may increase the inmates' mindfulness and job prospects. But when the state wishes to treat an offender via *coercive medical treatment* such as MPA, the treatment must be narrowly tailored to address an aspect of an offender's psychology that was a primary cause of their crime and, further, is a cause for extraordinary worries that the offender will commit the same type of crime once he is released. Again, this is because any coercive rehabilitative punishment must be a narrowly targeted response to the crime committed such that it constitutes a proportional response to the criminal act that is likely to actually reduce the likelihood of recidivism with regard to the type of crime committed.

Assessment of drug court programs indicate that they do indeed reduce rates of recidivism (Bahr et al., 2012). This may be because they are designed to target rehabilitative treatment more carefully at a group of offenders who suffer from a common psychological disorder. This targeted psychological disorder, addiction, is quite likely to be a primary cause of their crime and also a likely cause of recidivism. This may also be due to the multifaceted approach to treatment of addicted offenders, where offenders are also given drug tests and therapy or because drug-addicted offenders are more likely than sex offenders to be willing participants in their treatment program. Drug-addicted offenders can choose to reject their treatment and go to prison to serve their regular sentence, whereas sex offenders subject to MPA orders may face a significantly increased sentence, such as life in prison.

Thus, while chemical castration bears some surface-level resemblances to the treatment model of the drug courts, the latter succeeds as a rehabilitative treatment (and reduces recidivism) because it narrowly targets the psychological states that led to an offender's crime, encourages offender "buy-in" and supports medication with other forms of treatment, such as therapy. Chemical castration statutes lack any of these features and therefore cannot be justified as rehabilitative punishment.

But readers at this point may be forgiven for thinking I have forgotten an important aspect of the Florida and Louisiana statutes: the required medical evaluation. Isn't this part of the statute precisely meant to require a psychiatrist to identify a sex offender's primary reasons for committing their sex crime and then to use this information to determine eligibility for MPA, in the same way a drug court may use medical professionals to determine who is a drug addict? I think it isn't at all clear that the statutes were written to include a medical examination for this purpose, and in practice, it seems unclear that courts and court-ordered psychiatrists understand this to be the aim of medical evaluations under the castration statutes. The Florida statute (§794.0235(2)(a)), for example, provides that "an order of the court sentencing a defendant to medroxyprogesterone acetate (MPA) treatment under subsection (1), shall be contingent upon a determination by a court-appointed medical expert, that the defendant is an appropriate candidate for treatment." As Spalding (1998) notes, there is no stipulation as to who counts as a medical expert (any MD? a MD with a certain specialization? a nurse? a psychologist?), nor any information on what qualifies an offender as an "appropriate candidate" for treatment. Is the medical experts just looking to see if the offender could physically tolerate the treatment, or is he or she looking for whether the treatment will be effective—and if yes, effective in what sense?

Consider again Phu Tran's case. Tran was convicted of digitally penetrating two clients of the nail salon where he worked. The court record doesn't make it at all clear *why* he assaulted the women: he could have experienced overwhelming sexual desire and acted upon it, or he could have hated the women and wanted to violate them due to this hate, or he could have desired the women and not really understood his actions were unwanted (or at least criminal). Tran's reasons for breaking the law aren't really relevant to his guilt: if he sexually penetrated the women by force or without consent, Tran committed a crime. But Tran's reasons for committing the crime *are* relevant to whether or not Tran should be considered a good candidate for the rehabilitative treatment of MPA. If Tran committed the crimes from overwhelming sexual urges MPA might be a useful tool for his rehabilitation, by diminishing his sexual urges in such way that he might be able to make better sexual choices. But if Tran committed the sex crimes from an overwhelming hatred for women or out of a misguided attempt to secure a date or a sexual experience, application of MPA will address a part of Tran's psychology that is irrelevant to his crime and unrelated to his likelihood of recidivism.

Dr. Thomas, the psychiatrist who examined Tran to determine eligibility for administration of MPA testified that Tran exhibited signs of having a sexual disorder and that he was likely to commit sex crimes again after his release (Franceschina, 2005). Remember that Dr. Thomas also testified that Tran might suffer from psychopathy, saying "I'm not prepared to say he's a dyed-in-the-wool psychopath, but he certainly has some of the characteristics." A journalist present reported that Dr. Thomas offered evidence of Tran's psychopathy as relevant to his candidacy for MPA. Dr. Thomas indicated that MPA would make Tran "similar to a eunuch" by "shutting down his testosterone"—presumably with the idea that would make him less dangerous—and in the end, Dr. Thomas recommended Tran be castrated permanently (although the court sentenced him to five years of MPA).

Dr. Thomas' testimony seems to support chemical castration of Tran as either a retributive or incapacitative punishment, not as rehabilitative treatment. A recommendation for permanent administration of MPA indicates she did not think she was performing a medical evaluation of Tran to determine if MPA might help him tone down overwhelming sexual urges, such that he could learn to make better sexual decisions. If Dr. Thomas did think there was any chance that Tran would be rehabilitated by the administration of MPA, she probably wouldn't have recommended Tran be made a "eunuch" for life: this sort of recommendation does not offer any hope that Tran will be reformed by MPA so as to make better sexual choices. A eunuch is a male whose external genitals are removed, often before puberty, so that secondary male characteristics fail to develop. Dr. Thomas' use of this term indicates that she viewed MPA as a means to incapacitate Tran from sexual choices. And although Dr. Thomas stated that Tran suffered from a "sexual disorder," there is no indication she testified that Tran suffered from overwhelming sexual urges that led to his crime—urges that might be dampened with the administration of MPA.

Dr. Thomas's testimony regarding Tran's psychopathic characteristics is especially worrying. If Tran assaulted his victims due to lack of empathy for his victims or from a desire to violently control them, then administration of MPA may have little impact on the psychological causes of Tran's crime. Dampening sexual desire will have little to no impact on his psychopathy, and if psychopathy or narcissism (which often coexists with psychopathy; Paulhus & Williams, 2002) were the primary cause of Tran's crime, MPA may have little effect on his likelihood of recidivism.

Finally, note that there is no indication that Dr. Thomas recommended therapy or any other treatment in conjunction with the MPA. Just like medication to reduce cravings for illegal drugs, medication to reduce sexual or aggressive urges is most likely to have a rehabilitative effect when therapy is utilized in conjunction with medication.

It might be that other medical health professionals performing examinations under the Florida and Louisiana's chemical castration statutes ware more attuned to the idea of chemical castration as rehabilitative treatment aimed at persistent and overwhelming sexual urges. But there is nothing in either statute requiring a medical professional to make a finding that some disordered aspect of the offender's psychology will be treated with MPA or that the offender may be less likely to recidivate due to the treatment. Instead, the statutes leave courts and medical professionals free to determine what it means for an offender to be a "good candidate" for castration, such that the examiner may look solely for ability to tolerate the medication, or worse, feel they are asked to determine whether an offender *deserves* MPA. And because California doesn't even require a medical evaluation before the administration of MPA, there is no chance that offenders castrated under the California statute will be screened with regard to whether MPA might have a rehabilitative effect.

Further, in Florida and California, an offender may choose surgical castration instead of administration of MPA. It seems exceedingly unlikely that offenders who choose surgical castration ought to be considered "rehabilitated" with regard to sexual choices. Due to the permanency and stronger effect of surgical castration, it is more likely to achieve the forward-looking end of (permanent) incapacitation than rehabilitation, although it is unlikely surgical castration would lead to complete incapacitation with regard to sex crimes, and in most cases, permanent incapacitation will violate the upper limits of retributive proportionality.

To sum up the argument: the state can't target any aspect of offenders' psychology it doesn't like for rehabilitation when rehabilitative treatment is mandatory or coerced. To be justified as rehabilitative, coercive medical treatment must be narrowly tailored to address a primary psychological cause of an offender's crime and address extraordinary worries about recidivism with regard to the type of crime for which the offender is being punished. This means that the statutes that allow for such coercive rehabilitative treatment must clearly articulate a means for identifying those offenders who have a psychological problem, such as addiction or overwhelming urges, that were a primary cause of their crime and that might be rehabilitated via medication or other treatment. As such the Florida, California, and Louisiana statutes are not written so that they might be justified in mandating chemical castration as rehabilitative treatment. The two states that require a medical evaluation, Florida and Louisiana, do not make clear that these evaluations are meant to determine candidacy for rehabilitative treatment, and California does not require a medical evaluation and instead applies castration purely based upon aspects of the crime, not the criminal offender. Finally, none of the three statutes provide for other common aspects of the drug court's rehabilitative programs (that are likely correlated with their efficacy): a component that would allow offenders to "opt out," other treatment options provided in conjunction with medical treatment such as therapy, and a lessening of penalties if the treatment program is successfully completed. Thus, none of the three statutes can be justified by the forward-looking aim of rehabilitation.

Conclusions

To be a legitimate use of state power, punishment statutes must be written so as to achieve one or more of the primary functions of punishment. I have argued here that chemical castration of criminal offenders does not achieve the punishment aims of retribution, deterrence, or incapacitation and that the most likely justification of the practice is rehabilitation. However, the Florida, California, and Louisiana chemical castration statutes cannot be justified as providing rehabilitative treatment because they qualify offenders for chemical castration based upon features of their sex offense and do not provide a method for parsing out the small subset of offenders who possess a psychological symptom or disorder that MPA might treat. Further, these statutes fail to put into place other aspects of a treatment program likely to make rehabilitative medical treatment more successful, such as therapy.

I think the previous discussion supports the claim that any state-imposed coercive medical treatment of criminal offenders, including any direct brain intervention, must meet three criteria. First, the state may only target an offender's psychological states for rehabilitative treatment where such states are directly tied to a psychological disorder or symptom—there must be a disorder or symptom present to justify medical treatment. Second, because rehabilitative treatment of offenders is applied as punishment, the state may only target psychological states that (a) act as a primary cause of the offender's crime and (b) give rise to extraordinary worries that the offender will recidivate with regard to a similar type of crime. Third, the state must have some confidence that the rehabilitative treatment imposed will be effective in treating the offender's mental disorder or symptom such that the offender will be less likely to recidivate with regard to the same type of crime for which he is being punished.

Further, state-enforced medical rehabilitative treatment programs are more likely to be effective if they also have a voluntary component and where treatment includes a nonmedical component, such as therapy. Drug court rehabilitative treatment programs for drug-addicted offenders meet all of these requirements: they target cravings for illegal substances, a symptom of addiction, where such symptom is a cause of an offender's crime and are also likely to cause him or her to recidivate; medical treatment programs for addiction have been shown to be effective; and finally, drug court treatment programs, including medical treatment, have been shown to be effective in lowering rates of recidivism. Chemical castration programs such as the ones in Florida, California, and Louisiana meet none of these requirements. Thus, the chemical castration statutes in these states represent an unjustifiable use of state power.

References

Abbott, A. (2012) *Chemical Castration and Retributive Justice: the girl with the dragon tattoo*, NYU Forum on Law, Culture, and Society, published on October 3, 2012, accessed on 10/29/14. http://www.forumonlawcultureandsociety.org/2012/10/03/chemical-castration-retributive-justice-the-girl-with-the-dragon-tattoo/

Allen v. Illinois, 478 U.S. 364 (1986).

Bahr, S. J., Masters, A. L., & Taylor, B. M. (2012). What works in substance abuse treatment programs for offenders? *The Prison Journal, 92,* 155–174.

Bentham, J. (1996). *An introduction to the principles of morals and legislation.* Oxford, England: Clarendon Press.

Blackstone, S. W. (1879). *Commentaries on the laws of England: In four books. Vol. 2.* Chicago, IL: Callaghan.

Bomann-Larsen, L. (2011). Voluntary rehabilitation? On neurotechnological behavioural treatment, valid consent and (in)appropriate offers. *Neuroethics, 6*(1), 65–77.

Brooks, Thom. (2012). *Punishment.* London: Routledge.

Brown, D. K. (2002). What virtue ethics can do for criminal justice: A reply to Huigens. *Wake Forest Law Review, 37,* 29–50.

Francheschina, P. (2005, September 2). Judge orders molester to undergo castration. *South Florida Sun Sentinel.*

Frase, R. (2003). Limiting retributivism: The consensus model of criminal punishment. In M. Tonry (Ed.), *The future of imprisonment in the 21st century.* Oxford, England: Oxford University Press.

Furman v. Georgia, 408 U.S. 238, 309–310 (1972).

Hart, H. (1961). *The concept of law.* Clarendon Law Series. Oxford, England: Oxford University Press.

Hart, H. L. A. (1968). *Punishment and responsibility: Essays in the philosophy of law.* Oxford, England: Clarendon Press.

Jefferson, T. (1778). A Bill for Proportioning Crimes and Punishments. *The Founders' Constitution* (Vol. 5, Amendment 8, Document 10). Retrieved from http://press-pubs.uchicago.edu/founders/documents/amendVIIIs10.html

Kaplow, L., & Shavell S. (2002). *Fairness Versus Welfare.* Cambridge, MA: Harvard University Press.

Kahan, D. M. (1996). What do alternative sanctions mean? University of Chicago Law Review, *63*(2), art. 4.

Matusow, H., Dickman, S. L., Rich, J. D., Fong, C., Dumont, D. M., Hardin, C., . . . Rosenblum, A. (2013). Medication assisted treatment in US drug courts: Results from a nationwide survey. *Journal of Substance Abuse Treatment, 44,* 473–480.

Melella, J. T., Travin, S., & Cullen, K. (1989). Legal and Ethical Issues in the Use of Antiandrogens in Treating Sex Offenders. *Bulletin of the American Academy of Psychiatry in Law, 17*(3), 223–232.

Morris, N. (1974). *The future of imprisonment.* Chicago, IL: University of Chicago Press.

Morris, N., & Tonry, M. (1991). *Between prison and probation: Intermediate punishment in a rational sentencing system.* Oxford, England: Oxford University Press.

National Institute of Justice (2010a, May 14) Overview of Drug Courts http://www.nij.gov/topics/courts/drug-courts/Pages/welcome.aspx

National Institute of Justice. (2010b, October 25). Reporting of sexual violence incidents http://www.nij.gov/topics/crime/rape-sexual-violence/Pages/rape-notification.aspx

NYU Forum on Law, Culture, and Society. (2012, October 3). Retrieved accessed on October 29, 2014 from http://www.forumonlawcultureandsociety.org/2012/10/03/chemical-castration-retributive-justice-the-girl-with-the-dragon-tattoo/

Paulhus, D. L., & Williams, K. M. (2002). The dark triad of personality: Narcissism, Machiavellianism, and psychopathy. *Journal of Research in Personality, 36,* 556–563.

Scott, C., & Holmberg, T. (2003). Castration of sex offenders: Prisoners rights versus public safety. *Journal of the American Academy of Psychiatry and the Law, 31,* 502–509.

Sifferd, K. (2016). Virtue ethics and criminal punishment. In J. Webber & A. Masala (Eds.), *From personality to virtue.* Oxford, England: Oxford University Press.

Simpson, T. (2007). "If your hand causes you to sin . . .": Florida's chemical castration statute misses the mark. *Florida State Law Review, 34,* 1221–1246.

Smith, K. L. (1998). Making pedophiles take their medicine: California's chemical castration law. *The Buffalo Public Interest Law Journal, 123,* 1–42.

Spalding, L. H. (1998). Florida's 1997 chemical castration law: A return to the dark ages. *Florida State University Law Review, 25,* 117–139.

Stinneford, J. F. (2005). Incapacitation through maiming: Chemical castration, the eighth amendment, and the denial of human dignity. *University of St. Thomas Law Journal, 3,* 559.

Tonry, M. (2008). Learning from the limitations of deterrence research. *Crime and Justice, 37,* 279–311.

Tran v. State, 965 So. 2d 226 (Fla. Dist. Ct. App. 2007). https://www.4dca.org/content/download/157978/1397466/file/4D05-3933.op.pdf

Tyrer v. United Kingdom, 2 Eur. Human Rights R. 1, 58 I.L.R. 339 (Eur. Ct. Human Rights 1978).

Washington v. Harper, 494 U.S. 210 (1990).

14

Foundational Facts
for Legal Responsibility

Human Agency and the Aims
of Restorative Neurointerventions

Paul Sheldon Davies

> If humans are not conscious and intentional creatures who act for
> reasons that play a causal role in our behavior, then the foundational
> facts for responsibility ascriptions are mistaken.
>
> —Stephen Morse (2008)

Restorative Interventions

One intended function of neurointerventions is the enhancement of certain capacities. Call these *ampliative* interventions. A more modest intended function is the *restoration* of diminished capacities to some baseline, either modest or ambitious. We may aspire modestly to restore a person's competencies to reduce the risk he poses to the community. Or we may aspire ambitiously to render a person not merely safe but also practically rational, so she may be held responsible for future actions. The focus of this essay is the latter inventions, those that aspire ambitiously to restore a person to responsibility.

My thesis is that we should be skeptical that this intended function can be fulfilled. Not because of anything peculiar to persons who might benefit from such interventions, but simply because some of the competencies we regard as integral to correct attributions of legal responsibility appear to be competencies that human beings in general do not possess. If so, then the alleged foundational facts for legal responsibility fail to apply to organisms like us, including persons whose capacities have no need of restoration.

Advocates of restorative interventions, in consequence, face at least three substantive challenges. The first is whether currently available interventions actually restore the targeted competencies. It is not clear, for instance, that chemical castration is causally efficacious in reducing recidivism among convicted rapists (see Chapter 12 of this volume). The second challenge is whether the imposition

Paul Sheldon Davies, *Foundational Facts for Legal Responsibility* In: *Neurointerventions and the Law.* Edited by: Nicole A Vincent, Thomas Nadelhoffer, and Allan McCay, Oxford University Press (2020). © Oxford University Press 2020 DOI: 10.1093/oso/9780190651145.001.0014

of available interventions, even if effective, is ethical. The third challenge—the topic of this discussion—is whether the competencies we intuitively judge as integral to legal responsibility are instantiated in capacities we in fact possess. Even if we have excellent evidence that restored competencies are ones we judge to be integral to responsibility, we face the further questions: Are those competencies implemented in capacities we in fact possess, and, if so, are we capable of exercising them in our day-to-day interactions? I argue that, on balance, our best current evidence converges on a negative answer to these questions.[1]

If my thesis is correct, the most obvious response might be to withhold the concept of responsibility and to suggest alternative concepts with which to regulate human behavior. A quite different response, however, is to endeavor to change the kind of organism we are until the concept correctly applies to us. After all, if we anticipate having the technology to intervene on a person's brain to restore him to current baseline capacities, may we also anticipate developing technology with which to improve that baseline? If so, we may anticipate *ampliative* neurointerventions that will enhance our responsibility-relevant capacities and thereby create an important role for *restorative* neurointerventions. I will briefly address this possibility in the penultimate section of my discussion.

Criminal Responsibility, Folk Psychology, Practical Rationality

For concreteness, I shall focus on the definition of criminal responsibility in the Model Penal Code, Section 2.01:

> A person is not guilty of an offense unless his liability is based on conduct that includes a voluntary act or the omission to perform an act of which he is physically capable. The following are not voluntary acts within the meaning of this Section: (a) a reflex or convulsion; (b) a bodily movement during unconsciousness or sleep; (c) conduct during hypnosis or resulting from hypnotic suggestion; (d) a bodily movement that otherwise is not a product of the effort or determination of the actor, either conscious or habitual.

According to the Code, a person is criminally liable only if the person's action results from his or her own effort or determination. Now, it would be nice if the Code told us what constitutes "effort" or "determination" in the relevant sense, since both terms are strikingly nonspecific.

---

[1] If we possess the relevant capacities but we cannot exercise them on a regular basis, then they cannot suffice for attributions of legal responsibility for our day-to-day actions.

However, some legal theorists claim this nonspecificity is unobjectionable, even virtuous. According to these theorists, the law presupposes, and is intended to codify as far as possible, our shared folk psychological intuitions regarding our capacities as rational agents, including capacities that distinguish between actions caused by "effort" and actions caused by something else. On this view, legislators create laws that capture these intuitions, and judges and jurors rely on the same intuitions in case-by-case application of those laws. This allows judges and jurors to be sensitive to the multiple ways in which "effort" and "determination" can be manifested.

Stephen Morse (2011), a proponent of this view, is explicit on the relationship between folk intuitions regarding our psychological capacities and the law:

> Brief reflection should indicate that the law's psychology must be a folk psychological theory, a view of the person as a conscious (and potentially self-conscious) creature who forms and acts on intentions that are the product of the person's other mental states. We are the sort of creatures that can act for and respond to reasons. The law treats persons generally as intentional creatures and not simply as mechanistic forces of nature. (p. 116)[2]

It is this dependence of the law on our folk psychological view of ourselves that leads Morse to say what he says in the epigraph to this essay, namely, if progress in science reveals that we are not responsive to reasons that play a causal role in our actions (in ways suggested by folk intuitions), then the foundational facts for responsibility are mistaken. Here is the larger passage:

> At present, the law's "official" position—that conscious, intentional, rational and uncompelled agents may properly be held responsible—is justified unless and until neuroscience or any other discipline demonstrates convincingly that humans are not the creatures we think we are. That is, if humans are not conscious and rational creatures who act for reasons that play a causal role in our behavior, then the foundational facts for responsibility ascriptions are mistaken. (p. 19)

Well, then, what does folk psychology (and thus the law) posit about the capacities required for criminal responsibility? Let us begin with Morse's answer to this question. Responsibility for an action, he says in the passages just quoted, requires that the person be endowed with

---

[2] Excerpts of Morse (2011) are reprinted in Jones, Schall, and Shen (2014). Morse makes the same point in several places, including in Vincent (2013).

- a capacity for practical rationality that is
- unencumbered by internal or external compulsion, and that includes
- consciousness and potentially self-consciousness, as well as
- the capacity to form intentions derived from other mental states, that is,
- a decision-making capacity that is responsive to reasons and, in particular,
- responsive to reasons that play a causal role one's actions.

This list, though a fine beginning, calls for elaboration. Setting aside the vagueness of "consciousness" and "self-consciousness," we need, at a minimum, to specify what, according to our folk psychological intuitions, is required for a "decision-making capacity that is responsive to reasons that play a causal role in one's actions."

To that end, consider a case in which we must judge whether a person is responsible for her action—let us imagine that you have stolen your neighbor's car and are now on trial for theft. Part of the prosecution's task is to establish beyond reasonable doubt that your thievery was a result of your own "effort" or "determination." What, according to our folk intuitions, must the prosecution establish?

One requirement is that, at the time you stole the car, or at some earlier time, your rational, deliberative capacities were free from internal and external compulsion. Weak compulsion may diminish, and strong compulsion eliminates, responsibility for one's action. A further requirement is that your deliberative capacities were, at the relevant time, functioning above some minimal threshold. But what kinds of capacities are minimally required for you to qualify as practically rational?

It seems that, at minimum, you must have possessed of at least two operative capacities. The first is an operative capacity for relevant forms of *knowledge* and *motivation*, and the second is an operative capacity for *drawing practical inferences* (i.e., the capacity to infer that a specific action is called for, given what you know and what you desire).

I will elaborate on each of these capacities presently, but I pause to explain the importance of the qualifier "operative" in the previous sentence. I take it as obvious that you are responsible for stealing your neighbor's car only if your action resulted from a deliberate decision to steal the car, or, at the very least, from *some* deliberate decision causally implicated in your act of stealing—including, perhaps, the deliberate decision to refrain from deliberating and to instead act on a whim.[3] The reason is simple: if the lineage of decision-making that resulted

---

[3] We can leave open exactly *when* a person must have exercised her practical reasoning capacities. In some cases, it will be imperative that she reasoned immediately prior to acting; in others, it will suffice that she reasoned at some point prior to acting.

in your stealing includes *no* deliberate decision about the theft or *no* deliberate decision about whether to deliberate about the theft, then it is difficult to see how you, the agent, can be legally or morally responsible for that act.[4] But this means that, at the time of whatever deliberations led to your theft, your knowing, motivational, and inferring capacities must have been intact *and* operative. The mere possession of some "general capacity for rationality" is *not* sufficient. If it were, then you would be legally responsible for acts you perform while sleepwalking or while hypnotized, and you clearly are not.[5]

Let me now elaborate on both capacities, beginning with knowledge and motivation. In the case of your theft, it seems intuitive that your deliberative capacities met the minimal threshold for practical rationality only if, at the relevant time,

   i. You knew, or you reasonably should have known, that stealing was illegal and that you might be deprived of liberties if convicted of theft.
   ii. You knew that, by stealing your neighbor's car, you might satisfy some desire, for example, the desire to sell it for profit, or to experience the adrenaline rush that comes from risk-taking, and so on.

If (i) does not obtain—if you failed to understand that taking your neighbor's car is theft and thus subject to legal sanction—then the intuition that you are criminally responsible may be diminished. If (ii) does not obtain—if you held no belief, no recognition at all, that taking the car might benefit you in some way—then your status as a minimally rational agent is called into question.[6]

In addition to the capacity for knowledge, you must have had the capacity to be motivated in the relevant ways. Your capacities exceeded the threshold only if

   iii. The prospect of losing your liberties was an incentive for you to refrain from stealing your neighbor's car.
   iv. The prospect of having the car, and thereby satisfying some desire, was an incentive for you to steal it.

---

[4] This can be contested. Some theorists claim we can be morally responsible for an action in the absence of any decision concerning that action, so long as the action expresses or reflects our "real" selves (e.g., Smith, 2005). To make such a view plausible, however, either the concept of moral responsibility must be drained of much of its content or we must smuggle in precisely the kind of prior deliberate decisions as previously described—namely, prior decisions that somehow contributed to the formation or maintenance of one's "real" self.

[5] This is why Morse (2011) is mistaken in claiming that possession of the "general capacity for rationality" suffices for criminal responsibility (p. 117).

[6] This is true even if your theft was externally coerced, even if someone put a gun to your head and ordered you to steal the car. The salient belief in that case would be that stealing your neighbor's car would significantly reduce the chances of your being murdered.

If either motivation is missing, your alleged responsibility is in doubt. If (iii) is missing—if you knew that theft would put you at risk of losing your liberties but you nonetheless had no motivation to refrain—that is prima facie evidence of some sort of affective malady that may attenuate your responsibility.[7] If (iv) is missing—if you had no motivation to do the deed you in fact did—that is evidence that your taking the car did not truly derive from your own deliberative capacities, and that too attenuates your responsibility.

The second requirement draws directly on both components of the first. Your capacities exceed the minimal threshold for rationality only if

v. You had the operative capacity to consciously infer (from the relevant knowledge and motivation stated in i–iv) the conclusion that you ought to refrain from stealing or the conclusion that you ought to steal, where the conjunction of your knowledge and motivation would have functioned as reasons that played a causal role in your action.

Condition (v) captures what I take to be the heart of our folk psychological intuitions regarding ascriptions of responsibility. The intuition is that we are responsible only if we have the requisite inferential capacities and only if we are responsive to reasons that are causally efficacious. Thus, in the case of your theft, you must have had the capacity to draw a practical conclusion—to form the conscious intention to perform some specific action—from premises in which the competing actions (to steal, not to steal) are assigned some kind of evaluative weighting, based on the knowledge and motivations in (i)–(iv). This inference, moreover, must have been a causal factor in your action.

Insofar as our folk intuitions can be articulated, and insofar as they are stable, each of (i)–(v) is plausibly necessary for the correct attribution of criminal responsibility. If one or more fails to obtain in our day-to-day activities, the ascription of criminal responsibility is without foundation. More modestly, if condition (v) fails to obtain, attributions of criminal responsibility are surely without foundation.

Accordingly, I shall argue that the inferential capacities required in (v) are inoperative—they fail to generate a conclusion that plays a causal role in the relevant action—whenever the agent's knowledge and motivation fail to function together as reasons. As we will see, the range of cases in which our knowledge and motivations fail to function together is far from trivial.

---

[7] More generally, if knowledge of a possible sanction does not provide some motivation to refrain, that is prima facie evidence of some type of affective deficiency that may diminish responsibility.

In Defense of Skepticism

There are several strategies with which to substantiate my claim that the ambitious function of restorative neurointerventions cannot be fulfilled. For brevity, I offer evidence for just the following two claims[8]:

(1) Some of our actions are due to affective processes that are action-relevant but cannot figure in our practical reasoning because they do not rise to conscious awareness.

(2) We sometimes "know" things—believe them at the level of conscious awareness—in ways that fail to engage our affective capacities. Such "knowledge," therefore, is action-irrelevant and thus plays no causal in our practical reasoning.

If either (1) or (2) is true, then our actions sometimes result from affective processes that, one way or another, fail to engage our conscious knowledge and, in consequence, fail to engage our practical reasoning (described in condition v).

Some of the best evidence for (1) and (2) comes from integrating two seemingly disparate neuroscientific theories. According to Jaak Panksepp (1998), Panksepp and Biven (2012), the mind of modern humans is comprised in part by a subcortical ancestral mind that is largely affective. The effects of this ancestral mind are clearly action-relevant—they causally influence our decisions and actions whether or not they rise to conscious awareness. At the same time, according to Dehaene and Naccache (2001), Dehaene, Charles, King, and Marti (2014) and Dehaene and Naccache (2014), our subcortical affective processes are architecturally incapable of sending signals directly to brain areas responsible for conscious awareness. We become aware of our subcortical lives indirectly, if at all, and only by way of interpretation.

Affective Neuroscience

Panksepp hypothesizes that the ancestral mammalian mind implemented in subcortical processes is endogenous and autonomous[9] in the following senses. It is endogenous in that it comprises a set of capacities that do not require any learning for their operations; these capacities are built into the subcortical mammalian brain. It is autonomous in that its operations require no signals or

---

[8] The arguments herein are meant to complement those in Davies (2013). Both arguments, taken together, result in a consilient conclusion stronger than the conclusion of either argument on its own.
[9] I borrow these terms from Bechtel (2008), as they are apt for describing Panksepp's view.

feedback from cortical capacities; it is demonstrably operative in mammals with no cortices. Here is a glimpse of relevant evidence.

First, a young rat that has never seen or interacted with a cat will freeze in fear if a tuft of cat fur is placed nearby. What triggers the behavioral and autonomic symptoms of fear is the olfactory reception of certain molecules from the fur, and such fear is triggered without any prior exposure to cats. The rat's fear system can be turned on as if by a simple neural switch.[10]

Second, this neural switch can be flipped by external sensory stimuli, such as cat fur, but also by internal stimuli, including a bit of electrical current. Stimulate any of the relevant brain areas—the central and medial amygdala, the medial hypothalamus, parts of the brain stem—and the animal will freeze at low levels of current and try to flee at higher levels. This holds for rats, cats, and every mammal species tested thus far. Freezing and fleeing are also accompanied by autonomic responses typical of fear. In addition, associative learning occurs as a result of stimulating the fear system. These animals learn, for instance, not to return to the locations where they received the fear-inducing stimulations (see Panksepp, 1998, Chapter 11; Panksepp & Biven, 2012, Chapter 5).

In addition to discovering the rather extensive subcortical fear system, Panksepp has discovered six other such systems. He describes them as "primary-process affective systems," where a process is "primary" insofar as it is an effect of subcortical systems built into the structure of the brain that operate more or less autonomously. It is worth pointing out that six of Panksepp's seven systems are functionally dedicated to social interactions.[11]

Third, Panksepp's primary-process systems are indeed autonomous as well as endogenous. This is clear from experiments in which the entire cortex of an infant mammal is surgically removed and the animal is raised along with its intact siblings. When Panksepp, or when Sergio and Vivien Pellis, studied the emotional profiles and social behaviors of these decorticated animals, they found it difficult to distinguish the decorticate animals from their intact peers. Rough and tumble play, for instance, is nearly indistinguishable between decorticated and intact rats (Pellis & Pellis, 2009, p. 48). Moreover, when Panksepp showed his students a decorticated and an intact rat playing together and asked them

---

[10] This seems, incidentally, a simple counterexample to the view that emotional states are necessarily intentional states.

[11] As many readers know, Panksepp's primary-process systems comprise FEAR, RAGE, LUST, CARE, GRIEF, PLAY, and SEEKING. (For compelling evidence of an eighth primary-process affective system, a SOCIAL DOMINANCE system, see van der Westhuizen and Solms (2014, 2015). System names are given in uppercase to indicate that these subcortical systems produce effects that may not match the typical effects associated with our nontechnical use of the same terms. For example, there are known cases in which cortically based processes are causal factors for what we normally call fear. That, however, is compatible, with Panksepp's claim that our endogenous subcortical FEAR system is integral to our fear experience and, indeed, to all fear learning (see Panksepp & Bivens, 2012, Chapter 6).

to identify the one with no cortex, 75% picked the wrong animal. Panksepp speculates that the decorticated animal, being less inhibited and thus emotionally more expressive, strikes us as more normal.[12]

These experiments make clear that emotional profiles and social behavior are effectively implemented in subcortical structures and do not depend for their operations on any cortical structures. This is not to deny that cortical structures interact with subcortical structures in intact organisms; surely they do. But it is clear that the subcortical capacities of these animals are sufficient on their own for a range of emotional and social competencies. This is why I say that such systems are not only endogenous but autonomous as well.

Fourth, and crucially, these endogenous, autonomous subcortical systems exist not only in nonhuman mammals. They exist is us as well. We know this in part because subcortical systems in humans are functionally homologous with those in other mammals. But we also know this from the study of human children born with little or no cortical tissue.

Figure 14.1 contains six images of the brain of a three-year old girl born with virtually no neocortex. Bjorn Merker describes the child's brain this way: "spared

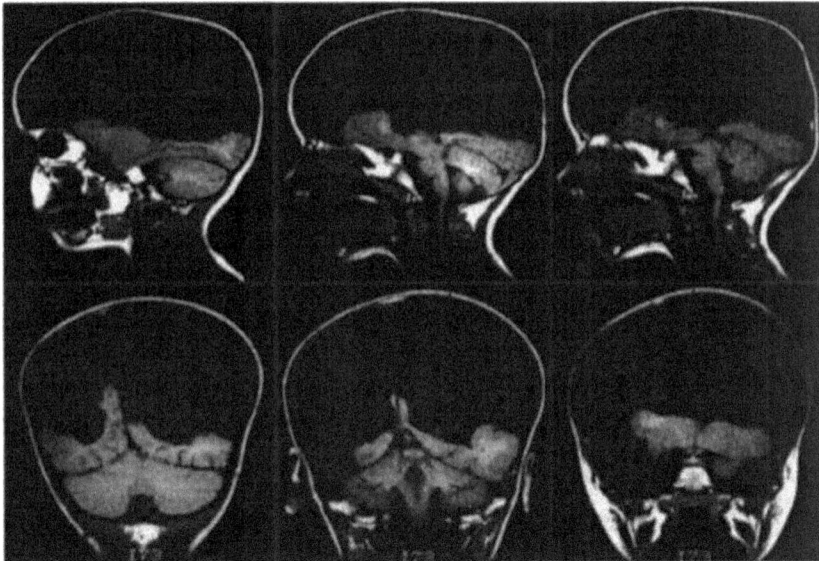

Figure 14.1. Six magnetic images of the head of a child with hydranencephaly. Reprinted with the kind permission of the American College of Radiology (ACR Learning File, Neuroradiology, Edition 2, 2004).

---

[12] These are data from an unpublished study (Panksepp, personal communication, March 2012).

Figure 14.2. Two photos of the same child, Heather Joy, as her baby brother is placed on her lap. Reprinted with permission from Cambridge University Press from Merker (2007).

ventromedial occipital and some midline cortical matter overlies an intact cerebellum and brainstem, whereas the rest of the cranium is filled with cerebrospinal fluid" (Merker 2007, p. 78). Merker goes on to point out that remnants of cortical tissue in anencephalic children typically develop no radiating connections to mid- and lower-brain structures and, in addition, may be found on autopsy to be gliotic (p. 78). Such remnants are likely possessed of little or no function.

Yet the two photos in Figure 14.2 of the same girl—her name is Heather Joy—show Heather just as her father is setting her baby brother on her lap (left photo), followed by her reaction a second or two later.[13] We can quibble about how to best describe Heather's reaction. It looks to be an expression of intense pleasure, even joy. At the very least she is experiencing an affective state with a very positive valence. All this in a child whose brain is probably devoid of cortical function.

Finally, we may generalize from the case of Heather Joy thanks to the clinical studies of Alan Shewmon (Shewmon, Holmes, & Byrne, 1999). Shewmon studied four children, two with anencephaly and two with severe cortical dysgenesis. Physicians and neurologists attendant at the birth and early days of these children predicted permanent vegetative states. Yet, once the children were placed in supportive home environments, they all developed clear discriminatory, emotional, and social capacities.

One child, for instance, with severe anencephaly, despite having no occipital cortex, was able by age four to visually track objects. She would become upset if her view was blocked, and her adoptive mother became convinced that the girl, at least on some days, could identify her by visual cues alone. By age five, the child consistently recognized her mother and familiar persons nonvisually and became tense in the company of unfamiliar persons. By 12 she enjoyed music. She would orient her heard toward the sound, and she would smile. She showed a preference for ballads and for rhythmic dances—she would vocalize during her

---

[13] Both parents are facing Heather, and one is helping hold the baby boy in place on Heather's lap.

favorite pieces—and when the music therapist changed pieces, the child's facial expression would change, and she would stop vocalizing.

Shewmon claims that all four children were "conscious" insofar as they were aware of their bodies and of specific features of the environment. In particular, the behavior of these children revealed clear and stable preferences for specific persons and features of their environment. What is important for my purposes is that the capacities of these children were sufficient for coherent and predictable discriminatory, emotional, and social behaviors, despite being implemented subcortically. That they were implemented subcortically is quite clear: "Primarily, these children's consciousness can be inferred to be mediated sub-cortically, not because there were absolutely zero cortical neurons, but because the few that were present could not plausibly subserve the totality of their conscious behaviors" (Shewmon et al., 1999, p. 371).

In sum, the study of intact and decorticated rats, the fact that subcortical structures appear to be functionally homologous in all mammal species studied thus far, and the study of anencephalic children all converge on Panksepp's larger view. The mind of modern humans comprises, in part, an ancestral mammalian mind implemented in subcortical structures. This ancestral mind is endogenous and autonomous. It causally influences our discriminatory, emotional, and social capacities whether we realize it or not. It is, as Panksepp puts it, a gift for living.

Cognitive Neuroscience of Consciousness

Dehaene studies conscious awareness of a specific sort, what he calls "consciousness-as-reportability." His goal is to discover the neural processes that give us the capacity to notice and report on the contents of our experiences. Dehaene's hypothesis is that this form of awareness is implemented in cortical structures that interact dynamically. The main components of his model are threefold.

First, the human cortex comprises a set of functionally distinct areas, some more or less localizable, others distributed. Each area is functionally specialized; each receives a specific range of information as input, processes that information, and sends the results to other brain areas. One such area is the global workspace—the second main component in Dehaene's model. The workspace receives signals from functionally specialized brain areas and "broadcasts" them. It functions as a kind of central switching station, making incoming signals available to other specialized areas capable of receiving and processing them. The auditory cortex, for example, receives information produced by perceived speech sounds and, after processing that information, sends the results to the workspace where they are broadcast and perhaps received by other areas—including, in some instances, Broca's area, where further processing may result in verbal responses.

The third component is a top–down attention mechanism capable of amplifying a proper subset of signals that reach the workspace. When this mechanism amplifies a given signal, and when the amplification crosses a certain threshold, a self-sustaining processing loop emerges—or, as Dehaene sometimes puts it, a self-sustaining loop "ignites."[14] When this happens, the content of the amplified signal becomes the object of conscious awareness. In addition, this amplified signal is then broadcast to other specialized areas, and when these other areas receive the amplified signal, their activity might increase, thereby expanding the object of one's conscious awareness. (See Dehaene et al., 2001, and Dehaene et al,. 2014, for elaboration.)

On this model there are several ways a neural signal can fail to rise to conscious awareness. These failures are of particular importance here. One is due to excess load. If our attention mechanisms are overrun with heavy traffic of incoming signals, the majority may fail to rise to awareness. Another is signal weakness. If the outputs of functionally specialized areas are weak or intermittent, there may be too little incoming information in those signals for our attention mechanisms to process.

The most decisive way in which a signal may fail to rise to awareness is architectural. When a specialized brain area bears no architectural connections to the workspace, its outputs have no chance of rising to conscious awareness. Dehaene gives the following examples:

> the activity of many neurons, for instance, in the subcortical and brainstem nuclei, is excluded from conscious mobilization (e.g., circuits for respiration and emotion). In many cases, we become aware of those circuits only through their indirect effects on other representations, such as in somatic cortical areas. (Dehaene & Changeux, 2004, p. 1148)

On this model, emotional or affective capacities implemented in subcortical areas cannot rise directly to conscious awareness, due to the very architecture of the brain. At most, the effects of these capacities may rise to awareness, but only indirectly.

To appreciate the indirectness, consider that our respiratory processes never send signals to the global workspace. We become aware of respiratory distress only after the fact, by way of downstream somatic effects. We experience shortness of breath, for instance, only after we have been exerting ourselves for several

---

[14] We might refer to Dehaene's model affectionately as the "combustion theory of consciousness."

seconds or minutes. The same is true, according to Dehaene, of our subcortical affective processes. Direct outputs from these affective systems never reach the workspace. Instead, a subcortical system such as fear might produce a range of outputs that cause somatic changes. If these changes are represented cortically and those representations are broadcast in the global workspace, then we may become conscious of them. In such cases, however, what reaches the workspace are not outputs from the fear system, but representations of somatic effects caused by fear. In so far as those representations are ambiguous—insofar as multiple affective systems can produce similar somatic effects—they require interpretation. (More on interpretation presently.)

This concludes my integration of the theories of Panksepp and Dehaene. If this integration is correct, then, as a consequence of the architecture of our brains, some subcortical affective capacities produce action-relevant effects with no direct route to conscious awareness. This fact alone suffices for the truth of claim (1).

But the truth of (1) is also clear regarding the *indirect* effects—that is, the downstream somatic effects—of subcortical, affective systems that *can* reach the global workspace. Some somatic effects fail to reach conscious awareness not because of gaps in our neural architecture, but merely from signal weakness. Still others are strong enough to reach the workspace and thus be broadcast, but must be interpreted due to their nonspecific nature. Our interpretive capacities, however, are demonstrably prone to error, and this generates a kind of skepticism that also lends support to thesis (i). I will discuss each possibility in turn.

Action-Relevant but Nonconscious

Consider, then, the downstream somatic effects produced by any of Panksepp's primary process systems. As mentioned, if these somatic effects are represented cortically, they might be sent to and broadcast by the workspace. Within this general category, now consider the subset of downstream somatic effects too weak to reach the global workspace. This may include effects produced by several, perhaps all, subcortical systems, including low-level anxiety, stress, fear, frustration, anger, depression, lust, etc. These effects no doubt influence our moods, energy levels, motivations, activities, decision-making, and actions in ways we fail to notice. These effects, that is, are sometimes action-relevant, despite failing to reach conscious awareness. Thesis (1) is true, therefore, in cases where somatic effects could have risen to awareness but failed to do so due to signal weakness.

We have, of course, known of such cases for quite some time. We need only recall social psychological research from the 1970s and 1980s, including, for instance, the so-called mere exposure effect. Robert Zajonc, together with

William Kunst-Wilson, exposed subjects subliminally to a series of octagons. Afterwards, when explicitly (not subliminally) shown pairs of octagons in which one octagon was reproduced directly from the subliminal series, subjects were asked two questions: whether they thought they had seen either of the octagons before, and whether, for each pair, they preferred one octagon over the other. The results were striking. Recognition was at chance (48%), but preferences were skewed toward the octagons previously "seen." That is, 60% of subjects said they preferred certain octagons (those to which they had been subliminally exposed), even though less than half recognized any of the octagons explicitly seen. Mere exposure to visual stimuli too weak to reach conscious awareness nonetheless provoked an affective preference (Kunst-Wilson & Zajonc, 1980).

Years later, Piotr Winkielman and colleagues wondered whether subjects in Zajonc's experiments had any conscious awareness of the affective changes that occurred (Winkielman, Berridge, & Wilbarger, 2005). The stimulus—the subliminal exposure—was clearly outside subjects' awareness, but what about the change in affect caused by that nonconscious stimulus? Were subjects aware of feeling differently after the subliminal prime? To find out, subjects were exposed subliminally to either a happy, neutral, or angry face, followed by a masking stimulus. Immediately after the mask, half the subjects were asked to rate their mood on a short survey (to determine whether their conscious feelings had been altered by the subliminal prime). They were then given a fruit beverage to drink. Subjects were free to pour and drink as much beverage as they liked, and the quantity consumed by each subject was monitored. By contrast, the other subjects were first given a limited quantity of the same fruit beverage and asked to rate how well they liked it. They were then given the same short survey to determine their consciously reportable feelings.

Winkielman and his colleagues obtained two important findings. First, the ratings of the fruit beverages correlated positively with the type of face to which subjects had been subliminally exposed. Those exposed to a happy face rated the beverage higher than those exposed to an angry face. Second, the conscious feelings reported by subjects did not correlate with the type of face subliminally perceived. Those exposed to a happy face reported conscious feelings indistinguishable from those exposed to an angry face.

These results, and similar results from many other experiments on the affective effects of nonconscious primes, may appear pedestrian. But they are significant. They demonstrate that a stimulus of which we have no awareness can causally influence our affective processes in ways we do not consciously notice and that this influence exerts a demonstrable causal effect on our judgments and our actions. Subjects exposed nonconsciously to a happy face judged differently (they rated the fruit beverage differently) and acted differently (they consumed more of the fruit beverage) than those exposed to an angry face.

When we combine these experiments with the integration of Panksepp and Dehaene, we are faced with a convergence of evidence for claim (1). Some somatic effects fail to reach conscious awareness not because of gaps in our neural architecture but merely from signal weakness. Such effects, despite being too weak to be processed in the global workspace, nonetheless exert discernible causal effects on our actions. In such cases, we are moved by affective processes about which we have no reportable, conscious awareness. We are moved by factors about which we cannot practically reason.

Action-Relevant, Conscious, but Ambiguous

Now consider the subset of somatic effects strong enough to reach and be processed by the global workspace. To distinguish these effects from the relatively weak effects such as low-level anxiety, depression, etc., consider the following scenario. You are scheduled to give a professional talk in one hour. You believe the success of your presentation will influence your chances of receiving a job offer you strongly hope to receive. You feel butterflies in your stomach, your palms are sweaty, your bowels uncertain. You are feeling the somatic effects of one or more subcortical affective systems. But which system(s)? Are you afraid? Are you excited? Or are you feeling the combined effects of both a negatively valenced fear and a positively valenced excitement? Or are you feeling the somatic effects of other affective systems?

These are important questions. Without reliable answers—without a reliable method for interpreting the downstream somatic effects of our subcortical systems—we cannot specify the motivations required for practical reasoning. The problem, however, is that we have no such method. Of course, we make all sorts of inferences to what may *appear*—from our conscious perspective—to be the best explanation, but we have no reliable grounds to distinguish correct from incorrect inferences.[15] To see this, recall Michael Gazzaniga's split-brain subjects (for a wide-ranging review, see Gazzaniga, 2000). We can be confident, in light

---

[15] More modestly, we have no interpretive method that is reliable in situations where the potential causal factors are relatively opaque and/or complex. Situations in which the potential causes are few and transparent are subject to less skepticism. Timothy Wilson makes a related point (although, on my view, he is perhaps overly optimistic that we can reliably interpret affects such as anger and sadness): "It might be difficult to discern how the deep-seated facets of our personality have shaped our behavior, but easier to tell that we are angry at John for forgetting our dinner date, sad because we just heard that our grandmother is ill, or nauseous because we just ate the entire bowl of clam dip" (Wilson, 2002, p. 98; see also Davies, 2009, pp. 146–150).

of Gazzaniga's experiments, that the following partial model of our practical reasoning capacities is highly plausible:

The Neural Damage Deprivation Model of Giving Reasons
　　Whenever our left hemisphere operates in the absence of causally relevant (i.e., information isolated in the right hemisphere), it invents a "reason" for the agent's action based on whatever information it can access.[16]

Yet, if this model is plausible, it should be easy to generalize to a model with much greater scope, a model that applies to all persons:

The Structural Deprivation Model of Giving Reasons
　　Whenever our conscious, reason-giving capacities operate in the absence of causally relevant, nonconscious information, or in the presence of indirect, conscious information, they invent a "reason" for the agent's action based on whatever information they can access.

The structural deprivation model is compelling precisely because, in one crucial respect, we are all like Gazzaniga's subjects. As a result of surgery, they were deprived of architectural connections between the two hemispheres. But all persons, if Dehaene and Panksepp are right, are constituted by an ancestral brain nestled inside modern cortical capacities, where some causally relevant effects of at least some parts of the ancestral brain bear no architectural connections to our capacity for consciousness-as-reportability.[17] Such direct connections are simply absent from our neural architecture.

Although the interpretations produced by Gazzaniga's subjects were sensible, at least from the first-person perspective, they were nonetheless mistaken. They were mistaken due to incomplete information, information that was neurally isolated despite being action relevant. Yet all persons, including those with intact corpora callosa, are prone to similarly incomplete interpretations, due to structurally analogous causes. We are all victims of neurally isolated information that is action-relevant. That, indeed, is one of the main lessons to be drawn from my integration of Panksepp and Dehaene.

---

[16] In one experiment, the subject's left-hemispheric linguistic capacities had no access to information in the right hemisphere about a perceived snow scene. As a result, the left hemisphere had no idea—none at all—why the subject's left hand had pointed to a snow shovel. Why asked why he pointed to the shovel, the subject confabulated a "reason" that cohered with his limited but available information, but that was factually incorrect nonetheless.

[17] Just to be clear, I am not asserting our ancestral brain bears no connection to our neocortex. That would be silly. The claim is that some of our ancestral, subcortical emotions bear no direct connection to our specific capacity for consciousness-as-reportability.

Given this isolation, we must interpret the indirect effects of our subcortical capacities. In doing so, we do what Gazzaniga's subjects did: we concoct an account by trying to make as much sense as possible of the information that happens to be available. Available information of course includes not only the felt downstream somatic effects, but also information about the immediate environment, patterns of past behavior, recollections of past interpretations, etc. Yet all these additional forms of information were available to Gazzaniga's subjects as well! Those persons did a competent job weaving narrative interpretations of their actions based on all available information. The problem was that the totality of available information was critically incomplete and critically ambiguous.

Since we, like Gazzaniga's subjects, are faced with the task of making as much sense as possible of information that is incomplete, or ambiguous, or both, we must accept that our interpretations have the same status, namely, interpretations that may feel utterly correct from the first-person perspective, but that nonetheless may be partially or wholly mistaken. Precisely this is why we should accept claim (1) even in cases where the somatic effects of our affective systems are strong enough to reach conscious awareness. Unless we can be reasonably confident that we know why we are moved to perform a given action—unless we can be confident that our interpretation of our somatic effects is correct— we cannot engage in any practical reasoning that is informed about our actual motivations. Our practical reasoning is stultified due to an intransigent bit of self-ignorance.

It is worth pointing out that this form of self-ignorance, in addition to supporting (1), also raises a unique problem for attributions of criminal responsibility. On Morse's view, the reasons one employs in one's practical inferences must be among the actual causes of our actions.[18] Yet, if you reason to the decision to steal your neighbor's car on the basis of factors that misrepresent the actual causes of your action, then the account you give is a confabulation. In such a case, the factors that actually cause you to act are outside your field of deliberative awareness. They are, in fact, akin to a form of internal coercion, since you, the consciously aware decision maker, are impotent with respect to them.

In cases such as this, attributions of responsibility are out of place. If our folk psychological intuitions lead us to withhold such attributions in instances of coercion—and they do—then those same intuitions should lead us to withhold them here. Therefore, except when we have reasonable evidence that the agent's

---

[18] Here, again, is the relevant passage: "If humans are not conscious and rational creatures who act *for reasons that play a causal role in our behavior*, then the foundational facts for responsibility ascriptions are mistaken" (Morse 2008, p. 19; emphasis added).

expressed reasons match the actual causes of her actions, we are in no position to claim that the conditions of practical rationality are met (especially condition v).

Conscious but Action-Irrelevant

I turn now to claim (2), that we sometimes know things that fail to engage our affective capacities. This is trivially true of knowledge that bears little or no relation to human motivation. Our knowledge of spatially remote facts is illustrative. That the moon is approximately 384,400 km from earth, although interesting, is not among the things that move most of us to act. Knowledge of temporally remote facts is also illustrative. My knowledge that I did not attend the world premiere of Beethoven's Ninth Symphony has little bearing on any action I might perform. It sometimes causes me to feel something akin to regret, but it rarely moves me to think or speak of it.

By contrast, (2) is far from trivial regarding knowledge of things spatially and temporally proximate, especially things that bear on our needs and desires. The scope of human practical rationality is, in the main, restricted to things within our grasp that we need or desire—immediate things such as food, freedom of movement, and social attachments—and more mediate things such as education, financial stability, and good health. The question, then, is whether claim (2) applies to our knowledge of these sorts of things. Are we sometimes endowed with knowledge of things we need or desire that nonetheless fails to engage our affective capacities? The answer, I shall argue, is undoubtedly affirmative.

To begin, consider the all-too-frequent patterns of human action in which persons knowingly put their safety, health, or liberty at risk. Consider the 20-year old male who drives his car recklessly despite being able to recite from memory all the risks of such behavior. Not all 20-year old males drive recklessly, to be sure, but given the vividly documented risks to oneself and others, what explains why any do? Or consider the person who deliberately cultivates the habit of smoking cigarettes. Not all persons who take pleasure in the taste of cigarette smoke or the effects of nicotine cultivate the habit, but, given the widely publicized health risks, what explains why anyone does?

What seems most salient, or as salient as any other factor, is knowledge that, as a matter of neurological fact, fails to connect with the agent's affective capacities. Such failures may result from either (a) the absence of requisite neural anatomy due to genetic, developmental, and/or environmental factors or (b) factors that compete with and prevent one's knowledge from engaging with one's affective capacities, even when the requisite neural anatomy is in place. There is compelling evidence that both failures are quite real and perhaps even ubiquitous. I will briefly describe evidence for each.

(a) The Absence of Requisite Neural Anatomy Due to Genetic, Developmental, and/or Environmental Factors

Action-irrelevant knowledge resulting from absent neural structure can occur in one of two ways. The first occurs when normal neural development is thwarted by genetic, developmental, and/or environmental factors. Some of the best-studied cases involve top–down neural deficiencies, in particular, diminished function in the prefrontal cortex (PFC) that renders persons unable to do the things they know they should do. Other well-studied cases involve bottom–up neural deficiencies, including diminished function in affective capacities that result in a similar disability. For brevity, I will describe a single instance of the first sort.

Consider the study of persons suffering from selective damage to the PFC. In one well-known study, Antoine Bechara and colleagues examined Elliot, a patient with damage to the ventromedial sector of the PFC caused by a tumor and its surgical removal. Post-surgical testing revealed that Elliot's memory, language skills, and IQ were normal; his capacity for propositional knowledge was intact. Yet, in Bechara's famous gambling experiment, Elliot failed in spectacular fashion. Despite explicitly knowing which decks of cards were most risky, Elliot persisted in choosing cards from those decks, gambling himself straight into bankruptcy (Bechara, Damasio, Damasio, & Anderson, 1994).

Persons with an intact PFC behave quite differently. Even before they become consciously aware of the risks presented by decks A and B, they change course and refuse cards from those decks, thereby avoiding bankruptcy. When Bechara and his colleagues repeated these experiments while measuring galvanic skin responses, they discovered a critical difference in affect. Persons with an intact PFC, in the course of learning the high costs associated with decks A and B, gradually began to experience a spike in galvanic skin response *prior* to deliberating about whether to select from those decks. They began to experience an *anticipatory* affective flash when contemplating one of the risky decks. Persons with damage to their PFC, by contrast, showed no such anticipatory affective spike (Bechara, Tranel, Damasio, & Damasio, 1996).

Exactly how to best characterize this difference is perhaps up for grabs, but it is consistent with the data to conclude that persons with compromised PFCs may "know" that a given action is not in their interest—"know" in the sense that they can articulate the risk involved—yet nonetheless not feel or register the threat involved. The felt sense of threat is not among the factors that cause them to act. This is so, despite the fact that these persons demonstrably "know" (i.e., can recite) the threat posed by the risky decks. We could hardly ask for a clearer exemplar of knowledge that is action-irrelevant.

Now, the obvious rejoinder is that cases like Elliot's provide scant evidence for claim (2). Why? Because the Bechara et al. (1994, 1996) experiments show that persons with *intact* prefrontal cortices *do* have a connection between knowledge and affect—that is how they avoided bankruptcy—and that includes most of us. So the evidence proffered for claim (2) applies at best to a very small fraction of all human agents.

Not so. It turns out we already have compelling evidence that, for instance, a fairly significant portion of the U.S. population is afflicted with structural deficiencies in the PFC that correlate with diminished executive function. The structural deficiencies are not nearly as dramatic as those studied by Bechara, but they are far from trivial. These deficiencies, in fact, provide striking confirmation of Robert Sapolsky's (2004) prediction that future improvements in brain scanning technology will reveal substantial variation in PFC functioning across the human population.

The compelling evidence comes from an experiment performed by Adrian Raine and colleagues (Raine, Lencz, Bihrle, Lacasse, & Colletti, 2000; see also Raine, 2013, pp. 137–143). Begin with the fact that approximately 15% of the adult U.S. population is known to suffer from some form of personality disorder, with over 3.5% suffering specifically from antisocial personality disorder.[19] When Raine used anatomical magnetic resonance imaging to study the brains of persons diagnosed with antisocial personality disorder, and then used sophisticated software to create detailed topographical representations of prefrontal cortical areas, he discovered an 11% reduction in gray matter in the afflicted persons! Persons diagnosed as antisocial have 11% fewer neurons in their PFC than persons without that disorder!

As Raine points out, this reduction in gray matter is not visually perceptible to the naked eyes of anyone, including experts, for it amounts to a mere half millimeter in thickness. That is why it has not been observed earlier. Yet, as Raine also notes, the correlation between antisocial personality disorder and this prefrontal cortical reduction in neurons is compelling. And since this initial study in 2000, Raine has conducted a meta-analysis of 12 similar studies, and the robust finding is that a diminished PFC is positively correlated not merely with antisocial individuals, but also with individuals diagnosed with psychopathy and individuals who have committed violent crimes. This, of course, means that the percentage of persons demonstrably afflicted with diminished PFC function is

[19] See the National Institute of Health (2004). That report was published in 2004. If the same percentage holds today, given the current population of nearly 322,000,000 people, approximately 11,270,000 people in the United States are afflicted with antisocial personality disorder. Hardly a small or insignificant number. And as I point out in the following text, that number increases if we include persons diagnosed with psychopathy and persons who have committed violent crimes.

larger—perhaps much larger—than the 3.5% who suffer from antisocial personality disorder (Yang & Raine, 2009).

These latter studies provide compelling neurological evidence that there are structural PFC deficiencies across some nontrivial portion of the human population and that these structural deficiencies diminish function. Therefore, we are *not* justified in assuming that the connection between knowledge and affect is intact in most people; perhaps it *is* intact in most of us, but these advances in knowledge undermine our justification for assuming it to be. This conclusion, moreover, increases in strength when we consider the structural deficiencies in brain areas other than the PFC that also affect the connection between knowledge and affect, especially deficiencies in the subcortical areas comprising what Panksepp dubs the SEEKING system.[20]

Thus far I've described just one way in which absent neural structures can give rise to knowledge that is action-irrelevant. Another way involves no deficiencies of structure—no deviations from what is statistically normal—but simply absences of structures that never evolved in the first place. I offer one brief example.

Consider recent research on our sense of self. In these experiments, subjects' brains are scanned while they engage in self-referential thought, such as thinking about whether they possess a specified personality trait. They then engage in thoughts about other persons, such as whether a specific person has the specified personality trait. These studies have produced three noteworthy results. First, when subjects think about themselves, a particular area in the PFC lights up differentially, namely, the ventral medial PFC. Second, when they think about some person other than themselves, there is a spike in a different part of the PFC, namely, the dorsal medial PFC. Third, and crucially, when subjects think about themselves not in the present tense but with regard to some future time—when they think about what preferences they might have one year or five years from now—it is the second part of the PFC, the dorsal medial part, that lights up (e.g., Mitchell, Schirmer, Ames, & Gilbert, 2011; Wagner, Haxby, & Heatherton, 2012).

When combined with a variety of nonscanning experiments that converge on a similar conclusion (Pronin, Olivola, & Kennedy, 2008; Pronin & Ross, 2006), these experiments suggest the following hypothesis: When we think about ourselves performing a future action, we conceptualize our future self the same way we conceptualize another person, namely, from the third person point of view. More specifically, when thinking about our present selves, we mobilize our

---

[20] Panksepp's subcortical SEEKING system—the affective-motivational system par excellence—runs along much of the lateral hypothalamus, with clear projections to various cortical areas, including the PFC (see Panksepp, 1998, Chapter 8; Panksepp & Biven, 2012, Chapter 3). Also, for an account of the structural and functional deficiencies that occur in the amydala and hippocampus of psychopaths, see Raine (2013, Chapter 5).

current subjective resources, including our affective states, but when thinking about our future selves, we do not do this. Just as we do not impute our current affective states to others,[21] we likewise refrain from imputing them to our future selves. To the extent we think of our selves in the future, we do so in a way that is affectively disconnected to our present selves.

This affective disconnection provides a potential explanation of the reckless behavior of some 20-year old male drivers, as well as persons who deliberately cultivate the habit of smoking cigarettes. At the very least, it provides prima facie evidence of knowledge that is action-irrelevant, due not to some genetic or developmental deficiency, but due entirely to the actual structure and functioning of intact human brains.

(b) Factors That Compete With and Prevent One's Knowledge From Engaging With One's Affective Capacities

Yet action-irrelevant knowledge does not require the absence of requisite neural structures. It can occur when our knowledge is forced to compete with other factors that engage our affective capacities. When these other factors are highly salient, their effects can swamp our knowledge, rendering it action-irrelevant. This can occur, so far as we know, even when the requisite neural anatomy is functioning normally.

The salience of our social relations comes to mind. At nearly every stage of human development, we are all subject to a variety of social pressures; our need for social affiliation appears to be as neurologically entrenched as any other need.[22] Such pressures appear to be particularly potent from adolescence and into our twenties. Indeed, the PFC, the home of our capacity for social judgment, is not fully developed until we reach our mid-20s. This may explain why a 20-year old male's knowledge of the risks of reckless driving can be so irrelevant to his actions. Relative to the affective potency of perceived social incentives, many of which are operating nonconsciously, the risks of reckless driving appear too remote, too unrelated to one's current affective assessments. The young driver conscious "knowledge" is swamped by his nonconscious, social affective urges.

---

[21] Of course, sometimes we do impute our own affective states to others; that, at any rate, is the main thesis of simulation theories of mind. In the studies cited, however, subjects were not asked to attribute a mental state to another person, but to judge whether that person possesses a given personality trait.

[22] For evidence, consult virtually any work in the growing subfield of social neuroscience. For a good review of work on intergroup relations and the workings of the brain, see Cikara and Van Bavel (2014).

A similar point may hold for at least some persons who take up cigarette smoking. Based on a telephone survey of over 800 smokers,[23] Paul Slovic (2001) reports the following facts. When asked whether, in deciding to smoke, smokers thought about the health effects, nearly 90% of respondents answered either "a little" or "not at all." When asked what they thought about when deciding to smoke, approximately 62% said they wanted to try "something new and exciting." When asked whether, if they had the chance to do it all over, they would start smoking again, 82% said "No." All this suggests that a significant majority of smokers did not think, or did not recall thinking, about the future effects of their decision to smoke. Knowledge of the risks involved was, at best, weakly engaged with their affective capacities.

We can sketch a possible neural explanation of this kind of action-irrelevant knowledge by extrapolating from my integration of Panksepp and Dehaene. Recall that, on Dehaene's model, none of Panksepp's primary-process systems send signals directly to the neuronal workspace. Only the downstream somatic effects of our subcortical systems can rise to conscious awareness. Now consider how, on this model, information might flow in the other direction, from our cortical to subcortical structures. How might our consciously reportable beliefs trigger and engage our affective systems?

Well, if we are consciously aware of the risks of smoking cigarettes, then that informational content is being broadcast in our global workspace. How might it reach our subcortical affective systems? One plausible route is via affective learning.[24] Imagine a person who learns to associate the felt fear of incapacitation and death with the thought of smoking or the thought of driving recklessly. For that person, let us assume, the mere thought of smoking or driving wildly is likely to trigger a negatively valenced affect.

Even so, this conditioned negative affect will have to compete with other affective forces and, at least in some instances, it will be comparatively weak. The youthful driver may experience some degree of discomfort while driving recklessly, but if incentives concerning his social standing are in play, the latter may once again swamp the former. Everything will of course depend on the particulars of the case. The point is simply that our neurologically entrenched needs for social affiliation are likely to have far greater affective potency, at least for some persons in some circumstances.

This point about the relative strength of our social affects must be combined, moreover, with the previous point that we tend to form judgments about our future selves from a third-person point of view. We tend to see and feel our future

---

[23] The survey was conducted in 1999 by the Annenburg Public Policy Center at the University of Pennsylvania.
[24] See Panksepp and Biven (2012, Chapter 6) for an intriguing discussion of affective learning.

selves in a way that is affectively anemic, and, at the same time, we tend to see and feel our immediate selves through the powerful lens of our socially-based affective capacities.[25] This is a virtual blueprint for the construction of "knowledge" that fails to engage our action-relevant affective capacities.

These then are some grounds for claim (2). We can know things in ways that are action-irrelevant due to severe neural damage, as Elliot's case illustrates, or due to more subtle neural deficiencies of the sort detected by Raine. Yet even in cases of no known neural impediments, a person's knowledge can fail to engage one's affective capacities if the requisite neural structures do not exist or if the knowledge is swamped by competing concerns, especially concerns as neurologically entrenched as social affiliations. If this line of reasoning is correct for some range of actual cases, then claim (2), like claim (1), supports my thesis that we are not endowed with the day-to-day capacities required for criminal responsibility.

Ampliative Neurointerventions?

If my thesis is correct—if our concept of criminal responsibility does not apply to organisms like us—two responses appear open to us.[26] One is to withhold the concept, to refuse to apply it to our selves. The other is to change the kind of organism we are, to alter or amplify our capacities until the concept correctly applies. Are there good reasons for thinking that either of these responses is wiser than the other?

No, not in the abstract, for they are by no means incompatible. If our concept of criminal responsibility does not apply to organisms like us, it is rational to refuse to apply it to organisms like us. This is consistent with applying that concept to organisms that are not like us, to organisms possessed of responsibility-relevant capacities we presently lack. Rejecting a concept on grounds of its inapplicability is compatible with accepting that same concept if and when it is applicable.[27] So the second response to my thesis, that we strive to make our

---

[25] Two observations are relevant here. First, as mentioned previously, six of Panksepp's seven primary-process affective systems are dedicated to social relations (Panksepp 1998). Second, one of Robert Zajonc's (1980) many pointed insights is relevant: "Because affective judgments are inescapable, they cannot be focused as easily as perceptual and cognitive processes. They are much more influenced by the context of the surround, and they are generally holistic. Affective reactions are thus less subject to control by attentive processes" (p. 156).

[26] This section is a response to searching questions from Nicole Vincent, for which I am most grateful.

[27] As I explain in elsewhere, withholding dubious concepts—concepts that plausibly do not apply to their intended targets—is distinct from eliminativism concerning those concepts. Eliminativism is surely in order in some cases, but to insist in general on the elimination of concepts that presently fail to apply to organisms that are known to evolve over time would be an egregious form of anti-intellectualism (Davies, 2009, pp. 43-44).

selves more responsible by altering or expanding our capacities, does not conflict with the first response that we withhold our concept of responsibility in light of our actual capacities.

Less abstractly, however, the two responses are far from equal. With respect to the second, and as I explain in a moment, we are ignorant of what is possible and, in consequence, of what is desirable. With respect to the first response, by contrast, as the discussion above attests, we know (or believe with justification) that our current concept of criminal responsibility does not apply to us. Thus, the first response is preferable, at least for the foreseeable future.

Our ignorance regarding the second response is readily apparent from a distance. First, we have limited knowledge of the extent of our neural plasticity. This is a problem with several dimensions. To illustrate, consider an analogy to hearing. Our auditory sensitivities, if amplified beyond a certain threshold, would cause us to hear the circulatory and muscular processes that occur in our necks and skulls. That would interfere with and probably defeat the auditory system's function of enabling us to hear accurately things in our environment.[28] In cases like this, amplifying the capacity defeats the systemic function of that very capacity. Are amplifications generally subject to this sort of self-defeat? The answer, I take it, is that we cannot know except on a case-by-case basis in light of experimental evidence. Second, we have limited knowledge of the technological innovations yet to be developed. We know, for instance, that the splitting of atoms was judged impossible as late as the 1890s and that other innovations, such as the manipulation of genes, were probably not in the imaginative field of most biologists during Mendel's lifetime. We apparently have no reason to think that our present predictions regarding future innovations would fare any better.

The breadth and depth of our ignorance, moreover, blocks our ability to make judgments of desirability. If we cannot describe in an informed way the kinds of amplifications that are possible and the good and ill effects that would accrue to us, we are in no position to judge whether any of the actual but presently unknown possibilities are desirable. And this should give us pause when considering the second response to my thesis.

The extent of our ignorance is perhaps better illustrated in light of the specific capacities and limitations as previously discussed. Consider the evidence offered in support of claim (2), that we sometimes "know" things in ways that are action-irrelevant. We know from recent brain scan and behavioral experiments that

---

[28] This phenomenon occurs even without amplifying our auditory sensitivities. Some people hear internal noises produced within their heads as a result of hearing loss. This condition is usually labeled "pulsatile tinnitus," a relatively rare form of tinnitus. Even without hearing loss, persons with carotid artery disease or other vascular conditions may hear the flow of their own blood, and persons with muscle disorders may hear noises produced by muscular contractions in the head ("Tinnitus," n.d.).

when we make predictions about our selves in the future, we conceptualize our selves as we conceptualize another person. Just as we do not attribute our current affective states to other agents, we likewise do not attribute them to our imagined future selves. We are affectively disconnected from our future selves. As a result, at least some judgments we make about what we might do or prefer in the future qualify as knowledge that is action-irrelevant.

Now, is this a consequence of neural processes upon which we can successfully intervene? Among the interventions available today, or future interventions for which we currently have credible evidence, are there any that might give us the ability to judge our future selves in ways that are not affectively anemic? The correct answer, I take it, is that we do not know. We do not know what kinds of interventions might cure us of our affective anemia because we do not know exactly why we suffer such anemia in the first place. We do not know which neural processes we have, or which we do not have, that make our judgments concerning our future selves so disconnected.

What we do know is that the amplifying effects of currently available pharmaceutical interventions—modafinil, donepezil, etc.—are not plausible cures for what ails us. These drugs appear to heighten wakefulness, vigilance, attention, and memory, and in the absence of relevant experimental evidence, we have no reason to think that amplifying any or all of these capacities would enable us to conceptualize our future selves in ways that are affectively related to our present selves. The same is true of currently available neuroprosthetics. Research in this area, although tantalizing, focuses almost entirely on sensory and motor deficits—on interfaces between the environment and perception (e.g., cochlear implants) and on interfaces between motor intentions and external action (e.g., moving a robotic limb).[29] It is difficult to see how enhancements in sensory or motor capacities would ameliorate our affective anemia.[30]

I am not suggesting that ampliative neurointerventions are impossible or even unlikely. To the contrary, the scope and power of such interventions appears all but inevitable. I am making the banal point that the two responses to my thesis as previously described are by no means on a par. Not yet, anyway. The most rational response to my thesis is to withhold our present concept of criminal responsibility, since it fails to apply to organisms like us. Whether it might apply to

---

[29] There is, in addition, some research on brain stimulators that improve concentration in gamers (see Leuthardt et al., 2014, for a nice overview).

[30] What makes this case particularly vexing is that we are epistemically, as well as affectively, unconnected to our future selves. Even if some intervention endowed us with the ability to impute our current affects to our imagined future selves, the accuracy of such imputations would be up for grabs. Our affective capacities change in the course of development; how I respond to a given situation today may be a poor guide to how I will respond five years hence. So perhaps our affective anemia in such cases is beyond curing?

our amplified future selves or descendants, we simply do not know. It is this lack of knowledge that makes the first response the wiser of the two.

Conclusion

I conclude that conditions (i)–(v), derived from our alleged folk psychological intuitions, do not reliably obtain in the day-to-day actions of organisms like us. This conclusion is based in part on the evidence given for claims (1) and (2). If this is correct, then our current conceptualization of criminal responsibility fails to apply to us.[31] I further conclude that restorative interventions, even if effective and ethical, cannot fulfill one of their main intended functions, namely, the restoration of competencies sufficient for correct attributions of criminal responsibility.

If relevant ampliative interventions cannot yet be seen on the horizon, then the foundational facts for legal responsibility need to be recast. They need to reflect not what some theorists think we ought to be, but what we actually are. That is no small task. We presently know what kind of practical agent we are not, as the evidence discussed here attests, but we have no clear, comprehensive view of what we are,[32] and even less of what we might become.

References

Bechara, A., Damasio, A., Damasio, H., & Anderson, S. (1994). Insensitivity to future consequences following damage to human prefrontal cortex. *Cognition, 50*, 7–12.

Bechara, A., Tranel, D., Damasio, H., & Damasio, A. (1996). Failure to respond autonomically to anticipated future outcomes following damage to prefrontal cortex. *Cerebral Cortex, 6*, 215–225.

Bechtel, W. (2008). *Mental mechanisms: Philosophical perspectives on cognitive neuroscience*. Hove, England: Lawrence Erlbaum.

Cikara, M., & Van Bavel, J. J. (2014). The neuroscience of intergroup relations: An integrated review. *Perspectives on Psychological Science, 9*(3), 245–274.

Davies, P. S. (2009). *Subjects of the world: Darwin's rhetoric and the study of agency in nature*. Chicago, IL: University of Chicago Press.

Dehaene S., & Changeux, J.-P. (2004). Neural mechanisms for access to consciousness. In M. Gazzaniga (Ed.), *The cognitive neurosciences* (3rd ed., pp. 1145–1157). Cambridge, MA: MIT Press.

Dehaene, S., Charles, L., King, J.-R., & Marti, S. (2014) Toward a computational theory of conscious processing. *Current Opinion in Neurobiology, 25*, 76–84.

---

[31] For additional considerations in support of this claim, see Davies (2013).
[32] This is the thesis of Part 3 of Davies (2009).

Dehaene, S., & Naccache, L. (2001). Towards a cognitive neuroscience of consciousness: Basic evidence and a workspace framework. *Cognition, 79*, 1–37.

Gazzaniga, M. (2000). Cerebral specialization and interhemispheric communication: does the corpus callosum enable the human condition? *Brain, 123*, 1293–1326.

Jones, O., Schall, J., & Shen, F. (Eds.). (2014). *Law and neuroscience.* New York, NY: Wolters Kluwer Law and Business.

Kunst-Wilson, W. R., & Zajonc, R. (1980). Affective discrimination of stimuli that cannot be recognized. *Science, 207*, 557–558.

Leuthardt, E., Roland, J., & Ray, W. (2014). Neuroprosthetics. *The Scientist.* Retrieved February 22, 2015, from http://www.the-scientist.com/?articles.view/articleNo/41324/title/Neuroprosthetics/

Mayo Clinic. (n.d.). Tinnitus. Retrieved from http://www.mayoclinic.org/diseases-conditions/tinnitus/basics/causes/con-20021487

Merker, B. (2007). Consciousness without a cerebral cortex: Challenges for neuroscience and medicine. *Behavioral and Brain Sciences, 30*, 63–134.

Mitchell, J., Schirmer, J., Ames, D., & Gilbert, D. (2011). Medial prefrontal cortex predicts intertemporal choice. *Journal of Cognitive Neuroscience, 23*(4), 1–10.

Model Penal Code. (n.d.). Retrieved from http://wps.prenhall.com/wps/media/objects/13023/13335893/downloadables/model_penal_code_sel_sec2.pdf

Morse, S. (2008). Determinism and the death of folk psychology: Two challenges to responsibility from neuroscience. *Minnesota Journal of Law, Science, and Technology, 9*(1), 1–36.

Morse, S. (2011). Neuroscience and the future of personhood and responsibility. In J. Rosen & B. Wittes (Eds.), *Constitution 3.0: Freedom and technological change* (pp. 113–129). Washington, DC: Brookings Institution Press.

Morse, S. (2013). Common criminal law compatibilism. In N. Vincent (Ed.), *Neuroscience and legal responsibility* (pp. 27–52). Oxford, England: Oxford University Press.

National Institutes of Health. (2004). Landmark survey reports on the prevalence of personality disorders in the United States. *NIH News.* Retrieved from http://www.nih.gov/news/pr/aug2004/niaaa-02.htm

Panksepp, J. (1998). *Affective neuroscience: The foundations of human and animal emotion.* New York, NY: Oxford University Press.

Panksepp, J., & Biven, L. (2012). *The archeology of mind: Neuroevolutionary origins of human emotions.* New York, NY: W. W. Norton.

Pellis, S., & Pellis, V. (2009). *The playful brain: Venturing to the limits of neuroscience.* Oxford, England: Oneworld.

Pronin E., Olivola, C., & Kennedy, K. (2008). Doing unto future selves as you would do unto others: Psychological distance and decision making. *Personality and Social Psychology Bulletin, 34*(2), 224–236.

Pronin, E., & Ross, L. (2006). Temporal differences in trait self-ascription: When the self is seen as another. *Journal of Personality and Social Psychology, 90*(2), 197–209.

Raine A. (2013). *The anatomy of violence: The biological roots of crime.* New York, NY: Pantheon Books.

Raine, A., Lencz, T., Bihrle, S., Lacasse, L., & Colletti, P. (2000). Reduced prefrontal gray matter volume and reduced autonomic activity inn antisocial personality disorder. *Archives of General Psychiatry, 57*, 119–127.

Sapolsky, R. (2004). The frontal cortex and the criminal justice system. *Philosophical Transactions of the Royal Society London, 359*, 1787–1796.

Shewmon, A., Holmes, G., & Byrne, P. (1999). Consciousness in congenitally decorticate children: Developmental vegetative state as self-fulfilling prophecy. *Developmental Medicine & Child Neurology, 41*, 364–374.

Slovic, P. (2001). Cigarette smokers: Rational actors or rational fools? In P. Slovic (Ed.), *Smoking: Risk, perception, and policy* (pp. 97–124). Thousand Oaks, CA: SAGE.

Smith, A. (2005). Responsibility for attitudes: Activity and passivity in mental life. *Ethics, 115*, 236–271.

"Tinnitus." (n.d.). *Mayo Clinic*. Retrieved from https://www.mayoclinic.org/diseases-conditions/tinnitus/multimedia/tinnitus/img-20007277

van der Westhuizen, D., & Solms, M. (2014). Social dominance and the affective neuroscience personality scales. *Consciousness and Cognition, 33*, 90–111.

van der Westhuizen, D., & Solms, M. (2015). Basic emotional foundations of social dominance in relation to Panksepp's affective taxonomy. *Neuropsychoanalysis, 17*(1), 19–37. doi:10.1080/15294145.2015.1021371

Vincent, N. (Ed.). (2013). *Neuroscience and legal responsibility*. Oxford, England: Oxford University Press.

Wagner, D., Haxby, J., & Heatherton, T. (2012). The representation of self and person knowledge in the medial prefrontal cortex. *WIREs Cognitive Science, 3*, 451–470. doi:10.1002/wcs.1183

Wilson, T. (2002). *Strangers to ourselves: Discovering the adaptive unconscious*. Boston, MA: Harvard University Press.

Winkielman, P., Berridge, K., & Wilbarger, J. (2005). Unconscious affective reactions to masked happy versus angry faces influence consumption behavior and judgments of value. *Personality and Social Psychology Bulletin, 31*(1), 121–135.

Yang, Y., & Raine, A. (2009). Prefrontal structural and functional brain imaging findings in antisocial, violent, and psychopathic individuals: A meta-analysis. *Psychiatry Research: Neuroimaging, 174*, 81–88.

Zajonc, R. (1980). Feeling and thinking: preferences need no inferences. *American Psychologist, 35*(2), 151–175.

PART IV
CHANGING PEOPLE

15

Make Me Gay

What Neurointerventions Tell Us About Sexual Orientation and Why It Matters for the Law

Andrew Vierra

Introduction

This chapter challenges the restrictive definition of *gay* used in legal discourse, argues for the adoption of a broader definition that is inclusive of more individuals within this broader class, and demonstrates that the adoption of a broader definition would help frame arguments for gay rights in a way that is both stronger and more inclusive of the entire gay community. Current legal arguments for gay rights use *gay* primarily to refer to individuals that have same-sex erotic desires. However, as I argue below using a thought experiment based on a neurointervention that would alter the orientation of one's erotic desires, the term *gay* should be understood in a broader sense to include a more diverse group of individuals, including some individuals that do not have same-sex erotic desires and some individuals who do not take their erotic desires to be an important part of their identity. I argue that, for this reason, legal arguments for gay rights presume a definition of *gay* that is overly restrictive and excludes individuals that we should want to extend rights to—such as lesbian feminists that choose to be romantically involved with members of the same sex despite not necessarily having same-sex desires. To rectify this problem with the way that arguments for gay rights are being framed, I suggest that we expand the use of the term *gay* in legal discourse to encompass a more heterogeneous population than the one picked out by same-sex–attracted individuals. I argue that doing so would help frame arguments for gay rights in a way that is more inclusive of what, on my account, is the entire gay community and would strengthen arguments for gay rights.

I begin by outlining some views about what it is to be gay. In particular, I draw attention to what I call the "common intuition"—the view that being gay is a matter of having same-sex erotic desires—and argue that this is the definition of *gay* that is presupposed in legal discourse. I then argue against this definition by proposing a counterexample to holders of the common intuition based on

Andrew Vierra, *Make Me Gay* In: *Neurointerventions and the Law*. Edited by: Nicole A Vincent, Thomas Nadelhoffer, and Allan McCay, Oxford University Press (2020). © Oxford University Press 2020
DOI: 10.1093/oso/9780190651145.001.0015

the idea of a neurointervention that gives individuals same-sex erotic desires for a period of one day or longer. I begin this section by overviewing the science about what causes sexual preference to show that, in theory, we could develop a neurointervention that changes sexual preferences for one day or longer. I then argue that even holders of the common intuition—including those in the legal arena—would not believe that the users of such interventions would necessarily become gay. I will take this to show that being gay is not simply a matter of having same-sex erotic desires. Finally, I argue that, in light of my argument to this point, arguments for gay rights are being framed incorrectly. I propose that a broader definition of the term *gay* should be adopted in legal discourse and explain some of the advantages of doing so.

What Is Gay?

Philosophers, scientists, and sociologists' views on what it is to be gay can be roughly divided into four camps: the self-identification view (Kushner, 1992, pp. 45–46), dispositionalism (Dembroff, 2016; Stein, 2001, Kinsey, Pomeroy, & Martin, 1948; Kinsey, Pomeroy, Martin, & Gebhard, 1953), social constructionism (Ward, 2015), and what I have called the common intuition. There is variation within each of these camps as to whether sexual orientation is binary (gay or straight), bipolar (a continuum between gay and straight), or composed of multiple discrete categories (Wesleyan University uses LGBTTQQFAGPBDSM[1]). For the sake of this discussion, I will assume that the binary model is the correct view, largely because that is a tacit assumption in the current legal debate over gay rights with which I shall engage.

Self-identification views hold that the way one identifies determines one's sexual orientation, regardless of one's behavior, sexual desires, or the opinion of others. As Edward Stein (2001) puts it, the self-identification view is "a view that gives weight to a person's own assessment of his or her sexual orientation . . . ." (p. 44). On this view, one could, for example, be exclusively erotically attracted to members of the same-sex and married to a same-sex partner but still be straight if that is how one identifies. Self-identification views are thus radical departures from the common intuition. They deny the importance of erotic desires altogether and focus solely on the way one identifies.

Dispositional views hold that "a person's sexual orientation is based on his or her sexual desires and fantasies and the sexual behaviors that he or she is disposed to engage in under ideal conditions" (Stein, 2001, p. 45). The focus on

---

[1] Lesbian, gay, bisexual, transgender, transsexual, queer, questioning, flexible, asexual, genderfuck, polyamorous, bondage/discipline, dominance/submission, and sadism/masochism.

erotic desires resembles the common intuition, but the dispositional view differs in its focus on counterfactuals and the addition of behavior as a determinant of sexual orientation. According to some dispositional views, one is gay if one would engage in sexual behaviors with members of the same sex in a variety of different ideal situations, where the word *ideal* is intended to capture such clauses as that one is not forced to have sex, one has different sexual partners to choose from, and there are no social pressures to choose one sex over the other. Put another way, if one would have sex with members of the same sex in the majority of a sufficiently large number of ideal circumstances and would decline sex with opposite-sex partners in similar circumstances, then one is gay. Dispositionalism allows that under some counterfactual circumstances, straight individuals will have sex with and maybe even feel erotically attracted to members of the same sex—for instance, when incarcerated individuals who previously had exclusively opposite-sex partners enter sexual and romantic relations with other incarcerated individuals of the same sex. But it holds that one's sexual orientation cannot be defined by circumstances that account for only a small percentage of one's dispositions.

Social constructionists—to give a broad generalization—argue that what it is to be gay is the result of contingent social and historical processes. The concept *gay*, or so the argument goes, need not have existed at all and need not be at all as it is. Some lesbian feminists, for example, argue that lesbianism in the United States is defined as a matter of same-sex erotic desires because "male society defines lesbianism as a sexual act . . . [and] this reflects men's limited view of women as sexual objects" (Faderman, 1984, p. 87). In addition to noting that gay is a social construct, some social constructionists take the further step of rejecting the way society defines *gay* on the grounds that the definition is both contingent and harmful. Some lesbian feminists take the contingency of male society's definition of the term *lesbian* and the negative normative consequences that arise from viewing women as sexual objects as grounds to reject the notion that lesbianism is a sexual identity. Instead, lesbian feminists offer alternative, women-oriented, definitions of lesbianism such as "a lesbian is the rage of all women condensed to the point of explosion" and lesbianism is "a political choice" (Faderman, 2015, p. 234).

Throughout this chapter, though, I focus on the common intuition—the position that being gay is a matter of having same-sex erotic desires—because that is the definition that I will argue is presupposed in legal discourse. I begin by overviewing the prevalence of the common intuition in arguments for gay rights and in U.S. Supreme Court rulings to demonstrate that the common intuition is the definition of *gay* used in legal discourse. I then outline the argument proponents of the common intuition put forward to defend their definition.

The Common Intuition

The common intuition has been presupposed in many arguments for gay rights—for instance, that being gay should not be a ground for being discharged from the military, that gay people should be allowed to marry one another, adopt children, or be recognized as one another's legal guardians in situations where, for example, medical treatment decisions need to be made by a substitute decision maker. One example is the immutability argument. Proponents of this argument (American Psychological Association [APA], American Psychiatric Association, National Association of Social Workers, & Texas Chapter of the National Association of Social Workers, 2003; Lady Gaga, 2011; Schwarz, 2015) begin from the premise that gay individuals cannot choose or change their sexual orientation (i.e., their erotic desires are immutable). They then argue that one should not be discriminated against on the basis of what one cannot choose or change, so gay individuals should not be discriminated against on the basis of being gay—for instance, they oughtn't be discharged from the military purely on grounds of being gay or denied the right to marry a partner of the same sex, adopt a child, etc.

In making this argument, gay rights activists presuppose that being gay is a matter of having same-sex erotic desires (i.e., the common intuition). This definition of *gay* fits well with their argument. In contrast, self-identification views and some social constructionist views (e.g., those put forward by lesbian feminists) do not fit as well with their argument because on those views at least some individuals can *choose* to be gay. Erotic desires, on the other hand, are largely unchangeable. Gay conversion therapies like "pray the gay away," for example, are not successful at reorienting or extinguishing same-sex erotic desires even when the individual in therapy genuinely wants to be attracted to members of the opposite sex (Anton, 2010; Halderman, 1991). Definitions of *gay* that center on same-sex erotic desires, like the common intuition, are thus a good fit for proponents of the immutability argument.

Recent U.S. Supreme Court cases provide several examples of the common intuition and the immutability argument playing a role in legal discourse. In their amicus brief for *Lawrence v. Texas* (2003),[2] APA et al. (2003) repeatedly stressed that for most gay men[3] and women, being gay (i.e. having same-sex erotic desires) is not a choice (pp. 4, 8, 9) and sexual orientation is "highly resistant to

---

[2] The Supreme Court case that ruled that a Texas statute (§21.06) that made sodomy a crime was unconstitutional.

[3] The APA et al. (2003) says "most" and not "all" because "in the Kinsey studies of the 1940s and 1950s" some gay individuals reported having "incidental attractions to or behaviors with the other sex" (p. 8). I assume that they took this finding to suggest that some gay individuals have a limited degree of choice.

change" (p. 4). APA et al. used these claims to argue that people should not be discriminated against for being gay, because being gay is a matter of being same-sex attracted, and this is a feature that people do not get to choose and cannot change. Further, in the majority opinion of the Court in *Obergefell v. Hodges* (2015), the landmark Supreme Court ruling that the Constitution requires states to issue marriage licenses to same-sex couples, the Court twice noted that sexual orientation is immutable (pp. 4, 8), writing that for gay individuals, sexual orientation's "immutable nature dictates that same-sex marriage is the only real path" to the "profound commitment" of marriage (p. 2594).

The common intuition also played a role in the Department of Justice's decision to recommend that Edie Windsor's case against the Defense of Marriage Act be considered under heightened scrutiny,[4] which was critical in getting the case heard by the Supreme Court (Holder, 2011). One of the criteria for giving a case heightened scrutiny is that being a member of the group that is being discriminated against (in this case, people who are gay) "is not a choice (and is) immutable" (Kaplan, 2015, p. 142; Bowen v. Gilliard, 1987, p. 602-03). Unlike other definitions of what it is to be gay, which often include individuals that choose to be gay, the common intuition holds that sexual orientation is simply a matter of having same-sex erotic desires and thereby supports arguments for heightened scrutiny in a way that other definitions of what it is to be gay do not.

The prevalence of the common intuition in these high-profile cases and arguments for gay rights suggests that the common intuition is the definition of *gay* that is presupposed in legal discourse. Further, the prominence of the common intuition in successful arguments for gay rights suggests that the definition of *gay* that is used in these cases matters.

Arguments for the position that being gay is a matter of having same-sex erotic desires tend to center on the definition's intuitiveness. Edward Stein (2001, pp. 44–45), for example, argues against the self-identification view of what it is to be gay by claiming that the self-identification view leads to unintuitive consequences. He argues that some individuals that self-identify as straight may have same-sex erotic desires that they are not aware of, or are repressing, and in his view, the most intuitive thing to say about these people is that they are gay. He then claims that because the "self-identification view does not seem to capture our notion of sexual orientation," the view is not sound (p. 45). A sound definition of *gay*, according to the common intuition, is thus one that the folk find intuitive (this is indeed precisely why I refer this position as the "common intuition"). And, in line with the common intuition, the most pervasive definition of what it

---

[4] Under heightened scrutiny, "the assumption is no longer that the law is constitutional; the burden is now on the government to show that the law furthers an 'important' government interest and that the law is 'substantially related' to that important issue" (Kaplan, 2015, p. 141).

is to be gay in the United States is that being gay is a matter of having same-sex erotic desires. The first seven entries on Urban Dictionary (2016a; that do not define *gay* as "happy") define being gay as being homosexual, which in turn is defined exclusively in sexual and romantic terms such as "sexual preferences" for members of the same sex, "sexual attraction" to members of the same sex, and "guys who are into other guys." The Merriam-Webster (2016) dictionary likewise defines being gay as being "sexually attracted to someone who is the same sex." Even the APA (2008) defines being gay as having same-sex "erotic attractions and sexual arousal" (pp. 2–3). The American Psychiatric Association and the National Association of Social Workers purport the same definition (APA et al., 2003, pp. 4–5, esp. footnote 6).

Proponents of the common intuition, thus, hold that *gay* is by definition a matter of having same-sex erotic desires, not unlike the proposition that *table* is by definition a piece of furniture, typically with four legs and a flat top and typically used to place things on top like cups, glasses, plates, vases, ornaments, computers, and the like, but not typically used for such things as sleeping or sitting on. That is, when people use the word *gay* to refer to a person, what they mean is that that person has same-sex erotic desires. If this is right, then individuals, like some lesbian feminists, who self-identify as gay despite not having same-sex erotic desires, are just misunderstanding the meaning of the word *gay* like an individual who calls a chair a *table*.

In the next section, I will explain why even if this is the definition of *gay* that most people actually have in mind, or perhaps what they would say if they were asked what *gay* means, there is nevertheless good reason to suppose that after reflecting on the considerations that I will discuss, they would subsequently retract their view as not accurately capturing their view on what *gay* means. That is, I will show that even holders of the common intuition would find it intuitive that under some circumstances an individual can have same-sex erotic desires without being gay. In doing so, I will demonstrate, contra the common intuition, that being gay is not simply a matter of having same-sex erotic desires.

Gay for a Day? Being Straight with Same-Sex Erotic Desires

In this section, I develop a counterexample to the proponents of the common intuition's claim that being gay is a matter of having same-sex erotic desires. I intend for this to be a counterexample that engages with views and commitments that proponents of the common intuition will recognize as their own—that is, I intend to engage with them on their own terms—rather than merely offering yet another different definition of *gay*. In this way, I hope to convince them that on reflection they do not after all endorse the claim that being gay is a matter of having same-sex erotic desires. I argue that thinking critically about the possibility of a "gay-for-a-day" pill—an intervention that would give a straight individual same-sex erotic desires for one day—and how common intuition holders, including the person taking the pill, would perceive such a person post-intervention reveals that even people who thought that they would endorse the common intuition would, on reflection, recognize that being gay is not after all simply a matter of having same-sex erotic desires. I begin by explaining how this neurointervention might work. I then look at the social scripts straight people use to engage in homoerotic behavior without taking themselves or others taking them to be gay, and I use these observations to motivate my counterexample before generalizing my argument to long-term interventions to show that my claim (that being gay is not just, and perhaps not even, a matter of same-sex attraction) applies not only to the contrived scenario of a short-duration change in sexual attraction induced through the use of a medical intervention, but that it applies to ordinary situations as well.

Making the Brain Gay

In this section, after describing recent developments in neuroscience and genetics and how they inform our understanding of the neurophysiological factors that underpin sexuality, I argue that it is plausible that a neurointervention may at some stage be created that will give people same-sex erotic desires. The vast majority of neuroscientific and genetic research focuses on the prenatal conditions correlated with same-sex erotic desires in males, so that will be the example discussed in this section. I will begin with the neurohormonal studies that link the development of same-sex erotic desires with the exposure of the fetus to certain hormones, and conclude with twin studies and research on the "gay gene."

Neuroscientific research on sexual orientation focuses on the hypothalamus, the brain's hormone center. The hypothalamus plays a key role in determining the strength of individuals' sex drives and the frequency that individuals have sex, so many scientists hypothesize that it plays some role in orienting erotic desires. Simon Levay (1991), for example, examined the cadavers of 41 males of varying sexual orientations to see if there were any morphological differences between the hypothalamus of gay and straight men. He found that the third interstitial notch of the anterior hypothalamus (INAH-3) is the same size in gay men and straight women (half the size of straight men). Because most women appear to be attracted to men, and women have smaller INAH-3s than straight men, Levay reasoned that the size of the INAH-3 may indicate the sex/gender that one is erotically attracted to, and hormone levels might play a role in determining sexual orientation.

To discover the role that hormones play in directing erotic desires toward a specific sex/gender, researchers began investigating whether gay men and straight women share sexually dimorphic characteristics.[5] The idea was that if these similarities exist, then this may be interpreted as evidence that gay men are prenatally exposed to similar levels of the same hormones as straight women. If this is the case, then perhaps hormone levels predict the sex that one is erotically attracted to, and future studies could determine if hormone levels also to some extent determine the sex that one is erotically attracted to.

The 2D:4D ratio (the ratio of the length of the second and fourth finger) is one such sexually dimorphic trait; males have lower ratios than females, i.e. longer ring fingers (Manning, 2002; Gobrogge et al., 2008, & Loehlin, 2009). Higher exposure to androgens like testosterone is thought to cause male's decreased ratio, so if men with same-sex erotic desires, on average, have higher 2D:4D ratios than men with opposite-sex erotic desires, then they may have had less prenatal exposure to androgens. Researchers have performed twin studies across different ethnic groups to determine if men with same-sex erotic desires have different 2D:4D ratios than men with opposite-sex erotic desires. This research has resulted in two findings. First, the similarity in digit ratios between monozygotic twins is higher than in dizygotic twins, suggesting that genetic influences outweigh nonshared environmental factors. Second, as predicted, men with opposite-sex erotic desires have lower 2D:4D ratios than men with same-sex erotic desires. This result has been confirmed in Japanese (Hiraishi, Sasaki, Shikishima, & Ando, 2012) and White populations but does not seem to hold in Black and Chinese populations (Manning, 2007).

The differences in hypothalamus size and the variation in hormone levels are thought to result from genetic variations between straight and gay individuals. One study found that 52% of male identical twins and 22% of male nonidentical twins share concordant nonstraight sexual orientations (Bailey & Pillard, 1991), so assuming that these numbers are representative, nonenvironmental influences must play some role in determining same-sex erotic desires and their corresponding brain structures, or so the argument goes. With this thought in mind, a number of studies have been performed looking for what has come to be popularly referred to as the "gay gene." Dean Hammer (1993), for example, found that maternal uncles and cousins of gay men were more likely to be gay than fraternal uncles and cousins of gay men, suggesting that the "gay gene" is on the X chromosome, which males inherit from their mothers. Hamer, Hu, Magnuson, Hu, & Pattatucci (1993) later found that gay brothers share chromosomal region Xq28 at a higher rate than straight brothers (82% vs. 50%; Hu, 1995). Hamer

---

[5] Dimorphic characteristics are traits that the two sexes of the same species do not generally share.

et al. concluded that "at least one subtype of male sexual orientation is genetically influenced" (p. 321). More recently, computational geneticist Tuck Ngun created a predictive model for sexual orientation using genetic markers. The algorithm uses epigenetic information from five regions of the human genome to predict male sexual orientation with 67% accuracy (Reardon, 2015).

The upshot of this research is that same-sex erotic desires might be influenced by genes that determine brain structures. There is, thus, no in-principle reason to think that neurointerventions that alter what sex one is erotically attracted to will not become available in the not-so-distant future. They could work by, say, prenatally altering hormone levels or by activating transcription factors. Indeed, there are already medications that diminish libido—antiandrogen medications administered (sometimes forcibly) to convicted sex offenders are one example (see Chapters 12 and 13 in this volume)—this is also a common side effect of many antidepressant medications (Rosen, Lane, & Menza, 1999), and all psychological traits are at least in some sense neurologically based. So if a safe and effective way of changing one's same-sex erotic desires were ever discovered, it would likely stem from advances in genetics and neuroscience.

In the next two sections, I argue that if a straight individual took a neurointervention that gave them same-sex erotic desires, then even common intuition supporters would have reason to agree that they would not necessarily have become gay. If I am right that common intuition supporters would come to this conclusion, then I will take myself to have shown that being gay is not simply a matter of having same-sex erotic desires. I begin by looking at the various ways that proponents of the common intuition with social capital—that is, individuals who can break various social norms without negative social consequences—engage in homoerotic activities without considering themselves or being considered by others to be gay. I then extend this analysis from homoerotic behaviors to same-sex erotic desires by considering what I call a gay-for-a-day pill—a neurointervention that would give an otherwise exclusively opposite-sex-attracted person who uses it same-sex erotic desires for one day—before extending the analysis to long-term interventions. I argue that an individual that took such an intervention would not become gay, so being gay is not simply a matter of having same-sex erotic desires.

Social Capital Allows Sexual Norms to Be Broken

The term *gay* is often used in two different ways, especially in high school settings. One way is to jokingly emasculate someone who is popular and widely known to be straight. Call this *friendly emasculation*. Another way is to emasculate and express disdain toward someone who is gay or does not have social capital. Call this *hostile emasculation*.

Paradoxically, being the target of friendly emasculation can reinforce one's straightness if one has what C.J. Pascoe (2003) calls "jock insurance"—a form of social capital. Consider hazing rituals at fraternities. Pledges are sometimes forced to engage in what is called "the elephant walk" or the "limp biscuit."[6] The men who have the social capital to do these activities without becoming the target of hostile emasculation end up reinforcing their straightness by bonding with their fraternity brothers and demonstrating their commitment to their hypermasculine and straight fraternity. These men do not consider themselves to be gay. In fact, they sometimes take themselves to be showing off how straight they are. They are so comfortable with their straight identities that they can break sexual norms without worrying about others thinking that they are gay.

Laura Hamilton (2007) gives another example of jock insurance in her recent study of straight college women who kiss other women at parties. In her study, Hamilton found that college women's homoerotic acts were consistent with being straight. Unlike "real lesbians," these self-identified straight women used same-sex kissing to attract the male gaze. In doing so, they took same-sex kissing—often a lesbian act meant to express affection toward a member of the same sex—and redefined it as a flirtation device to attract members of the opposite sex. As one subject in the study explained the purpose of same-sex kissing, "You get guys that you just like to see their expressions. It's just so funny to see them be like, 'Oh my god, I can't believe you just did that, that was awesome'" (p. 164). Like the men in the fraternity example, these women did not take themselves to be lesbians, nor did the men who were watching them. They only kissed women that they were certain were straight while they were under the influence of alcohol—a drug commonly used by these women to make their same-sex kissing evidence of their spontaneity and a result of their transient state of mind instead of a genuine erotic attraction to the same sex. By kissing other women while using these social scripts, they separated themselves from what they called "real lesbians" (p.165).

C.J. Pascoe and Tristan Bridges give one final example of jock insurance in their analysis of the Warwick men's rowing team's annual nude photo calendar—a calendar designed to raise money for the team and (more recently) raise awareness about bullying and homophobia. Pascoe and Bridges (2014) note that at first it seems strange that these rowers would be willing to pose naked with other

---

[6] Urban Dictionary defines the "elephant walk" as a group of guys that "form a straight line and grab the erect cock of the guy in back of them with one hand and put their thumb in the sphincter of the guy in front of them then they walk in a circle" and defines the "limp biscuit" as a fraternity hazing ritual in which "Several guys stand in a circle around a biscuit (and) they all begin to jerk off, ejaculating onto the biscuit. The last person to cum, consequently, has to eat the soggy biscuit."

men. Men who engage in homoerotic activities are often seen as being gay—an identity that often results in hostile emasculation and a loss of social capital—so making an all-male nude calendar seems like a huge social risk. However, iron-ically, these men's actions may reinforce their straightness. Indeed, Pascoe and Bridges write that "the Warwick rowing team's gender and sexual practices and proclamations reinscribe their heterosexuality as so powerful and inevitable that even an anti-homophobia stance can't call them into question."

All of these examples share the following theme: proponents of the common intuition with social capital or jock insurance can "act gay" (i.e., engage in same-sex erotic behaviors) without considering themselves to be gay or being considered to be gay by their peers. In fact, they often reinforce their straight identities through their homoerotic activities. My aim in emphasizing this shared theme among these examples is to underscore the following point. Considering the amount of flexibility some straight individuals have within their straight identities and the tendency for individuals with jock insurance to reinforce their heterosexuality *even more* when they act in more extremely ho-moerotic ways—just consider the limp biscuit!—it is difficult to imagine what these individuals could possibly do to undermine or cast doubt upon their un-impeachable straightness.

Admittedly, I concede that another feature that all of the previous examples share in common is that, regardless of what one happens to be *doing*, none of the protagonists actually have same-sex erotic desires. In light of this, wouldn't the right conclusion to draw from the above examples be precisely that the common intuition is correct—that is, that being gay is a matter of having same-sex erotic desires—and hence that a gay-for-a-day pill would cross this boundary and that a user of this pill would become gay?

I see no reason to think that the gay-for-a-day pill would impinge on these individuals' straight identities when all of these other activities do not. And no-tice that rather than simply following the above trend of homoerotic *behaviors* being compatible with being straight, the gay-for-a-day pill would indeed go a step further. In the Warwick example, the athletes have the masculine capital and jock insurance necessary to act in homoerotic ways *without having same-sex erotic desires* attributed to them, but this is not what the gay-for-a-day pill would provide. Rather, high-tech short-lasting conversion therapy of this sort would by definition (my definition of what the gay-for-a-day pill would do) give a male athlete same-sex erotic desires. The athlete would not just be *acting* like they are attracted to members of the same-sex to support a cause or undergird their straightness; they would *actually have* the desires. However, rather than undermining my analogy, I argue that, paradoxically, this even greater contrast between what they would take themselves to still be (not gay) and their having same-sex erotic desires as well as any behaviors, makes my point even more salient—their straightness would only be underscored further if they still would not self-identify or be identified by their peers as now being gay.

Individuals with jock insurance already have sufficient social capital to get away with bending sexual norms. There is little reason to think that bending the norms further by taking the gay-for-a-day pill would diminish these men's perceived straightness, especially in certain hyper-masculine contexts like fraternities. Gay-for-a-day pills could be forced on individuals before they engage in activities like the elephant walk. But precisely because these individuals would only take the pill to access the hyper-heterosexual fraternity in the hopes of having sex with women, I suspect that few individuals (including, most importantly, the individuals taking the pill themselves) would consider these men gay. Rather, I propose that the gay-for-a-day pill would become just another vehicle through which straight men and women can reassert their straightness—by acting gay without being gay.

Here is another example to demonstrate the same point. Imagine a college-aged woman who is repulsed by people who are gay. She believes that being gay is morally wrong and has visceral disgust reactions when she observes homoerotic activities. However, on her boyfriend's birthday, she decides to take a gay-for-a-day pill so that she can act out one of her boyfriend's sexual fantasies and find it slightly less repulsive (she still considers what she is doing to be morally wrong, is disgusted by her actions, and strongly identifies as straight, but is wholeheartedly committed to giving her boyfriend the best birthday present ever). It seems unlikely to me that the folk would believe that this woman temporarily becomes gay. It also seems plausible to me that while under the influence of the gay-for-a-day pill she might exclaim something like "Wow, Johnny, how ghastly—I really feel sexually attracted to that girl! I'm so turned on by her, how repulsive!" explicitly distancing herself from her actual same-sex erotic attraction. After all, like the straight girls who kiss other girls at parties, she is only taking on these desires as a tool for the pleasure of a man, not to be gay.

If my conjectures are correct about how people who take the gay-for-a-day pill and others around them would view themselves or others[7] under the influence of the gay-for-a-day pill, then people who, I take it, are just like holders of the common intuition—ordinary folks, not some fringe group with idiosyncratic opinions and views—would indeed believe that at least some individuals under some circumstances could take the gay-for-a-day pill and yet not become gay. That is, some individuals *could have same-sex erotic desires without being gay,* which entails that being gay cannot after all simply be a matter of having

---

[7] Experimental philosophical work on whether the folk share my intuitions is beyond the scope of this chapter but would be a helpful supplement to the arguments I make in this section.

same-sex erotic desires, contra the presuppositions that permeate the current legal debate about gay rights, equality, and discrimination.

Long-Term Interventions

To address the foreseeable objection that perhaps my argument would not work beyond contrived scenarios where same-sex erotic desires last for only a short period of time (i.e. for just a day), I will now consider the possibility of a gay-for-a-year pill. Extending my argument to this longer case is essential because, after all, one can acknowledge that one cannot be gay for a day, and that it is not the case that same-sex erotic desire is sufficient for being gay and still consistently hold that being gay consists in having a *pattern of same-sex erotic desires* (POD). Put another way, one can claim that having same-sex erotic desires over an extended period of time is sufficient for being gay even if having same-sex erotic desires for just one day is not sufficient for being gay,[8] and, therefore, a long-term neurointervention that gave a person same-sex erotic desires for a sufficiently long period of time could make a straight person gay. Richard Pillard and J. Michael Bailey (1995) argue something like this, describing sexual orientation as "the sustained erotic attraction to members of one's own gender, the opposite gender, or both—homosexual, heterosexual, or bisexual respectively." I call this the *POD thesis*.

Gay for a Year
One version of the POD thesis holds that if one has same-sex erotic desires for one year, then during that one-year period, one is gay. I will argue against this position by providing a counterexample in which one has same-sex erotic desires for one year but does not consider oneself to be gay and is not considered by others to be gay. In doing so, I will demonstrate that having same-sex erotic desires for one year is not sufficient for being gay.

I previously overviewed three ways straight individuals engage in same-sex erotic activities without being gay. One shared characteristic of each of these activities was that they were infrequent; these heterosexual women did not kiss other women at every party, nor did the Warwick team pose naked every day (let alone for a year). There are, however, other circumstances under which straight-identified individuals can engage in same-sex erotic activities regularly for a year without considering themselves to be gay or being considered gay by others. One such example is prison relationships.

[8] I will not tie the POD thesis down to any exact length of time. POD thesis holders could coherently hold that the same-sex erotic desires have to last at least one week or that they have to last forever to be sufficient for making one gay. I will attempt to show that, whatever the length of time, having same-sex erotic desires is not sufficient to make one gay.

Prison comes with a variety of heterosexual scripts that enable straight men to have sex with other men without being identified as gay (Kunzel, 2002, 2008). For example, some incarcerated men argue that they are straight by appealing to their insatiable sex drive or the "agonizing call of biology" (Kunzel, 2002, p. 260). They claim that although they prefer to have sex with women, they have to make due with less than ideal circumstances. One incarcerated individual explained "These are men in their physical prime. They have the same drives that young men on the outside do, but they don't have the same opportunities for satisfaction. They crave sex, but there are no girls. So, of necessity, prisoners turn to each other" (p. 261). Author Louis Berg (1934) similarly appeals to the male sex drive in his description of male prisons: "in the end, all normal men (i.e. straight men) will find themselves torn by this natural hunger where satisfaction is denied for any length of time" (p. 143).

Other incarcerated individuals appeal to the need to protect themselves. They are not gay because they only have sex with other men out of necessity. These men agree to, say, have an exclusive same-sex sexual relationship with another inmate not because they are gay, but because they worry that if they don't, they will be harmed. They are straight men in nonideal circumstances.

I suspect that straight men that use the gay-for-a-year pill while incarcerated could appeal to similar social scripts. For example, men using the neurointervention could explain that they only took the pill because they knew that they would not have access to women—the gender they would prefer to have sex with if given the choice—and because they have an insatiable sex drive they knew that they would end up having sex with other men during their sentence. And if they are going to do that, why not enjoy it? Other users could argue that they are only taking the pill to protect themselves. They assume that they are going to have to have a same-sex relationship for their own personal safety, and taking the pill would make it easier to endure the relationship.

Under either justification, it seems to me very unintuitive to insist that the person concerned becomes gay after taking the pill despite the fact that they whole-heartedly disavow this claim, and they whole-heartedly insist on their straightness. In the former case, the intervention user continues appealing to masculine social scripts, like their sex drive, to buttress their identification as straight. As we saw in the fraternity and Warwick examples, appeals to masculinity are intimately tied with straight identities, and more masculine individuals can bend sexual norms without being identified as gay (especially in hypermasculine settings like fraternities, male athletics, or, indeed, prisons). In the latter case, the intervention users do not take the same-sex erotic desires to have anything to do with their sexual identity (indeed, they could be happily married to women outside of prison); rather, the desires are simply a means to an end (i.e., their protection).

If the conclusions I have derived from considering the possibility of a gay-for-a-year pill are correct, then having same-sex erotic desires for one year is not sufficient to make one gay, and being gay, contra its use in current legal discourse, is not simply a matter of having same-sex erotic desires. Although this argument alone does not prove that the POD thesis is not sound—recall that I did not tie the POD thesis to any specific length of time—I believe that this argument (in addition to my previous arguments) can be extended to cover any length of time that the POD thesis might deem sufficient to make one gay. The social scripts that allow straight men to use the gay-for-a-year pill while in prison without considering themselves to be gay or being considered by others to be gay may even become more credible as the prison sentence increases. Controlling one's sex drive for one year (i.e., not having sex with other men for one year) is far easier than remaining abstinent for, say, 10 years.[9] How people identify and what social scripts are at their disposal to describe what they do and how they feel play a critically important role in imbuing same-sex attraction with either gay or straight salience. Particular behaviors (e.g., intercourse with a person of the same sex) and feelings (e.g., same-sex erotic attraction) might even, by default, normally be associated with particular scripts and self-identifications. However, what is doing the conceptual work here—what turns homoerotic behavior and same-sex attraction into manifestations or evidence for a person *being* gay—are these social scripts and self-identification. By itself, the behaviors and feelings are neither gay, nor straight, nor anything in particular.

Legal Considerations

As I previously explained, the common intuition plays a critical role in many arguments by advocates for gay rights and even by U.S. Supreme Court Justices. One prominent example is the immutability argument as previously discussed. For the convenience of my upcoming analysis, this argument can roughly be standardized as follows:

1. Being gay is a matter of having same-sex erotic desires (i.e. the common intuition).
2. The orientation of one's erotic desires is predetermined, or at least strongly constrained by biological and social factors.

---

[9] None of the previous discussion rules out the possibility that individuals who take reversible long-term interventions could become gay. For instance, an individual who identified as gay, had a long-term relationship with a same-sex partner, and was invested in gay politics would likely become gay after taking the intervention (if they were not gay already). My point is only that a POD or even that plus same-sex erotic behavior is not sufficient to make one gay.

3. The biological and social factors to which one is exposed are largely out of one's control—that is, nobody gets to choose the biological and environmental factors that determine their own sexual orientation.
4. Thus, one cannot choose whether or not one is gay.
5. Nobody should be discriminated against on the basis of what they can neither choose nor change.
6. Therefore, nobody should be discriminated against on the basis of being gay.

I previously argued against premise 1. If I am correct that premise 1 is false, however, then the immutability argument no longer demonstrates that one cannot choose whether or not to be gay. At best, the argument shows that (with our present technology, which has not yet produced a gay-for-a-day or similar effective and presumably medically safe gay conversion therapy), one cannot choose whether or not one has same-sex erotic desires. And, from there, the argument can only derive the conclusion that nobody should be discriminated against on the basis of *having same-sex erotic desires*. That is, without premise 1, the premises no longer entail the conclusion that nobody should be discriminated against on the basis of *being gay*.

The distinction between being gay and having exclusively same-sex erotic desires has serious consequences for arguments for gay rights as they are currently being framed. For example, as I previously mentioned, one of the criteria for giving a case heightened scrutiny is that being a member of the group that is discriminated against (in this case people who are gay) "is not a choice (and is) immutable" (Kaplan, 2015, p. 142). This criterion is best met on the basis of the common intuition—other theories discussed did not hold that sexual orientation was immutable. So if, as I have argued, the common intuition is not correct and being gay is not simply a matter of having same-sex erotic desires, then it is not clear that the immutability criterion would count towards heightened scrutiny in cases involving members of the gay community that are not innately and exclusively same-sex attracted.[10] To demonstrate one practical implication of my argument, lesbian feminists—that is, women who are in sexual relations with other women but not because they are same-sex attracted (see previous discussion)—may not be entitled to protection from discrimination given the way that arguments for gay rights are currently being framed.

Equally importantly, distinguishing between being gay and having same-sex erotic desires reveals that arguments for gay rights are being framed incorrectly

---

[10] Even if the common intuition was correct, the argument would only work as long as we lack the technology to alter the orientation of one's same-sex erotic desires (see Vierra & Earp, 2015; Earp & Vierra, 2018).

and in a way that is underinclusive. The definition of *gay* currently used—what I have called the common intuition—does not encompass all gay individuals and only refers to one aspect of some gay individuals' identities. This is important not just because the way the term *gay* is currently being used in legal discourse is misleading, but also because of the sorts of ramifications vis-à-vis practical implications that I mentioned in the previous paragraph. That is, this has practical implications for arguments for gay rights that depend on the common intuition, such as those grounded in immutability.

Gay rights advocates should be troubled by the current framing of the legal debates about gay rights, discrimination, and equality. Most importantly, as it stands, the definition of *gay* presumed in legal discourse simply does not include all of the individuals whom we want to, or at least should want to, protect. The definition excludes members of the gay community who likewise face severe discrimination but do not take erotic desires to be a major part of their identity.

Take lesbian feminists, whom I briefly mentioned earlier, as one example. As I previously recounted, lesbian feminists are lesbians, but they "deny that their choice to be lesbians arises from sexual interest or sexual proclivity" (Faderman, 1984, p. 87). Instead, they identify as lesbians for normative and political reasons. "They believe that it is male society that defines lesbianism as a sexual act and that this reflects men's limited view of women as sexual objects" (p, 87). Thus, for lesbian feminists, being a lesbian is a political choice. As Faderman (2015) notes, "lesbians are not born. . . . Lesbians are women who have *chosen* to refuse to put themselves at the service of men" (p. 234).

Because lesbian feminists deny that same-sex erotic desires are an important part of their identity—if they have such desires at all—they do not fall under the purview of the common intuition. But progressives should not want to exclude lesbian feminists from the conversation simply because they are not included in an inaccurate definition of what it is to be gay. Lesbian feminists are met with many of the same injustices that gay individuals are because they choose to be with other women and want to fight against patriarchal norms that harm women generally. Excluding lesbian feminists not only unfairly treats lesbian feminists as if they are not a part of the gay community—a community they are strong advocates for—but also sends a message to the gay community that gay individuals only deserve protection from discrimination if they cannot choose whether or not to be with a member of the same sex. Put another way, only including some gay individuals in arguments concerning gay rights and excluding other gay individuals sends the message "gay is only okay for some gay individuals." This message starkly contrasts with "gay is good"—the simple slogan popularized at the beginning of the gay liberation movement in the 1960s—which was designed to lift up a united community comprised of all gay individuals. It is the latter slogan that we should endorse, and one way to begin doing that would be to expand the definition of *gay* used in legal discourse from the common intuition to one that includes all gay individuals.

Importantly, moving away from the common intuition could strengthen arguments for gay rights. In addition to making arguments more inclusive of the entire gay community, the move could also help focus arguments on the legal considerations that matter the most. Take arguments for heightened scrutiny as an example. The reason why the gay community should receive heightened scrutiny when courts consider the constitutionality of discriminatory legislation is not because being gay is immutable—after all, even if individuals could change their sexual orientation, they would still deserve protection from discriminatory laws. Rather, it is because there is a long history of discrimination against *all* gay individuals in the United States—including individuals that choose to be in same-sex relationships, like some bisexual and pansexual individuals. Accordingly, when legislation is passed that discriminates against gay individuals, the legislation almost certainly will be based on animus and will not have a rational basis. And it is for this reason that judges should look upon the legislation skeptically and question the government's motives using some form of heightened scrutiny. Put another way, the reason that judges should apply heightened scrutiny is not because of one trait shared by some members of the gay community but because of the discrimination that the gay community has suffered and continues to suffer from.

Conclusion

In this chapter, I used the possibility of neurointerventions on sexual orientation to challenge the common intuition that being gay is simply a matter of having same-sex erotic desires. In doing so, I demonstrated that there is a discrepancy between the individuals referred to by *gay* in legal discourse and the larger and more diverse gay community. I then argued that this discrepancy should be disconcerting because the definition of *gay* presupposed in legal discourse excludes members of the gay community whom we want, or at least should want, to protect. I concluded by suggesting that debates over gay rights should adopt a broader, nonexclusive, definition of *gay*.

Acknowledgments

This chapter has benefited greatly from comments from a number of colleagues at Georgia State University. In particular, Nicole Vincent's feedback throughout the development of this chapter has been invaluable. Comments from Brian D. Earp, Eddy Nahmias, Dan Weiskopf, Calvin Warner, and Jared Riggs have also greatly improved this chapter. Any errors are entirely my own.

References

American Psychological Association. (2008). Just the facts about sexual orientation and youth: A primer for school personnel. Retrieved from http://www.apa.org/pi/lgbt/re-sources/just-the-facts.aspx

American Psychological Association, American Psychiatric Association, National Association of Social Workers, & Texas Chapter of the National Association of Social Workers. (2003). Lawrence v. Texas, 539 U.S. 558. Retrieved from http://www.apa.org/about/offices/ogc/amicus/lawrence.aspx

Anton, B. S. (2010). Proceedings of the American Psychological Association for the legislative year 2009: Minutes of the annual meeting of the Council of Representatives and minutes of the meetings of the Board of Directors. *American Psychologist, 65*, 385–475.

Bailey, J. M., & Pillard, R. C. (1991). A genetic study of male sexual orientation. *Archives of General Psychiatry, 48*(12), 1089–1096.

Berg, L. (1934). *Revelations of a prison doctor*. New York, NY: Minton, Balch.

Bowen v. Gilliard, 483 U.S. 602-03 (1987).

Dembroff, R. (2016). What is sexual orientation? *Philosophers Imprint, 16*(3), 1–27.

Earp, B. D. & Vierra, A. (2018). Sexual orientation minority rights and high-tech conversion therapy. In G. Caruso (Ed.), *Handbook of philosophy and public policy*. New York, NY: Palgrave Macmillan.

Faderman, L. (1984). The "new gay" lesbians. *Journal of Homosexuality, 10*(3–4), 85–95.

Faderman, L. (2015). *The gay revolution: The story of the struggle*. New York, NY: Simon & Schuster.

Gobrogge, K., Breedlove, S., & Klump, K. (2008). Genetic and environmental influences on 2D:4D finger length ratios: A study of monozygotic and dizygotic male and female twins. *Archives of Sexual Behavior, 37*, 112–118.

Halderman, D. C. (1991). Sexual orientation conversion therapy for gay men and lesbians: A scientific examination. In J. C. Gonsiorek & J. D. Weinrich (Eds.), *Homosexuality: Research implications for public policy* (pp. 149–160). Newbury Park, CA: SAGE.

Hamer, D. H., Hu, S., Magnuson, V. L., Hu, N., & Pattatucci, A. M. (1993). A linkage between DNA markers on the X chromosome and male sexual orientation. *Science, 261*(5119), 321–327.

Hamilton, L. (2007). Trading on heterosexuality: College women's gender strategies and homophobia. *Gender & Society, 21*(2), 145–172.

Hiraishi, K., Sasaki, S., Shikishima, C., & Ando, J. (2012). The second to fourth digit ratio (2D:4D) in a Japanese twin sample: Heritability, prenatal hormone transfer, and association with sexual orientation. *Archives of Sexual Behavior, 41*(3), 711–724.

Holder, E. (2011). "Letter from the Attorney General to Congress on litigation involving the Defense of Marriage Act." Retrieved from https://www.justice.gov/opa/pr/letter-attorney-general-congress-litigation-involving-defense-marriage-act.

Hu, S., Pattatucci, A. M. L., Patterson, C., Li, L., Fulker, D. W., Cherny, S. S., . . . Hamer, D. H. (1995). Linkage between sexual orientation and chromosome Xq28 in males but not in females. *Nature Genetics, 11*(3), 248–256.

Kaplan, R., Windsor, E., & Dickey, L. (2015). *Then comes marriage: United States V. Windsor and the Defeat of DOMA.* New York, NY: W. W. Norton.

Kinsey, A., Pomeroy, W., & Martin, C. (1948). *Sexual behavior in the human male.* Philadelphia, PA: W. B. Saunders.

Kinsey, A., Pomeroy, W., Martin, C., & Gebhard, P. (1953). *Sexual behavior in the human female.* Philadelphia, PA: W. B. Saunders.

Kunzel, R. (2002). Situating sex: Prison sexual culture in the mid-twentieth-century United States. *GLQ: A Journal of Lesbian and Gay Studies, 8*(3), 253–270.

Kunzel, R. (2008). *Criminal intimacy: Prison and the uneven history of modern American sexuality.* Chicago, IL: Chicago University Press.

Kushner, T. (1992). *Angels in America: Part one, millennium approaches.* New York, NY: Theater Communications Group.

Lady Gaga. (2011). *Born this way* [Audio recording]. London, England: Abbey Road Studios.

Lawrence v. Texas, 539 U.S. 558 (2003).

LeVay, S. (1991). A difference in hypothalamic structure between heterosexual and homosexual men. *Science, 253*, 1034–1037.

Loehlin, J., Medland, S., & Martin, N. (2009). Relative finger lengths, sex differences, and psychological traits. *Archives of Sexual Behavior, 38*, 298–305.

Manning, J. T. (2002). *Digit ratio: A pointer to fertility, behavior, and health.* New Brunswick, NJ: Rutgers University Press.

Manning, J. T., Churchill, A. J. G., & Peters, M. (2007). The effects of sex, ethnicity, and sexual orientation on self-measured digit ratios (2D:4D). *Archives of Sexual Behavior, 36*(2), 223–233.

Merriam-Webster.com. (2016). Gay. Retrieved from http://www.merriam-webster.com/dictionary/gay.

Obergefell v. Hodges. 576 U.S. (2015).

Pascoe, C.J. (2003). Multiple masculinities? Teenage boys talk about jocks and gender. *American Behavioral Scientist, 46*(10), 1423–1438.

Pascoe, C.J., & Bridges, T. (2014). Bro porn: Heterosexualizing straight men's anti-homophobia stances. *The Huffington Post.* Retrieved from http://www.huffingtonpost.com/cj-pascoe/bro-porn-heterosexualizing-straight-mens-anti-homophobia-stancesb4386206.html.

Pillard, R., & Bailey, J. M. (1995). A biological perspective on sexual orientation *Psychiatric Clinics of North America, 18,* 71–84.

Reardon, S. (2015). Epigenetic 'tags' linked to homosexuality in men. *Nature.* Retrieved from https://www.nature.com/news/epigenetic-tags-linked-to-homosexuality-in-men-1.18530

Rosen, R., Lane, R., & Menza, M. (1999). Effects of SSRIs on sexual function: A critical review. *Journal of Clinical Psychopharmacology, 19*, 67–85.

Schwarz, H. (2015, May 21). A majority of Americans now think gays are born that way: That says a lot about same-sex marriage. *The Washington Post.*

Stein, E. (2001). *The mismeasure of desire: The science, theory, and ethics of sexual orientation.* Oxford, England: Oxford University Press.

Urban Dictionary. (2016a). Gay. Retrieved from http://www.urbandictionary.com/de-fine.php?term=gay

Urban Dictionary. (2016b). Homosexual. Retrieved from http://www.urbandictionary.com/define.php?term=homosexual.

Vierra, A., & Earp, B. D. (2015, April 21). Born this way? How high-tech conversion therapy could undermine gay rights. *The Conversation*.

Ward, J. (2015). *Not gay*. New York, NY: New York University Press.

PART V
ENHANCING PEOPLE

16

Neuroenhancement, Coercion, and Neo-Luddism

Alexandre Erler

Introduction

The ethical debate on the practice of neuroenhancement has become a major trend in the field of neuroethics in recent years. Neuroenhancement refers to the use of a range of techniques—often biomedical technologies, which will be the focus of this chapter—by healthy people with the aim of improving their mental abilities and affective dispositions (as opposed to treating a disease or mental disorder, the purpose for which these biomedical technologies were developed in the first place). One of the most widely discussed examples of such a practice has been the use of psycho-stimulants like amphetamine (Adderall®), methylphenidate (Ritalin®) or modafinil (Provigil®) by students on various University campuses looking for a study aid (see e.g., Greely et al., 2008). Such substances are sought for their purported beneficial effects on concentration, memory, and wakefulness, but also, as has recently emerged, because they increase some users' energy levels and motivation to engage in academic work (see, e.g., Vrecko, 2013; Ilieva & Farah, 2013).[1] In this regard, psycho-stimulants are proving more similar than previously thought to another kind of intervention that had been discussed even earlier, namely the enhancement of mood and personality using antidepressant drugs like Prozac®. Psychiatrist Peter Kramer kick-started the ethical debate on this latter practice with his book *Listening to Prozac*, in which he reported anecdotes of formerly depressed patients who, even after they had gotten better (or so he reports), requested to stay on the drug on grounds that it gave them (among other things) a more socially appealing personality—for

---

[1] To be precise, we ought to distinguish among such effects between those that involve performance *enhancement* and those involving performance *maintenance* (Ranisch, Garofoli, & Dubljevic, 2013). The former category of effects allow the user to reach a level of performance that she could not reach otherwise (e.g., to remember a greater amount of information than she could without the enhancement). Effects of the latter category, by contrast, prevent one's performance level from deteriorating in the face of detrimental factors like fatigue. For the sake of simplicity, I will use the term *neuroenhancement* to cover both performance enhancement and performance maintenance.

Alexandre Erler, *Neuroenhancement, Coercion, and Neo-Luddism* In: *Neurointerventions and the Law*. Edited by: Nicole A Vincent, Thomas Nadelhoffer, and Allan McCay, Oxford University Press (2020). © Oxford University Press 2020 DOI: 10.1093/oso/9780190651145.001.0016

instance, more extroverted and less prone to negative affect (Kramer, 1993).[2]
More recently, increasing attention has also been given to various forms of brain
stimulation, such as transcranial magnetic stimulation and transcranial direct
current stimulation (tDCS), which, in addition to their relevance for the treatment of conditions like depression and schizophrenia, show the potential to enhance both mood and cognitive functions like memory, mathematical ability,
and language learning (Coffman, Clark, & Parasuraman, 2014; Cohen Kadosh,
Levy, O'Shea, Shea, & Savulescu, 2012; Meinzer et al., 2014; Santoni de Sio,
Faulmüller, & Vincent, 2014). Other interventions have also been discussed, such
as the prospect of technologically improving people's *moral* dispositions, for example, by reducing racial bias or the propensity to violent aggression (Douglas,
2008, 2013; Focquaert & Schermer, 2015; Harris, 2011). More futuristic forms of
neuroenhancement include neural implants that would allow us to connect our
brain directly to computers, thereby allowing our cognitive capacities to benefit
from the exponential gains that have characterized machine intelligence for the
past half-century at least (Kurzweil, 2005).

One of the main ethical concerns that have been raised about neuroenhancement interventions, and the one on which the present chapter will
focus, is the issue of *coercion*. The notion of coercion comes in a variety of forms,
so a few conceptual clarifications are in order here. First, in the context of the
neuroenhancement debate, it is common to distinguish between *direct* and *indirect* coercion (Dubljevic, 2013; Farah, 2012; Greely et al., 2008). A paradigm
example of direct coercion to enhance would be an employer making the willingness to use neuroenhancers an explicit requirement of a particular position
(see Chapter 17 of this volume): imagine a job description stipulating that "the
successful candidate will be willing to use [neuroenhancer X] when necessary."
The requirement need not necessarily be explicit, however. As long as a company
manager, for instance, expected all of his employees to use neuroenhancers, even
if he never stated his expectation in an "official" manner (but, say, solely relied on
hints), direct coercion would be present. In cases of indirect coercion, by contrast, no one is enforcing an actual requirement to enhance, whether explicit or
implicit. The pressure to enhance does not come directly from a recognized authority, but is rather the by-product of something else, such as expectations about
productivity. Suppose that some neuroenhancer successfully boosts productivity in some particular activity and that a number of people are using it for that
purpose. If an employer tends to hire the most productive people in that area,

---

[2] Although Kramer's (1993) book raises fascinating philosophical questions and may well fore-
shadow what will become possible in the future, let me note however that his heavy reliance on
personal anecdotes (rather than on large-scale data from peer-reviewed studies) should make us cautious before assuming that the sort of durable personality enhancement he describes is truly something we can already achieve today, whether with Prozac® or any other current method.

while having no particular expectations about neuroenhancement use itself, all applicants for this type of job will nevertheless find themselves—indirectly—under pressure to take neuroenhancers to increase their competitiveness.[3] This second, indirect form of coercion is the one that a number of students report being faced with in relation to psychostimulant use, in their quest to get good grades (e.g., Forlini & Racine, 2009; Partridge, Bell, Lucke, & Hall, 2013).

Second, it is also useful to distinguish between what I shall call "unconditional" and "conditional" coercion. Unconditional coercion, as I shall define it, occurs when someone is forced or pressured to use some intervention in circumstances where one could not reasonably be expected to defy the pressures and refuse to use that intervention. Unconditional coercion on my definition does not entail that a person simply has no choice about whether or not to accept some form of neuroenhancement—this would represent *compulsion*, a more extreme scenario. Rather, in cases of unconditional coercion, one can still make that choice, but the alternatives to enhancement are all highly undesirable, to the point that one cannot reasonably expect the agent to embrace any of those alternatives.[4] To illustrate, suppose that, as some authors believe might become appropriate in the future (e.g., Persson & Savulescu, 2008), we were to make it a legal requirement for everyone to undergo moral enhancement using biomedical means, on the grounds that this were necessary to avoid a global catastrophe. There are various ways in which we could implement such a requirement. We could for instance punish non-compliance with imprisonment: this would be an example of unconditional coercion in my sense (one would still have the choice to resist the enhancement by going to jail, although hardly anyone could reasonably be expected to make it and face its consequences). Alternatively, although this would be even more difficult to defend, we could put a moral enhancement drug into the water supply, unbeknownst to consumers (so that no one could decide to escape the drug by drinking only bottled water), or we could force-feed it to those who refused to take it. These latter two courses of action would constitute compulsion (avoiding taking the drug would not be an option at all). Most would agree that compulsion to enhance would be ethically wrong, except perhaps in highly exceptional circumstances, which is why I will not discuss it very much at all in this chapter.

Conditional coercion, on the other hand, concerns cases in which the pressure to use the relevant intervention occurs in the presence of at least acceptable alternatives for the agent, so that an individual *can* reasonably be expected

---

[3] This would include all those who do not already enjoy (say, because of natural talent) a competitive advantage so great that they can expect to remain ahead even if their less talented competitors start using neuroenhancers, and they do not.

[4] I thank Nicole Vincent for helping me see the significance of this distinction.

to pursue one of those alternatives if she does not wish to undergo the inter-vention. The inability to work for a certain company because one refused to use neuroenhancers, in the previously cited example, would thus represent an instance of conditional coercion in my sense—provided that other acceptable careers that did not require the willingness to enhance were available to that person (otherwise, we would have crossed the line into unconditional coercion).[5] Let me add that it is only appropriate to talk about someone being conditionally coerced (or facing conditional coercion) in cases where the person does *want*, for example, to exercise the profession for which neuroenhancement is required. If someone had no interest in any occupation where such a requirement was pre-sent, it would seem inappropriate to say that this person was being coerced, even conditionally, to enhance herself, just because she would be ineligible for any such occupation given her rejection of neuroenhancement.

It is worth noting, however, that the distinction between unconditional and conditional coercion is not meant to imply the existence of a sharp dividing line between the two. Rather, paradigmatic cases of unconditional and condi-tional coercion represent two ends of a spectrum, with many intermediary cases in between. First, the number of acceptable alternatives to jobs that required neuroenhancement could be greater or smaller, and cases where many such alternatives were available would represent clearer instances of conditional co-ercion than cases where only one or two such alternatives were available (which would be much closer to unconditional coercion). Second, what counts as an "acceptable" alternative is certainly, to some extent, open to debate. For instance, imagine a situation in which neuroenhancement use has become a precondi-tion of getting a university degree, because it is now so widespread that the bar for what counts as satisfactory academic work has been raised—to a level that hardly anyone can reach without the help of neuroenhancers. Would we then be dealing with conditional or unconditional coercion to enhance? Some might claim that the latter is true, arguing that a university degree has become all but a necessity in modern society and that the lack of it entails costs one cannot rea-sonably be expected to bear, whereas others might disagree, pointing to var-ious careers that do not require a university education. Controversial cases are therefore possible. Still, the existence of a gray area does not mean that there

---

[5] Coercion to enhance could also come about *after* one had already embarked on a particular career, if the use of neuroenhancers gradually became expected from those pursuing such a career, even though this expectation wasn't present originally. The coercion could either be conditional, if the person subjected to it could still reasonably be expected to transition to a different, sufficiently desirable career where neuroenhancement was not mandated, or unconditional, if such a thing could not reasonably be expected from that person. Furthermore, what was originally conditional coercion could also gradually become unconditional, if acceptable alternatives to the agent's chosen career in-itially existed but eventually disappeared as enhancement made its way through society.

are no clear-cut examples of each kind of coercion, such as those described in the previous paragraphs. A further, interesting question which I cannot explore in depth here is the extent to which the subjective perspective of the agent herself might determine what counts as an acceptable alternative. I will limit myself to suggesting that the agent's own judgment need not necessarily be decisive in this regard. We should at least make room for the possibility that someone might suffer from either (a) false consciousness and fail to recognize that the only options available to her were very poor ones (e.g., working conditions involving mistreatment) or (b) expensive tastes, leading her to discount options that the overwhelming majority of us would regard as perfectly acceptable (think of someone who refused to acknowledge any other profession than that of supermodel as a desirable career path).

In a professional context, occupations where use of idealized (and in some cases, already existing) neuroenhancers might plausibly become mandated or at least expected by employers seem numerous, in view of the various ways in which it could improve job performance. To give but a few examples, one study found that the drug modafinil had a beneficial impact on the memory and decision-making capacity of sleep-deprived doctors (Sugden, Housden, Aggarwal, Sahakian, & Darzi, 2012). Similar benefits can be expected in other professions where sleep loss is a hazard, such as long-haul truck drivers, or where a sharp focus over extended periods is key, such as air traffic controllers.[6] U.S. military pilots who refuse to take amphetamines when asked to do so can already be denied the chance to fly combat missions, with potentially damaging consequences for their career (Mehlman, 2004)—although the military is now reported to be turning to the safer alternative represented by modafinil (Mehlman, 2015). A caveat we ought to add here is that the likelihood that people will come under pressure to use neuroenhancers like modafinil partly depends on future advances in artificial intelligence and the automation of tasks that they allow. For example, self-driving trucks, which could drive for many hours with no breaks and while maximizing fuel efficiency, are already at an advanced stage of development, leading some to expect massive job losses among truck drivers in the relatively near future (Meola, 2016). In areas where technology can thus substitute for human workers, concerns about coercion to enhance may well prove irrelevant. That said, all occupations are not equally vulnerable to automation,

---

[6] It is worth mentioning, however, that the extent to which currently available substances might be suitable in those contexts is a disputed matter: to take the example of truck drivers, stimulants like amphetamines are actually believed to *increase* the risk of traffic accidents (despite their benefits for wakefulness) due to their side effects, which can include agitation, tachycardia, and even hallucinations (Girotto, Mesas, de Andrade, & Birolim, 2013). Modafinil, by contrast, seems to hold greater promise in this context (Krueger & Leaman, 2011), although some remain worried about its addictive potential (Heinz, Kipke, Heimann, & Wiesing, 2012).

and as long as humans are needed in the workforce, especially for complex and cognitively demanding tasks, the prospect of neuroenhancement will retain its appeal. In fact, this appeal might be increased if neuroenhancement can help people keep up with the performance levels attained by machines and thereby preserve at least some of their competitiveness in the face of automation.

When it comes to the technological manipulation of affect and personality, the correlation between the display of positive emotion by employees and customer satisfaction in virtually all forms of customer service is well established (e.g., Pugh, 2001), although it is worth noting that the authenticity of such displays appears to matter as well (Andrzejewski & Mooney, 2016). Insofar as employees high in traits like agreeableness, extroversion, and low in negative affect tend to be preferred to others for such jobs, those who "naturally" fall short in those areas might feel the pressure to use neuroenhancers, which—should they prove able to produce such effects, at least in the future—would likely provide a more effective and reliable path to the desired qualities than more traditional methods of emotion management (Kramer, 1993). A conscientiousness enhancer might enjoy even broader appeal, given the demonstrated association between that trait and academic and job performance (Higgins et al., 2007).

When discussing neuroenhancement interventions in what follows, I shall assume that they are effective. Admittedly, as we have just seen, this is an assumption for which the current empirical evidence is mixed (depending for instance on the type of effect sought and on the context of use) when it comes to existing interventions, which means that my discussion will be speculative to some degree.[7] In principle, coercion (both direct and indirect) to undergo such interventions could occur even if that assumption were mistaken—or at least the perception of it could—with similar consequences. Suppose it turned out, for instance, that the stimulants currently popular among some university students do not in fact help them achieve better grades but simply create a false perception that they do. As long as this perception was widespread enough, students could feel pressured to take those substances. If this were the case, however, the natural way to alleviate such pressures would be to run large-scale information campaigns about the ineffectiveness of psychostimulants as study aids, which would also highlight the risks (if any) that they posed to health and could be combined with further disincentives depending on the magnitude of those risks. A further assumption behind my analysis is that the interventions in question

[7] In particular, there is currently little evidence that neuroenhancers like psychostimulants can be used by healthy people on a regular basis, rather than just occasionally, without ever losing their effect and fostering tolerance.

are undertaken by competent adults on themselves; I shall leave aside their use on children, which raises additional ethical worries. Even focusing on the adult context, some people—philosophers and nonphilosophers alike—worry that the spread of neuroenhancements throughout society could lead to the establishment of a "new normal" (Vincent & Jane, 2014), with most people coming under pressure to use those technologies, even if they would ideally prefer not to, on pain of facing significant social and economic penalties. The concern here seems to be that even indirect coercion of this kind would be ethically problematic in itself, which implies that we ought to take active steps to protect people from it, although this may not justify going so far as prohibiting others from enhancing themselves.[8]

Is this concern about indirect coercion justified? I will suggest that it is not—at least not insofar as it entails that such coercion to enhance should worry us per se. I shall proceed by highlighting our attitudes toward existing forms of coercion to use technology, and by arguing that our stance on neuroenhancement needs to be consistent with those attitudes. While the fact that pressures to use neuroenhancers limit people's freedom of choice does count in favor of countering such pressures, I will argue that this consideration is outweighed by the many benefits we could expect from a widespread adoption of neuroenhancement. If so, the value of personal freedom of choice and the badness of coercion are not sufficient, by themselves, to justify setting up any special safeguards to protect people against indirect coercion to enhance, whether conditional or unconditional. The advent of a "new normal" involving neuroenhancers thus need not, in itself, be of concern to us. That said, I will add two concessions. First, I agree that people's right to bodily integrity demands that they should be protected from *compulsion* to enhance, as well as from most instances of *direct* coercion to do so (although there might be exceptions in that latter case). Second, I will acknowledge that *other* important considerations, distinct from coercion itself, can, when present, give us good grounds for introducing special legal safeguards even against *indirect* coercion. Furthermore, even when such safeguards are not warranted, it remains desirable to encourage, whenever possible, gestures of good will (e.g., the adoption of special accommodations) toward those who for whatever reason might not wish to use neuroenhancers. I will then conclude by responding to a few possible objections to my analysis.

---

[8] Authors who raise the coercion worry also include Appel (2008), Caplan (2003), Chatterjee (2006), Dubljevic (2013), Farah (2002), Forlini and Racine (2009), and Mehlman (2004). Greely et al. (2008) also mention it, but suggest—correctly, as I will argue later—that the need for safeguards against such coercion depends on the safety profile of the relevant interventions.

Possible Strategies Against Indirect Coercion to Enhance

Before considering whether the importance of protecting people's freedom does warrant measures to forestall the rise of indirect coercion to enhance, let us briefly consider some measures that might be introduced to that effect. The most radical one would obviously be an outright ban on the use of neuroenhancers by the healthy (while still allowing of course for therapeutic uses of those same substances or devices). In effect, this is already how drugs like methylphenidate or modafinil are regulated in the United States, since it is illegal to purchase them there without a prescription.[9] While such regulation is chiefly the responsibility of governmental agencies like the U.S. Drug Enforcement Administration and the U.S. Food and Drug Administration, there have also been private initiatives. In the academic context, Duke University thus set a precedent in 2011 by modifying their official policy on academic dishonesty in precisely such a direction: the "unauthorized use of prescription medication to enhance academic performance" was added to the types of act constituting cheating (Duke University, 2011). The type of proposal we are considering would require extending such restrictive measures (which ultimately would have to be government-enforced, rather than left to the discretion of private actors) to all neuroenhancement interventions, including some, such as tDCS, which are currently commercially available to the public (as illustrated by the much-discussed headset sold by company foc.us).[10]

One ethical difficulty that has been pointed out about this strategy is that, to protect the freedom of those who do not want to have to enhance themselves, it impinges upon the freedom of those who would like to use those interventions (Farah, 2002; Hall, 2004). Why exactly should the freedom of the former be given more weight than that of the latter? I shall argue later that a persuasive justification can be offered for such a difference of treatment, but that it needs to appeal to considerations distinct from freedom. The attempt at a full-fledged ban on neuroenhancement use would also face implementation challenges, given that the already existing black market would likely further expand and that some people might still gain access legally to the relevant interventions for enhancement purposes either by faking the symptoms of a disorder or by finding a doctor willing to facilitate their nonmedical use. For the moment, nevertheless, let us keep in mind the possibility of outright prohibition for the sheer sake

---

[9] Even though they are not regarded as equivalent in terms of their abuse potential, with methylphenidate being classified as a schedule II drug, and modafinil only as schedule IV (Sahakian & LaBuzetta, 2013, p. 148).

[10] Whether such devices currently sold to the public do have enhancing effects has been contested. For instance, one study found that the foc.us headset actually had a *negative* impact on working memory (Steenbergen et al., 2016).

of preventing indirect coercion. What more moderate alternatives could we pursue?

Another option that has been suggested would involve some form of collective action: as workers and citizens, we could take a stand together against the demand for ever-increased productivity and the other social expectations that drive the use of neuroenhancers. Among other things, this would involve voluntarily refraining from using such interventions while the choice is still up to us (Forlini & Racine, 2009; Vincent & Jane, 2014).[11] However, given the strong interest that many have in becoming more effective at doing their job (and in having at least some other people become more effective too), whether for positional or nonpositional reasons, one might doubt that the necessary critical mass of people could be won over to prevent indirect and conditional (and ultimately, perhaps even unconditional) coercion from arising—at least on the assumption that the appeal of neuroenhancers were not diminished by concerns about safety, or by prohibitive prices that could not be brought down.[12] If such voluntary initiatives are not viable, we might have to turn again to laws and regulations.

Third, we could try to make the choice to enhance less appealing, while staying away from a ban, for instance by imposing financial (taxes) and regulatory burdens (licensing procedures) on those who chose to use the relevant interventions in the absence of a medical need (for such a proposal, see, e.g., Dubljevic, 2013). A possible challenge for that strategy is that the choice to enhance—by contrast, for instance, with the choice to smoke—will often be driven by expectations of economic benefits. If neuroenhancers led to better work performance, which led to greater opportunities for career advancement and eventually to a higher income, then the burdens to be borne to use those interventions might merely represent an investment which could be expected to yield a high return once the employee has started reaping the benefits of superior performance. The burdens in question would thus have to be very heavy to deter a high enough number of people so as to forestall coercion (in which case the threat of increasing socioeconomic inequalities might arise, if only the wealthy found it profitable to invest in neuroenhancement use). Furthermore, this proposal would again likely face the challenges of a black market and of some people circumventing the economic burdens either by faking symptoms or with the help of "liberal-minded" doctors.

---

[11] For the sake of accuracy, let me note that these two articles are focused on the specific issue of *cognitive* enhancement. However, the points they make about the need to prevent coercion seem to apply just as well to other forms of neuroenhancement.

[12] In the latter case, coercion might still affect the few wealthy people who could afford the relevant interventions. Others would strictly speaking be protected from such coercion by their insufficient means, given that being coerced into doing something arguably presupposes being able to do do that thing. This economically less advantaged group might instead simply suffer the consequences of such a new competitive disadvantage without being able to do anything about it.

On reflection, we may question whether any of those strategies (or further alternatives that I may not have considered) would be successful in staving off the rise of indirect coercion to enhance. Let us, however, set those doubts aside, and assume that at least one of these would work well enough (which particular one might be superior is not crucial to the rest of my discussion). Would we then be justified in implementing it simply for the sake of protecting people from such coercion? I now want to defend a negative answer to that question.

Freedom, Neo-Luddites, and the "New Normal"

Consider the attitude that our society appears to take toward those referred to as Neo-Luddites,[13] that is, people who, for ethical or religious reasons or simply out of personal preference disapprove of most modern technology, including computers, mobile phones, the Internet, and sometimes ATMs and cars. Examples of contemporary Neo-Luddites include, among religious groups, the Amish, and among secular figures, authors like Chellis Glendinning, Kirkpatrick Sale, and the infamous "Unabomber" Ted Kaczynski (a rather isolated case in his espousal of violent activism). Although Neo-Luddites differ in the specific grounds of their opposition to modern technology, they tend to accuse it of weakening communities, undermining worthy traditions, promoting warfare, destroying the environment, revealing human hubris in our pretension to achieve dominion over nature, and encouraging "a mechanistic approach to life" (Glendinning, 1995, p. 84; see also Sale, 1995). In our technologically oriented society, in which Neo-Luddites are presumably a minority, there is no doubt that many professional, economic, and political opportunities will be closed to them if they act on their dislike of modern technological devices. And while this loss of opportunity still does not, for the most part, translate into coercion in the case of the Amish, who form a largely independent community with—for the most part—no wish to join the broader society, the same cannot be said of secular Neo-Luddites who are part of the dominant culture. Many jobs in that culture thus require both the willingness and ability to use computers, email, and the Internet; in a number of cases, the only way to apply for a job is online. Even when no actual requirement to use them is present, rejection of those technologies will still put one at a competitive disadvantage by closing off important sources of information and channels for communication. Public libraries often

---

[13] Named after the original Luddites, a group of English textile workers who protested against the evolution of their working conditions in the early 19th century, including the introduction of technological devices that diminished the need for skilled laborers. One tactic they employed involved attacking loom factories and destroying machines (Banning, 2001).

offer computerized catalogues exclusively. Computers are found in virtually any car manufactured today. And so on. Secular Neo-Luddites thus face both direct and indirect coercion to use devices they would prefer not to use (and which, in fact, they would prefer to see eliminated). Even their most prominent activists have made concessions to the tech world for the sake of promoting their ideas: the books of Glendinning (1990) and Sale (1995) can thus be purchased on Amazon—some are even available in Kindle format.[14]

Nonetheless, I take it, most of us do not believe that the pressures bearing on all members of our society to adopt those technologies, and the costs to be faced for refusing to do so, are ethically unacceptable and that new antidiscrimination laws should be passed to protect Neo-Luddites from such costs. Imagine a committed—although perhaps not very pragmatic—Neo-Luddite who wishes to pursue an academic career, which he expects would help his views gain respectability and influence the thinkers of tomorrow, yet is unwilling to make any compromise with regard to his antitechnology convictions. It may well be *nice* if the institutions to which he applied for positions were willing to make special arrangements for him out of respect for his personal beliefs and allowed him for example to send only hard copies of his application documents or, assuming he were to be hired, to allow him not to use email (thereby becoming the envy of his colleagues besieged by messages) and to write his academic papers by hand, or on a typewriter, to be then converted into electronic format by another staff member when necessary. Yet it nevertheless does not seem that it would be *wrong* of the university, or discriminatory, to decline to consider this person's application if he refused to comply with their initial expectations—even though the fact that this person could not pursue an academic career due to his rigid personal convictions might still strike us as regrettable and as something it would be desirable to avoid when possible by allowing such special provisions to be made.

Does our attitude reflect mere prejudice, or can it be supported by argument? There is no doubt that the generalized use of computers, email, mobile phones and other instances of modern technology significantly facilitates communication and coordination within companies and other organizations, which helps further the legitimate goals that such entities pursue, such as greater efficiency and productivity. And in some cases, this can be expected to benefit not only individual organizations, but society as a whole. Greater efficiency in conducting medical research, for instance, means that new life-saving treatments or vaccines will take less time to arrive. The development of medical technology, from magnetic resonance imaging machines to clinical decision support systems, has

---

[14] In fact, Sale now appears to have resigned himself to the inexorable march of technology and to the coercive pressures that come with it: in a recent interview, he describes attempts to continue the Neo-Luddite battle as "futile" (Hill, 2014).

helped improve the ability of physicians to diagnose and treat their patients. Besides their positive impact in the practice of medicine, computers are also yielding precious assistance in other contexts, such as commercial aviation, which is now safer than it has ever been, partly thanks to the role of digital technology in preventing dangerous situations from arising. Computer simulations help us predict the weather and make breakthroughs in physics, engineering, and various other fields. It seems quite plausible to think that these numerous social benefits outweigh the badness of the pressures we are under to use those technologies, even if these pressures mean that some (the Neo-Luddites) must go against their own convictions to conform to them or face reduced opportunities if they refuse.

It seems to me that a similar argument could be made about indirect coercion to use neuroenhancers. Indeed, neuroenhancement interventions of the sort we have reviewed at the beginning would, *if* they could deliver on their promise, bring many of the same benefits as computers, for instance. By increasing productivity and improving the quality of service of some workers, they would promote the legitimate goals of the organizations that employ them. They would also have broader social benefits. Doctors who, thanks to neuroenhancers, reasoned better at the end of a long shift would be less susceptible to medical errors. Air traffic controllers and truck drivers with better focus and faster reaction times would make road and air travel even safer than they are today, potentially saving many lives. Were neuroenhancement to become the norm among scientists, the pace of research might accelerate, again meaning that crucial breakthroughs (such as new treatments for various diseases) would come sooner.[15] Here again, it seems that the expected social benefits outweigh the badness of the existence of indirect coercion to enhance. Therefore, ceteris paribus, our attitude to such coercion should be the same as our attitude to the kind of coercion experienced by Neo-Luddites in the Digital Age.

That said, since this last statement is only true ceteris paribus, it does not mean that, as a matter of fact, we have no reason whatsoever to take preventive measures against indirect coercion in relation specifically to neuroenhancement. Indeed, neuroenhancers of the type I am envisaging might still involve

---

[15] As mentioned previously, we should remember that whether or not neuroenhancement will bring such benefits depends to some extent on future advances in machine intelligence. It may be that many of these benefits will in fact be secured by delegating tasks to intelligent machines, rather than through a neuroenhanced workforce. However, we have also seen, first, that automation may not affect all professions equally, at least in the near term; in some fields, the introduction of neuroenhancement might be more relevant than in others. Second, even assuming significant progress in artificial intelligence, neuroenhancement might still help human workers avoid getting left behind by machines in terms of work performance. Any coercive pressures that these technologies might create should therefore be weighed against the fact that they might also contribute to protecting employment opportunities for people!

normatively relevant differences with the more familiar technological devices we have just discussed. When these differences are present, they will give us additional reasons—distinct from considerations of freedom and autonomy—to ensure that people are protected from indirect coercion to enhance, reasons that can in principle outweigh even the significant benefits to be derived from the general adoption of neuroenhancement. It is to this issue that I turn next.

Reasons Why Coercion to Enhance Might Be Objectionable

What considerations could make indirect coercion to use neuroenhancers morally more problematic than coercion to use the technological devices that represent the current "normal"? I will begin by considering one difference that quickly comes to mind: the invasive nature of neuroenhancers, in virtue of which any coercive pressure to use them might be said to violate people's right to bodily integrity. I will argue that while this consideration does show *compulsion* to enhance, as well as most cases of *direct* coercion, to be ethically objectionable, this does not extend to indirect coercion. I will then look at three other factors which I do take, when present, to render indirect coercion to enhance problematic and which might misleadingly suggest that such coercion is objectionable in its own right: these factors are lack of safety, fostering adaptation to oppressive circumstances, and having negative side effects that go beyond health.

The Right to Bodily Integrity

Neurointerventions of the sort previously described are arguably more invasive than the use of devices like computers. Both types of intervention, it may be noted, interfere with brain functioning in some way. Even the mere act of using a computer involves having certain sensory experiences (e.g., visual sensations of a computer screen) that form part of our brain activity, and learning, say, how to type on a keyboard produces synaptic connections in our brain that are different from those we would have developed had we only ever relied on pen and paper, for instance. Nevertheless, computers and similar devices typically affect brain functioning only indirectly, by means of the sensory organs, whereas neuroenhancement interventions do so directly, by introducing a foreign element into a person's body or brain. In the case of psychoactive drugs, a chemical substance is introduced into the person's body and crosses the blood-brain barrier. And even with an intervention like tDCS, which is often described as noninvasive, an electric current travels through a person's scalp and skull to certain areas of her brain.

Granting the greater invasiveness of neurointerventions, what are its normative implications? It might plausibly be argued that the right to bodily integrity—that is, the right to resist unwanted interferences with one's own body—represents a fundamental human liberty that ought to be protected by the law. The common acceptance of such a principle presumably explains, for instance, why vaccinations (another invasive procedure) are, in places like North America, not mandatory in most professional contexts. Many hospitals in the United States have made flu vaccinations mandatory for health-care workers (Tuttle, 2015), but a number of them also allow for exemptions, not just for medical reasons but also for religious or philosophical ones. Since the right to bodily integrity is arguably a very important one, it suggests that at least most employers should not be allowed to directly coerce their employees into using neuroenhancers.

That being said, the same rationale does not seem to apply to indirect coercion. Take again the example of vaccinations. Perhaps it would be wrong of most employers to indirectly coerce their employees into getting vaccinated, for example, by showing preference for candidates with no objections to vaccination in their hiring practices. But assuming this would indeed be wrong, it is presumably because employees who reject vaccinations present no serious risk of harming the functioning and productivity of the companies they work for (or the health of their colleagues). If so, their employers lack any strong reason to expect them to get vaccinated. However, if a person's objection to vaccinations could in fact be expected to significantly hinder her productivity (and thereby that of the company), for example, by causing her to take extended periods of sick leave, *and* if that person did not have valid reasons for her view[16] (but held it, for example, on the basis of mistaken empirical beliefs), then it would no longer seem problematic for an employer to be less willing to hire people holding such a view. In line with what I have argued to this point, I would treat analogous cases involving indirect coercion to enhance in the same manner.

What is more, even in the case of vaccinations, not all hospitals incorporate exemptions for health-care workers. In some cases, workers have been fired for refusing vaccination on nonmedical grounds (Tuttle, 2015). The reasoning of the employers in such cases is that such workers present a threat to those around them, particularly patients with already fragile health. In the case of neuroenhancers, we have seen that in some professions, they might be expected to save lives, for example, by reducing the number of medical errors among doctors. When the stakes are so high, it is no longer clear that people's right to bodily integrity should always trump the need to prevent serious harm to people to the greatest possible extent. It might therefore conceivably be appropriate,

---

[16] Valid reasons could for instance be medical ones (intolerance to some vaccines). I will consider such reasons in relation to neuroenhancement in the next section.

under certain conditions and in certain professional contexts to tolerate even direct coercion (although not compulsion) to enhance—even though such cases will presumably be the exception rather than the rule, as most professions do not involve stakes of that magnitude. The interest of a company in maximizing the productivity of its employees for the sake of profit clearly does not carry the same ethical weight as society's interest in avoiding preventable deaths in contexts like medicine or air travel.

For those who, at this point, might still have the intuition that even indirect coercion to use neuroenhancers is ethically problematic because it threatens bodily integrity, I now want to suggest that it might be possible to explain that intuition by appeal to a distinct consideration—namely, the implicit assumption that such invasive interventions present a serious risk for users.

Safety

Arguably, it is problematic when a person is coerced, even in an indirect manner, into using interventions that pose significant risks to her health. Very weighty considerations will be needed to justify such a practice, and it isn't clear that the expected benefits of neuroenhancement just listed will be weighty enough. The chronic use of psychostimulants like Adderall® is thus known to have a variety of side effects, from milder ones like dry mouth and insomnia to potentially serious conditions including addiction, psychosis, cardiovascular problems, and even sudden death (Lakhan & Kirchgessner, 2012). It would seem wrong to pressure doctors or air traffic controllers to compromise their health by taking such substances, even if this could be expected to yield significant social benefits. Similarly, if it were to turn out that Ritalin® and Adderall® use really had become necessary for many students to keep up with their peers in terms of academic performance (and was not merely perceived as such), this might provide a justification for an outright ban on the nontherapeutic use of those substances by students, to be enforced by drug tests if necessary. While such a system would certainly be coercive toward those who wished to use those stimulants despite the risks involved, it would be similar in spirit to, say, the widespread practice of banning smoking in public places to forestall harm from passive smoking. True, we have seen that, already today, U.S. pilots can be pressured to use substances like amphetamines or modafinil to complete long flight missions. But first, taking such drugs is to some extent in the pilots' own interest, insofar as it reduces their risk of having a crash due to fatigue,[17] and, second, one might argue that matters

---

[17] A similar argument would apply in the case of long-haul truck drivers, yet in their case there seems to be more room for adjusting work conditions so as to remove the need for stimulant use.

of national defense are weightier than even the sort of considerations I have adduced in favor of neuroenhancement in other contexts.

Importantly, however, our safety-based reason to protect people from coercion to enhance will only hold for interventions which, in light of our current knowledge, do not appear safe enough. While this likely applies to substances like amphetamine, the status of other drugs like modafinil or of interventions like tDCS is less clear. Modafinil has so far appeared to have a significantly better safety profile than amphetamine, although controlled studies of its long-term effects on healthy users are still lacking (Porsdam Mann & Sahakian, 2015). The safety of tDCS has already been demonstrated in controlled laboratory settings, but not yet in the "real" world (Dubljevic, Saigle, & Racine, 2014). It might be argued on that basis that no one should be pressured to become a guinea pig by undergoing interventions the long-term safety of which is still in doubt. Notice, however, that we seem willing to tolerate pressures of just that kind in relation to some familiar technological devices: the health effects of long-term mobile phone use are thus still not known with certainty, and in 2011 mobile phone radiation was classified as "possibly carcinogenic" by the International Agency for Research on Cancer (World Health Organization, 2011; see also Maron, 2016). Yet very few of us are protesting at the fact that avoiding exposure to cell phone radiation is virtually impossible in our society. This still doesn't mean that coercion to use modafinil or tDCS is necessarily acceptable—for instance, modafinil has a number of side effects that are absent from mobile phones, and as we have seen, some researchers are concerned about its addictive potential (Heinz, Kipke, Heimann, & Wiesing, 2012; Volkow et al., 2009). The line at which an intervention can be considered "safe enough" is a tricky one to draw, but wherever we choose to draw it, it is important not to set more stringent standards for neuroenhancers simply because they are recent and unfamiliar, or because some of them bear the bad name of "drugs."

So far I have been considering scenarios in which neuroenhancement posed a health risk for all or at least most people. However, we could also imagine a case in which the relevant interventions were only dangerous for a minority of people with a specific bodily constitution. The members of that unlucky minority would then find themselves pressured to take risks that most people in their society did not have to face to remain competitive on the job market (and perhaps other contexts, too). Would a ban on most neuroenhancement technologies be justified in that type of case as well? In light of the expected benefits of a wide adoption of neuroenhancement, adopting such a ban would seem difficult to defend and would be at odds with our existing practices. Consider, for instance, that people with certain disabling conditions (e.g., osteogenesis imperfecta, which causes brittle bones that are prone to fracture) may face a heightened risk of injury at their workplace or while commuting. As a result, it may be safer for these people to work from home. Many employers, however, may prefer their employees to be present at the workplace, creating pressures on members of the group with disabilities to face the associated risks. Still, our society does not try to counteract these pressures by forcing everyone to work at home, and neither does it forbid employers to expect nondisabled employees to travel to the workplace. Rather, people with disabilities are protected from such pressures from prospective employers in two ways. The first one is disability benefits, for those who have difficulty finding adequate employment and have limited resources to live on. Second, civil rights laws like the American With Disabilities Act require employers, in certain cases, to provide "reasonable accommodations" for people with disabilities. This could involve allowing an employee to work from home, to come back to the example previously described. That said, employers are only subject to such a requirement provided that the accommodation will allow the employee to perform all the essential functions of the job and that it will not create an "undue hardship" for the employer (Zackin et al., 2015).

If an unlucky minority were to emerge for whom neuroenhancement technologies presented a health risk, its members should be granted some of the same legal protections as those that people with disabilities enjoy today. Which protections exactly? Given that the job performance of workers who did not use neuroenhancers would usually be inferior to that enhanced workers (i.e., after all, one of the core purposes of neuroenhancement),[18] it might be difficult to make a persuasive case for requiring employers to show no preference for enhanced workers in their hiring practices. Offering a form of compensation akin to disability benefits to those who suffered from their inability to enhance themselves might be a more defensible proposal. Nonetheless, this issue is a complex one where the right conclusion might depend on a number of factors, including the magnitude of the health risks encountered by the unlucky minority and the opportunity costs that would be entailed by measures destined to secure equal employment prospects for the members of that minority. Depending on the details of the situation, we might decide that adopting such measures would in fact be appropriate.

I would maintain, however, that there would be no adequate grounds for extending such compensatory or protective measures to people who abstained from neuroenhancement purely out of personal preference or on the basis of

---

[18] Of course, this might not always be true, as it would partly depend on the magnitude of the enhancement, as well as on each person's "natural" level of performance; for example, a person of average intelligence who was able to boost her IQ to 130 thanks to neuroenhancement would still not match "natural" geniuses.

philosophical or religious beliefs hostile to technology, if they faced no health risks from the relevant procedures—just as people who might demand to work from home for similar, nonmedical reasons would not be entitled to any special compensation for, or protection against, the associated loss in their professional opportunities.

Fostering Adaptation to Oppressive Circumstances and Corrupting a Person's Affective Life

By oppressive circumstances, I mean circumstances in which a person's significant interests, potentially grounding corresponding *rights*, are being disregarded, with the result that the person is deprived of a significant component of a good human life. The interests in question can be varied. Consider someone who has just experienced the loss of a close relative. Even though there is no federal law in the United States requiring employers to grant "bereavement leave" to employees who find themselves in such a situation, many companies do have policies granting a number of days off work (usually around three) to bereaved employees, for the purpose of allowing them to attend funeral services but also to mourn their loss. (In some countries like Canada, this practice is actually legislated in most jurisdictions.) Suppose now that, due to the advent of a safe and effective mood and/or motivation enhancer, companies with a bereavement leave policy decided to shorten or even terminate it, on the grounds that it was no longer necessary for their employees to experience the feelings of dejection that normally accompany bereavement—and that tend to cost the company money by temporarily diminishing productivity. It would arguably be wrong of companies to deprive their employees of bereavement leave in this way (or even to be more willing to hire candidates who freely agreed to forfeit it), as, first, this would go against the employees' significant interest in expressing their love for the departed through mourning, and, second, it would pressure them to corrupt their affective lives by preventing themselves from experiencing fundamental human emotions that were appropriate to the situation they were in.[19]

---

[19] Admittedly, this second charge would especially apply if the relevant mood enhancer were to constantly affect the emotional state of bereaved employees as long as they kept taking it. It would have less force in a scenario where the effects of the enhancer were short-lived and dissipated once the working day was over (provided that one stopped using it until the next morning). In the second scenario, unlike the first, the bereaved person could still experience the "right" emotions outside of the work context. The employee's high mood level at work might still be troubling, and coercion to artificially induce it would still seem problematic, but the concern would be less pronounced.

Other examples could be given. Suppose for instance that the customer service advisors of a company came under pressure to use a new personality enhancer that would (safely) give them an unshakably agreeable disposition, one they would retain even when dealing with the rudest of customers, because their managers expected this to maximize customer satisfaction.[20] Here too, one might argue that such pressure from their employer was wrong because it required them to adjust to oppressive circumstances: circumstances in which their interest in defending themselves (with due politeness) against insults, thereby preserving their self-respect, would be frustrated. Furthermore, it would again have a corruptive influence on their character by making them overly docile. While agreeableness probably does constitute a reasonable requirement of positions of this kind, it does not follow that a customer service advisor should *always*, even when confronted with aggressive, racist, or otherwise disrespectful people, behave agreeably if she is to do her job well.

Admittedly, it is less clear that such a line of argument could be extended to employers who required their employees, whether directly or indirectly, to display the maximum degree of agreeableness, extraversion, or sunniness still lying within the "healthy" range of those traits (so that they didn't collapse into obsequiousness or gullibility), either with a view to promoting customer satisfaction or to satisfy their own individual preferences for certain personality traits. Indeed, talk of corrupting the users' affective dispositions would no longer seem appropriate in such cases. And it does seem appropriate to grant employers a certain leeway (although not an unlimited one) with respect to the personal qualities of applicants that they can base their hiring decisions on. There are at least two types of situation in which it could be legitimate for an employer to allow a candidate's personality to affect her hiring decision: first, if the candidate's personality could be expected to affect her future job performance, as well as that of the company as a whole, and, second, if her personality were likely to affect the atmosphere in the workplace. For instance, a very unpleasant person who did not get along with any of her colleagues could compromise the performance of her working group, even if individually she were very efficient. And even if she had no negative impact on anyone's performance, because others had learned how to put up with her bad attitude, she might still negatively affect everyone's mood at the office. If an employer had good reason to foresee any of these consequences, it seems that she would be entitled to decline to hire this person on account of her disagreeable personality.

Finally, suppose that some white-collar workers at a company started using a safe pharmaceutical that significantly boosted their motivation to

---

[20] From the perspective of the managers, the intervention would thus count as a personality enhancer, even though we may not regard it that way.

work and safely reduced their need for sleep to four hours a night, thereby enhancing their productivity. Thanks to the intervention, they find it easy to tolerate a 120-hour workweek, partly because they now need less sleep and partly because they have a diminished interest in nonwork-related activities, including social interactions with friends and family (to mirror an effect of Adderall® described by Vrecko, 2013, p. 9). Their personal life becomes impoverished as a result of this workaholic lifestyle, but since their foremost priority is career advancement, they are willing to pay the price. Their superior productivity soon earns them the favors of the management in the form of promotions and bonuses, inciting other workers to adopt the enhancement too. Soon, enough people at the company are working 100 hours or more a week with the help of neuroenhancers to put pressure on the rest of the employees to follow suit, on pain of being viewed as setting everyone back and eventually losing their job. Slowly, the 100-hour-plus workweek creeps into social expectations and becomes the "new normal." Most of us, I assume, would regard this as a nightmarish social development—as society having adapted to, and promoting, an oppressive workaholic mindset.[21] While we may very much welcome an enhancer that safely reduced our need for sleep, we would presumably still object to it if it also impacted our motivational set and lifestyle in this manner.

All of these examples involve the corruption of an employee's affective life, as well as an adaptation to oppressive circumstances in which a significant interest shared by all people gets frustrated, even though a different interest is being disregarded in each case. In the first (bereavement) case, this interest is the chance to mourn the loss of a loved one; in the second (customer service) case, it is the ability to act so as to protect one's self-respect; and in the third (workaholic) case, it is the enjoyment of an adequate work-life balance.[22] Perhaps we could take one step further and add that a corresponding right is also being violated in each scenario—that is, respectively, the right to mourn, to self-respect, and to an adequate work–life balance. The last of these putative rights, however, might elicit the objection that in contexts like the American one, it is agreed that some

[21] One might object that this scenario is implausible, because most people would object to such a social development, including many employers who desire work–life balance for themselves, which would prevent that state of affairs from ever becoming the norm. While I very much hope that this is correct, and that the course of action recommended by Vincent and Jane with regards to cognitive enhancement would be followed in relation to the workaholic pill, it nevertheless seems at least conceivable that the scenario I have described could occur: for instance, those at the top of the ladder might either regard minimal amounts of free time as adequate, or they might secure better conditions for themselves than for their employees, who in turn might feel they had no choice but to accept such an extreme work schedule (and might simply get progressively used to it).

[22] In addition to these, there is presumably another interest (or even right) being disregarded in all scenarios, namely, the interest in not being pressured to corrupt one's own affective life or character.

people, such as Wall Street bankers, can legitimately be expected by their employer to work 80 to 100 hours a week on a regular basis. Unlike most European countries, the United States does not have regulations stipulating a maximum number of working hours per week (Kaufman, 2013).[23] However, even recognizing such a practice as legitimate need not conflict with the view that everyone, including Wall Street bankers, has a right to work–life balance, one would then just have to add that people can permissibly waive that right, if they wish for instance to trade it for an extremely lucrative career.

At the regulatory level, I would argue that if a scenario like the workaholic pill were ever to become reality, maximum working hours, of the kind set out in the Working Time Directive (European Council, 2003) of the European Union (which sets the limit at 48 hours per week on average, although we could debate whether this amount is adequate or not) should be used as a tool to protect people from unconditional coercion to use such a neuroenhancer. However, I leave it open whether exceptions to that regulation should be allowed for certain occupations (as is the case in countries like the United Kingdom). Perhaps conditional coercion to take the workaholic pill could be tolerated, as long as we could be confident that it would remain confined to just a few specific domains and would not spread to the rest of society. If the risk of it spreading were sufficiently real, however, it would give us a reason not to allow any exceptions at all to maximum working hours.[24]

Similarly, when it comes to the bereavement and the customer service scenarios, I would support laws prohibiting employers from directly or indirectly coercing their employees into using the relevant neuroenhancers, in the spirit of existing laws meant to protect people with disabilities from discrimination. However, I would be less inclined to consider the possibility of exempting certain employers or professions from such regulations than in the case of working time, because the human goods that would then be sacrificed are arguably of even greater ethical importance than work-life balance is. While sacrifices of work-life balance are viewed as undesirable yet are commonly tolerated provided that they are only temporary, someone who sacrificed their self-respect, even temporarily, would usually be considered as having suffered a serious ill, not just an inconvenience.

---

[23] While some jobs do require employers to pay their employees more if they make them work beyond a certain number of hours per week (so-called overtime), there is no upper limit on overtime hours in the United States (Lee et al., 2007).

[24] Let me emphasize that this conclusion applies to the example of the workaholic pill as I have specifically characterized it. A few tweaks in the example might elicit quite different intuitions. For instance, in the case of a pill that safely cut our need for sleep by half, but had no impact on our motivational set, we might not necessarily object if part of the waking time thus gained were devoted to working a few more hours per week.

Negative Side Effects That Go Beyond Health

Even if the coercion to enhance did not foster adaptation to oppressive circumstances, it could still have serious negative side effects, impacting not the person's health but rather her well-being or interests.[25] These side effects could mean that the person now had maladaptive emotional and behavioral dispositions, but they could also simply consist in a large amount of unnecessary psychological suffering. Consider again the example of workers seeking to increase their productivity. Rather than resorting to a workaholic pill, they might use a neuroenhancer that gave them laser-like focus and cleared their thinking, allowing them to get more done within a given amount of time and with no loss of quality. Suppose, however, that the effects of the intervention do not dissipate as soon as the working day is over, but persist until late into the night, as a result of which users strike those around them as being constantly hyper-focused, lacking in spontaneity, and incapable of relaxing. Their social and personal life would therefore suffer, even though the length of their work week might not be excessive (unlike the workaholics, they don't work longer hours, just more effectively) and their general work conditions, not oppressive.[26]

Other, similar examples could be offered: for instance, one could imagine employees (say, waiters in busy establishments) being pressured to use memory enhancers to perform better at work, and then becoming tormented by unwanted, unpleasant memories they otherwise wouldn't have retained (Erler, 2011). Again, if the use of such interventions were to spread because of the competitive advantage they conferred at work, thereby putting pressure on people to use them and suffer the consequences, we would have a problematic scenario that might require imposing disincentives, or even a complete ban if necessary, on the use of the relevant interventions, to protect people from coercion to use them. The general thing to note about scenarios of this kind is that this particular reason to object to such coercive pressures would disappear if the interventions in question could be fine-tuned to the point where they no longer had such negative side effects. For instance, it might be possible to ensure that the effects of some neurointervention didn't last longer than the period of time during which they were desired (i.e., working hours), either by using an intervention that only

---

[25] Which by the definition given in section 4.3, would mean ultimately creating oppressive circumstances for the person—but this time would not foster *adaptation* to such circumstances.

[26] This contrast is sometimes overlooked. My impression is that the common worry that neuroenhancement will unavoidably promote oppressive imperatives of performance and productivity only derives plausibility from the fact that, usually, these imperatives demand sacrificing our work-life balance, or health (or both). But in principle, neuroenhancement need not demand sacrificing either: e.g. it might simply make us more effective and productive by making us smarter. There is nothing intrinsically oppressive about demanding that people use more rather than less effective tools to improve their job performance, provided that the use of these tools is safe enough.

had short-term effects and adjusting one's intake accordingly, or by using another intervention to cancel out the effects of the first when needed.[27]

There are, therefore, a variety of reasons why indirect coercion to enhance might prove objectionable, including, to recapitulate, the fact that it might pose a threat to the health of users; that it might foster adaptation to oppressive circumstances; and finally, that it might have harmful side effects other than health effects. Nevertheless, these reasons are distinct from the intrinsic badness of coercion itself. This means that, if an effective neuroenhancer turned out to be available that avoided these various ethical pitfalls (and any other I may have omitted), there would be no good grounds for regarding coercion to use that intervention as ethically problematic. Or at least, such coercion would be no more problematic than the one we already tolerate in relation to the technological devices to which Neo-Luddites are hostile.

Possible Objections

I will conclude by considering potential objections that might be leveled at the analysis I have offered. As I cannot pretend to be exhaustive, I will limit myself to three that come readily to mind.

Cognitive Liberty

First, it might be argued that the position I have defended neglects people's right to cognitive liberty—which has been characterized as "a right to (and not to) direct, modify, or enhance one's thought processes" (Sententia, 2013, p.356; see also Bublitz, 2013). Such an important right, it might be said, would be threatened by coercive pressures—even of the indirect kind—to use neuroenhancers, whereas that is not the case with the pressures to use computers and other similar technological devices that we already tolerate. Indeed, the argument would go, while neuroenhancers clearly involve the modification and enhancement of our thought processes (that is, after all, their very purpose!), one might find it less clear that tools like computers do so as well. After all, unless we accept the somewhat controversial thesis of the extended mind, we may doubt that the use of computers or smart phones improves, say, our concentration or memory (in

---

[27] No doubt, such a process may not be without its own complications. Counteracting the potential undesirable side effects of memory enhancement by blunting or erasing memories, for instance, would raise a number of issues: is there a risk that people might go too far in re-writing their own memories? How far is "too far"? And even if one only wished to mimic "normal", healthy forgetfulness, how would one even know what that concretely meant?

fact, we may fear that it impairs those capacities!), no matter how useful these devices might be in other ways. If there were indeed such a difference between neuroenhancers and more traditional technological devices, they would call into question my claim that indirect coercion to use the former should be regarded as ethically on a par with similar coercion to use the latter (which as we have seen is not usually considered problematic).

For the most part, however, this objection does not stand up to scrutiny. (I will add two caveats in a moment.) Working on a computer for many hours, by impacting our sensory experience, certainly modifies our thought processes (compared to what they would be if we were using different tools to do our work). Furthermore, computers that provide us with information we couldn't have obtained otherwise (such as those that allow us to run weather forecast models), or help us make complex decisions (such as clinical decision support systems), arguably enhance our thought processes or at least our ability to make decisions (e.g., whether to go for an evening walk, or to stay home because the weather is likely to turn inclement). Even if it became difficult and penalizing—as it already is to some extent—to avoid relying on those devices for the purpose of weather forecasting, making a medical diagnosis, and in other contexts, should we object to that state of affairs on the grounds that it constituted an illegitimate infringement on our cognitive liberty?[28] If not, then that notion does not justify objecting, either, to a "new normal" that involved neuroenhancers.

That being said, it should be acknowledged, first, that this objection may have greater plausibility when applied to *compulsion* to enhance. Physically forcing someone, against their will, to use a computer, or to watch a certain movie, would typically be wrong, and this might partly be explained by the fact that it would involve an interference with their thought processes to which they had not consented (not even implicitly) and were, on the contrary, opposed. In cases of indirect coercion, however, interventions are not imposed on users without their consent (even though they may resent the pressures that they face to use those interventions).

Secondly, there is one particular type of indirect coercion to enhance that would indeed raise legitimate concerns about potential infringements of cognitive liberty: namely, coercion to use neural implants that would be vulnerable to hacking. This would especially apply to implants that got connected—at least occasionally—to the internet, in order for instance to vastly expand the amount of information directly accessible to a person's mind, or to enable "telepathic" communication between the brains of two different people, who could be located

---

[28] There are various other ways in which people are expected to modify their minds for professional purposes: think of employee training programs, for instance.

in opposite parts of the planet. Hackers could conceivably break into such a system and gain access, say, to a person's private memories stored in digital form. Worse, they might even be able to tinker with those memories, or with some of the person's thought processes, and ultimately influence the person's behavior by taking control of her implant (a process that has been dubbed "brainjacking"; see Pycroft et al., 2016). Such actions would constitute serious violations of privacy and cognitive liberty, and there would be solid grounds for working to prevent even indirect coercion to use interventions that put one at a non-trivial risk of suffering such harms. Presumably, this concern only applies to a subset of neural implants, provided that it is possible to create hacker-proof implants (if only by confining them to offline use), yet it is an important one to bear in mind, nonetheless.

Isn't There Something to the Neo-Luddites' Arguments?

A second possible objection would be that I have been too quick to assume that there is nothing problematic about the sort of pressures we already tolerate in relation to technology use. Isn't there more to the Neo-Luddites' arguments than I have been willing to recognize? After all, the global increase in computer use has brought a number of health issues, such as visual and musculoskeletal problems. I have already mentioned the uncertainty surrounding the impact of long-term mobile phone use on health. Used laptops, mobile phones, digital cameras and other electronic devices are being dumped by the millions into developing countries, where they are dismantled in often unsafe conditions, leading to environmental damage and harmful effects on the health of local populations. As a result of the ubiquity of mobile phones, many employees are now expected to be reachable on an almost constant basis, allowing working time to seep into their private lives and elevating their stress levels. Finally, there is evidence that the use of computers and cell phones, while allowing people's social networks to spread out through geographic space, has simultaneously led to a reduction in the probability of face-to-face encounters with family and friends, and promotes a wider array of weak social ties rather than more localized yet stronger ties (e.g., McPherson et al., 2006), which some might interpret as vindicating the Neo-Luddites' concern about the weakening of community ties due to the spread of technology.

While these may all be valid concerns, two things should be noted here. First, it isn't clear that recognizing their force implies that we should accept the validity of the Neo-Luddite position on modern technology. For one thing, the Neo-Luddites fail to acknowledge the many benefits it brings, and which need to be weighed against its drawbacks; for another thing, it may be possible to address these drawbacks otherwise than through the radical solution of turning away from such technology. The musculoskeletal disorders experienced by many computer users can be prevented by, for instance, maintaining good posture and taking frequent breaks. The harmful effects of electronic waste could be dealt with by promoting recycling, as well as inciting manufacturers to design devices in a more environmentally-friendly way (so they can be repaired and recycled wherever possible) and discouraging planned obsolescence.[29] As for the negative social effects of computer and cell phone use, they can be mitigated by working to change our attitudes and behavior: e.g., by deliberately limiting our use of those devices (especially outside of work) to make time for real-life interactions, and by negotiating with employers so that expectations about being reachable remain as much as possible confined within certain limits and do not extend, for instance, into vacation time.

But more importantly, even if we assume that there is in fact more to the Neo-Luddite view than I have been willing to acknowledge, this still wouldn't contradict the central claim I have defended: namely that the sheer existence of coercion to use modern technology is not in itself bad enough to warrant taking measures to counteract it, whether in relation to technological devices like computers or to neuroenhancers. While adopting the Neo-Luddite pro-posal would admittedly eliminate coercion to use such technology, it neverthe-less wouldn't do so *for the sheer sake* of eliminating it, but rather on the basis of distinct considerations, such as those just listed (health, social harms, and en-vironmental damage). Set aside those considerations, and technology use again appears overall desirable in light of the expected benefits, even if it leads to some degree of coercion.

Wouldn't the "New Normal" Create Oppressive Circumstances?

This reply can help us answer a third and final objection, which would ask what prevents Neo-Luddites themselves from arguing that they have a sig-nificant interest in staying away from computers and also, presumably, from neuroenhancers. After all, whatever one thinks of their beliefs about tech-nology, they surely have a strong interest in being able to live in accordance with them. Such an ability does seem to represent an important component of a good human life. On my own account, then, can't the Neo-Luddites complain

---

[29] By its very nature, of course, technological progress makes the phenomenon of obsolescence unavoidable, and we may well be seeing it evolve at a faster rate today than it ever has previously. Still, this should not be equated with the notion of *planned* obsolescence, which involves deliberate efforts to shorten a product's lifespan so as to force consumers to buy a replacement sooner (even though the replacement product need not improve in any way upon its predecessor).

of being forced to adjust to oppressive circumstances? And won't the same be true of all the opponents to neuroenhancement, if it ever becomes the new normal?

Two things should be said in response. First, it is not clear that Neo-Luddites are completely unable to live in accordance with their personal beliefs, even amid the ubiquity of modern technology in contemporary society. Indeed, they can still avoid using such technology whenever possible, and express their condemnation of it in oral or written form, as authors like Sale and Glendinning have been doing. Admittedly, there is a significant cost to such avoidance, and sometimes avoidance is simply not an option, in which case compromises are required. But this is still not the same as having no leeway to follow one's Neo-Luddite beliefs. Similar remarks would apply to those who opposed neuroenhancement in a world in which it had become the "new normal."

It might be objected here that the compromises that people with such convictions would have to make would be very significant indeed, and that this would largely deprive them of the good of being able to follow these convictions. This leads me to my second point: the extent to which such people can be said to be facing oppressive circumstances and to be deprived of an important human good arguably depends on the plausibility of the beliefs that they want to follow. And I would claim that, because those beliefs are not supported by truly persuasive arguments in the case of the Neo-Luddites and of those who oppose neuroenhancement under any form, the good that these people might miss out on by living in a society where such interventions have become the norm is not of the same magnitude as the sacrifice of one's self-respect or the long-term loss of work–life balance. As a result, their circumstances are not plausibly characterized as oppressive, even though they may experience them as such. Being unable to fully live out one's personal philosophy is not necessarily enough, absent any constraints on the content of that philosophy, to count as finding oneself in oppressive circumstances. People whose personal philosophy or religion tells them that friendships are vicious, or that civilization is evil, arguably do not count as living in oppressive circumstances if they find themselves unable to avoid all friendships or all contact with the fruits of modern civilization—even though society should avoid hindering their pursuit of their own conception of the good, provided that this does not entail unacceptable social costs.[30]

---

[30] And if we suppose, again, that the Neo-Luddite position is in fact more plausible than I incline to believe, it might then become appropriate to say that Neo-Luddites are currently facing oppressive circumstances. But this would not simply be because they are unable to fully live in accordance with their personal philosophy; rather, it would be because they are (by hypothesis) suffering the harms from technology that that philosophy has identified.

Conclusion

If the central argument I have presented here is correct, the prospect of neuroenhancement becoming the "new normal" is not, in itself, a proper source of ethical concern, insofar as the coercive pressures it would create would be of the indirect type (as opposed to compulsion and most cases of direct coercion, which are indeed problematic in themselves and should be forestalled by appropriate regulation). Nevertheless, there are various distinct factors that could make the advent of this "new normal" problematic. I have tried to spell out what these factors might be.

The question then becomes: once we acknowledge the relevance of those factors, will we end up agreeing, when it comes to regulating neuroenhancement, with those who believe that coercion to enhance should be opposed as such? The answer will depend on whether neuroenhancers already exist, or at least can reasonably be anticipated in the near future, that are both effective, safe, and can be widely used without leading to the ethical pitfalls I have described. Further empirical evidence will be needed to establish this. At any rate, given the contingent nature of the link between these pitfalls and neuroenhancement use, it is important to be clear about what our justification is if we do decide that safeguards against indirect coercion are needed, so that we can identify what sort of future, improved interventions might in principle render that justification obsolete. Whether or not such safeguards are appropriate, however, it remains desirable for society to promote, within the limits of practicality, a spirit of tolerance for dissenters from technology that would mitigate the costs they will unavoidably have to bear as a consequence of their personal beliefs.

References

Andrzejewski, S. A., & Mooney, E. C. (2016). Service with a smile: Does the type of smile matter? *Journal of Retailing and Consumer Services, 29*, 135–141.

Appel, J. M. (2008). When the boss turns pusher: A proposal for employee protections in the age of cosmetic neurology. *Journal of Medical Ethics, 34*(8), 616–618.

Banning, D. (2001). Modern day Luddites. *Media Technologies and Society*. Retrieved from http://www.jour.unr.edu/j705/rp.banning.luddite.html

Bublitz, J. C. (2013). My mind is mine!? Cognitive liberty as a legal concept. In E. Hildt & A. G. Franke (Eds.), *Cognitive enhancement: An interdisciplinary perspective* (pp. 233–264). Dordrecht, The Netherlands: Springer.

Caplan, A. (2003). Is better best? *Scientific American, 289*, 104–105.

Chatterjee, A. (2006). The promise and predicament of cosmetic neurology. *Journal of Medical Ethics, 32*, 110–113.

Coffman, B. A., Clark, V. P., & Parasuraman, R. (2014). Battery powered thought: Enhancement of attention, learning, and memory in healthy adults using transcranial direct current stimulation. *Neuroimage, 85*(Pt 3), 895–908.

Cohen Kadosh, R., Levy, N., O'Shea, J., Shea, N., & Savulescu, J. (2012). The neuroethics of non-invasive brain stimulation. *Current Biology, 22*(4), R108–R111.

Douglas, T. (2008). Moral enhancement. *Journal of Applied Philosophy, 25*, 228–245.

Douglas, T. (2013). Moral enhancement via direct emotion modulation: A reply to John Harris. *Bioethics, 27*, 160–168.

Dubljevic, V. (2013). Cognitive enhancement, rational choice and justification. *Neuroethics, 6*, 179–187.

Dubljevic, V., Saigle, V. & Racine, E. (2014). The rising tide of tDCS in the media and academic literature. *Neuron, 82*(4), 731–736.

Duke University. (2011). Student conduct: Academic dishonesty. Durham, NC: Author.

Erler, A. (2011). Does memory modification threaten our authenticity? *Neuroethics, 4*(3), 235–249.

European Council (2003, November 4). Directive 2003/88/EC of the European Parliament and of the Council. Retrieved from https://eur-lex.europa.eu/legal-content/EN/ALL/?uri=CELEX:32003L0088

Farah, M. J. (2002). Emerging ethical issues in neuroscience. *Nature Neuroscience, 5*, 1123–1129.

Farah, M. J. (2012). Neuroethics: The ethical, legal, and societal impact of neuroscience. *Annual Review of Psychology, 63*, 571–591.

Focquaert, F., & Schermer, M. (2015). Moral enhancement: Do means matter morally? *Neuroethics, 8*, 139–151.

Forlini, C., & Racine, E. (2009). Autonomy and coercion in academic "cognitive enhancement" using methylphenidate: Perspectives of key stakeholders. *Neuroethics, 2*, 163–177.

Girotto, E., Mesas, A. E., de Andrade, S. M. & Birolim, M. M. (2014). Psychoactive substance use by truck drivers: A systematic review. *Occupational and Environmental Medicine, 71*, 71–76.

Glendinning, C. (1990). Notes toward a Neo-Luddite manifesto. *Utne Reader, 38*, 50–53.

Glendinning, C. (1995). Technology Can Be Damaging. In O. W. Markley & W. R. McCuan (Eds.), *America Beyond 2001: Opposing Viewpoints* (pp. 82–88). San Diego: Greenhaven Press.

Greely, H., Sahakian, B., Harris, J., Kessler, R. C., Gazzaniga, M., Campbell, P., & Farah, M. J. (2008). Towards responsible use of cognitive-enhancing drugs by the healthy. *Nature, 456*, 702–705.

Hall, W. (2004). Feeling "better than well." *EMBO Reports, 5*, 1105–1109.

Harris, J. (2011). Moral enhancement and freedom. *Bioethics, 25*, 102–111.

Heinz, A., Kipke, R., Heimann, H., & Wiesing, U. (2012). Cognitive neuroenhancement: False assumptions in the ethical debate. *Journal of Medical Ethics, 38*(6), 372–375.

Higgins, D. M., Peterson, J. B., Pihl, R. O., & Lee, A. G. (2007). Prefrontal cognitive ability, intelligence, big five personality, and the prediction of advanced academic and workplace performance. *Journal of Personal and Social Psychology, 93*, 298–319.

Hill, K. (2014), July 15). The violent opt-out: the Neo-Luddites attacking drones and Google Glass. *Forbes.* Retrieved from http://www.forbes.com/sites/kashmirhill/2014/07/15/the-violent-opt-out-people-destroying-drones-and-google-glass/-35d3c3913bb7

Ilieva, I. P. & Farah, M. J. (2013). Enhancement stimulants: Perceived motivational and cognitive advantages. *Frontiers in Neuroscience, 7*, 198.

Kaufman, G. (2013). *Superdads: How fathers balance work and family in the 21st century.* New York, NY: New York University Press.

Kramer, P. D. (1993). *Listening to Prozac.* New York, NY: Viking.

Krueger, G. P., & Leaman, H. M. (2011). *Effects of Psychoactive Chemicals on Commercial Driver Health and Performance: Stimulants, Hypnotics, Nutritional, and Other Supplements.* Washington, DC: Transportation Research Board of the National Academies.

Kurzweil, R. (2005). *The singularity is near : When humans transcend biology.* New York, NY: Viking.

Lakhan, S. E., & Kirchgessner, A. (2012). Prescription stimulants in individuals with and without attention deficit hyperactivity disorder: Misuse, cognitive impact, and adverse effects. *Brain and Behavior, 2*(5), 661–677.

Lee, S.-H., McCann, D. M., Messenger, J. C., & International Labour Organization (2007). *Working Time Around the World : Trends in Working Hours, Laws and Policies in a Global Comparative Perspective.* London; New York; Geneva: Routledge; ILO.

Maron, D. F. (2016). Major cell phone radiation study reignites cancer questions. *Scientific American.* Retrieved from http://www.scientificamerican.com/article/major-cell-phone-radiation-study-reignites-cancer-questions/

McPherson, M., Smith-Lovin, L., & Brashears, M. E. (2006). Social isolation in America: Changes in core discussion networks over two decades. *American Sociological Review, 71*(3), 353–375.

Mehlman, M. J. (2004). Cognition-enhancing drugs. *Milbank Quarterly, 82*, 483–506.

Mehlman, M. J. (2015). Captain America and Iron Man: Biological, genetic and psychological enhancement and the warrior ethos. In G. Lucas (Ed.), *Routledge handbook of military ethics* (pp. 406–420). New York, NY: Routledge.

Meinzer, M., Jahnigen, S., Copland, D. A., Darkow, R., Grittner, U., Avirame, K., . . . Floel, A. (2014). Transcranial direct current stimulation over multiple days improves learning and maintenance of a novel vocabulary. *Cortex, 50*, 137–147.

Meola, A. (2016). Self-driving trucks will hit the road more quickly than cars. *Business Insider.* Retrieved from http://www.businessinsider.com/self-driving-trucks-will-hit-the-road-more-quickly-than-cars-2016-4?IR=T

Partridge, B., Bell, S., Lucke, J., & Hall, W. (2013). Australian university students' attitudes towards the use of prescription stimulants as cognitive enhancers: Perceived Patterns Of Use, Efficacy And Safety. *Drug and Alcohol Reviews, 32*, 295–302.

Persson, I., & Savulescu, J. (2008). The perils of cognitive enhancement and the urgent imperative to enhance the moral character of humanity. *Journal of Applied Philosophy, 25*, 162–177.

Porsdam Mann, S., & Sahakian, B. J. (2015). The increasing lifestyle use of modafinil by healthy people: Safety and ethical issues. *Current Opinion in Behavioral Sciences, 4*, 136–141.

Pugh, S. D. (2001). Service with a smile: Emotional contagion in the service encounter. *The Academy of Management Journal, 44*, 1018–1027.

Pycroft, L., Boccard, S. G., Owen, S. L., Stein, J. F., Fitzgerald, J. J., Green, A. L. & Aziz, T. Z. (2016). Brainjacking: Implant security issues in invasive neuromodulation. *World Neurosurgery, 92*, 454–462.

Ranisch, R., Garofoli, D., & Dubljevic, V. (2013). "Clock shock": Motivational enhancement, and performance maintenance in Adderall use. *AJOB Neuroscience, 4*, 13–14.

Sahakian, B. J., & Labuzetta, J. N. (2013). *Bad moves: How decision making goes wrong, and the ethics of smart drugs.* Oxford, England: Oxford University Press.

Sale, K. (1995). *Rebels against the future : The Luddites and their war on the industrial revolution: Lessons for the computer age.* Reading, MA: Addison-Wesley.

Santoni de Sio, F., Faulmüller, N. & Vincent, N. A. (2014). How cognitive enhancement can change our duties. *Frontiers in Systems Neuroscience, 8,* 131.

Sententia, W. (2013). Freedom by design: Transhumanist values and cognitive liberty. In M. More & N. Vita-More (Eds.), *The transhumanist reader: Classical and contemporary essays on the science, technology, and philosophy of the human future* (pp. 355–360). Oxford, England: Wiley.

Steenbergen, L., Sellaro, R., Hommel, B., Lindenberger, U., Kuhn, S., & Colzato, L. S. (2016). "Unfocus" on foc.us: Commercial tDCS headset impairs working memory. *Experimental Brain Research, 234,* 637–643.

Sugden, C., Housden, C. R., Aggarwal, R., Sahakian, B. J., & Darzi, A. (2012). Effect of pharmacological enhancement on the cognitive and clinical psychomotor performance of sleep-deprived doctors: A randomized controlled trial. *Annals of Surgery, 255*(2), 222–227.

Tuttle, B. (2015). Workers are being fired for refusing to get flu shots. *Time.* Retrieved from http://time.com/money/4101787/flu-shot-mandatory-workers-fired/

Vincent, N., & Jane, E. A. (2014, June 15). Put down the smart drugs—Cognitive enhancement is ethically risky business. *The Conversation.* Retrieved from http://theconversation.com/put-down-the-smart-drugs-cognitive-enhancement-is-ethically-risky-business-27463

Volkow, N. D., Fowler, J. S., Logan, J., Alexoff, D., Zhu, W., Telang, F., . . . Torres, K. (2009). Effects of modafinil on dopamine and dopamine transporters in the male human brain: Clinical implications. *JAMA, 301*(11), 1148–1154.

Vrecko, S. (2013). Just how cognitive is "cognitive enhancement"? On the significance of emotions in university students' experiences with study drugs. *AJOB Neuroscience, 4*(1), 4–12.

World Health Organization, International Agency for Research on Cancer. (2011, May 31). IARC classifies radiofrequency electromagnetic fields as possibly carcinogenic to humans. Retrieved from http://www.iarc.fr/en/media-centre/pr/2011/pdfs/pr208_E.pdf

Zackin, R. S., Boyarsky, M., & Jarusiewicz, L. J. (2015). Telecommuting as an accommodation—A legal quandary for employers. *New Jersey Law Journal.* Retrieved from http://www.gibbonslaw.com/Files/Publication/8bce2eed-6b82-448e-80c3-2933fe125251/Presentation/PublicationAttachment/2c01d554-22b1-4422-8377-2db7cc27a5a4/NJLJ employment law supp Aug 2015.pdf

17

Neurointerventions and Business Law

On the Legal and Moral Issues of Neurotechnology in Business and How They Differ From the Criminal Law Context

Patrick D. Hopkins and Harvey L. Fiser

Introduction

In the past 30 years a great deal of thought has gone into looking at the relationship between law and burgeoning neuroscience. Much of that investigation has focused on criminal law. That is to be expected since criminal law is more popularly familiar, more widely addressed in entertainment media, and for many ethicists, legal scholars, and scientists goes to the heart of thorny and important issues of responsibility, guilt, causation, punishment, justice, and free will.

However, there is another important area in which neuroscience will interact with the legal world that is only beginning to be studied—business law, understood broadly as comprising commercial law, contracts, some parts of civil law, corporate law, and, for purposes of this chapter in particular, employment law. While the issues of business and neuroscience might at first seem to lack some of the luridness of courtroom drama there are good reasons to delve into them.

First, the sheer number of people directly engaged with the employment sector of society dwarfs the number of those directly engaged with the criminal justice sector of society, with, for example, in a recent one-year period in the United States, 7 million[1] people under correctional system authority and 140 million people under employment law authority (Bureau of Judicial Statistics, 2015; U.S. Census Bureau, 2014).

Second, work, employment, and commerce permeate culture in ways that organize and orient most people's daily life experience more profoundly than we

---

[1] In 2015, approximately 6.7 million people were incarcerated in U.S. prisons.

Patrick D. Hopkins and Harvey L. Fiser, *Neurointerventions and Business Law* In: *Neurointerventions and the Law.*
Edited by: Nicole A Vincent, Thomas Nadelhoffer, and Allan McCay, Oxford University Press (2020).
© Oxford University Press 2020
DOI: 10.1093/oso/9780190651145.001.0017

tend to realize. The necessity of work and the quotidian presence of the jobs we need, want, train for, avoid, lose, love, or hate makes the profound organizing presence of employment in our lives invisible precisely because of its ubiquity. With (roughly on average) a third of every week spent unconscious in sleep; a third spent scattered about in various leisure, chore, and social activities; and a third spent working, the experience most citizens have as workers forms the single largest block of adult experienced life.[2] To the extent that neurotechnology affects employment, neuroscience holds out a potentially much larger change for society than its effects on criminal justice.[3]

Third, although many of the same concerns that appear in neuroscience and criminal law appear in neuroscience and business law—concepts of responsibility, rights, autonomy, agency, and privacy—a different set of relationships, constraints, motivations, choices, and legal standards apply, which means both that analyses of concepts and concerns in criminal neurolaw do not necessarily apply to business neurolaw and also that the puzzles and problems of business neurolaw have their own fascinating character.

In other places, we have laid out the ways in which neurointerventions could affect employment law, policy, tort liability, and the culture of employment—sometimes in more extensive detail, sometimes in more summary detail (Fiser, 2016; Hopkins & Fiser, 2017). We do not want simply to repeat those analyses here but do want to provide an overview of neurointervention and employment law and emphasize its contrast to criminal law. To that end, we will explain the business and employment context, particularly as it is distinguished from the criminal justice system context. We will then survey what neurointerventional technology could accomplish in the business setting and show why various people might be motivated to use it. Next, we will lay out the basic options for law and policy dealing with employment-related neurointerventions. We conclude with an admonition to remember the importance of the psychological value of work and its proper place in human life.

---

[2] There is variation depending on age, location, financial status, and health status, but as an example, the U.S. Bureau of Labor Statistics (2015), in its American Time Use Survey of 2014, reported that for employed people between the ages of 25 to 54 with children, the average number of hour spent sleeping on a work day was 7.7 and the average number of hours working was 8.9, with leisure, sports, eating, household activities, and other tasks taking up 7.4 hours.

[3] The amount of time we spend on our jobs is amazing enough when compared with other life activities. The average full-time employed American is estimated to work for 47 hours per week, with 25% reporting working more than 60 hours per week (Saad, 2014).That compares to an estimate of roughly 18 hours of leisure (half of which is reported as passive television watching) and roughly 48 hours of sleep a week (Bureau of Labor Statistics, 2015; J. M. Jones, 2013; Saad, 2014).

The Business Law Context

Contrast to Criminal Law

Business law comprises a wide variety of legal matters. We are focusing on employment law here, but elements of various noncriminal and criminal law practices are imbricated throughout employment relations. In general, however, we will mark the largest differences between employment law and criminal law by highlighting the following areas and showing what an important difference they make for neurolaw analyses:

Contracts

Most of the relationships between employers and employees, companies and customers, and companies and other companies (including rights and duties of all involved) are mediated by way of contracts.[4] While in some oblique sense, criminal law operates with contracts in that voluntarily taking a particular position may subject an individual to specific criminal law restrictions and simply continuing to do business or just be a citizen of a particular state may implicitly commit one to following its laws, for the most part, people find themselves nonvoluntarily already situated within a criminal law setting. We do not sign on the dotted line to abstain from murder, theft, and rape in return for remuneration and health insurance benefits. We always already have certain justice system obligations and violations of those obligations are treated as offenses against society. By contrast, in employment law, one's obligations are largely generated by what one agrees to do and one agrees to those obligations in return for some form of consideration (such as payment). As such, the obligations can vary widely depending on the needs of the employer, the abilities and desires of the employee, and are adopted, avoided, or abrogated willingly and explicitly.

Privacy

As suggested by the importance of contract-regulated norms, employment law is mostly about private relationships between people (typically individual humans and the "artificial persons" of corporations).[5] While there are, of course,

---

[4] For a broad guide to U.S. contract law, see Rosenhouse (1992) and Farnsworth (2004).

[5] Unions form a different kind of agent relation in that unions are not corporations and not individual humans. However, labor organizations are included as "persons" under the definitions of the U.S. National Labor Relations Act of 1935 (National Labor Board, 1935) and are composed of employees who bargain collectively through organizational representatives. The bargain reached is treated functionally as a labor contract, but is still technically with each employee, not with the union as a corporate person. As Robert Gorman writes in *Young v. North Drury Lane Productions, Inc* (1976), "a labor agreement is not a contract of employment; employees are hired separately and individually, but the tenure and terms of their employment once in the unit are regulated by the provisions of the collective bargaining agreement" (p. 540).

criminal restrictions on what sorts of relationships individuals can engage in, the employment contract within those limits means that violations are treated as offenses against individuals and are typically governed by civil law systems. A wronged person files a lawsuit against a wrongdoer rather than a prosecutor filing charges (as an agent of the state) against a citizen, as in criminal cases. In general, this means that the desires, expectations, knowledge, and beliefs of the individuals involved have a primary effect on what counts as wrongdoing and being wronged.

Protections

Considered as a grave matter of justice and individual rights against the state, criminal law is replete with protections for the accused that limit the power of the state, but these protections do not shelter individuals in civil proceedings. Familiar criminal law concepts of double jeopardy, speedy trials, ex post facto law immunity, warrantless searches, the right to a lawyer, and safety from self-incrimination do not normally apply to civil employment disputes. There is typically far less concern for individual liberty and privacy in civil cases. The one area in which protection has been prominent in employment is discrimination law—although that concept can be both more and less restrictive than generally appreciated. Commonly people tend to think that employers cannot "discriminate" on the basis of sex, religion, race, etc. However, the notion of a job qualification is paramount. If a job requires a certain racial appearance, sex, or religious affiliation, then the employer can discriminate (it is important here to note that "discriminate" simply means to recognize differences between things or events and that there is a distinction between just and unjust discrimination in making decisions).

Burden of Proof

Not only are protections for defendants fewer and weaker in employment civil cases, the burden of proof for the accuser is lower. Whereas criminal culpability requires a "beyond a reasonable doubt" standard, civil cases require only a "preponderance of evidence" standard. In addition, criminal cases nearly always allow for a trial by jury but civil cases may often be decided by a smaller jury or even a single judge.

Vicarious Responsibility

Generally, in criminal law, the person charged, tried, and punished is the person who directly committed the criminal act. They have both the mens rea and the actus reus attached to them. While there are various degrees of intent, action, and conspiracy, the basic idea is that responsibility lies with the person who intended to act and then did act. In civil cases, however, especially as it pertains to employee behavior, the concept of vicarious liability is very strong. All kinds of third parties to an action can be held liable for what another person does. It is often the case that the employer of an employee who causes some harm is considered liable for training them badly, not monitoring them enough, or even for having hired them in the first place without accurately predicting potential bad behavior (foreshadowing the applicability of neurointerventions).

Punishment

Much of the difference in proof and protection standards arise from the perception that civil cases typically involve less serious punishments. In criminal cases, a defendant is charged by the state with an offense against the state and if found guilty, faces punishments ranging from fines to imprisonment to death. In civil cases, defendants are accused by other individuals (or classes of individuals) and may be found more-or-less liable for some wrongdoing. Punishments usually include only monetary damages or injunctions to cease or engage in some activity. Jail time or death are never options. Of particular note is that in criminal cases the issue is more about the state punishing someone for antisocial behavior. In civil cases, the issue is more about compensation for the person who was wronged rather than punishing the wrongdoer (although there is the exception of extraordinary punitive damages). This is why it makes sense in a civil case that a defendant might offer a plaintiff money to drop the suit, whereas a defendant offering money to the prosecutor's office to drop a criminal charge would be judged as far less acceptable.

The difference between the criminal and business law contexts are important in general and important specifically for issues of neurointervention. In criminal law, the primary issue is whether or not a punishable individual is innocent or guilty of competently, willingly, and knowingly committing an antisocial act as defined by a system in which they already exist. In employment law, the primary issue is what sorts of contracts individuals may voluntarily engage in, what obligations those contracts produce, and to what extent they are liable for actions that they or other parties perform related to that contract. These are very different sorts of things.

Types of Business Agents

While judges, juries, legal counsel, and defendants show up in both contexts, there are notable differences in the major roles they play in business and criminal law. Whereas main categories of agents in the criminal justice system include the state prosecutor, the police, and the accused, the business law system has its own set of major agents.[6]

Employers

The individual human, group, or corporation that has work that needs to be done and will provide compensation for that work is a primary agent in employment law. Employers both create the job and determine what the necessary requirements are for those who hold that job. As such they will rightly be interested in the abilities and capacities of job applicants, in predicting the suitability and performance of applicant, and in specifying expectations implicitly or explicitly through contracts and rules. Keep in mind that unless an employer is the sole and complete owner of a business, the vast majority of humans making decisions about employment will also themselves be employees, with their own set of contractual job obligations. Few people will be solely in the role of employer. With regard to the issue of neurotechnology, employers will be interested in improving verification of applicants' abilities, predicting performance, monitoring, and improving a worker's productivity.

Employees

The individual human who works for another entity in return for compensation is also a primary agent in employment law. An employee typically works under a specified job description, some form of contract (oral or written, implicit or explicit), and their work and position is constrained by a set of legally recognized rights and duties. Discussions of ethics and policy often treat employees as the subordinate member of an unbalanced power dyad with employers having the upper hand. Whether or not that characterization is accurate, however, is highly contextual and depends on the specific labor market's supply and demand. In many cases, employees (or applicants) competitively market themselves and select from a number of options and positions, with the employer just as much bound to the resulting negotiated contract as the employee. With regard to the issue of neurotechnology, employees will be interested in how extensive or invasive screening procedures might be, what the specific duties of their job would include, whether they themselves might be encouraged or required to modify themselves to qualify for or excel at the

---

[6] Nicole Vincent has made the interesting point that in criminal law the victim has a minor role. The very notion of "victimless crimes" (such as driving while intoxicated attests) to the conceptualization of crime as an offense against the state or the people. Victims of crimes do not even get mentioned in the names of cases—whereas in civil law a case might be named *Smith v. Big Company*, in criminal cases a case would be named *The State v. Jones* (personal communication, August 10, 2017). Also, see U.S. Federal Courts (n.d.).

position, and how they might independently use neurotechnology to modify themselves to improve their skills, abilities, competitiveness, mood, or satisfaction with work.

Legislators/Regulators/Enforcers

Although there are significant differences between them, the people who create the laws by which employment relationships are governed, who codify and specify the actual requirements of that legislation, and who enforce those laws and regulations are also important players. While all of these people are employees as well—of government typically, although possibly of trade unions or arbitration firms—and thus subject to the regulation and issues all employees are subject to, they also create the system in which those issues are framed. A wide variety of neuroscience information could be relevant to generating that system, particularly empirical information related to the psychology of work and economic productivity. Equally powerful in practice, however, empirical evidence shows that people are strongly biased to ignore empirical evidence and are instead motivated by various emotional reflexes and cognitive biases in making rules and enforcing them (Cooper & Kovacic, 2012; Eskridge & Ferejohn, 2002). Assumptions about work, freedom, satisfaction, and productivity are bound up in folk psychology and tradition. To the extent that legislators and regulators are responsible for creating more effective and healthy work systems, they would be professionally (if not also morally) obligated to consult the empirical literature.

Customers

Finally, people who purchase the goods and services that businesses provide are central agents in business law—although as customers per se they predominantly fall outside the realm of employment law and into the broader area of business and economic regulation. Ways in which customers participate in business law broadly include consumer protection acts, contractual relationships, and truth-in-advertising laws. With increasing information about neuromarketing techniques, customer behavior is likely to become something that could be more precisely predicted and affected, leading to concerns about psychological manipulation and, likely, expansion of consumer protection law to neurotechnology (Fiser & Hopkins, 2017). The specific way customers can interact with employment law as customers per se, however, is in negligent hiring and negligent supervision torts, in which customers can sue employers for having insufficiently screened or inadequately managed their employers. As we have argued elsewhere, negligent employment torts are likely to be a major vector through which neurointerventions are expanded in an attempt to reduce liability (Fiser & Hopkins, 2017).

Types of Employment Situations

A number of specific situations arise within the employment context that are very different from the criminal law context. The situations differ with regard to manner of their creation and to the variability in what legal obligations they engender. They will also provide a variety of points in which neurotechnological interventions could be applied.

Job Creation

Creating a new position and specifying the requirements and conditions of that job are usually based on an analysis of work needs and markets. This is typically done in response to either increased work or a change in the type of work. While many new job designs may largely copy existing roles from other businesses, it is possible to tailor something unique for a particular business. The key issue is laying out what tasks need to be performed and what traits and abilities an employee would need to perform that job—potentially including traits and abilities that could only result from neurointerventions, for example, better-than-normal memory, persistent alertness, better-than-normal vision, the ability to go without sleep for long periods of time without cognitive decline, higher- or lower-than-normal empathy, temporary elimination of implicit racial bias, or an enhanced ability to produce or detect lies (Hopkins & Fiser, 2017). There is nothing illegal per se about specifying that a job requires some ability no ordinary human has.

Hiring

Applying for a job, screening candidates, determining whether an applicant is qualified for the job, and ranking qualified applicants is largely about predicting specific job performance. It involves a variety of psychological and physical assessments—all things that neuroscience is increasingly providing more sophisticated tools for. Such assessment involves not only choosing the best candidate for the employer's needs, but also shielding the employer against direct and vicarious liability for having chosen a poor candidate—for example, an incompetent employee whose actions result in harm to a client.

Training and Assigning

This process involves educating and inculcating skills for both new hires and for existing employees (whose jobs are changing or who are moving to new positions) and selecting employees for specific tasks based on an assessment of their abilities and past work performance. The tasks may include specific physical, occupational, and intellectual skills but often include character traits, moral traits, and social skills. Although involving many of the same assessments as the hiring process, assigning work is subtler and typically involves those people who are already under the aegis of an employment contract.

Rewarding

This process involves evaluating existing employees for purposes of commending them, promoting them, or providing bonuses. The evaluation typically focuses on work performance but in many cases includes social and moral contributions to the business or group.

Disciplining

This process involves evaluating existing employees for purposes of reprimanding them, demoting them, docking them, or firing them. The evaluation process may include procedures similar to rewarding employees, but the legal ramifications are harsher and legal justifications more constrained than for rewarding. As a result, there is a stronger focus on demonstrated job performance, future job performance, job qualifications, failed remediation, and surveillance of employee performance. Assessments of the employee are generally held to a higher standard for firing than hiring since the employer already indicated a judgment of qualification and expectation of success—a situation that indicates how important initial assessment is. As negligent hiring lawsuits increase, however, hiring assessments are likely to increase in depth and thoroughness (Fiser & Hopkins, 2017).

Types of Employee Characteristics

Employers look for certain characteristics in potential employees. While some of the traits that are looked for are obvious, some are not quite so and it is useful to delineate them explicitly. In some cases, traits that might appear to be irrelevant to any job and not a legitimate axis of selection are in fact relevant and have been expressly ruled as legitimate considerations by regulation. In some cases, traits that might only rarely appear in job ads and job descriptions because they seem intangible become more explicitly relevant precisely because neurotechnology may be able to detect or modify them.

Appearance

This refers most commonly to the way a person looks—their attractiveness, their apparent gender or apparent race, their physiognomy, their size. More broadly speaking, it could include not only the visual but anything detectable by ordinary senses, such as the auditory (how a person's voice sounds), or olfactory (how a person smells). While there is sometimes a quick reaction to say that appearance should not be considered part of a job qualification, it is expressly clear in law and practice that it is. Whether only hiring women for jobs as lingerie models, only hiring people with certain racial appearance features for ethnic marketing, or only hiring physically attractive people for receptionist work, there are many cases in which appearance is a legally recognized requisite for employment. The purpose in pointing this out is not because appearance is particularly related to potential neurotechnological adjustment, but rather to show that what counts as a violation of legal labor rights is relative to the specific qualifications of a job.

Skills

This refers to the set of current abilities an applicant or employee possesses, in the sense that they can do something or perform some task. Skills do not have to be something that a person has learned. They may include any ability—learned or not—such as having 20/20 vision or being able to lift 100 pounds. Some skills may be explicitly related to the job (e.g., "Applicant must be proficient in SPSS software") while some skills may be directly related but less easy to quantify (e.g. "Applicant must be friendly and able to put people at ease"). We divide relevant skills into five subcategories (which ends up being important for potential neurotechnological and other bodily modification) each of which ranges from the general to the very specific: physical, intellectual, social, communication, and cognitive.[7]

Capabilities

This refers not to existing abilities, but rather the capacity a person has to develop new skills, knowledge, and physical traits that might be needed for future work. Similar to the difference between the storage capacity of a hard drive and the programs that are currently installed, capabilities indicate what an employee would be able to do in the future. They include the more familiar "mental"

---

[7] "Categories of skills include *physical skills*, which are bodily abilities that range from the specific task-oriented (must be able to lift 200 lbs., must be able to type 100 words a minute) to general (must be coordinated, have 20/20 vision, good hearing, endurance). *Intellectual skills* are facilities in thinking, understanding, and problem-solving involving mathematical, verbal, and analytic areas and include the specific (must be able to calculate specific mathematical functions) to general (must have an extensive vocabulary, must good at problem-solving and critical thinking). *Social skills* are a constellation of abilities that facilitate team work, interaction, and generally getting along with others. They are typically described in general terms (listening, collaborating, being respectful, being assertive) but in certain jobs can be specifically delineated (make frequent eye contact, does not fidget, has a firm handshake). *Communication skills* are related to social skills in interpersonal contexts but include a variety of abilities from general (good writer, good speaker) to specific (must be fluent in Spanish). Finally, *cognitive skills* are more akin to physical skills in that some are learned and some are part of the natural lottery. They are not the same as intellectual skills because they refer to more general abilities related to cognitive function such as alertness, attentiveness, recall speed, executive functioning, perception accuracy, fine motor control, spatial processing, and emotional self-regulation" (Hopkins & Fiser, 2016, 785–786).

traits such as memory capacity, learning speed, and focus, but can also include "physical" traits such as longevity, vitality, muscle responsiveness, and bodily coordination.

Attitudes

This refers to mental dispositions, moods, feelings, and evaluative tendencies that shape one's behavior and interpretation of events. Attitudes are not the same thing as beliefs—although they shape and are shaped by beliefs—but rather are conative and affective judgment tendencies.[8] They may be either explicit (consistent with beliefs) or implicit (and either consistent with or run counter to expressed beliefs) and there are instruments by which to measure their nature and strength.[9] Attitudes can run from the very general (trusting, optimistic, pessimistic, upbeat, gloomy, suspicious, aloof, practical, apathetic, passionate) to the more specific (racist, sexist, self-confident, self-defeating).

Moral Character

This refers to relatively persistent personality traits that are distinctly related to moral emotion, normative judgment dispositions, and the strength or weakness of personality.[10] Moral character is partly a matter of judging a person as good or bad but also partly identifying a set of psychological traits that contribute predictively to determinations of a person's future behavior, of their future normative judgments, and of other people's normative judgments about them. They involve dispositional qualities related to moral judgments and behaviors such as courage and cowardice, generosity and stinginess, arrogance and humility, kind and spiteful, and quarrelsome and friendly. It is important here to be aware that the traditional "virtue" is not always the trait an employer would want. In some cases—say, a loan officer responsible for evaluating loan applications—being

---

[8]   Attitude itself is a psychological construct that is somewhat debated, but most influentially, Eagly and Chaiken (1998, p. 1) describe attitudes as "a psychological tendency that is expressed by evaluating a particular entity with some degree of favor or disfavor." Hogg and Vaughan (2005, p. 150) describe it as "a relatively enduring organization of beliefs, feelings, and behavioral tendencies towards socially significant objects, groups, events or symbols." All of these emphasize the idea that attitudes contain enduring emotional orientations toward objects, not just propositional belief content or like/dislike. For a comparison and debate over the best models of attitude, see Gawronski (2007).

[9]   For information on the development of the concept of implicit attitudes and tests for measuring them, Greenwald and Banaji (1995), Greenwald, McGhee, and Schwartz (1998), Whitley (2010), and "Project Implicit" (n.d.).

[10]   Definitions of "moral character" typically emphasize the stability and enduring quality of personality traits and judgments dispositions. For example, "The virtues and vices that comprise one's moral character are typically understood as dispositions to behave in certain ways in certain sorts of circumstances. For instance, an honest person is disposed to telling the truth when asked. These dispositions are typically understood as relatively stable and long-term. Further, they are also typically understood to be robust, that is, consistent across a wide-spectrum of conditions. We are unlikely, for example, to think that an individual who tells the truth to her friends but consistently lies to her parents and teachers possesses the virtue of honesty" Timpe (n.d.).

ruthlessly dispassionate might be preferred over being empathetic and be a legitimate requisite for the position.

Propositional Content

This refers to the actual semantic content of a person's beliefs, not their attitudes toward beliefs. Using the term *"propositional"* in the logical sense of a claim, the idea here refers to the content of a person's belief set and in particular, their memory. While one's skills are supported by memory and while the capacity of one's memory constrains what could be learned in the future, the current propositional content of memory refers to what one actually currently believes in a dry, literal sense. Examples that demonstrate the relevance to the business context include the knowledge of the chemical formula of a new proprietary drug not yet patented, the details of secret negotiation, Chinese vocabulary, usernames and passwords, visual schematics of an engineering design, or the names of all the spouses and other family members of your coworkers.

Neurointerventions in the Workplace

Studying the role of neuroscience and neurotechnology in criminal law has often been concerned with issues such as lie detection, the relevance of exculpatory neurological evidence, the self-incrimination potential for brain scans, and prophylactically monitoring people who may be neurologically disposed to committing crimes. Other issues include inducing competency for accused persons to stand trial, making people psychologically fit for punishment or execution, altering the brains of those released back into society as an anti-recidivism measure, and implanting monitoring and modulation devices in brains. The first group of issues deal with neurotechnologies of *detection* while the second group deals with neurotechnologies of *intervention*.[11] Although neurointerventions are the focus of this volume, in both types of technology it is crucial to recognize that criminal law is a very specific context—a nonvoluntary system operating in which people are suspected of crimes, accused of crimes, found guilty of crimes, are treated as owing a debt to society that must be paid in terms of prison time or death, and as a result of the gravity of the situation are granted extensive protections against self-incrimination and investigative evidence-gathering, and are often offered state support for their defense (see, e.g., *United States v. Wade,* 1967).[12]

---

[11] Numerous examples of these technologies—existing, developing, and speculative—are given in Fiser (2016), Hopkins and Fiser (2016), and Fiser and Hopkins (2017).

[12] For a short discussion of criminal procedure and protections, see Legal Information Institute (n.d.).

The business law context is equally specific but very different—a voluntary system operating in which people engage in contracts for mutual benefit, consciously provide large amounts of personal information in order to be selected; eagerly give "neuroevidence" (sometimes of questionable evidentiary value) of their personalities, abilities, and backgrounds; can be fired for no reason; not only have no right to avoid self-incrimination but in some ways are expected to self-incriminate (e.g., the dreaded job interview question "What are your weaknesses?"); can only avoid testing that might provide medical information that could be used to discriminate against them; expect to be monitored regularly; can be charged as negligently liable for their own harmful behavior or the behavior of their employees; and are provided no state support for defense.

As a way to highlight how different these legal situations can be, let us give one contrasting example (from what could be many) of how a neurointervention could be treated. Consider a situation in which a neurointerfacing device could be functionally connected to a person's brain. There are several possibilities here that vary in terms of physical invasiveness and mode of operation—including brain implants that would be surgically placed deep into neural tissue (Regalado, 2014), optogenetic fibers implanted into tissue (Matveev, 2015; Unh & Arenkiel, 2012), nonpenetrating optogenetic wireless arrays placed on surgically thinned areas of the skull (Dixon Dorand, Barkauskas, Evans, Petrosiute, & Huang, 2014; Patel, 2013), injectable wireless optogenetic devices (Liu et al., 2015), electrode/stent hybrid devices inserted into neck veins via catheter and snaked up into cortical areas (Oxley et al., 2016; University of Melbourne, 2016), biometric record/broadcast contact lenses implanted in the eye (Chowdhry, 2016; Mochari, 2015; Solon, 2014; Tenderich, 2014), interactive microsensors injected into the bloodstream (Liu et al., 2015), and injectable neural mesh (Kim et al., 2013; Liu et al., 2015; Sanford, 2016).

For purposes of this chapter, we will use the example of implantable contact lenses. We choose this technology for several reasons. First, it is relatively simple with a low level of invasiveness and a concomitant relatively low risk of side effects. Second, it has wide application to both criminal and business contexts. Third, it also highlights how the notion of a neurointervention can be broader than expected. While the term *neurointervention* often elicits images of brain-in-the-skull implants or drugs passing the blood–brain barrier, the entire nervous system, which is distributed throughout the body, can be subject to intervention. The retina, for example, which some implantable ocular lenses could affect, is standardly understood as part of the brain—and not peripherally but as a genuine part of the central nervous system, referred to as the only part of the brain we can see directly (Gottlob, 2015). It is a thin sheet of neural tissue composed of several layers of neurons and—in an oft-remarked-upon biological oddity—light must pass through these neurons to photoreceptor cells deeper in the retina, which then send signals back up to the neurons. The retinal tissue it-self is not merely a conduit, but also begins processing, separating, and spatially encoding image information. Technologies that directly affect the retina then, are truly central nervous system neurointerventions. While many functions of an implantable lens would not need to interface with the retina, the ability to access neural tissue without involving skull manipulation is inviting.[13]

Versions of implantable lenses already in development could measure body temperature and blood alcohol levels, be used for authentication in accessing restricted areas and devices, transmit biometric information, track movement, receive information that the wearer could see, and connect to other electronic devices for control and interface functions (Chowdhry, 2016; Mochari, 2015; Solon, 2014; Tenderich, 2014). Versions being researched (and for which patents have already been filed) include cameras that could record and transmit images, providing both real-time and stored recordings of what occurs in the implantee's visual field (Chowdhry, 2016; Solon, 2014).

There are two elements to consider in examining the legal issues of such implants. One is the purpose of the implant. The other is the timing of the implant.

Regarding *purpose*, the goal of required lens implants would most often be to monitor, deter, and promote behavior. Anyone wearing the lenses could be monitored both in terms of location and in terms of (visually accessible) ac-tivity. The ability to record and transmit or store the images the person could see (and given video enhancement programs, even phenomena they could not see) could provide extensive information about what behavior they were engaging in and what behavior other people in the recording field were engaging in, which would be useful as evidence for determining both criminal culpability and civil liability. The lenses could also engender considerable motivation for deterring undesired behavior. Psychologically, just the knowledge that they were being recorded would make someone less likely to engage in criminal or negligent behavior, since there would always be a "policeman at the elbow." Physically, it could become possible to generate a feedback through the lens that could cause temporary visual interference, providing a long-distance electronic version of macing, tasering, or strobelight blinding (Santos, 2010). More speculatively, it might also become possible to send stimuli to the retina to produce specific images (say, WARNING! or CEASE AND DESIST!). Promoting behavior would also be a function, and not only in the negative sense that deterring unacceptable behavior would in many cases automatically imply increasing acceptable beha-vior. Employees using such lenses could interface with other devices for greater

---

[13] Some of the other technologies mentioned in this chapter do this as well, such as the stentodes, injectable neural mesh, and neural dust.

efficiency and would be able to make use of stored and replayable images for improving work performance. Criminals using such lenses during incarceration could be gauged for good behavior and postincarceration could have greater opportunities for employment because they could be constantly monitored, and if some illegal or suspicious activity did occur in their vicinity, they would have recorded proof that they were not the culprits, thus obviating much of the automatic suspicion that would otherwise fall on them.

Regarding *timing*, lenses could be required before any indication that a person specifically needed to be monitored, deterred, or motivated, or they could be required after some indication that a person needed to be monitored, deterred, or motivated in the future. In the *before* situation, a position might require employees to be fitted with lenses as a bona fide occupational qualification (e.g., if some brain–machine interfacing were needed for accuracy or speed), or as a condition to limit liability (e.g., if de facto "reasonable care" and "reasonable foreseeability" standards in negligent employment torts demanded it),or lenses might be required of everyone as a general preventive crime measure. In the *after* situation, a person might be required to be fitted with lenses because they have already failed in some aspect of expected behavior (e.g., job performance or rule infraction), because they have previously committed some crime or infraction and are now suspected of recidivism or work untrustworthiness (so this could be a requirement of penal probation, or parole, or prison release, or workplace probation), or because they have some detected neurological condition that indicates a statistically higher chance of criminal, negligent, faulty, or inappropriate behavior.

Although a great deal of parsing and subtle analysis could apply to these various possible situations, the basic point here is that criminal law and business law would treat them very differently.

In the criminal law context,

a. Requiring any kind of neurointervention as a preventive measure for crime would likely not even count as part of criminal law (since no crime has been committed) but would involve civil rights and public health law considerations, or it could be treated as a practice treading on the principle of treating people as innocent unless they are proven guilty of a crime.[14]
b. Requiring lens implants as part of incarceration could be challenged as cruel and unusual punishment.[15]

[14] "The principle that there is a presumption of innocence in favor of the accused is the undoubted law, axiomatic and elementary, and its enforcement lies at the foundation of the administration of our criminal law" (*Coffin v. United States*, 1895).

[15] See Carney (2012) for a discussion of monitoring technology challenges to pre- and postincarceration).

c. Only in rare circumstances can one party be vicariously criminally re-sponsible for another person's crimes and so there would be no need or motivation to immunize oneself by requiring another person to have lens implants (Kreit, 2008).

d. Everyone already finds themselves embedded in a criminal law system and so the restrictions or compulsions that are part of that system are typically held to need strong justification as a power of the state over individuals.[16] As such, neurointerventions would receive a high level of scrutiny.

In the business law context,

a. Requiring a neurointervention as a preventive or safeguarding measure for safety, quality control, and infraction prevention would be entirely consistent with business law—especially employment law. Employees are often monitored, assessed, recorded, and tracked using a wide variety of electronic surveillance methods, and this has nothing to do with whether they have already shown themselves to be untrustworthy. The principle of not treating someone as "guilty" when they have done nothing wrong is irrelevant in the employee context since the purpose of requiring neurointerventions such as implanted lenses is not about establishing or responding to guilt but is instead about efficiency, performance, preven-tion, safety, and liability reduction. Should something go to court about employment, it would almost always be a civil procedure, in which case liability would be the issue, not guilt or innocence.

b. Requiring lens implants for employees would obviously have nothing to do with cruel and unusual punishment, since the situation would not be one of punishment and would not be within the arena of criminal proceedings in the first place.

c. It is common in business for one party to be judged vicariously liable for another person's actions, so there is immense motivation to im-munize oneself against responsibility for other's wrongdoing. While in criminal people are rarely held criminally responsible for not fore-seeing and preventing a crime (Fiser & Hopkins, 2017),[17] employers are explicitly subject to vicarious liability for what employees do, even

---

[16] Unlike the employment context, the general population does not voluntarily subject themselves to our systems of criminal laws and various rights. The very nature of voluntarily accepting an em-ployment position is a contract which contains obligations and rights on each side of the contract. Rights to privacy in employment are very different than rights to privacy in a general population context (*Luedtke v. Nabors Alaska Drilling, Inc.*, 1989; Porter & Griffaton, 2003).

[17] Rare instances of "vicarious criminal liability" occur in situations where one crime is being committed but another potentially unforeseen crime ultimately occurs, such as felony murder (Guerra, 2015).

when not at the behest of the employer. Consider situations in which employees interact with customers or the public in ways that that could potentially cause harm (security guards, air traffic controllers, drivers, pilots, surgeons, childcare workers, nursing home staffers, home health workers, delivery persons, firearms sales staff; Fiser & Hopkins, 2017, pp. 55–65). In the type of tort know as *negligent hiring* and/or *negligent retention*, an employer is liable for an employee's criminal, negligent, or otherwise harmful behavior committed during the course and scope of employment if they do not exercise "due diligence" and use "reasonable care" in assessing and monitoring employees (Fiser & Hopkins, 2017, pp. 66–69).[18] If negligent hiring lawsuits sensitize the system to the point it is considered "reasonable" to constantly surveil employees, an employer might be effectively *required* to mandate lens implants to avoid being negligent. The simple *existence* of such technology (given safety and efficacy) can produce a new standard such that not requiring it places an employer at risk (Fiser, 2015; Fiser & Hopkins, 2017, pp. 447–449).

d. Everyone does *not* already find themselves embedded in any particular employment law context and must enter into those contexts through voluntary contractual relationships. As such, employees are not absolutely required to accept any potential neurointervention but are only conditionally obligating themselves as one party to a contract. As such, neurointerventions would find a much more individual and permissive atmosphere in business than in the justice system, and to compete more effectively in the job market, individuals might themselves volunteer or provide their own implants.[19]

This is just one hypothetical case. It is meant to show how different the criminal and business law contexts can be. What could generate a constitutional concern about state power and defendants' rights in the criminal context could just be a private contractual matter in the second, affected more by lawsuits than legislation. To speak of neuroscience and law only in terms of criminal law would miss a vast and influential area of the legal system.

---

[18] In some cases, even those who hire independent contractors may be liable for negligence (see *Noble v. Sears, Roebuck & Co.*, 1973).

[19] Already, competitive companies in Silicon Valley are seeing employees use pharmacological neurointerventions to enhance performance (Fiser, 2016, p. 476). One in four musicians have used beta blockers to improve their live performances, "with 70 percent getting the pills illicitly" ("Musicians Use Beta Blockers," 2013). Some argue that pitchers voluntarily undergo Tommy John surgery to repair damages "ulnar collateral ligament[s] in the elbow" to enhance performance of baseball pitchers (Berra, 2012).

Policy Options

As with questions of neurointerventions in criminal law, the issue of what policies should regulate these technologies quickly comes to the fore in civil and business law. However, the initial framings of the policy problems are distinct. In criminal law, the question is, How do neurointerventions fit into the existing obligations, liberties, and protections of the nonvoluntary system everyone finds themselves already subject to? In business, and particularly employment law, the question is, What limits should constrain people in voluntarily entering into contracts with others that create specific employment obligations and protections? The criminal law question is more about fitting new technologies into established legal system categories—the purpose of which system is to protect people from actions of others that endanger their life, health, property, and welfare. The employment law question is more about delimiting bounds of individual liberty to create labor contracts that make use of new technologies—the purpose of which delimiting is to protect people from excessively exploitative working conditions.

The different framing of the policy questions in these areas tends to pull on normative worries in different ways. In criminal law policy—at least in the U.S. context—there is an optimism that new neurointerventional (and other biointerventional techniques) could be used to improve prevention and detection of crime while simultaneously there is a concern among civil libertarians that techniques could be used to circumvent established protections for the accused or the imprisoned—a familiar tension between law, order, liberty, and state power. In employment law policy, the issues are newer and the worries less clear (Baird et al., 2012; Farah, 2015; Jones et al., 2013; Morse, 2011).

On the one hand, there might be an immediate reaction that employers should not be allowed to use neurointerventions because of safety and privacy concerns. However, keep in mind that companies are already constrained by numerous safety regulation standards that any neurointervention would have to meet, just as construction standards require fire exits and nonskid stair surfaces. Also, even if a company did want to use neurointerventions, they would not be unconditionally compulsory—they would only be conditional requirements for a person who wanted to apply for a job.[20] Companies can

[20] There may be a parallel to some criminal cases, for example, a convicted sex offender may be offered parole on the condition that they have the lens implants (or other biological alterations) or a violent schizophrenic might be offered release on the condition that they have ingestible drug delivery devices to force medical compliance. Interestingly, though, in both these cases, the neurointervention would be a public safety measure, not a punishment. It would also not be a crime to refuse the neurointervention. The choice to refuse would remain available. A response to this may be that being faced with the alternatives of either staying in prison or having a neurointervention, there is no real "choice" at all, but this would be factually incorrect. There is in fact a choice. It may be a hard choice, but it is a choice, and what is more, it is a situation in which there would be no choice at all without the neurointervention. If the danger posed by the sex offender or the violent schizophrenic

already quite legally require a great deal as a condition for taking a job—not only background checks, wearing certain clothes, using certain language, restricting social media postings, but also modificational requirements such as flu shots, prophylactic iodine, prophylactic salt tablets, wearing protective gear, biological testing, drug testing, and disallowing the use of legally available alcohol.[21] These all in some sense "intrude" on the employee's life—but only with the employee's agreement and in return for reciprocal obligations on the part of the employer.

On the other hand, there might be a reaction that employees themselves should not be allowed to use neurointerventions because this would create unfair competition or promote risking side effects of the interventions. This would be similar to arguments against the use of performance enhancers in athletics. However, in athletics, the performance and the competitive rankings are themselves the goals—to run faster than other people, to jump higher, to hurl farther, to lift more weight, to score more points. In business, however, the goal is not to stay alert for the sake of staying alert, or remember better for the sake of remembering, or to work longer hours for the sake of longer hours, nor even to work more hours than other people for the sake of being the person who works the most hours. The goal would be to improve function in those areas to succeed at work, with the concomitant benefits of salary, security, satisfaction, and status. It is largely for those reasons that people already pursue other ways to distinguish themselves and be more competitive—graduate degrees, attending prestigious schools, taking specialty courses to do better in standardized testing. Those attempts at improving performance and competitiveness are allowed and even admired.

The policy for how to deal with workplace neurointerventions will then be formed partially as a balancing act between the interests of the employers, the employees, and other stakeholders such as customers. Unlike the criminal justice situation, though, where the balance of interests is more characterized as between the state and the accused, the interests in the business situation is between individuals and other individuals (Santoni de Sio et al., 2016). The individual

---

is sufficient to keep them incarcerated or institutionalized (or both) then the neurointervention actually creates choice where there was none before.

[21] Hoffman (2001) discusses pre-employment testing and background checks. See Occupational Safety and Health Administration (2011) for the regulations requiring protection for "eyes, face, head, and extremities, protective clothing, respiratory devices, and protective shields and barriers . . ." when needed. Meister (2013) discusses the rights and obligations of employees in social media use, and Weiner (2014) discusses inoculations for employees; and Russo (2014) discusses regulation of off duty alcohol consumption by employers.

employer will obviously be interested in marketplace success—profitability due to improved competitiveness and efficiency and reducing liability due to improved screening and management practices. Individual employees and job applicants will be interested not only in liberty and privacy (as is everyone) but also with gaining a stable income, benefits, and satisfying work.

It is important not to assume that the only dynamic occurring here would be an employer requiring or pressuring an employee to use such technologies. So far—in its limited scope—the opposite has been more common. It is employees who are electing to use pharmacological enhancers to do better at work (Santoni de Sio et al., 2016), do better at training, and compete against others to get the jobs they want. It might actually be the case that employers would prefer that employees not make use of neurointerventions—because of worries about side effects, concerns about fairness, or because of bioconservative values. Although not a perfectly analogous context, anyone who teaches college students is aware of the widespread use of certain unprescribed stimulants for purposes of improved academic performance—a practice illegal (De Santis & Hane, 2010; Hanson et al., 2013; Webb, Valasek, & North, 2013), sometimes against school policy (Alpert, 2012), and almost entirely a "bottom–up" phenomenon. Similar dynamics arise in some areas of employment, with applicants (fresh from universities where perceived pharmacological enhancers were common; Alpert, 2012) eager to make use of whatever neurointerventions they believe will improve their work.

While there are many variations to the regulatory schemes possible, in basic terms there are three general options for governing workplace neurointerventions that differ both by how they weigh the importance of liberty for employee and employer and by how they weigh the importance of prevention of potential social harms.

Mutual Prohibition

Employers could not require neurointerventions nor could employees use them. This policy would weigh preventing the exploitation of workers most heavily (exploitation both by employers and the workers themselves) and weigh the liberty of the contractees the least. This would be more restrictive than current regulations. While U.S. employers are currently forbidden from pre-employment medical testing and asking about disabilities (ADA, 2009), the type of technology here is not medical. Its goal is prognostic, surveillance, and enhancement for job performance. Employees are not currently forbidden to use neurointerventions (other than drugs classified as illegal), so this would create a new set of restrictions and a complicated system for determining which alterations would be allowed, which would not, and why (caffeine yes, but modafinil no?)

Employer Prohibition/Employee Permission

Employers could not require neurointerventions but employees could use them. This policy would weigh employee liberty and privacy most heavily and weigh employers' interests the least. This would be somewhat more in line with current U.S. policy in that employers are limited in what medical information they can acquire about a job applicant. Presumably this policy would be motivated by a desire to minimize the exploitation of workers. However, unless employees were forbidden from telling employers about neurointerventional alteration (which would represent a greater level of restriction of employee liberty than currently in place), they could still open up to employers about such information, claiming it made them better qualified for the job and a much smaller liability risk than people without implants. In addition, employers would still have to assess workers' performance and if employees who were using neurointerventions were getting better evaluations, the standard for good performance might end up being effectively raised by the "invisible hand" of employee competition (Vincent & Jane, 2014).

Mutual Permission

Employers could require neurointerventions and employees could use them. This policy would weigh individual liberties in forming contracts most heavily and social worries about the potential complications of increased competition the least. This would practically result in a change in the kind of information employers can currently acquire (although again, mostly indirectly as a result of Americans with Disabilities Act violation fears) and a change in the dynamics of workplace assessment. Employers could use neurointerventions and require them for a job, which would give them a great deal of control over their employees. However, employers could also not prohibit employee use of neurointerventions (if employee permission-to-use were treated as a right) and as such might be forced to give higher evaluations to those employees who used neurotechnology. Who would be at the mercy of whom would not always be clear.[22]

---

[22] There would also be an employer permission/employee prohibition where employers could use neurotechnology for detection and monitoring but in which employees were not allowed to have implants. We leave out this category here because it would apply only to detection technologies, not actual intervention.

Conclusion

Neurointerventions (and other biointerventions[23]) in the workplace are likely to have profound cultural and legal effects. Those effects—and the thinking about those effects—will be different than what they are in the criminal justice system. There is a different set of expectations, necessities, liberties, and legal structures. In particular, there is a different impact on the voluntary associations of the parties involved. Employers are not compulsory philanthropies. Employees are not involuntary subjects. Even the relationship of employee–employer is one that only obtains as a result of mutual agreement. Policies regarding neurointervention and business law will have to deal with limiting what individuals can agree to contractually (and in many cases, unlike criminal law, these will be agreements about behaviors that would be entirely legal outside an employment context). With a host of not only legal and moral concerns but economic and psychological concerns as well, we will need to think at both a legislative and personal level about what is important in work. While neurointerventions might improve our work performance many times over, ultimately we need to ask a values question that is every bit empirical as it is normative—how much better do we need to be? After all, neurointervened rats in an updated rat-race are still in a rat-race. The race itself must be worth running.

References

ADA, 42 U.S.C. 12112(2)(A), 12112(4) (2009).

Alpert, D. (2012, January 20). *Viewpoint: Change honor codes to include abuse of non-prescription drugs*. USA Today College. Retrieved from http://college.usatoday.com/2012/01/20/opinion-change-honor-codes-to-include-abuse-of-non-prescription-drugs/.

Baird, A. A., Barrow, C. L., & Richard, M. K. (2012). Juvenile neurolaw: when it's good it is very good indeed, and when it's bad it's horrid. *Journal of Health Care Law & Policy*, *15*(1), 15–35.

Bartels, D. M., & Pizarro, D. A. (2011). The mismeasure of morals: Antisocial personality traits predict utilitarian responses to moral dilemmas. *Cognition, 121*, 154–161.

Berra, L. (2012, March 23). Force of habit. *ESPN*. Retrieved from http://espn.go.com/mlb/story/_/id/7712916/tommy-john-surgery-keeps-pitchers-game-address-underlying-biomechanical-flaw-espn-magazine

---

[23] Other types of interventions not specifically neurological in nature could include gene therapy, nanotechnological modification, prosthetic exoskeletons, prosthetic implants, steroids, growth hormone treatment, and cosmetic surgery.

Blasi, A. (2005). Moral character: A psychological approach. In D. K. Lapsley & F. C. Power (Eds.), *Character psychology and character education* (pp. 67–100). Notre Dame, IN: University of Notre Dame Press.

Bureau of Judicial Statistics. (2015). Correctional population in the United States. Retrieved from https://www.bjs.gov/index.cfm?ty=pbdetail&iid=5870

Bureau of Labor Statistics. (2015). American time use survey. Retrieved from http://www.bls.gov/tus/charts/chart9.txt

Business Dictionary. (n.d.). Attitude. http://www.businessdictionary.com/definition/attitude.html

Carney, M. (2012). Correction through omniscience: Electronic monitoring and the escalation of crime control. *Journal of Law and Policy, 40.* https://openscholarship.wustl.edu/law_journal_law_policy/vol40/iss1/8

Chowdhry, A. (2016, April 11). Samsung patent unveils idea for smart contact lenses with a camera and display. *Forbes.* Retrieved from http://www.forbes.com/sites/amitchowdhry/2016/04/11/samsung-patent-unveils-smart-contact-lenses-with-a-camera-and-display/#5b6da5ab67be

Coffin v. United States. 156 U.S. 432, 453 (1895).

Cohen, T. R., Panter, A. T., Nazli, Turan, N., Morse, L., & Kim, Y. (2014). Moral character in the workplace. *Journal of Personality and Social Psychology, 107*(5), 943–963.

Cooper, J. C., & Kovacic, W. W. (2012). Behavioral economic: implications for regulatory behavior. *Journal of Regulatory Economics, 41*(1), 41–58.

Cushman, F., Young, L., & Greene, J. D. (2010). Multi-system moral psychology. In J. M. Doris (Ed.), *The moral psychology handbook* (pp. 47–71). Oxford, England: Oxford University Press.

Danziger, S., Levav, J., & Avnaim-Pessoa, L. (2011). Extraneous factors in judicial decisions. *PNAS, 108*(17), 6889–6892.

Delgado, M. R., Frank, R. H., & Phelps, E. A. (2005). Perceptions of moral character modulate the neural systems of reward during the trust game. *Nature Neuroscience, 8,* 1611–1618. doi:10.1038/nn1575

De Santis, A. D., & Hane, A. C. (2010). "Adderall is definitely not a drug": Justifications for the illegal use of ADHD stimulants. Substance Use Misuse, 45(1–2), 31–46.

Dixon Dorand, R., Barkauskas, D. S., Evans, T. A., Petrosiute, A., & Huang, A. Y. (2014). Comparison of intravital thinned skull and cranial window approaches to study CNS immunobiology in the mouse cortex. *IntraVital, 3*(2), e29728.

Doris, J. (2002). *Lack of character: Personality and moral behavior.* Cambridge, England: Cambridge University Press.

Eagly, A. H., & Chaiken, S. (1998). Attitude, structure and function. In D.T. Gilbert, S. T. Fisk, & G. Lindsey (Eds.), *Handbook of social psychology* (pp. 269–322). New York, NY: McGraw-Hill.

Eskridge, W. N., Jr., & Ferejohn, J. (2002). Structuring lawmaking to reduce cognitive bias: A critical view. *Cornell Law Review, 87*(2), art. 12. https://scholarship.law.cornell.edu/cgi/viewcontent.cgi?article=2874&context=clr

Farah, M. (2015). Some optimism on brains, pain, & law—Let's see what we can achieve. Retrieved January 30, 2017, from http://blogs.harvard.edu/billofhealth/2015/07/29/some-optimism-on-brains-pain-law-lets-see-what-we-can-achieve/

Farnsworth, E. A. (2004) *Contracts* (4th ed.). New York, NY: Wolters Kluwer Law & Business.

Fiser, H. L. (2016). The treatment for malpractice-physician, enhance thyself: The impact of neuroenhancements for medical malpractice. *Pace Law Review, 36*(2), 438–476.

Fiser, H. L., & Hopkins, P. D. (2017). Getting inside the employee's head: Neuroscience, negligent employment liability, and the push and pull for new technology. *Journal of Science, Technology, and Law, 23*(1), 44–89. https://www.bu.edu/jostl/files/2017/04/Fiser-Online.pdf

Gawronski, B. (Ed.). What is an attitude? (Special issue). *Social Cognition, 25*(5).

Goodwin, G. P., Piazza, J., & Rozin, P. (2013). Moral character predominates in person perception and evaluation. *Journal of Personality and Social Psychology, 106*(1), 148–168.

Gottlob, I. (2015, March 20). The eye is the only part of the brain that can be seen directly: Here's what secrets it can reveal. *Business Insider.* Retrieved from http://www.businessinsider.com/the-eye-is-the-only-part-of-the-brain-that-can-be-seen-directly--heres-what-secrets-it-can-reveal-2015-3

Greene, J. D., Sommerville, R. B., Nystrom, L. E., Darley, J. M., & Cohen, J. D. (2001). An fMRI investigation of emotional engagement in moral judgment. *Science, 293*, 2105–2108.

Greenwald, A. G., & Banaji, M. R. (1995). Implicit social cognition: Attitudes, self-esteem, and stereotypes. *Psychological Review, 102*(1), 4–27. doi:10.1037/0033-295x.102.1.4, PMID 7878162

Greenwald, A. G., McGhee, D. E., & Schwartz, J. L. K. (1998), Measuring individual differences in implicit cognition: The implicit association test. *Journal of Personality and Social Psychology, 74*(6), 1464–1480, doi:10.1037/0022-3514.74.6.1464, PMID 9654756

Guerra, K. (2015, April 19). Elkhart Four: Teen murderers who didn't kill anyone. *Indy Star.* Retrieved from https://www.indystar.com/story/news/crime/2015/04/19/men-became-murderers-without-killing-anyone/26027173/

Haidt, J. (2001). The emotional dog and its rational tail: A social intuitionist approach to moral judgment. *Psychological Review, 108*(4), 814–823, 828–834.

Harman, G. (2000). Moral philosophy meets social psychology: Virtue ethics and the fundamental attribution error. In G. Harman, *Explaining value and other essays in moral philosophy* (pp. 165–178). Oxford, England: Oxford University Press.

Hartshorne, H., May, M. A., & Shuttleworth, F. K. (1930). *Studies in the organization of character.* Oxford, England: Macmillan.

Hanson, C. L., Burton, S. H., Giraud-Carrier, C., West, J. H., Barnes, M. D., & Hansen, B. (2013). Tweaking and tweeting: Exploring Twitter for nonmedical use of psychostimulant drug (Adderall) among college students, *Journal of Medical Internet Research, 15*(4), E62.

Helzer, E. G., Furr, R. M., Hawkins, A., Barranti, M., Blacki, L. E. R., & Fleeson, W. (2014). Agreement on the perception of moral character. *Personality and Social Psychology Bulletin, 40*(12), 1698–1710.

Hoffman, S. (2001). Preplacement examinations and job-relatedness: How to enhance privacy and diminish discrimination in the workplace. *University of Kansas Law Review, 49*, 517.

Hogg, M., & Vaughan, G. (2005). *Social psychology* (4th ed.). London, England: Prentice Hall.

Hopkins, P. D., & Fiser, H. L. (2017). "This position requires some alteration of your brain": On the moral and legal issues of using neurotechnology to modify employees. *Journal of Business Ethics, 144*(4), 783–797. doi:10.1007/s10551-016-3182-y

Jayawickreme, E., Meindl, P., Helzer, E. G., Furr, R. M., & Fleeson, W. (2014) Virtuous states and virtuous traits: How the empirical evidence regarding the existence of broad traits saves virtue ethics from the situationist critique. *Theory and Research in Education, 12*(3), 283–308. doi:10.1177/1477878514545206

Jones, J. M. (2013, December 19). In U.S., 40% get less than recommended amount of sleep. *Gallup*. Retrieved from https://news.gallup.com/poll/166553/less-recommended-amount-sleep.aspx

Jones, O. D., Marois, R., Farah, M. J., & Greely, H. T. (2013). Law and neuroscience. *Journal of Neuroscience, 33*(45), 17624–17630. doi:10.1523/JNEUROSCI.3254-13.2013

Kim, T.-I., McCall, J. G., Jung, Y. H., Huang, X., Siuda, E.R., Li, Y., . . . Bruchas, M. R. (2013). Injectable, cellular-scale optoelectronics with applications for wireless optogenetics. *Science, 340*(6129), 211–216.

Kreit, A. (2008). Vicarious criminal liability and the constitutional dimensions of Pinkerton. *American University Law Review, 57*(3), art. 3.

Legal Information Institute. (n.d.). Criminal procedure LII. Retrieved from https://www.law.cornell.edu/wex/criminal_procedure

Liu, J., Liu, J., Fu, T-M., Cheng, Z., Hong, G., Zhou, T., . . . Lieber, C. M. (2015). Syringe injectable electronics. *Nature Nanotechnology, 10*(7), 629–636.

Luedtke v. Nabors Alaska Drilling, Inc., 768 P.2d 1123 (Ak. 1989).

Matveev, M. V., Erofeev, A. I., Terekhin, S. G., Plotnikova, P. V., Vorobyov, K. V., & Vlasova, O. L. (2015). Implantable devices for optogenetic studies and stimulation of excitable tissue. *St. Petersburg Polytechnical University Journal: Physics and Mathematics, 1*(3), 264–271.

Meister, J. (2013, February 7). The future of work: Why updating your company's social media policy is required. *Forbes*.

Milgram, S. (1974). *Obedience to authority: An experimental view*. New York, NY: Harper & Row.

Mochari, I. (2015, October 15). 7 crazy things Google's solar-powered contact lenses might do. *Inc*. Retrieved from http://www.inc.com/ilan-mochari/google-patent-solar-powered-contact-lens.html

Morse, S. J. (2011). Avoiding irrational neurolaw exuberance: A plea for neuromodesty. *Mercer Law Review, 62,* 837.

Musicians use beta blockers as performance enabling drugs. (2013, August 16). *WQXR*. Retrieved from https://www.wqxr.org/story/312920-musicians-use-beta-blockers-relieve-stage-fright/

National Labor Relations Board, National Labor Relations Act, 29 U.S.C. §§151–169, 152 (1, 7) (1935).

Noble v. Sears, Roebuck & Co. 33 Cal. App. 3d 654, 662–663 (Cal. Ct. App. 1973).

Occupational Safety and Health Administration. (2011). 29 C.F.R. §1910.132.

Oxley, T. J., Opie, N. L., John, S. E., Rind, G. S., Ronayne, S. M., Wheeler, T. L., . . . O'Brien, T. J. (2016). Minimally invasive endovascular stent-electrode array for high-fidelity, chronic recordings of cortical neural activity. *Nature Nanotechnology, 34*(3), 320–327.

Patel, P. (2013, April 12). Injectable optoelectronics for brain control. *IEEE Spectrum*. http://spectrum.ieee.org/biomedical/devices/injectable-optoelectronics-for-brain-control

Porter, W. G., II, & Griffaton, M. C. (2003). Between the devil and the deep blue sea: monitoring the electronic workplace. *Defense Counsel Journal, 70*(1), 65.

Project Implicit. (n.d.). Retrieved from https://implicit.harvard.edu/implicit/faqs.html

Regalado, A. (2014, May 29). Military Funds brain–computer interfaces to control feelings. *MIT Technical Review.* Retrieved from https://www.technologyreview.com/s/527561/military-funds-brain-computer-interfaces-to-control-feelings/

Rosenhouse, M. A. (1992). American Jurisprudence 2d Volume 82 Workers' Compensation to Wrongful Discharge. Toronto ON: Lawyers Cooperative Publishing/Thomson Reuters.

Russo, K. J. (2014, September 18). Prohibiting off-duty alcohol consumption by alcoholic employees violates ADA, says EEOC. *National Review.*

Saad, L. (2014, August 29). The "40-hour" workweek is actually longer—by seven hours. *Gallup.* Retrieved from http://www.gallup.com/poll/175286/hour-workweek-actually-longer-seven-hours.aspx

Sanford, K. (2016, August 29). Will this "neural lace" brain implant help us compete with AI?, Nautilus. Retrieved from http://nautil.us/blog/with-this-neural-lace-brain-implant-we-can-stay-as-smart-as-ai

Santoni de Sio, F., Faber, N. S., Savulescu, J., & Vincent, N. (2016). *Why less praise for enhanced performance? Moving beyond responsibility-shifting, authenticity, and cheating to a nature of activities approach. In Cognitive enhancement: Ethical and policy implications in international perspectives* (pp. 27–41). New York, NY: Oxford University Press.

Santos, E. M. (2010, June 30). How to use a strobing flashlight. *Police.* Retrieved from http://www.policemag.com/channel/patrol/articles/2010/06/how-to-use-a-strobing-flashlight.aspx

Solon, O. (2014, April 15). Google embeds camera in smart contact lens. *Wired.* Retrieved from http://www.wired.co.uk/article/google-contact-lenses-camera

Tenderich, A. (2014, January 16). NewsFlash: Google is developing glucose-sensing contact lenses! *Healthline.* Retrieved from http://www.healthline.com/diabetesmine/newsflash-google-is-developing-glucose-sensing-contact-lenses

Timpe, K. (n.d.). Moral character. In *Internet encyclopedia of philosophy.* Retrieved from http://www.iep.utm.edu/moral-ch/#SH3a

Ung, K., & Arenkiel, B. R. (2012). Fiber-optic implantation for chronic optogenetic stimulation of brain tissue. *Journal of Visualized Experiments, 68,* 50004.

United States v. Wade, 388 U.S. 218 (1967).

University of Melbourne. (2016, February 9). new device to get people with paralysis back on their feet. Retrieved from http://newsroom.melbourne.edu/news/new-device-get-people-paralysis-back-their-feet

U.S. Census Bureau. (2014), Business dynamics statistics, Firm characteristics data table, economy wide. Retrieved from http://www.census.gov/ces/dataproducts/bds/data_firm.html

U.S. Federal Courts. (n.d.). Criminal cases. Retrieved from http://www.uscourts.gov/about-federal-courts/types-cases/criminal-cases

Vincent, N. (2014). Neurolaw and direct brain interventions. *Criminal Law and Philosophy, 8*(1), 43–50.

Vincent, N., & Jane, E. A. (2014, June 14). Put down the smart drugs: Cognitive enhancement is ethically risky business. *The Conversation.* Retrieved from https://theconversation.com/put-down-the-smart-drugs-cognitive-enhancement-is-ethically-risky-business-27463

Webb, J. R., Valasek, M. A., & North, C. S. (2013). Prevalence of stimulant use in a sample of U.S. medical students. *Annals of Clinical Psychiatry, 25,* 27–32.

Weiner, L. J. (2014, October 10). Hospitals battle unions over mandatory flu shots for nurses. *Health Leaders Media.* Retrieved from http://www.healthleadersmedia.com/nurse-leaders/hospitals-battle-unions-over-mandatory-flu-shots-nurses

Whitley, B. E. (2010). *The psychology of prejudice & discrimination.* New York, NY: Wadsworth Cengage Learning.

Young v. North Drury Lane Productions, Inc., 80 F.3d 203, 207 (7th Cir. 1996).

Index

Figures are indicated by *f* following the page number

For the benefit of digital users, indexed terms that span two pages (e.g., 52–53) may, on occasion, appear on only one of those pages.